STREAMS OF CIVILIZATION

Earliest Times to the Discovery of the New World

Volume One

Albert Hyma and Mary Stanton

• A PUBLICATION OF •
Christian Liberty Press
502 W. Euclid Avenue, Arlington Heights, Illinois 60004

2000 Printing

Printed in the United States of America

ISBN 1-930367-43-0

Introduction

The vast majority of ancient history texts written during the twentieth century contained an overwhelming bias in favor of interpreting history from a secular and evolutionary perspective. This bias explains why modern history books rarely attempt to show the relevance of the Bible to the interpretation of historical events or personalities.

Thankfully, many students of history in recent years have begun to question the validity of historical interpretations that deny the existence of a personal Creator and assume that all of history can be explained and examined solely on the basis of humanistic/scientific terms. The secular world view that has dominated the study of history for the last hundred years is now in trouble.

The humanistic approach to historical interpretation has begun to self-destruct primarily because it provides students with a host of questions that have no adequate answers. The study of history on purely secular terms forces a student to conclude that our planet, and mankind in general, has no ultimate meaning or purpose. History is therefore reduced to a study of arbitrary and random events that have no ultimate significance. A cosmos of change and chaos is all that secular historians can offer the minds of men. No wonder the secular world view is beginning to crumble.

The opening of the twenty-first century provides great opportunities for those who believe that the only adequate method for historical interpretation is through the spectacles of the revealed will of God—the Holy Scriptures.

Advancement in scientific technology and archaeology will continue to reveal the fact that the Biblical record is both reliable and authoritative for faith <u>and</u> <u>life</u>. The marvelous wonders of Creation and human history constantly remind us of the reality of our Divine Creator and force us to admit that He is the focal point of all history—not man.

The text that follows entitled *Streams of Civilization*, will present students with a wealth of historical data and information on world cultures. Each reader, however, will be challenged to accept the Biblical method of historical interpretation and will, therefore, be encouraged to worship the Creator of the earth rather than its creatures.

Michael J. McHugh
Arlington Heights, Illinois
2000

FOREWORD AND ACKNOWLEDGMENTS

Streams of Civilization represents the fruition of a four-year project sponsored by the Institute for Creation Research. This volume is designed to produce a truly objective textbook on world history, suitable for use in both public schools and private schools.

Practically all previous textbooks on world history have been written from a secular, evolutionary, humanistic point of view. Frequently texts contain an anti-Christian and even anti-American bias. Such books are offensive to many parents of public school young people and even more so to both parents and teachers in Christian schools. Furthermore, such texts have presented a distorted view of history that has contributed to a strong modern-day decline of interest in history as a subject for serious study, especially ancient and medieval history. Thus there has been a great need for an introductory textbook of world history which attempts to remedy these deficiencies.

A public school textbook should be objective, recognizing that parents and pupils represent a wide variety of philosophical, political, and religious beliefs. Every attempt has been made to present a balanced and objective perspective on world history which should commend itself to all types of school systems. For example, the evidences for both the creationist and evolutionist interpretations of prehistory are given. The Judaeo-Christian background of western history is presented objectively and thus not offensive to those of other faiths. Western civilization is emphasized, but not over-emphasized, with much space devoted to the important histories of African and Asian peoples. Throughout the book the writers and editors have conscientiously tried to give an objective view of the history of all the world in such a way as to satisfy the needs of both public and private schools.

These goals proved to be more ambitious than originally realized, and the project has, therefore, taken longer than anticipated. A great many people have participated in the project in one way or another, and it is hoped that this wide participation finally has produced a book of optimum benefit to all.

Dr. Albert Hyma and Dr. Mary Stanton are eminently qualified to serve as co-authors for such a book as this. Although others have written or rewritten various sections of the book, *Streams of Civilization* is pre-eminently the product of their experience and expertise. Dr. Hyma was Professor of History at the University of Michigan for many years and is author of numerous other text and reference works in history. The basic manuscript was originally from him and reflects his wide knowledge of history in general, and especially his unexcelled authority in medieval and Reformation history.

Dr. Stanton is an accomplished archaeologist, cultural anthropologist, and educator, as well as an historian. Outstanding among her contributions to the book are the numerous insights into the cultures and personal lives of ancient peoples, as well as her research into the history of the peoples of Asia and Africa and the pre-Columbian tribes in America. Both Dr. Stanton and Dr. Hyma are also experienced teachers in both public and private schools, and their writing manifests real concern for the interests and needs of young people.

In addition to the two main authors, Polly Hutchison did extensive research and writing for the final manuscript. Her experience as a history teacher in public schools and as a successful writer enabled her to make many valuable contributions. Certain sections, especially in Chapter 1, were written by the Director of the Institute for Creation Research.

Project Coordinator and General Editor was Marilyn Hughes. Assisting her in this herculean task were Annette Bradley, Nancy Eckis, Donna Schenk, and Evelyn Stephens. Publication of the book by Creation-Life Publishers was under the overall direction of George Hillestad, President, and Gilbert Tinker, General Manager. The Index was prepared by Henry M. Morris, III.

Jay Wegter was in charge of artwork and cartography. Others who participated in art and layout were Tim Ravenna, Gary Johnson, Joe Austin, Marjorie Kibbi, John Meitz, Donna Schenk, Brian Tinker, and Gil Tinker. Those who assisted Dr. Stanton in her initial research, proofing, and artwork included George Phillips, Ralph McEwen, Dorothy Standiford, Mary Day, Marguerite Day, Evelyn Halstrom, Ginny Pruitt, and David Burgher. Credits for photographs are listed separately.

Reviewers and consultants on the project have added greatly to the final book. Dr. Edna Parker read Dr. Stanton's entire original manuscript, making many helpful suggestions. Dr. Dean Gresham, Professor of History at Point Loma College, reviewed the entire completed manuscript. Several faculty and staff members at Christian Heritage College reviewed part or all of the manuscript at various stages, including Dr. Arnold Ehlert, Dr. James DeSaegher, Robert Lovell, Margarette Hill, William Low, Dr. Duane Gish, Dr. Harold Slusher, Carl Zimmerman, and Peggy Hansen. Dr. Norman Steinaker, Project Specialist for the Ontario-Montclair (California) Public School District, reviewed and corrected the entire completed manuscript.

The final manuscript was typed by Betty Braskamp. Other typists included Judy Bott, Mary Ann Baker, Sharon Stanton, and Gloria Hughes. We also appreciate the efforts of Ron Baker and Don Albert of the El Cajon Publishing Company who helped us meet our publication deadline.

The project has involved many participants, the above named representing only the more active contributors. Recognition must also be given to the supporters of the Institute for Creation Research, whose contributions make projects such as this one possible.

To a large degree, this textbook is breaking new ground. There is a need for truly objective textbooks in many other fields, fields that have been almost monopolized by humanistic emphases for many years. It is hoped that *Streams of Civilization* will prove to be a real turning point. Comments from users and readers will, of course, be welcome in order that future editions of this book as well as future textbooks in other fields will attain these objectives to the maximum degree.

Henry M. Morris, Ph.D.
Director, Institute for Creation Research
El Cajon, California

CONTENTS

Why History?

Every student at some time has asked the question: "Why is it important to study history? What difference can it make to me what a lot of people did thousands of years ago?"

History is important because it is the story of people, how they came into existence and what they did. People have always faced the same problems of food, shelter, social organization, political structure, and religious expression. By exploring the streams of civilization throughout time, we will have a better understanding of how the world came to be the way it is today. It will also help us to understand better the events that are happening today and the decisions being made that will change the future.

The Story of People

People have always had a strong desire to leave records about their activities. Those records, whether chiseled in stone, baked on clay tablets, written on parchment, or fed into a computer, give us a picture of how these people lived. History, then, has two functions: it reflects present experiences, and it reveals the life and culture of the past. Whether records were written yesterday or thousands of years ago, they are useful in helping us understand the world in which we live today.

People from many countries are helping to make information available about past cultures and civilizations. As the story of mankind unfolds, many questions come to mind. Was there one original language? Did mankind begin from one family? If there was only one family in the beginning, how did the different races begin? What effects did the fall of the Roman Empire and other powers have on future civilizations? Answers to these questions and many more are presented in the following pages.

In order to understand history, it is important to understand the difference between two basic terms that will be used again and again: civilization and culture.

Culture. The term culture, which comes from the Latin word *cultura*, meaning "care for," has many meanings. A culture includes all the things one uses to control, benefit from, or make use of the environment.

When we use the word culture in *Streams of Civilization* we will be referring to two basic

The National Archives in Washington D.C., one of the largest record-keeping centers in the United States, bears a strong resemblance to the Pantheon in Rome. Its records and documents, available for public viewing, provide a source of historical information to interested readers.

meanings: (1) People try to control their environment by changing it or adapting to its more permanent parts, such as climate and geography. For example, a people may change their environment by irrigating a desert area; they may adapt to their environment by wearing warm clothing in a cold climate. (2) People use materials found in their physical environment to develop their culture. One way they do this is by using available materials such as wood, mud, stone, and reeds to build homes.

The family is the basic unit of organization in any culture. Several families who are related and share a common need to work together for survival are known as a *clan*. As a clan grows in

size and influence, villages and cities are established.

As these people join together, they develop common geographic, economic, social, and political ties. These cultural characteristics and achievements are then passed on to future generations.

Japanese women stop for lunch during the rice planting season. Rice planting is a community experience; groups of men and women work together to plant each other's rice paddies.

Eskimos have developed the geographic, economic, and political characteristics necessary to make them a distinct culture.

The Bible As An Historical Record

Many sources of information such as ancient records, literature, and science are used by historians to tell the story of man. One reliable historical document is the Bible, which was written over centuries by the Hebrew people.

Some people try to prove that the Bible is inaccurate because it mentions historical facts, cities, and empires that are not recorded anywhere else. As archaeologists continue to uncover ancient cities and civilizations, their findings have proved the Bible to be true.

The recent discovery of the Dead Sea Scrolls also has supported the Bible's accuracy. Some of the ancient writings are books of the Bible. When these scrolls were translated, it was learned they were almost exactly the same as our modern Bible.

Since the Bible has proven to be as accurate as other records, the authors of *Streams of Civilization* have selected it as a major historical record. When used, the text makes statements such as "according to the Hebrew record" or "the Bible states."

Civilization. When a culture expands from villages and communities into more complex social and political cities, it is known as a civilization. The individual culture is always a part of the civilization, but there is advanced development in the arts and sciences. It is difficult to know exactly when the change occurs. In *Streams of Civilization*, groups of people are called a civilization when a culture begins to develop to the degree that it influences other cultures and deserves the term "city."

History's Building Blocks

People in many different fields of study, called *disciplines*, provide information on past civilizations and cultures. The historian takes this information, studies it, and decides what it means to him. Ancient records, current events, and information collected from other disciplines are called the building blocks of history. What are some of these disciplines that help the historian in his search for the past?

A Blend of Disciplines

Archaeology and Anthropology. Archaeology is the scientific study of the remains of relics, artifacts, and even lost cities, to learn about the way a people lived. Anthropology is the study of the physical character, environment, social relations, and culture of people. These two disciplines are closely related, but archaeology is older. Nearly three thousand years ago people wrote of their interest in digging up and studying the ruins of ancient civilizations. Excavations are a necessary part of both disciplines and these people have become very skilled in their work.

Discoveries made at archaeological sites are referred to as *finds* or *findings*. One of the ways information is provided through archaeology is in pictures of a people carved on their monuments. From these pictures we are able to tell what type of clothing they wore, the type of jewelry they used, and the skills and crafts they developed.

Throughout the world, archaeologists search for *tells*. A tell appears to be a flat-topped hill or mound, but actually conceals the debris-covered ruins of ancient cities. Many times a city was built upon the destroyed remains of a previous city. Ancient Troy, for example, had nine levels, each representing a different city.

The excavation of an ancient site is slow and difficult work. Great care must be taken to be sure nothing is lost or broken. Some archaeologists use toothbrushes and tablespoons

Flat-topped hills covering the ruins of ancient cities are called *tells*. They often resemble the cone-shaped hills surrounding them, as pictured here. Can you guess which one is the tell? (center front)

A trench cut is a method of excavating in which a cut is made through many levels of earth at one time. It is a quick way of determining the number of civilizations in that area. Megiddo, a well-known tell in Israel, has twenty-six levels of civilizations.

In early civilizations copper urns were made in many different ways. The body of this one was made from only one piece of copper, in Hittite fashion. The handle was attached later.

Egyptian jewelry, such as these earrings, was made of gold and was used as money or items of trade by early civilizations.

The Alps, mountains with nearly impassable peaks, have protected Italy from mass invasions. The lower slopes provide pastureland for goats and cattle. They are also the source of the Po River, in which valley civilization in Italy began.

to uncover the ruins of ancient cities. They carefully sift the soil through fine screens to be sure to recover the tiniest broken pieces of pottery.

Today, archaeologists use two major methods of excavation: (1) They remove one layer of remains at a time so they can study the complete civilization before digging deeper to uncover the next city. (2) They cut a trench through successive layers in a selected section, called a *trench cut*. This allows them to learn about all the civilizations that were located in a tell. However, it is not the best method because so much can be damaged by cutting a trench. Since it is sometimes difficult to raise money for archaeological work, this is often the method archaeologists are forced to use, as it is faster.

Anthropologists are more interested in the people of these ancient civilizations than in the ruins they left behind. They study physical features of any skeletal remains and attempt to trace their race and origin. People, whether living today or in ancient times, are of primary concern to the anthropologist.

Geography and Geology. Two companion disciplines which contribute a great deal to the historian's resource material are geography and geology. Geography is a science that deals with the earth and its life. It especially studies the physical description of land and sea and the distribution of plant and animal life in these areas.

Geography is an important key to understanding history. Almost every great civilization has had mountains nearby to provide sources of water for lakes and rivers, protection from enemy attacks, and resources such as iron and copper. For example, streams originating in the mountains of central Africa feed the White and Blue Nile Rivers which empty into the larger Nile River. The Nile River provides all the water for the people of Egypt, and without it the ancient civilization would not have survived.

The Po River originates in the Alps and is warmed from the air around the Adriatic Sea. Those living in the temperate zones were able to spend less time protecting themselves from the cold and more time developing the fine arts and culture. In these examples we can see that the area where people live helps to determine the direction their civilization will take. People who live on flat, fertile plains will form a different outlook and character from those people who live in barren mountains, isolated valleys, or in other geographic environments.

Geology is the science that deals with the study of the earth and life recorded in the rocks and fossils. A knowledge of geology helps us to know if an area is likely to have earthquakes, why river beds change, how glaciers move, if there will be enough water, and many other features of an area. It is through geology that we learn if a civilization had a natural foundation of minerals in the soil, a spongy soil, or a solid rock base. These conditions would determine whether the people of a civilization would be farmers, herders, hunters, or even nomads.

Biology. The science that studies living organisms is called biology. Biology helps the historian answer questions on how people developed different skin coloring and the effects of disease on a society. Biology also explains how people exist and survive in their environment. Since these are all questions related to a civilization's life style, they should be considered in the study of history.

Economics. The science that deals with the way goods and services are produced, distributed, and used is called economics. An economic system may be based on a simple exchange of goods, or it might be more complicated. Today we use money, credit cards, mortgages, and loans.

Different people have used many items for barter, exchange, or money. Such things as leather-backed turtle shells, semiprecious stones, bars of gold, and rings of silver have been used in various economies. The idea of minted coins was first introduced about 4700 years ago, with paper money coming into existence somewhat later. The rise, development, and fall of almost every civilization has depended greatly on its economic policies and trading problems.

Political Science. A study of political science tells how governments are established, the way they operate, and what different types of agencies exist within a civilization. The earliest form of government was the family unit. This expanded to the clan, village, city, and state as the population grew. Before understanding why people act the way they do, we have to know something about the political side of their history.

Many different types of government have been tried throughout history. *Streams of Civilization* discusses each type, such as a monarchy, democracy, or communism (and the nations that practiced them). By studying these governments and the way they have affected the peoples of the world, we are better able to understand the world around us.

Another study in the field of political science is *diplomacy*. Diplomacy is the study of the relationships between governments and peoples. It shows us actions which cause war, develop trade, and bring peace. The study of diplomacy helps us understand what we can expect as the result of actions taken by governments.

We have all heard the statement, "History repeats itself." Therefore, it is important to learn as much as possible about the way people lived in the past. Through political science we can understand why people and governments act the way they do. The one major lesson of history is that people have behaved in much the same way throughout the ages. Basic problems and human needs have remained the same.

Civilizations have always had some means of monetary exchange. These coins from Thebes in ancient Greece are decorated with a Boeotian shield on one side and a wine jar symbolizing the god Dionysus on the other. The shield was a symbol of the Boeotian League, a group of Greek cities with Thebes as the leader.

Mountains, rivers, and deserts form natural barriers of protection and influence the growth of civilizations. By looking at this map you can see for yourself the directions people would choose when migrating, and how the boundaries of the nations were decided upon.

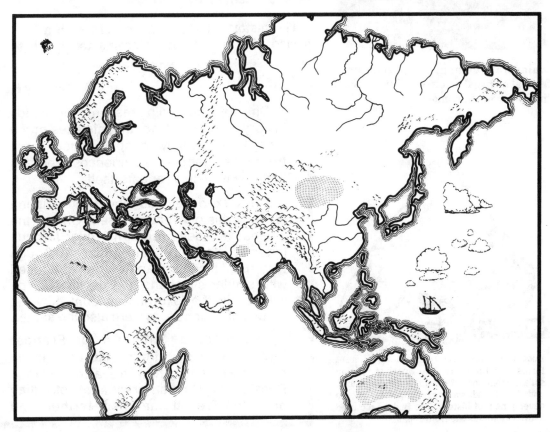

Malaysian demon; prepared for a festival or ritual ceremony. Buddists are firm believers in demons.

Buddha has been pictured in many different forms over the years. The Buddhist religion spread from India to Southeast Asia, China, and Japan and was very important in the development of history. The Buddha pictured above resembles one from Japan.

Religion. In this textbook the term *religion* refers to the worship of God or of gods and goddesses. From a civilization's religion came its ideas of what was right and wrong and its moral values. These religious ideas shaped the way people lived and treated each other, as well as how their civilization prospered.

We have also learned a great deal about education from a people's religion. From the earliest times to the present day, education was often handled by religious groups and organizations.

Historical Time Periods

The history of the world covers such a long period of time, it almost seems too much to learn. To make the study of history easier, historians divide history into three major time periods.

Creation to Current Events

Ancient History. This period begins with the appearance of the first human beings on our planet. Ancient history may be divided into two parts: (1) preliterate, or prerecords, the time before there were any written records; and (2) literate, the period after about 3000 B.C. when written records were kept. Most historians consider the end of the ancient period to be in the fifth century after Christ. The fall of the Roman Empire in the West (476 A.D.) was the final event in this time period.

History Repeats Itself

One of the main reasons we study history is to learn from the mistakes of the past. Unfortunately people seldom learn from other peoples' experiences. Perhaps that is why history repeats itself.

Many examples could be given pointing out how history repeats itself. One of the easiest to see concerns two famous leaders, Napoleon and Hitler. Although they ruled a century apart, they were faced with similar situations and decisions. You will see in the following account how the results of their actions were also the same.

Napoleon, as emperor of France, had conquered almost all of Europe except England. Then his army invaded Russia. The Russian army kept retreating and the French marched farther and farther into Russia. When the terribly cold Russian winter arrived, the French army was almost completely destroyed. Napoleon never recovered from this disaster and soon afterwards lost his throne.

Hitler was the dictator of Germany. He had conquered most of Europe except England. Then, instead of remembering what happened to Napoleon, Hitler invaded Russia. Once again the Russian armies began retreating and the Germans were pulled deeper into Russia. When winter arrived, the Germans were trapped in a conflict they could not win. Hitler was forced to continue sending men and supplies to Russia, which gradually weakened Germany's forces. Then Russia's allies invaded Europe. Like Napoleon, Hitler was defeated.

Medieval History. The Middle Ages, or the medieval period, has been so named because it falls between ancient and modern history. The date which often has been considered as the end of the medieval period is 1492. That was the year Columbus discovered America and the Moslems lost their last state (Granada) in Spain. Thus, the medieval period covers the years between approximately 500 A.D. and 1500 A.D.

Modern History. It is generally assumed in European and American schools that the beginning of the 1500s is the most suitable dividing line between medieval and modern history. All events occurring since that time are in the modern history time period.

Views of History

History is the study of things that are past. It also helps us understand what is happening in the world today. Some historians view history as a game with players, rules, and clever plans. The players are people of all civilizations. The rules are the many sciences, such as biology, geology, archaeology, and geography.

By studying people of the past and their planned "moves," we discover which moves lead to success or bring destruction. However, each person must first decide whether to be an active player in the game of history or a "pawn." As players, we try to improve the world in which we live. As pawns, we ignore the moves and decisions that others make which affect our lives.

Other historians see history as a stream. On the surface it appears to flow steadily onward, moving at will. Actually, however, it is slowed down, changed, and forced onward by strong undercurrents.

No matter what their viewpoint, historians agree that history *does* repeat itself. Human nature and life today are not much different from the way they were in the days of Noah, Caesar, or Kennedy. Decisions facing us today are much the same as ones that had to be made in the past.

The authors of *Streams of Civilization* realize the importance of examining the past. By doing this we are able to understand the present. In the pages that follow, we will explore many fields of study and ancient records. These are combined to present the story of man, beginning with his origin. It should become clear as you read this book that there are laws of the universe that always have been the same. You will also see that they are still operating today.

Some historians view world history as a game, illustrated here with the world as a chessboard. As portrayed by the players on the board, people from every civilization have participated in the game of history. Each player has used the various scientific disciplines, or fields of study, as rules. Throughout time players have studied the rules, developed strategies, and made their "moves." By studying these moves and the relationships of language, race, culture, war, and peace, players are better able to understand the world in which they live. Unlike chess game pieces, however, players in the game of history are not just "pawns," but are each responsible for their own actions.

New Perspectives

Historians are continually updating history textbooks to reflect the latest information. The pages entitled "New Perspectives" are designed to provide updated view points regarding previously held views of historical events or personalities.

The word, "History", came to us from the Greek scholars who went with Alexander the Great (pages 132-137) during his conquests of new lands. These scholars recorded details about the people in distant lands: their manners, dress, habits, foods, customs, and so forth. Among themselves, the scholars said, "This is exactly what we saw." That expression was given in one Greek word, "(h)istemi" which is pronounced "histame" with a long "a" and "e." "(H)istemi" meant "that which is" and in literature is translated by "is" or "are."

When the scholars made their final records for Alexander and the Greeks to read, they said, "History" referring to "that which is, or that is how we saw the people in various lands of conquest."

The science of Archaeology has changed our perspective in many areas. Bible scholars believe that man was intelligent from the day of creation. He communicated first with his Creator, and then with his wife and children (family). Archaeologists have <u>never</u> found a civilization wherein members did <u>not</u> communicate in some form of written patterns.

However, scholars who do not accept creation, believe that man had to learn how to communicate gradually, slowly, over the generations. So these writers use the word, "Preliterate" to tell readers that man did not (or could not) record his or her ideas from the beginning. Prior to the science of Archaeology, such teaching was largely unchallenged. But, now, artifacts from "digs" (archaeological excavations) have changed many ideas about man's past life styles.

Biblical history allows no time "before history began." There are no "pre-humans" on any records. (See pages 15-18 for a discussion of "Missing Links".) Remember: "A bone, whether whole or a fragment, is not a civilization unless culture is found with it." From the science of Archaeology, we learn that man always used fire, built houses as family homes, had music, used a written communication and practiced a belief system, or religion.

As archaeologists are uncovering civilizations farther away from the present, they are finding brilliant cultures with written communications as far down as they go. (See page 19 for a discussion about dating past civilizations.) Several ancient civilizations are dated to 8000 B.C. and even 10,000 B.C. as archaeologists dig level-by-level and identify artifacts. Archaeologists had to dig through a flood layer of water-laid silt at some sites in order to reach lower civilizations. Now that archaeologists are interpreting signs and symbols from ancient civilizations (as among the Olmecs, pp. 91-93), they are revising their perspectives of history. For example, archaeologists are now convinced that the Sumerians were not the first people to develop a written language. New perspectives on this topic are now found on page 33.

From these kinds of evidence, we know that mankind did not necessarily move through—the hunting stage—to pastoral—to domestication of animals—to sedentary and eventually to the age of technology. The Biblical record teaches how man left Noah's "Houseboat," immediately planted vineyards, established communities, built cities, and had the technology to build a high tower from bricks that were held together by bitumen. However, as groups of families migrated away from a crowded community, they carried tools with them. When those tools wore out, they used whatever materials they found to build a culture that controlled the environment around them. (For example, it may have been several generations before the families who settled around the Baltic Sea found iron and developed furnaces to design iron tools again.)

Modern archaeologists are continually finding data that supports the Biblical record regarding ancient civilizations. As usual, the ancient writings of the Bible are far ahead of those who are seeking to uncover the mysteries of past civilizations.

HOW DID IT ALL BEGIN?

Projects

1. Find at least three stories on how the earth and life began from either ancient cultures like the Egyptians and Greeks or from the American Indians, Chinese, or Africans. Compare these stories. Are they based on creationist or evolutionist beliefs? Explain.

2. Make a scale model, or drawing to scale, of Noah's Ark.

3. Do a study on floods, earthquakes, tornadoes, hurricanes, and volcanoes. Are they occurring as often or more often than they have in the past? Does this support the evolutionist's viewpoint that natural occurrences are continuing in the same way as they always have?

4. Write a story about cave people based on the facts given in this chapter. At the end of your story, state whether you agree that they were "barely human." Explain.

5. Do a study on "stone age" people who have been discovered in modern times. Check newspapers and magazines for reports. Why have these people not advanced further than they have?

6. Do a study on unusual events in the heavens, such as eclipses and Halley's Comet. How often do they reoccur? How do these past occurrences help scientists predict future events?

7. Do a study on the Great Redwoods of California. How old are they? Research any tree whose rings were marked after it died, to show its age and the historical events that happened while it lived. Tell about this tree, bringing pictures, diagrams, or models to explain.

8. Do a study on the Ice Caps. How do evolutionists say they were formed? How do creationists say they were formed? What do scientists say will happen if they melt? Where did water for Ice Caps come from? Explain.

9. Class project. Have a class debate on evolution and creation.

Words and Concepts

uniformitarianism
law of entropy
history's building blocks
clan
missing links
creationist
disciplines
civilization
catastrophism
omnivorous
evolutionist
tell
culture
king lists
carnivorous
diplomacy
trench cut
history's two functions
sediments
**Second Law of
    Thermodynamics**

How did it all begin? The system of Evolution claims that everything in the universe evolved by chance. The concept of special creation teaches that all matter and life was created with a purpose and in order by God. Above, the earth is seen photographed from the Apollo 13 spacecraft.

Fossil Ferns

In the Beginning

In studying the story of man, it is important to start with his origin—his beginnings on earth. There are many viewpoints about where the first person came from because no written records have been kept. There are also many questions which remain unanswered about this period of early history.

What happened to the dinosaurs and other strange creatures? Why has the earth changed so much? Who were the "cave men" and where did they come from? These are not easy questions and even scientists disagree on the answers.

In this chapter we will explore the facts of science and other fields of study in an attempt to answer these questions. We also will compare the two major ideas about man's beginnings—evolution and creation. As we travel through very early times, each person must make his own decision and answer for himself the question: "How did it all begin?"

Time Before Our Known Records

Before written history began, the world must have been very different from the way it is today. There were probably no arctic areas with freezing temperatures and no arid desert areas. Strange creatures, such as giant dinosaurs and great flying reptiles, lived on the earth. How do we know about these very early things? Remains of these and other extinct animals have been discovered by archaeologists.

Fossil Findings. We know the arctic regions were once warmer because bones of thousands of animals have been excavated from now frozen soils. Fossils of elephants and other such animals have been found, in some instances,

with flesh still on their bones and food still between their teeth.

Fossils are any remains or traces of animals or plants that have been preserved in the earth's crust throughout the ages. Fossil remains of tropical plants also have been found in these arctic regions. Surely there have been great changes in the world.

Two Explanations—

Beliefs Not Theories

There are two major explanations about very early events and how the earth began.

Giant elephants, called mammoths, once roamed the forests and grasslands of the earth. Remains of these extinct animals have been found in arctic regions, the United States, and parts of Europe.

They are known as Special Creation and Evolution.

In *Streams of Civilization* we will not refer to either viewpoint as a theory. A scientific theory can be proved or disproved by actual testing and measuring. This is not possible with either evolution or creation. Scientists cannot see or test events that took place in the distant past. They cannot prove without a doubt how the earth and all life began. Therefore, we will refer to creation and evolution as concepts, models, beliefs, or systems. Those who believe in evolution are called evolutionists, and those who believe in creation are called creationists or creationist scientists.

Since neither evolution nor special creation can be proved by science, a person must simply believe in one or the other. Each, therefore, is a *faith*. Both require faith or belief because they are based on events of the past that cannot be verified one way or the other. It is just as scientific to believe that God created the earth as it is to believe that it was not created by God. Neither belief can be tested scientifically.

Evolution. The general concept of evolution has been found in many religions and philosophies of the world, both ancient and modern. In its current form, however, it dates back to 1859 when Charles Darwin, a young theological graduate, published the famous book entitled *The Origin of Species by Natural Selection*. Since then, scientists and non-scientists have tried to find ways to prove his ideas.

According to leading evolutionists, matter in some form has always existed. They believe that many changes have been occurring slowly over aeons of time. The earth, they believe, was formed from some kind of cosmic dust

The concept of Evolution claims that all life came from one cell. Evolutionists believe that this one cell gradually changed over billions of years into man and into every kind of plant, bird, and animal in the world.

cloud about four and a half billion years ago. Then by some unknown process, non-living chemicals in the seas evolved into a simple living cell about three billion years ago. This first cell has since evolved into the cells of every plant and animal that ever existed.

This evolutionary process in plants and animals is said to happen because of the processes of mutation and natural selection. A mutation is an accidental and unpredictable change in the reproductive material of a cell. Natural selection is the process by which nature weeds out individuals who in one way or another are less fit than others to survive and reproduce. Evolutionists estimate that perhaps four million years ago, one of these evolving lines produced human beings. Since that time, changes have been more in the cultures and economic systems of mankind than in man's body and brain.

When we use the term evolution in this book, it refers simply to the process of evolution. According to evolutionists, this process involves aeons of slow changes, mutations, and natural selection.

There are three main points that evolutionists use to support their beliefs:

1. Living things are similar in many ways. These likenesses include similarities in body form, in the first stages of embryonic growth, and in the chemicals of the blood and reproductive cells. These similarities exist, for example, between apes and men.

2. Changes in nature have always occurred. There are many examples of this. Varieties of dogs have been produced during the past 4,000 years from an original dog "kind."

Great numbers of mutations have been produced in the fruit fly, as well as in other plants and animals. The color of the "peppered moth" is known to have changed from a dominantly light color to a dominantly dark shade. This change occurred in England during the Industrial Revolution. As the trees became darker from the soot in the air, the moths' color gradually changed.

These changes were possible because of the different characteristics located in the gene pool of the moth. Other changes have occurred in some animals who seem to have some organs that have no useful function. Such organs are believed to be the remains of organs that were once useful to their ancestors. There is no doubt that there is a great amount of change taking place in nature.

3. The fossil record. Remains of plants and animals have been preserved in the rock formations of the earth's crust. These are said to represent former geological ages. Evolutionists

Charles Darwin wrote about the evolutionary process in his work, *The Origin of the Species by Natural Selection.*

Evolutionists claim the peppered moth of England is an example of evolution. The moth has changed from a light color to a dark one, as pictured here.

Evolutionists claim a fish gradually turned into a bird over a long period of time. The fossil record, however, has never revealed remains of any of the in-between, or *transitional*, stages of development that are pictured here.

believe that old rocks contain fossils from an early stage of evolution, and young rocks contain more recent, more complex life. Thus, evolutionists say, the fossil record shows the evolution of life over the ages.

Special Creation. Unlike evolutionists, creationists claim there is no natural process that explains the origin of earth or of life. The creation model defines a period of Special Creation. During this time all the stars and planets, all the plants and animals, and the first man and woman were supernaturally created by God.

The creationist agrees that many changes have taken place since that time. He knows that some of the created kinds of plants and animals even have become extinct. The creationist believes, however, that it is not possible for one living thing to evolve into a completely different kind of organism.

Interestingly, creationists use the same three main points as the evolutionists to support creation. They claim, however, that the evidence for creation is more substantial than the evidence for evolution. Creationist scientists explain their beliefs as follows:

1. The many likenesses in living things are to be expected if everything was created. Such a

Evolution vs. The Gospel of Christ

During the twentieth century, a number of scientists and religious leaders have sought to reconcile the teachings of Biblical Christianity with the teachings of Darwinian evolution. However, a growing number of people who believe in the gospel of Jesus Christ are finding that evolutionary beliefs undermine their Christian faith.

When a person accepts the theory of evolution they are forced to conclude that the story of Adam and Eve's fall into sin, as recorded in the Holy Bible, is a myth. Consequently, Jesus looks very foolish for coming to the earth to save people from the myth of original sin. Indeed, evolutionary teaching requires individuals to fictionalize major portions of the Bible that talk about sin, creation, and Jesus as Savior.

It is proper to conclude, therefore, that the teachings of true Biblical Christianity are incompatible with the teachings of evolution. Individuals must ultimately accept the Biblical view of origins or the evolutionary view of origins by faith. However, professing Christians would do well to remember the words of Jesus as he declared, "He who is not with me is against me;" Matthew 12:30a

(1)

(2)

Artists throughout the centuries have been fascinated by the creation and have pictured the beginning of life in many forms of art. These engravings, representing an unusual decorative style of the 1700s, were originally published during that time in a Bible. The engravings realistically present the creationists' view that God spoke the world into existence by saying: (1) "Let there be light," and (2) "Let the dry land appear."

Many varieties of dog "kinds" exist today. There is no scientific evidence, however, of a dog evolving into a different kind of animal.

master design would have to use similar organs, such as eyes and ears, if they were to be used for similar purposes, such as seeing and hearing and communicating with one another.

In addition to explaining the likenesses, the creation model also answers the question of why there are so many differences in living things. So far, evolutionists have not been able to show how such completely different features could have evolved by accident from the same ancestor.

2. Changes in nature do occur and the process of natural selection does operate. Such changes, however, take place within a "kind"; that is, dogs change into many varieties of dogs, but never into cats. These changes are horizontal, not vertically upward toward more complex kinds. Creationists agree that mutations also occur, but there never seem to be any "good" ones.

Natural selection operates to conserve the kinds of organisms as they were created. This process keeps the injuries which result from mutations from gradually affecting all the other individuals in a particular group of living things.

3. The many fossils that have been uncovered over the years are known as the fossil record. This record reveals to the creationist that there always have been differences between kinds of organisms. Nobody has ever found a series of fossils showing a gradual change of one kind of animal or plant into a different kind. Fossils have shown variations within a kind, but never stages of development into new kinds. These situations—variations within kinds and differences between kinds—are exactly what one would expect if creation were true.

In addition to their argument that the very evidences claimed by evolutionists are really better evidences for creation, creationists point to two important additional scientific evidences for creation. One is the scientific law of decreasing order (also known as the Second Law of Thermodynamics or the law of increasing "entropy"), according to which *every* system in nature tends to go downhill from order to disorder *unless* it has available (1) some kind of special "motor" to take in a surplus of ordering energy from outside and; (2) some kind of "blueprint" to guide this energy into orderly growth. Since the evolutionary process has neither such a mechanism to energize it nor program to direct it, creationists maintain that this scientific law makes evolution impossible. However, the law of decay is quite consistent with the idea of an originally perfect creation which is now running down, and so it fits the creation model easily.

The other special evidence for creation is the great complexity of living organisms. Even the simplest one-celled animal is far more complex than the most complex computer or spaceship or any other invention of mankind. It can be shown mathematically that such highly-organized systems almost certainly could never—in all the history of the universe—organize themselves by chance. That is, the number of different "events" of any kind that could ever happen anywhere in the universe in all of its history turns out to be far less than the number of events that would have to take place before even the simplest living thing could ever arise without anyone or anything to guide it.

Summary. Which belief—evolution or creation—fits these facts of science best is a decision you will have to make for yourself. Remember that neither belief actually can be _proved_ by science. In the following sections there are additional facts about evolution and creation. This information will give you a good foundation for your study of history.

Men, Monkeys and Missing Links

Regardless of when the universe came into being or how life began, people are interested in the nature of man's beginnings and early history. Evolutionists believe that apes and men evolved over many millions of years from some unknown apelike ancestor. Creationists believe that the first man and woman were created by God as human beings and that all people are their descendants.

To better understand man's beginning, scientists look for pieces of bone and other remains that might have belonged to a very early man. By examining these bones, scientists try to determine whether they came from an animal or a human. Bone findings reveal much information to scientists.

For example, if a skull or fragments of a skull are found, they are measured to determine the size of the brain. Even if only a very tiny piece is found, the size of the skull can be estimated. Also, the opening at the base of the skull (where the spinal cord is attached) shows whether or not the head was held upright. The eye sockets indicate what the face may have looked like. The shoulder sockets show whether the specimen walked upright or spent most of its time on four legs.

A jawbone and teeth are very important because no two animals have exactly the same kind of teeth or jaws. The size of the jawbone and teeth help the scientist determine what the specimen ate. It could be either _vegetarian_ (eating only vegetables), _carnivorous_ (eating only meat), or _omnivorous_ (eating both plants and animals).

The Cave Men

Since Darwin's time, many people have felt that the cave men of very early times proved the concept of evolution. If these early people seemed to be less than human, people thought they were in a stage of evolution between an apelike creature and man. For example, many books show the early cave people to be stooped and apelike in appearance. They claimed these cave men were the "missing links" in man's development. That is, they were believed to be an in-between, or _transitional_, stage in man's development.

Scientists today are aware that incorrect ideas about these early people have been published. They are taking a close look at the remains of these very early men. We will now examine some of the interesting evidence about these so-called cave men.

Neanderthal Man. The unmistakably human remains of the Neanderthal Man were first discovered in 1857 in Germany. Later other remains were found in France and Spain. In the past, the Neanderthal Man was thought to be the missing link between the ape and modern man.

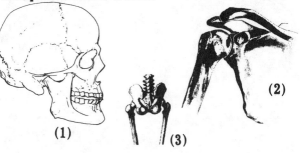

(1)   (2)   (3)

The stooped posture of some early men known as "Neanderthal" came from disease, not from ape-like ancestors.

Neanderthal Man (Skhul V). From Rusch's _Human Fossils_, in _Rock Strata and the Bible Record_, P.A. Zimmerman, Ed., Concordia Publishing House.

The shape of a skull (1) is not evidence of human intelligence, but its size can determine if it is _hominid_, or human. If a part of the skull is found, specialists can estimate the size of the brain capacity. Shoulder sockets (2) illustrate the position of the arms and whether the specimen walked upright on two legs or moved on four legs. The pelvic bones (3) indicate the sex and approximate age of a specimen. If parts of a thighbone socket are found, it can determine whether the specimen walked upright or spent most of its time on four legs.

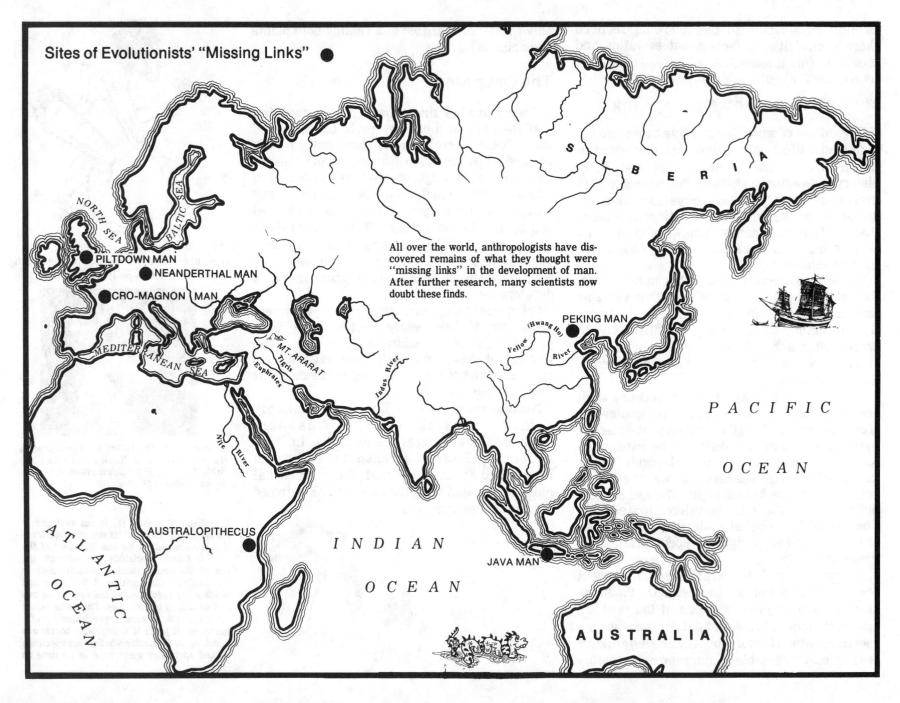

Sites of Evolutionists' "Missing Links" ●

All over the world, anthropologists have discovered remains of what they thought were "missing links" in the development of man. After further research, many scientists now doubt these finds.

Today both evolutionists and creationists agree that the Neanderthal Man is not that link. The remains of bones indicate he had a full-sized human brain. Evidence suggests he raised flowers, designed tools, painted pictures, and practiced a religion. Most anthropologists believe his stooped posture was due to a combination of arthritis and a lack of Vitamin D in his diet.

The Cro-Magnon Man. Another early cave dweller was the Cro-Magnon Man. Remains of this tribe were first discovered in 1868 in southern France. Other findings were discovered later in Switzerland, Germany, and in the province of Wales in Great Britain. Again, scientists now agree that Cro-Magnon is not a missing link, but a human being that looks much the same as we do today.

The Java Man. For many years the Java Man was considered to be the first human to walk upright on two legs. Bones were found by Dr. Eugene Dubois in old river gravels about a mile from Trinil, Java, in southeast Asia. About 1890 he found two teeth; the next year he found a skull cap and a thighbone at a different location. From these few remains, he concluded that he had found an ape-man, which he named *Pithecanthropus erectus.*

For thirty years anthropologists, including Dr. Dubois, studied and debated these findings. He and others finally decided the teeth were from an orangutan and the skull from a giant gibbon. A close look at the thighbone showed it came from a modern man.

The Peking Man. Between 1920 and 1930 a number of teeth and skull fragments were discovered near Peking, China. Only a few people examined them and they were thought to be very old. These bones disappeared while being shipped during World War II and there is little information about their age or origin.

Of those who examined the bones of the Peking Man, some believed they were from animals. Many anthropologists, however, believed that Peking Man and Java Man were both primitive human beings, living in a very primitive state of culture. They had a smaller brain than people today. These two early peoples walked upright on two legs and are, therefore, both often classed in the genus *Homo erectus.*

The Piltdown Man. In 1911 a discovery near Piltdown, England, created a sensation in the scientific world. Someone found ancient bones, and many thought that the supposed missing link between ape and man had been uncovered.

After almost forty years, however, it was discovered that some of the remains of this Piltdown Man had been chemically treated to make them appear old. It was also discovered that the different parts of the skeleton did not even come from the same creature.

Additional fossils of *Homo erectus* have recently been found in Australia. According to the standard evolutionary methods of dating, these findings are about 10,000 years old. This means they are younger than either the Neanderthal Man or the fossils of modern man.

Australopithecines. Much attention has been given to the work of Dr. Louis Leakey, his son Richard Leakey, and other scientists. While working in Africa, they have found many old bone fragments—portions of jaws, skulls, and many teeth. They claimed that they had found a prehistoric creature, a "near-man," whom they believed was the forerunner of man as we know him today.

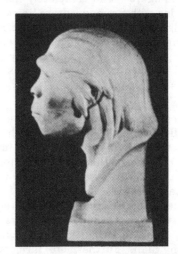

The tree-dwelling tarsier, a small mammal native to Southeast Asia, is known for its owl-like eyes and nimble hands. Because of its keen sight and facial structure, many evolutionists claim the kitten-sized tarsier is the common ancestor of apes and men.

Sinathropus pekinensis (so-called Peking Man). From Rusch's *Human Fossils,* in *Rock Strata and the Bible Record,* P.A. Zimmerman, Ed., Concordia Publishing House.

Zinjanthropus drawn by Neave Parker for Dr. L. S. B. Leakey. Copyright, *The Illustrated London News & Sketch, Ltd.,* 9/1/60.

The Leakeys found completely human remains with fire and culture items two levels below the Australopithecines. [Remember: Archaeologists dig down through levels. The artifacts they find level-by-level are dated older as the levels go deeper.]

Peking Man, according to authorities in the Beijing Museum, started with one tooth found in an apothecary shop (drug store). Davidson Black bought the tooth, traced it to caves near Chou-k'ou-tien, China where he discovered other kinds of teeth, bones and primitive tools. However, modern chinese men have the same kind of tooth as the so-called Peking Man. Furthermore, farmers in the rural areas of China today use the same kinds of tools that are now on display with the Peking Man exhibit in the Beijing Museum.

The so-called man that the Leakeys found was called *Australopithecus.* It supposedly lived two to three million years ago, walked erect, and used crude tools. Its brain was about the size of a gorilla's. Thus, people believed this was a true missing link between man and his apelike ancestors.

The archaeological work in Africa continues to attract much attention. Many anthropologists were convinced that *Australopithecus* was an evolutionary ancestor of man. More recent discoveries, however, have raised serious doubt about this belief. For example, Richard Leakey discovered more complete fossil remains which showed *Australopithecus* as having long arms

---

Piltdown Hoax

In Piltdown, England, some bones were found that scientists believed were the remains of the oldest man yet discovered. After studying these bones for almost forty years, the British Natural History Museum was forced to admit that the find was just a clever hoax. They announced that the jawbone was from a modern ape, probably an orangutan, that had been doctored with chemicals to make it look old.

Even though they now realize the jawbone was from an ape, scientists still believe that the skullcap is from an ancient man. Before they discovered the hoax, they thought the skull was 500,000 years old. Now they think it is 50,000 years old. Other scientists, however, believe that the dating methods are not accurate beyond 4,000 years B.C. For this reason they believe the skull is only a few thousand years old.

---

and short legs. He was not able to stand erect, but walked on the knuckles of his hands. Later a scientist named Oxnard made extensive studies of the *Australopithecines*. He claimed *Australopithecus* was some kind of extinct animal unrelated to man or ape.

Many very recent (1970-76) discoveries have been made in Africa. They reveal that creatures much like men of today were living in Africa at the same time as the *Australopithecines*, or possibly even earlier. They walked erect, used tools, were more than 150 cm (five feet) tall, and had fully human-type hands.

Summary. Evolutionists, such as the Leakeys, believe man's ancestors will be found someday. They agree that those once thought to be "missing links" do not actually fit in that category. Creationists, on the other hand, say that missing links have not been found because they never existed. Man was created as man and is not related to any animal.

Dating Methods

To record history it is important to know when a civilization or culture existed. The methods used to give ages to the many things found by archaeologists are called *dating methods*. By using several methods, historians can tell the dates of objects and artifacts back to about 1000 B.C. with reasonable accuracy. Beyond this, to about 2500 B.C., artifacts can often be dated with an accuracy of about 100 years (written 2500 B.C. ± 100 years). In this way events related to the artifacts can be given dates.

There are some serious problems involved in using dating methods, however. When scientists attempt to date objects before 2500 B.C., they often make major errors in the dates. Let us

The Metric System

The metric system, an international system of weights and measures, was legalized in this country by an Act of Congress on July 28, 1866. It was first established in France in the 1700s and has undergone many changes since that time. The SI (Systeme Internationale) method has replaced the more traditional metric systems and is the one currently approved by most countries of the world.

As the United States joins other nations in converting to the SI metric system, every effort is being made to introduce the system to the American public. It has been adopted by schools throughout the country, and students are learning to use metric measurements as they would a new language. The metric system, although difficult and confusing at first, is supposed to be simpler in the long run.

The following table of measurements give the metric symbols used in this textbook:

m - meter (1 m = 3.281 feet or 1.10 yards)
km - kilometer (1.609 km = 1 mile)
m t - metric ton (1 m t = 1.102 short tons)
cm - centimeter (2.54 cm = 1 inch)
ha - hectare (1 ha = 2.471 acres)
m² - square meter (1 m² = 10.764 square feet)
kg - kilogram (1 kg = 2.205 pounds)
°C - °Celsius (or Centigrade)
   $[°C = (°F - 32)(0.5556)]$
km² - square kilometers (1 km² = .386 square mile)

take a brief look at some of the major dating methods.

Sequence Dating. The method of dating a civilization by studying its pottery is called *sequence dating*. Sir Flinders Petrie found that every civilization's pottery was different, either in design, shape, or texture. When archaeologists are excavating a new site, they sometimes uncover pottery from a period of civilization they recognize. This can give them a fairly accurate idea of the age of the new culture. Sequence dating also tells how much trade went on between civilizations that existed at the same time.

Artifacts. An *artifact* is any simple object showing a person's workmanship. Many types of artifacts help historians date civilizations. For example, scarabs (signature seals used in Egypt) carried the name of the ruling pharaoh. Therefore, cities where these

Scarabs were used in Egypt as the pharaoh's signature on personal letters and government documents. Because these beetle-like seals bear the name of the ruling pharaoh, historians use them to help date events.

Sequence dating is a method of telling the age of civilizations. It is done by comparing the ages of pottery and other items discovered in various levels of a tell with items in other tells. For example, in this drawing pottery located in level two of tell A (counting from the top), level five of tell B, and level four of tell C indicates the civilizations that existed at the same time and probably traded with each other.

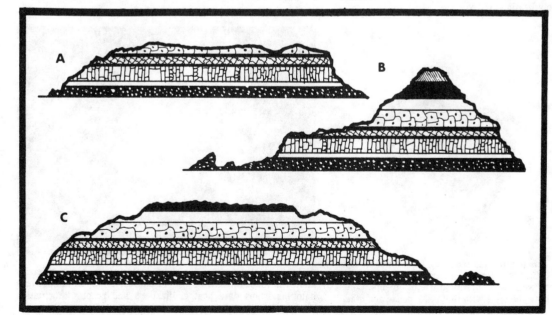

Historians in ancient civilizations recorded information by carving a document called a "king list" on a stone prism. This prism from Sumer in modern Iraq names ten kings — those who ruled before the Flood and those who ruled after the Flood. By comparing this list with king lists found elsewhere, historians and archaeologists can usually tell when a civilization existed.

This painted jar from Khafaje, dated c. 1900 B.C., indicates the potter's desire for beauty as well as his practical use of objects. Compare the style with that of Mycenae and other civilizations.

scarabs were found would have existed around the time of that pharaoh. Coins, stone tablets, or papyrus rolls also recorded information about rulers or events.

King Lists. King lists and orderly lists of events with dates (chronologies) reveal many stories about kings. King lists were written by historians of ancient civilizations and cultures. Comparing lists from different historians and areas has helped to develop more accurate dates for events. Some modern historians, however, have found reason to question the purposes and accuracy of these records. Many ancient historians exaggerated the facts because they wanted to make their ruler appear great and powerful. That is one reason why errors sometimes occur in modern accounts of ancient history.

Astronomy. Many ancient civilizations kept records of the movements of the stars and planets. This was done for religious reasons

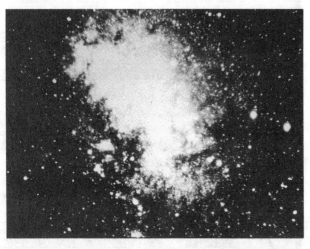

Astronomy, the study of the stars, is one of the oldest sciences known to man. Ancient records of unusual events in the heavens help historians date past civilizations and record information useful to us today.

> **The "Circa"**
>
> Archaeologists and historians often are unable to be exact when dating ancient artifacts and civilizations. This is especially true for objects that are older than 2000 B.C. When there is much doubt as to the age of their findings, scientists use the word *circa*, or c. with a date. This means "approximately" or "about" and the date given is the closest estimate.

rather than for science. Modern astronomers (scientists who study the stars), however, have found these old records very helpful. Unusual events such as eclipses of the sun or moon have always occurred and have been recorded throughout the world. A comparison of these records may help us decide which cultures existed at the same time.

Carbon-14 Dating. Scientists often help historians and archaeologists date civilizations by examining their findings. For example, when they are given remains of living things, certain scientists can estimate their age by a process called the *carbon-14 dating method*. Scientists have learned that all living things absorb a radioactive substance into their system from the air. This is called carbon-14 or radiocarbon. After anything dies, this radiocarbon decays at a known rate every year. The amount of radiocarbon left in the remains at a given time tells scientists how long it has been dead. For many years this seemed to be a good and accurate way to date ancient findings with only a five percent margin of error.

Today, however, many scientists are questioning the use of carbon-14 as a dating method, especially for very old remains.

The method may well be wrong. Many still use the radiocarbon method; however, some scientists and historians do not accept this method for dating items beyond 1000 B.C.

Potassium-Argon Dating. The decay of radioactive minerals in rocks provides another way of dating civilizations. Many of the objects found by archaeologists are in and around rocks. By showing the age of the rocks, people assume the deposit had the same age. One widely used way of determining how old rocks are is known as the *potassium-argon dating method*. Potassium is a metal-like element found in nature and argon is a gas. This method

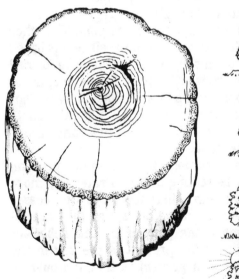

Tree-ring dating is one method scientists use to determine and date past events. The annual rings reveal many things in the growth of the tree itself. As this drawing shows, wounds, droughts, winds, and the thinning of woods all affect the life of a tree. Such factors make tree-ring dating less than perfect.

can only be applied to rocks that were formed by great heat, such as volcanic action.

The potassium in lava rocks and other igneous rocks changes slowly into argon. Scientists measure the amount of argon in a rock and compute how long it took the potassium to decay. Then they give an age to the rock. This method is widely used and many of the fossils found by the Leakeys have been dated in this way.

As with the carbon-14 dating method, however, scientists have learned that this potassium-argon dating method is also subject to great error. By studying the formation of new volcanic rocks, they have found that free argon gas often gets trapped in the rock. This happens when it is first formed and is not a result of the decay of the potassium. Therefore, many rocks appear old, but are not.

Tree-ring Dating. When a tree is cut down, you can see its growth in the form of circles, or rings, around the inside of the tree trunk. Scientists count and compare the growth rings of living trees with those found in trees used in ancient villages. From this information they have developed the *tree-ring dating method*. It is based on the findings of the long-living tree known as the bristlecone pine.

Today the tree-ring dating method is being used to double check and revise the carbon-14 method. Even this method, however, is subject to error. Two or more rings may grow in a single year. Also, it is hard to compare patterns of rings from timbers of different times and places.

Summary. As you can see, it is difficult to determine the age of bones and other fossil remains. Many other factors also affect the accuracy of dating fossils. For example, bones found in a river bed or gravel pit may not be the

Any method of dating depends on the basic presuppositions or beliefs of the person who is designing and using the measuring system. No one gave the measurements of archeological levels, tree rings, potassium-argon levels in lava rock, or radiocarbon at the time of destruction. Formulas, created to suit the measurement, are designed with basic assumptions. One of them says, "All things today are the same as they have always been." This does not allow for the Flood and attendant changes. As discussed under "Uniformitarianism" on page 22, some scientists forget that rock "levels" are all mixed up with no rhyme or reason. Scientists who designed carbon-14 apparently based their formula on charcoal from cloth found at Jericho, which they thought was the oldest city. But archaeologists know that many cities in the Tigris-Euphrates River Valley are much older than Jericho. Furthermore, rays from the sun, moon, cosmic elements, or from water change chemical ratios for potassium-argon and carbon-14 dating.

The Leakeys did not date bone fragments by carbon-14. They dug lava rock from beneath bones and measured the rock by the potassium-argon method. Then the bones were given the same age as the date of that rock. Furthermore, the Olduvai Gorge where the Leakeys site was located is a watershed and all of the bones had been washed to the site by surging water which causes minerals to seep from objects.

So what do historians do with these problems? Historians gather all the data they can find, measure artifacts by as many methods as possible, compare with Biblical data as the foundation for time frames up to 100 A.D. and draw conclusions.

same age as the rocks around it. Erosion and earthquakes could have changed the landscape and the bones could have been washed there from another place. In general, the only really dependable way of determining dates is careful analysis of written records.

The History of the Earth

There is another aspect of history about which evolutionists and creationists have different beliefs. Evolutionists believe the earth is very old, with the records of many billions of years now found in the rocks of the earth's crust. These records are called the "geological ages," and they are believed to record the earth's long evolutionary history prior to the appearance of man on the earth.

Creationist scientists believe, on the other hand, that these rocks and the fossils found in them were formed by a great worldwide flood that occurred sometime after man had been created. In this view, the fossils do not tell of the gradual evolution of life over many ages, but rather of the rapid destruction of life in one age, the age before the flood.

Uniformitarianism / Catastrophism

Since the scientific method can be applied only to repeatable and observable events, it is not possible to prove scientifically which view is correct. One must study the rocks and fossils closely in order to decide which concept seems to explain the facts better. The first belief is called *uniformitarianism* because it depends on the idea that present-day geologic processes, acting more or less uniformly as they do at present, can explain how all these rocks were slowly formed over long ages in the past. The other belief is called *catastrophism* since it is based on the idea that a worldwide catastrophe formed most of these rocks. The most important part of the catastrophe was a great deluge of water, but it was also accompanied by gigantic earth movements, volcanic eruptions and other violent phenomena.

The main argument for the uniformitarian "model" is the feeling that it is safer and more scientific to assume that the earth's processes have always been more or less as they are today. A slogan made popular by this school of thought is that "the present is the key to the past." A second argument is that it would be necessary to have long ages in order for the evolutionary process to function adequately.

Catastrophists, on the other hand, insist that present-day processes could never account for the great mountains of the world, the vast expanses and thicknesses of sedimentary rocks, and numerous other features of the

Evolutionists believe the present is the key to the past. As pictured here, rainfall, erosion, volcanoes, and earthquakes similar to those today are believed to have formed the strata (layers) over billions of years. Creationists studying the erosion of the earth and formation of sediment in the oceans believe it occurred in a much shorter period of time.

earth—especially the great masses of fossilized plants and animals that were buried in these rocks. Only a worldwide flood could explain them, they maintain. They show that no normal modern process is sufficient to cause any of the earth's geologic features and, therefore, that just about every rock formation in the earth must have been produced by at least a local flood or other catastrophic event. Furthermore, they point out that, since the geologic data do not show any worldwide time-breaks in rock-forming processes, such processes were going on at least somewhere in the world all the time. Since each particular unit was formed rapidly, and since each unit is followed by another one without a time gap, therefore, the entire assemblage of rocks supposedly representing the geological ages must have been formed rapidly, in what would amount to a worldwide flood.

According to the uniformitarian system, man completed his physical evolution perhaps about three million years ago during the famous Ice Age, which is believed to be the most recent of the geological ages. During this period great sheets of ice crept over much of North America, down as far south as the northern states in the United States and corresponding latitudes in Europe. Most geologists believe that the continental glaciers advanced and retreated three or four times during this period.

The Paleolithic ("Old Stone") Age. One strange aspect of the evolutionary model is that, although man completed his biological evolution perhaps three million years ago, he did not begin his cultural evolution until about ten thousand years ago, after the last retreat of the glaciers. Perhaps the rigors of the Ice Age kept him from making more progress. During all this time, he lived merely by hunting animals and gathering fruits and nuts, using only the crudest of chipped-stone tools and weapons. This period of culture is called by archaeologists the Paleolithic ("Old Stone") Age.

The Neolithic ("New Stone") Age. This period of time started perhaps ten thousand years ago at which time people began to raise crops, domesticate animals and live in organized villages. Their tools were now made of shaped stone and they began also to make pots and other utensils of clay. Soon afterwards they learned how to use metals; the Bronze Age and Iron Age then quickly followed. Writing was invented and great cities began to be organized. After over a million or more years of evolutionary stagnation, civilization suddenly appeared.

The Flood. The uniformitarian beliefs do not include a worldwide flood. However, early nations and tribes from all parts of the world have traditions of such a flood at the beginning of their histories, and creationists believe these records must be taken seriously. Such a flood would explain the geological evidences of

Named for George Bird Grinnell, this glacier was discovered by him in 1887. Located in Glacier National Park, its estimated thickness is 122-152 m (400-500 feet).

Explosive Evidence for Creation

An extremely important geological event happened in the year 1980, as a major volcanic eruption took place in the state of Washington at Mt. Saint Helens. The eruption of this volcano was so violent that it knocked down millions of trees, laid down numerous tons of strata, changed the flow of rivers, and formed several large canyons. These massive geological changes, which took place in just a few days, provided geologists who believed in catastrophism with significant evidence to prove that formations such as the Grand Canyon, did not require millions of years to develop. Creation scientists have long believed that the complicated geological formations that are now present in the earth, were created by sudden and violent catastrophes.

However, it was not until after scientists had studied the results of the Mt. Saint Helens eruption that conclusive evidence was available to support the theory that complicated geological formations could be formed in days versus millions of years. This new data directly challenges the fundamental principle of evolution that presupposes that organic and inorganic matter developed gradually over millions of years.

worldwide catastrophism that were mentioned previously.

The most complete record of the flood, and the one evidently least changed by later word-of-mouth transmission, is the one found in the book of Genesis, in the Hebrew Bible. Certain flood stories preserved on stone or clay tablets, such as those of the Babylonians and Assyrians, have been excavated by archaeologists and dated earlier than the time of Moses, the traditional author of Genesis. However, these contain obvious mythological additions, and it is much more likely that the Genesis record contains the original and true account.

According to this Hebrew record, all the basic kinds of plants and animals, as well as the first man and woman, were directly created in the beginning. The original world was a perfect world, with abundant provision for every need of man and the animals. This all changed, however, when the first man and woman (named Adam and Eve, according to the Hebrew record) rebelled against their Creator, and God had to introduce the law of decay and death into the world, partly as punishment and partly to make men and women recognize their helplessness without God. This law is a universal law which scientists have in modern times called their "law of entropy," describing how every system tends to go down from order to disorder. Everything tends to wear out, run down, grow old and die.

As human populations grew, their wickedness became so great that God finally had to destroy them all with the great flood. Only the patriarch Noah and his family survived the flood, in a great vessel built by him at God's direction. From his three sons and their wives, according

to the Genesis record, all modern tribes have descended.

Most modern scientific creationists believe that the flood is a better explanation for the great fossil beds and sedimentary rock deposits than is the evolutionary system of geologic ages. By this explanation, all the great animals that have been found as fossils—even the dinosaurs—lived together with man in the pre-flood world. The different zones in these strata do not represent different evolutionary ages, as uniformitarians believe, but different ecological communities in the age before the flood.

It is not possible to discuss in this book further details of geological data and how they are explained in the two systems. Interested students can learn more about the evolutionists' interpretations in any of numerous standard textbooks on evolution or historical geology. The alternate interpretation — based on special creation and a worldwide catastrophic flood—can be studied in any of a number of modern treatments of scientific creationism. Both types of books should be available in your school library.

That the Genesis accounts of creation and the flood can be used as a scientific model does not necessarily mean they are divinely inspired. The question of their religious authority is an entirely different problem, which must be settled elsewhere. The point we should notice here is simply that creationist scientists are convinced that these historical accounts are at least as scientific as the idea of evolution in their ability to fit all the actual facts, regardless of whether or not the Bible has any religious authority.

The Dispersion. In contrast to the evolutionary belief that the cultures of early people evolved slowly during several million years, creationists believe the evidence indicates human tribes and nations are only several thousand years old and that man was civilized right from the start. Immediately after the flood, human populations were very small, so it was not possible to develop complex societies. Even though people knew how to raise crops, work metals and build houses, they could not do any of these things for several generations. They first needed to have a large enough population and also to find new sources for metal, building materials and other resources. Furthermore, as people gradually migrated and spread out around the world, each tribe would have to go through the same cycle. First they would have to live off the land by hunting and gathering, living in whatever shelters they could find and using only crude wooden and stone tools. After some time, the tribe would be able to develop stable food supplies, both crops and herds. They would also locate metallic ores, suitable clays and other materials, and eventually establish a stable, self-sufficient society. This would take many years, and possibly several generations. It is not surprising, therefore, that archaeologists often find evidence of an "Old Stone Age" first, then a "New Stone Age" after that, and then a "Bronze Age" and so on. This need not mean an evolutionary growth in intelligence, but only the growth of a tribe in numbers and resources.

Furthermore, evidence is growing to support the idea that even the so-called "Old Stone Age" people had much more technical skill than many people have thought in the past. Although they may have lived in caves, they painted excellent pictures, raised flowers, used medicines, wore complex clothing, and used involved symbols in their inscriptions. In fact, there is so much

Noah's Ark

An Artist's Rendering of Noah's Ark

An important link to ancient civilizations, Noah's Ark is believed by many people to be hidden in a glacier on Mt. Ararat in eastern Turkey. Extremely large and unusually made, this ark would be a sensational find. The Bible says that Noah was divinely directed to build a boat in an area where there was no known water. The dimensions of the boat were to be approximately 140 m (450 feet) long, 23 m (75 feet) wide, and 14 m (45 feet) high (assuming that the "cubit" mentioned in the Hebrew record was 18 inches, or 46 cm) with three levels of deck space. A window opening was to be placed around the top of the ark for air and light. These dimensions indicate that the ark was large enough to hold 569 railroad stock cars. Figures have shown that two of every known species of land animal, living or now extinct, could have been housed comfortably in less than half of the ark's space.

This fragment of an ancient tablet, found in Nineveh and dated c. 650 B.C., gives the Assyrian version of a worldwide flood. Similar accounts of a flood have been uncovered in the literature of every major civilization since 1400 B.C.

evidence now to show that very ancient people were highly skilled that some people have jumped to the conclusion that they must have come by spaceship from some more civilized planet out in space. This idea, however, is not accepted by scientists, either creationists or evolutionists, because of the overwhelming problems it entails. It is also a needless idea if we accept the possibility that ancient men on the earth were very intelligent and skilled, as the creation model suggests.

The Ice Age. Many of these early tribes lived during the Ice Age, and for those who lived near the ice sheets, life must have been very difficult. For those who were able to establish their settlements in warmer regions, there was evidently plenty of rain, and great civilizations developed in regions that now tend to be very arid.

In the creationists' view, the Ice Age was caused by the change in worldwide environment brought about by the flood. They feel there is no good reason to think the Ice Age lasted more than about a thousand years—not several million years, as evolutionists think. The continental ice sheets covered the lands nearer the arctic at the same time that great civilizations such as those of ancient Egypt and Sumeria developed nearer the equator.

The book of Genesis in the Bible, as well as ancient traditions from a number of other sources, has an interesting explanation of what caused the first group of people after the flood to break up into different tribes and nations scattered throughout the world. This migration has been difficult for evolutionists to explain since it would have been to their advantage for early peoples to stay close together and cooperate if they could.

However, they could only work together if they could communicate with each other. According to the Hebrew record, people lived together after the flood for several generations, finally settling on the Euphrates River and building the first city at ancient Babylon. Because of their wickedness, especially in building a great temple tower where they could worship the stars and sun, God miraculously "confused" their languages so that only the members of each family could talk with each other. When they could no longer work together, they finally scattered by clans into different parts of the world where each group could then develop its own distinct culture.

Evolutionists do not accept this record. However, they do not yet have any other satisfactory explanation as to how different tribes and languages could ever develop from the common ancestral population of early people. To believe that each nation—and especially each "race"—developed its own language and distinct physical features by being separated from others for scores of thousands of years (as the usual ideas of evolutionary change would require) would lead to *racism,* the belief that some "races" have evolved further than others.

The Beginning of Written History. Once we reach the time when the first written records began to be made, there is no longer much question about the further course of history. Both creationists and evolutionists work with the same records, although their interpretations of them differ somewhat.

The rest of this book tells about the different groups of people—or "streams of civilization"—that made and recorded history after the very early dispersion. The way in which we interpret the meaning of all these

Flood stories told by every known society in the world is one of the greatest evidences for Noah's Flood. There had to be a common source. As you read about migrations at different places in this text, remember that the people carried the "Flood Story" with them. Each group of people eventually modified the boat into one like their style. One of the more interesting remnants of the Flood story is found in Sulawesi, Indonesia. (The Toraja community in and around Rante Pao.) The Toraja people believe that Noah was one of their ancestors. He and his family--there are always eight people who lived through the Flood Story-- landed in the Toraja area. So they have built their homes in the shape of a boat resting on beams as though it is on water.

The Dinosaur Mystery

Dinosaurs have fascinated people since their gigantic bones were first discovered over a century ago. Evolutionists believe the dinosaurs died out about 70 million years before people evolved, although they have never been able to figure out what caused their extinction.

However, there are many evidences that human beings lived at the same time as the dinosaurs. Most ancient nations have traditions of great dinosaur-like reptiles called dragons that lived at the beginnings of their histories. Pictographs of dinosaurs have been discovered on walls of canyons and caves.

Along the Paluxy River in Texas, many fossil footprints of dinosaurs have been found in the same limestone rocks where human footprints have been found. In some places the trails of human footprints and dinosaur prints cross each other, and there are even a few places where the human tracks are directly on top of the dinosaur tracks.

Most creationists believe that the dinosaurs were directly created at the same time as men, so that humans and dinosaurs did live together for many years. However, they believe most of the dinosaurs died in the great Flood.

records of migrations, wars, the rise and fall of different nations, and other events of history will depend largely upon what we believe about the very beginnings of history.

That is, were people originally created by God or did they evolve naturally from some animal ancestor? The answer to this question largely determines whether or not we can discern real meaning and significance to history, or whether it is all essentially a record of chance happenings and struggles for existence with no particular goal except what man can make of it for himself.

In this chapter we have tried to outline some of the evidences on each side of this vital question, so that each person can decide for himself or herself what to believe and how to live.

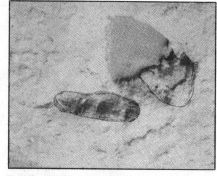

Fossils found in rock formations are evidence of the past. The above man and dinosaur tracks were found side by side in limestone along the Paluxy River in Texas, indicating both lived at the same time.

After the year-long Flood, the Ark landed on dry land in a drastically changed earth. As depicted in this drawing, the animals were freed to start life on the earth again.

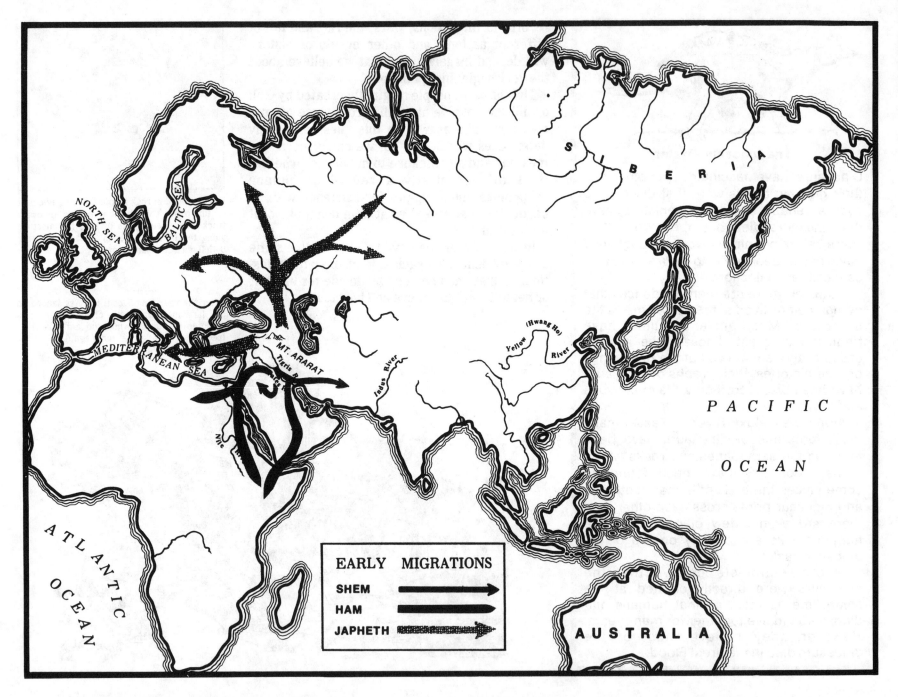

DAWN OF CIVILIZATIONS

Projects

1. Read a book or do a study about the search for Noah's Ark. Give a report on what you have learned. Why is the ark so hard to find?

2. Write a story based on the events at the Tower of Babel.

3. Invent a written language. Use symbols for letters like we do in our alphabet, or use pictographs or cuneiform symbols to represent entire words. Use your new language to write a letter to your teacher.

4. Do a study on the importance of laws. Why do the poor need special laws to protect them? Do rich people in the United States get better treatment?

5. Examine the Sumerian custom of having more than one wife. Do you feel this is a good idea?

6. Do a report for the class telling about Queen Shubad. Who was she and what is known about her life?

7. Do a report on Alexander Cunningham's life and work. Do you think we would know as much about ancient India if he had not lived?

8. Do a report on Imhotep. For what was he famous besides building pyramids?

9. What were the Seven Wonders of the Ancient World? Why do you suppose these monuments were chosen and not others? Are there other things you feel should be added? Draw or make a model of your favorite.

10 The Nile River flows north. Is this unusual? Name other rivers that flow north. What causes rivers to run in a certain direction?

Words and Concepts

Mesopotamia
dispersion
aristocrat
Vedas
dynasty
Fertile Crescent
ziggurat
polytheism
cataract
hieroglyphics
city-states
Sargon
Sanskrit
Etesian Winds
cartouche
cuneiform
exposure
scribe
nomes
sphinx

Double-headed, spiral pins have become a guide to the direction of the western migrations. They have been found along the shores of the Black Sea and in central Europe.

The first homes for Noah and his descendants would have been the available caves in the Mt. Ararat region as shown in this photograph.

The search for Noah's Ark has been made difficult because Mt. Ararat consists of two mountain peaks — greater and lesser Ararat. At the base of the mountain the remains of cultures not yet identified have been discovered.

This picture was taken by John Morris, who led the Institute for Creation Research expedition in 1972 to look for Noah's Ark.

Dawn of Civilizations

As we have seen, there are two views of the origin and early history of life on earth, evolution and creation. The evolutionary viewpoint sees man as the product of natural causes and chance. His further development through social and cultural changes is, therefore, also brought about fundamentally by operation of natural causes.

The creationist viewpoint, on the other hand, sees history in terms of God's purpose for the world and mankind. The first man and woman were specially created, and the events of human history can all be studied in terms of their relation to this plan.

In this book you will see how civilization and nations came into existence, flourished, and then faded away or were taken over by others. Whether their respective histories were controlled by chance or by a divine plan, it will be helpful for us to study them in relation to the future of our own nation and the other nations of

the modern world. This will help us to recognize our own problems and then, perhaps, to avoid the weaknesses that destroyed great nations of the past.

Two Models of Human Development

According to the evolution "model," man had completed his biological evolution from one to four million years ago. Further changes have produced the different races of men, as well as changes in cultures and technology. Evolutionists have interpreted the anthropological and archaeological findings to teach that human societies have evolved successively through a very long Stone Age, and then through much shorter Bronze and Iron Ages into a fully civilized state, perhaps about 6 to 8 thousand years ago. Occupation sites have been found in all continents which have been dated by the radiocarbon or other dating methods at well over 10,000 years old. It is significant, however, that all these older sites reflect a Stone Age culture. The earliest evidences of real civilization seem to be in the Middle East, somewhere near the Tigris-Euphrates Valley only a few thousand years ago.

The creationist agrees with the evolutionist that the earliest civilizations began a few thousand years ago in the Middle East. However, as discussed in the last chapter, he does not believe that the Old Stone Age lasted a million or more years. Rather, he interprets the archaeological and anthropological data as teaching that there was a very brief "stone-age" type of culture at each new occupation site as the different tribes of men were migrating around the world following the great Flood. As soon as each tribe could settle down in a more or less fixed location, it would usually, in only a few generations, develop its own civilization.

To the creationist, all such archaeological sites and evidences of developing civilizations should be dated since the Flood, which destroyed all earlier people and their civilizations, leaving any possible remains buried deep in the sedimentary rocks of the earth's crust. The large ages inferred from potassium and radiocarbon dating for such sites are all corrected to dates since the Flood.

For those who accept the validity of the Biblical histories, all the inhabitants of these ancient archaeological sites, as well as all present-day men and women, are descendants of the three sons of Noah (Shem, Ham and Japheth) who, with their wives survived the Flood in a great Ark built by Noah. The Ark landed on Mount Ararat (located on the eastern border of modern Turkey) and it is from that region that human migrations began.

Migrations

Since fossil remains of true man have been found in all continents dated far earlier (by evolutionary methods of dating) than the earliest written records or other evidences of civilization, evolutionists have not yet been able to develop a clear picture of the dates and routes of early migrations. There is still a difference of opinion as to where the first men evolved, although probably most evolutionists believe it was in southeast Africa. Dr. Richard Leakey has dated fossils of *Homo* found in this region as four million years old or more.

Neanderthal and Cro-Magnon sites in Europe have been dated at over 50,000 years ago, occupation sites in North America at over 15,000 years ago, and even in Australia at 10,000 years ago. There is evidence that migrations followed the Bering and Malaysian land bridges when the sea levels were lower during the Ice Age. Otherwise, however, there are few definite indicators of such prehistoric migrations, as far as evolutionary interpretations are concerned.

The highly questionable nature of Piltdown Man (England), Peking Man (China) and Java Man (Indonesia) has convinced most modern evolutionists that man completed his evolution

Games and toys from ancient Babylon tell about the life of people living at that time. All people have games and forms of recreation.

Reconstruction of the *Australopithecus robustus (Zinjanthropus)* skull.

in Africa shortly before the Ice Age and then spread around the world fairly rapidly during the Ice Age. However, the development of the first real civilization took place among the peoples in the Middle East. After this, civilization spread almost immediately into Europe, North Africa and Asia, and soon after that into America.

The creationist interprets these data in almost the same way as the evolutionist, as far as the spread of civilization is concerned. However, he believes all the "earlier" sites (Neanderthal, etc.) can likewise be included in the migrations from Ararat and Babel after the Flood and the Dispersion. The first waves of migration included those people who were less capable of rapid cultural advances, since the stronger and more industrious groups had settled in the fertile regions nearer the center of dispersion. The great ages used by the evolutionists, of course, must all be drastically reduced to fit within the post-Flood period, but scientific reasons for believing this can be done have been discussed in the preceding chapter.

Zinjanthropus drawn by Maurice Wilson for Dr. Kenneth P. Oakley. Used by permission of Dr. Oakley.

As far as the Biblical histories are concerned, these migrations took place primarily after the confusion of tongues at the Tower of Babel. There were three main streams of civilization flowing out from this region—the Semitic, the Hamitic and the Japhetic. Even evolutionists recognize these three groups of peoples, but they do not regard them as including all the peoples of the world. The Bible record does say that *all* men are descended from Shem, Ham and Japheth, but it is difficult now to be sure which nations correspond to each of these.

Genetic Changes in Early People

One of the most difficult problems for evolutionists to explain is the evolution of the different races. Assuming that all the modern tribes and races developed from a common ancestral stock that evolved, say, in Africa, how did the original population develop into such distinctively different varieties of men?

Evolution is believed to proceed through the processes of mutation, natural selection, recombination and segregation. If races developed in this way, it would seem to require a long period of segregation of the population before the mutation and selection processes could generate the new racial characteristics in order to get these really established in the population. Many evolutionists estimate that at least 50,000 years of segregation would be required to get a new race established.

The problem with this is that such a long period of segregation—long enough to generate a new skin color, say—would also be long enough to generate different mental and physical abilities. Thus, some races might well have so evolved as to be superior to others. This concept can easily lead to racism. Very few evolutionists are actually racists, of course, and there is no evidence that the different races do indeed show different mental or physical abilities. Nevertheless, this seems to be a serious problem for evolutionary theory.

The creation model seems to provide an easier explanation. According to this view, all the potential physical characteristics of all peoples were already present (by creation) in the genetic systems of the survivors of the Flood. Most of these characteristics were not outwardly expressed, however, as long as the entire population lived together and intermarried, with a free flow of genes. Only the "dominant" characteristics would be apparent, with the "recessive" characteristics being merely carried in the genes.

However, it has been shown in scientific studies in genetics that there are three factors which are able to cause the rapid appearance of new varieties in a species: (1) rapidly changing environment; (2) small population; (3) inbreeding. No mutations are required at all, and therefore, no great length of time is required. Under these conditions, characteristics which were recessive in the large population can quickly become dominant in a small population.

As the different family groups dispersed from Babel because of the confusion of tongues that God produced there, all three of the above factors would have been operating. It would have taken only a few generations for each clan (later to become a tribe or nation) to develop distinct physical characteristics of its own to go with its own distinct language.

These tribal characteristics may well have included distinct skin colors, eye colors, physical stature, etc. It is not really proper to call them *racial* characteristics, however since the term "race" suggests an evolutionary unit in the process of evolving into a new species. It is significant that the word "race" does not appear in the Bible. As far as the Bible records are concerned, all men are closely related by common descent from Noah only a few thousand years ago. There is only one race—the human race.

The Fertile Crescent

The area of Mesopotamia was part of a great curving plain known as the Fertile Crescent. This plain was one of the few areas in the Middle East with enough water to allow successful farming. Three rivers provided water for the Fertile Crescent. The two major rivers were the

New Perspectives

Records from archaeologists keep changing history textbooks. From the documents of archaeologists, we learned about Urartu, a civilization that was started at the base of Mt. Ararat circa 3500 B.C.. They had a language, rulers, laws and a highly developed culture showing skills of people. Urartu was in the northern Tigris-Euphrates Rivers valley (present Iraq and Iran). Other smaller nations with their own government and rulers, homes and education, cities and laws were in Haran (Aram in Armenia), the Mari, and Nuzu.

All the people on the earth have different facial characteristics and skin coloring. However, because of their many similarities and other findings, scientists have concluded that everyone has a common origin.

Some people believe the Tower of Babel described in the Hebrew record was spiral shaped. The above tower located in Iraq stands as a reminder of the original one. Renaissance painters used this tower as their model for depicting the Tower of Babel, as illustrated in the etching below, taken from a medieval Bible.

Tigris and Euphrates, while the tiny Jordan River watered the area known today as Israel. The climate in the Fertile Crescent was hot and there was little rainfall. Only the waters from the rivers enabled farming to flourish there.

Old Sumer

It was in the southeastern corner of the Fertile Crescent that Sumer, the oldest known civilization in the world, developed. Many scholars believe that Nimrod, one of Ham's grandsons, founded this civilization.

Government. At first Sumer was a group of independent *city-states*. This means that every city was an independent state with its own ruler. The different states had no loyalty or unity with each other, and in many cases they would go to war against each other.

Early Culture. As the first civilization, the Sumerians are thought to have invented many things that were used by later civilizations. They were the probable inventors of the wheel, later used by potters to shape clay. They also were first to use a wheeled vehicle to help them move heavy objects and to put wheels on chariots of war.

The Sumerians were the first people after the Flood to develop a written language. About 3300 B.C. they drew pictures and symbols in a style called *pictograph*. By 2800 B.C. these picture-symbols had been changed into signs which represented syllables. They had around 600 different syllables. A scribe would write by pressing a pencil-like writing stick, called a *stylus,* into a soft clay tablet. The different symbols appeared rather wedge shaped and for that reason their writing is called *cuneiform*, which means wedge shaped.

From this early civilization came thousands of literary works, including myths, epics, narrative poems, hymns to the gods and heroes, writings on wisdom, proverbs, fables, and essays on many subjects. Perhaps one of their more interesting works was the Epic of Gilgamesh, which in many ways resembled the Hebrew record of the Flood.

Each Sumerian city was ruled by its local priests. The priests were not worshiped as gods, but the people believed they

The Tower of Babel

According to the Hebrew record, when descendants of Ham, Shem, and Japheth arrived at the Tigris-Euphrates, everyone spoke the same language. A great Hamitic ruler named Nimrod unified the peoples of the valley. They began to build a tower and a city that would keep all the people together. It is believed that Nimrod thought this tower would make him powerful enough to rule the world.

Suddenly something happened that stopped the construction. Men began speaking in different languages and could no longer understand each other. As a result, groups that spoke the same language moved to many different places in the world. The unfinished tower and city were later called Babel, meaning "confusion." Is it in this place that the famed city of Babylon was later built?

Creationists believe the confusion of languages was an act of God because He was displeased with what the people were doing. This supernatural event resulted in migrations and the beginning of other nations.

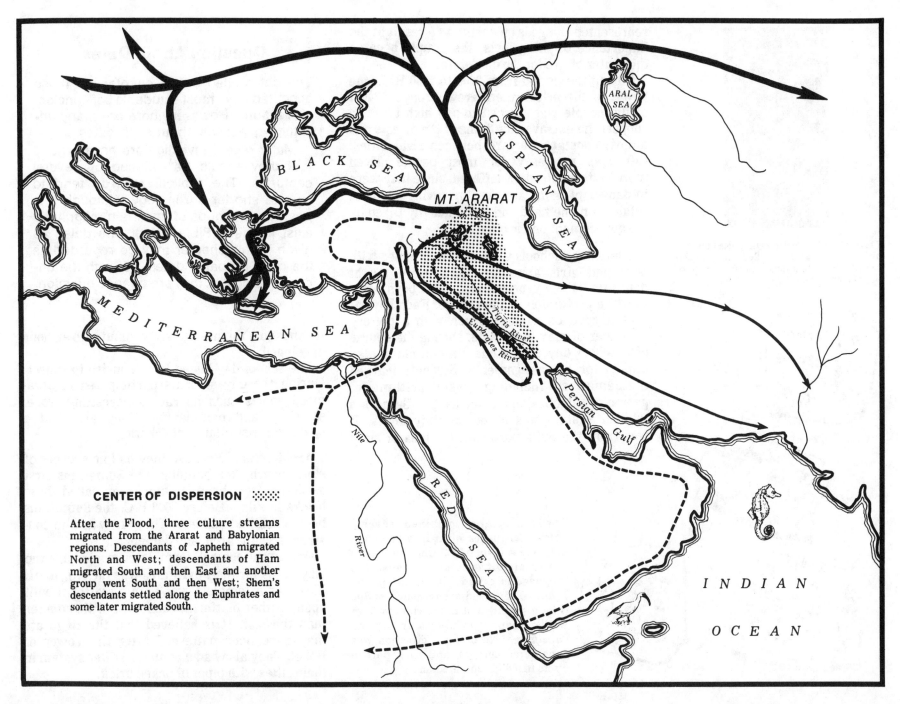

CENTER OF DISPERSION ::::::::

After the Flood, three culture streams migrated from the Ararat and Babylonian regions. Descendants of Japheth migrated North and West; descendants of Ham migrated South and then East and another group went South and then West; Shem's descendants settled along the Euphrates and some later migrated South.

MT. ARARAT

BLACK SEA

CASPIAN SEA

ARAL SEA

MEDITERRANEAN SEA

Tigris River

Euphrates River

Persian Gulf

Nile River

RED SEA

INDIAN OCEAN

The earliest Sumerian writing used pictures and symbols, a style called *pictographic script*. These limestone tablets were found near Babylon and are dated c. 3300 B.C.

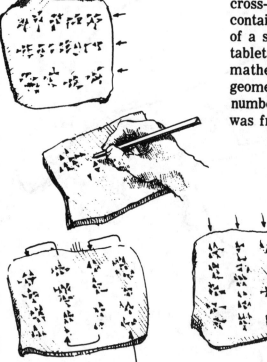

The Sumerians combined several written languages when they became a nation (See map, p.37). Chaldeans were the dominant scholars, because the language is called "Chaldean" in the Bible. They used a sharpened stylus (like a pencil) and damp clay, to form wedge-shaped symbols known as *cuneiform*. No uniform direction was considered correct, and each person wrote in a different direction.

represented the gods on earth. As a result of the importance of the priests, the temple became the center of life for the city-states.

During the period from 2800 to 2350 B.C., the power of the priest-rulers grew stronger. Most of the people were forced to pay high taxes to support the extravagant living of the priests and almost constant warfare between rival cities. Life was not easy for most people. Even merchants and traders suffered since they were in danger of being attacked by roving bands of soldiers on one hand and being heavily taxed by the government on the other.

Education. Schools were held in temples with boys and girls attending. Girls were taught domestic jobs by priestesses. The boys were taught a profession by the priests. Each boy sat cross-legged on a stone bench with a pottery container of clay at his side. During the course of a school day each student made many clay tablets for his assignments. Students learned mathematics, including basic arithmetic, geometry, algebra, and calculus. The Sumerian number system was based on sixty digits. It was from the Sumerians that the idea of sixty

Question About Dates

The dates cited in this chapter are those accepted by most students of ancient civilizations. However, there are many unsettled questions about such dates.

Many recent investigators have argued that they should be reduced by several centuries. The Biblical records tend to favor a shorter chronology, although it is possible that gaps of uncertain magnitude exist in these Bible dates. The dates as given in this chapter may be regarded as the most probable dates, but with the understanding that they are open to question.

seconds to a minute and sixty minutes to an hour developed.

The school day lasted from sunrise to sunset. During the day students participated in organized sports such as racing, wrestling, rope=skipping, and ball-playing. They also had a board game similar to checkers.

Architecture. Because they had no sources of stone nearby for building, the Sumerians first used sun-dried bricks. Later they baked these bricks in kilns. Before 3000 B.C. the Sumerians became skilled builders. They knew how to construct a vault, arch, and dome.

One architectural form later copied by the Egyptians for their pyramids was the *ziggurat*. This was a temple tower with a platform built upon another platform, each one a little smaller than the last. It is believed that the ziggurats may have been patterned after the Tower of Babel. They also had a complex sewer system in their cities with pipes of baked brick.

The Akkadian Empire

Sargon, A Great Leader. The first Sumerian states were conquered by the Akkadians, led by Sargon. This great ruler was once an orphan. In those days the custom of "exposure" was practiced; that is, if a child was not wanted by his family for some reason, he would be abandoned and left to die.

Sargon's mother, unable to keep him, placed him in a basket and left him in the Euphrates River around 2400 B.C. The baby was found by a gardener who raised him to be a soldier. Sargon grew to manhood and quickly rose to power in the Akkadian army, fighting in many wars. When the opportunity came, Sargon became the king of Akkad.

The area of the Fertile Crescent needed a strong ruler, and Sargon established the first empire in history—the Akkadian Empire. The power of the priests was broken during Sargon's rule.

Sargon was a great lawgiver and never forgot the rights of the people. He puts laws into effect, making it easier for poor people to go to court if they were mistreated. He also encouraged the merchant class to compete in trade. To insure the free flow of trade, he made sure no bands of outlaws or soldiers disturbed commerce.

While Sargon ruled his empire, it was strong and prospered. His children, however, were unable to hold what he had won. By 2230 B.C. Sargon's house had ceased to rule.

The Second Sumerian State

The Capital of Ur. When the Akkadian Empire was overthrown, the Sumerians once again became the dominant rulers of the Fertile Crescent. The Sumerian cities were united under strong leadership of kings and priests forming a new empire.

The major city and capital of this Sumerian state was the thriving seaport of Ur. Over the thousands of years since Ur was an active city, the river has built up silt at the mouth of the Persian Gulf. Today all that remains of this once rich and mighty city are huge mounds of dirt, six miles from the Euphrates River and almost a hundred miles from the Persian Gulf.

The Sumerians were excellent architects and builders. Their capital city, Ur, had a massive royal palace with huge staircases, large columns, and paneled walls. On these walls were beautiful paintings of humans and animals. Other public buildings and residences of the rich made the city attractive and beautiful.

Sumerian Society. Society classes in the empire were aristocrats, traders, freemen, and

A typical Semite, Sargon of Akkad had a prominent nose and determined mouth. He was a strong leader in the Euphratian civilization c. 2400 B.C. Apparently he was the first king to unify several groups of people into a kingdom.

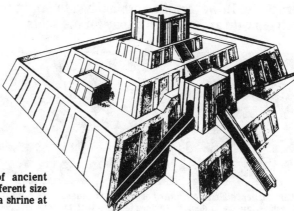

A temple-tower, or ziggurat, of ancient Babylon. Each platform was a different size and usually a different color with a shrine at the top.

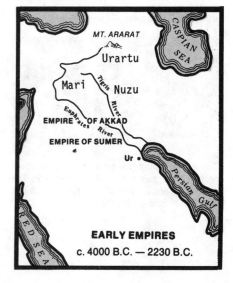

EARLY EMPIRES c. 4000 B.C. — 2230 B.C.

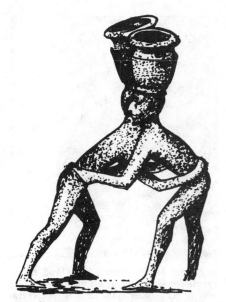

Wrestling was a natural sport in ancient civilizations. The above drawing is of a statue found in the Tell Agrab temple in Mesopotamia. It shows the unusual style of wrestling with participants balancing a pot on their heads. Some claim the pots were used as a "handicap"; others believe it was a religious ritual. Later, wrestling developed in the schools, and in c. 2500 B.C. it became a profession and a public entertainment.

Games have played a part in the lives of all people. The game above was found in the tomb of Queen Shubad of the city of Ur in the kingdom of Sumer (Iraq today).

slaves. Government officials and priests were the aristocrats, the privileged or high class. The lives of the working freemen and traders differed little, however, from the lives of the slaves.

Aristocrats lived in homes that were at least two stories high. Homes were built around a courtyard where families could enjoy the sunny weather. Some of these homes were richly furnished with lovely chairs, tables, chests, baskets, and beds. Beautiful items were made from copper, silver, gold, ivory, fine stone, and precious woods.

The poorer people lived in low houses with roofs of mud or reeds. Few decorations graced their homes. One interesting way of life, or custom, was how the people baked bread. They built dome-shaped brick ovens. A fire was built on the inside and the dough was pasted on the outer sides of the oven where it would be baked by the heat. In some parts of the Middle East bread is still baked in much the same way by rural tribesmen.

Marriage and family relations were governed by law; poor men were only allowed to have one wife. Women had some freedom to own property. However, the husband had the right to sell his wife and children to pay for his debts.

This banner, called a *standard* or *frieze*, is a masterpiece of early Sumerian art. It depicts a prince feasting with his courtiers and receiving booty from enemies. Dated c. 2500 B.C.

Religion. The Sumerian people practiced *polytheism*, or the worship of many gods. Their priests used the flights of birds, various sacrifices, omens, and rites to foretell the future and to hold their power. They had some idea of a life after death. but did not believe in heaven or hell.

When someone died, he was buried with many of his favorite personal belongings. It was hoped this would please the departed spirit. If he were not pleased with the burial, they believed he would haunt his former home and the people living there.

The Sumerians had a form of astrology in which they associated the planets and stars with their gods and goddesses. They kept careful records on the movements of these heavenly

The above artifacts are from ancient Sumer. On the left may be a representative man of that time period. People would carve these little statues of themselves, place them before their gods, and expect them to continually pray for them.

The bull-shaped base of a harp, on the right, was found in Queen Shubad's life-after-death dwelling. The head was made of gold and lapis-lazuli on wood and it is dated c. 2700 B.C.

bodies, and those records have been used by modern scientists in their studies of the heavens.

Fall of Ur. The Second Sumerian State ended in 2000 B.C. About that time Ur was destroyed by a large group of wandering peoples who invaded the Fertile Crescent. For 200 years Mesopotamia was plunged into chaos and warfare. During this time a new city, Babylon, was growing. This city soon dominated the entire Middle East. Although the Sumerians ceased to control the Mesopotamian area, their culture greatly influenced every civilization that followed.

The Indus River Valley

India thrusts like a giant triangle into the Indian Ocean. It was here that another ancient civilization grew and flourished. Cut off from the rest of Asia by the high and rugged Himalaya Mountains, India can be entered through the narrow Khyber Pass in the northwest. Through that famous route came the first settlers in India and successive waves of invaders. India's fertile plains below the mountain barrier were watered by the river systems of the Indus and Ganges. There is uncertainty whether the first colonists in India were descendants of Shem, of Ham, or a mixture of both.

Mohenjo-daro and Harappa

Civilization Develops. It was on the fertile plains of the Indus River Valley that civilization first developed in India. About 3000 B.C., 500 years after Sumer developed, people migrated there. They brought with them the knowledge of architecture and building they had

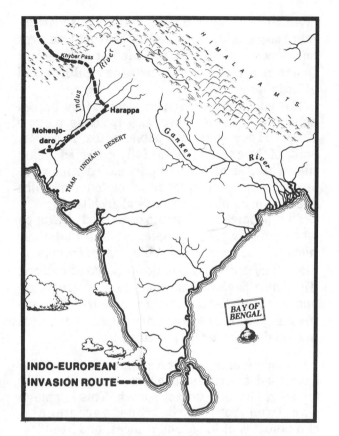

Like many ancient civilizations, the Sumerians buried people with personal possessions after death. The above headpiece, dated c. 2700 B.C., was of gold and adorned Queen Shubad in her elaborate tomb in Sumer. She was also buried with many beautiful pieces of jewelry and musical instruments.

learned in Mesopotamia. They built the cities of Harappa and Mohenjo-daro.

Life in Early Indian Civilizations. These ancient towns, in gridiron fashion, were mapped out with streets running at right angles and parallel to each other. The buildings were all made of sun-dried bricks. Both homes and businesses were built around courtyards with their outer walls facing the street. Those who could afford to lived in two-story homes built around open patios much like those in distant Ur. These homes had conveniences that might surprise us to discover in such ancient

Mohenjo-daro was a well-planned city on the banks of the Indus River. It was built by descendants of Shem and Ham who migrated from the upper Euphrates River Valley. The model below is based on archaeologist's findings in the area of Mohenjo-daro.

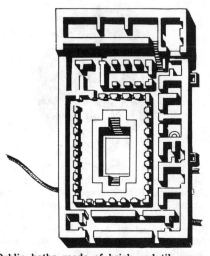

Public baths made of brick and tile were built in Mohenjo-daro for the comfort of the poor people c. 3000 B.C. These baths had dressing rooms around the center pool and drainage systems to carry the water into the public sewers, as this sketch shows.

Stone tablets, called seals, were used by ancient tribes and civilizations for identification when conducting trade and business. These have been dated c. 2800 B.C. Seals may have had a meaning to Indus River Indians similar to one the totem pole symbol has to the American Indians.

civilizations. Such modern luxuries as swimming pools, sewers, forced air heating, and even hot showers were a part of life in those ancient Indian cities, even though only the wealthy could afford them.

The poor people lived in single story homes built side by side, lined closely along narrow streets. They could use public baths, however, built of bricks and beautifully designed inlaid tile. The use of tile designs, called *mosaics,* spread across the world and even today mosaics are a favorite of decorators and architects.

The people in Mohenjo-daro and Harappa were not a warlike people. Feeling that their mountain barrier would protect them from invasion, they built an agriculturally based culture. They also began to develop the arts, language, and literature. At a very early time they became master weavers and produced beautiful materials from cotton and linen.

Language and Literature. Early Indians also developed a written language, using a symbol for each phonetic unit of speech. This language was used to record trade agreements, chronologies of kings and princes, and beautiful literature. In these ancient epics are recorded references to a flood that destroyed the earth. In their version the man who survived the flood was called Satyauata. He had three sons named Iyapeti, Sharma, and C'harma. Notice how closely the story of the flood parallels the Hebrew record, even to the similarity in the names of the children of Noah.

Iy a p e ti Sh a (r) m a C' ha (r) ma
J a ph e th Sh e m   Ha m

The Indian legend is similar to the Hebrew record in still another way. C'harma laughed at his father who had become drunk; in the Hebrew account Ham laughed at Noah for the same reason. Descendants of the children of Noah certainly remembered these events and passed them on to their children. With the great number of stories about a flood coming from so many cultures, this certainly was an event which had great impact on human history.

Education and Trade. Schools were held in the temples of the cities. Students learned reading, mathematics, writing, and history. Many young men hoped to become scribes when they finished school. This job was similar to an executive secretary today and scribes were in great demand. They were needed to keep trade information, personal records, and correspondence.

Ancient Cities Discovered By Workers

While a beautiful civilization developed in Mesopotamia, others also existed in ancient India—Mohenjo-daro and Harappa. However, no one knew how significant they were until 1922.

In 1856, while the first railroad through the Indus River Valley was being built, two brothers found the ruins of ancient cities in a jungle area. The workmen used stone from these ruins to provide coarse gravel for their roadbed.

Then, Alexander Cunningham, Director General of the Archaeological Survey of India, saw characters written on a seal that had been found in the rubble. He knew the ruins must be important. It was almost sixty-six years later, however, before it was discovered that the cities of Mohenjo-daro and Harappa were the centers of a widespread civilization.

Merchants did much business with Mesopotamia, Egypt, and even with the cities along the shores of the Mediterranean. Goods were carried in caravans by donkeys, camels, horses, cows, and even elephants.

The Aryan Invaders

Mohenjo-daro and Harappa Destroyed. The developing civilization of the Indus River Valley was overwhelmed by the fierce and warlike, nomadic Aryans who swept into India through the unguarded Khyber Pass. The wealth of Mohenjo-daro and Harappa was in striking contrast to the tent cities of the Aryans, located on the windswept steppes of central Asia. The conquest was quickly accomplished since the people of India were not prepared to defend themselves. By 2500 B.C. little remained of Mohenjo-daro and Harappa except ruins of buildings and a few frightened people striving to remain alive.

The Aryans. Tall, fair-skinned people from the area of West Turkestan in central Asia, the Aryans were nomads. They lived off the meat of their herds and what loot they could gather from pillaged and conquered cities. They were not builders. They preferred the nomadic life and caring for their herds of cattle. Cattle meant wealth to the Aryans. Even their word for war meant "a desire for cows." Their amusements and entertainments, like their daily life, were active and physical. They were fond of horse-racing, chariot-racing, dancing, gambling, and wrestling.

The family and the tribe were important social units to these wandering Aryans. Marriage was a serious step and divorce was not allowed. The tribe was like a large family and the tribesmen were fiercely loyal. Sometimes several tribes united together, but this was not a frequent occurrence.

The Aryans believed in an afterlife, and their ceremonies surrounding death were important to them. Bodies of the dead were burned on funeral pyres because they believed that fire freed the soul so it could soar upward to heaven.

Aryan Heritage. Although the Aryans destroyed the cities of India, they later stopped their nomadic life and settled there. The Aryans wove their own rich heritage of legend and history into that of the Indian people. They developed a new written language called *Sanskrit*, a language of beautiful sounds and descriptive words and terms. Even today it is considered the classical language of India.

Great literature flowed from the pens of the Sanskrit writers. Among these works are the *Vedas* which give their ideas on religion, life, death, philosophy, and music. Some of the

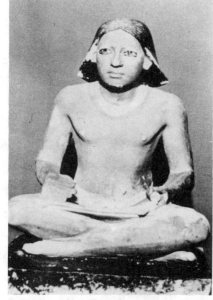

A scribe, such as the one pictured here, was similar to an executive secretary today. Many held responsible positions in ancient civilizations as early as 2750 B.C.

जातस्य हि ध्रुवो मृत्युः ध्रुवं जन्म मृतस्य च ।
तस्मादपरिहार्येऽर्थे न त्वं शोचितुमर्हसि ॥

अव्यक्तादीनि भूतानि व्यक्तमध्यानि भारत ।
अव्यक्तनिधनान्येव तत्र का परिदेवना ॥

Jātasya hi dhruvo mrityuh dhruvam janma mritasya cha,
Tasmād aparihāryerthe na tvam shochitumarhasi.

Avyaktādīni bhūtāni vyakta madhyāni Bhārata
Avyakta nidhanānyeva tatra kā paridevanā.

For certain is death for the born, and certain is birth for the dead; therefore over the inevitable thou shouldst not grieve.

Beings are unmanifest in their origin, manifest in their midmost state, O Bharata!; unmanifest likewise are they in dissolution. What room then for lamentation?

(II. 27-28)

The Sanskrit language, originated by the Aryans, is still the classical language of India. The Sanskrit text and translation (left) are from the *Bhagavad Gita, The Song Celestial*, an epic that reveals a great deal about ancient Hindu or Aryan culture.

Vedas (which means knowledge) are poetry, others are prose instructions on life. In the introduction to the *Vedas*, called the *Rig-Veda*, there are many questions on the meaning of life. One such question is, "Why does a red cow give white milk?" We may wonder why this question is asked, but we must remember these people saw cattle as wealth and were very curious about them. They also wondered about the world around them. Think of your world—have you ever wondered where the television picture comes from? Maybe their curiosity was not so foolish after all. We know much about our world today because throughout history people kept asking questions and trying to find answers.

Ancient Egypt

Egypt was protected from invasions mainly because of her location and geography. As a result, her people were able to develop a distinct culture and stable civilization that lasted for almost 2,000 years. There were times when Egypt's government was weak and disorganized, and for short times they were conquered by outside invaders. During all this time, however, Egyptian art, religion, government, and life continued much the same as always. To make Egyptian history easier to understand, historians have divided it into three major periods. The first two, the Old Kingdom and the Middle Kingdom, will be discussed in this chapter. The New Kingdom, the third phase, will be discussed in Chapter 3.

If you could have flown over ancient Egypt you would have noticed vast desert regions. Through them a narrow green strip of land on either side of the Nile River struggled to maintain itself against the desert. This was Egypt, a

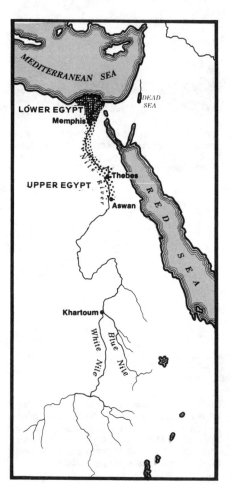

narrow green valley alignment between 10 km and 48 km (six and thirty miles) across.

Influence of Geography

Egypt had a great advantage over the other civilizations we have studied. It was protected on all sides by natural barriers. Deserts to the west, south, and east, and the Mediterranean Sea to the north, gave the Egyptians protection from outside invasions.

The Nile River. The Nile is the longest river in the world, extending 6,592 km (4,037 miles). It starts at Lake Victoria in central Africa and ends in the Mediterranean Sea. From its source, until it reaches the city of Khartoum, the river is called the White Nile. This is because it has a milky-gray color. At Khartoum it blends with the clear waters of the Blue Nile.

Between Khartoum and Aswan, the Nile flows northward through six *cataracts*, or rapids. In the cataracts the water rushes over rough rocky beds, while dropping as much as 38 cm/km (two feet each mile).

North of the First Cataract is a valley 16 km to 48 km (ten to thirty miles) wide called Upper Egypt by historians. As it approaches the Mediterranean Sea almost 960 km (600 miles) further north, the Nile divides into seven

Egypt's Ancient Name

Many historians believe the first settlers of ancient Egypt were the descendants of Mizraim, Ham's son.

The ancient Arabic name for Egypt, Mizraim, is still used today by Egyptians when referring to their country. For example, modern airplanes there have the insignia "Mizraim" printed across their tails.

branches, forming the Nile Delta. This area is hot and humid and is known as Lower Egypt. Some people are confused by Upper Egypt being in the south and Lower Egypt being in the north, but the Nile flows north, not south.

The Gift of the Nile. About 3000 B.C., the same time Sumer, Harappa, and Mohenjo-daro were established, the Egyptian civilization had its beginning. Early wanderers, descendants of Ham, came across the Red Sea and were attracted by the rich, fertile Nile Valley.

The famous Greek historian Herodotus was one of the first to call Egypt "the gift of the Nile." There is very little rainfall in Egypt so all water, whether for drinking, farming, cleaning, or bathing, comes from the Nile River. Perhaps even more important than the water itself are the yearly floods that cover Egypt from May to October. As the river creeps over its banks, it spreads a rich new layer of soil across the Nile Valley and provides a base for agriculture.

Etesian Winds. As people settled in the area and cities formed, the Nile River became a major source of transportation. This was made easy because of the natural winds. The hot desert air produced a low pressure area in the south, pulling in strong, cool breezes from the Mediterranean Sea. These breezes, called the *Etesian Winds*, enabled a merchant to raise his sails and be pushed upstream against the current. When he was ready to return downriver, all he had to do was lower the sail and float downstream on the current.

Water Control by Governments. The early people who arrived along the Nile Valley were quick to see the importance of working together to set up irrigation projects. They also built dikes to hold the water long after the yearly floods. Since everyone needed water, some type of governmental control was necessary to see that everyone got their fair share. These early governments were called *nomes*. Each nome was responsible for water distribution and repair of the equipment in their district.

The Old Kingdom

Upper and Lower Egypt. The geography of Egypt naturally divides the country into two sections—Upper Egypt and Lower Egypt.

The narrow Nile Valley in the south separates Upper Egypt from Lower Egypt, the broad Delta plain in the north. The ruler of Upper Egypt wore a white crown. His kingdom reached from the First Cataract of the Nile at Aswan to the southern border of Egypt. The ruler of Lower Egypt wore a red crown with a cobra symbol on the front. This kingdom reached from Aswan to the Nile Delta on the Mediterranean Sea.

Egypt United. About 3100 B.C. the first great ruler in Egypt's history, Menes, united Upper and Lower Egypt. The two royal crowns were combined to make one symbol of Egyptian

A Felucca on the Nile River.

The Etesian Winds made two-way navigation on the Nile River easy for commerce and communication. Ships would raise their sails and be pushed against the up-river current and would lower their sails and drift downstream to return.

authority. Menes wore a white crown with a cobra symbol. The rule of Menes and his descendants is called the First Dynasty. (A *dynasty* is the continuous rule of a country by the same family. We will see this term again when we study China.)

Religion. As the people began to fear their ruler, they no longer used his name. Instead they called him *pharaoh*, which means "great house," referring to the magnificent palace in Memphis, Egypt's capital. As government became more complex, the pharaoh appointed his brothers, sons, and favorite nobles as assistants to help him govern. However, the pharaoh always gave the orders and retained final control over everything.

The Pharaoh, A "Divine" Ruler. To establish their authority, Menes' descendants claimed he was the son of the sun god, Ra. This meant that the ruler of Egypt was considered almost a god, giving him more than earthly authority. If anyone disobeyed the ruler, they believed it would anger the gods. As a result the rulers of Egypt had *absolute* power over every portion of Egyptian life.

There were two important results of the pharaohs' claim to being divine. First, there was the development of a strange custom. The pharaoh would marry his own sister. The pharaohs could have as many secondary wives and concubines as they wished. However, in order to keep the divine blood of the sun god as pure as possible, the pharaoh would always have his sister as his major wife. If the pharaoh and his major wife only had daughters, the eldest daughter would marry the most promising son of the many concubines. In this way the royal family would continue and could claim divine descent. The marriage of a brother and sister was not wise since weak physical or mental characteristics had a greater chance of appearing in their children.

Afterlife Tombs. The other result of the belief in a divine pharaoh was that great amounts of time and energy were spent on tombs, called life-after-death homes. The early Egyptians believed the pharaoh returned to the sun when he died. There he would see to it that the Nile would continue to flood every year and

Embalming, Egyptian-Style

When people in ancient Egypt died, many were *embalmed* and their bodies formed into a mummy to prevent decay. Although the embalming process is no longer used today, it was commonly used by ancient Egyptians.

First, they pulled the brains out through the nostrils with an iron hook. Then they cut into the body's side and took out the vital organs. The stomach cavity was rinsed with palm wine and filled with perfume and spices before being sewed up. The body was soaked in a solution of sodium and aluminum sulfate for up to seventy days. At the end of this time, the corpse was washed and wrapped in bandages of waxen cloth to form a mummy. It was then smeared with gum, which the Egyptians commonly used instead of glue, and painted with makeup. Many mummies were decorated with jewelry, covered with elaborate clothing, or encased in gold, as in the case of King Tutankhamen. As many as five elaborately decorated encasements have been found on one mummy.

Egyptian Mummy

that the crops would grow. For this reason the people would do everything they could to please the pharaoh.

During the Old Kingdom, the Egyptians believed that only the pharaoh and those nobles he selected would share in the life after death. The common people were still willing to work on tombs because they believed their pharaoh would help them after he died. The earliest tombs were rather small, but as the wealth and power of the pharaoh grew, larger and larger tombs were built.

The Great Pyramids. The first pyramid was built when Pharaoh Zoser commanded his chief minister, Imhotep, to build him a tomb. Imhotep copied the idea of the ziggurat from Mesopotamia and designed the *step pyramid*. Although his was the first of the pyramids, other pharaohs were quick to build even larger homes for their life after death.

During the Fourth Dynasty, c. 2600 B.C., Pharaoh Khufu (Cheops) had the Great Pyramid built. The Greeks considered this one of the Seven Wonders of the Ancient World. The farmers did the construction work during the non-agricultural season. This gave them work to do when they otherwise would have been unemployed. Around 100,000 men worked on this project for 20 years. They were paid out of the government granaries. More than two million limestone blocks, weighing 2268 kg (two and a half tons) each, were cut out of the quarries on the east bank of the Nile River. They were then ferried across the river and pulled up the west bank on rollers. The base of the pyramid was 230 m (755 feet) per side and it reached 147 m (481 feet) into the sky

This pyramid was facing due north. In the absolute center was the pharaoh's chamber. His

Spelling of Names

When studying Egyptian history, the pharaohs' names sometimes cause confusion. Over the years, as people translated Egyptian hieroglyphics into our alphabet, they recorded different spellings for the same name. For example, the pharaoh who established the Egyptian Middle Kingdom is called Amenemhet I in one source, Menthuhotep I in another, and Menthotpe I in yet another.

Because of these varied spellings, it is very important to learn the dates and time periods. This will help you recognize which pharaoh you are reading about, no matter how his name is spelled. In *Streams of Civilization* we have used the most common spellings of these names.

The Great Pyramid was built by the Egyptian Pharaoh Cheops. Near this pyramid his son, Chephren, built the Great Sphinx, shown above. The sphinx had a lion's body and Chephren's head, showing his power and authority as pharaoh. The body is 73 m (240 feet) long and 20 m (66 feet) wide. The face is 4.0 m (13 feet) wide. Centuries later the Egyptians forgot the original purpose of this sphinx and began to worship it as a representation of the sun god.

Huge life-after-death tombs, called *pyramids*, were built to house and honor pharaohs of early Egypt. To keep the body and personal possessions safe, they were designed with many hidden passageways and sections, as shown in this sketch of Pharaoh Khufu's pyramid. Over the years, however, graverobbers have discovered and taken the jewels and other riches from these ancient monuments.

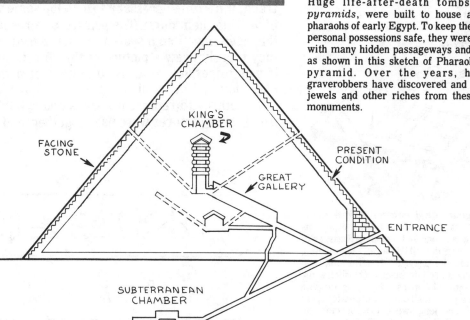

KING'S CHAMBER

FACING STONE

GREAT GALLERY

PRESENT CONDITION

ENTRANCE

SUBTERRANEAN CHAMBER

The Step Pyramid is the oldest existing building in Egypt. It was copied after the Ziggurat of Sumer. The small temple rooms around it have become buried in the desert sand.

The Egyptians are given credit for making the world's first paper. Made from the papyrus plant, it was a long and tedious process, as illustrated and described here: (1) selecting and cutting the papyrus, (2) trimming and cutting the stalk into pieces, (3) slicing the papyrus into thin strips, (4) laying the thin slices on a pounding board in alternate layers crosswise and lengthwise, (5) pounding the papyrus until it becomes pulp and later a sheet laid out to dry.

wife's chamber was about 9.14 m (30 feet) below. The entire pyramid was tightly sealed, except for a passage for food to be brought to the couple. The pyramid was then covered with a white limestone coat of paint to reflect the brilliance of the sun, representing their god Ra.

Although every care was given to provide protection against graverobbers, almost every tomb in Egypt has been disturbed and its treasures stolen.

Achievements. When the Nile River overflowed every year, all traces of family boundaries would be lost. In order to re-establish these boundaries quickly and accurately, the Egyptians developed a mathematical system for surveying boundaries. They also learned to add, subtract, and use the square root.

Hieroglyphics. Because so many records had to be kept on taxes, the water districts, and trade, it became necessary to develop some way of writing them down. The priests, as a result of this need, invented a system of writing. At first they merely drew a picture of the object. Since it was impossible to draw a picture of a word like "lovely" or "finish," they developed certain pictures to represent sounds and syllables. All of these pictures were used together, and the

result was an interesting but difficult system of writing. Because they stored the records in the temples, this type of writing was called *hieroglyphics*, which means "sacred carvings." These hieroglyphics were used for all formal records which were carved on buildings, walls, monuments, or wherever wanted.

Later a more simple form of writing was developed for use in keeping everyday records and in letter-writing. Called *hieratic* writing, this was a combination of abbreviated pictures and a series of hooks and marks.

Papyrus Paper. The Egyptians developed the world's first writing paper from papyrus reeds that grew in abundance along the banks of the Nile River. Papyrus reeds were also used to make rope, roofs, sandals, and even light fishing boats.

The early books and records were not bound on the side like our books today. Instead the sheets of papyrus were joined together to form one long sheet. The end of this sheet was fastened to a spool and the entire document was rolled up in what we call a scroll. These scrolls were stored in clay jars where many have been found, preserved because of Egypt's dry climate.

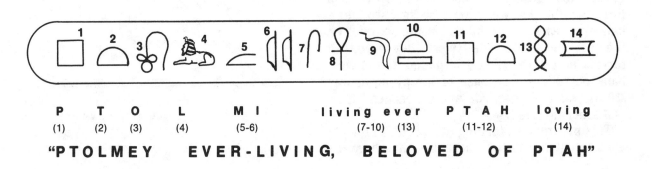

P	T	O	L	MI	living ever	PTAH	loving
(1)	(2)	(3)	(4)	(5-6)	(7-10) (13)	(11-12)	(14)

"PTOLMEY   EVER-LIVING,   BELOVED   OF   PTAH"

The Decline and Fall of the Old Kingdom. The leaders of the Old Kingdom built great monuments and made great advances in science, art, and government. Although the Old Kingdom ended after about five centuries, the type of government it established continued to rule Egypt for almost 2,000 years.

In the Old Kingdom the government owned all the land and decided how to best use the irrigation systems. The common people were given land where they could build a home and farm. They were expected to give a third of their harvest to the government, and the priests demanded a share of what was left.

The priests had gained great riches and large amounts of land. No one dared to criticize what they were doing or how they lived for fear of angering the gods. At the same time, the rich nobles were refusing to pay taxes and beginning to break away from the authority of the pharaoh. The common people, caught between these powerful groups, found their world was no longer secure and peaceful. The pharaohs were no longer able rulers and the Old Kingdom began to decline.

The Middle Kingdom

For two hundred years conflict within the kingdom continued. Invaders crossed the deserts and disrupted life. Irrigation projects fell into ruin and civil war raged as three ambitious families tried to set up their own government.

Egypt's Middle Kingdom. About 2100 B.C. Amenemhet I reunited Egypt. He was not able to bring all the nobles under his control. He did, however, win their support because of the good foreign trade contacts he made.

Under the rulers of the Middle Kingdom, Egypt's government moved in a different direction. Instead of spending large sums of money to build mighty monuments, the pharaohs began rebuilding the country. An irrigation project was completed, adding thousands of square meters (acres) of farmland.

Trade Brings Prosperity. Foreign trade was very important. The Egyptians developed four main trade routes. The first was, of course, the Nile River itself. Another was in the Mediterranean Sea where Egyptian merchants stopped at Cyprus, Crete, Rhodes, Sicily, Sardinia, Ugarit, and other commercial ports. Overland, caravans traveled to the cities in the Tigris-Euphrates Valley area and from there into Europe. Finally the pharaohs built two canals, one at Wadi Hammamot near Thebes and the

Early Egyptian art was creative and animal-oriented since hunting was their primary occupation. They introduced the *sphinx*—a huge lion having a man's head, a symbol of strength. (Usually the head was that of the reigning monarch who commanded its construction.) The above drawing is an alabaster sphinx in Memphis, Egypt, that measures 3.7m (12 feet high) and 5.5m (18 feet) long. This particular sphinx was in existence when Abraham and Sarah traveled to Memphis and when Joseph was the Prime Minister of Egypt.

MAIN TRADE ROUTES ■■■
OVERLAND MAN-MADE CANALS ....

Musicians were in great demand by Egyptians. Both men and women entered the profession, as represented in this painting.

An ankh is a symbol of eternal life. It was originated by the Egyptians who believed that life continued after death.

Egyptian life decorated the inner walls of tombs to surround the dead with daily activities.

other at Wadi Tumilat, the northern tip of the Red Sea. These marvels of engineering genius connected the Red Sea to the Nile River and opened Arabia and eastern Africa to trade.

As a result of trade and wise leadership, Egypt prospered. The fine arts were encouraged, and once again colossal buildings, statues, and monuments were built all over the country.

Grain coming to the government as taxes was stored at special storage cities. When other countries suffered famine, the Egyptians would sell surplus food to them. This added greatly to the wealth of the country.

Rise of the Middle Class. Perhaps one of the greatest social changes to take place during the Middle Kingdom was the rise of the middle class. As trade became more important, the pharaoh needed men to help him with all the records and the organization of trade. The rich

nobles thought this work too humble and refused to help. From the middle class came ambitious men, trained as scribes, who were anxious to help the pharaoh and gain wealth and position.

As a result of common people taking important roles in government, a significant change was made in the religion. (You will remember that only the pharaoh and his favorite nobles were allowed to build homes for their life after death.) It was decided that everyone could join in the afterlife and could build a tomb to provide for this future life.

Those in the middle class who could afford them began to build small tombs in the desert area around the pyramids of the great pharaohs. In this way we have been able to discover how the common people lived, in addition to the life style of the pharaohs.

One of the reasons we know so much about the lives of the early Egyptians has to do with the location of their pyramids and tombs. Built on the desert sands, the dry heat has acted as a preservative. Furniture, writings, clothing, artwork, and even food, has been found in much the same condition as it was thousands of years before. Other civilizations, developed in wetter climates, have left little more than rotted fragments of what their culture may have been.

Egypt Invaded. Egypt had become rich, but she had neglected her defenses, depending upon the deserts to keep her enemies out. The Egyptian army was poorly armed and badly trained. In addition, the last pharaoh of the Middle Kingdom was not an able ruler. Rich but weak, Egypt was a prize too tempting to be left alone by her neighbors.

Out of the desert area of what is now Arabia and Syria came a fierce, warlike people called the Hyksos. This tribe's name means "Asiatics"

Canaan — The Promised Land

It was probably during the Middle Kingdom that Abraham's grandson Jacob left the land of Canaan (present-day Israel) and moved to Egypt because of a famine. Jacob learned that his son Joseph, who was thought to be dead, was Prime Minister of Egypt. Joseph gave land in Goshen, a fertile area along the Nile Delta, to the seventy members of his family.

Almost 400 years passed before Jacob's descendants left Egypt and returned to Canaan. They had progressed greatly over the years and in Canaan started a new civilization. These people, descendants of Abraham, will be called Israelites, Hebrews, or Jews in this book.

and the Egyptians had never faced such enemies. They had war chariots pulled by horses, the likes of which the Egyptians had never seen before. They also used a two-edged dagger and sword and shot a powerful, double=curved bow with bronze-tipped arrows.

The Egyptians with their clumsy spears and heavy armor were no match for the warlike Hyksos as they swept through Egypt. Cities were quickly conquered and looted. To the Egyptians the Hyksos were like the locusts that stripped their farmlands of grain.

Then, instead of taking their loot and leaving, the Hyksos settled in Egypt and made their headquarters at Tanis-Avaris in the Nile Delta. For a time they allowed a puppet pharaoh to sit on the throne of Egypt, but he took his orders from the Hyksos. By 1785 B.C. the Hyksos were in absolute control of Egypt.

Hyksos Influence. The Hyksos introduced many new changes to Egyptian life. The army was completely changed and new weapons were used. The Hyksos made changes in the Egyptian language, simplifying it. They also introduced a simpler form of mathematics. New laws were introduced and a strict moral code was set up. It became law that a man could have only one wife.

Under the Hyksos the spinning and weaving trades were encouraged. Also, there was more freedom in allowing artists to make things in gold and precious stones. One big change was that the building of large monuments, pyramids, and other religious structures stopped. The Hyksos introduced new gods and did not allow the Egyptian priests the special privileges they had enjoyed under the pharaohs.

Although the Hyksos ruled Egypt from 1785 to 1580 B.C., they were always considered outsiders and were hated by the Egyptians. During their rule there were many rebellions and uprisings. In 1580 B.C. a confident young ruler, Ahmose I, raised a powerful Egyptian army and drove the Hyksos out of Egypt. The Nile Valley was once again ruled by its own people.

Egyptian tombs were elaborately painted with scences to show how dedicated the deceased person was to certain gods. Here, the pagan god, Osiris-Khenti-Amentiu is honored.

New Perspectives

Can you imagine people building civilizations all around the world at the same time? Normally, we think of history as following a sequential, step-by-step forward pattern. Nevertheless, we should understand that the civilizations of past centuries were actually built by different people at the same time. The various "families" of the earth eventually became so dispersed that they developed into the following distinct groups of people:

Families of the Earth

Eastern Asia: Mongolian, Chinese, Korean, Ainu

Southern Asia: Indians, Islanders of the South Pacific, Malaysians, Vietnamese, Thai, Aborigines of Australia

Africa: Egyptian, Cushites, Nokians, Bushmen, Hottentots

Europe: Italians, Gauls, Celts, Russian, Slavic, Finns

Americas: Eskimos, Canadians, Mayans, Incans, Pre-Columbians

Each family group used what tools they took with them when leaving "home." When they settled again in new lands, they started over by locating resources like wood or metals.

EXPANDING CIVILIZATIONS

Projects

1. Do a study on nationalism. What countries today are trying to gain freedom from foreign rulers? Choose one of these countries and report on its past history and its struggle for self-rule.

2. Read a book about one of the following people and give a report on his or her life: Queen Hatshepsut, Thutmose III, Akhenaton, or Ramses II. What kind of people were they? Would you have liked them for friends? Explain.

3. Pretend you were living during Moses' time. Write a story in which you are either Moses' sister, an Egyptian during the plagues, or a young person leaving Egypt during the Exodus. Be sure to say what you saw, did, and felt.

4. Compare the pharaohs we have studied with American presidents. Match those who were similar. For example, which pharaoh and which president founded their countries? Was there a president like Akhenaton who showed love for his family in public? Was there a warrior-type president?

5. Give a report on the man who discovered one of the following: King Tut's tomb, Troy, or Crete. Who was he and why did he conduct his search? What did he discover and how did this affect his life?

6. Build a working model of an irrigation system like the Euphratian one pictured in this chapter. Or, make a model of a Greek merchant ship or a wattle-and-daub house.

7. Find and read the story of the Trojan War. How did it start? Who won? Who were the major heroes? Draw a picture of your favorite scene.

8. Class project. Take a field trip to a nearby museum or place where Indian culture can be found. Give a report on the Indians from your area.

Words and Concepts

Huaca Prieta
Folsom point
minos
Divine Right of Kings
kohl
Exodus
Poverty Point
Llano Man
dowry
Hapiru
subsidies
Danger Cave
Acropolis
Code of Hammurabi
heretic
satellites
Clovis point
citadels
irrigation
theocracy
nationalism

Expanding Civilizations

Cultures began to spread from the Tigris-Euphrates Valley area about 2100 B.C. Many archaeologists and historians believe that people migrated throughout the world from this area as a result of the confusion of languages at Babel. Some civilizations came into existence and developed early in history; others took longer. This happened because of differences in geography and climate.

Egypt, overturning the foreign rule of the Hyksos, developed her civilization into one of unmatched splendor. In Mesopotamia the early civilizations of Sumer and Akkad were replaced by the more advanced civilization of Babylon. Another great civilization came into existence in the Mediterranean area. Since it centered around the Aegean Sea, it was known as the Aegean civilization.

Meanwhile, as civilizations spread and progressed in the Middle East, a group of sturdy hunters ventured northward. They crossed a land bridge and entered into the area known today as the Americas. In these remote areas, cut off from trade and the exchange of ideas, civilization developed slowly.

In 1545 B.C. Egypt's New Kingdom began. During this time huge palaces, monuments, and temples once again were erected throughout Egypt. A campaign of foreign conquests followed and Egypt became a world power for many centuries.

Many historians believe that it was during the New Kingdom that the Hebrew people, Jacob's descendants, were removed from their homes to serve the Egyptians as slaves. Certainly there was a need for slaves because of the massive building programs. Later, also during the New Kingdom, Moses led the Hebrew people out of Egypt in what is known as the Exodus.

Egypt was recovering from the Exodus when a pharaoh tried to introduce a new form of worship to the Egyptians. This almost destroyed this country and shortly afterwards Egypt was conquered by the Assyrians. In 670 B.C. the New Kingdom came to an end.

Egyptians Regain Their Freedom

After nearly a hundred years of Hyksos domination, a young Egyptian prince named Ahmose I drove the Hyksos from Egypt. The Egyptians were not satisfied until every foreigner was removed from government office.

Nationalism—A Love of Country

Nationalism, a word we often hear about in the news, means a great love of country and a desire for self-rule by the people of a nation. Those fighting for nationalism are usually under the government of a foreign ruler.

We usually think of nationalism as a modern idea, something unique to Africa or Asia. Today, however, we recognize that people have loved their countries from earliest times. The first nationalists were the Egyptians who fought against the Hyksos. Time and again we will see how nationalism played an important role in the affairs of nations.

Amenhotep's unfinished sarcophagus and tomb reveal how he died unexpectedly. Normally, an Egyptian completed a smaller tomb if he thought he would die early. King Tut knew he was going to die young, so he built and completed a child-size sarcophagus.

The Hyksos army retreated into the Taurus Mountains near the Caspian Sea. The hated Hyksos were driven out of Egypt and the Egyptian army got to taste the excitement of conquest outside of its borders at the same time.

Nationalism and Anti-Foreign Policy. Once Ahmose I set up his rule, he began to remove all foreigners from public office. All of Egypt was filled with a spirit of *nationalism*. This means they wanted to rule themselves and to be free of all foreign influences.

When Amenhotep I became pharaoh, he further erased traces of foreign domination. All positions of authority were taken away from foreigners and given to trustworthy Egyptians. Non-Egyptian owners of business and industry were stripped of their hard-earned savings and all non-Egyptian ideas and influences were suppressed.

A Period of Rebuilding and Growth

Ahmose I and his son Amenhotep I spent most of their time rebuilding Egypt. The next pharaoh, Thutmose I, concentrated on invading and conquering other countries. Egypt soon controlled most of the Middle East to the north, including much of the area which is now Syria.

Apparently the unfortunate effects of brothers marrying their sisters appeared in Thutmose I's family. Although the royal couple had sons, none of them were mentally capable of being rulers. With the support of the major nobles and the priests, Thutmose I had his daughter Hatshepsut crowned queen before he died.

Queen Hatshepsut. As a child Hatshepsut wore the short pleated skirt of a prince and attended the temple school—usually attended by only boys. She was trained to rule Egypt. Portrayed in a statue carved during her reign, she wore the traditional beard always worn by the pharaoh.

While Thutmose I was alive, Hatshepsut was co-ruler with her father. At his death she married one of her half-brothers, Thutmose II. Hatshepsut and Thutmose II had no children, and therefore no heir from the gods.

Thutmose II died at an early age. Thutmose III, the son of a concubine who was selected to rule after him, was still a child. Then Hatshepsut did something no other queen of Egypt had ever done before. Claiming that the sun god, Ra, had commanded her to rule Egypt, Hatshepsut declared herself pharaoh. She even appeared in public with the mace and royal collar and wore the false beard of the pharaoh.

Under Hatshepsut's rule Egypt prospered. Her reign is considered one of the most successful in Egypt's history. She maintained

Egypt's Queen Hatshepsut, the only woman to reign as pharaoh, appeared in public wearing a false beard and men's clothes.

Since Queen Hatshepsut was preparing Moses to be the next Pharaoh, and he was "learned in all the wisdom of Egypt" (Acts 7:22), Moses probably accompanied the queen through the canals to Egypt's turquoise mines in the Sinai.

Dier-el-Bahari, a temple in Egypt, was designed for Queen Hatshepsut by her favorite minister and architect, Senmut. When Hatshepsut died, Thutmose III tried to destroy the temple and had her name removed.

54   Chapter Three

order, encouraged trade, and for most of her rule, kept Egypt at peace. As queen and pharaoh, Hatshepsut ruled Egypt well for more than 20 years.

A Bitter Prince Becomes Pharaoh. As Thutmose III passed from his teens to adulthood, he began to worry about becoming pharaoh. Although he led Egyptian armies on many successful campaigns, "Pharaoh" Hatshepsut still maintained control of the kingdom. She included him in public ceremonies, but he was forced to remain in the background. His bitter resentment grew into hatred over the years.

In 1479 B.C. Hatshepsut died and Thutmose III was pharaoh in his own right. Many historians strongly suspect that Thutmose III had her murdered so he could rule in her place. His hatred for her was so extreme that he did not allow her to be buried in the tomb that was prepared for her. To the Egyptians this was a terrible act because it cut her off from any possibility of an afterlife. Archaeologists are still searching for the place where she was buried. This search is more difficult because Thutmose III had her name removed from all monuments.

With Hatshepsut out of the way, Thutmose III showed his anger to her supporters. He defaced

Thutmose III was prevented from ruling as pharaoh by Queen Hatshepsut. After her death, he became pharaoh and led many successful military campaigns against Egypt's enemies.

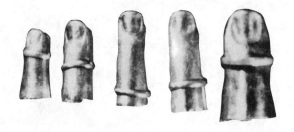

Egyptian pharaohs were believed to be Ra, the sun god, in human form. During public ceremonies they wore gold finger caps, such as these, to reflect the sun.

the tombs of those already dead. Those living, including Moses, were in danger of losing their lives.

Military Expansion. Thutmose III's reign was marked by great military campaigns. He began his rule by suppressing a Hittite rebellion at Megiddo. During the rest of his reign he conducted seventeen campaigns in the Euphrates River Valley. He defeated all the kings in the Fertile Crescent, making them pay tribute and accept his rule. In these newly conquered territories, called *satellites*, he always left strong fortresses under the leadership of Egyptian soldiers and governors. Thutmose III developed a strong army as well as a large navy.

In 1447 B.C. Amenhotep II became pharaoh. He continued fighting against the Hittites in Syria and Egypt became even more powerful. The next pharaoh was Thutmose IV. Very little is known about this ruler, although it is believed that Egypt's beliefs and power were severely shaken during his reign. He left the throne to his brilliant son, Amenhotep III.

Under Amenhotep III's leadership Egypt reached the peak of her splendor. By 1390 B.C. the capital of Thebes was one of the most magnificent of its age. Tribute poured into the country from all over the known world. This was all lost, however, when Amenhotep IV became pharaoh. He not only failed to provide leadership, but also tried to change Egypt's religion.

Cultural Growth. Under the dynamic leadership of Egypt's New Kingdom pharaohs, the people and the country prospered. Egypt became the center of trade in art and luxury goods.

In addition to the building programs of the New Kingdom, beautiful works of literature appeared. Many proverbs, hymns, stories of heroic adventures, and tales of life at sea were also written. In order to encourage writers, the government helped to support them while they worked. (Such government payments are known as *subsidies*. The United States gave a few subsidies to writers during the Depression of the 1930s and today pays subsidies to farmers and some businesses to keep them operating.)

Spacious villas and artificial lakes were built by the upper classes, providing magnificent surroundings. A favorite form of entertainment for the noble's family was the lavish banquet with many guests. Both the noble and his wife dressed in pleated, white linen skirts. They wore broad collars set with semiprecious stones, gold bracelets, and heavy, perfumed black wigs. Egyptian nobles also spent their time hunting on their large estates.

Egyptian women used many cosmetics, such as rouge, perfume, and eye makeup. They painted their eyelids with a black powder called *kohl* which made their eyes look bigger. It also protected them from the brilliant glare of the sun. They used highly polished copper mirrors for grooming.

Merchants from every country crowded the streets of ancient Thebes where life was interesting and active. There the buildings surpassed anything in the known world at that time.

Challenges to Egypt's Religion

Egyptians were greatly influenced by their religious beliefs. In fact they were almost controlled by them. They worshiped animals, bugs, the Nile River, their ruler, and hundreds of other gods and goddesses.

During the New Kingdom, the power of the Egyptian gods was challenged in two ways. One was by the God of the Hebrew people as Egypt was struck by ten destructive plagues. The other challenge came from Pharaoh Amenhotep IV who tried to introduce a new religion to the Egyptians.

The Hebrew Challenge. During the early part of Thutmose I's reign, harsh laws were passed against foreign slaves. This included laws against the Hebrews who had become slaves under Ahmose I. In an attempt to reduce the large Hebrew population, the Pharaoh sent out orders for them to work overtime at their construction work. When this failed, another harsh law was passed. Women who helped in childbirth were ordered to kill all Hebrew boys at their birth.

These harsh laws only united the Hebrews in thought, faith, and purpose. They looked for a leader to rescue them from slavery. They wanted to go back to the land of Canaan, where their ancestor, Jacob, had lived so many years before.

A Leader Is Born. The Hebrew record tells of one child, later called Moses, who was not killed at birth. His mother had placed him in a basket and put it in the Nile River. Then, while bathing in the Nile River, a daughter of pharaoh found the basket among the papyrus plants on the banks of the river. The child was taken to the palace to be raised as her son. His real mother, a Hebrew slave, learned where the baby had been taken and offered to act as his nurse.

Moses was trained to help govern Egypt along with the other children of the royal family. His schooling included astronomy, literature,

This makeup kit was found in the tomb of Queen Hatshepsut, showing her love for beautiful things. Egyptian women used such toiletries as eye shadow, mascara, lipstick, and powder. They also styled their hair by teasing.

Anubis was the jackal-headed god who the Egyptians believed judged the souls of people after death. This wall mural shows a pharaoh receiving power from the sun god and Anubis.

Sand flies were among the many creatures of nature worshiped by the Egyptians. Their likenesses were made into necklaces such as this one from the 18th Dynasty.

When Did Moses Live?

There are no records that give the exact dates when Moses lived. The authors believe he lived between the reigns of Queen Hatshepsut and Pharaoh Akhenaton, roughly between 1520 and 1378 B.C. Amenhotep II, then, ruled as pharaoh between 1447 and 1411 B.C. He was the pharaoh whom Moses asked repeatedly to free the Hebrew slaves. When he refused, his reign was shaken by the well-known plagues of Egypt. Akhenaton would have been the ruler when the Hebrews entered Canaan.

Amenhotep II's rule is used as the central point of reference.

There are two factors that support the theory that Moses lived during the above time period:

1. We know that Moses was 80 years old when he led his people out of Egypt. Subtracting 80 years from 1447 B.C., we come to the time when Hatshepsut ruled Egypt. This means Moses was born during her reign.
2. The Hebrews, led by Moses, wandered in the wilderness for 40 years before entering Canaan. Add this 40-year period of time to 1447 B.C. and you come to the approximate time of Akhenaton's rule. It was during the end of his reign that records claim a people called "Hapiru" invaded Canaan. Many historians believe "Hapiru" actually means Hebrew.

architecture, mathematics, agriculture, military skills, business, and trade economics. In addition he mastered all the known languages of his day.

As a member of the Egyptian government, Moses served as an overseer of building projects in the Nile Delta. While there, he killed an Egyptian. Moses then fled to the Sinai peninsula where he found refuge for forty years.

Egypt and the Ten Plagues. Moses became an Israelite leader. According to the Hebrew record, one day Moses stood before Amenhotep II, demanding that the Hebrew slaves be set free. When Pharaoh refused, ten plagues struck Egypt, one after another, almost destroying the country.

Some historians question whether Amenhotep II was the pharaoh who opposed Moses. There are two things, however, that indicate that he was the ruler. First, we know that Amenhotep's tomb was never finished, probably because he died suddenly. The Hebrew record explains this. It states that the pharaoh, who opposed Moses,

An Egyptian royal family stroll outside their palace. Most homes of royalty and of the wealthy were surrounded by lavish gardens filled with flowers, plants, and birds. There peacocks, deer, dogs, and cats roamed freely.

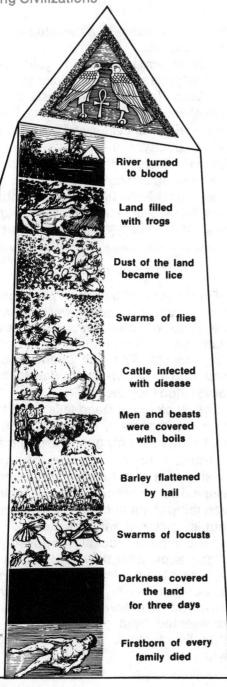

River turned
to blood

Land filled
with frogs

Dust of the land
became lice

Swarms of flies

Cattle infected
with disease

Men and beasts
were covered
with boils

Barley flattened
by hail

Swarms of locusts

Darkness covered
the land
for three days

Firstborn of every
family died

and his army drowned while pursuing the Hebrews when they left Egypt.

The second point indicating that Amenhotep was the ruler at this time is that Amenhotep II's son and heir never ruled Egypt. We know from the records that he had a son, but nothing has been recorded about his life. Since the last plague to strike Egypt called for the death of the oldest son of *every* family, this would explain what happened to Amenhotep II's son. He probably died at a very young age.

Few records have been found of Egyptian history following the plagues. It is believed that Amenhotep III and Thutmose IV succeeded each

A Prophetic Dream

Some months before the death of Amenhotep II, his nephew Thutmose IV was hunting in the desert. On his way home, he fell asleep while resting between the paws of the Great Sphinx. He dreamed that the sphinx told him he would become the next pharaoh. He argued with this because his uncle, Amenhotep II, already had a son, heir to the throne. Amenhotep's son disappeared, however, from Egyptian history and Thutmose IV was later crowned pharaoh. As a memorial to the dream, he recorded it in stone and placed it between the paws of the sphinx.

According to the Hebrew record, the ten plagues were a series of supernatural signs brought against the Egyptian people as a result of pharaoh's refusing the Israelites the freedom of worship. Each plague was related to nature, the source of all Egyptian deities, and would seem to be a direct attack on their gods. The fact that Egyptian magicians were unable to imitate the plagues proved the power of the true God.

The ten plagues, in order of their occurrence, are depicted from top to bottom on the obelisk illustrated here.

other as rulers. Perhaps Egypt was recovering from the terrible destruction of the plagues.

The Heretic Pharaoh. Until this time all the pharaohs worshiped the same Egyptian gods. They claimed to be deities, the sons of the sun god, Ra. As a result, Egypt's government was a *theocracy*. This means the people believed their rulers were guided by their gods in decision-making. Usually a theocracy was governed by priests.

Pharaoh Amenhotep IV, the son of Amenhotep III, was different. He disagreed with the officially accepted religion of Egypt. Such a person is called a *heretic*. It is possible that he was influenced by the writings of the Hebrews or by the power of the Hebrew God shown during the ten plagues. Whatever the reason, Amenhotep IV changed his name to Akhenaton and changed Egypt's religion.

Instead of worshiping many gods, Akhenaton wanted Egyptians to worship one god, whom he called Aton. Naturally the priests opposed this change of religion. Akhenaton moved his capital from the religious center at Thebes to Amarna, a newly built city.

Akhenaton was different from previous pharaohs in other ways. He only had one wife, the beautiful Nefertiti. Many paintings and statues have been found of this couple, portraying them as happy and loving. This was the

This picture of Egyptian servants, painted on the wall of a tomb, shows the type of people who served the nobility. Notice their wigs and transparent clothing, typical of this time period. Because they had little importance in rank, the servants were all pictured alike.

The Book of the Dead

The Egyptians' beliefs in many gods and in a person's afterlife were detailed in *The Book of the Dead*. People believed death was a continuation of the pleasant things in life. The rich spent much time preparing a tomb which was to be their home when they died.

The Book of the Dead tells that Ptah was the most important, all-knowing god, and that he was the only god who could appear in human form. The Egyptians also worshiped a ram-headed sphinx, the god believed to be responsible for seeing that everything continued as it was created. Anubis, pictured with the body of a man and the head of a jackal, supposedly would judge people after they died. The sun god, Ra, was always pictured as a round orb, surrounded by its rays. Hathor was the cow-goddess of love and childbirth. Amon, represented by a goose, serpent, or any other living thing, was the invisible life-giver.

first time a pharaoh had been pictured in a relaxed, natural pose.

Akhenaton Loses Power. Although Akhenaton tried to bring a period of peace and growth to Egypt, disturbing clouds were gathering all over his empire. Angry priests were determined to destroy him and his new god. At the same time, cries for help were heard from the area of Canaan. A powerful people were invading the country and the local governors were calling on Akhenaton to send help.

Many historians believe these people, called *Hapiru*, were, in fact, the Hebrews. They were then led by Joshua who had replaced Moses. Many letters like the following were sent to Akhenaton:

"Your Majesty should also know that enmity against me is very, very great. All the towns which the king has placed under me have joined the Hapiru-brigands. Would that the king would place me under the protection of the man who will lead the archers of the king, so that I might reclaim the towns which have joined the Hapiru-brigands and put them under me again. Then I would be able to serve my lord the king just as our forefathers did before. . ."

The Hebrews, or Hapiru, did conquer Canaan. But they did not have to fight against Egyptian armies since Akhenaton was unable to send help to the rulers of Canaan. Akhenaton's reign was short. It is possible that he was murdered by the priests or by other enemies who were determined to regain their former authority.

Discovery of El Amarna Tablets

Egyptian peasant women of the late 1880s made their own fertilizer. One day as a woman was crushing baked tablets into the soil, it was discovered that she was destroying ancient tablets of cuneiform writing. She did not realize that they contained messages from Canaan's puppet kings in Palestine to Egyptian pharaohs. In them Amenhotep II and Amenhotep IV (also known as Akhenaton) were asked for assistance against Hapiru invaders.

Once the value of the tablets was realized, museum curators began to search for their source. It was learned that they came from an area around Amarna and were written c. 1470 B.C. In 1891 Sir Flinders Petrie began excavating this site. Since that time hundreds of tablets, known as the El Amarna Tablets, have been uncovered.

This section of *The Book of the Dead* shows a judgment taking place in the Hall of Osiris. If the deceased was found guilty, the heart was devoured by Ammut who waited with bared teeth on the pedestal. From left to right are the gods: Osiris, Four Sons of Horus, Ammut, Thoth, Horus and Anubis, and Maat, goddess of truth. *The Book of the Dead,* illustrates a great deal about Egyptian civilization c. 2000 B.C.

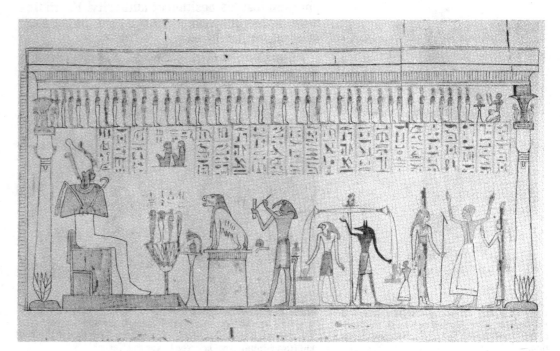

The baboon, Egypt's symbol for the god of wisdom, was painted on the wall above King Tutankhamen's sarcophagus (coffin).

Ramses II was the last powerful pharaoh in Egyptian history. During his reign trade increased and Egypt became a conquering nation.

Fall of the New Kingdom

The challenges to Egypt's religion had greatly weakened the nation's power. Before long, however, the priests were given special privileges once again. They regained their position as the religious power in Egypt. After this, however, Egypt never returned to her former greatness.

Tutankhamen — "King Tut." Akhenaton and Nefertiti did not have any sons to become pharaoh after Akhenaton's death. Since the powerful nobles controlled the kingdom, they arranged a marriage that would protect their power. Tutankhamen, believed to be the son of Amenhotep III born shortly after his father's death, married Akhenaton's daughter. The capital was moved back to Thebes and the pharaoh lost his position of authority. From this time on the pharaoh no longer held the position of speaking for the gods.

Tutankhamen died at the age of 18 or 19 after a reign of only nine years. He was buried in the

A sphinx was an Egyptian mythological figure that was half-man, half-animal. Here a double row of ram-headed sphinx line the 30.58 km (three-mile) drive between Luxor and Karnak.

Valley of the Kings. His tomb, nestled between those of Ramses I and Seti, somehow escaped grave robbers. Then in 1922 Lord Carnavaron of England discovered this tomb with over $100,000 worth of gold buried in it. Tutankhamen's mummy had been placed inside three gold cases and put in a stone sarcophagus. This coffin was found enclosed in four gilded, wooden outer cases.

Egypt's Last Great King. Ramses II, who ruled between 1292 and 1225 B.C., was the last great pharaoh to rule Egypt. He lived to be ninety and had a remarkable reign. He led his army against the Hittites in Syria and against the people of Canaan. Wherever he led his armies, they conquered. He also used his navy as an instrument of war.

For a brief time, Ramses II brought glory back to Egypt. Trade flourished and Egypt became mighty and rich. Ramses II built many monuments, but nobody knows which ones were actually constructed during his reign. This is because he often had the names of other pharaohs removed from monuments and his own name put in their place.

Records claim Ramses II had 100 sons and 50 daughters. For the next 400 years, descendants of these people made up a special class in Egypt. During many of those years, Egypt's rulers were chosen from this group of people.

Under Ramses II large portions of the spoils of war and most of the taxes gathered were given to the priests. This practice was increased under Ramses III, his successor. Finally the royal treasury was empty and workmen could not be paid. While the common people starved, the priests' purses bulged. One-third of Egypt's population was enslaved to the priests. The priests owned one-seventh of all the farmland in the country and their property was free from taxes.

Egypt's Decline. Finally, as the priests became more influential, the pharaoh was overthrown. A priest began to rule in his own right about 1200 B.C. This was bound to happen since the priests had continued to gain power after the death of Akhenaton. The kingdom decayed because new thoughts and changes were forbidden. Egypt's theocratic government was dying.

Another cause for Egypt's decline was the rise of the ambitious Assyrian and Chaldean Empires. The forcefulness of these people caused merchants to transport goods by water for safety. Trade routes shifted to the north through the Caspian and Black Seas into the Mediterranean.

Once again the streams of civilization had turned in a new direction, leaving Egypt to await new conquerors. For the next 2,000 years, Egypt was dominated by foreigners.

The Old Babylonian Kingdom

When invaders destroyed Ur, as we learned in the last chapter, the Sumerian civilization in the Tigris-Euphrates Valley came to an end. This was about 1960 B.C. and for almost 200 years there was no strong government in the Fertile Crescent. Prices rose and the ordinary people who were farmers suffered the most. Merchants were able to make great fortunes because there were no government controls on prices or interest rates. The Old Babylonian Kingdom was established about 1760 B.C. by a king named Hammurabi.

Hammurabi, An Absolute Ruler

Hammurabi conquered the lower end of the Tigris-Euphrates Valley and named Babylon as his capital. Under his leadership, the Old Babylonian Kingdom rose to greatness. After his death, invaders brought the kingdom to an end.

Religion. Much of the Sumerian culture had been adopted by the Babylonians, especially their religious customs. The gods and goddesses whom the Sumerians worshiped were given new names by the Babylonians. For example, the Sumerian goddess of love and war, Innana, was called Ishtar.

The people in the Old Babylonian Kingdom believed that everything was controlled by a god or goddess. They worshiped thousands of deities.

The chief god of the Babylonians was Marduk. Hammurabi claimed that he was Marduk's chief representative on earth and that he ruled because Marduk wanted him to rule. He also claimed that he received guidance from Marduk.

Demons have been real to people of all civilizations. This drawing, found near the Zagros Mountains, is typical of what the early Mesopotamian people thought demons looked like.

Figure of ancient lion tamer from Sumer.

Hammurabi paying homage to Awil-nannar. Hammurabi lived about the same time as Jacob and Joseph.

To make the land more usable, early settlers in the Tigris-Euphrates Valley area developed a system of *irrigation*. As a horse turned a wooden wheel in a circle, a waterwheel located in a river scooped up water into a man-made ditch. Through this ditch the water traveled to areas where it did not normally flow. By controlling the water supply in this way, people were able to live and to grow food in more areas, an important cultural development. This photograph shows a "modern" metal irrigation system that is used by Euphratians today.

Hammurabi believed he did not have to answer to anyone except Marduk for his actions. The idea of ruling with the special approval of the country's god is called *The Divine Right of Kings*. This means kings have the right to do anything they want because they are the chosen representative of the gods or God. We will come across this idea many times during the course of history. Because of the Divine Right of Kings, Hammurabi was the religious authority as well as the political authority in his kingdom.

The Babylonians also copied the Sumerian customs of naming the stars after the gods and goddesses and trying to foretell the future by studying the stars. When important decisions had to be made, soothsayers examined the inner organs of freshly killed animals to tell the future. Believing there were demons everywhere who could gain control of people, the Babylonians tried to cast them out with special chants and magic charms.

Government. By declaring himself the representative of Marduk, Hammurabi was able to gain the support of the people he governed. After getting their support, he brought order to the war-torn area and improved their living conditions.

One of Hammurabi's first acts was to bring the merchants under government control. They were not allowed to charge more than twenty percent interest on loans. He helped trade by building a highway system throughout his kingdom and was the first ruler in history to set up a postal system. The major function of this system was to keep Hammurabi informed about events in all areas of his kingdom. The postal system also helped the merchants conduct business throughout the country.

Hammurabi did not forget the farmers who had suffered great hardships during the years of warfare. An elaborate network of irrigation canals was built to provide water for land not previously farmed.

Every city in Hammurabi's kingdom had individual laws. In many areas the government was not responsible for enforcing laws and there were no policemen. If someone was injured by another person, the matter was settled by feuding and revengeful actions. This was known as "law by vengeance." Nobody was satisfied to let a quarrel die and the feuds became bitter. The influential people, however, could do whatever they chose because nobody had the power to punish them.

Code of Hammurabi. King Hammurabi's most valuable contribution to world history is the set of laws he wrote. Hammurabi had his scribes travel throughout the kingdom, collecting laws. His advisers helped him decide which were the best laws to keep and what new laws to add.

When they finished, they had a set of some 300 laws controlling every aspect of life. These laws, called the Code of Hammurabi, were carved on a large stone pillar so everyone could read them. This system of law brought order and unity to the Old Babylonian Kingdom.

When we compare the Code of Hammurabi to our modern laws, it seems very rough and cruel. It is important, however, to realize that even harsh laws were better than the lawlessness that had existed. One of the most important regulations introduced by this code was that even the king had to obey the laws. This put limits on how the king could treat people and gave them the right to complain if he acted unfairly.

Under the Code of Hammurabi, every person was "frozen" in his social class. If your father was a farmer or a merchant, you would have to be a farmer or a merchant. Nobody, except the slaves, could ever change social position. When people were captured in war and enslaved, they were allowed to own property and to buy their freedom. A person who became a slave to pay a debt had to serve three years before being freed.

The main principle behind this code was that of "an eye for an eye and a tooth for a tooth." This means if someone harmed a person, he had to suffer the same injury in return. There were also degrees of punishment according to social position. If someone in the lower classes harmed a person in the upper classes, his punishment would be greater than if he had harmed someone in his own class. But if a person in an upper class committed a crime, his punishment would be greater than if he belonged to the lower classes. The upper classes were expected to have more respect for the law and to set a good example for the rest of the people.

Women were given rights under Hammurabi's code. They were allowed to own property and engage in business. There are records proving that women hired for jobs usually performed by men were given equal pay.

A woman was given a contract when she married and she was protected by the terms of this contract against abuse from her husband. She usually brought a sum of money called a *dowry* to her husband. The terms of her contract usually depended on the size of the dowry. If she did not have a dowry, she often was treated as a slave.

The Code of Hammurabi provided for every man in the kingdom to serve in the army, work on public projects, or pay a fine. It set basic prices for doctors and other specialists so they could not overcharge their customers. If someone's farmland was destroyed by a flood, he was given an extra year to pay his debts.

Fall of Old Babylon. Under Hammurabi the Old Babylonian Kingdom prospered for forty-two years. Trade became a very important profession and contacts were made with civilizations all over the known world. Goods poured into Babylon and the kingdom prospered.

When Hammurabi died, his heirs were unable to protect the kingdom from invasion. In 1600 B.C. a mountain tribe known as the Hittites captured Babylon. A short time later another tribe conquered the rest of the Old Babylonian Kingdom.

The history of Mesopotamia then shifted to the northern part of the Fertile Crescent. But, as we will see in the next chapter, the city of Babylon again became the center of a great empire, controlling more territory than Hammurabi ever dreamed of ruling.

The Aegean Civilization

The streams of civilization also moved westward from the Middle East to the northern areas of the Mediterranean Sea. It was there

The Code of Hammurabi was a combination of the existing law codes from four Mesopotamian city-states. There are 282 laws carved on this black stone which is 2.3 m (seven and one-half feet) tall. Hammurabi had them gathered and inscribed c. 1750 B.C. At the top of the monument, Hammurabi is shown receiving the symbols of authority from the god Marduk.

This ancient urn, found near the Hittite capital in the Anatolia, was made from one sheet of copper. It was heated and pounded into shape with a metal hammer by a coppersmith. The handle and cover were added later.

that the Aegean civilization had its beginning. Centered around the Aegean Sea, this civilization consisted of two separate cultures—the Minoans and the Mycenaeans. The Minoan culture began first on the island of Crete and the Mycenaean culture developed in the area known today as Greece.

Greece is the country in the southernmost part of the Balkan peninsula that extends into the Mediterranean Sea. No matter where you stand in Greece you are never more than 120 km (75 miles) from the sea. On the eastern coast is the Aegean Sea and on the west is the Ionian Sea. Hundreds of islands are located off the coast in the Aegean Sea, the largest and most important being Crete. This island is approximately 240 km (150 miles) long from west to east and 56 km (35) miles) wide.

Early Migrations

According to the early records of the Hebrew people, descendants of Japheth first settled on the shores of the Black and Caspian Seas. Then, they migrated across the peninsula of Turkey where they built the city of Troy. Located at the crossroads of both land and sea trade routes, this city became wealthy and powerful. Later, descendants of these people crossed the Dardanelles Strait and migrated to Crete and Greece. Archaeologists have found the remains of gold jewelry, cups, offering vases, and religious objects in tracing this migration.

Early settlers in the Balkan peninsula found a mountainous country. There were no great rivers and no fertile valleys for farmland like other civilizations have had. The mountains were very important, however, to the later development of Greek civilization because they isolated the different city-states.

The Minoans

The first Aegean civilization developed on the island of Crete probably because it was safe from invasion. The Aegean Sea formed a natural boundary. Crete became the center of the Aegean world and dominated the people living on the mainland. The people of Crete were

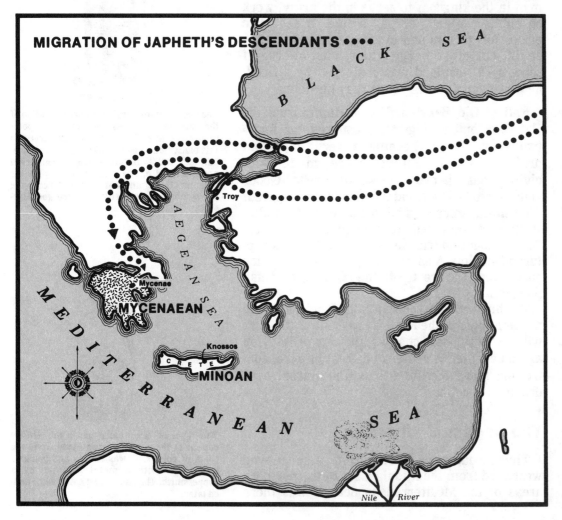

MIGRATION OF JAPHETH'S DESCENDANTS ••••

BLACK SEA

Troy

AEGEAN SEA

Mycenae

MYCENAEAN

Knossos

CRETE

MINOAN

MEDITERRANEAN SEA

Nile River

called Minoans because the king was called "minos." This title was similar to the Egyptians' use of the title "pharaoh."

A Sea Culture. It was only natural that the people of Crete relied on the sea for their living. They were skilled enough to develop ships capable of making long voyages. By 2100 B.C. there was a brisk trade among the Mycenaean cities of Greece, Crete, and the city of Troy. Cretans also traded with the Egyptians and with the cities along the coast of Palestine.

The major items of export were olive oil, wine, pottery, and artifacts made from metal. The Cretans also traded beautiful jewelry of gold and copper which they were skilled in making.

The Mystery of Cretan Writing

The Minoans developed three types of writing during their history. They first used pictures and later scripts representing spoken syllables.

Archaeologists call the first script Linear Script A. The third type of writing was a combination of Cretan and Greek scripts and is known as Linear Script B. Although many records have been found of all three of these forms of writing, only Linear Script B has been translated. Since this writing was developed late in Cretan history, records give little information about the Minoan civilization.

Linear Script B

The Minoans seemed to rely on their sea boundaries to protect them from attack. Their cities show no signs of fortifications, according to findings. There are no war scenes on their *frescoes* (paintings drawn directly on the fresh plaster of the walls). This indicates that war and fighting were not considered very important. Their sea boundaries, however, did not protect them from invaders as we shall see.

Religion. Apparently there were no powerful priesthoods on Crete as there were in other civilizations. It is hard to tell whether the Minoans considered their king a god. We do know they worshiped a "mother goddess" and a "snake goddess" because many small statues of them have been found. The Minoans also are credited for introducing Zeus and some of their other gods to the Greeks.

Most civilizations built huge monuments and temples for their rulers and their gods; the majority of the painting and sculpture was designed to glorify the gods or to picture religious themes. The Minoans built no such monuments or temples for their gods.

Everyday Life on Crete. The climate was very warm on Crete and the people dressed accordingly. The women wore long, low-necked dresses that often were open almost to the waist. Their hair was worn long in very tight ringlets. They wore as much jewelry as they could afford. The men dressed very simply in short boots, a loin cloth, and sometimes a jeweled waistband.

The people in Crete had many of the conveniences used in the cities of Mesopotamia. They had indoor bathrooms and plumbing

Women of Knossos wore revealing dresses similar to those of the nineteenth century in the United States. They imported linen from Egypt, cotton from India, and wool from Turkey. Many women designed their own clothes.

People have always looked for faster ways to copy messages. Today people use carbon paper, xerox machines, or quick printing. In Crete, cylinder seals were used. These seals were made of baked clay with messages in pictures or writing on them. The seal was then rolled over soft clay to duplicate the message quickly. Cypriots and Minoans from Crete used silver cylinders.

systems with running water. (The drain pipes for their sewer system were built so expertly that they can still be used today.) Sun-dried bricks and wooden frames were used to build homes.

The most impressive building on Crete was the beautiful palace at the capital city of Knossos. The palace, approximately five stories high, had so many rooms, courtyards, stairways, and halls that it resembled a maze. The entire building covered 2 ha (6 acres.)

Minoan artwork, rather than being stiff and formal, was full of rhythmic motion. People were pictured in almost every activity of life. The walls of the palace of Knossos were covered with lovely frescoes.

Minoan Civilization Disappears. About 1400 B.C., one-hundred years after the Hyksos took over Egypt, the Minoans were conquered by Mycenaeans from mainland Greece. The beautiful palace at Knossos was destroyed by fire. (This might have happened later during a revolt against the Mycenaean conquerors.) The palace was never rebuilt and civilization on Crete slowly disappeared until it was only remembered in myths.

It was not until 1905 that Sir Arthur Evans, an English archaeologist, investigated the source of these myths. He discovered the ruins of the palace at Knossos and unearthed this forgotten civilization.

Theseus and the Minotaur

For many years all that was known about Crete was in a popular Greek legend. It told how Greek boys and girls were sent to the island of Crete as tribute. There the king of Crete, who controlled all of Greece, offered them to Minotaur, a Cretan god who was half man and half bull.

Theseus, the son of a Greek king, volunteered to go to Crete to kill the Minotaur. The Minotaur was protected by a labyrinth (maze), but Theseus was able to find a way around the winding passages and killed the Minotaur.

It is interesting to note that the favorite sport in Crete was bull-jumping, similar to present-day bullfighting. It may be that Greek young people were brought to Crete to participate in this dangerous sport.

We also know that the king's palace at Knossos on Crete resembled a maze, which may be where this part of the legend developed. Often the king of Crete wore a golden mask of a bull, and it is possible that Theseus, after finding his way through the labyrinth, killed the king who looked like a minotaur.

Bull-jumping was a favorite sport of the Minoans on Crete c. 2800 B.C. As this drawing shows, a person would run toward a bull, grab its horns, and do a somersault flip over its back. Bull-jumping was primarily a spectator sport like bull-fighting is today.

Minoan life is depicted in this reconstruction of the Grand Staircase approaching the palace of Knossos, Crete. As slim Minoans shepherd their flocks up the ramp, a man and woman dressed in court attire enter the building.

The Mycenaeans of Early Greece

Unlike the Minoans on Crete, the Mycenaeans settled in an area that lacked natural boundaries. On the mainland they were separated from one another by the rugged mountains. As a result of trade, their culture was greatly influenced by the civilizations existing in the Middle East and Egypt.

During the early part of their history, the Mycenaeans were controlled by the Minoans. Then, as we have seen, the Mycenaeans overthrew the Minoans and destroyed their culture. They overtook the island's trade and Mycenaean seaports thrived.

A Wealthy, Warlike Culture. The Mycenaean civilization, rich from trade and drawing heavily from other peoples' ideas, provided much gold and riches for its citizens. Archaeologists have discovered a mother and child wrapped in gold foil. They also have found gold cups and dishes.

The Mycenaeans, however, were in constant civil conflict. They proved to be more warlike and aggressive than the Minoans. The early inhabitants developed fortified centers at Pylos, Thebes, Mycenae, and other sites. These places were never cities like Knossos or Babylon. The people lived in small farming villages around these administrative centers which were ruled by kings.

Although the Mycenaeans produced no great cities, they did build fortresses, called *citadels*, on the tops of high cliffs for protection. Each fortress, called an *acropolis*, had a temple for the gods and a palace for the king within its walls. The name "acropolis" is derived from the Greek words *kros*, meaning "highest," and *polis*, meaning "city." Therefore an acropolis is a "high, protected place."

It was probably due to rival trade routes that the Mycenaeans joined forces and attacked the wealthy trade city of Troy about 1200 B.C.

Search for Ancient Troy

For thousands of years people reading the *Iliad*, Homer's epic of how the Greeks destroyed Troy, considered the story a myth. In 1870 a German archaeologist named Heinrich Schlieman determined to discover Troy. For the next fourteen years, he excavated the ancient site in northwestern Asia Minor until he discovered the ancient city of Troy that the Greeks destroyed. Since then archaeologists have learned Troy was built and destroyed nine times.

The Dorian Invasion. Not long after the attack on Troy, the Mycenaeans were invaded by a group of northern people called the Dorians. Although the seaport citadel of Pylos made every effort to defend itself, it was overcome and destroyed. The remaining Mycenaean citadels fell one after another, ending in 1120 B.C. with the fall of Mycenae.

The Dorian invasion is a turning point in history. After this invasion, Greece was again isolated from the rest of the world. During this time the Greek civilization developed on its own with new ideas about government. Many Greek political concepts have been adopted by the United States government.

The first acropolis was built by Mycenaeans. It was a fortress on top of a cliff, designed by these early Greeks for better protection.

Greek merchant ships, such as this one, sailed the Mediterranean Sea, taking the Greek culture to other lands and bringing back merchandise.

Eskimo ritual mask with ermine tail decoration. This mask came from the Tlinqit Indians who live in southeast Alaska.

The Western Hemisphere

While civilizations competed for power in the Tigris-Euphrates Valley area, in Egypt, and in India, people also lived in North and South America. Where did these people come from? How did they happen to be living on a continent separated from the rest of civilization by oceans?

Migrations to the Americas

The latest studies in anthropology indicate there were two major paths of migration from the Eastern to the Western hemispheres: 1) across the Bering Strait from northeast Asia to Alaska and down the Pacific Coast; 2) across the Atlantic Ocean to the Caribbean area—a feat recently accomplished in an Egyptian-like boat.

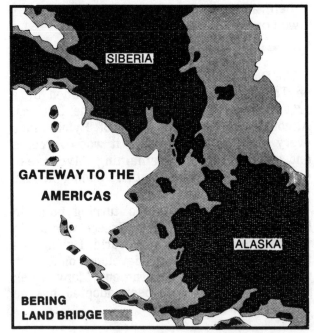

SIBERIA

GATEWAY TO THE
AMERICAS

ALASKA

BERING
LAND BRIDGE

The Land Bridge. A large portion of land connected the extreme northeastern part of Russia to the land known today as Alaska. People crossing the Bering Strait, however, did not realize they were crossing from one continent to another. At the time of these migrations, the area looked much different than it does today. There was much more land—in some places it was as wide as the distance from the Great Lakes to Texas. People following game spent many years crossing this area.

Parallel soils and vegetation in Western Africa and eastern South America may indicate the two hemispheres were one land mass and the continental drift was more recent than supposed. Cultural patterns such as the ziggurat, negroid facial features, and artistic perspectives were often "Old World."

A Question of Arrival Time. Although scientists agree that the first settlers in the Americas came from Asia, they disagree about when they arrived. Scientists who follow the concept of evolution date the findings of the first people discovered in the Americas at about 12000 B.C. The first villages and cultural remains have been dated about 3000 B.C. According to these dates, primitive man roamed the Americas approximately 9,000 years before he learned to do anything more than make a chipped spear point.

Scientists who believe in creation and the flood believe people progressed faster than this in building civilizations. They believe descendants of Noah migrated to the east after leaving the Tower of Babel. Gradually moving northward, they crossed the land bridge and entered the Americas about 3500 B.C. After a five or six hundred-year period of hunting, they formed villages. Other descendants of Ham crossed northern Africa and set out across the ocean until they, too, came to land. (Refer to page 35 and a world map.)

Early American Cultures

The earliest people in the Americas faced harsh conditions. There were glaciers covering much of the north central portion of North America. After the tools and equipment they had brought with them from the Tigris-Euphrates Valley wore out, they were forced to invent new tools and weapons from whatever materials were available. They made spear points from chipped stone and flint. They used them to hunt elephants, bison, mammoth, tapir, and camels, and smaller game, including deer, rabbits, and others.

Llano Man. The earliest traces of these primitive hunters have been found in what is now the Great Staked Plains area of Texas. Called Llano men by scientists, these people made tools from bones and hammerstone. The first big advance in their culture was the development of a more effective spearhead called the *Folsom point* (named for the area where it was discovered by archaeologists). This and another type spearhead called the *Clovis point* made it easier to hunt larger game. The knowledge of how to make these points was shared by migrating hunters and spread throughout the Americas.

Culture spread from one group to another in the Americas, basically as a result of the migrating hunters. As people settled in villages, cultures sprang up in many areas at the same time. They would not have had much influence on each other had it not been for the migrating hunters.

Danger Cave People. While Llano men using their Folsom point hunted mammoth, a different culture developed in what is now the Great Basin Desert in the Southwest United States. These people lived in an area called Danger Cave. They wandered across the desert gathering wild grasses and plants for food. They developed a shallow milling stone for grinding parched, wild plant seeds into flour. Woven baskets, some of the oldest samples ever found, were made by the Danger Cave people. They also made traps, nets, and snares to capture porcupines, rats, mice, and gophers which they roasted and ate with a gruel (porridge) made of ground seeds.

Poverty Point. Recently, archaeologists discovered remains of an early civilization at Poverty Point in Louisiana. Today Poverty Point is composed of six circular ridges shaped like an octagon, 1.2 km (3/4 of a mile) across. Across these mounds are ridges and on the outer edge is located a huge irregular mound.

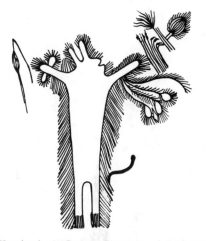

Hunting in the Danger Cave area of the Great Basin Desert is depicted by this cave painting found in present-day Texas.

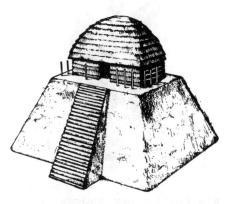

One of the earliest North American Indian cultures, the Mound Builders, built religious and civic centers of wood and thatch on top of mounds of dried mud. As shown in this drawing of a temple mound, stairways were made of logs. Notice the resemblance to the pyramids of Mexico and South America, two civilizations which greatly influenced the North American Indian.

Llano men used primitive weapons to spear the great North American elephant.

Between the ridges deep pits have been discovered, resembling those usually used for garbage around a large town. Archaeologists estimate that at least 600 homes were located there and were built about 1000 B.C. This makes Poverty Point the oldest North American civilization of any size yet discovered.

Poverty Point was a stone culture. The people ground and polished hematite and other stones into balls, weights, and small ornaments. Flint, chert, and quartzite were chipped to form blades, points, and delicate punching and cutting tools. Although not much pottery has been uncovered, small crude figurines, always female, have been discovered.

Tens of thousands of small, baked clay balls and cylinders have been discovered. The Indians heated these balls in a fire, dug a pit, and buried the hot clay with meat they wished to cook. These clay "fire balls" were also used to heat water. Clay balls such as these were used for cooking because early Indians did not have pans to place over the fire. The clay was often decorated by grooving, punching, or squeezing and each housewife had her own favorite decorations.

Wild corn was first cultivated by the American Indian in Mexico as food. Unlike modern ears of corn, the cob was believed to by only an inch long, as illustrated here in its actual size.

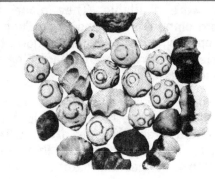

Foods of Early Indians

Many foods that might otherwise have been overlooked were introduced to the world by the American Indian. A partial list of these crops include lima beans, tomatoes, peppers, pumpkins, avocados, cocoa, pineapples, and white and yellow squash. The Indians were also responsible for discovering a popular, but inedible, crop—tobacco.

The Spearthrower

The spearthrower, called Atlatl by South American Indians, was a stick about 61 cm (two feet) long with a small hooked tip at one end. The end of the spear was placed in this hooked tip, in effect giving the hunter a longer arm. This made it possible for the thrower to hurl the spear with greater force. In this way he was able to kill larger animals such as the mammoth.

Archaeologists have uncovered the early American Indian artifacts pictured here in Poverty Point, Louisiana, where a civilization existed c. 1000 B.C. The clay balls (top) were decorated and then heated. Called "fire balls," they were put in ovens to cook food. The artifact collection (bottom) of this primitive stone culture includes crude jewelry, art objects, and weapons.

At least thirty-three smaller sites similar to Poverty Point have been found at different places along the Mississippi River. Each has the major features of the Poverty Point site, although archaeologists do not know if there was any relationship between the two areas.

Early Mexican Culture. As we have learned, the people in the Americas gathered seeds and plants for food, but did no farming. The earliest villages where crops were grown have been found in Mexico along the Gulf Coast. These crops were gourds, chili peppers, and pumpkins. Later, kidney beans, sweet and white potatoes, and peanuts were also harvested.

It was in Mexico that a small vegetable no bigger than a kidney bean was first planted. Cross-bred with similar wild plants, this vegetable became the New World's most important crop—corn. Corn is one plant that will not grow wild. The art of planting corn has been passed from culture to culture across both North and South America.

By 2000 B.C. farming was a way of life and villages became more common. Early farmers used the "slash-and-burn" technique. Every few years they cleared off an area by burning down the trees and vegetation. Crops were grown there until the soil became exhausted of its minerals. Then the land was left alone and a new area was cleared off.

The earliest farmers lived in "pit" houses with floors below ground level. Later, simple "wattle-and-daub" houses were built. These homes were made of a framework of poles, interwoven with cane or brush, and plastered with clay. The thatched roofs were made of grass, palm leaves, or other similar materials.

In the early Mexican sites, thousands of tiny, female figures, 10 to 13 cm (four to five inches), have been found by archaeologists. These figures were so abundant that even today farmers' plows frequently dislodge them from the ground. Nobody is really sure why the clay statues were sculpted, but they have been helpful in dating civilizations.

Huaca Prieta. About 1000 B.C. several hundred people formed the village of Huaca Prieta along the Pacific coast of Peru in South America. They lived in pit houses that had one or two rooms and whale bones and wooden beams for roofs. These people made their living by net-fishing and farming. Their main crops were lima beans and squash. Instead of pottery they used gourds which were decorated with figures carved into their sides.

The people of Huaca Prieta were artistic weavers. They learned to dye yarn many different colors. They wove figures of men, sea creatures, and animals into cloth with the multicolored yarn. They also wove beautifully decorated baskets.

Other Early American Cultures. Most of the early cultures of North America were very primitive compared to the civilizations we have been studying. The earliest remains yet found are those of the Mound Builders. Mounds of earth were used by these people for tombs, defense, homes, and possibly religious purposes. The Mound Builders, although they sometimes hunted big game, gathered seeds, nuts, and other wild plants for food.

In the woodlands of eastern North America, mammoths and other large leaf-eating animals moved south. At the end of the Ice Age the weather was too cold for them. The people living in this area were then forced to change their

Throughout history primitive people have used interwoven poles, reeds, and branches (called wattle) covered with soft clay or mud as daub to construct simple homes. The early people in Mexico used techniques similar to those of the Middle East peasants pictured above to build their wattle-and-daub homes.

The Story of a Mastodon Named "Sue"

The story of "Sue," a Mastodon discovered in Florida, is an example of the way a historian put details of a "Dig" into history.

A drag-line operator was digging a canal through empty land to control water. He was getting dry land ready for a contractor to build new homes west of West Palm Beach, Florida. The operator saw some huge bones in the bank of the canal he was digging. He called the owner who, in turn, called Dr. Mary Stanton, an historian and archaeologist, to identify the bones.

When she asked to preserve the site for excavation, the operator dug a canal around the bones and set pumps to drain the water for digging. She trained students to assist with the excavation. They kept records of every detail.

Identified bones included: mastodon, mammoth (three varieties), bison, dog, alligator, sloth, bird, turtle, capybara, fish, dog, and horse.

Why were carnivorous and herbivorous animals buried at the same place--in one level--all together? Probable answer: all the animals went to their place of security--a watering hole--during an impending catastrophe. Conclusion: Dr. Stanton concluded that the catastrophe fit the time and results of the Universal Flood and all dating methods supported the position.

way of life. They began fishing, hunting deer and other small game, and gathering edible plants. It was during this time that these North American people began making more com-

At one time this mastodon, a member of the elephant family, wandered around Florida. Its bones were found with the remains of all types of fish, birds, and animals during an excavation in Palm Beach County, Florida. This reconstruction, done by the Gem and Mineral Society under the direction of Dr. M. Stanton, is on view at the Science Museum and Planetarium of West Palm Beach.

plicated tools. They invented a perforated spear-thrower and made grooved axeheads, crude soapstone bowls, and pottery.

Along the region of western Tennessee, from the Mississippi River to Florida, lived a people now called the Shellfish-Eaters. Huge mounds of empty shells, dated about 1000 B.C., mark the places where these early people lived.

In the Lake Superior area of northern Wisconsin, people discovered copper deposits and began making copper tools and spear points. Adzes and gouges (developed for carving wood) and slate knives have been discovered in the area now known as the state of New York.

Summary. The history of the Americas began as a struggle for survival in a new environment. After the Indians began to grow their own food supply, the story changed. People struggled against each other. As they learned to control their food supply, people had more time to turn their creative talents into works of art. The stage was then set for the flowering of more involved civilizations.

Migrations to the Orient and Africa

Descendants of Ham traveled south from Mt. Ararat to the Persian Gulf, followed the Persian Gulf and Arabian Sea, and crossed the Strait of Aden into Africa. (Refer to Map on page 35.) Archaeologists and anthropologists have traced them through the worship of the moon and elements of astrology.

The Orientals descended from the sons of Japheth who turned east after crossing the Caucasus Mts. (See page 28.) As families continued eastward, groups broke off to start communities. Once east of the Altai Mts., they dispersed to the Bering Strait and south to the Yellow River. These people were primarily traced through their peculiar pottery styles.

RISE OF SMALL KINGDOMS

Projects

1. Do a study on punishment for crimes. Is it true that the more civilized people become, the better they treat criminals? How many states have the death penalty today? What are some new ideas being tried to rehabilitate prisoners? Are these methods working? Are crime rates going up or down? Explain.

2. We have seen that purple dye came from the murex shell. What other colors did ancient people use and where did they get them?

3. Give a report on Joshua and his battles after entering Canaan, or report on the lives of one of Israel's judges.

4. Build a model of a yurt.

5. Give a report on Amazons. What did the Greeks say about them? Find at least one story about Amazons. Are there any people today who could be called Amazons? Explain.

6. Read the story of Odysseus' (Ulysses') return home from Troy. What were your two favorite parts? Why?

7. Select a Greek myth dealing with any of the strange creatures mentioned in the text. Draw a picture showing your favorite part of the myth.

8. The Greeks solved their overpopulation problem with colonies. What are experts saying about the population explosion today? What is being done about this problem?

9. The Olmecs worshiped a "werejaguar." What other strange creatures have people believed in throughout history? How do you think these ideas came about?

10. Do a language study. List ten English words that came from the Greek language and ten English words that came from the Latin language.

Words and Concepts

Mount Olympus
murex
colony
myths
yurt
Homer
Great King of the Sun
primogeniture
aristocracy
steppes
first horsemen
Chavin de Huantar
oracles
politics
compensation
Ten Commandments
Magna Graecia
mythology
agora
Mursilish I

A Hittite warrior wore a cone-shaped helmet made of iron, as illustrated here.

The Hittites were descendants of Heth, a grandson of Ham. They built a fabulous civilization on the Anatolia (high plateau) of what is now called Turkey.

Rise of Small Kingdoms

As major civilizations were flourishing and declining, many smaller nations and tribes also were becoming a part of history. Some of these tribes had very little influence on the course of world history. Others played important roles, even though they never became powerful nations. Although it is impossible to study all of these people, we will discuss those cultures which have had the greatest influence on our way of life.

Many groups, such as the Philistines, Hittites, Israelites, Amorites, Canaanites, Edomites, and Moabites, lived in the general area of Mesopotamia. Tribes such as the Cimmerians, Scythians, and Sarmatians settled the vast spaces of southern Russia. On the Balkan peninsula, the Mycenaean peoples had been scattered by the Dorian invaders. There a new culture came into being, eventually becoming the glorious civilization of Greece. In the Western Hemisphere, the Olmecs of Mexico and the Chavin people of Peru established the first civilizations in that area.

The Middle East

The area of the Fertile Crescent and the area along the Mediterranean coastline that is now Israel is often referred to as the Middle East. Many kingdoms tried to rule this area during its early history. First one kingdom dominated, perhaps even overran the territory. Then another would take its place. Often the loser in the power struggle disappeared from the pages of history. The Middle East was, and still is important to world history.

The Hittites

According to Biblical records, the Hittites were descendants of Canaan, one of Ham's sons. They migrated into the Anatolia, the area now known as Turkey, where they found people already living. These people were descendants of Japheth who had entered Turkey from the Black Sea area. The two groups joined together and were called the Hittites. As they conquered the other tribes living in the area of Turkey, they became the dominant civilization.

Achievements. The Hittites were a warlike people. Their greatest contributions were the development of agriculture, trade, and iron. They were also noted for their code of laws which was more humane than those of other civilizations we have seen. The Hittites made few cultural contributions; their art and architecture were copied mostly from other peoples.

The Hittites were the first people after the Flood to rediscover the uses for iron. By 2000 B.C. they had developed an improved method of refining iron that made it stronger. They used this method to develop iron weapons. Since all the other civilizations in Mesopotamia had copper weapons, the Hittites had a great advantage in warfare. Their iron weapons could cut through the copper shields and swords as if they were made of wood. Soon the Hittite warrior in his conical helmet and boots with sharp, up-turned toes was feared all over the Mesopotamian area.

Hittite Rulers. A Hittite king was also the religious leader. He was called the "Great King of the Sun." Both the king and queen led the people in worshiping Teshub, their great god, and Arinna, the sun goddess. When a king died, the Hittites believed he became a god and they worshiped him.

The most famous Hittite king was Mursilish I. Under his leadership the Hittite armies conquered North Syria and parts of the Euphrates Valley. It was Mursilish I who destroyed the city of Babylon in 1600 B.C., bringing the Old Babylonian Kingdom to an end.

Babylonian Influence. Once they were in control of the Mesopotamian area, the Hittites began to trade with their neighbors. As a result the Hittites copied many of Babylon's styles. Hittite architects, for example, modeled the capital at Hattusas after Babylonian architecture. On rock walls around the capital were bas-relief carvings of musicians, artists, farmers, warriors, and many other people in everyday activities. From these carvings we have learned something of how the Hittite men and women dressed and lived.

The Babylonians influenced the Hittites in other ways too. The Hittites used Babylonian

cuneiform writing and copied the literature, art, and religion of Babylon. Their laws were much like the famous Code of Hammurabi, except that they were not as harsh in their punishments. Instead of "an eye for an eye," the Hittites allowed people to make a payment, called *compensation,* to the injured person.

The Kingdom Falls. Internal problems caused an almost lawless period in the Hittite Empire. Thutmose III, the forceful and warlike pharaoh who succeeded Hatshepsut, conquered Syria.

Much of what we know about the Hittites comes from studying the carvings in rock walls around their capital. The carving illustrated here shows Hittite men and women in everyday activities.

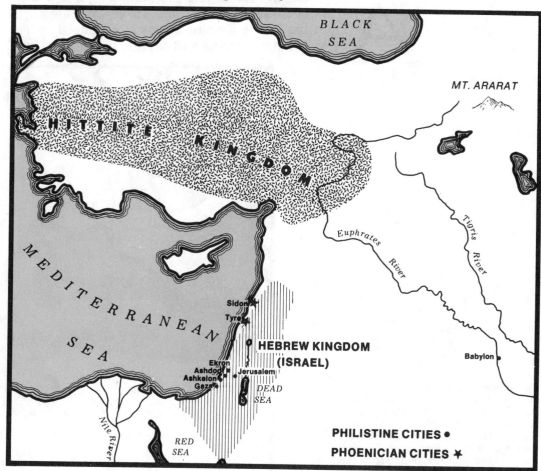

"HOW WE GOT THE LETTER 'A' "

Egyptian Apis

Phoenician Aleph

Greek Alpha

Roman A

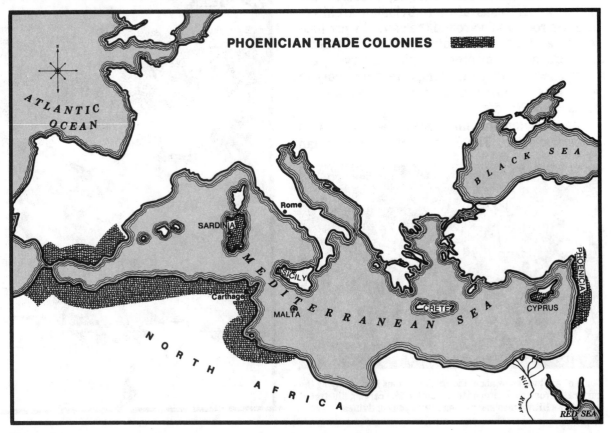

For many years the Egyptians remained in control of this area. Finally, in 1470 B.C., during the reign of Pharaoh Akhenaton, the Hittites were able to break away from Egyptian control. Two centuries later Ramses II tried to recapture Syria. When he was unable to defeat the Hittites, he made a treaty with them in which the two agreed not to attack each other.

With their fierce army the Hittites should have been able to set up a powerful and lasting empire. About 1200 B.C., however, a new wave of invaders poured into Turkey and destroyed the Hittite Empire. It was so completely wiped out that for thousands of years the only record of the Hittites was in the Bible. Finally, late in the nineteenth century, archaeologists began uncovering the ruins of Hattusas, rediscovering this almost forgotten people.

The Phoenicians

There are no records showing where the Phoenicians came from. Their major cities, Tyre and Sidon, have the same names as two of Ham's grandsons. For this reason some scholars believe these people were Hamitic. Their greatest contributions were in navigation and trade, as well as a written alphabet.

PHOENICIAN TRADE COLONIES

ATLANTIC OCEAN

BLACK SEA

Rome

SARDINIA

MEDITERRANEAN SEA

SICILY

Carthage

MALTA

CRETE?

CYPRUS

PHOENICIA

NORTH AFRICA

Nile River

RED SEA

This decorative mascara holder from ancient Phoenicia shows the people's skill in metal artwork and love of beauty. Made of bronze, the head contains a stem for applying the mascara. This holder also reveals that people have not changed much over the years; women used makeup to improve their appearance, just as they do today.

Early Settlers. About 2000 B.C. the Phoenicians settled along the coast of the area known today as Lebanon. Because other peoples living in the Fertile Crescent were more powerful, the Phoenicians were limited to the territory along the coast. Their country was too mountainous for them to make a living by farming. So, like the people of Crete, they turned to the sea for their livelihood.

As the Phoenicians traveled the entire length of the Mediterranean Sea, they established trade cities along the coast. Phoenician cities flourished in Cyprus, Malta, Sardinia, Sicily, and in North Africa, including the powerful city of Carthage. Long after the Phoenician cities in Canaan had been conquered, North Africa's Carthage challenged Rome for leadership of the Mediterranean area.

A Great Trading Nation. The Phoenicians developed a strong merchant marine and their ships carried trade goods to every part of the known world. Phoenician sailors were brave and adventurous. They sailed past Gibraltar into strange and unexplored waters and began trading with British tribes. From Britain they brought tin, furs, and hides. Their ships also reached the southeastern coast of Africa where it was profitable to trade jewels, spices, and other goods.

The Phoenicians were also famous for their woven cloth. Their fabrics, particularly a beautiful purple-colored cloth, were in demand all over the known world. The Phoenicians discovered that they could get a purple dye by crushing the murex shellfish. These shells were found along the coast of the Mediterranean Sea, but were rare. For this reason only the rich could afford clothing dyed purple. Most of the kings of the time claimed the privilege of wearing this color, and thus it became known as "royal purple."

Religion. Phoenicians worshiped many of the same gods that most of the peoples of Canaan worshiped. Only the Hebrews of Canaan are known to have worshiped one God.

Each Phoenician city had its own god, called Baal. The king was usually considered a descendant of this god, making him a half-god. The goddess of love was called Ishtar, or Astarte. Women often cut off their long hair and placed it on the altars as an offering to her.

The most terrible god the Phoenicians worshiped was named Moloch. He supposedly demanded human sacrifices, so parents offered their children to show their devotion. Trumpets and flutes played loudly to drown out the cries of the babies as they burned in the blazing fire in the god's lap.

The Written Alphabet. For centuries the Phoenicians have been credited with developing the written alphabet. In recent years, while working at the site of Lachish, an ancient

The Phoenicians—Brave Sailors

Recent archaeological findings in South America lead scholars to believe that the Phoenicians sailed to the Western Hemisphere almost 2,000 years before Columbus. Whether they were blown off course or sailed there purposely to look for new trade markets and goods is not known. The brave Phoenicians, however, sailed completely around the coast of Africa. This feat was not repeated by any civilization until centuries later.

The murex shellfish was crushed by the Phoenicians to get a beautiful purple dye for cloth. Only kings and emperors could afford to buy this dyed cloth, and purple became known as a "royal" color.

Canaan means "Land of red-purple" from the industries developed by makers of dye from the murex shell fish.

Phoenician trading ships, like the one pictured here (of c. 900 B.C.) sailed to many parts of the world. Merchants traveled to England, around the tip of Africa, and may have even landed on the coast of South America.

Moloch, one of many Phoenician gods, viciously awaits the sacrifice of a living child in his flaming, hollow stomach.

Hebrew city, archaeologists have discovered evidence which suggests the Hebrews were the source of the first written alphabet. It was developed by Hebrews in the Sinai peninsula and, therefore, it is known as *Sinai script.* Historians are not certain, however, whether the Hebrews or the Phoenicians were the first to invent the alphabet.

The Phoenicians were responsible for spreading the written alphabet throughout the Mediterranean area through trade. Cuneiform and hieroglyphic methods of writing were too clumsy and time consuming in keeping trade records. The Phoenicians simplified the alphabet which was very useful. It was copied first by the Greeks, who added vowels. Later it was adopted by the Romans. The Romans passed it on to modern European languages. The English language today takes eighty percent of its vocabulary from either Greek or Roman sources.

The Hebrews

The Hebrews had been forced into slavery in Egypt for some 400 years until Moses led them out, as we have seen. For forty years these people wandered in the wilderness around Sinai. During that time, their laws were written down and their religious customs developed. Moses then brought them back to Canaan, a land which they believed had been promised by God to their forefathers, Abraham and Jacob.

From Egypt to Canaan. The Hebrews came out of the wilderness to invade Canaan about 1440 B.C. The rulers of the cities there asked Pharaoh Akhenaton of Egypt to send troops to their aid. But Akhenaton was unable to help them. So under Joshua, the leader who followed

Moses, the Hebrews soon got control of much of Canaan.

When the Hebrews invaded Canaan, many tribal groups already lived in the area. The people there worshiped many gods and, in some instances, offered human sacrifices to those gods. When cities were founded by these tribes, children, even babies, were buried alive under the cornerstones of the city gates. Such human sacrifices were often made to get the gods' approval before beginning the construction of major public buildings and temples.

Moreover, religious celebrations barely resembled worship. They were occasions where people were encouraged to get drunk and behave in ways that today are considered immoral. Pornography, sex symbols, and both male and female prostitution were accepted parts of Canaanite society. The Hebrews believed that God had directed them to conquer Canaan and that the people living there would be defeated because of their lack of morals.

The Rule of Judges. The Hebrews came into Canaan and conquered city after city. Early

Mt. Sinai, on the Sinai peninsula, is the site where Moses received the Ten Commandments from God.

Hebrew society was set up on a tribal basis. After Joshua died, there were no outstanding leaders to unite all of the Hebrew people. When they were threatened by serious danger, they united under the leadership of a judge. A judge at that time was not like a judge of today. He not only settled problems among the Israelites, but also served as the military and religious leader. Once the danger was past, the Hebrews again returned to tribal government.

The most powerful enemies the Hebrews had to face during these early years of their lives in Canaan were the Hittites and the Philistines. The Philistines had come into the Middle East from islands in the Mediterranean. They knew how to make iron weapons and were fierce warriors. Marching along the coast of the Mediterranean Sea, they conquered every city they attacked. It seemed as if no one could stop them. As they approached Egypt, Ramses III defeated them and they retreated from Egypt to Canaan. There they established five strong city-states—Gath, Ashkelon, Gaza, Ashdod, and

Ekron. Because the Philistines had iron weapons and the Hebrews did not, they prevented the Hebrews from becoming a strong power for many years.

Finally the Hebrews were united under King Saul and the nation of Israel was formed. Israel was not a strong country, however, until 1005 B.C. when her second king, David, defeated her enemies.

Israel Under Solomon. Solomon, David's son, ruled Israel from 965 to 925 B.C., the country's most prosperous and powerful period. King Solomon married Hittite and Phoenician princesses in order to make peace treaties with those countries. He also married an Egyptian princess. For a wedding present, her father conquered Canaanite territory and gave it to them.

Tribute and trade made Israel one of the richest nations in the area. Members of royalty

The Philistines were fierce fighters. They controlled the land of Canaan until King David defeated them and set up the Hebrew Kingdom. Philistine warriors often wore feathered headgear like the ones pictured above.

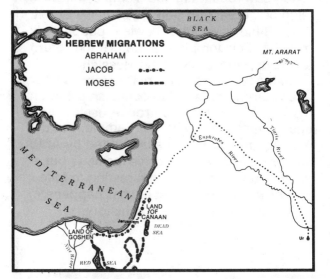

HEBREW MIGRATIONS
ABRAHAM ·······
JACOB ·-·-·-·
MOSES ━━━━━

David—Shepherd, Poet, King

King David, second king of Israel, is probably best known as the shepherd boy of fifteen who killed a giant with a stone and a sling. The Hebrew record tells us that David, a member of the tribe of Judah, was directed by God to face Goliath, the fearful Philistine warrior. The giant was reported to be 297 cm (9' 9") tall and was covered with armor. But David's stone entered a small opening in his headgear and killed him. Thirty years later David became king. He united the Hebrew people and, under his leadership, Israel became a powerful and prosperous nation.

David is also known for writing most of the book of Psalms found in the Bible.

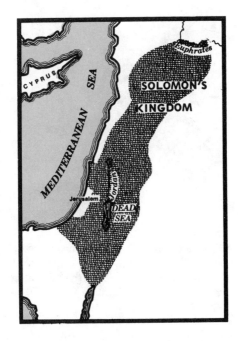

Solomon's Temple, a magnificent structure built to worship God, took seven years to complete. Porches for housing priests who were serving in the Temple were located on both sides of the Temple. Solomon's Temple was destroyed by Babylonians in 586 B.C. and again by Romans in 70 A.D. when Titus conquered Jerusalem.

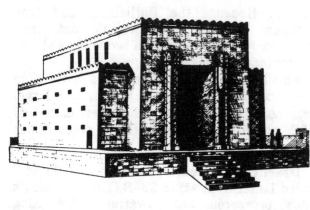

came to Israel from other countries to see for themselves if the reports of the wealth and wisdom of Solomon were true. One such visitor from a country along the Gulf of Arabia was the famed Queen of Sheba.

During Solomon's reign, beautiful cedar trees were imported from Phoenicia and a magnificent temple was built for the worship of God. This temple plays an important role throughout Israel's history.

Decline and Fall of Israel. When Solomon died, Israel was divided into two kingdoms. One

Since Jews have no temple, they worship at the Western Wall. Jews believe that the lowest rocks are from the retaining wall King Solomon built in Circa 970 to 963 B.C.

Arabs and Jews Vie for Temple Site

The site where Solomon's Temple was built is very important to three major religious groups — the Hebrews, the Moslems, and the Christians. When Solomon built the Temple, he asked God to bless it. So whenever the Jews displeased God, they turned toward the Temple and prayed believing God would forgive them.

Solomon's Temple was completely destroyed two times. It was rebuilt twice. The last time it was destroyed, the Hebrew (Jewish) people were sold as slaves throughout the Roman Empire. For nearly 2,000 years, the Jewish people have dreamed of returning to Israel and rebuilding their sacred temple.

When the power of the Jews weakened, Arabs moved in and took control of Israel and the city of Jerusalem. In the next thousand years, a new religion known as Islam developed among the Arab tribes. The Arabs, also called Moslems, believed the spot where Solomon's Temple had stood was sacred. It was there that their

forefather Abraham offered to sacrifice his son and had seen an angel of God. It was on this site that the Moslems built an elaborate place of worship known as the Mosque of Omar.

Some Christians attach another importance to the site of Solomon's Temple. They say rebuilding the Temple will be a sign of the Second Coming of Jesus Christ. The Bible says the Jewish people will rebuild their temple just before the return of Jesus, who is called the Messiah.

In the twentieth century the Hebrew people returned to Israel to establish a Jewish nation. Today they control Jerusalem and many want to rebuild their temple. But the tiny nation of Israel is surrounded by Arab nations which want to drive the Jews out of their country. It will be interesting to follow the news of Israel to see what happens in this important part of world history.

was called Israel and the other Judah. These kingdoms were not strong enough to defend themselves from enemy attack. The Egyptian army, led by Pharaoh Shesonk, attacked Jerusalem and carried off the city's riches. Then the Assyrian Empire came into existence and its armies completely overpowered the Hebrews. The nation of Israel came to an end about 722 B.C. For centuries Israel was dominated by a variety of people and nations. It was not until 1948 A.D. that Israel once again became an independent country.

Hebrew Influence. Although the Hebrews were a powerful people for only a very short time, they had a great influence on world history. Their most important contribution was their belief in one God. While other civilizations worshiped many different gods, the Hebrews were the first early people to continue their worship of just one God throughout their history.

The laws that Moses introduced after bringing Israel out of Egypt have influenced the law codes and way of life of all the countries of Europe and the Americas. These laws, known as the Ten Commandments, are found in the Old Testament of the Bible.

The Early Russians

Russia is a very large area covering nearly one-eighth of the world's land surface. It includes many different land forms and climatic

New Perspectives

During the years of 1990-1992, many changes occured in the area labeled "Russia" on the map. The Union of Soviet Socialist Republics no longer exists. The area is now (April, 1992) broken into separate countries held together by the political term, "Commonwealth of Independent States." Muslims are gaining a greater influence in this new Commonwealth. We are all watching history in-the-making in the former Soviet Union.

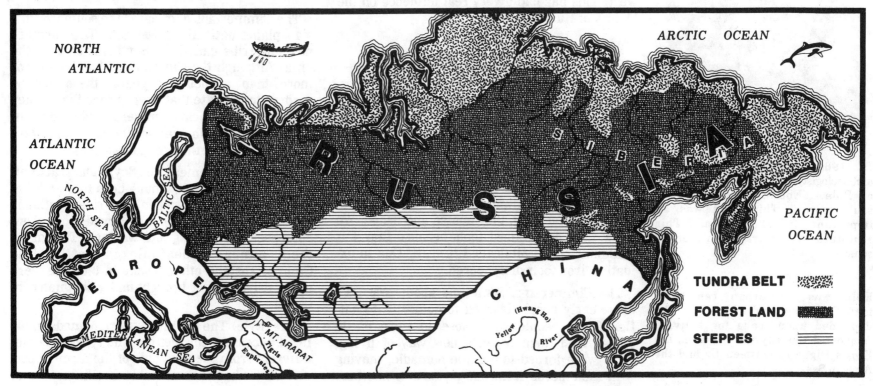

NORTH ATLANTIC

ATLANTIC OCEAN

ARCTIC OCEAN

NORTH SEA

BALTIC SEA

RUSSIA

SIBERIA

PACIFIC OCEAN

EUROPE

CHINA

MEDITERRANEAN SEA

MT. ARARAT

Tigris

Euphrates

Yellow (Hwang Ho) River

TUNDRA BELT

FOREST LAND

STEPPES

In 1964, Matthiae, an Italian archaeologist, uncovered the ancient city of Ebla. Eblahites were skilled sculpturers. This head was an important official or priest. This sculpture was portrayed in the city square.

Ebla was an urban center of manufacturing, and merchants who depended upon trade for a living frequented this city which was on the King's Highway between Ur and the Arabian Sea.

areas within its boundaries. Parts of the country are forests, dense with pine, fir, and birch trees. In the far north there is a region of frozen marshland called *tundra*. Reindeer herds can survive the harsh conditions found there, and for centuries they have been herded like cattle. In the south central area is rolling prairie land called the *steppes*. There are also coal and salt mines, black farmlands, and great stretches of desert.

A major factor in Russia's geography is its lack of mountain barriers, except in the south. Unlike the other countries we have studied, Russian territory has been open to invasion throughout its history. We will see that invaders have swept into the country from both east and west. This has had a very real influence on the history of Russia.

The Earliest Settlers

The first people to live in Russia settled in the area between the Black Sea's eastern shore and the Caucasus Mountains. By 3000 B.C. these people were living in small villages by the seashore and on river banks. Their homes were often semi-sunken sod houses much like those built by the early pioneers, who settled on the plains. In addition to farming, they hunted and fished. We know they had refined tools because they left well-built burial pits called *tumuli*. Due to oxidation, iron tools disappeared.

The Cimmerians. Sometime about 2000 B.C. these early people learned to domesticate cattle. Those people who chose to raise cattle rather than farm began a new way of living. They were forced to become nomadic, moving with their herds from one pasture to another.

These nomads became part of a group known as the Cimmerians.

The Cimmerians roamed Russia's southern plains, breeding horses and cattle. They lived off the milk and meat of their herds. They also grew rich by attacking the farming communities and forcing them to pay tribute.

Historians have not yet identified any written records from the Cimmerians other than the animal-pictographs found on their tombs. Gold and metal objects have been found in their graves. This indicates trade existed between the Cimmerians and civilizations located further south along the Mediterranean Sea.

The Scythians

The Cimmerians dominated the southern Russian plains until about 800 B.C. Then another nomadic tribe called the Scythians entered the area. Although the Cimmerians had horses for more than a thousand years, there are no records to indicate that anyone rode them. They were used to pull carts or were herded like cattle. From every indication, the Scythians were the first people in the area to ride horses.

The First Horsemen. The Scythians practically lived on horseback. Young boys four and five years old had their own ponies to ride. Scythians learned to shoot a double-curved bow from horseback for hunting and warfare. This made them almost unbeatable in battle. The Cimmerians and other people in the area were either driven out or brought under Scythian control.

Life Style. The Scythians were nomads, making it necessary for them to find types of homes different from the mud huts of the farming people. Theirs had to be movable dwellings. So they

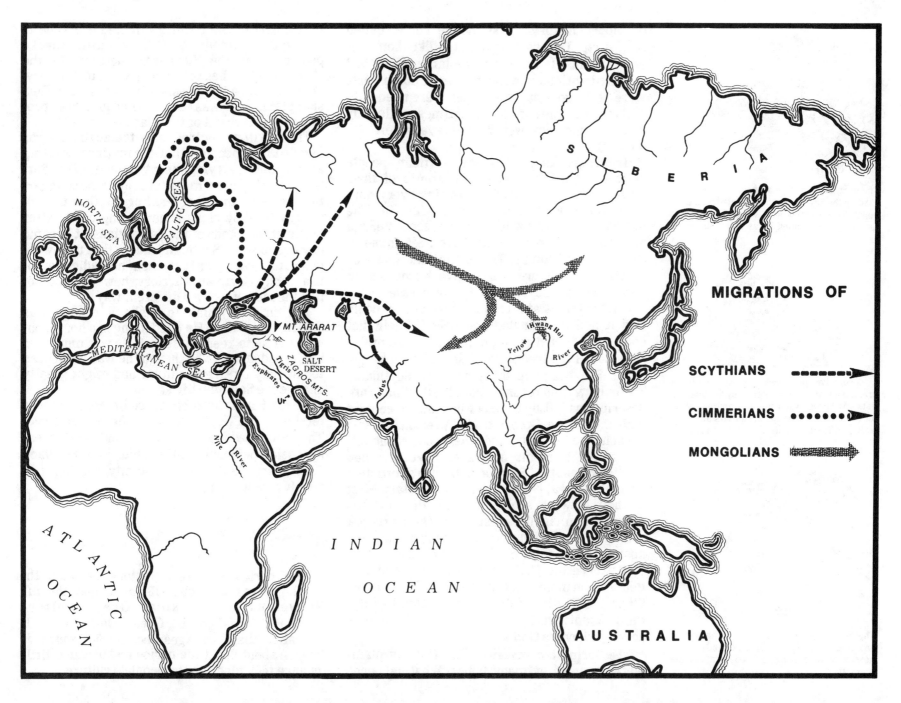

The yurt, the first type of mobile home, w a s used by the Scythians who migrated with their herds. These homes were sometimes so large that they were pulled by as many as twelve oxen.

A decorative pin, such as this one, was created out of precious metals by Scythian artists. Although beautiful, the animals were not realistic. By lengthening antlers and combining different animals, the Scythians created the world's first abstract art.

The Scythians developed a technique of shooting over their shoulders while riding horseback, and became good warriors and marksmen.

developed history's first mobile home, called the *yurt*. The yurt was a tentlike home of animal skins. It was built on a large wagon bed mounted with huge wooden wheels. Some yurts were so large that twelve oxen were needed to pull them. They were sometimes pulled by women when there were no oxen available.

Historians know that the Scythian people believed in a life after death. Tombs of their leaders have been found, containing everything they would need or want in an afterlife. The bodies of a leader's wife, favorite servants, and as many as 25 to 50 horses have been found in some leaders' tombs. The clothes and weapons that have been discovered give historians an idea of how the Scythians lived and dressed.

The Scythians ate fresh fruit when they could find it and they hunted and fished. Their diet consisted of dried grains, horse meat, and milk.

By 400 B.C. Greeks living in cities along the Black Sea began to trade with the Scythians. The only written records about the Scythians are descriptions left by Greeks who came in contact with them. The Greeks traded precious metals in exchange for grains and other food products.

Art. As a result of trade, Scythians had precious metals. Soon artists were creating designs of great beauty from these metals. Most of their artwork showed animal life, but they pictured animals unrealistically. Their artwork remained a pleasing blend of realism and the abstract. Their art pieces were traded further west where the Goths, a tribe which later settled in Germany, began to copy the designs. When the Scythians disappeared from history, their traditional art forms were further developed by the Goths.

The Sarmatian Invasion. The Russian plains were occupied by many tribes. What happened in one part of the country affected everyone in the country. About 300 B.C. a fierce, warlike people called the Huns were defeated by the Chinese. They began moving west to find new lands and invaded Russia. Soon the entire Russian plains area was in motion as groups of people were driven out of their lands by invaders.

The territory controlled by the Scythians was invaded by a people called Sarmatians, wearing armor and carrying heavy lances. The Sarmatians also used metal stirrups which helped them stay on their horses. For the first time in history the Scythians began losing battle after battle at the hands of the Sarmatians. It became obvious to some Scythian leaders that they were going to have to change their nomadic way of life. Many Scythian warriors, however, did not like the idea of living a different way.

The first Scythian to make a change was Scyles, their ruler. He tried living in a house, but was unable to keep it a secret. He was murdered by his bodyguard who thought he was influenced too heavily by Greek culture and might greatly change the Scythian life style.

As the Sarmatians conquered more and more territory, the Scythians were forced to move. They migrated into the area around the Crimea, a Russian peninsula that extends into the Black Sea. There they built a new city and began a totally new way of life.

The Greek Dark Ages

The period of Greek history between the Dorian invasion about 1150 B.C. and the full flowering of classical Greek culture c. 750 B.C. is called the Greek Dark Ages. It is called the Dark Ages because not much is known about this time period and because little change took place in the people's culture.

The records we have of the Dark Ages were written later, based on oral stories and songs of traveling bards, minstrels, and storytellers. These men passed on traditions and values of the period. Stories of strength, courage, skills, family relations, and love passed from one generation to another. Adventures of heroes and warriors were written down by later poets. The greatest of the Greek poets was Homer who told the exciting story of the Greek war with Troy and the great adventure of Odysseus' (Ulysses) return from that war.

When the Dorians defeated the Mycenaeans in 1200 B.C., a totally new type of civilization rose in its place. The people who survived scattered across the peninsula, setting up new cultural units. The Dorians founded a city called Sparta. Refugees from Mycenae moved to Athens where their love of freedom and beauty became a major aspect of that city's culture. Another city, Corinth, was built by people of many different backgrounds.

Homer, a popular poet during the Greek Dark Ages, entertained young and old alike with vivid stories of wars and heroes. These stories, such as the *Iliad* and the *Odyssey*, recorded history for future generations.

As villages and, later, cities were built, the people of different villages rarely saw one another. Travel was difficult and the various cities developed unique cultures without being influenced by each other.

Greek City-States

As the population increased, the major cities, along with the villages in the surrounding plains and valleys, became city-states. Each city-state was a government unit, independent of the other Grecian city-states. The people were loyal to their own city-states, but did not feel a loyalty to the idea of a Greek nation.

Greek Bards, Ancient Historians

Poets in ancient Greece were called *bards*. Unlike poets of today who write and publish their works for everyone to read, bards traveled from city to city telling their stories. Most of their tales were adventures of wars and heroes. When crowds no longer gathered to hear them, they moved on to another city. Their stories were passed down from generation to generation and were finally written down.

The most popular of the Greek bards was Homer. His major works include accounts of the Trojan War, the *Iliad* and the *Odyssey*.

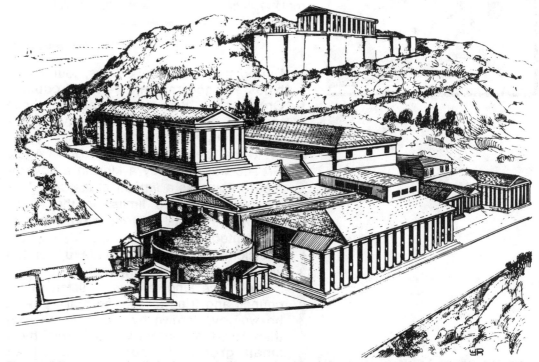

The Acropolis, or "upper city," of Athens was built on a rocky pinnacle, as shown in this photograph of its ruins. It has been called Pericles' Acropolis because he made it a place of beauty. Notice the buildings of the agora at the base of the cliff.

GREEK DARK AGES

There was a great rivalry between the city-states for economic alliances with smaller nearby villages which they often controlled. The city-states often warred with each other as a result of their rivalries.

Early Development. The city centers that developed during this time were different from the citadels of the warlike Mycenaeans. They still used the tops of hills and cliffs for protected areas where they could find safety from attack. Over the years more temples were added to the acropolis which became the center of their city-state. By 600 B.C. a center developed below the acropolis where the people lived and traded. This business section was called the *agora* or marketplace. In this "downtown" section of the city, people bought and sold all kinds of products. People gathered in the agora to discuss important business and to give speeches concerning their government. Such speeches became known as their *politics*.

Social Classes. During the Dark Ages of Greece, society was set up with definite class divisions. The upper classes, called the *aristocracy,* were the rulers. The ordinary, or common people, could be punished for questioning an order given by a member of the aristocracy. Most of the little villages and towns were ruled by a king who generally had a council to advise him. When war threatened, the ordinary people were drafted into an army.

A few rich people had spacious gardens and

Greek Influence on World Governments

During the Greek Dark Ages, four major types of government were introduced. Greeks have been ruled by each of these forms of government at one time or another throughout their history.

At the beginning of the Dark Ages, Greece was ruled by a king in a government known as a *limited monarchy.* This means there were limits on the king's authority. He was not free to do whatever he wanted. The king was guided in his decisions by a council made up of the wealthy people in the kingdom.

When the king refused to listen to his council and tried to take on more power, he was overthrown by the council which then ruled the country. Such rule by a small group of people is called an *oligarchy.* Many times the only laws the oligarchy passed were those to help the rich. Because the common people were being disregarded, they were quick to support another type of ruler called a *tyrant.*

Tyrant has a different meaning today than it had in ancient Greece. Then the tyrant was a ruler with absolute power to do anything he wanted. He ruled with the consent of the people and tried to help them. Today we think of a tyrant as someone who overthrows the government and rules by using secret police and terror. Examples of twentieth-century tyrants are Hitler, Stalin, and Mao Tse-tung.

When a Greek tyrant abused his power, he was overthrown and the people governed themselves. This form of government was called a *democracy.* When the Greek people grew tired of running their government, they usually allowed another tyrant to take control.

their homes were airy with large columns and open courtyards. Most people, however, lived in simple homes which lined narrow, crooked streets. At the foot of the acropolis were the fields where the people grew their food.

Greek Mythology

During the Dark Ages, Greeks developed ideas about their gods and life. To the Greeks, life was not the grim waiting-for-death that dominated other civilizations. Greeks did not develop the cult of worshiping their rulers, and they did not believe in making human sacrifices. Although some of their gods were originally introduced by the people living in the Fertile Crescent and Egypt, they took on different personalities in Greece. Stories of the lives and actions of the gods and goddesses are still read today. These stories are called *myths* and the study of myths is called *mythology*.

Women Warriors

When people read Greek myths, they usually think of them as fairy tales. As a result of archaeologists' discoveries, however, historians believe much of what the Greeks wrote was based on fact. A good example of this is the Greek reference to *amazons,* women warriors.

It is possible the Greeks got the idea of amazons from the Sarmatians, who defeated the Scythians in southern Russia. The Sarmatians had a custom which said their young women could not marry until they killed a man in battle. Therefore, they fought alongside their men until they married.

The Greeks did not actually believe that their gods were divine. They thought they were humans, more beautiful than most, who had become immortal. Because they were still human, the Greek gods did not sit in judgment of the world. Instead they became involved in the affairs of the world, often acting just like spoiled, overgrown children trying to have their way. Greek myths tell of gods and goddesses taking different sides in quarrels and actually fighting with each other over events on earth.

The Greek gods were thought to live in splendid palaces, high atop the cloud-covered peak of Mount Olympus in northern Greece. They did not spend much time in their mountain homes, however. Supposedly, they often came to earth, taking the form of ordinary people. They came in contact with the people of earth. Occasionally a woman was so beautiful, or a man so brave, that the gods allowed him to come to Olympus, joining the gods and becoming immortal.

Major Greek Gods. According to Greek mythology, the king of the gods was Zeus. He was often pictured with lightening bolts which he hurled at anyone who offended him. Although Zeus was king of the gods, he was a hen-pecked husband who often tried to hide what he was doing from the sharp eye of his wife, Hera.

Zeus had two brothers. Poseidon was the ruler of the seas and oceans and the god of horses. Hades, his other brother, was ruler of the underworld kingdom where people went when they died. Hades married Proserpine, the lovely daughter of Ceres, goddess of the harvest. He had carried her off against her will. She only remained with him three months out of the year. During those months her mother punished the earth by making it turn to winter.

The favorite goddess of the people of Athens was Zeus' daughter, Athena. She was supposed to

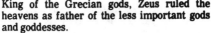

King of the Grecian gods, Zeus ruled the heavens as father of the less important gods and goddesses.

Athena, daughter of Zeus, was the goddess of wisdom and the arts. People believed she also protected warriors and the city of Athens.

According to Greek mythology, a centaur was a part man, part animal creature who battled with their heroes.

have sprung, full grown and in armor, out of Zeus' forehead. She supposedly protected warriors in battle, but she was also the goddess of wisdom.

Another child of Zeus was Apollo. It was one of his jobs to drive the chariot of the sun across the heavens from sunrise to sunset. A Greek myth claims that when Apollo's son, half-man and half-god, tried to manage the wild horses that pulled the chariot, he almost set the world on fire.

Oracles and Strange Creatures. The Greeks had special places where they believed the gods spoke to them through the help of priestesses. These places were called *oracles,* and people went to the oracle when they wanted to know the future. The oracles answered any question they were asked, but they answered in a way that seemed obvious. Usually their answers had a hidden, or double, meaning. Thus, people tried

to foresee their own fate and often made the wrong decisions after hearing the oracle. The most famous oracle was the Oracle of Delphi where Apollo was supposed to give the messages.

In addition to gods and goddesses, the Greeks had myths and legends about who their heroes fought. They believed there were many strange creatures such as *centaurs,* creatures with the head, shoulders, and chest of a man and the body of a horse. Other creatures were *cyclops,*

Medusa, was a woman in Greek mythology who had snakes for hair and eyes that turned people to stone. She was one of three sisters who were known as Gorgons.

Oracle at Delphi Causes Conflict

People in ancient times often visited an oracle, which is a person or shrine believed to have divine knowledge. Their advice, however, usually had double meanings.

An interesting story about an oracle concerns King Croesus of Lydia. King Croesus had been watching the rise of a powerful new empire called Persia and wanted to conquer it.

Lydia, located in Asia Minor, was one of the richest kingdoms the world has ever known. She was one of the earliest countries to mint coins and this money was used throughout the Middle East. Even today, the phrase "rich as Croesus" means unequalled wealth.

Croesus, who ruled Lydia from 570 to 546 B.C., visited the famous Oracle at Delphi to get advice about whether or not to attack the Persians. The oracle's answer was that a mighty kingdom would be destroyed if he did attack. Confident of victory against the powerful Persians, he declared war. A mighty kingdom was destroyed; but it was King Croesus' own kingdom of Lydia.

giants with only one huge eye in the center of their foreheads, and also a dreadful woman named *Medusa* who had a nest of snakes for hair.

Legend tells that Medusa was so fearful that anyone who looked at her face would turn to stone. There were also other strange creatures who could help or hinder the god or goddess. Among them were the winged horse Pegasus, and the various local deities, such as nymphs, oreads, and dryads.

Like other civilizations, the Greeks built temples to their gods. Before many centuries passed, however, the people stopped worshiping the gods. The temples lasted long after belief in the gods had ceased. Although they no longer believed in them, the gods and goddesses remained close to their hearts. Even today people enjoy reading the exciting, funny, and always fascinating stories of Greek myths.

The Greek Colonies

As the years passed, a grave problem faced the Greeks. Their land was becoming overpopulated. This meant there were more people than the land could support. Food shortages were causing serious problems. In addition to this, the early Greeks practiced *primogeniture,* meaning that the eldest son inherited all the property. Any other sons were forced to remain on the land as servants to their brother or to go out to try to earn a living somewhere else.

Early Migrations. The Greeks had already turned to the sea for foods. Fishermen learned they could sail to nearby islands and distant lands where good farmland was available. Many families began to see migration as the solution to their problems. Money was raised to build sturdy boats and fill them with supplies. Then the people who were willing to risk everything they possessed on a chance for a new life set sail. These ventures were called *kolons,* meaning limbs. The travelers were considered to be an extension or outgrowth of the mother city-state. It is from the Greek word *kolon* that we get our modern word colony.

The various groups sailing from Greece settled in many different countries. Once established, they began to grow crops and to trade with their mother city-state. Food and raw materials were shipped back to Greece. Vases,

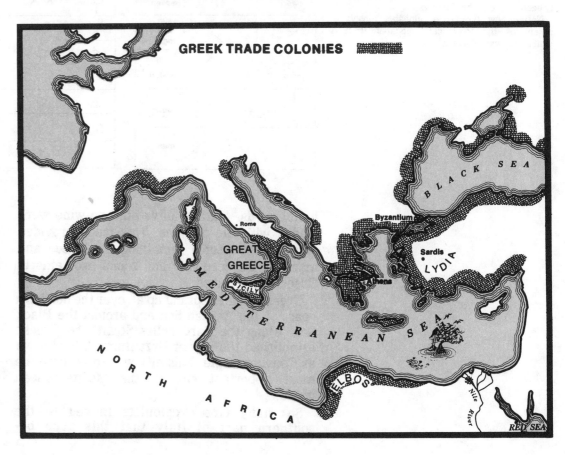

This chart compares the alphabets of four civilizations, showing how one civilization passed along its knowledge to another.

Before the alphabet was developed, people communicated with pictures and symbols called pictographs. These forms, however, were too detailed and time consuming to meet the growing need for a speedy written language.

Cuneiform, a system of writing common to several ancient civilizations, was developed by the Sumerians. About the same time, another system of writing known as hieroglyphics was taking shape in Egypt. The Egyptian hieroglyphics were still in the form of pictures.

The origin of our modern alphabet, formerly traced to the Phoenicians, has more recently been traced to the Hebrews.

Notice how the Greek alphabet closely resembles the Phoenician alphabet from which it was derived.

ORIGINAL PICTOGRAPH c. 3500 B.C.	SIMPLIFIED CHARACTER c. 3000 B.C.	MEANING
		fish
		ox
		donkey
		grain
		god heaven
		sun day light
		to till plough
		house
		man

EGYPTIAN HIEROGLYPH	SINÁI SCRIPT c. 1500 B.C.	REPRESENTS	PHOENICIAN c. 1300 B.C.	EARLY HEBREW c. 600 B.C.	GREEK c. 500 B.C.	ROMAN c. 100 A.D.	PHONETIC VALUE
		ox-head	K	K	A	A	'
		house	9	9	B	B	b
		throw-stick	⌐	⌐	Γ	C	g
		door	◁	◁	Δ	D	d
		man with raised arms	⅃	ⅎ	E	E	h
		hand	𝖸	𝖸	I	I	y
		palm of hand	V	𝖸	K	K	k
		water	𝖲	𝖲	M	M	m
		snake	𝖸	𝖸	N	N	n
		eye	O	O	O	O	'
		mouth	⌐	⌐	Π	P	p
		head	9	9	P	R	r
		papyrus clump	W	W	Σ	S	s
		cross	X	X	T	T	t

metal goods, textiles, olive oil, and wine were traded with the colonies. This trade provided jobs for the people remaining in Greece and many of the economic and social problems in Greece were solved.

Greek colonies sprang up all over the northern coast of the Aegean Sea and around the Black Sea. Along the Dardanelles Strait, the Greeks established the city of Byzantium, later known as Constantinople. This city was to become the most important city in the Mediterranean world.

So many Greek colonists moved to the southern part of Italy that this area be-

came known as *Magna Graecia* (Great Greece). Greek colonies were also established on Sicily, on the island of Elba, on the northern coast of Africa, in Spain, and in France. In addition to trade between the Greek city-states and their colonies, a lively trade developed between Greek, Egyptian, and Phoenician cities. The Egyptian government even allowed the Greeks to build a trading city in Egypt where they could have their own governors, laws, and courts.

On the coast of Asia Minor, the colonial cities of Ionia became so important to the Greeks that they were considered a part of Greece. Greek culture developed in Ionia, making this area as important as the city-states of Athens, Sparta, and Corinth. Ionia served as a bridge between purely Greek culture and the cultures of the Middle East.

A New Form of Government. As the colonies added to the wealth of Greece, the rulers of the city-states found them useful in another way. Whenever people became dissatisfied with the government and tried to bring about changes, they were banished to the colonies. In this way the aristocrats were able to keep a tight control on their city-states and run things to suit themselves. This prevented rebellions and uprisings among the common people for many years.

People with a hunger for freedom and good government, however, will not remain under the harsh rule of bad government forever. A series of revolutions took place in which the government was removed from the power of the aristocracy. By 550 B.C. tyrants took over the city-states and divided the land more widely among the citizens. Trade was increased and people were encouraged to manufacture trade goods. As jobs, farmland, and food became available for everyone, the major need for colonies came to an end. As a result, few new colonies were started after the sixth century B.C.

Summary. The Greek Dark Ages were the foundation for the development of one of the world's most important cultures. Later we will see how each major city-state developed its own unique culture within the Greek state. We will see how the Greeks came up with a simpler written language than the world had ever known. This language allowed Greek culture to spread to all parts of the world. Greek became the official language of most of the world's civilizations. When we next study Greece, we will learn about this flowering of Greek culture known as Classical Greece.

The Earliest American Civilizations

After much careful searching and study, archaeologists have decided that two of the earliest civilizations in the Western Hemisphere were the Olmecs in Mexico and the Chavin in Peru. There are some basic similarities between these civilizations, indicating that one may have developed first and then spread to the other area.

Other cultures existed in the Western Hemisphere before this. Historians now are fairly certain, however, that the Olmecs were the first major civilization to emerge in present central America. There are many ruins that have not been studied and there are areas where nobody has yet searched. Later discoveries may turn up an older civilization that was the founder of both or something may be discovered to prove which came first. Until then, we will study the Olmecs first, assuming it was the civilization which came first and influenced those that followed it in Mexico.

The Olmecs

The Olmec civilization began on the shores of Mexico about 1200 B.C. Farming techniques of these people were still primitive. They could not grow enough food to support a large city. Instead, everyone farmed, hunted, and fished to provide food for their immediate families. Families were scattered throughout the area, living near the land they farmed.

Religion. The one thing that seemed to unite the Olmecs was their religion. They were the first people to construct huge buildings which they used as centers for their civilizations. But these centers were not cities as we think of them today. They were huge religious centers where people came to worship from miles around.

Not very much is known about the Olmec religion. Archaeologists believe the Olmecs must have worshiped the jaguar since pictures of this animal appear so frequently in their art. Realistic pictures of jaguars, as well as figures that appear to be part-man and part-jaguar have been found. These images have flabby, childlike bodies with cleft or deformed heads and snarling, fanged mouths. From the figures left by the Olmecs, we can gather that religion had a big influence over their lives.

Historians believe these people first worshiped the jaguar because of its strength and power. Over the years, however, fantasies developed and the animal began to take on supernatural traits. Finally a sort of "were-jaguar" developed.

Although the unearthing of Olmec figures tells us this religion and culture spread from Mexico to Guatemala and Honduras, it is not known how the religion was spread. It could have been spread by colonists, merchants, or missionaries.

Three Religious Centers. Three important Olmec sites have been discovered by archaeologists. They are San Lorenzo, La Venta, and Monte Alban. Each center was in a different type of location, but all three are easily recognized as Olmec by their sculpture.

San Lorenzo was apparently the first center, built about 1150 B.C. The temple complex was on top of a man-made mountain which rises 46 m (150 feet) above the river valley. It was 1.2 km (three-fourths of a mile) long and .81 km (a half mile) wide. This flat-topped mountain was painstakingly built. Baskets filled with dirt were carried to the site and emptied until the mound grew to an enormous height.

On top of the man-made mountain at San Lorenzo were temples, plazas, reservoirs, and

This Olmec seated figure was discovered near present-day Veracruz. Although this statue is of a complete person, it still resembles a jaguar. The snarling thick lips and catlike slanted eyes were typical features of Olmec sculpture produced sometime between 1200 B.C. and 500 B.C.

Beasts of Burden in the Americas

The people living in the Americas were faced with a different situation than the people of Europe, Asia, and Africa. They had no large animals that could be trained to pull or carry loads as did other civilizations we have studied. Evidently the pulling, lifting, and carrying that was necessary to build the pyramids, temples, and cities in the Americas had to be done without the help of teams of animals.

The huge stone head and headdress pictured here is the lightest of six found at San Lorenzo; it weighs *only* 5440 kg (six tons). The heads were buried carefully by the Olmecs. It was hundreds of years later that erosion washed the earth away around the site and they were discovered by archaeologists. The man in the picture is Matthew Stirling, the archaeologist who made this San Lorenzo discovery.

huge sculptures. San Lorenzo was a major center for almost 200 years and then it was abandoned. Everything was carefully destroyed. The monuments and sculptures were damaged and then buried in rows. It wasn't until the twentieth century that this cultural center was rediscovered. Soil erosion had uncovered parts of six gigantic heads that had been buried.

La Venta was built sometime between 1000 and 600 B.C. on a low island in the middle of a swamp. There were four huge stone heads at this site, one of them more than 2.4 m (eight feet) high.

Some of the stone heads and other monuments weigh between 41 and 51 m t (40 and 50 tons). There is no stone on the island and the nearest source is some 130 km (80 miles) away. This means that all the stone used on La Venta was cut in the mountains, dragged to the nearest river, loaded on rafts, floated to La Venta, and unloaded. All this was done without modern equipment, carts, wheels, or animals. The project probably required many people to work many hours. There is no evidence, however, to suggest that force was used to make the people work. It seems they were willing to work for their gods.

Monte Alban is located 320 km (200 miles) southwest of La Venta on a mountain that towers over three fertile valleys. There three stone pyramids and other ceremonial buildings were built sometime about 500 B.C. Nobody is sure how long Monte Alban remained an Olmec center. While the Olmec culture was being replaced by other groups, Monte Alban remained a religious center. The stones and materials used by the Olmecs were later used to build pyramids and temples for other people. Monte Alban remained a religious center until 900 A.D.

Summary. Although the Olmec culture ended, its mark was left upon the Middle American area. All of the civilizations that came after it seemed to copy the Olmec idea of religious centers with massive temples, pyramids, and monuments. The Olmecs also developed a very crude form of hieroglyphic writing that became the model of all forms of writing in Middle America.

The Chavin

About 1200 B.C., at the same time the Olmec culture was developing in the Middle American area, another culture was beginning to spread

Below is an artist's reconstruction of the great ceremonial center, Monte Alban. These ceremonial buildings, built around 500 B.C., were used by the Olmecs as a place of worship. The Olmecs were replaced by other cultures, but Monte Alban remained a religious center until 900 A.D.

The jaguar, native to tropical America, was worshiped by the Chavin people of Peru and the Olmecs of Mexico. Elaborate centers were built with stone figures carved to look like this wildcat, as the sculpture below indicates. Notice the similarity between the two jaguar's faces.

over a wide area of northern and central Peru. Today this Peruvian civilization is called Chavin. It was named after the ruins found at Chavin de Huantar on the high eastern slope of the Andes Mountains.

Geography. The early settlers in Peru found a mixture of desert, mountain and valley areas in which to live. People were able to settle around the oases in the deserts where water poured down from the Andes Mountains. They also lived in the fertile valleys between the mountain ranges where temperate climate allowed them to grow plenty of tropical fruit. Along the oases of Peru's coastline, people had learned to farm and there large villages began to develop.

Religion. As with the Olmecs, religion unified the people of Peru into an organized culture. The Chavin religion, like that of the Olmecs, centered around the jaguar.

As the jaguar religion began to spread from village to village, it acted as a bond to draw these people together. Local medicine men were quick to see the advantage of serving this new god so they became priests. Some of the larger villages became religious centers where impressive ceremonies were performed.

Certainly the people who worshiped the jaguar in Peru had no central government to unite them. There were no major migrations of people to new areas. When the people felt the need of supernatural help, they traveled great distances to the religious centers. They brought expensive gifts to the priests who served their gods.

Life Style. Finally elaborate ceremonial centers like the one at Chavin de Huantar were built. An enormous stone building dominated the site known today as the Castillo. It is 23 m² (250 square feet) and contains a maze of small rooms, ramps, and connecting stairways. It is believed that no people actually lived in the Castillo, but that it was a gigantic home for the gods. In the remains of a dim gallery, a figure with the fanged grin of a man-jaguar still stands.

At Chavin de Huantar and other ceremonial sites, artists, craftsmen, and traders from all over Peru met to exchange artistic ideas, as well as merchandise. With the interchange of ideas, the culture of the Chavin people spread widely. Then suddenly about 500 B.C. the Chavin culture came to an end. Nobody knows what happened. Perhaps the jaguar-god somehow failed his people and they stopped going to his temples.

Summary. Although the domination of the Chavin culture ended, civilization in Peru did not die. It simply separated into many individual cultures, each cut off from the other. Dozens of these cultures have been discovered and there are probably dozens more that are still hidden. In a later chapter we will study the most important of these civilizations.

The Origin of An Oriental or A Black

Anthropologists show from data that the genotype (the outward features) of a group can be altered by three factors:

1. A drastic climate change;
2. A drastic diet change; or
3. A drastic emotional stress.

But these changes can only take place as far as the existing gene pool allows; that is, the lateration cannot go beyond the latent genes within the gene pool.

CHAPTER 5

SUNSET OF MESOPOTAMIAN INFLUENCE

Projects

1. Make a model of an Assyrian chariot, the Assyrian bull-king, the Ishtar Gate, or the Hanging Gardens of Babylon. After reading our description of the Hanging Gardens, determine if they looked different from the illustration and draw them as you believed they looked.

2. Do a study on a major terrorist group, either one operating in the world today or at some other time in history. Explain its aims, methods, and success patterns. How do their methods compare with the Assyrians'?

3. Research the many types of armies a country can have, such as mercenary, draft, volunteer, and others. What are some advantages and disadvantages of these types of armies? How have they worked in the past?

4. Write a report on the building techniques used by ancient people. How did they discover bitumen and bricks? How did they cut, move, and lift heavy stones? You may want to build a model demonstrating how this was done.

5. In this chapter we study two social systems: slavery and caste. What are the advantages and disadvantages of these systems? How do they affect the people involved? Are slaves more efficient than hired workers? Explain.

6. Many leaders of countries have believed in astrology, for example Hitler and Napoleon. Give a report on one or two leaders who used astrology or other methods of foretelling the future. Did their use of future-forecasting help them? Explain.

7. Write a report on the life of Daniel. What things about him would make you want to have him for a friend? Are there things about him that would make you not want to know him? Explain.

8. Do a study on Buddhism and Hinduism. How do these religions differ? How are they similar? Explain why Buddhism is no longer popular in India.

Words and Concepts

reincarnation
caste
Law of the Medes and Persians
Cyrus
Nebuchadnezzar
terrorism
Upanishads
Vedas
"eyes and ears of the king"
Zoroaster
Hanging Gardens
astrology
Battle of Carchemish
Tiglath-Pileser I
brahmins
Zend Avesta
satrapies
astronomy
mercenaries
rajah
regent
absolute ruler

Sunset of Mesopotamian Influence

Ever since the earliest civilization was founded in Sumer, culture centered in the Middle East area of Mesopotamia. As we have seen, people migrated from this area to other parts of the world. But the major events of ancient history continued to take place in Mesopotamia.

At first, three major civilizations dominated the Middle East—the Assyrians, the Chaldeans, and the Persians. Then, when the last of these empires fell about 331 B.C., the major center of historical influence shifted to the West.

While empires were rising and falling in Mesopotamia, India entered an important period of her history. Known as the Vedic Ages, it was a time when the major structure of Indian life formed. It is in the area of religious thought that the Indians have made their greatest contribution to world history. During the Vedic Ages the complex ideas of the Hindu religion developed and the Buddhist faith was born.

ASSYRIAN EMPIRE 750-625 B.C.

The Assyrian Empire

About 1500 B.C. the city of Ashur, located along the banks of the Tigris River in northern Mesopotamia, became the capital of the Assyrian Empire. Its warlike ruler, Tiglath-Pileser I, conquered forty peoples, including the Hittites, Armenians, and the Hebrews in northern Israel. Tiglath-Pileser I founded an empire which became so powerful that it controlled the city of Babylon and even received tribute and gifts from the Egyptians.

The city of Ashur was not in a pleasant location. Once the Assyrian Empire grew, the king moved the capital to a new city, Nineveh. Nineveh remained the capital until the Assyrian Empire was destroyed. Two other Assyrian cities were also important. Nimrud, an ancient city mentioned in the Bible, was believed to be

Assyrian soldiers had a great advantage in warfare because of their light, fast chariots with spoked wheels that made them easier to handle. Here the charioteers appear to be making a quick turn on one wheel, as the sharp blade of the spoke keeps them from overturning.

built by the great hunter Nimrod. The other city, Arbela, was a great trade city.

The Assyrian Army. Assyrian soldiers, whose major occupations were warfare and hunting, were held in great respect. The Assyrians adopted the Hittites' iron weapons, including iron-tipped spears and arrows. They also wore bronze helmets and breastplates. The Assyrians had one weapon that gave them a great advantage in warfare. They used spoked wheels on their chariots, making them lighter, faster, and easier to maneuver on the battlefield.

A Terrorist Government. The Assyrians were the first people to conquer and control people by *terrorism*. This term means they used brutality and violence against the common people in order to control the government. The Assyrians were so brutal that everyone was afraid to fight them or to rebel once they had been conquered. No act seemed too cruel or too heartless for the Assyrians when a city refused to surrender. Mounds of dead bodies often lay in front of city gates. In other cities hundreds of prisoners were locked in buildings that were then burned to the ground.

The Assyrians used an unusual method of keeping their subjects under control to prevent rebellions. Once they conquered a people, the Assyrians moved the entire population to a different territory. Other people were brought to the conquered area. In these strange countries, people were usually more easily governed. They had no sense of nationalism, such as the Egyptians had for their country when they were taken over by the Hyksos.

Most of the people in the Mesopotamian area trembled with fear when they heard the Assyrians were coming. Nobody seemed strong enough to defeat them. For years the Egyptians bought their freedom by paying tribute to the Assyrian kings.

The Samaritans—A Despised People

The Hebrews in the northern kingdom of Israel were defeated by the Assyrians. All but the sick and elderly were transported to a new territory. Other people were brought to these conquered areas and intermarried with the remaining Hebrews. Thus, a new group of people called the Samaritans began. When the Hebrews finally returned to Israel hundreds of years later, they always looked down on these people as being inferior.

The Assyrian king was an "absolute" ruler. This means that his word was law and he could do anything he wished. He might have a council to advise him, but he did not have to follow its advice. If anyone displeased the king, he could be killed without a trial. There was no court of appeals and no second chance; when the king gave an order, it was obeyed.

Destruction of Babylon. When Babylon rebelled against the Assyrians about 721 B.C., King Sennacherib completely destroyed the city. Babylon was burned to the ground. Most of the population, regardless of age or sex, was put to death. So many people were killed that bodies blocked the streets. Babylon lost much of her importance; but, as we shall see, she was quick to recover.

Architecture. Although the Assyrians destroyed the city of Babylon, they were greatly

Powerful Assyrian kings, like the one pictured above, ruled an empire that included all of Mesopotamia, Israel, and what is today known as Turkey. Even the Egyptians sent tribute and gifts to the Assyrian court.

Illustrated here is one of the few existing samples of Assyrian sculpture. The king is shown with the body of a winged bull, symbolizing his godlike power.

influenced by the Babylonians. Nineveh was designed with the same architectural style used in Babylon. The major difference was that the Assyrian buildings were made of stone instead of brick, mainly because so much stone was available.

In addition to temples for their gods, the Assyrians built huge palaces for their kings. The royal palace at Khorsabad covered 10 ha (25 acres) and housed 80,000 guests. On the walls of the temples and palaces, the different kings left records of their rule. Most of these records proudly told of cutting off soldiers' hands, blinding enemies' eyes, and skinning traitors alive.

Art and Literature. The Assyrians spent little time on sculpturing and other types of artwork. They did make huge statues with their king's face on the body of a large, winged lion or bull. These elaborate statues were designed to show that the king was all-powerful and godlike.

The walls of Assyrian palaces also displayed bas-relief carvings. Almost all Assyrian artwork pictured realistic scenes of warfare or hunting.

An artist's idea of what Assyrian men and women looked like, drawn from descriptions found in letters and on rock carvings.

Assyrian bas-reliefs depicted animals more realistically than humans, as this stone carving from Ashurbanipal's palace shows. In this hunting scene, the lion seems to be crying out in great pain.

Astrology—A Game or A Religion

Early civilizations of Assyria, Babylonia, and Medo-Persia carefully studied the stars and planets, a science called *astronomy.* This information was combined with the worship of their gods to form what is known as *astrology.* These ancient people believed that the movements of the stars and planets affected the lives and fortunes of people on earth. They tried to predict the future by them.

As people learned more about science and the natural laws of the universe, astrology was no longer considered important. People felt that only the superstitious and foolish could believe it. But all through history there have been people (some of them very famous like Hitler) who believed strongly in astrology. Many would not do anything without consulting an astrologer to learn whether the stars predicted a good or bad day.

Today, astrological "forecasts" are printed in most daily newspapers, books, and many other publications. Some believe in them "religiously," others think they are fun. Unfortunately, interest in astrology has moved into areas of the occult and witchcraft.

While most early religions adopted astrology as a part of their worship and belief, it is interesting to note that the Bible states that God specifically condemns this practice. He commands people who believe in Him not to have anything to do with astrology.

The human figures were stiff and formal, but the animals were very lifelike.

The Assyrians did not create much literature. One Assyrian king had scribes collect and copy many of the literary works of Babylon. Archaeologists have discovered a royal library with over 20,000 clay tablets neatly catalogued and filed in baskets. Most of them were copies of Babylonian literature.

Religion. The chief god of the Assyrians was Ashur. When they conquered countries, they added other gods to those they worshiped. But the Assyrians always believed Ashur was the great god who protected their empire. In fact, King Ashurbanipal even had this god's name as part of his name.

Like the other civilizations we have studied, the Assyrians were interested in astrology. They kept careful records of the movements of the stars and planets in an effort to foretell the future.

Development of Economy. The Assyrians soon developed a thriving trade with the rest of the Middle East. They invented a monetary system, using bars of silver as money with the weight of the bar stamped on each one. It was not until Lydia became an empire many years later that these clumsy bars were replaced with minted coins.

Assyria's Decline and Fall

Under King Ashurbanipal, who ruled around 631 B.C., the Assyrian Empire was geographically the largest it had ever been. Even Egypt had been conquered and was an Assyrian province.

A Wealthy, But Unstable Empire. The very conditions that contributed to the rise of the Assyrian Empire led to its destruction. Over the years its bravest and strongest men had been killed in wars, decreasing the population. The people of conquered provinces were shifted around and, as a result, there was a large and somewhat disloyal minority. These captives were waiting for an opportunity to rebel.

Meanwhile, riches and tribute poured into the Assyrian Empire. The upper class people preferred to stay home and enjoy themselves rather than protect their country. King Ashurbanipal was forced to hire *mercenaries*, soldiers from foreign countries who fight for money.

Throughout history mercenaries have not been the best soldiers because they have not been willing to die for the country that hired them. On the other hand, soldiers who have fought to defend their own homes and countries were more willing to die for these causes. They often have defeated an army made up of mercenaries.

Nineveh and the Assyrian Empire Destroyed. Assyria was ripe for destruction. The dynamic rule of Ashurbanipal ended with his death in 626 B.C. His successors were unable to withstand the hostile forces. The mighty Assyrian Empire was conquered by the Chaldeans and their two allies, the Medes and the Scythians.

By 612 B.C. Nineveh was destroyed. Desert sands covered the ruins. The city of Nineveh disappeared from history until centuries later when archaeologists uncovered this once great civilization.

Ashurbanipal, a famous king of Assyria, ruled the vast Assyrian Empire when it was a great military power.

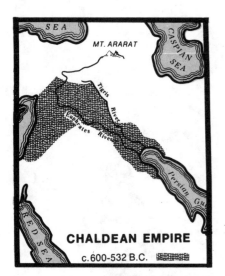

CHALDEAN EMPIRE

c. 600-532 B.C.

Two stone bulls from inside King Ashurbanipal's palace.

The Chaldean Empire

While the Assyrian Empire was weakening, a group of people known as the Chaldeans united into a strong force. These people came from the southern end of the Tigris-Euphrates Valley. Led by Nabopolassar, they rebuilt the city of Babylon which became the capital and most important city of the Chaldean Empire. The Chaldeans replaced the Assyrians as the major power in the Mesopotamian area.

Rise of the Chaldean Empire

Assyria Defeated. Nabopolassar made a treaty with a fierce, mountain people from the territory of Media, located along the Caspian Sea. To insure this treaty would continue, the king of Media arranged for the marriage of Ametis, his daughter, to Nebuchadnezzar, heir to the Chaldean throne.

King Cyaxares of Media conquered Assyria's northern territory and other small kingdoms in Asia Minor. The Medes took control of the highland area of the Assyrian Empire. Meanwhile, Nebuchadnezzar led a Chaldean army against Nineveh and completely destroyed that city in 612 B.C. The Chaldeans set out to conquer Canaan and the other Assyrian territories, including the Fertile Crescent.

The Battle of Carchemish. With the Assyrians defeated, the Egyptians saw an opportunity to recapture Canaan, a country they once controlled. They faced Nebuchadnezzar's Chaldean army at Carchemish, a city of Canaan. Historians consider this one of the major battles in world history. The Egyptians were so terribly beaten that they never invaded any territory outside of their boundaries again.

Nebuchadnezzar was stopped from conquering Egypt by the death of his father. He returned to Babylon to claim the throne. Later his armies did invade Egypt, and Lower Egypt became a province in the Chaldean Empire.

The Middle East Conquered. The Chaldean armies swept through the Middle East, making conquests everywhere they went. The southern Hebrew kingdom of Judah was defeated and the city of Jerusalem captured. King Solomon's Temple was completely destroyed, and all the leading people in the kingdom were taken to Babylon as prisoners of war. It would be seventy years before the Hebrews, or Jews, would be allowed to return to the land of Israel.

The City of Babylon

The city of Babylon has played an important role in Mesopotamian history. The capital of Hammurabi's kingdom centuries before, Babylon had been destroyed by the Assyrians. When the Chaldeans rebuilt the city, she regained her importance.

A Trade Center. Because of its location on the lower end of the Euphrates River, Babylon became an important trade center. Nebuchadnezzar encouraged trade by improving the highways throughout Mesopotamia. The city of Babylon was filled with goods and merchants from all over the empire. The majority of Babylon's written documents found by archaeologists have been contracts, loans, promissory notes, and other items dealing with trade. Soon Babylon was the capital of a great empire.

Nebuchadnezzar's Building Program. When Nebuchadnezzar became king in 604 B.C., he began rebuilding and adding to the size and beauty of Babylon. This city became one of the most beautiful and magnificent of its age. The King surrounded Babylon with massive walls that were 26 m (85 feet) thick. This means they were so large that seven Volkswagens could have parked end-to-end between the inner and outer edges. The city inside these walls covered some 520 km² (200 square miles), about the same size as the city of Chicago.

Unlike those in Nineveh, city structures were built of brick since there were no stone quarries nearby. These bricks were coated with bright enamel of different colors. Almost every brick

was inscribed with the statement: "I am Nebuchadnezzar, King of Babylon."

The Euphrates River flowed through the center of the city and was used as a roadway for transporting goods and people. The streets were laid out neatly at right angles to each other. The major street, called the Processional Way, entered the city through a huge gate, called the Ishtar Gate. This gate was made of beautiful blue tiles and decorated with animals of yellow tiles. Through this massive entrance victorious armies passed when returning from war with captives and tribute.

The structure that dominated Babylon was a seven-story ziggurat, or temple-tower. Some

The Ishtar Gate of Babylon (in present-day Iraq) is built of blue enameled bricks and is decorated with mythical animals in yellow tile. The gate towers 18 m (60 feet) high and is 12 m (40 feet) thick. Prisoners of war were led through this gate when the Babylonian kings had their Victory March after conquering new territory.

The Colorful Ishtar Gate

The Ishtar Gate was the main entrance into Babylon before Nebuchadnezzar built a second wall and enlarged the city. All prisoners of war, including the Hebrew Daniel, were forced to parade through this gate behind the triumphant conqueror.

The Ishtar Gate was a beautifully made structure of bright blue glazed bricks with more than 100 life-sized mythological animals set into the walls in yellow as decorations. Called a *shirush*, each animal had the claws of an eagle and the head of a serpent. The gate towered about 18 m (60 feet) high and was at least 12 m (40 feet) thick with guard towers built into it. It opened into the Processional Way that led to the Great Temple the Babylonians dedicated to their god Marduk.

Ruins of the ancient city of Babylon. The prophet Daniel probably walked through this gate.

This piece of brick is from the Hanging Gardens of Babylon. Notice the cuneiform writing inscribed on it.

historians have suggested that this unusual ziggurat was the remains of the ancient Tower of Babel and that it had been rebuilt by Nebuchadnezzar. The tower reached 200 m (650 feet) into the air, making it taller than the pyramids in Egypt. Each of the seven stories was colored red, blue, or orange, supposedly representing different heavenly bodies.

Nebuchadnezzar's palace covered 2.8 ha (seven acres). Huge stone lions guarded the entrance. The banquet hall was 52 m (171 feet) by 20 m (65 feet), with yellow walls and white floors. The walls of the palace were decorated with bas-relief sculpture.

The Hanging Gardens of Babylon. When Nebuchadnezzar's wife, Ametis, became

homesick for the hills and mountains of Media, the king had an elaborate ziggurat and terraced garden built for her. Known as the Hanging Gardens of Babylon, it is one of the Seven Wonders of the Ancient World. The ziggurat had five stories. The outside was coated with a tarlike substance called *bitumen* and a layer of lead for waterproofing. Over this covering was a thick layer of soil where shrubs, flowers, and trees from all over the empire were planted. In addition, there were fountains and aviaries for birds.

The lavish garden was watered by a special irrigation system. On the roof was a reservoir where rainwater was stored. When the reservoir went dry, it was refilled from the Euphrates River by a movable bucket system. Water from the reservoir was carried downhill to the gardens through pipes of baked clay.

From the ground the gardens seemed to hang suspended in the air. In the garden, 23 m (75 feet) above the city's heat and dust, the queen and her ladies walked around the splashing fountains and were shaded from the sun by trees.

The Hanging Gardens of Babylon were dedicated to Nebuchadnezzar's wife, Ametis, who longed for the hills and mountains of her homeland. This artificial mountain, covered with greenery from all over the empire, provided a beautiful playground for the queen and her ladies. Today it is considered one of the Seven Wonders of the Ancient World.

Life in Babylon

Babylonians lived in much the same way as others throughout Mesopotamia. The common people earned a living as farmers, soldiers, or merchants. Children attended schools that were held in the temples. The style of homes was similar to that of the Old Babylonian Kingdom.

Slavery. As a result of all the wars, slavery was more common in Babylon than in other cities. Most of the slaves were prisoners of war and, as a general rule, their life was difficult. If an owner felt his slave was not earning his keep, he could sell or kill him. Often slave masters were ordered to loan their slaves to the government for building projects or army service.

Although the life of a slave was usually harsh, there were a few opportunities for a male slave to improve his life. He could marry a free woman (if she was willing) and their children would be free. Also, if a slave was clever, his master might allow him to operate a business. Sometimes the slave was allowed to keep enough profit to buy his freedom. This, however, did not happen very often.

Unlike male slaves, women had little hope apart from getting a kind master. If they were pretty, they usually were added to a household as concubines. Otherwise, they married other slaves and their children continued in the same hopeless existence. There was little chance of a free man marrying a slave.

Religion. Along the city walls of Babylon, there were niches in which statues of gods were placed to guard the city. Altars were built on many city street corners. People could stop there during their busy day and make special offerings to their gods, the major ones being Baal and Marduk. The priests for the Babylonian gods were very rich and powerful.

There also were many ziggurats throughout the city. These were not merely places of worship, but were also places from which the priests could study the universe. We have already seen how the people in Mesopotamia practiced astrology, trying to foretell the future by the movements of the stars and planets. Today some historians believe these early studies led to naming some of the days of the week. Sun-

day was named for the Sun, Monday was for the Moon, and Saturday was for Saturn.

In addition to astrology, the Babylonians tried to foretell the future in many other ways. They interpreted dreams, examined the internal organs of animals, and studied drops of oil put in water. They believed in demons and nearly every part of their lives was associated in some way with sorcery or magic.

The Handwriting on the Wall

The capture of Babylon by the Persian king Cyrus is a good example of history being recorded in the Bible. After conquering most of the Babylonian Empire, Cyrus' armies marched on the city of Babylon. Inside the city walls the ruler Belshazzar was giving a party instead of preparing his armies for war. Belshazzar insulted God by using the golden cups from the Temple in Jerusalem to drink toasts to other gods during the party.

According to the Hebrew record, suddenly a hand appeared from nowhere and wrote a message on the walls. Daniel, one of the Hebrew prisoners of war, was brought in to translate the writing. It said, "God hath numbered your kingdom, and finished it. You are weighed in the balances, and are found wanting. Your kingdom is divided, and given to the Medes and Persians." That very night the priests of the city opened the gates and let Cyrus and his army into the city.

Even today the phrase "the handwriting is on the wall" means that time is running out unless major changes are made.

The Fall of the Chaldean Empire

When Nebuchadnezzar died in 562 B.C., his son Nabonidus became king. He did not, however, remain in Babylon to rule his country or lead his armies to conquer more territory. Like many people who want to know more about the past, King Nabonidus preferred to dig in the ruins of ancient Sumer. He was one of the first archaeologists in history.

A Weak Regent. With Nabonidus away in Sumer, his son Belshazzar ran the empire. He was a poor ruler, more interested in pleasure than in good government. Under his rule the judges and government officials became corrupt. The army, no longer fighting wars of conquest, lost its ability and desire to fight. The priests gained more and more power, but were unhappy with how the empire was governed.

Babylon Falls to the Persians. The government of Babylon became more and more unstable. Meanwhile, the Persians gained power and began conquering territory once controlled by the Babylonians. Then in 539 B.C. the Persian army, led by Cyrus, was at the gates of Babylon and the city was captured. Within thirty years after Nebuchadnezzar's death, the Chaldean Empire came to an end.

The Persian Empire

In the hills of what is known today as Iran, a group of shepherds were united by an aggressive leader named Cyrus. They were called Persians. At first they were controlled by the Medes who had helped Nebuchadnezzar overthrow the Assyrians. Then the Persians became a dominant force and the Medo-Persian Empire was

The Cyrus Cylinder, so named because it recorded King Cyrus' conquest of Babylonia, was made c. 538 B.C. The barrel-like stone cylinder tells how Cyrus spared the city and allowed the captive people to return to their homeland and rebuild their temples.

established. By the time the ruling house of Darius I began, the Medes had lost their importance. The kingdom became known as the Persian Empire, a power that would later dominate Mesopotamia and threaten the Greeks.

Development of The Persian Empire

After the Assyrian Empire was overthrown and before Babylon fell, King Cyaxares of Media conquered other small kingdoms in Asia Minor. He was a wise ruler and during his reign great wealth flowed into his kingdom.

The Medes, however, did not handle the riches and power well. When Cyaxares died, the people forgot the moral teachings that had given them strength. The men of Media began to dress like women and no longer trained for warfare. The government became corrupt as officials began to accept bribes.

Meanwhile, as the kingdom of Media was decaying, the Persians rebelled. Under the leadership of Cyrus, they overthrew the Medes. The people of Media, tired of their government's corruption, helped Cyrus take over their country. By 550 B.C. Cyrus had united the Medes and the Persians into an unbeatable fighting force.

The next enemy Cyrus faced was Croesus, king of Lydia. Their armies clashed at the Halys River in 547 B.C. Cyrus' troops, mounted on camels, defeated the Lydian army. This win also brought Lydia and Ionia under Persian control.

After conquering all of the territory as far east as the borders of India, Cyrus turned toward Babylon. As we have seen, the rulers of Babylon were without strong leadership. In this time of crisis, the Babylonian priests opened the gates and led the Medo-Persian army into the city. Cyrus added Babylon to his conquests and the Medo-Persian Empire was well established.

King Cyrus was not satisfied with the kingdoms of Assyria, Babylonia, Lydia, and Media that he controlled. He continued expanding his territory, but was killed while fighting an unknown tribe on the southern shore of the Caspian Sea.

Darius I — A Dynamic Ruler. The new king of the Medo-Persian Empire was Cambyses, Cyrus' son. He also set out to enlarge the empire and conquered Egypt. While in Egypt, however, he learned there was a rebellion at home. Cambyses started back, but died on the way. Legend says that he killed himself.

For a short time there was a struggle for power in the Medo-Persian Empire. As we have learned, the Medes had lost their importance and the empire was known as the Persian Empire. Then in 522 B.C. Darius I became king. Immediately, many of the provinces of the empire rebelled. Darius, however, was a dynamic ruler and an able general. His armies quickly stopped the rebellions. To prevent others from

Persian soldiers, such as this one, conquered the Babylonian Empire and Egypt. Until faced with the Greek armies, the Persians never lost a battle.

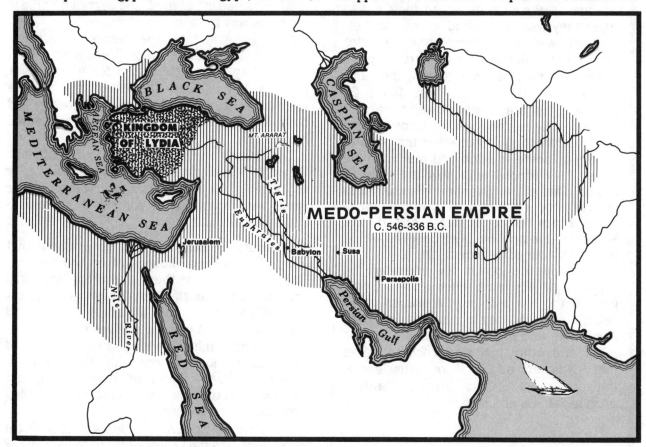

KINGDOM OF LYDIA

BLACK SEA

CASPIAN SEA

MT. ARARAT

MEDITERRANEAN SEA

AEGEAN SEA

Tigris

Euphrates

MEDO-PERSIAN EMPIRE
C. 546-336 B.C.

Jerusalem

Babylon

Susa

Persepolis

Nile River

RED SEA

Persian Gulf

rebelling, Darius treated the people with cruelty. In Babylon, for example, three thousand important people were crucified.

This ancient clay tablet from Assyria tells the story of creation. Dated about 650 B.C., its text is similar to Babylonian and Sumerian versions recorded hundreds of years earlier.

A Prophecy Fulfilled

Immediately after capturing Babylon in 483 B.C., the Persian king, Cyrus, passed a law allowing the many prisoners of war to return to their homelands. These captives were important people who had been taken to Babylon after Nebuchadnezzar conquered their countries. In their native lands they were permitted to rebuild their temples and the government paid for them. When the many Hebrews returned to Jerusalem, they began rebuilding the Temple. It was not until early in 445 B.C., however, that they were allowed to rebuild Jerusalem once destroyed by Babylonians.

It is interesting to note that the facts of history coincide with the information in the Bible. This record tells how the Hebrew prince Daniel, a prisoner of war from Jerusalem, received a special message from God. It was about the Messiah—the one the Jews believed would be the Saviour of the world.

Daniel wrote down the message. It stated that 476 solar years after Cyrus passed the law allowing Jerusalem to be rebuilt, the Messiah would ride into Jerusalem and proclaim himself King. The Bible and other historical records agree that Jesus entered the city of Jerusalem on that exact day. This proved Daniel's prophecy to be accurate.

Once Darius established control, he ruled wisely until his death in 486 B.C. Under his leadership the Persian Empire prospered as never before. He kept the army powerful by making his men fight such warlike tribes as the Scythians in southern Russia.

Life In The Persian Empire

The life style of the Persians was very similar to that of the common Mesopotamians. Generally, the peasants lived in the same style of home, ate the same kind of food, and earned a living in the same way as their ancestors.

Like the Assyrians, the Persians made few contributions to civilization. They were a warring society with little regard for literature or the arts. For this reason, most of their authors were hired to write literature and poetry, and their artwork was brought in from conquered provinces.

The priests were doctors of a sort, although they did not understand the nature of diseases or the effects of drugs. They combined magic spells with drugs and the combination frequently resulted in death.

Government and Law. The government that King Cyrus established after conquering Babylon was one of the best Mesopotamia had ever seen. It was the first time a government controlled people of different races and backgrounds. Everyone was given equal responsibilities and rights. As long as the people paid their taxes and were peaceful, they were allowed to keep their individual religions, customs, and trade contacts. In some cases they even had their own rulers.

The Persian Empire was the largest political organization in the known world until the time of the Roman Empire. In order to provide good government, the empire was divided into twenty-one provinces, called *satrapies*. Each satrapy was ruled by governors and inspectors were appointed to check up on them. These inspectors were called "the eyes and ears of the king," and it was their duty to report corruption and bad government. If a governor was cruel or unfair, he could be removed from office or hanged.

Persian law, called "The Laws of the Medes and Persians," was different from that of all the other countries. Once a law was passed, it could never be changed. This served two good purposes. First, it strengthened the idea that the law was above all people. Even the king was not as powerful as the law. Once a law was agreed to and written down, the king could not change it. Second, it made the kings very careful about what laws were passed. They wanted to be certain a law was just before passing it since it could never be changed if it proved to be wrong.

Three Capitals. The kings of Persia traveled throughout their empire, rarely staying for long in any one place. The empire had three capitals: (1) Susa was used in the wintertime. In the summer it was so hot there that some said a snake would fry if it crossed a street in the daytime. (2) Persepolis was built by Darius I and later was improved by his son Xerxes. (3) Ecbatana, located in a cool, mountainous area, was the summer capital.

Achievements. Persian rulers did all they could to encourage trade. They produced a standard minted coin for use in their empire, similar to coins used in Lydia.

The rulers also improved the roads. To protect travelers, troops were stationed in posts along the roads. It was said a woman could travel across the country in safety, accompanied only by her ladies-in-waiting.

Since horses had become the major land transportation, the king set up a type of "pony express" system. Every 23 km (14 miles) along the road, there was a station where messengers could change horses. A royal messenger could travel the 2600 km (1600 miles) between Sardis and Susa in one week. In this way the king could be well informed about all parts of his empire.

Homes and Architecture. The upper class people lived in beautiful homes with large gardens. Imported decorations and furniture inlaid with gold and silver were added to the luxurious surroundings. Some of their dishes were made of precious metals. Both men and women wore a lot of jewelry. Some of the rulers even had private hunting parks and zoos.

King Darius had an interesting hair style!

Darius the Great of Persia left this inscription on the side of a mountain, telling of his conquests throughout nine nations. It can be seen today above the main highway between Ecbatana and Susa in Iran. (See page 108 for the historical account.)

The Persians developed their own style of architecture. Many historians feel that Persian palaces were the most beautiful structures ever built. A great flight of stairs would rise from an open plain to the top of a hill where a palace stood. The rise was gradual, making the stairs more lovely to look at than practical. Some stairways were so wide that ten horsemen riding side by side could fit across them.

In King Xerxes' palace, the main hall had more than 9300 m² (100,000 square feet). It had seventy-two columns that were taller and more slender than those found in Egypt or Greece. The doorjamb and window frames were of a black stone that was shiny like ebony. The crossbeams in the roof rested on the backs of carvings of two-headed bulls or unicorns.

Religion. The Persians, like the Hebrews, thought it foolish to worship many gods and goddesses. They turned to the worship of one god whom they called Ahura Mazda, the Wise Lord. The Persians believed in this god as the result of a wise teacher named Zoroaster, who lived sometime around 600 B.C.

Zoroaster taught that Ahura Mazda created

the earth. He believed that the world contained both good and evil spirits. The good spirits, symbolized by light, were guided by Ahura Mazda. The evil spirits, symbolized by darkness, were guided by a spirit named Ahriman. Humans were involved in a warfare between these good and evil spirits. Zoroaster taught that at the end of time there would be a final judgment. Then those who were on the side of good would be rewarded with eternal life in a heavenly

This two-headed animal supported the beams across the doorway of King Xerxes' government palace at Persepolis.

This decorative *frieze*, a band of sculptured art, shows that Persian men and women from the twenty-one provinces brought yearly gifts and taxes to the emperor.

Translating—A Risky Business

Translating records written in Babylonian has baffled scholars for centuries. Then, in 1835 Henry Rawlinson, a British diplomatic officer stationed in Persia, discovered the names of Hystaspes, Darius, and Xerxes in an inscription written in Old Persian. Rawlinson tried to find an inscription with the same text written in both Old Persian and Babylonian.

He found it 91 m (300 feet) high on an almost inaccessible rock in the mountains of Media at Behistun, Iran. There, Darius I had the record of his wars and victories carved in three languages—Old Persian, Assyrian and Babylonian.

Day after day Rawlinson copied every character carefully. He even made plaster impressions of all the engraved surfaces while suspending himself by a rope or climbing over the rocks. In 1847, after 12 years of work, he finally succeeded in translating both the Babylonian and the Assyrian texts. Through his work, history was enriched with an understanding of another ancient civilization.

Hebrew Influence on Zoroaster

There are many similarities between the beliefs of Zoroaster, the Persian religious leader, and the teachings of the Hebrews in the Bible. The first five books of the Bible give the laws God expected His people to follow. They were written hundreds of years before Zoroaster. In addition, the beautiful Psalms contain many references to the final judgment, the resurrection of the dead, and the conflict between good and evil. These were written by David in 1000 B.C.

These writings were probably carried by Hebrew prisoners of war into the northern area of Mesopotamia after they were captured by the Assyrians. Zoroaster came in contact with the Hebrew teachings there, and they no doubt influenced his thoughts and life.

place. Those who were on the side of evil would be tortured forever.

The ideas and teaching of Zoroaster were contained in over twenty-one volumes entitled the *Zend Avesta*. When Darius I ruled, he made Zoroastrian beliefs the official religion of the Persian Empire.

Summary. The rest of Persian history is closely tied to the history of Greece. In the next chapter we shall see how the entire power of the Persian Empire was directed toward the divided city-states of Greece. Had the Greeks been defeated, their ideas on government, art, and philosophy would have died. The future of European history was greatly influenced by the outcome of the Greek-Persian Wars.

The Indian Vedic Ages

The period following the Aryan invasion of India is called the Vedic Ages by historians. This name came from a collection of writings known as the *Vedas* that were written by the Aryans. (See page 41.) The Vedic Ages are roughly divided into two periods: the Early Vedic Age, lasting from 1500 to 900 B.C., and the Later Vedic Age, from 900 to 500 B.C.

The Early Vedic Age

Immediately following the Aryan conquest of India, the nomadic Aryan tribes settled in villages. Agriculture became as important to the people as cattle. Each village was made up of family groups with the most important person in the village known as the "headman." In some villages he was elected; in others the office was passed on to other members of the family.

The Caste System. The Aryans were quick to see that their race would be absorbed by the dark-skinned Indians. To prevent intermarriage between the two groups, the practice of *caste* came into being. This term refers to separating people according to race and class. The caste system became a part of Indian life.

Only the Aryans were allowed to become priests, warriors, or craftsmen. The Aryans thought the Indian people were inferior and it was against the law for Aryans and non-Aryans to marry.

The Later Vedic Age

City-States Established. As the Early Vedic Age came to an end, there was a major shift in the population from the Indus River Valley to

Elephants are sacred to both Hindu and Buddhist religions. This temple in Delhi shows reverence to elephants.

the Ganges River Valley. Although the majority of people still lived in villages, a new type of government and politics developed. Small, isolated city-states were founded and each ruler, called a *rajah*, controlled the surrounding villages in his territory.

Each city-state was completely independent of the others and they were often at war with one another. The epic poems written during that period describe constant warfare between the cities. Moats and walls were built around the cities for defense.

In the center of the city was the palace of the rajah. The rajah had more power than a village headman. But he usually had a royal coun-

cil made up of his relatives and nobles to help him rule. The rajah was considered owner of all the land and received taxes from the villages. Actually the villages controlled their own property, but paid taxes in exchange for defense from raiders.

Indian Society. Indian society was divided into three major groups—the village, the caste system, and the joint-family. These strict groupings, combined with the difficult Hindu religion, greatly influenced the Indian culture we know today.

The Village. Each village had a council that was elected by the people to help the headman govern. Women were allowed to be members of this council. The council was responsible for distributing land and collecting taxes.

The Caste System. We have already discussed how castes developed to prevent the people of Aryan blood from marrying Indians. During the Later Vedic Age, the caste system developed into an even more complex system.

The Aryans themselves were divided into different castes according to their occupation. These castes were: the *brahmins*, or priests; the *kshatriyas*, or warriors; the *vaisyas*, including traders, merchants, and bankers; the *sudras*, made up of farm workers and serfs; and the *untouchables*. The last two classes were made up of non-Aryans. If a person of higher caste was touched by just the shadow of an untouchable, the people believed he was defiled.

The major purpose of the caste system was to keep the different groups of society separated. No one was allowed to associate with a person of lower caste. People were not allowed to change caste. Over the years these five major castes

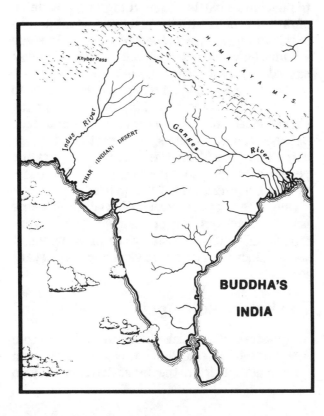

BUDDHA'S INDIA

gradually divided into thousands of groups according to social status, occupation, and religious position.

When this new caste system began, the warriors were the most important class. As fighting and warfare became less important, however, the brahmins became the most important caste. They were the teachers and historians, as well as the people's messengers to their gods. Once they took over as the highest caste, they kept this position even until modern times.

The Joint-Family. The joint-family in a village consisted of all the people who descended from the same ancestor. A family's eldest son became the new family leader following his father's death. All property belonged to the family, and all earnings were put into a common fund. Before any major decisions were made which would affect the family, all of the men met together to reach a common decision. The individual was not considered important. As a result, marriages were arranged by the family rather than according to the wishes of the people involved.

Indian Values. The people of India have different values today than the people in the United States or Western Europe. In India there has been more emphasis on the security of the group than on the interests of the individual. Indian society has been more concerned with stability and with keeping things the way they have always been. Western society has been more concerned with progress. Indians seem to be more passive about their lives than people in the West. Therefore, they seem more likely to accept whatever comes their way, even when it is harsh and unpleasant.

The Hindu Religion

Early Aryan Beliefs. Religion has always played an important role in Indian society. When the Aryans first arrived in India, they had several gods. Their favorite was Indra, an active, noisy god. Indra supposedly threw thunderbolts, ate dozens of bulls at a single sitting, and gulped down lakes of wine. Like other cultures, the Aryans offered sacrifices to their gods. They believed that when a person died, his soul went on to eternal punishment or to everlasting happiness.

Beginning of Hindu Beliefs. No particular person started the Hindu religion. During the Later Vedic Ages, an idea formed which held that there was a moral law higher than the gods themselves. This high ideal was called the *World Soul*, or *Brahma*. The people believed that the soul of each person was part of the World Soul. The goal of everyone was to join their souls with Brahma's which would bring them complete happiness and absolute peace.

These new thoughts were the beginning of the Hindu religion. Its basic beliefs about the meaning of life are found in the *Upanishads* written between 800 and 600 B.C. Although many of these Hindu ideas are discussed in the Upanishads, there is no written theology which tells exactly what the Hindus believe. For this reason, almost every time a new religion was introduced in India, it was absorbed by Hinduism.

Reincarnation, the Heart of Hinduism. One unusual Hindu belief is that of *reincarnation*, meaning a person's soul goes into a different body after death. Hinduism teaches that if a person leads a selfish, greedy, or otherwise wicked life, his soul can be "reborn" into the body of a

Vishnu, one of the chief gods of India, is believed by the Hindus to have appeared in the flesh ten times to save the world from destruction.

person of lower caste. Or he might even be "reincarnated" into the body of a dog, pig, or snake. Likewise, if a person leads a good life, his soul will be "reborn" into the body of someone of a higher caste.

The purpose of living many lives is supposed to teach the soul how to become perfect. The major idea behind Hinduism is that life is full of sorrow and misery. The ideal experience, then, is to be reincarnated into a person of brahmin caste. When this happens, a person's soul merges with Brahma at death and does not have to be reborn anymore.

Hindu Gods. Over the years thousands of gods and spirits were added to the original group of Hindu gods. All of them were considered part of Brahma, but were still worshiped separately. The major god was Trimurti, thought to be three gods in one. These gods were Brahma the creator, Vishnu the preserver, and Shiva the destroyer.

Vishnu was believed to be a kind god, working continually for the welfare of the world. Hindu followers claim he has appeared in the flesh ten times to save the world from destruction.

Influence of Hinduism. Hinduism affected every part of Indian life. One important area it influenced was the caste system. People were taught to accept their caste as their just reward or punishment for their past lives. If they rebelled against their caste, they believed they could be reincarnated into that same caste or a lower one. One of the Hindu sayings was: "Just as he behaves, so he becomes." This means that if people accepted who they were and lived a good life, they could be reincarnated into a better life.

The Hindu religion was (and still is) a harsh religion, offering little comfort or hope to its followers. The priests kept strict control over the people and religious ceremonies were very important. People were expected to make sacrifices and offerings even when they couldn't afford them.

Buddhism

Sometime about 563 B.C. a man was born who later founded Buddhism, one of today's three major world religions. His name was Gautama and he was the son of a ruler.

The Life of Buddha. Gautama was raised in the luxury of his father's kingdom, located at the foot of the Himalayas. At nineteen he married a beautiful princess and they had a son.

When Gautama was thirty years old, he was driving through one of the villages his father ruled. Suddenly, for the first time, he became aware of the misery, disease, and sorrow in which the ordinary people were forced to live. When he returned to his palace, his own happiness made the world's misery seem worse.

One day Gautama left his palace, his wife, and his son and set out to discover the answers to his questions about life and death. At first he tried to find them among the holy men in the Hindu religion. For a time he punished his body by only eating one bean a day. He lost so much weight that his health failed, and he realized that was not the way to find answers.

After seven years of searching, Gautama sat down beneath a tree one day, determined not to leave until he understood the meaning of life. For forty-nine days he sat there. Finally, he discovered the truth, which he called *enlightenment*. From that time on his followers called

Trimurti is India's "three-in-one" god. The heads symbolize Brahma the creator, Vishnu the preserver, and Shiva the destroyer.

him Buddha, which means "the enlightened one."

Buddha's Teachings. For the rest of his life, Guatama Buddha traveled around the plains of the Ganges River Valley, telling his new truths to the villagers who flocked to hear him. He spoke mainly to the peasants and social outcasts. He taught them that many reincarnations were unnecessary and that by living an unselfish life, anyone could be released from the cycle of rebirths. Buddha claimed all men were brothers and for that reason should not lie, steal, kill, or hate. He believed the main purpose of life was to deny personal desires and to help others.

Buddha accepted the major Hindu teachings that life was miserable and that a person's actions determined if they would have a better life. But he disagreed with the Hindu belief that a person must belong to the highest caste, the brahmin, before he could escape into Brahma. He changed the name of Brahma to Nirvana.

Lesser and Greater Vehicles

Buddhism spread throughout the world and gradually divided into two separate groups. One group tried to follow Buddha's strict teachings of purity and self-denial in their individual lives. The other group was more concerned with worshiping Buddha and following emotional rituals.

About 78 A.D. a council of 500 monks met to work out the differences between the two groups. The meeting failed and Buddhism became permanently divided into the Lesser Vehicle and the Greater Vehicle. The majority of Buddhists followed the ritualistic form of worship, claiming this was the "great vehicle" that enlightened the greatest number of people. Those people who followed the more disciplined teachings called their faith the Lesser Vehicle.

Buddhist tradition states that when Buddha traveled around the country to teach, he wore a simple saffron-colored robe. No matter what country they are from, Buddhist priests still wear the same type of robe today.

Buddha's teachings are called the *Four Noble Truths*. Basically, these four truths are as follows:

1. A person's life is full of misery and suffering.
2. Sufferings are caused by a person's own selfish desires.
3. Sufferings end when a person completely overcomes his desires and gets rid of all jealousy, greed, and selfishness.
4. Nirvana could be achieved by right living.

Buddha's Death. Buddha had many disciples who followed his teachings. When he was eighty years old, a poor blacksmith invited him to dinner. The food was spoiled, but Buddha didn't want to hurt the man's feelings so he ate it anyway. He became sick and died.

Influence of Buddhism. Buddha had not meant to start a new religion. At first he wanted to improve Hinduism so it would be easier for the poor to follow. He always taught that he was not a special person, but over the years his followers forgot this. Many people thought of him as a god and worshiped him.

As Buddhism spread from India to other countries, many different kinds of Buddhist temples and statues were built. Priests began to take over the leadership of this new religion which soon became known for its rituals, legends, and magic charms. People worshiped other local gods that they also called buddhas, as well as the people who led outstanding lives as Buddhists. It seemed easier to follow a ritual than to live by the moral teachings of Buddha.

In India, Buddhism was eventually absorbed into Hinduism and disappeared. Before this happened, however, it spread into the rest of Asia. The Buddhist religion has influenced the lives of millions of people for almost 2500 years.

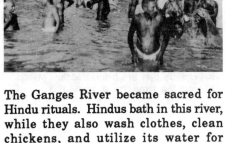

The Ganges River became sacred for Hindu rituals. Hindus bath in this river, while they also wash clothes, clean chickens, and utilize its water for drinking.

Orient	Africa
China had built major civilizations for nearly 2,000 years by this time. As noted previously, their distinctive pottery has been traced from the Caucasus Mts. to the Yellow River. A Yang-Shao people made reddish pots with geometric designs, while the Aung-Shan culture had shiny black pottery. Both groups made a three-legged pot for cooking three foods at one time. The potter's wheel was used and ancestor veneration was practiced, illustrating social structures.	African trade routes are being identified through Egyptian, Ethiopian, and Arabic records: 1. Across North Africa to the Atlantic Ocean; 2. Along the Indian Ocean; and 3. From Egypt to the Niger River region for salt and gold. Recently discovered caves in South Africa reveal a highly intelligent civilization in that area. Subsaharan people were farmers as well as traders.

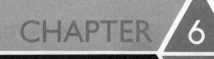

CLASSICAL GREECE AND HELLENIZATION

Projects

1. (a) Study Athens' government and the way her people lived. Is there a country today with a similar type of government and society? Explain and compare them. (b) Study Sparta's government and society. Is there a country today with a similar type of government or society? Explain and compare them.

2. According to their ideas on government, politicians can be divided into three groups—liberals, moderates, and conservatives. What do each of these groups believe? List three men in United States politics who represent each group.

3. Compare the membership and duties of the Greek Popular Assembly to the membership and duties of the United States Congress. How do they differ? How are they similar?

4. Do a study on the Olympic games. Why were they discontinued? Why were they started again? What new games have been added? Tell about unusual Olympic years. Tell about unusual or outstanding athletes.

5. Make costumes for dolls showing the different clothing worn by the peoples already studied.

6. Make models of one of the following: the pontoon bridge Xerxes built, Greek and Persian ships, or the Parthenon.

7. Do a study on Xerxes or Alexander the Great. What type of people were they? How many wives did they have? What interesting things did they do? Tell about their wars. Would you say they were good rulers? Explain your answers.

8. Read one of the Greek plays mentioned in the text. Did you think it was interesting? Explain. Compare it to a modern play. What differences do you notice?

9. Find a copy of the Hippocratic Oath. Doctors today still take this oath. What would you add to the oath? What would you remove? Explain.

Words and Concepts

Epicureans
Euripides
trilogy
Philippides
helots
Hellenistic Age
Stoics
Sophocles
Herodotus
Marathon
orators
Hellenic Age
Socratic Method
Hippocratic Oath
Delian League
Thermopylae
ostracism
Archimedes
Aeschylus
confederacy
hoplites
banishment

Classical Greece and Hellenization

While the Assyrians, Babylonians, and Persians took turns dominating the Mesopotamian area, a new civilization was developing in the area now known as Greece. This culture had little influence on nearby civilizations, however, until a Macedonian military general named Alexander united the Greeks. He then set out to conquer the world and became known as Alexander the Great. Greek language, philosophy, government, art, literature, and architecture became the model for all of the new cities of his empire. These Greek standards were upheld for many years by those who ruled after his death.

As we shall see in this chapter, the Greek Classical period included both the Hellenic Age and the Hellenistic Age. The Hellenic Age refers to Greece's early cultural development, including the period we call the Golden Age of Greece. It covers only that culture inside of Greece. The Hellenistic Age is the period after the conquests and death of Alexander the Great. This time of hellenization, when Persian and Greek culture merged into one, lasted for almost two centuries.

Greek City-States and Colonies

The land of Greece, divided by rugged mountain ranges, was slow to develop a single, unified government. Instead, a competitive life style unfolded in the city-states of Athens, Sparta, and Corinth. This was also true among the Greek colonial cities of Ionia in Asia. As a result, when threatened by invaders, the Greeks found it difficult to face the common enemy. In order to understand how the Greek culture emerged as the major influence in western history, we will first study how the people in the different city-states lived.

Athens

When the Mycenaean civilization was destroyed, you will remember that people from Mycenae fled to Athens. They brought their culture with them and greatly influenced the arts, literature, philosophy, and architecture of Athens. Therefore, when we think of early Greek civilization, we think of life in Athens.

Monarchy Ends. Athens was ruled by a king and the Athenians did not believe in complete democracy for everyone. But they did develop ideas of government that were quite different from the other civilizations we have studied. About 700 B.C. the monarchy was overthrown and a king no longer ruled Athens. The Athenian people never again allowed one person to rule with unlimited power.

The king was replaced by a council of noblemen who ran the government. The nobles owned most of the good farmland. The peasants were forced to rent the land, giving most of their crops to the landlord as payment. The high rental forced many peasants to either sell themselves into slavery to pay their debts or to run away. The peasants wanted the land taken away from the nobles and divided among them. There was much unrest between the nobles and the peasants and some feared open conflict. The ordinary people felt they had no voice in the government and were unhappy.

Solon, the Reformer. About 594 B.C. a nobleman named Solon convinced the ruling class that something had to be done to correct

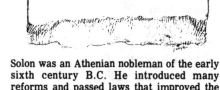

Solon was an Athenian nobleman of the early sixth century B.C. He introduced many reforms and passed laws that improved the lives of the lower classes.

the problems. He told them the peasants might rebel if they were not given more rights and a better way of life. As a result, Solon was named head of the government. He was given the task of putting together a new set of laws to settle the conflicts between the rich and poor.

The first thing Solon did was cancel all debts. Then he passed a law that prevented people from becoming slaves because they owed money. He encouraged the peasants to earn money through trade and industry by developing a plan to help them learn new skills. Solon offered full citizenship to any skilled artist or craftsman who would come to Athens and teach the people.

Tyrants Rule Athens. The nobles refused to support Solon in the reforms he was making.

The peasants took matters into their own hands and a civil war erupted. Then in 560 B.C. a military hero named Pisistratus took control of the government as a tyrant. He solved many of the problems by banishing nobles from Athens and dividing their lands among the peasants. During Pisistratus' reign artists were encouraged and Athens became the cultural leader of Greece.

Solon, An Early Moderate

Solon, the famed Greek reformer, would be referred to today as a political moderate. This means he did not want too many changes in government, but tried to please everyone with a middle-of-the-road policy. As is often the case with moderates, Solon was condemned by both sides. The nobles believed he threatened their power and position by giving too many rights to the peasants. The peasants felt he was not doing enough to improve their living conditions and was primarily out to help the members of his own class.

Today historians look at what Solon tried to do and see how wise he was. When someone says "he is as wise as Solon," it means that person is doing a great job in government.

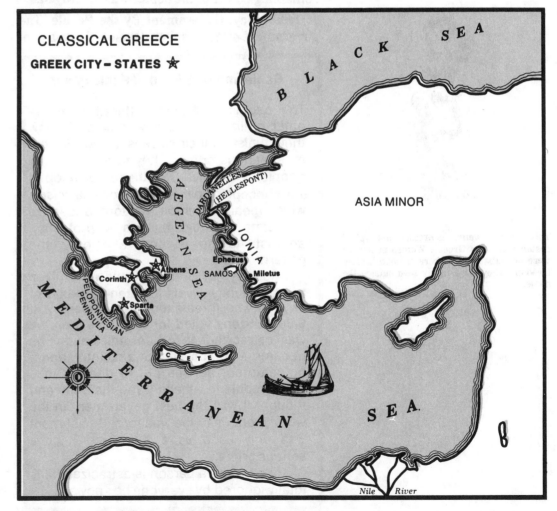

CLASSICAL GREECE

GREEK CITY – STATES ☆

BLACK SEA

ASIA MINOR

AEGEAN SEA

DARDANELLES (HELLESPONT)

IONIA

Ephesus

SAMOS

Miletus

Corinth

Athens

PELOPONNESIAN PENINSULA

Sparta

MEDITERRANEAN SEA

CRETE

Nile River

Although Pisistratus was a good ruler, his sons were not. They tried to rule after their father's death, but one was assassinated and the other was banished.

Following the death of Pisistratus and his sons, the banished nobles tried to reconquer the city. When they failed, another tyrant, Cleisthenes, took over. Under his rule the remaining power of the nobles was destroyed.

Democracy, Government By the People. The government of Athens then developed into a popular democracy. This means that all citizens could have an active part in the government. When a citizen became twenty years old, he could belong to the Popular Assembly, the body which passed laws, tried cases, and even elected the generals who led their armies. It was considered a citizen's duty to serve in the Popular Assembly, as well as to serve on the Council of Five Hundred.

The Council of Five Hundred advised the Popular Assembly. Every year the citizens of Athens were given a chance to serve on this council. They were not elected, but were chosen by lots and everyone had an equal chance. The laws were determined by the Popular Assembly, which usually met once a week.

The Athenians believed in freedom of speech. Almost every day men gathered in the agora, or marketplace, for speech-making and debates on major issues of the city. Greek audiences, however, were not polite. When someone spoke who was not skillful, he was often jeered at or pelted with olive pits and garbage.

The best public speakers, or *orators,* became the most influential men in Athens. Pericles, for example, an outstanding Athenian leader, was also one of the greatest of all Greek orators. He used his speaking ability to control the government, convincing people his ideas were best. Another famous orator was Demosthenes. He lived after the Peloponnesian War which we will be studying later. He was well known for his fiery speeches and often warned the Greeks that King Philip of Macedonia planned to invade Greece.

Athenian women had fewer rights than women of other cultures. They could not own property or take a case to court. Once married they were

This Athenian woman is dressed in a typical costume of early Greece. Women of Athens were not citizens and therefore had limited freedom. They were rarely seen outside the home.

Banishment, A Form of Punishment

The people of Athens differed from the other civilizations we have studied in how they punished their citizens. Except for the most serious crimes, they rarely executed people. The ruler Cleisthenes developed the concept of *banishment,* or *ostracism,* which meant a person was forced to leave the state. He did this as a protection against having nobles take over the government.

Once a year, all the citizens were given an opportunity to vote for a ten-year exile of anyone who threatened the democracy. If 6,000 citizens voted for the same man, he was ostracized. In Athens this meant he became a person without a country, and if he returned, he was put to death. Since most people in Athens loved their city and thought it was the best government in the world, serious crime was rare. Banishment was only used as a punishment for a serious crime.

Today when a person is ostracized he is totally ignored by everyone he knows.

Practice Makes Perfect

In ancient Greece public speaking was considered an important skill. Many young men tried to become good speakers. One of them, Demosthenes, had weak lungs and was unable to speak loudly or clearly. But he was determined not to allow this to ruin his career. He went down to the seashore, put pebbles in his mouth, and practiced speaking over the sounds of the waves. Demosthenes greatly improved his speaking ability and he became a great Athenian orator.

expected to stay home. They rarely went out except to go to the temple or to the theater.

Athens developed a type of government similar to the one we have today in the United States. Although most slaves, women, and most foreigners were not citizens, Athenians had a greater degree of individual freedom than any civilization we have studied so far. They did not worship their rulers and when a ruler threatened their freedom, he was banished.

Education. The purpose of education in Athens was to train the whole man—body, mind, and spirit. Boys began training at the age of seven. From sunrise to sunset their days were filled with activities. Gymnastics and music were two main areas of study. But the gymnasium was more than just a place where a boy got exercise, it was also a cultural center. As boys trained in all types of sports, they also discussed philosophy and the major events of the day. Boys' education included poetry, drama, history, science, mathematics, music, and public speaking.

Sparta

Athens' greatest rival for control of Greece was the city-state of Sparta. As we know, Sparta was settled by descendants of the Dorians who had destroyed the Mycenaean civilization. The way of life they developed was much different from that in Athens. Sparta was a warring society. Everything about its culture was aimed at teaching the young men to be fierce fighters.

The Olympics, An Ancient Ceremony

The Olympics is one of today's greatest athletic events. The Olympic games began thousands of years ago in Greece as part of Greek worship services. The Greeks believed the gods and goddesses liked to see healthy bodies and athletic skills. So, every four years the best athletes competed in racing, boxing, wrestling, discus, and javelin. At the start of the games, they honored Zeus, king of their gods.

An Olympic winner received no money. The winner of each sports event was given a crown of laurel leaves. Winning the Olympics was considered the highest honor a man could earn. When Greece fell, the Olympic games were discontinued.

Then in 1896 they were renewed. This time, however, the worship of Greek gods was no longer a part of the competition. Athletes competed for the honor of their country. Today, of course, the Olympic games are telecast all over the world for people of every nation to see.

Demosthenes of early Greece trained to become a good speaker. He filled his mouth with pebbles and practiced speaking over the sound of the crashing waves.

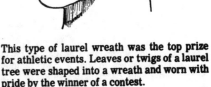

This type of laurel wreath was the top prize for athletic events. Leaves or twigs of a laurel tree were shaped into a wreath and worn with pride by the winner of a contest.

The Greeks introduced chariot racing to their sports-minded citizens. This chariot racing scene was painted on a huge urn.

The Helots. When the Dorians took over the territory of Laconia they founded the city-state of Sparta. They forced the people there to become slaves. These slaves were called *helots* and lived under such terrible conditions that they often revolted. The Spartans conquered neighboring city-states and made their people helots too. To prevent the helots from rebelling, the Spartan leaders developed good soldiers.

Sparta's Totalitarian Government. The Spartan government was headed by two kings, a small council of elders, and the Popular Assembly. The actual power to govern was in the hands of five overseers, called *ephars*. Although these men were elected by the Popular Assembly, they did not allow individual freedom.

Spartan shields were large enough to carry the dead or wounded. In Sparta a good soldier either came back carrying his shield or lying on it.

Sparta's government was *totalitarian*. This means it controlled every area of its citizens' lives. Citizens were not allowed to criticize the government. In order to keep the people from being influenced by foreign ideas, the government discouraged trade. One way they did this was to issue lead instead of gold or silver as money. Merchants would not trade with Sparta because they used this worthless money. The Spartan leaders were afraid that their citizens would be corrupted if they had luxuries.

A Military Society. From the moment a boy was born in Sparta, his life was controlled by the government. While still a baby, the boy was taken before leaders of the community and carefully examined. If he seemed weak or deformed, he was taken into the surrounding hills and exposed. Sometimes a child was found by a shepherd or a passing stranger and raised as a helot. Usually such a baby died of exposure or was eaten by wild animals.

If a baby was judged healthy, his parents were allowed to take him home until he was seven years old. Then he was taken to a barracks and began his training to become a warrior.

A boy's training was designed to teach him how to endure hardship and pain. He was forced to sleep outside in all kinds of weather. Even in cold winter weather he was allowed to wear only one garment and was never permitted to wear shoes. His diet consisted mainly of a black soup that tasted horrible. If he wanted something else to eat, he had to steal it. If caught, he was whipped, not for stealing, but for allowing himself to be caught. Once a year, until a boy was old enough to join the army, he was beaten in public. He was supposed to endure the pain in silence.

Spartan girls also received athletic training. They were taught to be totally loyal to the state. When they married, they were expected to encourage their sons to fight in the army. If any, or all, of a woman's sons died in battle, it was considered a great honor. Spartan shields were so large and heavy that if a soldier wanted to run away during battle, he would have to leave it behind. In wartime wives and mothers would hand shields to the men with the instructions, "Come back with your shield, or on it."

Sparta's major efforts were aimed at producing good soldiers. They made very few contributions in art, literature, or architecture. Although Sparta had one of the strongest armies in Greece, Athenian soldiers later proved to be as good as Spartans on the battlefield.

Corinth

The city of Corinth was located on the isthmus joining the peninsula of Peloponnese to mainland Greece. A seaport was built at either end of the isthmus. Shipbuilding and shipping became Corinth's major sources of income.

Ruled By A Dictator. The people of Corinth had a system of government somewhat similar to Athens. They were aware that a king threatened individual freedom, so they selected a dictator. The dictator remained ruler as long as he could keep the support of the citizens of Corinth.

One of Corinth's greatest dictators was Periander. He developed businesses and encouraged trade relations between Corinth and the coastal cities. He also built a paved highway across the isthmus.

Corinthian Hoplites. Citizens of Corinth who fought in their army were called *hoplites*. When they went into battle they wore heavy, protective armor, including a helmet, breastplate, and *greaves* (lower leg armor). They used an oval shaped shield and a 2.7 m (nine-foot) spear with an iron spearhead. An iron sword was used for close fighting. When the hoplites were not fighting, they often were engaged in trade, shipbuilding, or farming.

Corinth, although an important trade center, was never a major power in Greece. But Corinthian hoplites fought in the many wars between Sparta and Athens, as well as against foreign invaders.

Ionia

A Greek Influence. The cities of Samos, Miletus, and Ephesus made up the territory known as Ionia, located on the coast of Asia Minor. These colonies were founded by Athens. Ionia shared the Greek ideas on freedom. Greek culture spread throughout Mesopotamia as a result of athletic and music festivals in these cities. Ionia was also responsible for improving Greek culture by adapting the Phoenician alphabet to the Greek language.

Greek Freedom Threatened

From c. 750 B.C. to 550 B.C. the city-states of Greece were developing their separate cultures. Meanwhile, in Mesopotamia the Persians had conquered Babylon and had become a mighty empire. The Greek cities of Ionia also had been taken over. Their desire for freedom brought the Persian Empire and the Greek city-states into

Greek pottery made from black clay of Corinth.

direct conflict. As we shall see, the Greeks survived this foreign threat to their freedom. Athens, strengthened by the wars, then set out to establish an empire in Greece, but civil war erupted. It was called the Peloponnesian War because most of the fighting occurred on the Peloponnesus peninsula in southern Greece.

The Greek-Persian Wars

All the Ionian cities came under Persian control when Cyrus of Persia defeated King Croesus of Lydia. Under Persian rule the Greeks lost their freedom and democracy.

The Persian Threat. In 500 B.C. the Greek cities in Ionia rebelled, hoping to overthrow Persian rule. Darius I, the king of Persia at that time, sent troops to suppress the rebellion. Men and supplies came to the Ionians from fellow Greeks in Athens. But in spite of this help, the Ionians were defeated. The city of Miletus was burned as punishment, destroying a library and almost all of their artwork.

The Battle of Marathon. Darius was angered by Greek interference in the Ionian revolt, so he decided to bring all Greece under his control. In 490 B.C. the Persian army sailed across the Aegean Sea and landed on the plains of Marathon, north of Athens. Realizing they were outnumbered ten to one, the Athenians sent Philippides, a long-distance runner, to Sparta for help. He traveled the 241.4 km (150 miles) over hilly, rocky territory in two days. But the Spartans were having a festival and refused to send help until the celebration was over. The Athenians, badly outnumbered, attacked first. Under the leadership of Miltiades, Greek forces broke through the Persian lines and scattered their army.

Herodotus, the Greek historian who recorded the Persian Wars, stated that 6,400 Persians were killed while only 192 Greeks died. We must understand that this report may be slanted in favor of the Greeks, but the fact remains, it was a great victory. When the Spartan soldiers finally arrived, the Athenians were already celebrating their success.

The Battle of Marathon was important because it stopped the Persians from conquering Greece. A Persian victory would have greatly changed world history. It also gave the

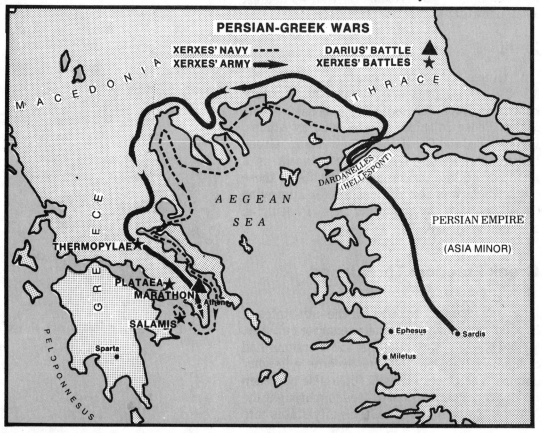

PERSIAN-GREEK WARS

XERXES' NAVY ----
XERXES' ARMY ⟶

DARIUS' BATTLE ▲
XERXES' BATTLES ★

MACEDONIA

THRACE

DARDANELLES
(HELLESPONT)

AEGEAN
SEA

PERSIAN EMPIRE

(ASIA MINOR)

G R E E C E

THERMOPYLAE ★

PLATAEA ★
MARATHON ▲
Athens

SALAMIS ★

P E L O P O N N E S U S

Sparta

• Ephesus
• Sardis

• Miletus

Athenians the necessary confidence and leadership to make them the most powerful Greek state of all.

Xerxes Continues the War. Needless to say, Darius was furious at his army's defeat. He immediately began training a new army in order to retaliate, but died before he could attack Greece again. His son Xerxes, determined to carry on his father's plans, gathered an army from every part of the Persian Empire. Each province had its own colorful uniform and armor for its troops.

To prepare for his attack, Xerxes had a pontoon bridge built across the Dardanelles Strait in 480 B.C. It spanned the waters, resting across the tops of 674 small boats. While the Persian army began its march to Greece, the Persian fleet followed along the coast to furnish supplies and support.

Miss Persia Beauty Contest

During the rule of King Xerxes in ancient Persia, there was a beauty pageant much like the Miss America and Miss Universe contests of today. After divorcing his wife for disobeying him, Xerxes wanted to select a new queen. He held a Miss Persia contest in which all the most beautiful girls in the Persian Empire entered. The winner, a lovely Hebrew girl named Esther, married Xerxes and became queen of Persia. Later she saved all the Hebrews from death when an evil advisor tricked the king into ordering them killed. This fascinating story is recorded in the book of Esther in the Bible.

Two Famous Battles. At first the Greeks wanted to defend only the Peloponnesus peninsula, allowing the Persians to destroy the rest of Greece. The Athenians finally convinced their allies to try and stop the Persians wherever they tried to enter the country. A group of 300 Spartan soldiers led by King Leonidas blocked the Persian army at a narrow mountain pass called Thermopylae. For three days this small force held off the Persian army. Then a Greek traitor showed Xerxes a secret pathway around the pass and the Persians attacked from the rear. The Greeks did not have a chance, but they preferred to die fighting rather than surrender. Today we associate Thermopylae with gallant bravery.

Once through Thermopylae, the Persians marched unhindered through Greece. They attacked Athens, burning this beautiful city to the ground as her citizens fled. Then the Athenians who had a fleet of lightweight, three-tiered ships, tricked the Persians.

The Athenian admiral Themistocles led his fleet into the shallow, narrow Bay of Salamis. The huge Persian ships followed, but once inside the bay, they could not be maneuvered. While

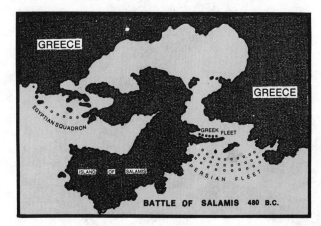

BATTLE OF SALAMIS 480 B.C.

A pontoon or "floating" bridge, extending across the tops of fishing boats, was constructed by King Xerxes. The Persian army of some 250,000 men was able to cross the waters of the Hellespont (Dardanelles Strait) by this means.

the Greek ships attacked, Xerxes watched in helpless anger as 200 of his 350 ships were destroyed. With his navy defeated Xerxes retreated to Persia before the rest of his empire rebelled. He left a strong force in Greece, but they were defeated at the Battle of Plataea in 479 B.C. This victory left Greece free from the threat of foreign invasion.

Summary. The Persian threat against Greece was ended. The Persians, however, still controlled the Greek cities in Asia Minor. These two powers again faced each other in battle, but the next time the Greeks invaded Persia.

The Persian Wars are very important to world history. The Greek victory kept their ideas about freedom, democracy, and individual rights alive. If the Persians had won, these ideas might have been lost and the history of the world would probably have been very different. It was many hundreds of years, however, before Greek concepts were put into practice. Nevertheless, they were recorded by the Greeks and influenced many people through the years.

Athens, A Threat From Within

The Greeks had united briefly to defeat the Persians. Once the direct threat of invasion was gone, the city-states again went their separate ways. Since the Persians still controlled Ionia, there was always the possibility of another attack on Greece. To prevent this, Athens formed a league with several smaller cities which later were forced to be a part of the Athenian Empire. Afraid of Athen's power, the other Greek cities

The Battle of Salamis, fought during the Greek-Persian Wars, was a major victory for the Greeks. The heavy Persian ships could not move freely in the narrow, shallow bay of Salamis. This battle marked the beginning of the end for the Persian King Xerxes.

A Confederacy, A Weak Government

When several cities or states join together for some reason, but do not give up their independence, a government called a confederacy is formed. The leaders usually agree to act together in certain matters, including trade, defense, and natural disasters. In every other way such cities or states continue to act independently from each other and the confederacy. It is a very weak form of government, however, and seldom works.

Immediately after the United States won its independence, a confederacy was established under the Articles of Confederation. It was not effective in governing the states so the Constitution was drafted. Each state gave up most of its individual powers to join the United States. Together they placed themselves under the authority of the federal government.

united. The civil war that resulted has been called the Peloponnesian War.

The Delian League. With Persians stationed across the Aegean Sea in Asia Minor, the Greeks feared another invasion. If this happened, they realized that a strong navy could keep the invaders from landing an army in Greece. With this in mind Athenians persuaded the other Greek cities along the Aegean Sea to form a confederacy against the Persians. (A *confederacy* is a group formed for mutual benefit or action. But each independent group remains in control of its own government and affairs.)

About 173 cities eventually became members of the Delian League. Athens was the largest and most powerful member. She furnished ships and the other cities furnished money. The confederacy treasury was kept on the island of Delos, from which the league took its name.

The Athenian Empire. By 468 B.C. the unified Greeks defeated the Persians in a naval battle near the Ionian coastline. As a result the Greek cities in Asia were freed from Persian control. Since the Persians no longer seemed to be a threat, many cities in the Delian League wanted to discontinue the confederacy. To their surprise and dismay, Athens forbid them to do so. Those who tried to withdraw were quickly brought under control by the Athenian fleet. Instead of being a confederacy, the cities discovered they were part of the Athenian Empire.

The Peloponnesian War. Sparta and Corinth were quick to see that their freedom and trade were endangered. They became allies with other free Greek cities, forming the Spartan League. The Peloponnesian War began in 431 B.C., lasting (with short truces) until 404 B.C.

Historians have divided the Peloponnesian War into two phases.

At first it seemed as if Athens would easily be the winner. She possessed a large empire, a navy that had never been beaten, and the rich Delian League treasury. Athens also had an outstanding leader, Pericles.

In the first phase of the war, the Spartan League raised a large army and besieged Athens. Pericles wasn't worried because the Athenian fleet brought in food and the siege did little harm. Then in 429 B.C. disaster hit Athens. A plague struck the city and one-third of the population died. To make matters worse, Pericles was one of the victims.

After Pericles, the tyrants who governed Athens were foolish crowd-pleasers. Under their leadership Athens attacked the city of Melos in 416 B.C. This city was fighting against being a part of the Athenian Empire. Melos lost and all of the men that were old enough to be soldiers were killed. The women and children were sold as slaves. This action brought the first phase of the war to an end.

Athens regained her strength and opened the second phase of the Peloponnesian War by attacking Syracuse in 415 B.C. Syracuse was located on the island of Sicily near Italy. By conquering this city Athens hoped to control all of the trade in the Mediterranean Sea and to rule all of the Greek world, including the Greek colonies.

After two years of fighting, Athens had lost two fleets and a large army. The Peloponnesian War continued for eleven more years. The Spartans received money from Persia and were able to build a strong fleet. In exchange they gave Persia the cities of Ionia. They defeated Athens' last fleet and Athens was forced to surrender.

Pericles, a brilliant Athenian statesman and orator during the Golden Age of Greece, is shown here in his general's helmet. He led Athens' army to victory in the early part of the Peloponnesian War.

She also had to give up her territories and her army was disbanded.

Influence of the War. Once Athens was defeated, the Greek city-states thought they were free to govern themselves. Much to everyone's horror, Sparta became a worse threat than Athens. Spartan troops tried to force their oligarchic form of government on everyone. Again the city-states united. They attacked and defeated Sparta. By then, however, it was too late for a democratic government.

The wealthy people were more convinced than ever that they were the only group able to govern. Intellectuals also had lost faith in democracy. The constant wars and uprisings made people look for a strong ruler to bring order and security to Greece.

The Golden Age of Greece

A period of great cultural growth followed the Persian Wars and lasted until the second year of the Peloponnesian War (460 to 429 B.C.). This part of the Hellenic Age is known as the Golden Age of Greece and centered around the city of Athens. It also is called the Age of Pericles since this great statesman ruled Athens at this time.

It was during this Golden Age that some of the world's most outstanding artists, philosophers, scientists, architects, and writers lived and worked. Although Greece was troubled by civil war, the cultural development continued. Throughout the Peloponnesian War there were many other great additions to culture.

Great historians also lived during the Golden Age of Greece. Herodotus, called the "Father of History," is known for his vivid descriptions of the Greek-Persian Wars. Many legends and exaggerated stories are also included in his works.

Another famous historian, Thucydides, wrote about the Peloponnesian War. He tried to keep his personal opinions out of his work. Much of what we know about this period of history comes from the work of these two men.

Architecture and Art

After the Greeks defeated the Persians, the people of Athens were faced with rebuilding their city. Money poured into Athens as a result of trade. The city they built was one of the most beautiful ever seen. Overlooking the city was the Acropolis. There stood the Parthenon, a graceful, majestic temple to Athena.

Architecture, A Reflection of Greek Life. Greek architecture was a reflection of their entire culture. The buildings were spacious with open sides. This was because the Greek weather was almost always sunny and clear and the Greeks preferred to be outdoors. They even worshiped and made sacrifices to their gods outside. Their temples were not built to hold

This drawing of Myron's famed *Discus Thrower* shows how Greek sculpture portrayed both freedom of movement and lifelike subjects.

The Parthenon, a masterpiece of fluted columns, still stands in the Acropolis as a major tourist attraction of Greece.

worshipers, but merely to house the god or goddess.

Early Greek architecture was very creative. Its magnificent style still can be seen today in the ruins of the Parthenon and other buildings. High, slender columns often decorated the buildings throughout Greece. Sometimes the Greeks used statues for columns, such as those found in the beautiful Erectheum. The three major types of columns were the Doric, Ionic, and Corinthian. In Athens the Doric column was the most popular. The Ionic column, similar to those used by the Egyptians, was developed in Ionia. The most decorative column was the Corinthian column.

Art Takes on Life and Movement. Greek sculpture was different from that of other ancient civilizations. Their statues displayed life and movement rather than the usual unrealistic, stiff style used by others in portraying their pagan gods. One of the most famous Greek sculptors was Phidias, known for his two beautiful statues of the goddess Athena. One

stood inside the Parthenon and was made of gold and ivory. The other was outside, standing 21.3 m (70 feet) high and overlooking Athens. The reflection of the sun on its spear tip served as a beacon to sailors. Another famous sculptor was Myron, best known for his statue, the *Discus Thrower*.

No Greek paintings have survived the centuries. We have learned something of Greek love of beauty and their ability to capture it in art through their designs on pottery. In them we find stories from Greek mythology and pictures of different festivals skillfully painted in bright colors.

Greek Drama

Greek drama has always been recognized as great literature. Other civilizations had stage productions, but they were not what we think of today as drama. They were part of a worship service and told the story of a god or goddess without any personality, conflict, or originality. They were performed according to strict ritual.

Doric columns were the simplest of the three Greek column styles. They were later copied by the Romans in their architecture.

The Acropolis, or "upper city," of Athens was built on a rocky pinnacle, as shown in this photograph of its ruins. It has been called Pericles' Acropolis because he made it a place of beauty. Notice the buildings of the agora at the base of the cliff.

The Erectheum, one of the buildings on the Acropolis, was original in its use of statues as columns.

In Greece, two major types of literature developed—tragedy and comedy.

Early Beginnings. Dramatic plays in Greece also were part of worship services. They were always performed during religious festivals. Like everything else in Greece, however, there was great freedom given to the writers and actors. The personality and motives of the characters were developed and exciting plots made them interesting. Since most festivals lasted for three days, many plays were written in groups of three. Each play followed the previous one, continuing the same basic story or theme from one play to the next. Each group of three plays was called a *trilogy*.

Theater productions of Greece were usually held outdoors. The stage faced a hill on which rows of stone seats rose in a semi-circle. The actors wore elevated shoes and large masks so all of the people could see them. This type of stage is called an *amphitheater*.

Many of the plays were based on Greek mythology or history. Being familiar with these stories, the people could then make their own interpretations.

Themes of Tragedy. Although most Greek plays were very exciting and dealt with such emotions as love, hate, anger, and pride, no violence was actually permitted on the stage. The viewer was told what was happening by different actors and by the chorus.

Three Great Writers. One of the major themes of Greek tragedy was fate. The Greek people believed that if anyone broke the natural laws, even when they did not know it, they would suffer endless misfortune. Sometimes this misfortune would be passed on to their children. In spite of this, however, the message of man's

free will comes through strongly in Greek drama.

Aeschylus is called the "Father of Greek Tragedy." During his life, from 525 to 456 B.C., he wrote 90 plays. Only seven of these have survived. One of his most famous was *Agamemnon*, a play dealing with pride. King Agamemnon refused to turn back from his plan to invade Troy, even when he knew a goddess didn't want him to go. To force the goddess' support, Agamemnon sacrificed his daughter to her. He broke the natural law forbidding willful pride. His wife never forgave him and when Agamemnon returned from the wars, she had him murdered.

Another great writer was Sophocles, who lived from 496 to 406 B.C. He believed that a certain amount of suffering comes to everyone. He also believed all people have a tragic flaw in their character, causing them to make wrong decisions. In his play *Antigone*, the king ordered the body of a traitor not to be buried even though he was his nephew. (The Greeks believed a person's soul wandered forever if he was not buried.) The king wanted to encourage loyalty. His decision, while noble, went against the laws of the gods. Antigone, engaged to the king's son, was the traitor's sister. Even though it meant death, she buried her brother. The king, disregarding the advice of his citizens and the pleas of his son, sentenced her to death. At the end of the play, the king sees that his foolish decision and pride cost him everything he valued in life.

Euripides, called "The Poet of the World's Grief," lived between 480 and 406 B.C. His main theme was that there has never been a completely happy man since life began. He tried to portray people's emotions and feelings. In his play *The Trojan Women*, he brings to light the

Large masks, such as this, were worn by actors of the Greek stage. They enabled performers to depict character traits and to change roles during a play. They also enabled people sitting in the back rows to see the actor's expression better.

misery and suffering of war through the lives of the Queen of Troy and her daughters after the fall of Troy.

Greek Comedy. Greek comedies often had subjects or actions that were immoral. Because there were no libel laws, playwrights often made light of leading citizens. Aristophanes, who lived from 445 to 385 B.C., pictured leading citizens as crooks, fools, and corruptors of good people, much to the delight of his audience. Slowly the quality of Greek drama declined. This was most evident in comedy plays.

Greek Science

The Greeks were among the first to reject the idea that spirits or gods were responsible for everything that happened in the world. They began to explore the world around them, searching to find out what made the world the way it was. As a result, some great scientific truths were first discovered by the Greeks.

Astronomy. After studying the universe, the Greeks claimed that the movements of the heavenly bodies were governed by natural laws. It was a Greek astronomer who first predicted when eclipses would occur. Other Greek astronomers discovered the world was round, not flat.

Some years after the Golden Age, a Greek named Eratosthenes (280 to 195 B.C.) combined astronomy and geography to draw a map of Europe, Asia, and Africa. This map was the most accurate one available until the sixteenth century A.D.

Mathematics. Three of the world's greatest mathematicians were Thales, Pythagoras, and Euclid of Greece. Thales of Miletus discovered

two new theorems in geometry. Pythagoras, a master of arithmetic and numbers, discovered that even musical notes had a mathematical relationship. Adding to the work of these scientists, Euclid wrote a book called *Elements of Geometry*. This book is still the basis for modern textbooks on the subject.

Archimedes (290 to 212 B.C.) was well known for his work in physics. He discovered the idea of the *lever*, a long stick used to help lift heavy objects. A modern use of the lever is the jack. Even a tiny woman can lift a car and change a flat tire. Archimedes once said in referring to this principle, "Give me a place to stand, and I will move the world."

Medicine. Perhaps the Greeks' greatest scientific advances were made in the field of medicine. In ancient Greece people used drugs to cure diseases, but they still believed illnesses were caused by evil spirits. Many put more faith

A muse player of Greece.

An Untimely Death

The life and work of Archimedes, a great scientist and mathematician, was valued by many countries of the ancient world. When Syracuse was captured by the Romans, a general warned his men not to harm the famous Archimedes.

Roman soldiers ran through the city looting and killing, while Archimedes sat in his courtyard unaware of what was happening. He was trying to solve a difficult problem and was unaware of the noise and confusion. A Roman soldier entered his home and killed him, not realizing that he was Archimedes, the man he had been ordered to capture alive.

in magic spells and chants than they did in the drugs.

After much study and observation, Hippocrates of Cos discovered that illnesses were caused by natural, not supernatural, causes. He recommended proper rest, diet, exercise, and drugs to cure his patients. He also believed doctors should be more concerned about the health of their patients than whether they paid their bills. Before his students could practice medicine, he required them to swear an oath of ethics, called the Hippocratic Oath. This oath is still taken by medical students before they become doctors.

Summary. Although the Greeks discovered many scientific principles, they did not make practical use of them. The Greeks were more concerned with theories and why things happened. It was several centuries before Arab and European scientists invented ways to put these Greek principles into action.

Philosophy

The word philosophy comes from the two Greek words *philos*, meaning "love of," and *sophos*, meaning "knowledge." Therefore a philosopher is a seeker, or lover, of knowledge. During and after the Golden Age of Greece, there were many philosophers, but the best known were Socrates, Plato, and Aristotle.

Socrates. One of the most famous philosophers of Greece was a man named Socrates, who lived around 400 B.C. Shabbily dressed and barefooted, Socrates wandered through the streets of Athens. He told people that they needed to know what true justice was in order to act wisely and be good citizens. Rather than giving speeches to change people's

Plato, a student of Socrates, was also a famous philosopher. He is well known for his literary work called the *Dialogues*.

minds, Socrates wanted people to think for themselves. He felt they should draw their own conclusions about what was right. To help them do this, Socrates would stop people and ask them questions. To answer his questions, they would have to think. Today the process of asking questions, or answering a question with a question, is known as the Socratic method. This is done to get people to think for themselves and is still used by teachers.

Many people felt that Socrates was a great teacher; however, others resented his questioning. Then one of his students tried to overthrow the democracy. Socrates was arrested for treason and for corrupting young men with his ideas. He was tried, found guilty, and condemned to death. His friends arranged for him to escape, but he refused to go. He believed a good citizen should always obey the law, even when the law seemed wrong. His friends stood by in sorrow while Socrates drank a cup of hemlock, a poisonous drink used by Athenians to execute condemned prisoners.

Plato. Socrates did not write down any of his ideas, but his most famous student Plato did. In his *Dialogues* conversations between Socrates and various people were recorded by Plato. This work reflected Socrates' ideas and his teaching style. Later, Plato wrote other dialogues in which he used the Socratic method to present his own ideas. He even used the name of Socrates as a speaker in the dialogue.

Plato started a school where his ideas could be taught. Called the Academy, this school was teaching Platos' philosophy and science 900 years after his death. While Socrates believed in democracy and in educating Athens' citizens so they could govern themselves wisely, Plato did not. Discouraged at the poor quality of Athenian rulers, he felt a philosopher-king would be a better leader.

Aristotle. Many historians feel that Aristotle was one of the most intelligent men who ever lived. He did not limit himself to one subject of study. He was an authority on astronomy, biology, mathematics, physics, poetry, politics, and ethics. For 20 years he attended Plato's Academy and then he established his own school.

When Philip, the king of Macedonia, wanted a teacher for his son Alexander, he sent for Aristotle. Since Aristotle, like Plato, believed that a properly educated king would make the best ruler, he accepted the job. Alexander later became a great military leader and conquered all the known world. Whether Alexander would have been a wise ruler will never be known because he died before having a chance to show his governing abilities.

Stoics and Epicureans. The ideas of early philosophers influenced life in Early Greece and world history. As people joined together in their beliefs on philosophy, two major groups emerged—the Stoics and the Epicureans.

Stoics believed everyone should live simple lives without luxuries. They felt people should be able to accept the hardships of life without complaining. The early Romans were one group of people who followed the Stoic philosophy.

The Epicureans followed the philosopher Epicurus. They believed that the good things in life were to be enjoyed, but never to excess. People should be moderate in their eating, drinking, and all other activities. Later followers of this philosophy were known for their "easy living." They were the ones who always seemed to have the best wine and food and who often overindulged. People have been influenced by these teachings all through history. As we study other civilizations, we will come across Stoicism and Epicureanism again.

Spread of Greek Culture

The final portion of Greece's Hellenic Age was dominated by the powerful figure of one man, Alexander the Great. He inherited a little-known kingdom, the small, northern country of Macedonia, from his father, Philip. Alexander later became emperor of the largest empire ever ruled by one man up to that time. Alexander is an exciting person to study because he was heroic in every way. Only his early death at the age of 32 stopped him from completely unifying his empire.

The period of history beginning after Alexander the Great's death is known as the Hellenistic Age. It ended when the Romans took over the Middle East around 146 B.C. During the Hellenistic Age, Greek culture no longer stayed within her borders. It blended with Persian culture and the influence of the Greeks was felt throughout the world.

Macedonia Conquers Greece

As we have seen, the Greek city-states found it difficult to unite, even when faced with outside invasion. The end of the Peloponnesian War found both Athens and Sparta defeated. These once-powerful city-states never again regained their strength or importance. The Athenian orator Demosthenes tried to warn his countrymen that they were in danger of attack from their northern neighbor Macedonia. But no one seemed to listen. The Greeks were too busy

Aristotle was a Greek philosopher. Like his teacher Plato, he supported the belief that a government should be ruled by a well-educated man. He was able to test his theories of government when he became Alexander the Great's teacher.

Alexander the Great, king of Macedonia, has been called a military genius. His empire was the largest the world ever had known.

fighting each other to worry about dangers outside of their borders.

Philip II of Macedonia. Macedonia, more rugged and mountainous than Greece, was not united politically under one man's leadership. Whenever a new king came to the throne, the different territories rebelled and tried to establish independent countries. Then Philip II became king of Macedonia and he brought all the territories under his control.

Philip II had always admired Greek culture. Before he became king he had been held hostage by the Greeks for a short time and became familiar with their way of life.

With Macedonia finally united, Philip II turned his eyes toward Greece. The Greek city-states seemed to be destroying themselves with almost constant fighting and he realized they could be easily conquered.

Athens was the only city-state which tried to stop him, but her weak army was quickly defeated. The rest of Greece surrendered to the Macedonians without fighting. Once Philip II was in control of Greece, he began making plans to invade Persia. He was assassinated in 336 B.C., however, before he could carry out his plans.

Alexander Takes Command. Alexander was only 20 years old when he became king. As was expected the territories in Macedonia and the Greek city-states rebelled.

First Alexander conquered Macedonia and then demanded that the Greeks recognize him as their king, just as they had his father. He marched into the city of Thebes, but they refused to acknowledge him. Alexander ruthlessly destroyed the city and the rest of Greece quickly surrendered.

Alexander seemed to fit the Greek ideal of a perfect ruler. He was extremely handsome, intelligent, brave, and a natural leader. He had learned about government and leadership from his teacher Aristotle. Historians have called him one of the greatest military geniuses the world has known.

Alexander The Great

Once Alexander had regained control over the Greeks, he revived his father's plan to take over the Persian Empire. It was Alexander's idea to unify all the people in the world under one ruler. He believed that if people were joined together through intermarriage and mingling of culture, they would have no reason to fight each other. With this great dream in mind, Alexander crossed the Hellespont and entered Asia Minor two years after he became king.

Alexander Tames A Horse

A legend about Alexander the Great tells how he tamed his horse, Bucephalus. The horse seemed too wild and untamable for anyone to ride. Alexander, still a young lad, watched the horse rear and lash out with its powerful hooves. He quickly realized that the high-spirited horse was spooked by its shadow. The palace courtiers were horrified as Alexander darted to the horse's side and grabbed the reins, changing its position. Horror and fear changed to amazed wonder as the horse immediately became quiet and easily manageable. Bucephalus became Alexander's favorite mount.

Alexander's Army. Traveling with Alexander was an army made up of both Greeks and Macedonians. Along with 30,000 foot soldiers, Alexander took 5,000 cavalrymen, engineers, surveyors, and a secretarial force. The engineers built equipment for besieging walled cities and the surveyors decided which routes the army should take.

Alexander's large secretarial force kept careful records of everything that happened and of everything they saw. The description we have of the Hanging Gardens of Babylon was made by writers who traveled there with Alexander. In addition to all of these people, Alexander also had a staff of scholars who looked for and studied plant and animal life. Samples of their findings were sent back to Aristotle in Greece.

A Military Genius Builds an Empire. Wherever Alexander's soldiers went, they made conquests. The Phoenician cities of Sidon and Tyre were captured, Canaan fell, and Egypt was conquered. By the time the Persian cities of Susa and Persepolis were taken, Alexander had put together the greatest empire the world had ever known.

Alexander abolished the tribute the people of Persia had been forced to pay their rulers. As a result they welcomed him as a liberator rather than a conqueror. Everywhere he went, Alexander established cities and introduced Greek culture to these Middle Eastern countries. At the time of his death, 70 of these cities had been established. Thus, Alexander hoped to bring about the unification of all peoples into one culture. Two of these cities, Antioch in Asia Minor and Alexandria in Egypt, became great trading and cultural centers.

With the Middle East under his control, Alexander decided to add the territory of India to his empire. His soldiers marched as far as the Indus River, winning battles as they went. Then tired and homesick, they refused to march any further into India.

Alexander felt betrayed by his army and their mutiny marked a change in his attitude toward the Greeks. Nevertheless, he agreed to stop fighting and appointed one of the defeated Indian kings as his governor. Alexander decided to make Babylon the capital of his vast empire because it was centrally located. He sent the sick and wounded there by ship. He and the rest of his army traveled the long trip to Babylon by land so they could explore more territory.

Alexander's Brief Rule. When Alexander arrived in Babylon, he began the difficult task of uniting the territory already under his control. He first organized an administrative staff. With his training and background, Alexander the

This is "(h) a Odos" or "The Way" that Alexander's army marched to Persia. It remains an unpaved path across grain fields beside the Aegaean Sea.

Alexander's Macedonian army pounded the high walls of Tyre with catapults and battering rams until a weak spot collapsed. Then they climbed over the rubble and engaged in hand-to-hand combat, during which 8,000 Syrians were massacred. With the victory, Alexander gained control of the entire eastern Mediterranean.

Great should have been one of the most able rulers in history. He had little time to prove his leadership, however, because he died within a year after his return from battle.

In an effort to blend the Greek culture with that of his subjects, Alexander began copying many customs of the people he ruled. From the Egyptians he took the idea that the ruler was a god. He adopted the Persian custom of having everyone who came into his presence kiss his feet.

The Persians and other people of the Middle East could not see anything wrong with Alex-

ander's customs. They had always treated their rulers as gods. The Greeks, however, with their love of freedom were shocked and angered. A wider gap was made between the Greeks and Alexander when he ordered his men to marry Middle Eastern women. The Greeks considered themselves superior to the people they had conquered and did not share Alexander's dream of creating a single, unified race.

Although Alexander claimed he wanted to unite his empire with Greek culture, he began to act more like a Persian ruler. He also became a drunken tyrant. Several times while drunk he

Alexander's sarcophagus shows a winged leopard and a goat with one mighty horn coming out of its head. These are the same symbols used by the prophet Daniel almost 300 years earlier to describe Alexander's kingdom.

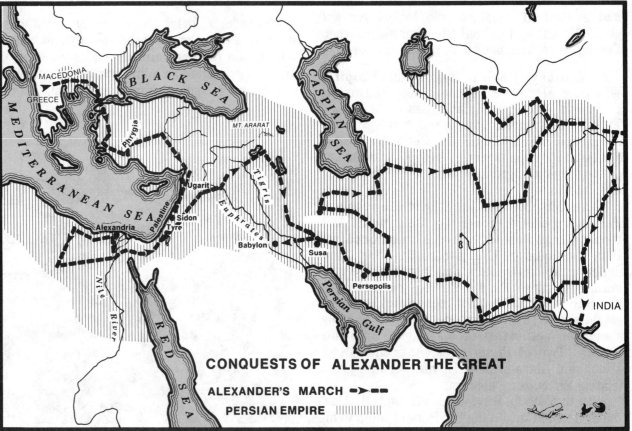

CONQUESTS OF ALEXANDER THE GREAT

ALEXANDER'S MARCH ➤━ ━

PERSIAN EMPIRE ||||||||||||

ordered the death of Greek officers who questioned his behavior. At one banquet he personally killed a general who had once saved his life. Although Alexander said he was sorry he killed the officer, his Greek soldiers wanted to leave him and return to Greece. Alexander persuaded them to stay, but there was constant tension between the Greeks and their leader. In 323 B.C. Alexander died of a fever.

Alexander's Empire Divided. Alexander's son was only an infant when his father died, and no provision had been made for an administrator to govern. With Alexander gone, his generals saw their chance to become rulers of Alexander's empire. These men were both ruthless and power-hungry. Everyone with any real claim to the throne was murdered. This included all of Alexander's wives, his baby son, mother, and brother Philip.

For seven years men struggled for control of the empire. Then four outstanding leaders divided the empire among themselves. Antigonus controlled Greece and the territory from the Mediterranean Sea to central Asia. Cassander ruled Macedonia; Ptolemy Lagi ruled Egypt and southern Syria. Lysimachus took over leadership of Thrace.

The struggle, however, was not completely over. Ptolemy gave Syria to his favorite general, Seleucus. Seleucus then captured Antigonus' Asian territory, establishing the Seleucid Kingdom in Mesopotamia and Syria.

The Hellenistic Age

Before Alexander's death, the Greek and Persian cultures began to blend together. This combination of customs and learning is known as Hellenistic culture. It spread as a result of

Daniel, A Great Prophet

In the land of Babylon, years before Alexander the Great was born, a Hebrew captive named Daniel lived. He was known as a great prophet of God. Daniel was often called upon by the leaders of his day to interpret or explain events, dreams, or messages.

According to the Hebrew record, Daniel once had a dream in which he saw strange and fearful animals fighting each other. God then revealed to him that the animals represented kingdoms and events that were going to happen in the world. The first animal in the dream, a ram with two horns, represented the kings of Medo-Persia. The second animal, a goat with one mighty horn, represented Alexander, the king of Greece. In the dream the goat suddenly appeared to defeat the ram. He then saw the goat's horn break and become four horns. Daniel prophesied that Alexander's kingdom would be divided into four kingdoms.

We know from historical records that Alexander, the king of Greece (the goat), did conquer the Medo-Persian Empire (the ram). When he died Alexander's empire was left to his young son (the goat's single horn). This son died and the empire was divided into four kingdoms, just as Daniel had prophesied many years before.

Except for future events every prophecy which appears in the Bible has come true. Even today we can see things happening that fulfill prophecies made more than 2,000 or 3,000 years ago.

The Rosetta Stone, found by one of Napoleon's soldiers in 1799, has three scripts (Greek, Demotic, and Hieroglyphic) inscribed on it. It was used to decode Egyptian writing.

trade between the new cities of the empire and the rest of Asia. Historians refer to the great movement of this culture throughout the known world after Alexander's death as the Hellenistic Age. The greatest areas of Hellenistic influence were in the Middle East and Egypt.

Hellenistic Cities. The men who ruled Alexander's empire established this culture as a way of life in the many new cities they built. These Hellenistic cities were carefully planned with long straight streets and a grid pattern for the blocks. Fine libraries, museums, and Greek temples were constructed.

Alexandria in Egypt was an outstanding example of a Hellenistic city. Located on a good harbor, her three-storied, stone lighthouse was famous throughout the world. The library there contained some of the rarest books of the world at that time. (It later was destroyed along with its priceless contents when Julius Caesar took over Alexandria.) More than one million people lived in Alexandria and ships from all over the world traded in her ports.

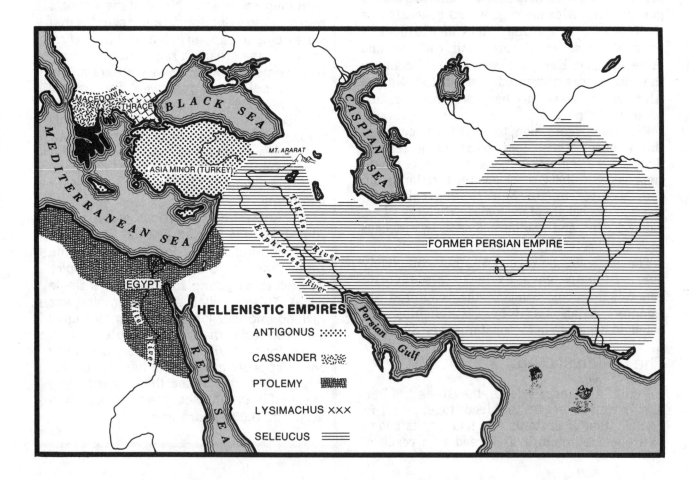

Influences of Greek Culture. Greek was the common language for merchants. This language continued to influence the world long after the Hellenistic cities ceased to be important. Greek became the language spoken by the educated men of Rome. The common people had their own version of Greek, called *koine*.

The Greek language has been a valuable help to historians. The New Testament of the Bible was first written in koine. From Greek words historians learned to read the Egyptian hieroglyphics. This was made possible when the Rosetta Stone was discovered by archaeologists.

The message on the stone was written in three languages: hieroglyphics, Demotic (a combination of Greek and hieroglyphics), and koine.

Hellenistic sculpture introduced Greek realism to Middle Eastern and Indian artists. The many advances made by Greek scientists were available to the Arabs after the Moslems took over the Middle East. These scientific ideas were documented and later used by universities in France, Italy, and Germany. Greek ideas on government and politics have had a great influence on the political history of Europe and the United States.

THE STARTING SLAB *at Olympia (below), divided to give each runner four feet of lateral room, accommodated 20 men. The racers, who wore no shoes, lined up by positioning their feet according to the grooves that are cut into the stone slab.*

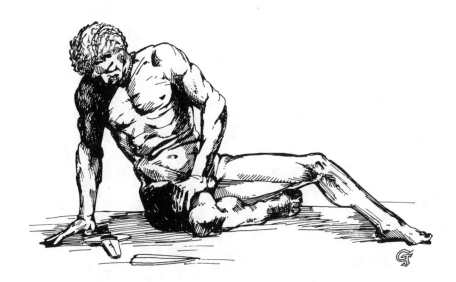

Hellenistic art was intense and realistic in every detail. This sculpture, called The Dying Gaul, captures the suffering and tragedy of a gladiator.

RISE OF THE ROMAN REPUBLIC

Projects

1. Study at least four civilizations and prepare a report on women's rights. Are there certain conditions that make a civilization favor stricter controls or more freedom for women? Why do you suppose this is true?

2. What were some of the unusual Etruscan religious customs? How did they mark boundaries of their cities and bury their dead? What influence did their religion have on the development and decline of their civilization?

3. Compare the differences between a democracy and a republic. Which form of government do we have in the United States? Which form do you feel is better? Why?

4. Draw a picture or make a model of the Roman Forum or the Senate.

5. The Plebeians worked hard to win rights in Rome. In the United States the Irish, Chinese, Negroes, Chicanos, Indians, and other minority groups have had to work for rights. Compare the struggle of one of these groups with that of the Plebeians.

6. Research how indemnities have been used in more recent times. Study how the indemnity Germany was forced to pay after World War I led to the outbreak of World War II. What is your conclusion on the use of indemnities?

7. Compare the welfare system in the United States with Rome's system of giving free food to the mobs. How do these systems of helping the poor operate and what are they supposed to accomplish? Is public welfare accomplishing these goals in the United States?

8. Do a report on one of these men—Hannibal, Julius Caesar, Pompey, or Mark Antony. Compare their goals and aims in their early life with their goals, aims, attitudes, and actions of their latter years. Did their successes and failures cause their personalities to change? How?

9. Do a report on Cleopatra. How did she become queen of Egypt? What other Roman besides Antony was in love with her? Do you think she really loved Antony? Why or why not?

Words and Concepts

gladiator games
plebeians
indemnity
grain speculation
Julius Caesar
Battle of Actium
consuls
tribunes
protectorate
civil war
Gaul
class struggle
Punic Wars
Scipio
Sulla
"crossing the Rubicon"
patricians
Hannibal
Gracchus Brothers
Triumvirate
Ides of March

Rise of the Roman Republic

The major stream of civilization moved from the Middle East toward western Europe. In the area now known as Italy, the Roman civilization developed. These people played a major role in world events for more than a thousand years. Roman leaders imposed one system of government upon the people, establishing first a republic and then an empire.

How the great Roman Empire came into existence is the subject of this chapter. The features that made Rome a great power, however, were developing long before it became an empire. Like the Greeks, the Romans were first ruled by a king. They became a republic in 509 B.C. and an empire in 31 B.C.

Early Beginnings

The Roman Empire had its beginning in the area of Italy. A narrow, boot-shaped peninsula, Italy appears to have "straps" in the Alps Mountains and a "toe" pointing into the Mediterranean Sea. It is about 1126.3 km (700 miles) long and is four times larger than Greece. The island of Sicily is located off the tip of Italy's "boot."

Early settlers in Italy found a mountainous country. The Apennine Mountains extend down the center of the peninsula. Unlike Greece, however, the mountains of Italy did not divide the country into separate units. Three nearby islands, Elba, Sardinia, and Corsica, provided raw materials and land for expansion.

Italy was a rich land. The broad, fertile plain along the west coast, as well as the area around the Po River Valley, was good pastureland and farmland. The mountain areas contained rich deposits of copper ore.

About 2000 B.C., while the first people were developing Greece, groups of Indo-European peoples wandered into the Po River Valley. From then on other groups also moved into the territory. They all mingled together, adding to each other's culture. One of these groups, the Italics, gave their name to Italy. Another, the Latins, gave their name to the language later used by the Romans.

The Etruscans

The groups that first settled in the Italian peninsula did little to build a civilization. This changed, however, when they were conquered by a group called the Etruscans. Until relatively recent times, there was not much information available about these people. Then archaeologists began piecing together Etruscan history and culture from their findings. They believe these conquerors were from the East, possibly Mesopotamia. The Etruscans introduced many customs and ideas to the people that were once thought of as Roman. We now know that they established the first city-state civilization in this area.

Early Settlements. The Etruscans settled in northern Italy about 800 B.C., taking over the peoples already living there. This was easy because the Etruscans were much more advanced than the people they conquered.

Romulus and Remus

One of the most popular legends about the founding of Rome comes from a tribe called the Latins. They settled along the Tiber River on the future site of Rome. The legend involved twin boys, named Romulus and Remus, who were thrown into the Tiber River by a wicked uncle. They were pulled out of the river by a mother wolf who had lost her cubs.

When the boys were grown, they killed their uncle and started the city of Rome. Each man wanted the city named after him. In the argument that followed, Romulus killed Remus. Romulus became the first king in 753 B.C. and the city was named Rome in his honor. This story is interesting because it shows the violence and harshness that became a basic part of the Roman character.

The Etruscans built many cities, including Pisa, Siena, and Assisi, which are still in existence today. Rome was already an established city when the Etruscans took it over.

Etruscan Culture. The cities founded by the Etruscans developed an independent culture. There was little influence from other civilizations. Most of the cities were relatively isolated from the rest of the known civilized world. This was because the best harbors were on the western side of Italy. The civilization they developed was distinctly Etruscan.

About 700 B.C. Greek colonies began to take shape on the southern end of Italy. As we have seen, these colonies were so large they were referred to as Great Greece. The Etruscans, quick to appreciate the value of Greek culture, began to adapt it to their own. Trade between the Greeks, Phoenicians, and Etruscans became very important. Nearly all the gold and silver in Italy at this time came in through trade. In exchange, the Etruscans traded copper, lead, iron, zinc, and tin.

Etruscan women, like the women in Mesopotamia, were respected and given rights

This statue in the Capitoline Museum of Rome shows a she-wolf nurturing the twins, Romulus and Remus. According to mythology, the orphaned boys were kept alive by the mother wolf.

The elaborate dress of this goddess of sleep is typical of the dress style of Etruscan women. This goddess, thought to bring peace during sleeping hours, was worshiped by the Etruscans and later by the Romans.

Unfortunately, many ancient civilizations vanished when later people, who had no sense of historical concern for the past, built upon ruins of previous cultures. Little-by-little, archaeologists found remnants of the Etruscans and have been reconstructing their brilliant civilization. Descendants of Japheth first settled along the Po River about 2500 B.C.; they expanded their civilization by following the river West, across the Apennine Mountains. Eventually, the Etruscan civilization extended from the Po to the Arno Rivers.

A man and his wife are depicted in sculpture as they recline in a loving pose, perhaps during a banquet. Etruscans had a love for banquets and the finer luxuries of life.

Many of the Etruscan superstitious customs, such as the practice of "marking the bounds," were carried over into Roman life. People marked the boundary lines of a field, home, or city with a plow, as shown here. Often the plowman was led by a priest over the boundary to be dedicated. The Etruscans believed the boundaries were sacred so all plowed dirt had to fall inside the boundary line. They also believed the plow should be carried over the place where the city entrance gate was to be located.

and freedoms. They attended banquets with their husbands and sculpture depicts them together in loving poses. Etruscan women were allowed to own property and some were involved in trade. Such freedom for women was unheard of by the Greeks who placed women only slightly above slaves.

Art and Religion. When the Etruscans first established themselves as a power in Italy, their artwork depicted large, sturdy, athletic men. They were active, joyous, and music lovers. Over the years, as luxury items from all over the world flooded their markets, their artwork changed. Pictures showed overweight, flabby

---

Myth or Reality

The Greek historian Herodotus recorded how the Etruscans may have been descendants of Lydians. He tells of a severe famine that struck the country of Lydia. In order to save lives, the king of Lydia divided the people into two groups. They cast lots to see which group would be allowed to stay in Lydia. The group which lost had to find a new place to live.

Tyrrhenus, the king's son, led that group to Smyrna where they built ships. They sailed away until they arrived in northern Italy. They settled there and changed their names from Lydians to Tyrrhenians after their leader. The Tyrrhenian Sea in Italy is perhaps named for them.

Many people say this story is only a myth. In recent years, however, archaeologists have made many discoveries which seem to back up many of the ancient myths. Some historians now believe this story could be true.

---

men and their faces showed disinterest in their surroundings. The artwork reflected a decline in their physical well-being, a factor which later resulted in the Etruscan's downfall. (We will see how the Romans later followed the same course of action, going into physical decline after becoming rich and prosperous.)

The Etruscans were controlled by religious rules on just about every subject, from founding their cities to burying the dead. The Etruscans always feared they would overlook an important omen, sign, or ritual and, by so doing, make some god or spirit angry. They were not concerned about right or wrong. Their primary interest was in understanding all the signs and performing all the rituals correctly.

The three primary Etruscan deities were Jupiter, Juno, and Minerva, which the Romans also worshiped later. The Etruscans also believed in demons. Pictures of them in all their ghoulish splendor have been found on the walls of tombs. One demon, named Charun, was pictured with horse ears, a beaked nose, and decaying flesh. His face was an eerie blue and he towered above his trembling victims, carrying a big mallet.

Emergence of Rome

Although the Etruscans conquered Rome, the Romans were always looking for a chance to throw off Etruscan domination. In 509 B.C. they succeeded in gaining political freedom, but they retained many Etruscan customs.

Decline of the Etruscans. From 700 to 500 B.C. the Etruscans controlled the western Mediterranean Sea. Etruscan fleets either traded or pirated, whichever seemed best at the moment. They fought the navies of the Greeks and the

Phoenicians who had set up the powerful trading center of Carthage in North Africa.

The Etruscans claimed that nations, like people, had a time of birth, growth, and death. They believed the average life of a nation was between 80 and 120 years. When their 120th birthday as a nation approached, Etruscan soldiers lost the will to fight. This lack of interest, along with additional collapse of their physical fitness, weakened their power. It is no wonder that the Etruscans fell before the strength of the Roman soldiers.

Etruscan Influence. The Romans adopted many things from the Etruscan civilization. One of them was the men's main garment, the *toga.* This was a loose outer coat or robe worn by men in public. The toga had been introduced by the Etruscans for use during their religious ceremonies.

The Romans also copied Etruscan homes, building covered walkways, called *porticos.* These walkways led to pillared courtyards. All rooms of the house opened into an inner courtyard, called the *atrium.* On the inside walls the Etruscans painted frescoes depicting lively everyday life. Many of these frescoes showed people at parties similar to the wild orgies later held by Romans. The practice of lying on low couches while eating from small tables was also introduced by the Etruscans to the Romans.

One of the most typical Etruscan characteristics—their harsh almost bloodthirsty concept of life—influenced the Romans. The Etruscan soldiers were the bravest and best fighters in the world. The Romans copied Etruscan weapons, armor, and fighting techniques. As a result, the Roman army became almost unbeatable. The Etruscans also invented the gladiator games which were later enjoyed by the Romans. In these competitions, performed mostly during funerals, armed men fought to the death. The Romans later turned the gladiator games into circuses where people spent an entire day watching men kill each other.

Rome Gains Independence. In 509 B.C. the Romans overthrew the Etruscan king and gained their freedom. Then Roman troops began to take over the Etruscan cities one at a time. By 250 B.C. the territory once controlled by the Etruscans was absorbed by Rome's political system. This was the beginning of the Roman Republic.

The Early Roman Republic

When the Romans broke away from the Etruscan king, they did away with the rule of one man and established a more democratic form of government, called a republic. The leaders, called *consuls,* ruled Rome and the territory they later conquered until it became an empire hundreds of years later.

This statue shows that the Etruscans were a sturdy, well-trained people. They migrated across the Apennine mountain range and established the kingdom of Etruria in the west-central part of Italy. The Etruscans greatly influenced Roman life.

Etruscan warriors were fierce, hard-fighting men whose long spears and individual shields were later copied by the Romans.

This *fasces,* a bundle of rods tied around an axe, was a symbol of authority carried before the magistrates in Rome.

Roman territory expanded with each conquest. The republic became more and more difficult to govern under the laws of a republic. We will see how the strain of controlling most of the known world finally destroyed Roman freedom and democracy.

The attitudes and customs of the Roman people made the early Roman Republic strong. The father headed each Roman family, including his servants and slaves. He had unlimited authority within the household and he was obeyed by all members. The atmosphere that prevailed in the homes taught all Romans to respect authority and obey government officials.

All citizens of Rome, whether rich or poor, belonged to the General Assembly. Only members of the nobility, however, could be members of the Senate. The Senate was the ruling body which elected men to govern the republic. Two consuls were chosen to rule the republic for one year. To prevent them from getting too much power, they were not supposed to be reelected for ten years.

Class Struggle. The Romans were divided into two classes of people: the nobility, called *patricians,* who were usually rich and owned large amounts of land; and the lower class, or *plebeians,* who were small, independent farmers and artisans.

Because the Senate was dominated by the patricians, the plebeians often were treated unfairly. At first the laws were vague because they were not written down. When a plebeian brought a case to court, a patrician judge most likely would rule against him. After many years of struggle, however, the plebeians finally won the right to have laws recorded. The laws were written on 12 bronze tablets to protect them from theft or change. They were placed in the Roman Forum (marketplace) for everyone to read. Memorization of these laws became part of every boy's schooling.

The Fasces — A Timeless Symbol

The fasces—an axe, bound in a bundle of rods—symbolized strength in unity to ancient people. Each rod, taken separately, could easily be broken; but tied together, they were unbreakable. The axe symbolizes the power of the state over life and death.

The fasces symbol has represented the government of Rome since the time of the Etruscans. During World War II, when Mussolini was dictator of Italy, his government was called a fascist government. This name originated from the fasces, the emblem he adopted for his symbol.

This reconstruction of the Forum of ancient Rome shows city life of the past. People shopped in the marketplace or worshiped in the temples. It was in the Senate building, located in the midst of the Forum, that Rome's major ruling body passed laws and held elections.

The plebeians also won the right to elect their own representatives, called *tribunes,* who were to protect plebeian rights. At first the tribunes were not allowed in the Senate. Later they had the right to stand in the doorway of the Senate and shout "veto" ("I forbid") to any laws they felt were unjust.

The plebeians worked hard to win more individual freedoms. Because they were needed to fight in the army, they were successful. The Senate was willing to give in to their demands to keep them happy.

Finally members of the plebeian class were allowed to hold important government offices. But instead of helping the lower classes, these

Roman Citizens Willingly Serve

Roman legend tells of an eighty-year old retired general who helped to save his country. The general, Lucius Quinctius Cincinnatus, was plowing his land when members of the Senate came to his farm seeking help. The republic was in danger and Cincinnatus was needed to lead the Roman armies. Although he could easily have used his age as an excuse to stay home, Cincinnatus quickly answered his country's call. Under his leadership the Romans won and Cincinnatus returned to his farm.

This story shows the dedication of Roman citizens, a virtue that helped make Rome great. People were willing to drop everything to help their country in battle. Then they humbly returned to their small farms, allowing others the glory of ruling them.

plebeians intermarried with the rich class. As a result, the old struggle of low against high class peoples and the rich against the poor continued.

Roman Expansion

The rulers of the Roman Republic were not as powerful as those in the empires we have studied. Roman leaders were not power-hungry, and they had no strong desires to conquer lands just to increase their strength. Nevertheless, the Romans found themselves engaged in war after war. They achieved many victories, adding many new lands to the republic.

The Romans had a strong and patriotic love for their republic. When danger threatened, they left their farms and businesses to fight in the army. These citizens were able soldiers and soon all the territory on the mainland of Italy was controlled by Rome.

Italy Conquered

The Romans conquered the Etruscans, Latins, and Greeks. They took over the entire territory of Italy and began to attach conquered territories to the Roman Republic. The conquered peoples were expected to pay taxes, but many of them were allowed to keep their own ruling families. When the new cities proved their loyalty, their inhabitants were allowed to become Roman citizens. It was considered a great privilege to be part of the Roman Republic. The new citizens thought of themselves as Romans and were fiercely loyal to their new state.

The Romans did not set out to conquer the world. New territory was added as a result of meeting emergencies. When the Romans dethroned their Etruscan king, they had to conquer the other Etruscan cities so they would not become a threat. Once the Etruscan cities were under Roman control, other Latin cities began to fear Roman power and tried to destroy it. The Romans met this threat by defeating the Latin cities and adding them to their growing republic.

The only part of Italy that remained in foreign hands was Great Greece. Once again the republic was threatened, but in 270 B.C. this enemy was defeated. As the Roman Republic gained control of the entire Italian peninsula, it was faced with its greatest threat yet—the Carthaginian Empire in Africa.

The Punic Wars

Carthage was started as a Phoenician colony about the time the Mycenaeans ruled the area of Greece. Although the Phoenician mother cities were captured by enemies, Carthage continued as a free city. Because of its location, Carthage became a powerful trade empire with colonies on Sicily and in Spain.

The Romans also had developed a flourishing trade. There was room for only one large trade

New Perspectives

Communities of family groups also became societies of people in Europe. The name "Europe" came from the Greek eu meaning "good", and rope. a special kind of twine or heavy string made from certain hemp. Apparently, the people north of Greece made a strong rope for their seafaring activities-hence, Europe, or the place of good rope. The societies of people who settled in the country known as "Portugal/Spain" were Celts. They also migrated by boat to the British Isles.

North of the Pyrenees Mountains that divided Spain from France, the societies became known as "Gauls". You will meet them on pages 152-154.

Also, remember that strong civilizations developed in Asia--especially China. During this era of Greco Roman history, the Chinese began transcontinental trading with Greece and Italy along the Silk Route.

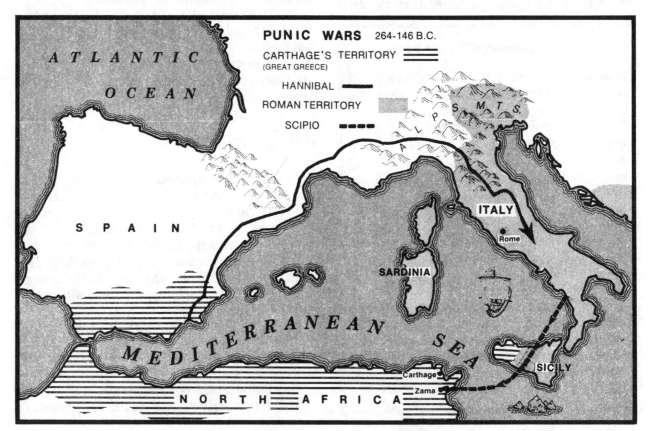

PUNIC WARS   264-146 B.C.

CARTHAGE'S TERRITORY
(GREAT GREECE)

HANNIBAL

ROMAN TERRITORY

SCIPIO

ATLANTIC OCEAN

SPAIN

ITALY

Rome

SARDINIA

MEDITERRANEAN SEA

SICILY

Carthage

Zama

NORTH AFRICA

A L P S   M T S.

capital in the area, so the Phoenicians and the Romans were bound to clash. Wars between Carthage and Rome followed. They are called the Punic Wars, from the Latin word *Punicus,* meaning Phoenician. There were three phases to these wars and they lasted a total of almost a hundred years.

The First Phase. The first clash came about 264 B.C. over the territory of Sicily. The people of Carthage had been merchants for centuries, traveling all over the Mediterranean Sea in their ships. They had a powerful navy which was an advantage in war.

The Romans, located across the Mediterranean Sea from Sicily, had no knowledge of ship-

---

A Clever Princess

There is an interesting legend about the founding of Carthage by a Phoenician princess named Dido. Dido's brother, the king of Tyre, killed her husband during a struggle for power. Fearing for her life, Dido fled with a band of followers until she came to North Africa.

The original inhabitants, led by Iarbus, objected to having new settlers in their territory. Not wanting to appear openly hostile, Iarbus told Dido she could have as much territory as could be contained by the skin of an ox. Iarbus was certain he had fooled the strangers since such a small amount of land could not support a colony.

Dido had the ox hide cut into one long, thin strip, which, when laid out, provided enough territory for a city. Realizing he had been outsmarted, Iarbus allowed the strangers to stay and Carthage was born.

---

building. They copied the ship designs of their enemy and Roman crews practiced rowing while the ships were on the beach. The hastily trained Roman fleet was no match for the Carthaginians. But they invented a hooklike object that tied the Carthaginian ships to their ships. This enabled the Roman soldiers to board the Carthaginian ships, demonstrating their superior hand-to-hand combat. Soon Carthage was forced to make peace, and Sicily, Sardinia, and Corsica fell to the Romans.

The Second Phase. The people of Carthage longed to avenge their defeat. Then Carthage and Rome got into another disagreement over territory. This time the territory claimed by both countries was in Spain. About 218 B.C. the second phase of the Punic Wars began.

A young Carthaginian named Hannibal thought of a daring plan to settle the disagreement between Carthage and Rome. Hannibal had been reared by a father who hated the Romans. He decided to cross the Alps and invade Italy from an unexpected direction. He was sure that when his army arrived in Italy, all the conquered Etruscan and Latin cities would join with him in fighting against Rome.

Hannibal took 40,000 men, 9,000 cavalry men, and 37 elephants and began the dangerous crossing of the Alps. Storms, snowslides, and a difficult path caused Hannibal to lose almost half his army and most of the elephants. Certainly Hannibal breathed a sigh of relief when he came out of the mountains into the lush sunshine of Italy in 218 B.C.

The Romans were panic-stricken. Time after time they sent armies against Hannibal. Although he was outnumbered, he won great victories. The one thing he had counted on was the revolt of the Italian cities, but it did not come to

In his attempt to add the Roman Republic to the Carthaginian Empire, Hannibal decided to cross the Alps and invade Italy from an unexpected direction. Because of severe weather conditions, many men and elephants died along the icy, snowy pathway.

pass. Hannibal was disappointed to learn that the people of Italy were loyal to the Roman Republic and would not join him. No reinforcements or supplies were sent from Carthage, so Hannibal's army was not strong enough to attack the city of Rome. For 15 years they ravaged the countryside of Italy, burning farms and small cities and defeating Roman armies.

For a long time it seemed that Rome was powerless in stopping Hannibal. Then the Romans put their army under the leadership of a brilliant general named Scipio. Instead of trying to attack Hannibal, Scipio and his army sailed across the Mediterranean Sea and attacked Carthage. Immediately Carthaginian rulers ordered Hannibal to come home and defend them. Hannibal hated to leave Italy because he felt he had Rome to the point of surrendering. He obeyed his orders, however, and returned to Africa.

Scipio and Hannibal met at Zama in 201 B.C. There Hannibal was defeated for the first time and was forced to flee. He went to Mesopotamia to live at the court of the Seleucids. Carthage was forced to disband its army and pay Rome an *indemnity*. This means they were required to repay the country for losses to property as a result of war. Under this agreement Spain was given to Rome as a part of its expanding territory.

The Third Phase. Carthage was recovering her strength and many Romans felt she was still a threat to Rome. Cato, the famous Roman statesman and orator, ended every speech with the cry: "Carthage must be destroyed." As a result, there was one more Punic War.

The Romans sent the Carthaginian government a series of impossible demands. One re-

Roman youths from wealthy families enjoyed dating. Here a maiden is being rescued by a young soldier.

quired that the entire city be moved 16.1 km (10 miles) from the coast. When the Carthaginians refused to comply with these demands, the Romans declared war. The Carthaginians were defeated and only ten percent of her population survived the massacre. The city was destroyed completely and even the city's ground was plowed with salt. Only a wasteland remained in the place where a bustling city of more than a million people had once lived.

The Republic Expands

Through the Punic Wars, the Romans also became involved with the problems of other countries outside the geographical area of Italy. At first their motives were a combination of self-interest to protect themselves and the unselfish desire to help people win their freedom. They felt both the Macedonians and the Seleucids were a threat to Roman trade interests. Later the Romans' motives became selfish as more territory was added to the republic.

Macedonia, Mesopotamia, and Egypt. Between the Second and the Third Punic Wars, the Romans began a series of attacks that led to the conquest of Greece. The ruler of Greece at that time was Philip V of Macedonia who had supported Hannibal when he invaded Italy. When Carthage was defeated about 200 B.C., the Romans turned on Philip. He was trying to capture all the territory around the Aegean Sea. The weaker Hellenistic cities of Pergamum and Rhodes had asked Rome for help. In 197 B.C. Philip was defeated and the country of Macedonia became a Roman province.

The Romans were then forced to fight the Seleucids who controlled all of Mesopotamia.

The Seleucids had also supported Hannibal by giving him a place to stay after his defeat at Zama. Hannibal tried to help the Seleucids capture Macedonia, but the Romans again defeated him. Hannibal took poison rather than be captured.

In 168 B.C. the Seleucids tried to conquer Egypt. The Romans stopped them and made Egypt a Roman *protectorate*. This means that the Romans had partial political control over Egypt and were responsible for protecting Egypt from enemy powers.

Conquest of Greece. The Romans were angered when the Greek city-states became anti-Roman and demanded that they leave the Aegean area. Instead of returning to Italy, the Romans destroyed the city of Corinth in 146 B.C. They took over all of Greece and placed the people under the Roman governor of Macedonia.

Although the Romans conquered Greece, Greek culture nevertheless played a very important part in Roman history. Greek culture had already been introduced to Rome earlier in the Greek colonies of southern Italy and Sicily.

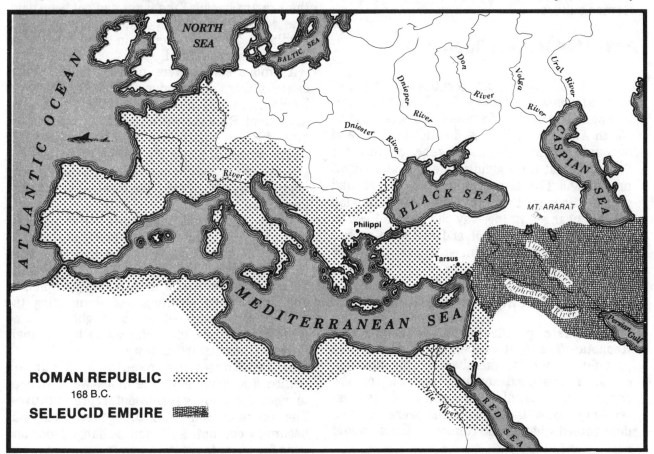

ROMAN REPUBLIC
168 B.C.
SELEUCID EMPIRE

Roman architecture was modeled after Greek styles. The major difference was that the Romans built gigantic buildings, preferring size to style. Most Roman sculpture and artwork was created by Greek artists.

There were no public schools in Rome. Those who could afford it sent their children to private schools to learn from Greek teachers. Others had Greek slaves to teach their children. The Roman patrician class spoke Greek, preferring it to Latin. Soon the Greek language, philosophy, literature, art, and science became a part of Roman culture.

Fall of the Roman Republic

By 146 B.C. the Roman Republic had acquired large amounts of territory. The Romans actually controlled Sicily, Sardinia, Corsica, Spain, North Africa, and Greece. In addition they had encouraged the Hebrews to rebel against the Seleucids and were giving Palestine and Egypt protection. The large number of slaves and tribute flowing back to Rome was making serious changes in the way the people lived in Rome. Trying to control and maintain such a large territory was almost more than the republic could handle.

Problems Facing the Republic

Two basic problems faced the Roman Republic. The first concerned governing and providing work for members of the plebeian class. The second involved defense of the republic and maintaining control of its vast territory. How these problems were handled determined whether the Roman Republic would survive or fall.

Unrest and Unemployment. Great changes were taking place in the plebeian class. You will remember that a loyal group of farmers were the strength of the Roman Republic When their country was endangered, they left their farms to defend their homeland. When the danger had passed, they returned to their farms. As long as the Romans fought in Italy, this system worked well. Things changed, however, when the fighting was in foreign territory.

When the farmer-soldiers returned home after years of fighting, they learned that they had lost their farms because the taxes had not been paid. The good farmland was controlled by patrician landlords. They had brought in large numbers of slaves to work the land.

As more slaves were brought to Rome because of wars and conquests, jobs for free men became few and far between. Many proud, independent Romans were forced to move to the city of Rome where they roamed the streets in angry mobs. Most of them seemed to feel the government owed them a living. During the day noisy crowds wandered the streets, unruly and discontent.

A law was passed which outlawed transportation of goods in the streets during the day. So from midnight until sunrise, while people tried to sleep, heavy wagons rumbled through the streets. The sounds of drivers' whips cracking and angry men shouting and demanding the right-of-way rang out in the night. It is no wonder that the rich preferred to live in their villas on the outskirts of town.

Since Rome supposedly was run on democratic principles, the mobs were allowed to vote for their government representatives. The problem was that the government was becoming corrupt. Evil men exchanged food and wine for the votes of the hungry people.

Ruins of the Corinthian temple to Jupiter. The stone pillars are about fifty feet high. How did these ancient people lift these heavy pillars into place?

Most patricians were pleased with things as they were, but some people realized that improvements were needed. The independent farmers were no longer the strong middle class of the Roman Republic. The virtues of hard work, honesty, and love of country were dying out.

The Gracchus Brothers. Many people wanted something done about the situation in Rome. One man who tried to start reforms was Tiberius Gracchus, a member of one of the most respected families in Rome. His grandfather was General Scipio, who had defeated Hannibal in the Punic Wars. Tiberius Gracchus was elected tribune in 133 B.C. and immediately set out to pass laws that would help the plebeians.

His first law limited the amount of land a person could own. All extra land was to be divided among the poor. The law was passed, but a tribune who supported the patricians vetoed it. While the veto was first introduced to protect the plebeians, it was then used by a tribune *against* the plebeians.

Tiberius Gracchus had the support of the Roman mobs. He demanded that the Senate remove the title of tribune from the man who had vetoed his bill. Many thought it was wrong to punish the tribune because he disagreed with Tiberius Gracchus. But the Senate was afraid of the mob, so it did what Tiberius asked.

Tiberius thought the bills he introduced were so important that he could do anything to get them passed. After serving his one-year term as tribune, Tiberius decided to run for office again. According to the law, he was supposed to wait ten years before running again. Tiberius evidently felt his program was important enough to justify disobeying the law.

The patricians could see that Tiberius was going to win his bid for another term. In order to stop his campaign, the people who opposed his reforms staged a massacre. Tiberius Gracchus and 300 followers were murdered and their bodies thrown into the Tiber River. This was the first time in Roman history that laws and governmental changes had been opposed with force and bloodshed.

When Tiberius was killed, his younger brother Gaius took up his cause. Gaius was elected tribune and again began to distribute land to the plebeians. He also encouraged plebeians to relocate in southern Italy, hoping to move some of the masses of population out of Rome. To encourage this, Roman leaders gave full Roman citizenship to the people of cities all over Italy. This means they were allowed to vote in the elections of Rome.

Another evil Gaius tried to stop was grain speculation. Rich people bought up all the wheat crop. When there was a grain shortage, they raised the price of grain and sold it at much more than its fair market value. Through Gaius'

At the expense of the poor, rich Romans built elaborate estates like this one belonging to the Gracchus family. Later Tiberius Gracchus fought for reforms to prevent the wealthy from oppressing the poor.

reforms the government bought and stored grain which was sold or given to the poor people. Eventually the government bought the grain and gave it to the plebeians in an effort to keep them from trying to overthrow the government.

Gaius was widely hated because his policies weakened the power of the patricians and the Senate. Finally the Senate hired men to kill him. In the fighting that followed, 3,000 of his followers were killed. Gaius killed himself in 121 B.C. to keep from being captured.

Problems Outside Rome. As a result of the Gracchus brothers' reforms, people began to see some of the weaknesses of the Roman Republic. It was becoming difficult to decide who was entitled to citizenship. Decisions had to

be made about how to rule the conquered territories as part of the republic. Reforms had failed and the common people were angry. Everyone realized things could not continue as they were.

If the Roman Republic was going to keep all its conquered territory, changes were necessary. Between 111 and 105 B.C., Roman armies fighting in North Africa and Gaul (France) were defeated. People rebelled in many of the territories and something had to be done.

Gaius Marius, one of two consuls elected at that time to govern Rome, came up with an idea for Rome's first professional army. Up to this time only citizen landowners were allowed to serve in the army. Very few of these men were actually available to serve in the army, so a new method of recruitment was needed. Marius formed a new army by hiring landless citizens for long terms of service. There were some drawbacks to the professional army, however, and it turned out to be a trouble spot throughout Roman history.

The main problem with the new army was that the soldiers' loyalty was not primarily to Rome. Instead they gave their support to the commander who paid their salary. Marius was loyal to Rome, but generals who followed him used the power given to them by the army to promote their own ambitions.

The First Civil War. A power struggle between Rome's Senate and the General Assembly led to a *civil war*. This means that the citizens in the territories rebelled and fought each other instead of a foreign enemy. The Senate chose Cornelius Sulla to suppress the people. In an attempt to keep the Senate from making decisions concerning the army, the General Assembly chose Marius to do the same

Simple Virtues Triumph

History repeatedly shows us that people become selfish and morally loose when they get money and power too quickly. At the same time, when people are poor and unemployed, they tend to lose their self-respect. They begin to lose their values and they grow angry and resentful of those who have plenty.

In the country of Media, people were strong, simple, and hard working. They united with the Babylonians to overthrow the Assyrian Empire. Then as they began to grow rich from their conquests, the people forgot the simple virtues which had made them strong.

These extremes also dominated the Roman Republic. Many honest people sought reform, but Rome was destroyed before any changes were made.

job Sulla had been chosen to do. The two generals clashed and the civil war broke out. First one general and then the other captured Rome and thousands of citizens were killed. When the fighting ended, Sulla was dictator of Rome.

Roman law allowed a dictator to rule the republic during an emergency, but at the end of the crisis he was supposed to resign. If a crisis continued, the dictator was supposed to resign after six months. Sulla broke this law and remained dictator for three years.

As dictator, Sulla attempted to strengthen the Roman government so it could govern its entire territory without problems. He attempted to make the Senate the supreme governing body. In 79 B.C. when he thought the government would run smoothly without him, Sulla stepped down as dictator.

The Republic Comes to an End

Sulla's reforms did not last and there was much unrest and fighting throughout the republic. People wanted a strong leader to bring order to the republic and to solve their problems. They were even willing to lose some of their freedoms.

The Second Civil War. While the Romans were looking for a leader, three men became consuls in Rome. They were Pompey, a famous general who had fought successfully in Italy, Africa, and Spain; Julius Caesar, who had added Gaul to the republic; and Crassus, an ambitious politician. The government established by these three men in 60 B.C. was called the *Triumvirate*. Each man served as consul for one year.

While Pompey was consul, Julius Caesar led his troops into the southern part of Gaul (France). The people there lived under primitive conditions, compared to the Romans. While Caesar was away, he sent written reports of his victories back to Rome so the people would not forget him. As a result, Caesar became a great hero to the common people. Pompey became jealous of Caesar's popularity and was afraid of his power.

Power Poisons People

As the English poet Shelley once said, "power poisons every hand that touches it." History is full of stories about men who were willing to take advantage of problems and disorder to gain unlimited power. Roman history is a perfect example.

Money and power gained as a result of conquest were often misused by the Romans. The common people were troubled by unemployment and hunger, but their leaders simply ignored the problems. As a result, the people began to lose confidence in their democratic government. With no way to earn a living, these once-independent and hard-working people lost their values and self-respect.

In the years before the fall of the Roman Republic, a growing number of people believed it was alright to break the law so long as it helped people. This idea of the "end-justifies-the-means" opened the door for even more lawlessness. The laws that once protected the masses no longer were effective. The virtues of loyalty and hard work which made the Roman Republic great, now vanished. The fall of the republic followed close behind.

Julius Caesar, a general-turned-dictator, improved conditions for the common people during his short five-year reign. As a result of laws he passed, debtors were no longer sold as slaves and farmers were given relief.

Pompey the Great was a Roman statesman and rival of Caesar.

In the meantime, Crassus was killed while leading his army in Asia. Pompey felt the time was right to get rid of Caesar. In 49 B.C. the Senate sent Caesar an order to disband his army and return to Rome. Caesar realized if he obeyed the order, he probably would be killed. He disobeyed and took his army across the Rubicon River into Italy. It was an act of direct rebellion against the Senate. The term "crossing the Rubicon" has come to mean taking a step from which there is no turning back.

Julius Caesar—Dictator For Life. In the fighting that followed, Pompey fled to Egypt where he was killed. Palestine became a province of the Roman Empire. Caesar became dictator for the rest of his life, claiming that his office was hereditary and that his heirs should succeed him.

In this drawing, Julius Caesar lies dead on the Senate floor after being murdered by his enemies. Cassius and Brutus stand in the foreground, holding the murder weapons.

Caesar ruled only five years, but during that time he accomplished many good things. He passed laws prohibiting the selling of people into slavery for debts and gave relief to small farmers. He changed the calendar to resemble the one we use today and named the seventh month, July, after his family name, Julius. In addition, he improved the coinage system, took a census, drained marshes, and built many public buildings.

In spite of all the things he accomplished, there were two groups of people who hated him and wanted him out of the way. One group consisted of people who had used their government offices to get rich. When Caesar cleaned up the corruption, they resented him. The other group was made up of people who wanted to go back to a republican form of government. They believed this would be possible if Caesar were out of the way. The two groups united in a conspiracy to kill Caesar. On the Ides (15th) of March in 44 B.C., Julius Caesar was stabbed to death in the Senate.

The Final Civil War. Caesar's heir was an 18-year old named Octavian. He joined with Caesar's friend, Mark Antony, to defeat the men who killed Caesar. In the rioting and fighting that followed, Cicero, a famous orator, was killed. After defeating their enemies, Antony and Octavian ruled the empire for ten years. Their relationship weakened, however, as the years went by.

Antony traveled to Egypt, where he fell in love with Queen Cleopatra, even though he already was married to Octavian's sister. It became obvious that Antony was planning to rule an independent empire made up of the Roman territory formerly ruled by Alexander the Great. Octavian decided to get rid of his rival.

Antony was a very popular leader so it was necessary for Octavian to turn public opinion against Antony before attacking him. Octavian produced a paper which he claimed was Mark Antony's will and read it to the Senate. The will stated that Antony wanted Cleopatra and her children to rule the eastern part of the Roman Republic. When the Senate heard this, they voted to send an army to stop Antony before he ruined the republic.

Octavian's forces met Antony in a naval battle known as the Battle of Actium. Both Antony and Cleopatra deserted their navies before the fighting started. Antony's fleet was destroyed in 30 B.C. Both Antony and Cleopatra committed suicide to avoid being taken as prisoners. Two of Cleopatra's children were murdered and three younger ones were taken to Rome as prisoners.

The Power of Public Speaking

In his famous play, *Julius Caesar,* William Shakespeare shows us the great influence of public speaking on the masses. At first the people were happy that Caesar had been murdered. After hearing a speech by Mark Antony during the funeral, however, they completely turned against Caesar's assassins.

Rulers and great leaders always have used eloquent speeches to get public support for their programs. *Propaganda,* slanted or one-sided information on a subject, is a favorite tool of dictators. It is important, therefore, for people to listen carefully to the statements of their leaders so that they can separate facts from emotions.

Octavian then was sole ruler of the Roman world. The Roman Republic had developed into the Roman Empire. Octavian took the name Augustus, became the first Roman emperor, and was known as Caesar Augustus.

Summary. The major trends established during the years of the republic survived throughout the period of the Roman Empire. The number of slaves in Rome continued to grow. The independent, small farmer became a thing of the past. The term plebeian, formerly used to refer to the middle class, then referred to the unemployed people crowding into Rome. There they were entertained by free circuses and given free bread. Such handouts helped wealthy patricians keep the common people from rebelling and demanding changes in government.

The patrician class, with the riches of the world at their fingertips and slaves to handle all their work, became cold-hearted, selfish, and cruel. The patricians drew upon the customs of the Etruscans and were entertained by orgies and gladiator contests.

Before very long, Rome became known throughout the world as a place of moral corruption. The Roman Empire enjoyed many years of peace and prosperity and it greatly influenced the rest of the world as we will see in the next chapter.

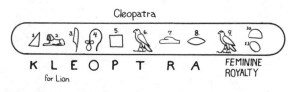

A cartouche is an oval area inscribed with the name of the country's ruler. This cartouche shows the hieroglyphics for Cleopatra's name and indicates she was a powerful ruler.

THE **ROMAN EMPIRE**

Projects

1. Do a study on the United States Civil Service. What are some United States laws regarding Civil Service employees? Do you feel these laws are fair or unfair? Explain. Is the United States Civil Service more complex than the one Augustus set up?

2. Write a report on volcanoes. What makes them erupt? Can extinct volcanoes come to life again? How do new volcanoes form? What are some major volcano disasters? Is Mt. Vesuvius the worst?

3. Compare Juvenal's Rome with the residential areas of New York City today. In what ways are they similar, in what ways different? Are people as rude? Is garbage thrown into the street from apartments? Which city would you rather live in? Explain.

4. Research aqueducts, what they are and how they work. Make a model or drawing to explain.

5. Give a report on ancient sports from earliest times until the Roman Empire. How do they compare with the major forms of sports around the world today? What are the major characteristics of these events? Consider boxing, bullfighting, sports car racing, as well as football, etc. Why do people enjoy these sports?

6. Do a research report on International Law. Where is the World Court located? How are the laws made and enforced? Have they been successful in the past? Explain. Do you believe these courts should have more power? Explain.

7. When the Germans were invading the Roman Empire, the Romans had a policy of containment. When the communists took over Russia, the United States and powers of western Europe began policies of containment. Compare the two policies. How effective were they? If the western powers had studied the Romans, what lessons could they have learned about containment?

Words and Concepts

containment
hearth
procurator
grammaticus
tablinum
Pax Romana
valkyries
crucifixion
tetrarch
Colosseum
atrium
Walhalla
resurrection
International Law
aqueducts
Mt. Vesuvius
comitatus
Latin Right
Virgil
peristylium
imperator

Augustus, "first citizen" of Rome, brought peace and unity to the Roman Empire. This sculpture, done about 20 B.C., shows Augustus in a reflective mood.

The Roman Empire

When Caesar Augustus became the first Roman Emperor in 30 B.C., the Romans began to enjoy a period of peace and prosperity. This period was known as the *Pax Romana,* or Roman Peace. It continued until the death of Marcus Aurelius in 180 A. D. During the reign of Augustus, the government of Rome changed from a republic to an empire.

The Pax Romana

The *Pax Romana* was marked by a strong administrative system concerned with the rights of the individual. Large-scale trade and culture flourished. The seaways were secure and the roads and highways were excellent. Fears of war and violence subsided as ordinary men turned to peaceful pursuits and the middle and upper classes became thoroughly civilized. A vastly improved legal system also contributed to the people's general well-being. The early emperors had unlimited power, but were not always good rulers. They ruled at the height of the empire, so prosperity continued in spite of them.

There were only four good rulers among the empire's first ten emperors. Seven of the ten died violent deaths. They all ruled in the midst of jealousy and hatred. There was peace throughout the Roman Empire, but it was peace brought about at the price of tyranny, bloodshed, and slavery. Under the rule of the last five emperors of the *Pax Romana,* however, things changed.

Rome was regarded by many as the "Eternal City" during the years of the *Pax Romana.* The empire seemed like a natural form of government, destined like Rome to live forever. Rome's influence was felt widely throughout the known world at that time.

Meanwhile, Germanic tribes in western Europe were becoming a threat. By the end of the second century A.D., these barbarians were pressing in on the empire's borders. Who could have possibly foreseen that they would one day take over the Roman Empire? Who could have predicted that the democratic freedom and stability of the *Pax Romana* would become a thing of the past and be replaced by the semi-anarchy and structure of the Middle Ages? We will see in the next chapter how the advances of these unruly tribes eventually led to the fall of Rome.

The Early Roman Emperors

Caesar Augustus. After defeating Mark Antony in 27 B.C., Caesar Augustus (Octavian) returned to Rome to restore the republic. He realized the Romans were slow to change and that many people would be opposed to the idea of the rule of an emperor. His title of *Augustus,* meaning "honored," was often used with reference to the gods.

Caesar Augustus ruled within the framework of the old republic's government. He took the power of a tribune, giving him the right to veto laws. He also took the military title of *imperator,* meaning "victorious general," which gave him control of the army. The words emperor and empire came from the Latin word *imperator.* With control over the army and veto power, Augustus had enough power to do anything he believed necessary. Instead of using the title of emperor, he preferred to be called "first citizen."

Augustus was a wise ruler and knew the empire needed a better form of government. So he set up a form of civil service within the royal household, giving power to men he trusted. Thus, talented free men and even slaves ran the empire as part of their household duties. The man in charge of buying grain for the royal palace, for example, also bought grain for government granaries. The man in charge of the royal treasury was also responsible for collecting taxes throughout the empire. Since the patricians in the Senate were too proud to accept these humble "household" jobs, Augustus had absolute control over the empire with little trouble from the Senate.

Augustus ruled the empire for 45 years. His reign was so successful that his subjects were willing to accept the one-man rule. His successors were able to use the title of emperor without objections. The system of government was so efficient that things continued to run smoothly even under the inferior rulers who followed him.

The Julio-Claudian Dynasty. The four rulers who succeeded Augustus were known as the Julio-Claudian emperors. Tiberius, this dynasty's founder, was from the Claudian family by birth. He was adopted by Augustus into the family of Julius Caesar. Two of the Julio-Claudian emperors, Tiberius and Claudius, were fairly good rulers. The other two, Caligula and Nero, stand out even today as examples of the corruption of absolute rule.

Tiberius was an able emperor in the beginning. His personal life, however, was filled with bitter disappointments. As he grew older, his bitterness turned to suspicion and hatred. The end of his reign was marked by terror in Rome. Tiberius had informants report plots to him, and he arrested and often executed the accused without ever checking to see if they were guilty When Tiberius died, everyone rejoiced.

An Unhappy Ruler

The Roman emperor Tiberius was a bitter, ill-tempered, stingy ruler. Perhaps he allowed situations in his life to make him this way. When Tiberius was a young man, he married a lovely girl named Vipsania. But Caesar Augustus wanted Tiberius to be his heir, so he ordered him to divorce Vipsania and marry his own daughter Julia. Tiberius had loved his wife and he never recovered from losing her. His new wife, Julia, was a sharp-tongued, loose-moraled woman. In later years she was involved in more than one plot to assassinate Tiberius.

The next emperor, Caligula, had been raised with the army. At first the young Caligula justified the people's hopes by making wise decisions and ruling well. But absolute power soon went to his head and he became cruel and immoral. The people no longer felt safe.

Little Boots

The ruler Caligula received his name in an unusual manner. As a little boy, he spent much time in military camps where his father was a general. His soldiers made him a small pair of boots like the ones they wore. The child was so proud of his new boots that the soldiers named him Caligula, the Latin name for "Little Boots."

Senators were forced to fight in the arena as gladiators, and women were frightened by the attentions of the emperor.

It became obvious that Caligula had mental problems when he made his favorite horse a consul. Finally after a reign of only four years, Caligula was murdered by a special group of bodyguards who were supposed to protect him. When news of Caligula's death reached the people, they were afraid to show their joy. They thought he might have started the rumor himself and that he would punish anyone who showed happiness at the news.

Claudius, Caligula's uncle, was the next ruler. It is believed that he survived his nephew's murderous reign by pretending to be feeble-minded. He was chosen emperor by the guards who had murdered Caligula. Nobody objected because he did not seem capable of being a powerful ruler. The people were surprised to discover, however, that Claudius was a wise and able ruler. His reign was cut short by his wife, who murdered him by feeding him poisoned mushrooms so her son Nero could become emperor.

This model of the Julio-Claudian emperors shows how many times intermarriage occurred between family members. Follow the "blood lines" from generation to generation. Eventually intermarriage merged four families into one, resulting in instances of insanity.

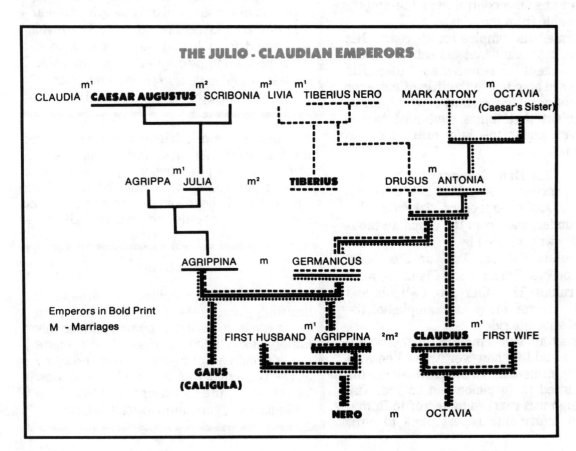

THE JULIO - CLAUDIAN EMPERORS

CLAUDIA m¹ CAESAR AUGUSTUS m² SCRIBONIA m³ LIVIA m¹ TIBERIUS NERO MARK ANTONY m OCTAVIA (Caesar's Sister)

AGRIPPA m¹ JULIA m² TIBERIUS DRUSUS m ANTONIA

AGRIPPINA m GERMANICUS

Emperors in Bold Print
M - Marriages

FIRST HUSBAND m¹ AGRIPPINA ²m² CLAUDIUS m¹ FIRST WIFE

GAIUS (CALIGULA)

NERO m OCTAVIA

Nero has the reputation of being one of the worst rulers in history. He was only 16 when he began to rule. Seneca, the great Roman philosopher, was his teacher and advisor in the early years of his rule. Despite Seneca's help the power of his position went to his head. He had his wife and mother murdered and ordered Seneca and the poet Lucan to kill themselves.

In 64 A.D. a terrible fire swept Rome. Roman historians claimed that Nero set the fire. Everyone knew that he wanted to rebuild the city. It was rumored that Nero watched the fire while singing about the burning of Troy. Before the people rose in rebellion, however, another rumor spread throughout the city. It said that Christians, not Nero, had set fire to Rome.

For several months innocent Christians were executed for this terrible crime. Men, women, and children were put into an arena to face wild animals as huge crowds watched and cheered. Nero staged evening "entertainment" in which Christians were soaked in tar, tied to tall poles, and then set on fire to provide light. This stopped when the people began to sympathize with the dying Christians. It is believed that the two great apostles, Peter and Paul, were executed during that time.

Nero began rebuilding the city of Rome. When he tired of the project, he set out to tour his provinces. Nero went to Greece where he put on a series of concerts, believing his artistic talents would be appreciated there. But his troops rebelled and he returned to Rome where he committed suicide. Nero's death brought the Julio-Claudian Dynasty to an end.

The Flavian Dynasty. Throughout the Roman Republic and the Julio-Claudian Dynasty periods, rulers had been members of the patrician class. After Nero's death in 69 A.D.,

however, the situation changed. Vespasian, the next ruler, came from the plebeian class. He had been a general in the army, stationed in Spain. Vespasian was a wise and practical-minded man who made many good changes in the government. The empire prospered under his rule.

Both of Vespasian's sons ruled before the Flavian Dynasty came to an end. Titus, the eldest, ruled for only two years, but three major disasters occurred during his reign. First, a fire broke out in Rome and burned for three days, destroying many important buildings. During the same year, the volcano on Mt. Vesuvius erupted and the cities of Pompeii and Herculaneum were destroyed. The next year one of the worst plagues in history swept through the Roman Empire, killing thousands of people.

Nero, the crazed and cowardly emperor who brutally murdered Christians, was responsible for burning the city of Rome. It is said that while the city was engulfed in flames, he casually played his fiddle.

The Arch of Titus in Rome was built to celebrate Titus' victory over the Jews and the destruction of Jerusalem in 70 A.D.

This ancient sculpture depicts Vespasian, a man of poor parents, who ruled the Roman Empire wisely for nine years. He made many changes in Roman government during his reign.

When Titus died, his brother Domitian became emperor. Domitian had been jealous of his brother all of his life. When he became emperor, he tried to outdo everything Titus had done. Finally the power of his position drove him to insanity and he declared he was a god. Christians and Jews alike were persecuted because they refused to worship the emperor. Domitian was finally killed by his wife, who, along with the members of his household, were afraid he would order their own deaths.

The Five Good Emperors. When Domitian died in 96 A.D., the Senate appointed a senator named Nerva as emperor. He had a short rule, but he initiated a plan to provide the empire with excellent rulers. Instead of passing the throne automatically to his children, Nerva looked for someone whom he believed would make the best emperor. He selected a man named Trajan and adopted him, so he became heir. The new system worked well and the next four emperors were probably the best ever in Rome.

The Emperor Trajan had been a general. During his rule the borders of the empire were expanded to their greatest limit. When Trajan died, his adopted son Hadrian came to power. Hadrian felt the empire was much too large so he pulled the Roman armies back to more defensible boundaries. He then had stone walls built in strategic locations to protect the new borders. The one that was built in England still exists and is known as Hadrian's Wall. It looks like a smaller version of the Great Wall of China.

When Hadrian died in 138 A.D., Antonious Pius became emperor. He was one of the greatest Roman emperors. During his rule there were no disasters and no persecutions. He refused to accept a salary and turned his personal fortune over to the government to help pay expenses.

Marcus Aurelius was the last of the good emperors. Although he was more of a philosopher than a soldier, he had a strong army. When his victorious soldiers returned from Mesopotamia, they brought a plague with them. It spread throughout the entire empire and in Rome alone more than 2,000 people died in one day. As a result, entire villages were wiped out and the army was greatly weakened.

Under Aurelius' rule the Germanic tribes to the north became a grave threat. The plague had weakened the empire and the Germanic tribes

This statue of Marcus Aurelius, the last of the good emperors, was sculpted in ancient Rome. Aurelius led his troops to war against the northern Germanic tribes to protect Rome. When he became ill the job fell into the less capable hands of his son Commodus.

Scapegoats in History

Throughout history rulers have used small groups of people as "scapegoats" to escape the anger of the majority. The scapegoats were either an unpopular minority or person who got the blame for bad government situations or disasters. The people took out their anger and frustration on the scapegoats rather than on the ruler. The Emperor Nero, for example, blamed the Christians for setting fire to Rome. This prevented an uprising which might have cost him his throne.

This scheme was also used by leaders after World War I. The Jews were the "scapegoat" for the Nazis when Germany lost the war. The Russian government let its citizens attack Jewish areas and kill the people living there whenever there were crop failures and other natural disasters. The people's attention was directed to the scapegoat instead of the real cause of their problems.

attacked, Aurelius recruited gladiators, policemen, and even criminals, to form an army. He pushed back the invaders, but his army was too weak to completely defeat them.

The tribes invaded the empire on two other occasions. The last time the Romans were strong enough to defeat them, but Aurelius became ill. Before his death in 180 A.D., he appointed his young son Commodus as the next emperor.

Instead of following his father's instructions to defeat the Germans, Commodus preferred living in Rome where he could enjoy being emperor. As a result, he made peace with the tribes, leaving a dangerous enemy on the Roman frontier that would one day destroy the empire.

Life In The Roman Empire

The Roman Character. As we have seen, a great change came over the Roman people as a result of their victories outside Italy. The old

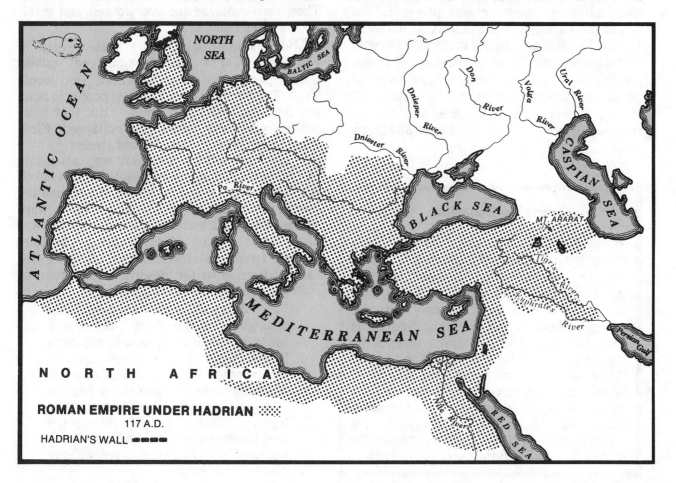

ROMAN EMPIRE UNDER HADRIAN
117 A.D.

HADRIAN'S WALL

virtues of hard work and patriotism had vanished. The masses that crowded in Rome received free food and entertainment so they were unwilling to work.

The rich people did not want to work either. The only occupation a patrician would consider was a position in government service. When the emperors began using their special civil service, the Senate became less important as a governing body. The patricians owned slaves who did all of their work. Thus they entered a period when all they lived for was pleasure. They staged lavish feasts, spent time at the baths, and attended games and chariot races at the arena.

The slaves made up about one-third of Rome's population. These people had been forcefully taken from their homes, herded like cattle to the slave markets, and sold. Some of the slaves were highly educated people. Hatred and discontent boiled within them and there was the constant fear of a slave uprising.

Slavery slowly changed however, after the Jewish uprising in 70 A.D. Slaves in large numbers were no longer brought in to be sold. Conditions for those already in the empire improved. Some slaves were allowed to buy their freedom. Others began to take pride in the household to which they belonged. The slaves who worked in the mines or on government construction projects were exceptions to the rule. They were underfed and overworked, and usually died after short, bitter lives.

Living Conditions. Rome was a city of contrasts. There were magnificent public buildings centered in areas where poor people lived. The Romans were the first people to build multistoried apartment houses. But they were overcrowded and sometimes collapsed. Fires often swept through the crowded streets.

It was difficult to find your way around in Rome. More than a million people lived in the city. There were no names on the streets and the houses were unnumbered. The streets were narrow and there were no sidewalks. There was always the danger of being hit by garbage thrown from upstairs windows. Juvenal, the famous Roman writer, described the streets of Rome around 100 A.D. like this:

"... Hurry as I can, I am blocked by a surging crowd in front, while a vast mass of people crushes onto me from behind. One with his elbow punches me, another with a hard litter-pole; one bangs a beam against my head, a wine-cask someone else. With mud my legs are plastered from all sides. Huge feet trample upon me, and a soldier's hobnails are firmly planted on my toes.

Gladiators performed in the Colosseum for the pleasure of the emperor. Here the gladiator with the net is about to defeat his opponent.

Spartacus' Rebellion

About 100 B.C. a gladiator named Spartacus led an army of more than 70,000 Roman slaves in an attempt to gain freedom. For three years or more, this army terrorized Italy. Finally internal problems divided the army and Spartacus was defeated. The Romans crucified the slaves and lined both sides of the road to Rome with them for 209.2 km (130 miles). Then a law was passed that prevented any more uprisings. It stated that if a slave killed his master, all the slaves in the household would be put to death, no matter how many there were.

That roof, from which a tile may crash down on my skull, how high it seems above us! How many times are cracked or broken crocks flung from the window! Look with what a heavy blow they dent and bruise the pavement! It may well be you'll be deemed an easy-going fool, improvident of sudden accidents, if you should go out to dinner intestate; for you have indeed as many dangers to your life to fear; at night there are wakeful windows open beneath which you must pass. You can but hope, and silently put up this piteous prayer that they may be content to pour down on you nothing worse than great pailsful of their slops."

Cultural Influences

The Romans made few contributions to culture because of their heavy emphasis on warfare and violence. Most of their art, architecture, literature, and science was copied from the Greeks. There were some areas, however, where the Roman influence was important to future world history. As we will see, the Romans' most important contribution was Roman law.

Homes and Architecture. The rich people had lovely homes on the outskirts of the city. When the city of Pompeii was discovered after being buried by lava from Mt. Vesuvius, archaeologists were able to get a good picture of Roman homes. They had been built around an *atrium,* a central court area with an opening in the roof. Sometimes the atrium had a pool that collected rain water. Near the atrium was the

tablinum, a room used as a study and small dining room.

The bedrooms usually opened into a lovely, landscaped courtyard. The courtyard, called the *peristylium,* often was lined with columns and contained statues and fountains. This was the family's favorite gathering place and they often ate there. The kitchens, slave quarters, and workrooms were located in the back of the houses. The floors were covered with beautiful tile mosaics. The walls were covered with decorative frescoes, usually depicting scenes from Greek mythology.

Roman homes did not contain much furniture. There were beds, chairs, tables, and chests that were richly decorated with gold and silver. Almost all the chairs were made for reclining and the people often preferred eating in this lounging position.

Although the Romans copied many ideas from the Greeks, they also developed some original building techniques. Their roads, bridges, and aqueducts were so sturdy that many are still in use today.

The Greeks, with their small population, did not need large buildings. In Rome, however, with its huge population, there was a need for large public buildings. The Romans developed two new styles of architecture, the vault and the dome, which allowed the roofs of their buildings to cover a larger space. The dome of the Pantheon, a building designed by Hadrian as a temple to the Roman gods, covered a room 43.3 m (142 feet) wide.

The Romans also invented a type of concrete. They constructed large buildings out of the concrete and covered them with thin slabs of marble. Thus the city appeared to be made completely of marble, when actually there was not enough marble for all the buildings.

An *atrium,* or inner courtyard, was built into Roman houses. The open roof allowed sunlight to shine through.

The Romans were skilled engineers as shown by the aqueducts they built. Aqueducts, like the one above, were elevated structures used for transporting water.

The gigantic open-air arena, known as the Colosseum, was built at the end of the first century A.D. It was the setting for circuses and public games which entertained Roman citizens.

The bridge over the Tiber River is another example of the advanced skill of Roman engineering. The bridge design bears a resemblance to bridges of the 18th and 19th centuries.

The Pantheon, dedicated to the Roman gods, was the first major building designed with a dome roof. The dome style of architecture filled the need for larger buildings.

Entertainment. The search for entertainment became the most important thing in the life of a Roman citizen. The major source of entertainment came from the circus. The Emperor Vespasian built the Colosseum, a gigantic public arena where gladiators fought each other and wild animals. The arena was large enough to be flooded so that naval battles could be staged for the enjoyment of the crowds. In addition to games, the Romans were great fans of the chariot races. The Roman citizens were as familiar with the leading gladiators and current racing champions as Americans are today with their favorite football players.

The wealthy loved to have dinner parties where every type of rare and unusual food was served. A dinner party could go on for hours. But the poor were more limited in their diet. They rarely ate meat of any kind. Their major meals included bread, olives, and grapes. Sometimes they used honey as a sweetener.

This marble carving shows a typical Roman chariot used for racing in the Circus Maximus and for transporting government officials.

The Roman public baths were like miniature cities. They offered poor people a place to go, away from the noise and confusion of city streets. One bath held more than 1,600 people. There were about 70 public baths in the city of Rome alone.

People went to the baths for many activities besides getting clean. There were games, lectures, musical performances, exercises, steam rooms, swimming pools, and people who gave massages. Merchants wandered through with all kinds of goods and foods for sale. When a man went to a bath, he could relax in comfort and enjoy the best of entertainment.

The Emperor Domitian built music halls where plays and concerts were performed. He also started a yearly contest known as the *capitoline games* where prizes were given for music and poetry.

Education. Under Vespasian public education was set up for Roman citizens. Government money was used to pay the teachers. Boys and girls went to school together until they were 12 or 13 years old. They learned reading, writing, and arithmetic. When the girls reached their teens, they were taken out of school. They then received training at home on how to become a good wife.

Since so many Roman homes had slaves to do the work, Roman women had lots of time for reading and continuing their education. Unlike the women in Greece, the Roman housewife was highly respected. She could eat with her husband and was allowed to leave home to go shopping. Women did not have the right to vote, but the historian Cato reported that they influenced elections during the last years of the Roman Republic.

When boys reached 13 years of age, they enrolled in the *grammaticus,* a school where they learned Greek and Latin grammar, history, geography, and astronomy. At the age of 16, boys went through a "coming of age" ceremony which symbolized that they had become men.

A boy could go to the Forum accompanied by his father and friends. There he exchanged his red-bordered child's toga for a man's plain white one. He also received his first man's haircut and shave. When the ceremony was over, he was publicly declared a Roman citizen and a special feast was held in his honor.

Literature. Most of the literature used by the Romans came from the Greeks. There were some exceptions. The Roman orator Cicero gave such beautiful speeches that they are still studied today in high school and college Latin classes. We have already discussed the papers Julius Caesar wrote about his wars in Gaul.

There were several Romans who wrote history, including Tacitus and Livy. Tacitus described Rome under the first five emperors. He is the only writer who gave us a picture of how the early Germanic tribes lived.

Three of the most famous Roman poets were Virgil, Horace, and Ovid. Virgil wrote the *Aeneid* which describes the journey of Aeneas from Troy to Rome. The poem was written to glorify the Roman Empire. Horace wrote *odes,* poems which were meant to be sung. His poetry was about love, friendship, and the duties of good citizens.

Ovid was influenced by Greek myths and the style of Greek poets. In his famous work, *Metamorphoses,* he wrote many ancient Greek stories that otherwise would have been lost. Three famous English authors, Milton, Spenser, and Shakespeare, were influenced by Ovid.

Roman Law. As you will remember, the early plebeians had the laws of the Roman Republic written down on 12 tablets so they could not be changed. As people of many different political backgrounds joined the empire, the laws had to be changed. As a result, equal justice laws were established in Rome and a body of laws was

International Law

Today there is a series of laws called international laws that protect the rights of countries. These laws, agreed upon by most of the countries of the world, concern problems that must be avoided to prevent wars.

In many ways these regulations are similar to ones we have at home. Rules are made by your parents which you must obey. Your neighbors each have different rules that must be followed. At the same time, there are city laws to insure that your neighbors do not interfere with your rights, even if their rules allow them to do so. The same principle applies to nations. There must be laws governing a country's coastal waters, airline hijacking incidents, and even treatment of prisoners of war and weapon limitations in times of peace.

Such laws had their start nearly 2,000 years ago when the Romans began combining the individual law codes of the territories they conquered. Roman laws were changed so that everyone in the empire was judged fairly. The body of laws they developed became the foundation of international law.

Virgil was a Roman poet and author. He wrote the epic poem called the *Aeneid* at the suggestion of the Emperor Augustus. It told of the greatness of the Roman Empire.

168

Chapter Eight

Greek		Latin	
A	A	A	A
B	B	B	B
Γ	Γ	C	CG
Δ	Δ	D	D
E	E	E	E
FIB	F Z	F	F
S	H	H	H
K	I	I	I
Λ	K	K	K
M	Λ	L	L
N	M	M	M
O	N	N	N
Γ	O	O	O
Φ	Π	P	P
R	Φ	Q	Q
E	P	R	R
T	S	S	S
Y	T	T	T
E	Y	V	V Y
	X	X	X
			Z

developed that has become the foundation of international law.

Some of these principles have been adopted into the United States' legal code, including equal rights for all citizens before the law and the concept that a person is presumed innocent until proven guilty.

Roman law is the basis for the law codes in Italy, France, Scotland, and Latin American countries. Laws set up by the Roman Catholic Church are also based on Roman law. We are all, to some degree, influenced by the Roman legal system.

Language. The Roman upper classes preferred to speak Greek, but the language of the ordinary Roman was Latin. As Roman soldiers and merchants traveled throughout the empire, they found it was easier to protect their rights and to help their trade if they could speak Latin. During the Middle Ages, Latin became the official language of scholars, the courts, and the Catholic Church.

As we shall see in the next chapter, because the Roman Empire fell, the countries that had been united by Latin developed their own languages. In Europe the languages of Italy, France, Romania, Spain, and Portugal are based on Latin. These languages are known as the "romance" languages, meaning they have come from the language of the Romans. Although English is not one of the romance languages, almost half of its vocabulary comes from Latin.

Roman Provincial Government

Government in the provinces was better under the empire than it was under the republic. Local rulers, using the title of king, or *tetrarch*, were allowed to rule their own territories. Local laws and religious beliefs also were observed. But a Roman governor, called *proconsul* or *procurator,* was placed in charge of the overall territory. He was responsible for keeping order, protecting his territory from attacks, and administering final justice. Only the Roman governor could order an execution. Temples to Roman gods were built in all the provinces.

The Roman governors were given salaries under the empire. This discouraged them from accepting bribes and collecting extra taxes from the people they governed. If there were too many complaints against a governor, or if he could not maintain order in his province, he lost his position.

The Latin Right. At first only cities in Italy were "free" cities. This meant that citizens of these cities were considered Roman citizens with all the rights and privilegs of a citizen of Rome. When Vespasian became emperor, however, he granted this privilege, called the *Latin Right,* to people in cities of Spain as well. Over the years other people throughout the empire were granted the same right, and their city's representatives were allowed to sit in the Roman Senate. The people were proud of their Roman citizenship and towns everywhere sought the coveted Latin Right.

The Empire—Prosperous and Protected. In sparsely populated territories, Roman-type cities were built. Each municipality had baths, forums, and an amphitheater. Temples to the gods also served as banks. There money-changers and merchants looked for customers. Crowds of people also gathered to learn the latest news, watch professional entertainers, and listen to philosophers.

Roads contributed to the general prosperity of the Roman Empire. Good thoroughfares were necessary to move troops from one part of the empire to another in case of attack. As bandits were captured, the roads became safer for travel and were used as major trade routes.

The territory along the northern European borders of the empire was always in danger of attack from the Germanic peoples living nearby. Troops were constantly on duty to protect the empire in these areas. Walls and protective forts were built along the frontier.

Once again the makeup of the Roman army changed. You will remember that under the early republic only Roman citizens who were landowners could be in the army. Later, however, the army became a unit of professional soldiers and any Roman citizen could join and receive a salary. People from the conquered provinces also were allowed to become soldiers.

Foundations of Christianity

Mesopotamia, once the center of civilization, had become an insignificant part of the Roman Empire. Although the area was no longer important in politics or trade, it became the location of one of the world's most significant events—the birth of Jesus. As a result of His life and ministry, Christianity became one of the world's major religions and changed the course of world history.

The Birth of Jesus. Shortly after Augustus became "first citizen" of Rome, he ordered everyone in the empire to return to their place of birth to be counted for tax purposes. Almost all governments have used a census to number their citizens. This gave officials some idea of the country's wealth and let them know how much tax to collect.

A humble carpenter and his promised wife from Nazareth, a small town in northern Palestine, made the difficult journey to Bethlehem for the census-taking. There she gave birth to a baby boy named Jesus. The mother's name was Mary, and the Bible record states that she was still a virgin at the time of the birth of Jesus. So the birth of Jesus was a miraculous sign that the promised Savior had come into the world. They returned to Nazareth where he grew up and later worked as a carpenter. Like other Jewish boys, Jesus studied the writings of the Hebrew prophets.

Jesus' birth was timely. As a result of Hellenization, almost everyone in the Roman Empire spoke Greek. This made it easier for the teachings of Jesus to spread throughout the empire. Another thing that helped Christianity to spread was the *Pax Romana.* Throughout the Roman Empire a peace existed that the world had never known. Travelers were able to go anywhere in the empire on the sturdy Roman highways without fear of bandits.

If Jesus had been born before Augustus' rule, the world would have been at war, and it is doubtful His teachings would have spread very far. If Jesus had been born a few years later, the political situation in Palestine would have lessened the impact of His teachings. Approximately 40 years after His death, the city of Jerusalem was completely destroyed and many people were killed. Roman troops swept through the province, taking almost every able-bodied person out of the country as a slave. When the massacre was over, there were few people left to teach.

Well-constructed roads, such as this one, were traveled in ancient times. Roman soldiers were able to move with great speed to areas under attack. Many of these roads are still used today.

Tiberius is a lovely seacoast city built in honor of the emperor with the same name.

ISRAEL
(At The Time of Christ)

Jerusalem, as viewed from Mount Ascension, is a center of religious life for Jews, Christians, and Muslims.

Jewish historians had foretold that a great prophet and deliverer would come and save the Hebrew people from their oppressors. He was to establish a kingdom like the great kingdom Solomon had ruled. From the time these prophecies were made until the birth of Jesus, the Hebrews were under the domination of a foreign ruler. The people waited anxiously for the appearance of the promised King, their Messiah.

The Bible states that Jesus was the Son of God and that He came to earth to save people from their sins. It was this claim that was responsible for His death. Even those who do not believe this, however, say that Jesus was one of the most remarkable teachers the world has ever known. His followers called Him the Christ, the Messiah. From this name came the names Christians and Christianity.

The Teachings of Jesus. It was during the reign of the Emperor Tiberius that the 30-year old Jesus began to teach. When Jesus began teaching, great excitement swept through Palestine. He performed many miracles, healing the sick and bringing hope to the troubled. His messages were simple and He used stories, or parables, to explain what He meant.

While Jesus agreed with the Jewish laws given in the Old Testament, His teachings were based on justice and love. He emphasized to the people that the ceremonies and rituals of Judaism were pointless without love and the proper attitudes. According to the Bible, Jesus taught that people should "love the Lord thy God with all thy heart . . . and thy neighbor as thyself."

Great crowds of people followed Him wherever He went. When news came that Jesus was coming, men left their fields or shops and women left their household chores to gather around Him. Twelve men were chosen by Jesus as His disciples, or followers, who later helped spread His teachings throughout the ancient world.

Religious leaders in Palestine were disturbed about Jesus and His followers. Although the Romans had given them religious freedom, the Romans expected them to keep peace. They were afraid the rulers would learn of the large crowds following Jesus and would take away their privileged religious positions in the temple.

But Jesus was not teaching ideas that would lead to overthrowing the Roman Empire. He was teaching people to be unselfish, to love one

Jesus gives His famous Sermon on the Mount from the Mount of Beatitudes. Wherever Jesus went people left their homes and businesses to hear Him. Many people were sick and crippled, hoping to be healed.

another, and to show love by the way they treated each other. He told them to live the kind of lives that would please God and not to worry about everyday problems because God would take care of all their needs. He told them to forgive others and God would forgive them for their own sins.

The Death of Jesus. Jewish religious leaders all agreed that Jesus had to be stopped. Because He claimed to be the Son of God, they thought He might declare himself King and disrupt the peace. Jesus was betrayed by Judas, one of His disciples, and was arrested after only three years of teaching.

Jesus was taken prisoner, but the trial that followed was illegal. Witnesses were bribed and gave false testimonies. The trial was held at night and only the judges who opposed Jesus were notified. The Jewish leaders found Him guilty and turned Him over to Pontius Pilate, the Roman procurator, for sentencing.

Pilate questioned Jesus and realized that He was innocent. He was faced with threats and blackmail and finally gave in to the demands of the leaders and people. Jesus was sentenced to die by crucifixion, nailed to a wooden cross on the hill of Calvary.

The Resurrection. Jesus' followers went into hiding, afraid for their lives. All their hopes for establishing a kingdom were destroyed. Jesus was buried outside of Jerusalem. The tomb was sealed by a huge stone and 30 Roman soldiers were ordered to stand guard, 4 at a time.

Then, shocking news rocked Jerusalem. The body of Jesus, buried three days before, was gone from the tomb. It is this one event that makes Jesus different from other religious leaders and great teachers. He was the only religious leader who was ever resurrected from the dead. More than 500 people saw and talked to Him after His resurrection. As a result, the teachings of Christianity are different from all other religions in the world today. Christianity is based on the death and resurrection of its founder, rather than on His teachings.

Thus, Christianity came to life during the reign of Tiberius. In the years that followed, it spread to every city in the Roman Empire. Christianity was accepted readily by the middle classes, many upper class people, and slaves. The teachings of Jesus began to have a tremendous influence on the social and political life of all people. Within a relatively short time, Christianity became the official religion of the Roman Empire as we will see in Chapter 9.

Christianity had its beginning in Israel—a country of little importance in those days. From there it spread to the Western Europe barbarian tribes. When Western Europe became Christian, education and culture began to flourish, making it the great civilization we know today. Christian teachings also had a great influence on the laws and ethics of the newly developing governments of Western Europe, Russia, and North and South Americas.

The Germanic Tribes

In this chapter we have mentioned the Germanic tribes several times. We shall see how they played an important part in the last days of the Roman Empire in the next chapter. For this reason, we will now discuss these people and learn who they were and how they lived.

Early Migrations

A group of people from northern India, southern Mesopotamia, and southern Russia began migrating to the area along the Baltic Sea in northern Europe. This happened about the

Golgotha was the hill of Calvary where Jesus was crucified. It gets its name from the Latin word for "skull." Notice the eye sockets and bridge of a nose in the rock formation.

This garden tomb, pictured as it is today in Jerusalem, is believed to be the place where Jesus Christ was buried after His crucifixion. Records say it was guarded by thirty Roman soldiers (4 soldiers changed every 3 hours) and was secured with a large stone and an official seal. There was a death penalty for removing this seal. Pilate's precautions were of no effect, however, for the heavy stone was rolled away and the resurrected Christ miraculously disappeared from the tomb.

same time that David was king of Israel. The New Egyptian Kingdom was ending and Assyria was rising to great power These early Germanic people did not leave any written records of their migration. But as a result of the work of archaeologists, we know about them.

Pottery, weapons, and tools belonging to these people have been discovered along the migration trail. Graves also have been found which enable us to know how these people dressed. Some of the dead were buried in hollow tree trunks and were found wrapped in beautifully woven cloth or in the skins of animals.

German Life

Life in Europe at this time was not easy. Unlike other civilizations we have studied up to now, the Germanic tribes did not live in year-around warm climates. They were forced to earn a living in a land that was cold and snowy in winter. For this reason, farming did not provide year-around food for the tribes, so they hunted wild game in the forests.

A Violent, Hard-Working People. Warfare became a major pastime of the Germanic peoples. The men used stone or iron

The Empty Tomb

Many people are uncertain as to what actually happened to Jesus' body. The one sure fact is that the tomb was empty. The following are explanations that have been given about this unusual event.

1. The 30 Roman guards claimed they all fell asleep at the same time and that Jesus' followers were able to roll away the heavy stone and take the body. This means that Jesus' followers stole the body from the tomb without awakening any of the soldiers. It is interesting to note that there was a death penalty for any Roman soldier who fell asleep while on guard duty. None of the guards, however, were punished.

2. Some claim that Jesus was not dead when He was put into the tomb. He then rolled the stone away and left. This theory ignores the presence of the guards who certainly would have arrested Him or killed Him. It also ignores the fact that Jesus must have been too weak from the crucifixion and loss of blood to roll away the stone.

3. There are those who suggest that Jesus wanted to be crucified in order to fulfill the prophecy, but that He expected to be taken down before He died. When His friends came to release Him from the tomb according to plan, they found Him dead. They carried the body away and hid it. The presence of the guards, however, is not explained, nor the fact they were all willing to die rather than stop preaching His resurrection.

4. Another explanation was given by the followers of Jesus. They said He was who He said He was—the Son of God. They believed He kept His word when He returned from the dead and promised the same eternal life to anyone who believed in Him. More than 500 of these people claim to have seen Him after the Resurrection.

battle-axes, swords, and long spears for fighting. They fought on foot, but when they could get horses, they fought on horseback. Later they began using helmets and shields of leather for protection.

When they were not fighting and hunting, the men spent most of their time gambling. Their favorite game was dice and many a man gambled away all his personal property, as well as the liberty of his wife and children. Some slaves in the Germanic tribes had been captured in fighting, but many of them were men who had gambled away their own freedom.

While the men hunted and fought, the women did the farming and housework. Life was hard for these tribes, but it strengthened the people. On their farms they grew oats, barley, hemp, and flax. They made coarse cloth and rope from hemp and wove linen from flax for soft underclothes. Sheep provided wool which the women spun to make warm outer clothing. Animal skins and hides kept out the cold winter winds, and the men wrapped strips of cloth around their legs for extra warmth.

The sheep and cattle were kept in pastures, but the hogs were allowed to run free in the

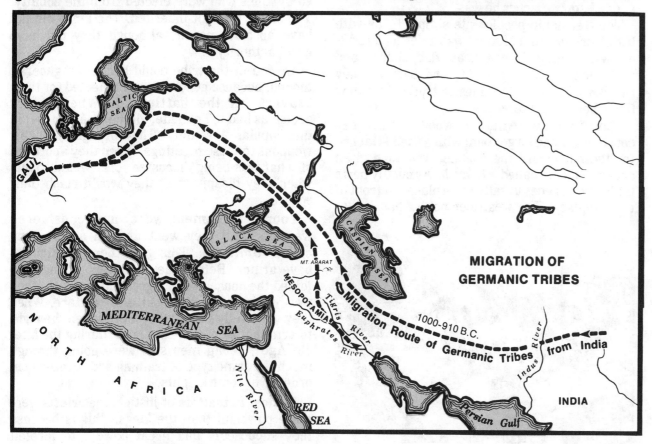

MIGRATION OF GERMANIC TRIBES

forests. There they ate beechnuts and acorns from the ground. While each family group owned its own fields, the forests and pastures were owned by the entire village and everyone could use them.

It is interesting to note that the cattle owned by these people did not look like the big, healthy cattle of today. They were tiny and undernourished by comparison. Even in the Middle Ages, when horses were large enough to carry a man wearing armor, the cattle remained small. Nevertheless, cattle were the main source of wealth for the Germanic tribes. The more cattle a man had, the richer he was.

The Germanic peoples ate simple foods with little variety. A lot of meat was eaten as a result of their hunting. They also ate fish, cheese, and a porridge made from oats and barley. They rarely had green vegetables or fruit unless they found berries in the woods.

Their homes were made of wood. Usually they consisted of one large room with a shed attached for the cattle. All the cooking was done in an open fireplace, called a *hearth*. A roughly hewn table and benches usually were placed in front of the fireplace. The wealthier nobles had larger

A German warrior of the Suevi tribe is portrayed here in a plastic model. Notice the unusual hairdo and dress style of the early Germans.

This German village scene shows the rustic simplicity of the early German life style.

homes. Sometimes they had a separate dining room where the walls were decorated with hunting and war trophies.

A German village was made up of 20 to 40 homes. The people liked to live in the villages rather than on the land they farmed. Even today many European farmers leave their homes in the morning and walk for 3.2 or 4.8 km (two or three miles) to their fields, returning home late at night.

Tribal Organization. The Germanic tribes developed a form of democracy. They were ruled by kings who were elected from the nobility. The office was not inherited. The kings did not have absolute power, although they did have great authority.

Anyone in the tribe could become a general, though, because generals were selected for their bravery on the battlefield. When major decisions had to be made, all the freemen met in the Popular Assembly. They brought all their weapons to these meetings. When they approved of what was being discussed, they would shout; when they disapproved, they would clash their spears.

Young noblemen were not considered warriors until they went through a ceremony called *comitatus*. This gave them the right to have armor. Before the comitatus, young men joined the household of a great noble where they were trained in all the skills of warfare. When they were fully ready, they were given the right to arm themselves. Years later, during the Middle Ages, young men still were going through much the same type of training and ceremony in order to become knights.

Justice. In matters of justice, the priests were more powerful than the kings. This is because they supposedly had great powers to foretell future events. When a person was accused of a crime, he was brought before the Popular Assembly. There he usually was forced to go through *trial by ordeal* to prove his innocence. This means he was tried with any type of ordeal, from taking a red-hot iron in his hand to engaging in combat.

Punishment for lesser crimes involved a fine, which was usually paid in cattle. The injured person received part of the fine; the rest went to the king or to the tribe as a whole. If a person was guilty of treason or desertion, he was hung. Bravery was considered one of a man's most important qualities. As a result, if a man was found guilty of cowardice, a hood was placed over his head and he was drowned in a swamp.

Religion. The early Germanic tribes worshiped nature, including the sun, moon, and stars. They had a chief god named Wodan from whom our day of the week, Wednesday, is taken. Wodan's wife's name, Frigga, became Friday, while Thursday was named for Thor, the god of thunder. One of the most important gods of these warlike people was Tiu, the god of war. From him we derive the name of Tuesday.

The German heaven, where only great warriors and brave men would go, was called Walhalla. When a warrior was dying, the Germans believed warrior maidens, called *valkyries* would come and take him to Walhalla. There the heroes would spend their days drinking wine from the skulls of their enemies.

The Roman Influence

The tribes close to the Roman Empire borders valued gold and silver because they could trade it for goods they could not make for themselves. They were not particularly interested in precious metals for their own use. In addition to these metals, a brisk trade in amber, hides, skins, goose feathers, and timber sprang up. Women even sold their hair to make blonde wigs for elegant Roman women. In exchange for these raw materials, the Germanic tribes received iron weapons, spices, glassware, and other items made of metal.

While many of the Germanic tribes were a constant threat to the Roman Empire, they were not all considered enemies. In the area now known as the Netherlands, the Romans made friends with a tribe known as the Frisians.

> ### Trial By Ordeal
>
> Ancient peoples used unusual tests, called trial by ordeal, to decide whether a person was guilty or innocent. Before someone was put to the test, he was assured by a priest that he would have the protection of the gods if he were innocent.
>
> Sometimes a person had to grab a hot iron; sometimes he had to place his tongue on it. Scientists have discovered that feelings of guilt, fear, and anxiety cause the mouth and skin to go dry. Therefore, a guilty person would be more likely to burn himself than someone who was confident because he was innocent.
>
> Another form of ordeal was a test for witches whereby persons were tied up and thrown into a pond. If they sank, they were thought to be innocent. If they floated, they were judged guilty because even the water rejected them. The main problem with this test was that many innocent people drowned before they could be rescued.

Thor, the god of thunder, was the most powerful of the Norwegian gods. Early poems describe how thunder and lightning clamored when Thor drove his he-goats or pounded his hammer.

The Romans taught these people how to make dikes along the rivers and seacoasts to keep their land from being flooded. They also taught them how to drain marshes and clear forests. All these things provided more good farmland so the Frisians could make a better living.

At first the Emperor Augustus planned to invade Europe and make the Germanic people part of the Roman Empire. But the Romans were defeated by a general named Hermann Arminius. There was never another serious attempt to make them part of the empire. There was, however, almost constant fighting between the Germanic tribes and the Romans.

The Romans' major policy against the Germanic tribes was one of *containment*. This means they did not try to conquer the tribes, but rather tried to hold or "contain" them in northwestern Europe. To do that, a chain of forts was set up along the Rhine River. Later these forts became cities that are still in existence today. Some of them are Coblenz, Cologne, Mainz, Utrecht, and Leiden.

In addition to forts, the Romans built a stone

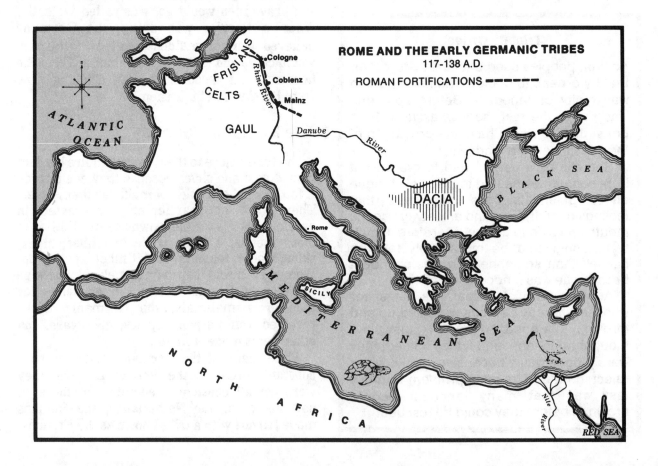

ROME AND THE EARLY GERMANIC TRIBES
117-138 A.D.

ROMAN FORTIFICATIONS ━━━━━━━

wall and wooden palisades along a 482.7 km (300 mile) stretch between the Rhine and Danube Rivers. The palisades were similar to those built by American pioneers for protection against Indians.

Another means Romans used to protect their frontier was originated by Emperor Trajan. Veterans of the army were granted land to the west and south of the walls, an area called *Dacia*. It was believed that these ex-soldiers would act as buffers between the tribes and the Romans. Sometimes, however, peaceful tribes crossed the frontier into Dacia where they would intermarry with the Romans.

As we have seen, the many Germanic tribes were basically similar. Some were more warlike than others, but their basic government, religion, and ways of life were the same. Some of them were merely destroyers, but they passed quickly from history. Some of the tribes were builders and they started the modern European nations.

As we move into the next chapter, remember the names of these different Germanic tribes, for you will come across them again and again: Frisians, Celts, Visigoths, Ostrogoths, Vandals, Burgundians, Franks, Angles, Saxons, and Lombards. We will see the important role these Germanic tribes played in the flow of civilization.

CHRISTIANITY, ROME, AND THE BYZANTINE EMPIRE

Projects

1. Do a study comparing persecutions of Christians during the Roman Empire with persecutions today. What is happening to Christians in communist countries? Are there other areas where people are persecuted for becoming Christian today?

2. Do a report on the apostle Paul. Are there any Christians today who remind you of Paul? In what ways?

3. Do a study on the economic relations between countries. Discuss balance of trade, balance of payments, inflation, and depreciation of currency. What did you learn about the United States' economic policies?

4. Reread the section on Rome before she was sacked by the Visigoths. Do a study on U.S. demonstrations, riots, and protests in the 1960s. What were the similarities or differences in these two situations? What lessons can the U.S. learn from what happened to Rome?

5. Research what happened to the Visigoths when they first moved into the Roman Empire. Were they justified in sacking Rome? Make a comparison of how Rome treated the Visigoths with how the U.S. treated the American Indians.

6. Do a report on the wives of the Byzantine emperors. What unusual things did you discover about these women?

7. Make a mosaic picture of something you have studied in this class this year.

8. Queen Zenobia led her soldiers to victory against Rome. Do you feel women should be drafted into the army if men are drafted? Are there countries that have women combat troops? How effective are they?

9. Class project. Take a field trip to a courtroom. Then prepare a report comparing the things you saw with what you have studied on Roman law in Chapters 7, 8, and 9.

Words and Concepts

The Dark Ages
icons
labarum
heresy
Coptic Church
balance of trade
mosaic
New Testament
archbishop
catacombs
Mamertine Prison
vandal
Gospels
bishop
martyr
Codex Justinian
"In this sign conquer"
Petrine Theory
deacon
gentile
Edict of Milan

Christianity, Rome, and the Byzantine Empire

When Marcus Aurelius, the last of the "Five Good Emperors," died in 180 A.D., the Roman Empire began a steady decline. During this time four major historical events occurred. These events were the development of the Christian religion, the fall of the Roman Empire, the founding of the Byzantine Empire, and the rise of Russia as a national state. Each of these events played an important part in making our world what it is today. It is important to study these events at the same time because each of them influenced the others.

The Development of Christianity

The Christian religion was centered around the life, death, resurrection, and teachings of Jesus, as we have seen. Jesus, his disciples, and most of the first people who followed Him, were Jewish. Many people thought Christianity was merely a branch of the Jewish religion. Immediately after Jesus' resurrection, many people became Christians after hearing the preaching of Peter and other disciples. More than 3,000 people became Christians as a result

The same Jewish religious leaders who had urged the Romans to put Jesus to death now worried about the popularity of this new religion. They convinced the Roman governor that the Christians were dangerous and should be punished.

Persecutions. The first Christian to die for his faith was a young man named Stephen. He was taken outside the gates of Jerusalem by an angry mob who threw stones at him until he died. Immediately after Stephen's death, religious leaders began a program of arrests and imprisonment of Christians. Many Christians left Jerusalem, hoping to escape persecution, and everywhere they went, they told people about Jesus. As a result, more and more people became Christians. Up to this point, however, most of the people who became Christians were followers of the Jewish faith, or Judaism. There had been no real attempt to bring the message to non-Jews, called *gentiles,*

The Jews have suffered more persecution than other religious groups. Christians have had more *martyrs,* people who die for their faith, than any other religious group in history, with the exception of the Jews. During the Roman Empire, there were ten major persecutions. The first was under Nero and was discussed in the last chapter. Nero's persecutions and those that followed did not occur outside of Rome until 250 A.D.

When the persecutions spread throughout the empire, laws were passed making it a crime to be a Christian. The emperors left the Christians alone, but they still could lose their property and

---

The Meaning of the Name Christ

The name Christ comes from the Greek word *Christos,* meaning "the anointed one." For centuries the Jewish people looked forward to the arrival of a Messiah, a Hebrew term meaning "Anointed of God." Jesus told His followers that He was the Messiah and Christians today believe that He was indeed the Messiah. For that reason those who believed in Christ were called "Christians" by the Greeks.

their lives if local governors wanted to persecute them. Anyone who found and reported a Christian could keep his property after he was convicted.

Today it is hard to understand why people who followed the teachings of Jesus were hated. But in those days, many people did not understand Christianity. The Roman Empire was falling apart and times were troubled. The Romans were convinced that their former Roman gods had made the empire great in the past. They believed it could be great once again, if only people would return to the worship of those gods. To the Romans, worshiping the gods was much the same as pledging allegiance to the flag in America today. Anyone who refused to do so was considered unpatriotic.

Since Christianity was against the law, Christians worshiped in secret. The non-Christians had many strange ideas about what went on in these secret services. Some people thought babies were murdered and eaten during the services. Others thought Christians were immoral and practiced free love while worshiping. Such rumors caused many non-Christians to fear the Christians and want to destroy them.

For many years the Christians in Rome hid in the *catacombs* to escape persecution. The catacombs were underground tunnels which the Jews used for burying the dead. There the Christians stayed, holding chapel services, marrying, and dying. Once the Romans learned where the Christians were hiding, the catacombs were cleared out. They remain today as evidence of the terrible sufferings the early Christians endured for their faith.

In spite of persecutions and competition from other religions, Christianity continued to spread. People were drawn to this faith in which members were willing to die for their beliefs. Christians faced persecution and death with quiet confidence and joy. This showed the world they had found something real, something that worked even during the difficult times. As the Roman Empire faced more problems and troubles, more people turned to Christianity—the only faith which offered them hope.

Christianity Spreads to the Gentiles. The credit for bringing the message of Christianity to the gentiles goes mainly to one man. Paul was his Roman name and Saul was his Jewish name. He was an avid believer in Judaism. Paul was a Roman citizen because he was born in Tarsus, a city with the Latin Right. While still a young man, he traveled to Jerusalem where he studied under Gamaliel, one of the greatest Jewish teachers.

While in Jerusalem, Paul saw the Christians, and like the other Jewish religious leaders, he

Stephen, an early Church leader, is stoned to death for refusing to renounce his beliefs. He is Christianity's first martyr.

Catacombs, or underground tunnels, were used by early Christians as hiding places to escape persecution. They also served as chapels for teaching and worship.

This photo shows the entrance to the Mamertine Prison where Paul was held captive before he was martyred for his faith. Some of the books of the New Testament were written by Paul while he was awaiting death in this prison. A church has since been built over this original entrance.

wanted to destroy them. He held the coats of the men who stoned Stephen to death and was one of the leaders who captured Christians and brought them to trial.

Paul's life suddenly was changed one day while he was riding to the city of Damascus with letters from Jewish leaders, giving him authority to arrest any Christians there. In later years Paul described what happened. He said a bright light, brighter than the sun, blinded him and caused him to fall from his horse. Then he heard the voice of Jesus telling him to stop persecuting the Christians.

As a result of this experience, Paul became one of the greatest missionaries Christianity has ever known. But he was different from other missionaries. He believed Jesus had told him to preach to gentiles, as well as to Jews. Most gentiles did not know anything about the Jewish faith or God's commandments. So Paul wrote letters to the churches showing the harmony between Judaism and Christianity. He also wrote about the doctrines that described Christianity and about Christian behavior. We are interested in this because some of his letters are a part of the Bible.

Paul of Tarsus, a persecutor of Christians, encounters Jesus on the road to Damascus. A blinding light, which blinded him for three days, changed his life and led him to become one of the greatest apostles of the Christian Church.

Paul was not the only missionary spreading Christianity, however. Churches were springing up in all the major cities of the Roman Empire. Even servants in Caesar's court became Christians and there was a church in Rome that was known throughout the Roman Empire.

The new faith was carried from city to city along the trade routes of the empire. Most of these cities were Hellenistic; Greek was spoken and Greek tradition was strong. Most of the influential Christian cities were located in the eastern part of the Roman Empire, including Antioch, Alexandria, Ephesus, and Corinth. Although Christian churches grew rapidly in the cities, the message was slow in spreading to the countryside where Greek was not spoken. Many of the major Greek cities rejected Christianity, preferring arguments of the philosophers to acceptance of a religion.

In Alexandria, Egypt, however, Christians translated the Bible into Egyptian and an Egyptian Christian Church was started. It was called the *Coptic Church* and it remained independent for hundreds of years. Through the Coptic Church, Christianity was taken into the interior of Africa, where Ethiopia became a Christian country.

In North Africa an Italian city was built where Carthage had stood, and Christianity became a strong influence there. Many of the truly great Christian writers came from this area. One of the most prominent was Augustine, who wrote the famous book entitled *The City of God* about the great troubles of Rome. Although non-Christians blamed the problems on the Christians, Augustine told how Christian prayers had prevented worse problems. He predicted that when the old city of Rome disappeared, a new and better Christian city of God would take its place.

Christianity also spread outside the boundaries of the Roman Empire. The king of Armenia became a Christian and all the people in this country followed his example. Its people endured terrible persecutions under Turkish rule, but this tiny area has remained Christian through modern times.

Organization of the Christian Church. During the early years, following the journeys of Paul and other missionaries, Christians met together for fellowship. There was little difference between the ordinary Christians and the people who did the preaching and teaching. As the number of Christians grew larger, there was a need for people who could spend all their time doing religious work. Before long the men in charge of larger churches had more authority than the men who ran the smaller churches. The early Christian Church was organized in much the same way as the government of the Roman Empire.

Deacons were chosen to care for the temporal needs of the local Church. *Elders* taught God's Word and provided leadership in the local churches—a position taken over by priests and ministers today. *Bishops* were overseers (or "shepherds") of the local Church, but this position changed the headship over several churches. An *archbishop* became the supervisor over churches in a distinct district or province.

It was this strong, dedicated organization that held the Christian people together when

(a)

Artwork by the Copts of North Africa is represented here by: (a) "Standing Man," Coptic sculpture in limestone and colored gesso, done in the sixth century A.D., and (b) A Coptic frieze of carved stucco, dated c. the 5th century A.D.

(b)

Early Monasteries

Before Jesus was born, there were groups of people in Israel called the Essenes, who lived in retreats. By 200 A.D. there were Christians in the East who wanted to prove their love for Jesus, so they became *hermits,* people who live alone and withdraw from society. They fasted and at times even tortured their bodies.

In Egypt, St. Basil founded the Christian monastic system in which men were allowed to strive for a common spiritual goal by living together in retreats under strict regulations. The Rule of St. Basil substituted hard labor and charitable works for the harsh punishments once practiced by the hermits. This concept has become the model for many of the monasteries which survive today.

In Western Europe St. Benedict established a monastery on a hill, called Monte Cassino, located between Rome and Naples. The men who lived there were called Benedictine monks. The strict Benedictine rules required the members of this monastery to take vows of poverty, chastity, and obedience to the *abbot,* the person in charge of the monastery. Monks took part in eight worship services a day, worked in the fields or workshops for six or seven hours a day, and spent two hours a day reading. Benedictine monasteries were established throughout Europe, and with other monastic orders survive today.

The Dead Sea Scrolls

The books of the Bible have been copied and recopied many times in the thousands of years since the Bible was first written. Today, in fact, none of the original Bible documents still exist. This has caused criticism from people who doubt the authenticity of certain portions of the Bible as it is today.

You can understand the excitement, then, when some shepherd boys discovered some ancient manuscripts hidden in a cave near the Dead Sea in 1947. Several years later others were found in caves nearby. Undoubtedly these documents were hidden in the caves for safe-keeping when the Romans destroyed Jerusalem. The writings were dated from 200 B.C. to 70 A.D. and included parts of the Bible. Called the Dead Sea Scrolls, these writings were compared with the modern Bible, and no major differences were found.

persecutions, trials, false doctrines, and the collapse of the Roman Empire might otherwise have destroyed their faith. As new ideas were brought to the attention of Christians, the bishops gathered in a council to discuss them. They decided whether or not the new teachings were true to Christian beliefs. Ideas that did not conform were thrown out.

The Triumph of Christianity. The only organization that continued to operate during the collapse of the Roman Empire was the Christian Church. The people, however, were beginning to look to the bishop of Rome for leadership. As a result of monasteries, learning was kept alive in the Church organization. In the countryside the people cared only about their survival. The feudal system was starting to develop as they turned to their local nobles and landowners for protection and security. Wandering bands of soldiers and bandits filled people with terror because there were no laws to protect them. The leaders of the Church became landowners and they rode at the head of small armies to protect people from raiders.

When Emperor Constantine became the absolute ruler of the Roman Empire, he considered himself the leader of the Christian Church as well. As soon as he declared himself to be a supporter of Christianity, everything began to change for the Christians. Formerly they were persecuted and considered enemies of the state. Then it became an advantage to be a Christian. Hordes of people began to call themselves Christians in order to get in on certain economic advantages.

At one time Christians were not allowed to teach at all; but then they not only were asked to teach, but also to write textbooks for use by teachers. In Constantinople, however, the schools were kept separate from the Church. In addition to Christian education, children were given a complete Greek education.

The Christian Church Divides. As we have seen, the Christian Church was well organized. But the same differences that caused the western part of the Roman Empire to break away from Constantinople were already at work to split the Christian Church. People began to come up with new explanations for the parts of Christianity they did not understand or believe. These new teachings began to cause arguments among Church leaders and threatened to destroy Christianity.

The Nicaea Council. One of the arguments resulted from the teachings of a priest named Arius. He found it hard to believe that God actually came to earth to die for people's sins. Therefore, he declared that Jesus was not God, but merely a lesser creation, like an angel. There was a lot of controversy about this and it soon became obvious that the leaders of the Church could not come to an agreement.

To settle the controversy, Constantine called together some 318 bishops and many lesser clergymen at the Council of Nicaea in 325 A.D. The teachings of Arius were declared to be *heresy,* or false teachings, and a declaration was written of the basic beliefs of Christians concerning Jesus. Another question that was settled at the Council of Nicaea was that of whether or not priests should marry. It was decided they could keep their wives if they were married before they became priests; otherwise they were not allowed to marry.

The Petrine Theory. As we have seen, conditions in the West became worse and the bishop of Rome became more and more important. Soon he was considered by the churches in the West to be the highest official in the Church. This idea was supported by a Bible quotation

The Nicene Creed

The Council of Nicaea was called together by Emperor Constantine in 325 A.D. Here Church leaders accepted the view that the Father, Son, and Holy Ghost were all equal and composed of identical substance. The power and spirit of the three are the same and they are known as the Holy Trinity.

From this council came the Nicene Creed, a detailed statement of Christian doctrine. Today this is part of the liturgy of some Catholic and Protestant churches. The creed in its entirety reads as follows:

"I believe in one God the Father Almighty, Maker of heaven and earth, and of all things visible and invisible: and in one Lord Jesus Christ, the only begotten Son of God, begotten of His Father before all worlds, God of God, Light of Light, very God of very God, begotten not made, (being of one substance with the Father), by whom all things were made: who for us men, and for our salvation came down from heaven, and was incarnate by the Holy Ghost of the Virgin Mary, and was made man, and was crucified also for us under Pontius Pilate. He suffered and was buried, and the third day He rose again according to the Scriptures, and ascended into heaven, and sitteth on the right hand of the Father. And He shall come again, with glory, to judge both the quick and the dead, whose kingdom shall have no end. And I believe in the Holy Ghost, the Lord and giver of life, who proceedeth from the Father and the Son, who with the Father and the Son together is worshiped and glorified, who spake by the prophets. And I believe in one Catholic and Apostolic Church. I acknowledge one Baptism for the remission of sins. And I look for the Resurrection of the dead, and the life of the world to come."

Early Small Churches

In addition to the dominant Eastern and Western Churches at Rome and Constantinople, there have always been various smaller Christian sects operating outside the main stream of organized Christian thought. These churches (Paulicians, Nestorians, Montanists, Novatians, Bogomilians, Albigenses, Waldensians, and others) were commonly branded as heretical and were persecuted by the established churches. Certain historians in several modern Christian denominations, such as the Baptists, maintain that their own origins can be traced back to these groups.

where Jesus tells Peter he gave him the keys to the kingdom of heaven and that he was to build the Church. Western churches believed that Peter had been bishop of Rome before he died. Therefore, the bishop of Rome should always be the head of the Christian Church. This was known as the Petrine Theory.

The bishop of Constantinople did not agree with the Petrine Theory. He felt he should be the supreme head of the Christian Church since the emperor lived in Constantinople and it was the most important Christian center. Gradually the two Churches grew further apart as new differences developed.

The Eastern Church of Constantinople used Greek in their services and the Western Church used Latin. The Eastern Church allowed their priests to marry and the Western Church did not. As other differences in worship arose, the two factions drifted still further apart.

The Western Church became the Roman Catholic Church and the bishop of Rome became known as the pope. The Eastern Church became known as the Eastern Orthodox, or Greek Orthodox Church, and the bishop of Constantinople became its patriarch. The heads of the two Churches met for the first time in 1964 when Pope Paul VI met the eastern patriarch in Jerusalem.

The Bible. The Hebrew Scriptures made up the Old Testament and at first this was the only Bible available to Christians. Although Jesus did not directly write down His own teachings, several of His followers did. Also, the Apostle Paul and others wrote letters of instruction to the various churches that were being established. Gradually certain of these writings were recognized by the early Christians as having the marks of divine inspiration. They were soon accepted as part of the Scriptures now called the New Testament.

Other early writings about Christ and the churches did not find such acceptance. Several centuries later, one of the Councils of the Church formally approved the documents comprising the New Testament.

Importance of the Church. The power and influence of the Church enabled the Church

After the division of the Christian Church, the Eastern Orthodox Church used Greek in their service. This church service is being held in Estonia, Soviet Union. Over the years changes have been made in the rituals used by the Greek Orthodox Church. The use of icons (such as the one being carried in the foreground) and the rich clothing of the church officials, however, are unchanged.

leaders to interfere in the politics and government of the newly emerging kingdoms we will be studying in the next section. We will see how the Eastern Orthodox Church played an important role in the history of Russia. The Roman Catholic Church was to play a great role in the history and development of Europe. It was priests in the Roman Catholic Church who kept education from dying out completely in Europe during the Dark Ages.

The Fall of Rome

As we have already seen, Germanic tribes were raiding across the Roman Empire's frontier while Marcus Aurelius was emperor. If his son, Commodus, had followed his father's advice and destroyed the enemy tribes, Rome might have had a chance for survival. But with this dangerous force on the frontier and all the other problems facing the empire, it was only a matter of time before the Roman Empire would come to an end.

An Unstable Empire

There were many factors leading to the fall of the Roman Empire. A major one was instability of the ruling class. Other factors involved the empire's economy, society, and size.

Unstable Leadership. There was no legal or efficient means to determine who would take over the throne when emperors died. For a time the method of adopting good men as their sons and preparing them to rule was used. But the plan was dropped when Marcus Aurelius left the throne to his real son Commodus.

Roman armies became a strong power in the empire and for the next 77 years, army leaders decided who would rule. At one point the crown was offered to the man who could pay the most. The army was divided into several strong units, each led by different generals. When one army declared someone emperor, another unit marched towards Rome and murdered him. They then put their own man in power. In the period following the death of Marcus Aurelius, 40 men were declared emperor. Only one of them died of natural causes.

Economic Instability. In addition to almost continuous civil war, many Italian cities were in economic trouble. During the height of the Roman Empire, the Italian cities were rich and flourishing. But it was a false prosperity, caused by riches and slaves that were brought home by the victorious Roman army. Few industries existed in these cities. A rich trade flourished between the Romans and the people in China and India. Silks, spices, and other luxury goods were brought into Italy. The Italians had only riches they had plundered from the conquered territories to trade. Over the years all of their riches were traded off and there was no way to replace them. The Italian cities became poor and the money used by the Romans became almost worthless. They had less and less gold and silver to put in their coins.

The Roman army was a threat to peace, as we have already seen. Even so, it was necessary to have a large army because the Germanic tribes were becoming more powerful as they began to break through the frontiers. But the troops had to be paid and taxes got higher and higher to provide money for their pay. Since only Roman citizens were required to pay taxes, it was becoming less of a privilege to be a Roman citizen. Many of those who were unable to pay the high taxes slipped across the borders and out of the empire.

Mosaics of Christian leaders portrayed them in the national dress of the country.

Social Instability. The cities were becoming terrible places in which to live. The number of unemployed city workers increased and they expected the government to provide them with food and entertainment. When things did not go the way citizens thought they should, they wandered the streets in mobs, looting and robbing. The stable citizens began to move to the country. Rich landowners built fortified homes for protection against raiders and allowed their workers to share their shelter when danger threatened.

More and more commoners moved to the countryside to farm the lands belonging to the rich. In order to bring things under control, a law was passed that made all people in the empire slaves of the state. Nobody was allowed to move or to change jobs without permission of the emperor. Citizens had to continue the work they were doing when the law was passed. Children were required to follow the same occupation as their fathers. Farmers belonged to the land instead of the land belonging to them. They were not allowed to leave their land, and if it was sold, they continued working for their new landlords.

Zenobia, queen of Syria and leader of that nation's army, being led through the streets of Rome after her defeat by Emperor Aurelius.

Balance of Trade

In many newspaper and magazine articles you read, you will see references to what we call the "balance of trade." This means that a country needs to sell as many items to foreign countries as it buys. If the country sells more than it buys, it is called a *favorable balance of trade.* If it buys more than it sells, it is considered to be an *unfavorable balance of trade.*

When a country has an unfavorable balance of trade, it must pay for the extra goods with gold. If this unfavorable balance continues for a long time, a country could lose all its gold reserves. Then money becomes worthless and other countries refuse to continue trading with that country. This situation causes unemployment, food shortages, and riots among people who lose faith in their government and the value of money. This is why it is important for every country to manufacture goods for trade. This was one of the reasons for Rome's decline. Trade with China was unfavorable to Rome, and Roman gold was flowing out of the country.

Queen Zenobia—A Great Leader

Immediately before Aurelius became emperor in 270 A.D., a fascinating woman came to power in Syria. She was a beautiful young queen named Zenobia. She tried to carve out an empire in the Middle East and personally marched at the head of the army to attack Roman garrisons. Soon the Middle East was under Zenobia's control and she attacked Alexandria with a powerful fleet. When Aurelius became emperor, he began attacking Rome's enemies. Zenobia was defeated and led through the streets of Rome in golden chains during Aurelius' triumphant victory parade.

Zenobia was highly educated and was a great teacher. She knew Greek literature and philosophy and spoke Latin, Egyptian, and Syrian. She also wrote a history of the Middle East.

A Divided Empire. It was becoming obvious to everyone that the Roman Empire, with all its problems, was too large for one person to govern. Many of the provinces were using the empire's confusion as an excuse to break away and gain independence or form a separate empire.

Diocletian Divides the Empire. In 284 A.D. Diocletian became emperor. He had a strong personality and made many wise decisions. He also realized that the Roman Empire was too large for one man to govern so he divided it into East and West sections. He moved his capital to the city of Nicomedia in the eastern portion of the empire. The man who ruled the western empire also moved his capital, choosing Ravenna.

Diocletian's soldiers were victorious in their wars and many provinces which had broken away from the empire now returned to Roman authority. Remember how Alexander wanted to be worshiped as a god when he began ruling his empire from the Middle East? Diocletian wanted the same thing, so he ordered everyone in his empire to worship him. When the Christians refused, they underwent one of the worst persecutions in the history of Christianity.

Constantine Reunites the Empire. Diocletian thought he had developed a peaceful way to introduce a new emperor. Both he and his co-ruler selected rulers to succeed them. Then they resigned to allow the new co-rulers to take over. Instead of the peaceful take-over Diocletian had planned, however, civil war broke out as six different men claimed the right to rule.

One of these men was Constantine. He had defeated all the other contenders for the throne and was facing his final enemy. On the afternoon before the battle, Constantine was thinking about the danger of fighting this general who

was expected to win. Constantine, whose mother was a Christian, said he saw a vision of a flaming cross in the sky and heard a voice say: "In this sign conquer." That night in a dream the same voice commanded him to have his soldiers mark their shields with the Latin symbol that spelled Jesus Christ. This symbol is known as the *labarum.*

Constantine won the battle and became emperor in 313 A.D. One of his first acts as emperor was to issue the *Edict of Milan* which ended all religious persecutions and allowed religious freedom for everyone. Thus, for the first time Christianity became legal.

Although Constantine reunited the empire, he did not feel that Rome was a good place for the capital. The only area that was still able to produce goods and maintain a favorable balance

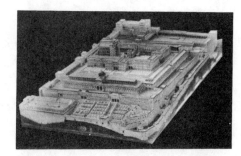

This reconstructed model of Diocletian's fortified palace at Spalato appears to be a forerunner of the medieval castles.

In this sculptured bust of Constantine, it is apparent that Roman art had begun to deteriorate by this time. A hero to the Roman Empire and the Christian Church, Constantine restored unity and prosperity to a divided empire. He also gave freedom and support to believers in Christ.

The symbols on the labarum were a Greek letter, CHI--X, that represented <u>Christ</u> and the Greek letter RHO--, that represented <u>King</u>. Thus, the labarum said, "Christ the King."

The labarum was a Christian banner adopted by Constantine after he saw a vision of a cross shining in the heavens. It remained a standard until the downfall of the western Roman Empire. The labarum is still used as a Christian symbol in the Roman Catholic Church.

of trade was in the east. Constantine decided to build a new city for his capital on the shores of the Dardanelles Strait. He named the city Constantinople (present-day Istanbul) and it became a great trade center.

Constantine walked around his new city and with his spear marked where the boundary wall should be built. His assistants were afraid he was making the city too big. But as the years passed, his city became even grander than Rome. Constantinople stood at the crossroads of three continents—Europe, Asia, and Africa. She had a perfect harbor for trade and controlled the entrance to the Black Sea.

The Empire Undergoes a Permanent Split. While the beautiful city of Constantinople flourished, Rome was having problems. The

The Byzantine Empire

When the first Greek colonies were established, a Greek city named Byzantium was built. This little city was still thriving when Constantine decided to build his new capital.

Although the name of the city was changed to Constantinople, the culture and surrounding territory are known as the Byzantine Empire. The people living there called themselves Romans and considered themselves to be part of the Roman Empire. When Rome fell, the people in Constantinople still considered this eastern empire to be the Roman Empire. In this book we will call it the Byzantine Empire to avoid confusion about which part of the Roman Empire we are discussing.

eastern empire, known as Byzantium, continued as a center for learning, culture, and trade until the 1400s. The western part of the empire, however, was declining fast.

When we refer to the Fall of Rome, we do not mean the total destruction of the city of Rome. This term means that the once-great Roman Empire had come to an end and the people in Western Europe were no longer united under a single government.

After the death of Constantine in 361 A.D., the empire once again was divided among his sons. When they died, the empire again plunged into civil war. As a result, in 395 A.D. the eastern and western portions of the empire were divided again and this time the division was permanent. Later in this chapter we will discuss the rise of the Byzantine Empire.

Germanic Tribes Invade the West

In the Western Empire, conditions were terrible. The government was harsh and cruel, taxes were heavy, and the government could not protect the people from the Germanic tribes. The provinces farthest from Rome began to break away and establish peaceful relations with the Germanic invaders. There were three major Germanic invaders, the Visigoths, Vandals and Ostrogoths.

The Visigoths. For a time the Visigoths were living in the territory that is now southern Russia. They had migrated there from Scandinavia. When the fiercely cruel Huns swept into Russia from Asia between 200 and 395 A.D., the Visigoths asked permission to enter the Roman Empire for protection. The Visigoths entered Roman territory; however, they were mistreated and some of their children were taken as slaves. The angered Visigoths no longer looked on the Romans as friends. They began attacking Roman settlements as they moved south. In 378 A.D. they defeated a Roman army in battle, and by 395 A.D., they had captured Athens and Corinth.

Rome was a city of fear. The Roman emperor in the West had his capital in Ravenna. With nobody left to protect Rome, the people there turned to the bishop of Rome for protection and leadership in running the city government. When Attila, the fierce Hun, camped outside the

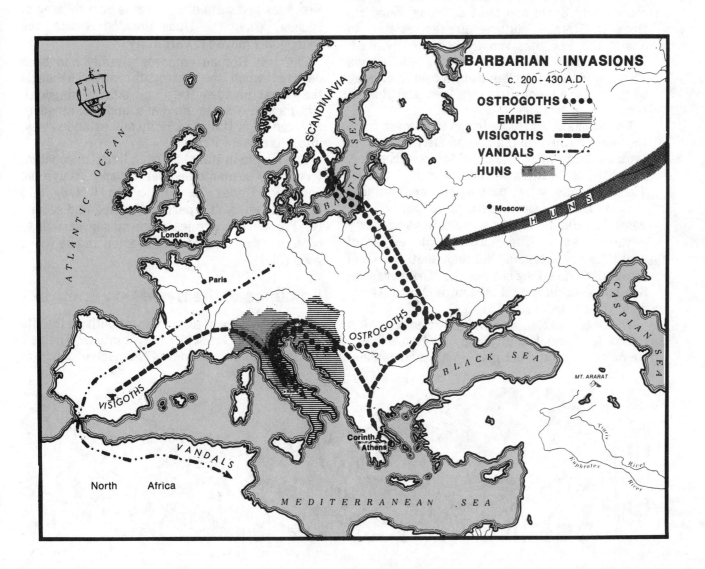

BARBARIAN INVASIONS
c. 200 - 430 A.D.

OSTROGOTHS ••••
EMPIRE
VISIGOTHS
VANDALS
HUNS

city, the bishop of Rome walked unarmed into his camp and persuaded him not to attack.

When the Visigoths arrived outside Rome, there was no protection. In 410 A.D. the entire world was stunned by the news that the once-proud city of emperors had been looted by barbarian armies. Carrying their loot, the Visigoths moved into Spain and built a strong kingdom. Because Roman culture already existed in Spain, the Visigoths rapidly became civilized. They learned Latin and became Christians. They ruled their kingdom using a combined code of laws made up of their own laws and Roman laws.

The Vandals. As Rome began to recover from the shock of invasion, a second Germanic tribe crossed the frontier into the old Roman Empire. This band of invaders was known as the Vandals. Their attacks were destructive and without reason. Hence, our modern word *vandal* has come to refer to anyone who destroys property without cause. The Vandals moved from southwestern Germany through southern Gaul into Spain. Then they crossed the Mediterranean Sea and established a kingdom in North Africa which lasted from 430 to 548 A.D.

The beautiful Roman cities in Africa served as a base for Vandal culture and they began to settle down. They did not give up all their lawless ways, however, for they still practiced piracy in the Mediterranean. They also attacked Rome from the sea, sacking the city for a second time.

The Ostrogoths. The last major wave of Germanic peoples to invade Italy before the final Fall of Rome was the Ostrogoths. This tribe moved south about the same time as the Visigoths and settled in the same general area of Russia. When the Huns invaded Russia, the Ostrogoths moved toward Italy.

The last Roman emperor already had been deposed when the Ostrogoth ruler Theoderic the Great invaded Italy and built a kingdom. His capital was in Ravenna and his kingdom covered all of Italy and Sicily and extended west into what is now France.

The people in Italy had been living in constant terror as Germanic invaders swept through the country. Under Theoderic the Ostrogothic Kingdom enjoyed a period of peace and security. Theoderic's armies were strong enough to protect his territory from invasion and he was a good ruler.

Influence of the Byzantine Empire

The city of Constantinople was built on the site of the ancient Greek city of Byzantium. The people living there considered themselves Romans

Greco-Roman fortresses like this one along the Black Sea shoreline housed soldiers who protected citizens from outsiders. Turks and Muslems added to the fortresses for their security.

Barbaric Visigoths sweep through the city of Rome, looting and killing the surprised citizens. The world was stunned when it heard that the former world capital had been sacked.

and called their empire the Roman Empire. Once the empire divided, it became too confusing to continue calling the eastern empire "Roman." To avoid confusion, historians call the empire, government, and the culture of this eastern empire "Byzantine."

Justinian—A Great Ruler

When Constantine's rule ended, the political history of the Byzantine Empire began to resemble that of the Roman Empire. For almost 200 years, there was fighting over who would rule.

Above we see Justinian faced with the most important decision of his life. As his city rebelled, his counselors advised him to flee for his life. Theodora, his wife, preferred to stay and fight, willing to die rather than return to the poverty she knew earlier in life. Her bravery gave Justinian the courage necessary to suppress the uprising.

Finally in 527 A.D., Justinian took the throne. He was to be one of the greatest rulers of the Byzantine Empire. Under his rule the artistic culture of the empire began to develop.

Emperor Justinian was a gentle, soft-spoken, average-looking man. One of his greatest dreams was to restore the Roman Empire to its former greatness. His army was well trained

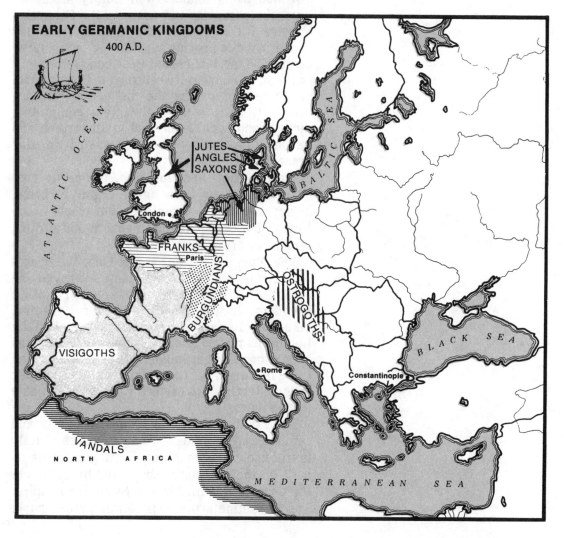

EARLY GERMANIC KINGDOMS
400 A.D.

ATLANTIC OCEAN
BALTIC SEA
JUTES ANGLES SAXONS
London
FRANKS
Paris
BURGUNDIANS
OSTROGOTHS
BLACK SEA
VISIGOTHS
Rome
Constantinople
VANDALS
NORTH AFRICA
MEDITERRANEAN SEA

and he used it to reconquer all the territory that had been lost. The army marched across North Africa and destroyed the Vandal Kingdom. Justinian's soldiers also conquered the Ostrogothic Kingdom in Italy. Ravenna became the western capital of the newly expanded Byzantine Empire.

Although his soldiers won victory after victory, the campaign did not help the Byzantine Empire. It cost a great amount of money to pay soldiers and to provide supplies for such a large army. The territories that were conquered were not rich, so no treasure returned to Constantinople to repay them for the cost of this military conquest. As a result, the men, equipment, money, and supplies needed to strengthen and defend Constantinople were wasted in this senseless adventure.

Shortly after Justinian died, the newly conquered territory once again began to break away. In these disruptive and troublesome times, it was impossible to govern and protect such large areas.

The European Dark Ages. Once the Byzantine armies entered Italy, they destroyed the effective government of the Ostrogothic Kingdom. It was shortly after the Byzantine take-over that a new Germanic tribe called the Lombards moved into Italy. Had the Ostrogoths been in control they might have been able to stop these invaders. But the Byzantines, also clinging to their territory in eastern Italy, were not able to stop them.

The Lombards took over northern Italy and set up a kingdom there. Today this area of Italy is still known as Lombardy. When the Lombards built up their strength, they tried to move into the territory claimed by the Byzantine Empire. The Byzantine army at first was pushed back.

Then, gaining strength, Byzantine forces attacked and pushed the Lombards out of the territory.

This constant struggle for control of Italy nearly destroyed the country. Farms were wasted and cities were destroyed. There was little chance to establish a government and it was centuries before Italy recovered from this destruction.

When the only firm government existing in Europe at the time lost authority, the period known to historians as the Dark Ages began. During this time the art and learning that had developed during the Roman Empire declined. Many libraries were destroyed, cities crumbled to ruin, and commerce and industry faltered.

Byzantine Culture

At this time, Constantinople developed into one of the greatest commercial cities in the world. When Rome was sacked by barbarian tribes and Europe entered the Dark Ages, culture continued to develop in Constantinople. There were new styles of architecture and new methods of artwork. This culture was passed on to the Russians.

At the same time, Greek knowledge and the best Roman achievements were kept safe in Constantinople. Centuries later, when the Turks were threatening to destroy the ancient city of Constantinople, this valuable knowledge was carried into Europe by fleeing scholars. There European scholars "rediscovered" this priceless heritage, starting a rebirth of knowledge and learning.

Art. Instead of using frescoes and bas-relief carvings to picture their art, the Byzantines perfected the *mosaic* art technique. Beautifully colored tiles were fitted together to portray scenes. Sometimes as many as 10,000 tiles were used in a single picture. Even portraits were done in mosaics. These lovely works of art are still as fresh and brilliant as they were when they were created. The colors in the tiles do not fade with age as paint does.

The Byzantine Church encouraged artists to create pictures and statues of saints and Biblical people. They believed the people would understand the Bible stories better if they saw them pictured in Byzantine dress and in local settings. Hundreds of these images, called *icons,* may be found in any Orthodox Church. The artists used the same techniques that had been developed in Constantinople many years before.

Architecture. The Romans had learned how to

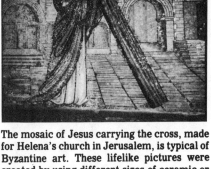

The magnificent Hagia Sophia reflects the beautiful architecture of the day.

The mosaic of Jesus carrying the cross, made for Helena's church in Jerusalem, is typical of Byzantine art. These lifelike pictures were created by using different sizes of ceramic or stone chips.

Icons in a church near Leningrad helped the people identify with the saints and Bible figures during their worship services.

Byzantine music was primarily Greek in style. Christians wrote hymns and festival entertainers wrote verses for special occasions. Many types of musical instruments were known including string instrument, the trumpet and several woodwinds.

build a dome over a round building, making some of their buildings the largest ever built. Byzantine architects learned how to put a dome over a square building. This enabled them to build churches in the shape of a cross, with a huge dome in the center and smaller domes at each extension.

The magnificent church of Hagia Sophia was built by Justinian. No other Byzantine building ever equalled its size and beauty. Beautiful churches in the Byzantine style also were built in Ravenna after Justinian's soldiers conquered Italy. When the Russians decided to build churches, Byzantine architects traveled to that land and taught them how to build according to Byzantine designs. In addition to churches, they built universities, libraries, public baths, forums, and recreation centers.

Roman Law. As we have seen, the Romans were a people with a deep respect for law. They had written the early laws on tablets and placed them in the Forum for everyone to read. As the empire grew, new laws were passed and some of the old ones were outdated. Many of the laws of the conquered territories were added to the Roman laws. One of Justinian's most important achievements as emperor was the preparation of a new code of laws. All laws, new and old, were checked and only those helpful in ruling the empire and protecting the rights of the people were kept. The new law code was called the *Codex Justinian.*

Through the years decisions of judges and their comments and interpretations of laws also were written down. Justinian had these papers put together in a work called the *Digest.* Today we say that our legal system is influenced by Roman law, but we really mean it is an outgrowth of the *Codex Justinian.*

St. Mark's Basilica in Venice, Italy, is a magnificent combination of Byzantine and Roman architecture. It is a reminder that the Byzantine influence was present in Italy as late as 1100.

Russia

Several groups of people took control of the area of Russia after the Scythians. These people gave up their nomadic life and settled in cities from 100 B.C. until about 700 A.D. Tribal groups like the Avars and the Finno-Ugrians drifted in from the East, intermarried with the Slavs, and became the ancestors of the modern Russians, Balkans, Czechs, Poles, and Hungarians.

The Khazars. Finally about 700 A.D., a semi=nomadic tribe called the Khazars established a kingdom. Although the Khazars ruled the local Slavs, they were not able to protect them from the fierce raiders who came in from the Asian plains. As a result of trading with Jewish merchants, the Khazars had accepted the Hebrew religion instead of pagan worship.

These Jewish merchants encouraged trade centers along the Don and Volga Rivers. Soon Slavs came from distant areas to trade for luxury items at the trade centers. Constantinople provided most of the lovely things that were traded in these centers. The Khazars also encouraged trade with the Varangian people who lived in what is now Sweden.

The Varangians. Varangian warriors were hired as soldiers to protect the trade cities of Novgorod, Polotsk, Smolensk, Lubeck, Chernigov, and Kiev from raiders. These fierce warriors were related to the Vikings that later invaded Europe. Many Varangians remained in Russia after their duties as soldiers were finished. One of these Varangian warriors, Rurik, became the founder of the first ruling house in Russia, as the king of Novgorod.

The Kingdom of Novgorod Expands. When Rurik died, his son was too young to rule. His guardian Oleg ruled for him. Oleg was responsible for capturing several other cities and making Kiev the capital of the new kingdom. Once the kingdom was strong enough, Oleg conquered the Khazars.

When the emperor in Constantinople refused to grant a trade treaty with the new kingdom, Oleg attacked Constantinople. His boats were unable to enter the harbor because the people had stretched chains across the mouth of the river. Oleg had wheels placed on the bottom of his boats, and the wind in their sails pushed

Varangian warriors, related to Swedish Vikings, were soldiers hired to protect the Slavic trade cities. Many of them stayed in Russia to live. The first Russian ruler was a Varangian and may have looked like this.

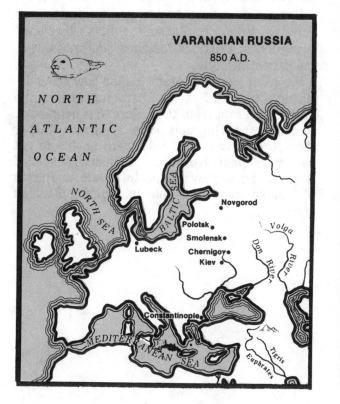

VARANGIAN RUSSIA

850 A.D.

NORTH ATLANTIC OCEAN

NORTH SEA

BALTIC SEA

Novgorod

Polotsk

Smolensk

Lubeck

Chernigov

Kiev

Volga River

Don River

Constantinople

MEDITERRANEAN SEA

Tigris

Euphrates

Vladimir's Decision

According to legend, Vladimir studied all major religions, including the Greek Orthodox, Islam, Judaism, and Roman Catholicism, before deciding to become an Orthodox Christian. Once he decided to become a Christian, he tried to live his life according to Jesus' teachings. He set free all the women in his harem. He fed the poor and, for a time, refused to punish the bandits in his country. He was in danger of losing his kingdom when the Church leaders in Constantinople finally pointed out that it was his duty to protect the people. He had all the people in his kingdom baptized. As we have already seen, this did not make them Christians since that is a personal decision each person must make for himself.

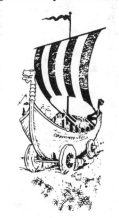

Russian Vikings, led by Oleg, reached Constantinople in a boat-on-wheels. Prevented from sailing the Dneiper River, they "sailed" across the meadows.

Onion-shaped domes grace the roof of a Russian Orthodox Church in Moscow. Architects from Constantinople copied the Byzantine style when designing many of the major buildings in Russia.

GREEK	SLAVONIC	CYRILLIC	RUSSIAN

Two monks from Constantinople developed an alphabet for the Slavic people. This alphabet was called Cyrillic and used Greek symbols. Modern Russian is based upon this alphabet and, as you can see, looks much like Greek.

them across the meadows where Constantinople's defenses were weak. When Constantinople agreed to trade with the new kingdom, the war ended.

Vladimir. The next ruler of the kingdom of Novgorod was Vladimir. Under his leadership the course of Russian history changed. His mother had traveled to Constantinople where she became a Christian. In 998 B.C. Vladimir became a Christian and set about making his kingdom a Christian country. Vladimir married a princess from Constantinople which greatly influenced Russia.

Before long, Russia adopted the beliefs of the Greek Orthodox Church rather than those of the Roman Catholic Church that had been adopted by the rest of Europe. Russians then looked to the East instead of to Europe for their ideas and culture. For a time even Church leaders in Russia were appointed by the head of the Church in Constantinople.

Byzantine Influence. Soon after he became a Christian, Vladimir ordered the first stone cathedral to be built in Russia. Workmen were brought in from Constantinople to build the church. Architects from Constantinople designed the major buildings and churches in Russia for many years. Russians worked as assistants on these projects until they learned to

build their own beautiful buildings. The basic designs of the churches were copies of Byzantine architecture.

Two monks from Constantinople traveled as missionaries to Moravia when they developed a written language for the Slavic people. They used Greek letters to represent Slavic sounds. This language is called Cyrillic after Cyril, the leader of the two monks. A form of this written language is still being used in Russia today.

The Cyrillic language made it possible for educated Russians to read the classical Greek works that were stored in Constantinople. They also began to develop literary works on their own. For the most part, the Russians were cut off from the literature being written in Europe.

Byzantine culture had a great influence on Russian artwork. Russian artists developed many icons, religious frescoes, and mosaics in the Byzantine style.

We shall see in a later chapter how other influences molded Russian character, making the people different from their European neighbors. Because the Russians were Orthodox rather than Roman Catholic, they were unable to get help and support from Europe when they needed it most. So the Byzantine influence in Russia played an important role in molding Russian character.

THE **DARK CONTINENT** AND THE **MYSTERIOUS EAST**

Projects

1. Prepare a report on the exchange of money in the world today. What is the European Common Market? Why was it formed? How is it affecting world trade?

2. Do a study on soil erosion. How do people add to erosion problems? What can people do to prevent erosion? Make a working model showing how some types of erosion work.

3. Explain in detail either of the following: Terracotta — what is it and how is it prepared? Silk — how is it made?

4. Research the role of women in India's government. Is Prime Minister Indira Gandhi's rule successful? Why or why not? Make a comparison between women rulers of ancient times and India's current leader.

5. Public welfare was introduced in China. How does this system work in the United States today? Describe.

6. Make a report on the life of one of the following: Confucius, Lao-tze, Candace, Piankhy, or Porus.

7. Price ceilings were introduced in China. How many times have they been introduced in the United States? Why were they introduced and how did they operate?

8. The first real printing press was invented in China. Make a working model based on this first printing press.

9. Give a report on the tsetse fly. What kind of disease does it carry? How does it infect animals? How was it brought under control?

Words and Concepts

Shuo Wen
Fayum Depression
Barabudur
Bantus
price ceilings
Olduvai Gorge
Mandate of Heaven
Angkor Wat
Nilo-Sudanic
Negro
Pygmy
catapults
legalism
tsetse fly
Fu Hsi
Kautilya
Mencius
Hottentots
Yang Shao
Nok
loess
Greater India
abdicate

The Dark Continent and the Mysterious East

We are now going to shift our attention from the Mediterranean civilizations to study three new areas—Africa, India, and China. There people lived and civilizations flourished at the same time the major civilizations we have already studied were at their peak.

While these three countries traded with other civilizations, they had little influence on the rest of the world until the 400s A.D. It was then that the Roman Empire developed an unfavorable balance of trade with these Eastern countries. This change in trade policies influenced the outcome of world history.

After 400 A.D. these three countries continued to develop outside the main streams of civilization, as we will learn in Chapter 14. We shall see how their ideas on life, their society, and government developed in entirely different directions from that of Europe. Over the years these countries dropped behind Europe in industrialization and in their standard of living. As a result, other nations have tended to ignore them.

Today these countries, once considered unimportant, are in a position to wield a strong influence on world affairs. China has become a communist country, and India and Africa are now drifting in that direction. As we study the history of these countries, we will better understand why these people think and act the way they do.

The Dark Continent

Africa has been called the *Dark Continent* because so little was known about its history and inhabitants. For years Africa was considered by Europeans to be a dark and mysterious place. It is only in more recent times that the secrets of Africa's past have been revealed.

To better understand Africa's history and the development of its civilization, we will divide the continent into three basic areas. The first is Egypt, the civilization that developed along the Nile River Valley. We have already studied this great civilization and its importance in the streams of civilization. Later in this chapter we will learn about still another civilization known as Kush, that was closely associated with Egypt and its history.

The second area of African development is North Africa, an area first settled by colonists from Phoenicia. When the Romans destroyed Carthage, they settled in this area and established many Roman cities. After the Fall of Rome, the Vandals built a kingdom there. The people of North Africa are racially Semitic and are lighter complected than other Africans.

The third area is the interior portion of the African continent. It can be divided into five basic population groups, including Negro, Nilo-Sudanic, Bantu, Pygmy, and Hottentot.

The true Negro people come from the West Coast of Africa. Most American blacks are descendants of these people. In the northeast, from the beginning of the Nile River southward into Kenya, there is a tall, slender mixture of Negro people known as the Nilo-Sudanics. In central Africa the Bantu people are found. They speak many different languages, but they all are related. They have increased in population and spread southward into Zimbabwe and South Africa. Also in central Africa, located deep in the rain forests, are the dwarf-like Pygmy people, many of whom are less than 152 cm (five feet) tall. The Hottentots, which include the bushmen, are found in South Africa.

These three heads are typical of peoples living in Africa, India, and China. In early times these three nations were fairly remote and unknown to peoples of the Western World. Today, however, the situation has changed to the point that all three nations occupy a vital role in world affairs. Black African woman (top) represents a country which is rapidly shedding foreign rule to become independent and modern; Indian man (center) comes from a nation whose starvation problems could soon determine whether India remains democratic or turns to communism; Chinese man (bottom) comes from largest communist country in the world which today influences all the rest of Asia.

African culture basically began in the area of Egypt, spread to North Africa, and then to the interior. It is important to realize, however, that there were people living in all these areas at the same time. It took longer for culture to spread to the African interior.

Although people began to settle and form colonies in North Africa very early, it was not until the 1700s that Europeans began to explore the interior regions. Much of Africa, therefore, remained a land of mystery until the eighteenth century.

The Influence of Geography

The geography of Africa has played an important role in its history and the development of its civilization. The great Sahara Desert divides the African continent and this has influenced its history.

When people became curious about the country that lay on the other side of the desert, they were told frightening stories by the nomadic tribesmen known as Berbers. These men handled all the trade between North Africa and the interior.

To stay in control of the gold, ivory, and diamonds of Africa's interior regions, the Berbers tried to prevent other merchants from trading with peoples in the interior. They told people it was too dangerous to cross the Sahara or that terrifying animals and fierce peoples waited to kill any strangers who dared enter their territory. Although the Berbers learned to travel across the hot, sandy wastes, the rest of the world was cut off from Africa's interior by this desert.

About 520 B.C. Phoenician sailors from Carthage sailed along the coast of Africa as far as the modern state of Sierra Leone. Although

WEST COAST "TRUE NEGRO"

NORTH AFRICA BERBER

CENTRAL AFRICA BANTU

NORTH EAST NILO-SUDANIC

RAINFOREST PYGMY

SOUTH AFRICA HOTTENTOT

Africa is a land of many people and tribes, each with a distinct language, customs, skills and total contribution to life. This map indicates only the major strains of inhabitants which migrated and settled into the various parts of the continent.

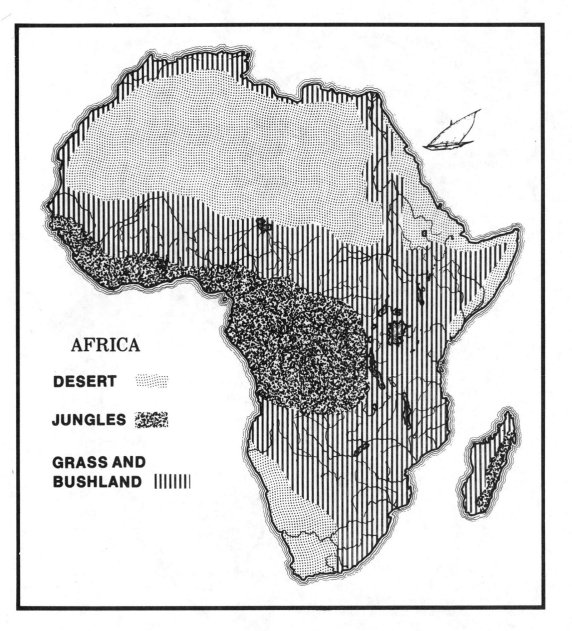

AFRICA

DESERT

JUNGLES

**GRASS AND
BUSHLAND** ||||||||

they sailed for almost 4827 km (3,000 miles), they could not find many good harbors where they could set up trading stations. Getting into the interior also was difficult for explorers because there were no good coastal harbors. Where there was a good harbor, thick jungles around it formed a wall that prohibited further exploration. The mighty rivers that rush downhill to the ocean are too violent to be used as water highways.

Land of Extremes. Africa is a land of extremes, making it difficult for the people to survive. The continent of Africa is three times as large as the United States. It contains every type of geographical condition in the world, including the Sahara Desert, the world's largest desert. The world's hottest temperature of 58.8°C (136°F) in the shade has been recorded there. In modern times rich oil deposits have been discovered under its barren sands.

While the desert area sometimes receives no rain at all for an entire year, there are other areas of Africa where 1016 cm (400 inches) of rain falls in a year. In the United States, 144.8 cm (57 inches) of rain in a year is considered unusually wet. You can see that areas receiving so much rain flooded easily, destroying crops and villages.

Africa also has grasslands, high mountains, swamps, and jungles. It seems as though soil rich enough to grow thick jungles also would be good farmland. But while the land at the southern end of Africa is good farmland, the jungle area is not.

The soil in jungle areas is different from that found in the rest of the world. When it is plowed, it packs so tightly that seeds do not sprout easily from the ground. The soil also lacks many of the minerals necessary for healthy food crops. Thus it is very difficult for people living in jungle areas to earn a living from farming. Because they could barely survive their harsh environment, the people in the African interior did not produce the strong civilizations we have seen in Mesopotamia, Greece, or Rome. Large crop surpluses are necessary to enable large numbers of people to live in a city. It was impossible for the people to maintain such a surplus from jungle land.

In the grasslands there also was a struggle for survival. Looking at the rich grass, it was easy to imagine herds of fat cattle grazing in peace and making their owners rich. The truth is that the African grasslands were plagued by the *tsetse fly,* a pest that killed or diseased most of the cattle. It was not until modern times that a cure was found and raising cattle has become profitable.

Discovering Africa's Past. Although it seemed almost impossible to survive in Africa, there were high levels of cultural development in the African interior. In recent years there has been a great interest in studying Africa's past. Newly formed African states have encouraged archaeologists, anthropologists, and other qualified people to explore Africa and learn about its history. In the United States, black studies are important courses offered on university and high school campuses.

Two completely different views have been formed of how Africa's history began and developed. One theory has been introduced by Dr. Louis Leakey. In the introduction to this book, we mentioned Dr. Leakey and his discoveries in Africa. For many years Dr. Leakey and his wife worked at the Olduvai Gorge in the country of Tanzania. This gorge is like a huge layer cake which shows layers of sediment. Dr. Leakey believes these layers represent the different geological ages in the slow evolution of the world. He believes the fossils and bones he discovered in this gorge were washed out of the layers and are millions of years old.

Dr. Leakey's son Richard, also working in Africa, has found the bones of what he claims is the oldest primitive man yet found. This primitive man is considered to be older than all other cave men, although there is little difference between these remains and modern man. This find makes it impossible for man as we know him today to have evolved from the cave men already discussed. Richard Leakey's findings are older than all of them.

As a result of the Leakeys' findings, many people now believe that all life began in Africa. When the population began to grow, people migrated from Africa into the rest of the world.

As we have already seen, many scientists believe that rock formations like Olduvai Gorge were formed as silt and debris settled during the year-long Flood. The Flood waters covered the earth for only a year. It is believed that bones found in the walls of the gorge are not older than the time of the Flood.

If the bones that have been found were washed from the walls, they would be old. But creationist scientists are not certain the remains washed from the walls. It is possible that they washed into the gorge from another area. They could, therefore, be much younger than the Leakeys claim. For these reasons not all scientists accept the conclusions the Leakeys have made about their findings.

African Beginnings

If all life did not begin in Africa, where did the African people come from? As we saw in our

In the past great numbers of livestock in Africa were killed by the tsetse fly. This healthy looking herd of cattle belonging to a modern Bantu tribe reflects the use of new pesticides, advancement of science, and improved farming methods.

World-renowned anthropologist Dr. Louis Leakey displays fossils he found in an African excavation.

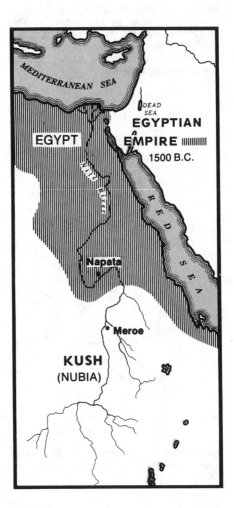

study of Egypt, the ancient name for this country was Mizraim after one of Noah's grandsons. Another of Noah's grandsons was named Cush. It is interesting to note that during the last years of Egypt's power, a kingdom named Kush existed south of Egypt. Many historians believe that Cush, or descendants of Cush, crossed the Red Sea into Africa about 3800 B.C. This would have been about the time the first people were settling along the Nile Valley.

The Sahara Desert was not as large then as it is today. In the area south of Egypt, there were large lakes that have since dried up. One of them is known today as the Fayum Depression. Here these descendants of Cush apparently settled.

From archaeologists' findings we can tell that there was plenty of fish and game in that area. Crops were plentiful and were harvested with stone sickles. The grain was stored in straw-lined holes. Fish hooks carved from bone were used for fishing and bows and arrows were used for hunting. The fibers of the flax plant were used for weaving fabrics.

These people left interesting drawings of cattle, herders, and strange-looking gods and goddesses on cliff walls. Their artwork shows an ability and sophistication above that of mere savages.

Sometimes too many cattle can overgraze the land, allowing desert sands to replace the grass. This may be what happened to the people living at Fayum. At any rate somehow the desert sands pushed in and they were forced to move away.

The Kingdom of Kush. By 2000 B.C. a thriving kingdom known as Kush had started south of Egypt in the area known in ancient times as Nubia. Today it is called the Sudan. These people were nomadic herders who later raided

Egypt, hoping to capture some of her rich grazing lands. As they became more settled, the Kushites established trade contacts with the people in Africa's interior. Kush grew rich on the gold and ivory trade.

About 1500 B.C. the Egyptians took over Kush and turned it into an Egyptian province. The Egyptians encouraged the Kushites to live in cities and gradually the old nomadic life died out. The capital of Kush was Napata and the Egyptians sent a governor to rule from there. Egyptian customs, architecture, and religion were brought into the new province. Because of trade contacts, Kush acted as a funnel through which Egyptian culture and ideas were passed into the interior of Africa.

The idea of pyramids was brought to Kush by the Egyptians. The Kushite pyramids were much smaller, however, and did not contain as many possessions as the Egyptian pyramids. Since little of their culture remains for us to study today, we know less about the everyday life of the Kushites than we do about the Egyptians.

Drawings on cliff walls in the Fayum Depression give an interesting view of two aspects of life: the Hunt and the Harvest.

The Kushites finally won their freedom after remaining under Egyptian control for almost 500 years. Egypt had entered its declining years and there was much corruption in government and religion. In 725 B.C. the great Kushite warrior-king Piankhy conquered Egypt. Egypt remained under Kushite control for 25 years. Then Piankhy sent military aid to the Phoenician cities which were being attacked by the Assyrians. The Assyrians defeated the Phoenicians and then swept into Egypt.

Egypt became an Assyrian province and the kingdom of Kush was pushed back to its original boundaries. During this time the Kushites learned the secret of smelting iron from the Assyrians. As a result, they were able to develop a rich trade in iron products.

The spreading fingers of the Sahara Desert already were choking the rich farmlands around Napata and soon it was necessary to move the capital. Meroe became the new Kushite capital. Meroe was located on the Nile River near the present-day city of Khartoum where trade routes had crossed for many centuries. Trade thrived between Meroe and China, India, Arabia, and the African interior.

About 250 B.C. Meroe was at its height. Because of its ample supply of trade goods, Meroe was constantly threatened by fierce Bedouin tribes from the North African Desert

Ethiopian Descendants

The people of Ethiopia claim their descendants came from Saba, or Sheba, as this country is known today. Menelik, their first king, was believed to be the son of King Solomon and the Queen of Sheba.

This forced her to keep a strong army for protection.

When the Roman Empire spread into Egypt, the days of the Kushite Kingdom were numbered. Roman ports offered better trade opportunities to merchants from China and India. At the same time, Bedouin raiders began attacking caravans traveling to and from Meroe and they even attacked some of the smaller Kushite towns.

Axum. About 1000 B.C., while the Kush kingdom was winning its freedom from Egypt, a new group of people migrated across the Red Sea. They settled in the area known today as Ethiopia, located on the northeastern coast of Africa. This area extended into the interior region, bordering the territory governed by Kush. It became the great trading nation of Axum.

In 300 A.D. an army from Axum attacked and destroyed Meroe, bringing the kingdom of Kush to an end. Survivors fled in all directions, but they carried the Kushite culture with them. Today archaeologists are discovering evidence of Kushite influence throughout west and central Africa.

By the end of the fourth century A.D., Ezana, the king of Axum, became a Christian. He made Christianity the official religion of his kingdom. Since most of Axum's trade was with the Christian countries along the Mediterranean Sea, ideas and goods flowed freely. Then the new Muslim religion spread across North Africa. Ethiopia (Axum) was cut off from her trade with Christian countries and became completely isolated.

The idea that a Christian country existed in Africa's interior became a legend in Europe. The search for Prester John and his golden city of African Christians began. Like the Seven

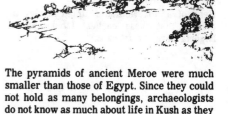

The pyramids of ancient Meroe were much smaller than those of Egypt. Since they could not hold as many belongings, archaeologists do not know as much about life in Kush as they do about Egypt.

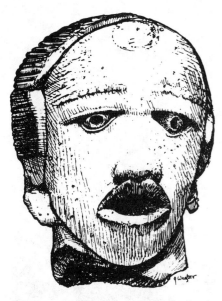

Head of a Nok woman sculpted in clay indicates that these earliest inhabitants of Nigeria were fine artisans.

Cities of Gold encouraged Spanish exploration in the Americas, this encouraged African exploration. It was not until the sixteenth century A.D. that this Christian country was "rediscovered."

The Nok Culture. The earliest African culture not influenced by outside civilizations was the Nok. We do not know much about this early African culture because there were no written records left behind. The knowledge we do have about the Nok and other African civilizations comes as a result of oral traditions and the findings of archaeologists.

The Nok culture developed about 800 B.C. in the area that is now northern Nigeria. It was a farming culture which had learned to make tools of iron and tin. The Nok people are famous for the beautiful, fired clay heads they made. Archaeologists have found many of these heads in recent times. In later years artists in Nigeria improved Nok techniques, making the heads of bronze, silver, gold, brass, and even terracotta.

Apparently the Nok people blended in with the other peoples of the area. In 400 A.D. they became part of the great trading empire of Ghana. We shall study Ghana and other African kingdoms in a later chapter.

The Indian Middle Ages

India has one of the oldest continuous cultures of any country in the world. When the Aryans invaded India, they introduced the caste system. They wanted to remain racially segregated from the people they conquered. They also developed the Hindu religion. Unlike other religions Hinduism allows all kinds of religious experiences. It even permits people to have entirely different beliefs on many subjects. As new theories and religions were introduced in India,

The Greek influence which dominated the cultures of North Africa and the Nile Valley is visible in this sample of the Ethiopian language. Earlier samples from Ethiopia reflect the influence of Egyptian hieroglyphics.

they were merely absorbed into the Hindu faith without really changing the basic religion.

Everyday Life

Hindu writers wrote rule books on every area of life, including how to fight wars, how to treat a wife, and others. The Hindus believed a person's reincarnation depended on how well he obeyed these rules. As a result, nobody tried to change or modify the religion over the years. For this reason people in India live today in much the same way they did thousands of years ago. A few modern inventions have made life more pleasant in recent years for the rich classes, however. It is important for us to study how the people lived before looking at the political history of India so that you may better understand why things happened the way they did.

Rural Villages. Most of the people lived in small rural villages and earned their living by farming. There were many things that destroyed their crops, including floods, drought, and insect pests. When things went well, some areas of India were able to grow two sets of crops in a year. During the rainy season, rice was grown. Later in the year, farmers used irrigation techniques to grow grain, cotton, or some other second crop.

The farmers had herds of cows, but as Hinduism absorbed Buddhist beliefs over the years, it became a crime to kill cattle. Then the people became vegetarians. Herds of sheep and goats were raised for wool and milk. Horses did not thrive in India due to the hot climate, although many kings did bring horses to India from the Hellenistic kingdoms in Mesopotamia. The common people were more likely to use

Farming methods in India have improved little over the years. Oxen are still used today as they were hundreds of years ago. Here modern Indian farmers crush sugarcane.

oxen to pull wagons. In some cases elephants and camels were also used for transportation.

Some of the crops grown by the farmers included rice, millet, wheat, barley, peas, lentils, beans, sugarcane, leafy vegetables, mangos, bananas, grapes, and fragrant woods. Many spices grew in India, including pepper, ginger, saffron, and cinnamon. Spices were a major export item. When silkworms and the secret of making silk were brought into India, silk became another important source of income for the villagers. Indian silk never was as fine a quality as Chinese silk, however, and the rich people in India continued to buy silk from China.

Cities. Most Indian cities were carefully laid out in a grid pattern, with the main street running north and south. There were some cities which were not carefully planned, but they were the exception rather than the rule. Every city had two main buildings, including the royal palace and the major Hindu temple.

The palaces of the kings were beautiful. They were adorned with gold-covered pillars and had many spacious rooms. Because they were made

out of wood, they have decayed over the centuries. Very little remains to tell us how they looked. The nobles and rich people had homes between three and six stories tall. They were miniature palaces and they all contained bathrooms with running water, gardens with pools for bathing, and balconies. Indians also invented a water machine for cooling air which worked much like a revolving lawn sprinkler used today.

While the rich people lived in luxury, the poor people lived in one room mud huts with thatched

Medieval Bathing Facilities

As we have seen, the people in ancient Sumer had plumbing and heated baths, as did the people in Mohenjo-daro and Harappa. The Greeks and Romans copied many of these conveniences. They furnished public baths where even the poor people could go and relax in hot water, steam, and luxurious surroundings. Although the people in India remembered how to build plumbing systems, the science was lost in Europe when Rome fell.

During the Middle Ages (which we will be discussing in the next few chapters), people in Europe had no running water. They could only bathe by hauling water or going to streams and ponds. Gradually the idea developed that too many baths would make a person sick. So the medieval European only bathed once or twice a year. It was not until hundreds of years later that Europeans rediscovered the science of plumbing and indoor bathrooms.

Due to the widespread poverty and disease in the overpopulated nation of India, it is often hard to tell the sleeping from the dead. Homeless people line the streets both day and night. Many of them are members of the beggar caste. There is little hope for these people to improve their lives as long as their caste system remains.

This snake-charmer's flute, looking rather like a snake itself, entices cobras from their baskets. It has been said that the charmer's body movements, more than his music, control the snakes.

roofs. People who could not afford them often slept in the street with their few belongings piled around them. Even today in the larger Indian cities, people sleep in the street when they cannot afford a place to stay.

Everyone in India loved flowers. The rich people had beautiful gardens next to their homes and spent much of their spare time enjoying them. There were lovely public gardens too where the poor people could get away from the pressure of the city.

The People. We have already seen how the caste system kept people locked into the same classes and occupations as their parents. There were not as many slaves in India as there were in other civilizations we have studied.

Some people became slaves when they could not pay their debts or when they were punished for crimes. Sometimes people even sold themselves to meet financial emergencies. Once a debt was paid, however, the debtor was free again. There were many laws to protect slaves and they could not be beaten or killed. When they grew old, their owner was required to provide for them.

The Hindu religion encouraged people to have large families. It was important for a family to have at least one son to perform the family's funeral rites. The more sons they had, the better.

Girls were not important and often were merely an economic hardship to their families. No matter how many daughters a family had, it still had to provide money for a dowry when they married. It was never important for women to be educated, although many upper class women were educated.

Although girls were a burden to a family, the practice of exposing babies was not used as much in Indian society as in other civilizations

we have studied. All children were spoiled and they were rarely spanked or punished.

Childhood ended at an early age for poor children. They were expected to help with the work of earning a living when they were old enough to walk. There were village schools attached to the temples for poor children who had time to attend. The rich children began their education when they were four or five years old. Their parents hired tutors to come in and teach their children in the home.

A young man went to school for 12 years and at the end of that time, he was supposed to marry. Girls were expected to marry young and it was not unusual for a girl to be married when she was eight years old.

Women in the noble families were not allowed to have more than one husband and divorce was not allowed. Even if the woman was a young child when her husband died, she could not remarry. The Hindus believed if the widow did not remarry and followed very strict rules, she would be reunited with her husband when they were reincarnated. They also believed that her actions would affect what station or caste her husband would be reborn into after death. For this reason the widow was forced to stay with her husband's family which kept a close watch on her at all times.

A widow had to sleep on the ground, shave her head, and go without jewelry, colored clothes, or perfume. She was considered to be bad luck and could not attend family festivals. Even servants avoided her and she had to serve herself. It is not surprising that many widows preferred to be burned alive on their husbands' funeral pyres, rather than live in this manner for the rest of their lives.

Indians did not wear many clothes because of the hot climate. Both men and women wore a long strip of cloth wrapped around the waist, extending down the legs. During this period the women did not wear anything above the waist, except in colder areas where they wore little jackets.

Both men and women wore makeup, including eye shadow and a form of lipstick. Rich men also wore sweet smelling oils and perfumes. Both sexes had long hair and women often wore theirs tied up in a bun at the nape of the neck.

Everyone wore lots of jewelry. The rich wore precious stones and metals and the poor wore glass and pottery beads. They wore jewelry hanging from their foreheads and running down the part in their hair. They had fancy necklaces and wore heavy earrings that stretched their ears. They also wore wide, gold girdles or belts with ropes of pearls hanging from them in long loops. Everyone had lots of bracelets, bangles, armlets, and anklets with tinkling bells.

Entertainment was simple in India. There was not much interest in athletic events because the hot climate made sports too tiring. Indians did have a form of bull wrestling, however, where men tried to throw a bull to the ground. There are pictures that were painted in ancient times showing a victorious bull after it gored the wrestler.

The Indians loved to gamble with dice. They also were responsible for developing the board game we call chess. There were musicians, bards, acrobats, jugglers, magicians, and snake-charmers who went from village to village entertaining the poorer people.

The Functions of Rulers. Very early in history, the people realized they needed rulers to maintain order, lead armies, and protect the working people from raiders and criminals. The noble people appointed the king, but they kept the right to revolt if he did not please them. For this reason the rulers of India always tried to keep their subjects happy.

The king was one of the few people of India allowed to have more than one wife. But there was always one queen who had power over the other wives and sometimes even the king was afraid of her. As a general rule, only the men were allowed to govern. But there were some women who did take over the rule.

The king was responsible for keeping law and order. If criminals were not caught, the king

---

Origin of Chess

The Indian civilization was the first to develop the board game, known today as chess. Their game required four players and dice. The game became popular in Persia and was changed to a game for only two. When the Muslims took over Persia, they also started playing chess. Christian knights, who fought against the Muslims during the Crusades, brought the game back to Europe. There chess underwent final changes and became the mind-challenger it remains today.

Today there is a sort of Olympic games competition in chess. Since 1969 the United States and Russia have been the major contenders. In 1969 Boris Spassky won the title; in 1972 Bobby Fischer won. In 1975 the Russian challenger won without playing when Fischer refused to accept the rules given for the match. As it now stands, Spassky remains the champion and is waiting for another challenger.

Indian women were extravagant in the use of makeup and jewelry. Gold and precious stones were fashioned into adornments to cover their heads and arms.

was required to repay the stolen items. The Hindus believed that any king who was an unfair judge would be reborn as a lizard or some other lowly creature.

Many times kings *abdicated;* that is, they voluntarily gave up their throne. When a ruler stepped down as king, he usually committed ritual suicide by starving himself to death or by drowning. There were many cases too when a son got tired of waiting for his father to die and murdered him for the throne.

Almost every part of life in India was controlled by the government. It controlled spinning and weaving factories where poor women with no support could earn a living. It controlled the manufacture of weapons and provided storage in government arsenals. There were state-owned shipyards where ships were built and rented to fishermen and merchants.

The Great Indian Kingdoms

The Mauryan Dynasty. After Alexander the Great conquered the Mesopotamian area, he invaded India in 326 B.C. At this time there were many royal states, and Alexander had little trouble defeating them. Alexander turned back to Mesopotamia when his soldiers mutinied and refused to go any farther. He left a local ruler named Porus in charge of India when he retreated.

Within five years this Indian section of Alexander's empire had broken away and the first Indian empire, known as the Mauryan Dynasty, was established. Although Alexander's territory in India was lost, Bactria, the territory on India's northeast border, remained under Hellenistic influence and later played an important role in Indian history. After Alexander left India, Chandragupta Maurya conquered his neighbors and established the largest and best Indian empire of all. For 24 years Chandragupta Maurya continued to add territory to his empire.

Kautilya, a wise counselor, helped Chandragupta Maurya run the empire. Kautilya is given credit for writing the lawbook *Arthashastra*.

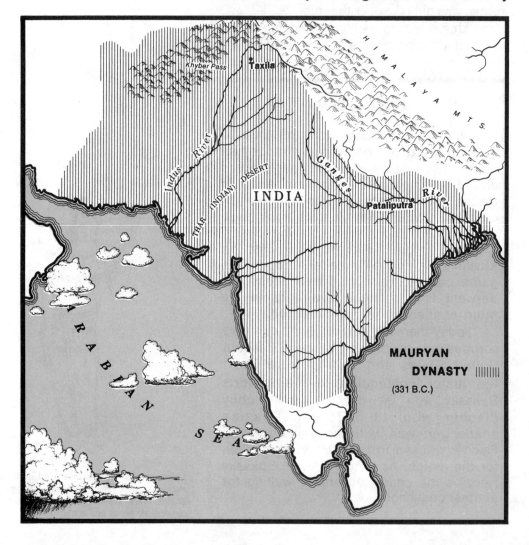

MAURYAN DYNASTY ‖‖‖‖‖

(331 B.C.)

Alexander's men defeated the army of King
Porus of India. An account of the bàttle at the
Ghelum River says that the king's elephants,
"maddened by the disaster, kept colliding
with the friends and foes alike."

Ashoka's testimonial—a column reflecting the combined influences of Greek architecture and Buddhist teaching.

This work comprises one of two sets of laws that governed the people of India for centuries, listing their duties and responsibilities in every situation. This book is a great help to historians because it shows us how the people lived and behaved.

Chandragupta Maurya was able to set up an empire because Alexander had already destroyed the power of smaller rulers. The merchants and farmers were in favor of a strong government because the constant fighting between the smaller kingdoms hurt trade and destroyed crops. Chandragupta Maurya proved to be a strong enough ruler to control the peoples he conquered.

Ashoka, Chandragupta Maurya's grandson, was the best ruler of India and one of the greatest kings in the world. Ashoka had been king for eight years when he converted to Buddhism. This made a great change in his character, causing him to put aside his warlike activities. He became determined to improve the lives of his subjects rather than kill people.

There were more than 2,000 cities in the Mauryan Empire. Many universities were established and scholars came from as far away as China to study the arts, science, and medicine. The capital city was Pataliputra which was 14.5 km (nine miles) long and 3.2 km (two miles) wide.

Under the Mauryan Dynasty, the government provided many public services for the people. It was responsible for sanitation, hospitals, and relief for the poor. (Today we call such relief *public welfare*.) During famines and emergencies, the government supplied the people with free food from state granaries.

Under Ashoka's rule the government cleared harbors, built and maintained bridges, provided ferryboat transportation, and built highways.

One of the highways was 1930.8 km (1,200 miles) long, almost half the distance across the United States. These ancient Indian highways had most of the conveniences of our modern interstate system. Every 1.6 km (one mile) there were road signs telling the distances to the many towns and villages. There were rest stops, complete with shady areas, hotels, wells, and police stations. People traveled these highways on everything from elephants to ox-drawn carts.

There was a flourishing trade between India and Mesopotamia, Greece, Africa, and China during this time. In addition to merchants, Ashoka sent Buddhist missionaries into Ceylon, Southeast Asia, and China. In these countries Buddhism took hold and it has since become one of the world's three great religions.

Ashoka enjoyed many of the Greek ideas and allowed Greek influences to come into his court. Buddhism did not require strict caste segregation, so foreigners were not considered unclean by Ashoka. The Hindu priests, however, hated Ashoka, his new religion, and foreign ideas. You will remember the kindly Pharaoh Akhenaton who was hated and finally overthrown by the

Epic Pillars

When Darius was king of Persia, he left monuments around his country. Carved in stone, they bragged about all the people he killed and cities he destroyed. Ashoka also left stone pillars scattered across India. Instead of bragging about what he had done, Ashoka's monuments encouraged people to treat each other fairly and told them how to live good and happy lives.

priests of the religion he had rejected. Ashoka was in the same position. Finally in 183 B.C., there was a palace rebellion. Ashoka was overthrown and a general took over the government. This was the last time India was solidly united under one government for 2,000 years. There were other kingdoms and empires, but none as great as the Mauryan Dynasty.

Greco-Bactrian Kingdom. You will remember that the territory of Bactria remained under Grecian influence after Alexander the Great conquered the area. In 185 B.C. Demetrius, the ruler of one of the Bactrian kingdoms, invaded India. India had not regained her unity after the death of Ashoka and Demetrius was able to take over a large amount of territory. Greek culture was introduced to India during the Greco-Bactrian Kingdom and Greek and Indian cultures merged.

One area in which Greek influence was felt was in sculpture. The Indians adopted the free, realistic style of the Greeks. They added purely Indian touches, creating some of the most beautiful Asian sculpture ever produced. Up to this time, there were no statues of Buddha. During the Greco-Bactrian Kingdom, many beautiful sculptures of Buddha and Buddhist saints were created.

Greek culture might have had a greater influence on India if the Greco-Bactrian Kingdom had lasted longer. But warlike tribesmen who were related to the Scythians began invading Bactria and India. For more than 300 years, there was terror and disruption as these tribes raided and plundered.

The Kushan Kingdom. About 78 A.D. a tribe of invaders took over the Greco-Bactrian Kingdom and set up the Kushan Dynasty. This new kingdom, which included northwest India and

the area currently known as Afghanistan, again opened up trade with foreign countries. It was a Kushan king who sent a trade embassy to Rome to congratulate Caesar Augustus on becoming emperor.

The Kushan rulers accepted the Buddhist religion. During the years their kingdom flourished, many missionaries and settlers were sent into Southeast Asia. There Indian culture greatly influenced the lives of the people. It was during this time that Buddhism split into the Greater and Lesser Vehicles.

The Kushan Dynasty collapsed in 225 A.D. Once again India was plunged into cultural

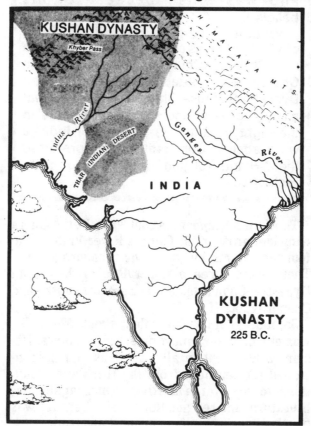

Combining the realism of Greek sculpture with the grace of India, this statue of Buddha is one of the most beautiful ever produced. Features reflect the Greek influence while the hairstyle and expression are pure Indian.

Coins bearing Demetrius' inscription were used in India after his invasion of that country.

darkness while many tiny kingdoms appeared. During the Kushan Dynasty there had been a revival of science, art, and medicine. Once again these cultural elements died out.

Gupta's version of Buddha shows the religious leader in the lotus position.

Early Christianity in India

There has never been any proof to support the legend that the Apostle Thomas went to India to preach the gospel. If he did go to India, he went during the Kushan Dynasty. Christian legend claims that he went there and was killed because of his beliefs.

Whether Thomas traveled to India, or whether it was some other missionary, a new Christian Church called the Martoma Church was started during the Kushan Dynasty. Because Christians believed that all people are brothers and sisters, equal in the sight of God, the majority of Indians were against Christianity. They preferred their Hindu religion with its rigid caste restrictions.

The Gupta Kingdom. About 300 A.D. the Gupta Kingdom arose in the Ganges River Valley. The founder of this kingdom was Chandragupta I. There were three major rulers in the Gupta Dynasty—Chandragupta I, Samudragupta, and Chandragupta II.

Samudragupta, who ruled about 320 A.D., was one of India's most outstanding rulers. His armies went out in all directions and he controlled the territory from the Himalaya Mountains to the Narbada River. Once again art, literature, and religion flourished. Treasure was pouring in as a result of conquest and trade.

The reign of Samudragupta is known as the "golden age of Sanskrit." King-sponsored writers appeared and *Mahabharata* and *Ramayana,* two great epics which are still read and enjoyed, were written at this time. One of the greatest writers of poetry and drama was Kalidasa who lived between 400 and 455 A.D. Many famous stories in literature came from India, including *Sinbad the Sailor.*

Under Chandragupta II, India became the happiest and most civilized country in the world. The Roman Empire was failing and the government in China was collapsing. By 388 A.D. Chandragupta II had conquered the last territory to be governed under the Gupta Dynasty.

The civilization that developed in India during these kingdoms was remarkable. There has never been another country where the government has treated its people better or where people treated each other better. It was not perfect and there were cases of cruelty and oppression, but compared to the other civilizations we have studied, it was mild.

The world owes a debt to India. In science Indians learned how to make soap, temper steel, and dye clothes. In medicine they introduced the practice of sterilizing a wound before operating, developed a type of plastic surgery, and made eyeglasses. Indians were the first to use cotton, calico, cashmere, and chintz.

About 480 A.D. India was invaded by some tribal people known as the Hunas. They took over northwest India. Although the Gupta Dynasty continued to rule until 550 A.D., the territory it controlled was tiny compared to what it had been.

Indian Influence in Southeast Asia

About 100 A.D. Indian merchants and later military conquests began to spread Indian culture into Southeast Asia. This area became known as Greater India in the same way that the early Greek colonies in Italy were called Great Greece.

Today historians divide Greater India into two sections, according to the amount of influence India had on their culture. The western section, including Ceylon, Burma, central Siam, and the Malay peninsula, was colonized by Indians. As a result of this close contact, their culture is a close imitation of Indian culture. The eastern section includes Java, Cambodia, and Champa in Indochina. These peoples were influenced by trade with India, but were far enough away to develop their own culture.

In the western section of Greater India, kingdoms rose up while a flood of Indian colonists dominated the government of this area. Even though the Indians intermarried with the local population, the rulers of these kingdoms had Indian names. Although India was conquered by the Muslims, some of these small kingdoms lasted many more years, carrying on India's culture.

There are many reminders of Indian influence in southeast Asia. Two outstanding ones are the Angkor Wat temple in Cambodia and the Barabudur Shrine in Java.

This photo depicts the beautiful temple of Angkor Wat in Cambodia. Notice the many detailed knobs, domes, and pillars that help to make this temple complex one of the most outstanding architectural achievements in the world.

GREATER INDIA
100 A.D.
WESTERN SECTION
EASTERN SECTION

BURMA
CHINA
INDOCHINA
CENTRAL SIAM
CAMBODIA
MALAY PENINSULA
JAVA

These three carved monkeys are located near the top of a wall of Toshogu Shrine in Nikko, Japan. They are generally interpreted as "see no evil, hear no evil, and speak no evil." They are probably from the writings of Confucius. Copies of this carving have been sold in all parts of the world. The shrine itself was built in tribute to the first of the shoguns. Legend states that when the artist finished this work for the shogun, his right hand was cut off so he could never work for a lesser person.

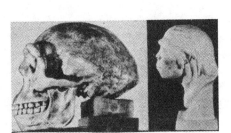

These photos show bones of a skull (left) believed to be those of Peking Man. Scientists assembled the bones and made a model of Peking Man's head (right) so that we can see what this man supposedly looked like.

Angkor Wat was built in long terraces with carved bas-relief scenes from the Hindu legends. It has five towers, including a central tower that rises more than 61 m (200 feet). The ashes of the king who built this temple rest under the central tower. The main gate faces east, the direction associated with death, which is very unusual in a Hindu temple. For these reasons archaeologists believe the Angkor Wat is a funeral monument something like the pyramids in Egypt.

The entire temple area is surrounded by a stone wall that is .80 km (half a mile) from north to south, and 1.1 km (two-thirds of a mile) from east to west. Not far from the temple are the remains of a large city that must have had a population of more than a million people.

The Barabudur is the most imposing Buddhist shrine in the world. It is built on top of a hill and rises nine terraces high. The shrine is covered with carvings of Buddha and other people described in the Buddhist writings.

The only way that the Barabudur and Angkor Wat differ from similar buildings in India is in their massive size. The Indians did not build for size, but for beauty. Although these two monuments are huge, it is easy to see the Indian influence in their architecture.

The Origins of Chinese Civilization

China covers more than one-fourth of the continent of Asia. It has more than 10,359,600 km² (four million square miles) of territory. Like Africa, China was cut off from the rest of the world by its geography. To the northwest is the Gobi Desert, to the southwest are the Himalaya Mountains, and to the east is the Pacific Ocean. Because of their isolation from the rest of the

world, the Chinese people developed a culture that was entirely different from any other in the world.

Two important rivers in China are the Yangtze River in the south and the Hwang Ho (Yellow) River in the north. The very earliest Chinese civilization developed along the Hwang Ho. This river runs through a great yellow plain that has been formed by dust blown from the central Asian deserts, called *loess*.

Chinese Beginnings

Historians do not agree about the origins of the people of China. In the 1920s and 1930s pieces of about 30 skulls, 11 lower jaws, and about 147 teeth were discovered some 40.2 km (25 miles) from the city of Peking. These remains were called Peking Man by the scientists who discovered them. They were said to be about half a

China's Imperial Color

The color yellow is very important in Chinese history. As we have seen, the soil along the Hwang Ho River is yellow and Hwang Ho means "Yellow River." Yellow became a special color reserved for royalty. The kings and emperors wore yellow robes and the roofs of the royal first Imperial palaces were made of yellow tile. Even the emperor was called Huang-ti, meaning the "Yellow Emperor." When the Mongols conquered China and outlying territories, they carried the imperial yellow color with them. In Russia the Mongol capital was called the Golden Horde because tents and the roofs were yellow.

million years old. As has already been discussed, these fragments were lost during World War II before they could be properly evaluated by other scientists. In addition the great age given to the Peking Man leaves a gap of 46,000 years until the next humans lived in China.

Many scientists believe that Peking Man either was an extinct ape or that the scientific dating methods used were inaccurate. Scientists now believe the first people to settle in China were descendants of Noah's son Japheth.

The earliest culture to be discovered in Asia is the Yang Shao culture of Inner Mongolia. This culture existed about 2500 B.C. Because of the cold and the lack of building materials, Yang Shao people lived in sunken pits with thatched roofs. They raised pigs and dogs for food.

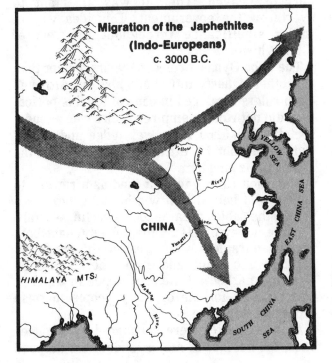

They discovered how to use a potter's wheel and made a thin, highly decorative pottery. They colored the pieces with striking designs in red, black, and white. But very little is known about these people. Official Chinese history does not begin until 1500 B.C. with the Shang Dynasty.

The Shang Dynasty. According to Chinese legend, the oldest dynasty to rule in China was the Shang Dynasty. For years people who studied China believed the Shang Dynasty was a myth and never really existed. According to legend, Fu Hsi, the first ruler, taught his people how to write, perform marriage ceremonies, play music, make instruments, paint lovely pictures, catch fish in nets, domesticate animals, and raise silkworms. The next emperor was supposed to have taught them how to use a wooden plow, market goods, and make medicine from herbs. Actually it must have taken several generations for the people to learn all of these things.

When archaeologists discovered the remains of this dynasty, they were able to open up a forgotten part of China's history. They learned

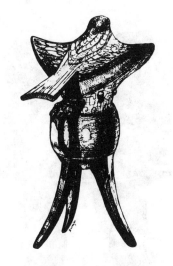

This beautiful piece of bronze, shaped like a bird, was used as a ritual vessel during the Shang Dynasty.

Oracle Bones

For centuries Chinese herb doctors prescribed ground dragon bones for many special ailments. In the 1800s scholars discovered there was writing on the bones being used by the doctors. It was learned that these bones were oracle bones, bearing messages from an oracle of a very old civilization. As a result, archaeologists discovered the Shan Dynasty, which up to that time was believed to be a mythical kingdom.

that the people living during the Shang Dynasty were very advanced. Although there were many farmers raising wheat, millet, rice, cattle, sheep, pigs, and horses, there also were people in specialized trades and jobs. They knew how to make silk and to produce beautiful pieces of bronze artwork. Even so their farming techniques were very primitive. One man had to hold a hoe made of a large stick while another man dragged it along.

The ruler of the Shang Dynasty was both priest and king. His role as priest was his most important job. He led the people in worshiping their ancestors which was done to keep the dead happy and in their graves. In addition to leading the people in worship, the king also helped foretell the future by use of oracle bones. Shoulder and leg bones of cattle were inscribed with a question and then thrown into a fire. The heat caused the bones to crack and the cracks

This handsome bronze ceremonial vessel was made to look like a guard dog. It was used in the rituals for ancestor worship during the Chou Dynasty.

Feudalism

Almost every area of the world has at some time in its history been governed under a feudal system. A feudal system was one in which powerful nobles were responsible for the protection of all the people on their land. They had their own courts, laws, and armies. The people owed the nobles service and money in exchange for protection. The nobles were supposed to be loyal to their king, but usually they had too much power to pay attention to him. Feudal systems were often warlike with nobles trying to capture more territory. As we shall see, a feudal system developed in Europe shortly after the Fall of Rome.

were examined by the priests for an answer to the question.

The Shang rulers claimed that heaven had given them the right to rule because of their position as priest-kings. The Shang Dynasty ran into trouble when a combination of domestic rebels and soldiers from another kingdom brought about its fall in 1027 B.C.

The Chou Dynasty. The ruler who took over the Shang Dynasty began a new dynasty called the Chou Dynasty. Since the Shang rulers claimed to be the "Sons of Heaven" who ruled with heaven's blessing, the Chou rulers had to come up with an excuse for deposing them.

They developed a new idea called the *Mandate of Heaven.* This was the idea that when a dynasty became corrupt and no longer ruled in the best interests of the people, it lost the support of heaven. Then it was all right to overthrow the government. This idea was of major significance throughout the rest of China's history.

The Chou Dynasty ruled 771 years, longer than any other dynasty in China's history. Although Chou rulers remained in control for this period, they did not rule an empire. Theirs was a feudal society. The Chou ruler was judge and priest. But he did not have much authority over the nobles in his kingdom.

The Chou ruler gave out land as a reward to nobles who helped him win his kingdom. As a result, the nobles became too powerful. Warfare became a way of life as the nobles fought both barbarian raiders who crossed the mountain barriers into China and each other. The Chou Dynasty marked a time of violence in which it was difficult for the ordinary people to raise crops and stay alive.

As weak states were conquered by stronger ones, the number of major landowners dropped from 1,700 to 55. These few landowners were as powerful as kings. When the final years of the Chou Dynasty arrived, new and improved methods of warfare had been developed. They now used mounted companies of archers and machines, called *catapults,* that hurled huge stones into fortress walls. Unable to control the nobles, however, the Chou ruler and his court became more concerned with pleasure than good government.

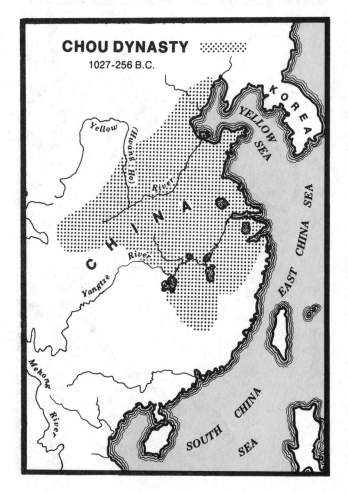

The Age of Philosophers. The Chou Dynasty brought with it two great philsophers, Confucius and Lao-tze, who influenced Chinese culture and thought. Chinese philosophers were more interested in practical matters than spiritual things. They were more concerned with answering the question "how" than "why."

About 551 B.C., a couple of years after Buddha, Confucius was born. The best known Chinese philosopher, he wandered from province to province with his students, teaching people to know their place and be happy in it. He thought that people should obey their rulers, parents, and older people.

Confucius was concerned with the warfare and disorder around him. He taught that the key to an orderly society was good behavior among the people and proper respect for those in higher positions. He said if a ruler behaved properly, his officials would follow his example. If government officials were honest, he said, people would be obedient and society would run smoothly.

Confucius, like Buddha, thought of himself as a reformer. He did not realize that someday he would be worshiped or that his ideas would play an important part in Chinese history. During his final years, he returned to his home province where he wrote *The Five Ching,* or *Canonical Books.*

At the same time Confucius was teaching, or possibly a few years after his death, another philosopher began to teach. He was Lao-tze, known as the "Old Master." Like Confucius, he was concerned about disorder in society, but disagreed with him on how to solve the problem. He came up with a philosophy called *Taoism,* a religion still practiced by the majority of Chinese people.

This portrait of philosopher-teacher Confucius has been reproduced from a rubbing of an 18th-century engraving. Confucius is remembered for his teachings on the virtues of obedience to family and rulers.

Lao-tze believed a person could learn the world's secrets by silently sitting and thinking about them. He believed everything in life had its opposite. This is known as the *yin* and the *yang*. For example, yin meant shady, female, dark, moon, weak, cold, or winter. Yang was sunny, male, light, sun, strong, warm, and summer.

The most important book on Taoist philosophy is the *Tao-te-Ching*, or *Book of the Way and of Virtue*. It was written by Lao-tze. Many people today are familiar with Taoism because it developed the martial art of Kung Fu.

Two hundred years after Confucius died, Mencius, another philosopher, became well known. Mencius studied the teachings of Confucius and added to them. He was mostly interested in finding a way to set up good government. He traveled throughout China, searching for a ruler who wanted to rule fairly and who was willing to be guided by a philosopher. Although he never found one, he still preferred kings to democracies.

When a country has a king, only the king needs to be educated in order to have good government, he thought. In a democracy everyone who has the vote needs to be educated in order to have good government. When Mencius could not find a good ruler, he began to teach the Mandate of Heaven, assuring people they had the right to overthrow bad rulers.

Although life during the Chou Dynasty was full of warfare and disruption, China's culture continued to develop. Literature flourished as rice paper was invented. Beautiful pottery and bronze work were created. Jade was considered so valuable that only sacred things could be made from it. Many lovely jade items have been recovered that were made during the Chou Dynasty.

The Everlasting Empire. A small kingdom called Ch'in became powerful on China's western border. It developed a strong army to fight off nomadic invaders. Once the army grew strong, it conquered many small kingdoms and finally took over all the territory claimed by the Chou Dynasty in 221 B.C. It is interesting to note that China got its name from the Ch'in Dynasty.

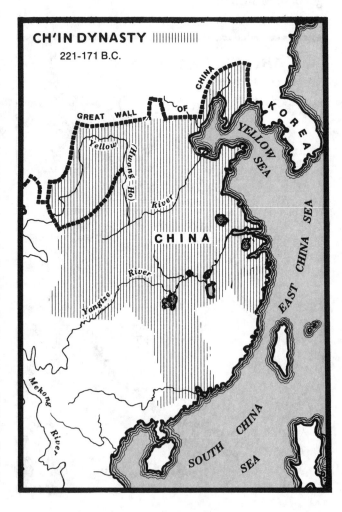

The first emperor of the Ch'in Dynasty was Shih Huang Ti. He took the title of the First Universal Emperor and planned for his empire to last for 1,000 years. The Ch'in Dynasty, however, only lasted 50 years. But the type of government organization he established to run his empire was copied by all future governments until 1912 A.D.

Huang Ti's government was organized along military lines. Each governor, official, and judge was responsible to someone of higher authority. The provincial governors were responsible to the emperor.

We saw how the Chou Dynasty came to power and developed a philosophy to justify its government. When the Ch'in Dynasty took power, a new philosophy came into being to support its new government. The philosophy was *Legalism,* which held that anything the emperor wanted was right. Under this system there were no civil laws to protect people. The Legalists believed people were basically selfish and needed absolute government, secret police, and strict laws to keep them from hurting each other and destroying the government.

The first thing Shih Huang Ti did was take away the power of the nobility and destroy the feudal system. He divided the land among the peasants and fixed taxes to be collected by his government.

The people were unhappy under the Ch'in Dynasty. Taxes were high and there were spies and informers everywhere. Everyone was forced to work on government and military building projects. To get workers for these projects, large masses of people were forced to pack up and move at the emperor's command.

One of the major projects undertaken by Shih Huang Ti was the Great Wall of China. There were many small sections of wall built by lesser rulers to hold back nomadic invaders. Huang Ti had these walls repaired and connected, forming one wall 2413.5 km (1,500 miles) long. Work on the wall was long, hard, and dangerous. Some 30,000 people died while working on it and were buried in the wall.

Mao-Tse Tung's Government

The Chinese have always been a people who turned to the past for examples of how they should live. When the Chou Dynasty overthrew the Shang Dynasty, a new philosophy developed. Called *The Mandate of Heaven,* it justified the act of overthrowing the government. For thousands of years Chinese rulers used this theory to justify their actions each time a new government came to power. When the Ch'in Dynasty took over, it developed a new philosophy called *Legalism.* This justified harsh government rule with no civil rights for the citizens.

When Mao Tse-Tung set up a communist system in China, the Western World waited for the Chinese to rebel against this foreign system. But Mao reached back into Chinese history. He used the Mandate of Heaven as his reason for overthrowing the government and the philosophy of Legalism to justify his type of government. The majority of Chinese supported Mao Tse-Tung's government. The fact that they have not rebelled shows that Mao understood history and his people enough to gain the necessary support.

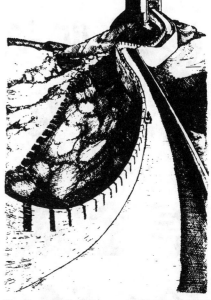

The Great Wall of China was begun in the mid-third century B.C. Because the construction project was so dangerous, the wall caused the deaths of thousands of the people who built it.

CHINESE ALPHABET

TS'ANG CHIEN

MODERN CHINESE

Huang Ti made many improvements in China. He set up a standardized monetary system for all of China. He also standardized weights and measures, so everyone knew how much they were buying without being cheated. He also required all wagons in China to have the same axle width. The roads were not paved and they often developed ruts. When all the wagons had the same axle width, they all fit in the ruts.

Highways landscaped by shade trees were built. They were built primarily so that soldiers could move quickly to any part of the empire. This also made it easier for the tax collector to travel around his territory.

A standard written language was permanently adopted. This was a written language with more than 40,000 characters which was already in existence. For the next 3,000 years, it remained much the same. No other language has managed to survive so long. The same language is still written and spoken today.

The Confucian scholars opposed all of these changes. To stop their criticism, Huang Ti passed a law making it an offense to own any history or philosophy books. Scholars who tried to protect their books were sent to work on the wall. Many historians believe it was during this time that all the historical records concerning the Shang Dynasty were destroyed. The works of Confucius survived because they were kept in remote monasteries and schools where they were not bothered. As a result of this persecution, Confucian scholars hated Huang Ti and when they wrote the history of China, they were very harsh in their judgment of him.

Huang Ti had hoped to build an everlasting empire. In 210 B.C., exactly five years after his death, his son's government was overthrown. **The Han Dynasty.** An army officer named Liu Pang established the new Han Dynasty in 171

B.C. During this time there were developments in the arts, religion, government, and in the size of the Chinese empire. Korea, Manchuria, Annam, and Indochina (today known as Viet Nam, Laos, and Cambodia) all came under the control of the Han Dynasty.

We know that the territory controlled by the Roman Empire was huge. It is interesting to note that the Han Dynasty Empire and the Roman Empire were about the same size. There was much trade between the Han Dynasty Empire and the Roman Empire.

The Han Dynasty realized that some type of qualifications should be necessary to get educated men into government office instead of simply giving important jobs to friends and family. A system of exams was set up based on Confucius' teachings and only people passing the exams could hold government office. This was the first civil service examination ever used. This method of choosing government workers lasted until 1904. It was during this time that the Chinese made sacrifices to Confucius as if he were a god.

The greatest Han Emperor was Wu Ti who ruled between 140 and 87 B.C. It was during his reign that the Huns tried to break through the Great Wall and invade China. Wu Ti's armies defeated the Huns in a terrible battle. The Huns then began moving westward away from China. We have already described the effects of this movement, as the Huns invaded Scythian territory and pushed tribes westward.

Wu Ti was a good emperor who was concerned about all the people he ruled. He tried to make conditions easier for the poor people by setting *price ceilings*. This means that merchants could not raise prices above a set figure. He also encouraged trade between the different parts of

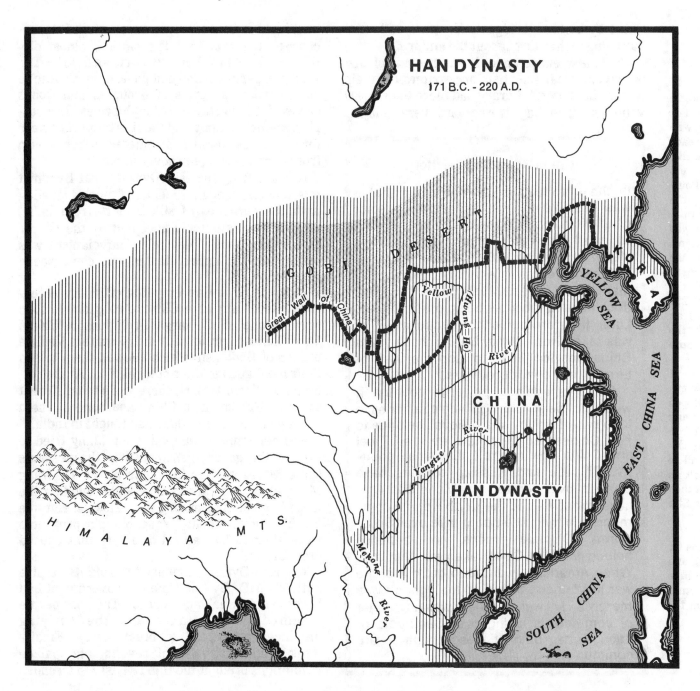

HAN DYNASTY

171 B.C. - 220 A.D.

GOBI DESERT

Great Wall of China

Yellow (Huang-Ho) River

KOREA

YELLOW SEA

CHINA

HAN DYNASTY

EAST CHINA SEA

Yangtze River

Mekong River

HIMALAYA MTS.

SOUTH CHINA SEA

New Perspectives

Countries in different parts of the world often experience similar events. For example, Rome (as a nation) was extending itself east in an effort to reach India where Delhi was becoming a city. Roman arches and Indian cupolas were blended into Delhi's architecture. Rome extended north to Britain, south up the Nile River, and west to the Atlantic Ocean. At the same time, China was also extending itself in all directions. The Chinese entered their Classical Age (600 B.C. to 200 B.C.). The fourth Dynasty of Tsin (Ch'in) took over the late Chou Dynasty; but then about 200 B.C. gave way to the powerful Han Dynasty. The Han Dynasty brought the many societies of Chinese people together.

Even as wrestling was a sport in Rome, so also the Mongolian youth developed wrestling skills to build character and confidence. Mongolian rulers often made war against China. So the Chinese rulers built the Great Wall to keep invaders out just as Rome built its walls in Britain and Europe. China then expanded its trade west along the Silk Route.

Chinese emperors built huge palaces for themselves, their wife (and harem), and children. The Quin Qing Palace illustrated typical Chinese architecture that was considerably distinct from the Romans.

China by building bridges and canals and standardizing money throughout the empire.

Wu Ti also encouraged literature and science by paying great scientists and writers for their work. The imperial library had more than 11,000 volumes, including works on every subject

---

China Regaining Territory

In the Introduction we mentioned that it was possible to use the past to predict what will happen in the future. In studying China's history, there is an example of this statement. From 202 B.C. China considered certain territory, including Manchuria, Korea, Mongolia, Annam, Indochina, and Tibet, as being part of China. Later this territory either broke away or was taken from China. During these years China was too weak to stop the theft of territory she considered hers.

China is again a powerful country. It would not be surprising if she again tries to take back territory she believes belongs to her. Chinese soldiers have invaded Tibet and China now controls that small country. Chinese and Russian soldiers have clashed over territory in Mongolia. Chinese troops helped the North Korean communists in their attempt to take over South Korea. Chinese troops and supplies helped the Viet Cong take over Vietnam. When Americans wanted to get out of the war in Vietnam, they said the fighting was merely a civil war and there was no danger of communists taking over Cambodia or Laos. Today both of these countries are communist.

---

imaginable. Other emperors continued to encourage the arts too. The world's oldest dictionary, the *Shuo Wen,* was written in 100 A.D.

This experiment in good government came to an end when a series of droughts and floods caused food shortages and high prices. The people became unhappy and the Han emperors were forced to use harsh punishments to keep them from overthrowing the government.

It was during the Han Dynasty that Buddhist missionaries began to enter China, traveling with the caravans of silk traders from India. Buddhism was quickly accepted by the poorer classes in China. They felt Confucianism was mostly for the upper classes who could spend time in school.

In 100 A.D. a Han emperor officially recognized Buddhism as a Chinese religion. It soon became one of the largest religions in China. The Chinese preferred the Greater Vehicle branch of Buddhism which allowed them to add their local gods to their new religion. At the outbreak of World War II, there were ten different sects of Buddhism in China and none of them was teaching what Buddha had taught in India.

Another emperor named Wang Mang tried to reform the government and help the peasants some 84 years after the death of Wu Ti. Wang Mang abolished slavery and began dividing the large landholdings among the peasants. But like Wu Ti's government, Wang Mang's programs were stopped by natural disasters that caused crop failures.

The Han Dynasty managed to rule its empire until 220 A.D. By this time the government had become both weak and corrupt. The poor people resented paying taxes and the outlying provinces attempted to break away. Finally weak emperors, peasant revolts, and palace revolutions brought the Han Dynasty to an end.

The Three Kingdoms. Following the collapse of the Han Dynasty, Turkish, Mongol, and Hun raiders began invading China. Many of these tribes stayed in China, intermarried with the Chinese, and adapted to the new culture. During the next 50 years, three major kingdoms replaced the once-powerful empire. There was almost constant warfare between the kingdoms and in 265 A.D., the Ch'in Kingdom conquered the other two. The enlarged kingdom did not last long, however. When it fell, 17 separate dynasties began fighting each other in order to set up a new empire. Of the 17 dynasties, only three were pure Chinese. It was 618 A.D. before the T'ang Dynasty built a new empire in China.

Although early Chinese history was a time of almost constant disruption, including the rise and fall of dynasties, some very real achievements were made in the areas of science. For example, the Chinese developed a printing press with movable type almost 400 years before the Europeans. They perfected a crossbow almost 1,300 years before the Europeans and were using a winnowing machine 1,400 years before the people in Europe.

Elderly women of distinction taught womanly virtues from perfectionist rules. They used books such as Admonitions of the Instructress to the Court Ladies. This text said, "Correct your character as with an ax, embellish it as with a chisel." A lady of the Emperor's court was loyal to her lord above all else. "A husband is heaven, and heaven cannot be shirked," wrote the masters of Chinese culture.

Thousands of paintings on silk paper have been preserved depicting these "Women of Grace." They were skilled in making silk and brocade fabrics, designing and sewing elaborate dresses (all sewing was done by hand), and in painting. The paintings they made centuries ago have helped to capture the spirit of Chinese women so historians could "feel ancient China."

Handscroll, ink on paper drawing from the Yüan dynasty. Early fourteenth century. Used by permission of the Metropolitan Museum of Art, New York.

A Timeline of China's History 220 A.D. - 1644 A.D.

The following timeline reveals the dynasties that came to power in China after the fall of the Han Dynasty in 220 A.D.

Hieu-Ti Dynasty 220 A.D. - 633 A.D.
Leader - Sui Dyn
Major Events - Started canals but was unable to calm
civil strife.

T'ang Dynasty 634 A.D. - 960 A.D.
Major Events - Conquered Turkestan and Korea - Renoum
poets
Li Po and Tu Fu - Invented a movable type
printing press

Sung Dynasty 961 A.D. - 1127 A.D.
Leader - Wang An Shih (a socialist reformer)
Major Events - Invented the magnetic compass and gun powder
Great advancements in printing, painting,
and porcelain

Sung South and Chin North 1128 A.D. - 1260 A.D.
Leader -   Genghis Khan and rival leaders from several
Mongol factions
Major Events - Genghis Khan unites the Mongols against China and
invades in 1211 - Chin is conquered - Kublai Khan
unites China under the Yuan Dynasty - Pax Tatarica
trade routes are established - Genghis Khan dies
in 1227

Yuan Dynasty 1261 A.D. - 1368 A.D.
Leader - Kublai Khan (Genghis Khan's grandson)
Major Events - Kublai Khan's armies finally conquered all of China,
Korea, and parts of Indochina in 1279. Invasion of
Japan by Kublai Khan fails - Marco Polo visits China
Kublai Khan dies in 1294 and the shaky Mongolian
power base begins to crumble - A Chinese rebel
faction seizes Beijing and the Ming Dynasty is born

Ming Dynasty 1368 A.D. - 1644 A.D.
Leader - Hongwu and his son Yunglo
Major Events - The religion of Islam is introduced and spreads
quickly throughout China - China develops its
merchant fleet and expands trade with the west -
Advancements are made in art and exploration -
Emperor Yunglo dies in 1424 and China begins to
become gradually more isolationist - Increasing
civil strife and conflicts with European powers
cause China to drift further into isolationism.

Summary

During the periods of peace between the warring Mongol armies, the Chinese people moved across Asia and made numerous trade contacts with European civilizations. These contacts greatly benefited China and the rest of the world as well.

From China, people in western Eurasia learned about gunpowder, printing, and the compass. Each caused dramatic changes in western Eurasia. The use of gunpowder led to new weapons. Printing revolutionized the spread of knowledge in Europe. The compass encouraged exploration in the search for trade because sailors could navigate even when they could not see the sun or stars.

China also benefited from exchanges with other people. From Egyptians, the Chinese learned how to refine sugar. Carrots, pistachio nuts, grape wine, and a grain called sorghum were introduced to China from western lands.

THE **EARLY MIDDLE AGES**

Projects

1. Research the lives of two early Christian women, such as Clovis I's wife, the king of Kent's wife, or Constantine's mother. Report on the influences they had on the events of history.

2. Make a detailed report on the life of one of the following: Clovis I, Gregory the Great, Charles Martel, or Charlemagne.

3. Do a study on your grandparents' last names. What country did your ancestors come from? Why did they come to America? How do you think they got their last names?

4. Since the building of the Tower of Babel, people have tried to achieve world peace by having one government rule the world. Are there any programs today designed to establish a one-world government? Would such a government be an advantage or disadvantage? Explain.

5. If you were a loyal Muslim, what would you do during a pilgrimage to Mecca? Compare this with what Christians do when visiting Jerusalem.

7. Mohammed founded a new religion and experienced severe persecution. Compare his life and the founding of Islam with the life of Joseph Smith and the founding of the Mormon faith.

8. Write a fiction story about a young person living in the Muslim Empire, or one living on a feudal manor. Include descriptions of family life, customs, and entertainment.

9. Make a cut-away model of a donjon.

Words and Concepts

tallage
tenants-in-chief
fief
Koran
shiek
Donation of Pepin
donjon
liege lord
arabesques
Hegira
lay investiture
Mayor of the Palace
serfs
knight service
muezzins
Islam
Papal States
Pastoral Care
aids
fealty
minarets
Allah
Dark Ages

The Early Middle Ages

Gradually the void resulting from the Fall of Rome was filled by four events that greatly influenced the Middle Ages. They were the rising of kingdoms in Europe, development of the Roman Catholic Church into a great power, development of feudalism, and the founding of a new religion called Islam in the Middle East. These four events dominated European history for more than 500 years and influenced history for almost a thousand years.

European Dark Ages

The collapse of the Roman Empire left a great void in Western Europe. Without an army or police, the people had nowhere to turn for protection. As the Germanic raiders destroyed cities and farms, the people were concerned only with survival. It was definitely not a time for reading, writing, or creating works of art. Most of the culture of the Roman Empire was lost. Thus, this early period of the Middle Ages was formerly referred to by historians as The Dark Ages.

Meanwhile, the Byzantine Empire flourished in Eastern Europe. The Persians were becoming a threat and Byzantine leaders pulled back the empire's eastern boundaries.

Christianity in Medieval Europe

After the fall of the Western Roman Empire, the people in Europe began the slow work of establishing some form of stable government that would give them security. The Roman Church played an important part in the new governments that evolved.

As we have seen, Christianity spread rapidly throughout the Roman Empire and several centers of Christian influence were established. The Coptic Church in Alexandria was the most important center of Christianity on the continent of Africa. Another Christian center arose in India. These churches continued to develop, completely unrelated to and uninfluenced by the other great Christian centers. The Greek Orthodox Church dominated the area controlled by the Byzantine Empire and was responsible for the founding of the Russian Orthodox Church. These Churches, which used the Greek language, continued to affect the world even after the fall of Constantinople to foreign armies.

As a result of the controversial Arian Heresy, beliefs which denied the idea that Jesus was the Son of God spread throughout

The Middle Ages

The Middle Ages refer roughly to that period of time between the Fall of the Roman Empire and the beginning of modern history. Sometimes the term medieval is used instead of Middle Ages.

The Middle Ages, then, is divided into several periods. The very earliest period of the Middle Ages is called the Early Middle Ages which extends from approximately 500 to 1050 A.D. The High Middle Ages extends from about 1050 to 1270 A.D. The Later Middle Ages, including the Renaissance and Reformation periods, lasted from about 1270 to 1660 A.D. Most of the material from here to the end of this volume deals with the Middle Ages.

Europe. Most of the Germanic tribes that became Christian accepted these Arian teachings. For a time it seemed as if these teachings would be the foundation of European Christianity. It was the Roman Catholic Church, however, that became the most important Christian institution during the European Middle Ages. Although this chapter deals almost entirely with the activities of the Roman Catholic Church, it is important to remember that other churches also existed in other parts of the world.

The Frankish Kingdom. We have not mentioned the Franks in discussing the Fall of Rome. This tribe lived far from the Roman borders and was almost untouched by Roman culture. For this reason the Franks were more backward than the Germanic tribes who had lived alongside the Romans for many years. The Franks moved south into the area of Europe that is now France.

Clovis I, of the Merovingian family, became the powerful leader of the Franks. Clovis wanted power and territory, and in order to gain it, he used every weapon that came to his hands. He used marriage alliances, treachery, assassination, and religious conversion to gain his goals.

After killing the other Frankish leaders, Clovis married the niece of the king of Burgundy, thus becoming his ally. In 496 A.D. Clovis declared himself a Christian and joined the Roman Catholic Church. Whether Clovis really became a Christian or not is open to question. Since the other Germanic tribes were Arians, Clovis was able to attack them with the support of the Roman Church. These conquests greatly added to his lands and power.

Clovis sent missionaries with the soldiers into each territory he conquered. He wanted to convert the people to Roman Catholicism.

Growth of the Roman Catholic Church. The Frankish Kingdom was established by Clovis at the same time the Ostrogoths built their kingdom in Italy. When Clovis died in 511 A.D., his kingdom was divided. For the next 50 years, there was a period of feuding between brothers and relatives. It was a time of cruelty, greed, and treachery, drunken kings and vengeful queens. While the Frankish Kingdom was losing strength, the Byzantine armies, sent into Italy by Justinian, destroyed the Ostrogoth Kingdom.

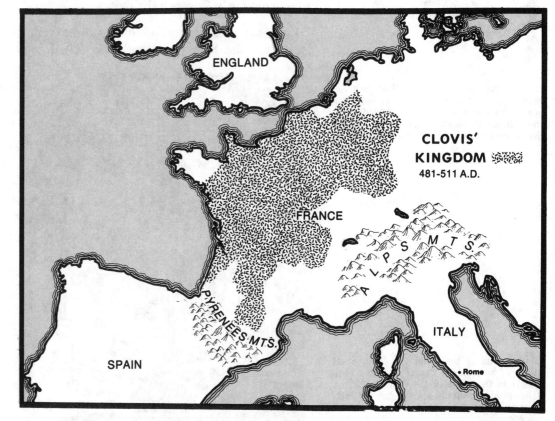

Gregory the Great left a brilliant political career to enter a monastery. As pope, he provided the strong leadership and authority the Roman Catholics needed to survive during the otherwise confusing period of the Middle Ages.

Clovis, chief of the Franks, is baptized at Reins as he joins the Church of Rome. Conquests in the name of the Catholic Church followed his conversion and the shrewd Clovis became a powerful leader of the Frankish Kingdom.

The pope in Rome lost much of his importance when the Byzantine armies conquered Italy, because he was forcefully put under the authority of the patriarch in Constantinople. The only time the pope received help was when Clovis became a Christian and captured the Arian kingdoms around him. The descendants of Clovis were so evil and corrupt, they were of no help to the Church.

Romans still looked to the pope, however, for guidance in their everyday affairs, matters of justice, and protection. Because there was no civil ruler in Rome, the Roman Church needed a strong pope. The Church later found such a leader in Gregory the Great.

Lombard Invasion. The only power left in Italy was the Roman Catholic Church. People

began to look to the pope for duties usually performed by kings. While the Church in Rome was trying to provide some measure of security and hope to the people of Italy, a new barbarian tribe called the Lombards invaded Italy from the north. Italy, already weakened by Byzantine invasions, civil wars, and plagues, was unable to stop these invaders.

The Byzantine emperor had been involved in a long war with the Persians and was too weak to send help to Italy. Thus in 568 A.D., the Lombards gained control of the great plain between the Alps and the Apennines. This area has been called Lombardy ever since.

Gregory the Great. Gregory the Great became pope in 590 A.D. He was a Roman noble who had given up a brilliant political career to enter a monastery. The leaders of the Church realized he had all the qualifications of a strong religious leader. Gregory had self-confidence and a strong will, and it was his desire to make the Roman Church powerful.

Gregory continued all the public works projects in Rome and the surrounding area. When the Lombards threatened to attack, he negotiated a treaty with them and they agreed to leave Rome alone. He announced that the pope was the main authority over all officials in the Roman Catholic Church. The pope had final authority over important church questions and the actions of Christians. He settled quarrels between Church officials and churches.

There were many men working in the churches of the smaller villages and outlying areas. They were unfamiliar with their duties, so Gregory wrote a book called *Pastoral Care* that told them what to do.

Gregory sent missionaries into the areas of Europe that were still backward and pagan. One of these missionaries was St. Augustine of Canterbury. St. Augustine went to England, which became a Roman Catholic country. Learning became so advanced there, that England soon was sending missionaries back to Europe.

When Gregory died in 604, the papacy and the Roman Church became one of the greatest powers of the Middle Ages. Future popes built on the foundation laid by Gregory and became more powerful and had more authority.

The Carolingian Empire

As we have already seen, the descendants of Clovis were wicked, cruel, and poor rulers. They were of little help to their people, spending most of their time in warfare and vices. These rulers became so degenerate as the years passed that they behaved like idiots and were unable to rule. By this time Clovis' kingdom had broken up into many smaller kingdoms. Since the kings were unable to rule, the actual authority for running each kingdom fell to a man known as the Mayor of the Palace.

Mayors of the Palace. The Mayor of the Palace was the king's chief minister. He had authority over all officials in the kingdom and made all the important decisions. He led the soldiers in wars against other kingdoms.

Pepin of Heristal was a Mayor of the Palace for one of the Frankish kingdoms in 687 A.D. He was so successful in leading his armies that all of the Frankish kingdoms were defeated and they united into one kingdom. For 27 years Pepin ruled this kingdom. He held the kingdom together by force, defeating rebellious nobles which added new territory to his master's kingdom.

When Pepin died in 714 A.D., his son Charles was only 20. There were other people who wanted to be Mayor of the Palace so Charles had to fight for the position. He won the name of Charles Martel, "the Hammer," because of his many victories against the rebellious nobles. By 720 A.D. Charles Martel was recognized by everyone as Mayor of the Palace for the Frankish Kingdom.

When Charles defeated the Muslims who were invading Europe from Spain in 732 A.D., he became the hero of Christian Europe. Charles

---

Medieval Surnames

During the Middle Ages people did not have first and last names as we do today. At first they were given only a first name. Later a last name was added to keep people from being confused with other people of the same name. People often were named after their profession, such as Matt the Tailor or Fred the Fowler. Sometimes they were named after some physical characteristic, such as Charles the Fat or Louis the Bald.

When a person's name appears in this text, its English translation follows, set off by commas. For example, Charles Martel, the Hammer, or Frederick Barbarossa, Red Beard. Sometimes men were named after their fathers as in the case of Ted, Eric's son, or were named after their home town, such as Tom of Cambridge. Over the years these names became surnames, which were passed on to their children and their descendants.

sent Christian missionaries from the Roman Church to the territories he conquered to teach Christianity. He learned quickly that the people were easier to govern if they already were Christians. When Charles died in 741, his son Pepin the Short became Mayor of the Palace.

Pepin and the Catholic Church. While Charles Martel was enlarging his master's kingdom, the Roman Catholic Church was having serious problems. The Lombard tribes which had been living peacefully in Lombardy were now invading Italy again and threatening to capture Rome. Pope Stephen III had nowhere to turn for help. He refused to accept the idea that the patriarch of Constantinople had authority over him or the Roman Church. He knew, therefore, that he could not depend on the emperor in Constantinople to send help.

At this time Pepin the Short decided he wanted to be king instead of Mayor of the Palace. He was afraid the nobles would rebel if he declared himself king, so he sent a

Gestures of praise and warm approval are given by the pope's representative as the newly crowned Pepin is declared king of the Franks.

messenger to the pope asking him to decide who should be king. Stephen III, realizing he needed a powerful friend, declared: "It is better that he should be called king who has the power, rather than he who has none." Pepin was crowned Pepin I in Soissons where a representative of the pope annointed him with holy oil.

As soon as Pepin was crowned, the pope asked him to help defend Rome against the Lombards. Pepin realized he owed the pope a favor, and in 756 A.D. he attacked the Lombards. He forced them to give up the stretch of territory that ran across central Italy from Rome to Ravenna. Once he had control of this territory, he presented it to the pope as a gift. The gift was called *The Donation of Pepin* and the territory became known as the *Papal States*. Pepin's donation had a great influence on European history and the history of the Roman Catholic Church.

The rents and other income from the Papal States made the Church independent, rich, and

---

Power of the Pope

When Pepin the Short asked the pope's judgment about who should be king, he conceded that the pope had power over him. He allowed a representative of the pope to anoint him when he was crowned king.

Later kings had major clashes with the pope over the question of whether the pope had the power to decide who could or could not rule a kingdom. These kings claimed they were earthly representatives of God, while popes were only spiritual representatives. The pope claimed the power to appoint kings and depose them.

DONATION OF PEPIN 756 A.D.
PAPAL STATES

Lombards. The Lombards were so terribly defeated by Charlemagne that they no longer were a threat to Rome. Charlemagne then became their king.

In the northern part of Charlemagne's kingdom, a tribe of pagan barbarians, called Saxons, were raiding his territory. It took Charlemagne 32 years, from 772 to 864 A.D., to conquer these people and add them to his kingdom. Like Charles Martel, he brought in missionaries to convert the people to Christianity before allowing them the rights and privileges of citizenship in his kingdom.

While his armies were fighting the Saxons, Charlemagne was busy in other parts of his kingdom. He put down revolts in Aquitaine and Lombardy. He conquered Bavaria and continually raided the Muslims in Spain. He became the overlord of a Mongolian tribe called the Avars who lived in Hungary.

The imposing Charlemagne is pictured here with the orb and other symbols of royalty after being proclaimed Holy Roman Emperor. Charlemagne's vast kingdom, with its many provinces, included most of the countries in Europe.

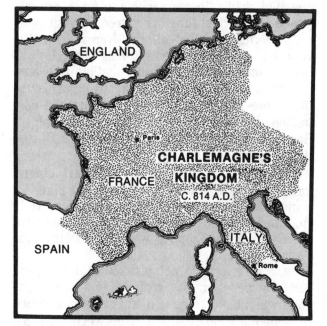

powerful. Since the pope ruled the Papal States as king, he had to be a strong secular ruler as well as a strong spiritual leader. The Papal States belonged to the Roman Church which prevented Italy from becoming a single united country until 1870.

Charlemagne—The Warrior-King. Pepin I's son, Charlemagne (Charles the Great), became king of the Franks in 768 A.D. Charlemagne was a large, active man who led the army well. Like most people in Europe during the Middle Ages, Charlemagne did not know how to write. He could, however, read some Latin and Greek.

After Charlemagne became king, he was called on by the pope to defend Rome from the

---

The Song of Roland

One of the most popular epic poems in the Middle Ages was *The Song of Roland.* This exciting poem tells about one of Charlemagne's raids against the Muslims. During the return from this raid, Roland, one of Charlemagne's best knights, was ambushed and killed before he could be rescued.

There was a great deal of violence and bloodshed after the Fall of Rome. People remembered the time of peace that had come at the height of the Roman Empire. As the Roman Catholic Church exercised its spiritual authority across Europe, people began to question whether a political authority could be reestablished. Charlemagne's efforts brought peace for the first time in hundreds of years.

Charlemagne ruled all the Roman Catholic countries in Europe except England. He was feared and respected by his heathen and non-Christian neighbors. He kept strong control over the nobles in his kingdom. Charlemagne controlled as much territory as the caliph in Baghdad and had more power than the Byzantine emperor.

On Christmas in 800 A.D., as Charlemagne knelt at a mass in Rome, Pope Leo III placed a crown on his head and proclaimed him Holy Roman Emperor. This act officially established the Carolingian Empire, which was named for Charlemagne.

Charlemagne was not pleased that the pope had crowned him. He realized this meant the pope was above kings and emperors in authority. This question of authority between pope and emperors would trouble Europe for hundreds of years. The idea of an empire failed because it was too late to reestablish the Roman Empire.

Life in the Carolingian Empire. Charlemagne, as emperor, was in absolute control of both the government and the Church. He appointed all the bishops and cardinals in the Church, a practice called *lay investiture*. Such appointments by secular rulers later caused a power struggle between popes and the European rulers.

Because he controlled so much territory, Charlemagne was not personally able to keep watch over the empire's government. He appointed counts to rule the separate provinces, which were called counties. To make sure the counts were honest, he sent two men, called *missi dominici,* meaning "those sent by the king." These men were to see that the king's orders were carried out and that everyone received justice. The *missi dominici* were

---

The Holy Roman Empire

When Pope Leo III crowned Charlemagne, he declared this ruler to be the first Holy Roman Emperor. Although Charlemagne's empire broke up shortly after his death, the name Holy Roman Empire was retained.

Rulers throughout the Middle Ages called themselves Holy Roman Emperors. Actually they had little power and they lost what power they did have by fighting Italy and the Roman Catholic Church. Historians jokingly say that the Holy Roman Empire was not holy, Roman, or an empire. The title only added prestige for the person who claimed it.

high-ranking nobles and bishops from the Church. As a result of the good government, there was peace throughout Charlemagne's empire and the common people farmed their lands without fear.

The one thing that concerned Charlemagne was the spiritual condition of the clergy. Many people had joined the Catholic Church out of fear of the rulers or because everyone else in their village had joined. Since there were no schools for the common people, they were unable to read the Bible even if they owned one. Most of

---

Education During the Middle Ages

As we have seen, every civilization had schools attached to their places of worship where the people could be educated. In the Muslim Empire, everyone attended school and the major cities had large public libraries.

In Europe, however, education was not considered important during the early part of the Middle Ages. The only people who learned to read and write were Church leaders. Even nobles and kings did not consider education important. They were more concerned with learning how to fight than with learning how to read. Many rulers of this period could not write their names and had to sign important documents with a mark. In the meantime, Latin was dying out as an everyday language, although the Church continued to use it.

It was not until the middle of the Middle Ages that nobles realized the importance of education for everyone. The common people were then allowed to attend school.

---

these people did not understand what it meant to be a Christian or what was expected of them as Christians. Many brought their old superstitions with them into the Church.

Most of the lower clergy were uneducated and unable to give proper Bible instruction. Charlemagne encouraged the bishops and abbots to establish schools for priests. He started a school in his palace and brought in leading European scholars to teach. The most famous teacher among these was Alcuin, who came from the famous school run by Bede in England. It was in Charlemagne's school that a simplified form of writing, called *Carolingian script,* was developed.

The Collapse of the Carolingian Empire. After Charlemagne's death in 814 A.D., his empire began to break up. There were several reasons why this empire did not survive. The main one was that the empire was too large. It included too much territory and there were people of too many different nationalities and languages to remain united. These people felt loyalty to Charlemagne, but not to their government. When he died and weaker rulers took over control, the peoples' loyalty faded.

A feudal system began to form before Charlemagne became king. But his strong rule kept the nobles under control. Once he was gone, however, the nobles ruled their own territories like kings. They resented any interference in their affairs from the rulers. As the nobles began to fight each other, the Carolingian rulers were unable to control them and the empire grew weaker as a result.

A new danger faced the people living in Europe after Charlemagne's death. The Vikings began raiding Europe's coasts and rivers. Fearless leaders were needed to protect the people from the Vikings. It was at this time,

Abbot in medieval monastery school prepares students for priesthood. Educators were rare and few people were lucky enough to receive an education in the Middle Ages.

This drawing depicts Louis the Pious, ruler of the Carolingian Empire. He ruled after the death of his father Charlemagne and before the vast empire was divided.

however, that the rulers were given names like "Pious," "Fat," and "Simple." We will be studying more about the Vikings in the next chapter. It is necessary at least to mention them now because of the destructive influence they had on the Carolingian Empire.

Before Charlemagne died, he crowned his son Louis the Pious as emperor. He hoped this act would tend to break up the precedent of having the pope crown the emperor. But after Charlemagne's death, Louis went to Rome to be crowned again by the pope.

When Louis the Pious died, his empire was divided among his three sons—Charles the Bald, Louis, and Lothair. Charles the Bald was given the territory that today is France. Louis became king of the territory that is now the nation of Germany. Lothair was made emperor and given the territory in between that of his brothers. The area controlled by Lothair has been absorbed over the years by both France and Germany.

The three brothers were not satisfied with their territory and were constantly at war. Finally in 843 A.D., they signed a peace treaty at Verdun which set up their permanent kingdoms. The Carolingian Empire had come to an end, although Carolingian kings continued to rule these territories for a while longer.

Islam—A New Faith Emerges

During the time when Rome rose to power and fell and Constantinople became the capital of a rich empire, the people in Arabia continued their nomadic life style. Most Arabs were members of tribes which followed their flocks and herds across the deserts in search of grass and water. Sometimes they added to their income by raiding merchant caravans and small settlements. The head of these nomadic tribes

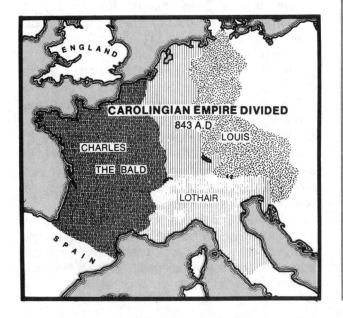

Father of Nations

The forefather of both the Jewish and Arab peoples was Abraham. According to the Hebrew record, Abraham had two sons by different women. Ishmael was the oldest, born of the concubine Hagar. Isaac, the younger, was borne by his lawful wife Sarah when she was 90 years old.

When Ishmael was unable to get along with his brother Isaac, Ishmael and his mother were sent away. Ishmael became the ancestor of the North Arabic peoples and Isaac was the ancestor of the Hebrews. It is interesting to note that the descendants of these two men are still fighting over the possession of the land of Israel today.

was called the *sheik.* He was elected as tribal leader by the head of each family in the tribe.

There were only a few cities in Arabia. The larger ones were located along the major trade routes. People of all faiths mingled in these cities. They were brought together by the riches from the trade in eastern goods. Although some Jewish and Christian merchants came to the cities, the majority of the people in Arabia were pagan. They worshiped many gods and spirits. The most popular spirits were thought to live in trees, wells, and stones.

While Mecca was a trade city, it was different from other Arabian cities. In Mecca there was a large square temple, called the *Kaaba,* which contained a sacred black stone. The Arabs believed the stone was sent from heaven and that many hundreds of pilgrims would come to Mecca to worship it. Since the pilgrims who went to Mecca to worship spent money while they were there, the merchants were eager to have as many people as possible come to the temple.

Mohammed

In 570 A.D. a baby boy was born who later changed the lives of most of the known world. The child's name was Mohammed. He was orphaned while very young and was raised by an uncle. At an early age he began to work in a caravan. When he was 20, he began working for a rich widow named Khadija. Five years later he married her even though she was 15 years older than he. Their marriage was a happy one and they had four daughters.

Mohammed often went alone to a cave where he prayed. One day he returned from the cave and told his wife he had heard a frightening voice tell him he was to be the messenger of *Allah,* his name for God. Mohammed was not sure whether he should believe the voice. But his wife convinced him he was to be a great prophet who would lead the Arabs away from the worship of idols.

The Islam Religion. Mohammed returned to his cave to pray. Each time he went home, he had new information about the religion he was starting. He called the religion *Islam,* which

---

Followers of the Islamic Faith

The followers of the Islam religion prefer to be called Muslims, not Mohammedans. This is because they do not want to imply that they worship Mohammed, Islam's founder.

Mohammed is considered by Muslims as being the last and greatest prophet from heaven. But they do not consider him to be different from any other prophet. Mohammedans, a general term that includes the religion, people, and teachings, is seldom used.

The term Muslim refers to a follower of the faith or a group who conquers and rules in the faith. Sometimes the term Moslem is used to refer to such a person. This name, however, is not preferred by the majority of members of the Islam faith.

It is important to remember that all Muslims are not Arabs, nor do all Arabs adhere to Islam. During the rise of Islam, the people of the Middle East were a Semitic people, called Arabs or Bedouins. But today some Arabs are Christians and other Mideast people are Muslims.

means "surrender to the will of God." Many of his ideas came from Judaism and Christianity, but many of his beliefs were entirely new. A follower of Islam is called a Muslim.

Mohammed taught that there was only one God. He believed that God had sent many prophets to earth to show people how to live in a way that would please Him. Almost all the prophets Mohammed believed in were Jewish. He taught that Jesus, too, was a prophet.

Mohammed believed there were many supernatural beings in the world. He believed in angels, but he also believed in spirits halfway between men and angels which he called *jinns*. Some jinns were supposed to be good and others were evil. He believed that Satan was an evil jinn.

There were five things every good Muslim was supposed to do. Everyday he was supposed to recite the Muslim creed: "I believe there is no god but Allah, and that Mohammed is his prophet." Believers were supposed to pray five times a day, going down on their knees and bowing toward Mecca. Wealthy Muslims carried prayer rugs with them so they would not get dirty while praying. They were also required to fast for one month out of every year. The month of the fast was called *Ramadan*. From sunrise to sunset during that month, no man or beast was allowed to eat or drink anything. All Muslims were required to give alms to the poor and to make at least one trip to Mecca during their lifetime.

Although the Arabs previously had not believed in a life after death, Mohammed taught them to believe in a hereafter. He believed that heaven was a delightful, cool garden with tinkling fountains and many beautiful women. If a man obeyed the five basic rules and did not drink alcohol, he could go there and enjoy all the delights forever. People who did not follow the rules, however, went to a place of scorching winds and black smoke, where there was only boiling water to drink.

When Mohammed began to teach people about his new religion, he was met by persecution. Merchants were afraid the new religion would stop people from coming to the Kaaba, causing them to lose money. At first the only people who accepted his religion were his wife, his cousin,

The Berbers, a Muslim tribe of North Africa, were nomadic peoples, shown here in search of food and water. These nomadic people traveled single file across the desert in companies called caravans. The famed Mohammed may have worked in a very similar caravan in his youth.

and a merchant named Abu-Bakr. Some slaves and poor people also were believers, but the rest of the people in Mecca stepped up their persecution.

The Hegira. Some merchants from a city called Medina did accept Mohammed's teachings and they invited him to come to their city. Since the persecutions in Mecca were getting worse, Mohammed decided to go. He left in secrecy with his few followers. His flight is called the *Hegira,* which means the "breaking of former ties." The Hegira took place in 622 A.D. Muslims designated this date as the beginning of their era, just as Christians started their calendar with the birth of Jesus. Medina was a rich city where good farms and handicraft industry provided adequate incomes. Mohammed's teachings were accepted in Medina. Soon he became the ruler of the city as well as its spiritual leader. His followers grew rich by raiding caravans from Mecca.

Mohammed's Death. Finally in 630 A.D. Mohammed returned to Mecca as the head of an army. One of his first acts was to clear all the idols out of the Kaaba. When the merchants realized that more people than ever would be coming to Mecca as a result of Islam, they stopped fighting it and became Muslim. By the time Mohammed died in 632, most of the Arab tribes had become Muslim. Islam was to become one of the world's three major religions.

Islam and the Muslim Empire

When Mohammed died there was a problem about who should take his place, because no provisions had been made for passing on the leadership. Three men who had been with Mohammed from the beginning claimed the position. They were Ali (Mohammed's cousin who was also married to his daughter, Fatima), Omar and Abu-Bakr. Omar was willing to step aside and support Abu-Bakr, who became the first *caliph,* the name given to Muslim rulers.

Mohammed had not put any of his teachings in writing during his lifetime. So when he died, his followers wrote down everything they could remember about his teachings. One of the first acts of Caliph Abu-Bakr was to have these beliefs compiled into a book called the Koran.

Muslim Conquests. Most of the tribes that had accepted Islam while Mohammed lived, tried to break away from the caliph's political control. After a year of almost constant warfare, Abu-Bakr got most of the tribes to accept his leadership again. He then set out to conquer the world.

The Kaaba in Mecca is the Muslims most holy temple. It houses a sacred black stone believed to have been sent from heaven. It is toward this spot that Mohammed's followers face when praying.

Mohammed's Successor

When a religious leader died, usually there was no need for a power struggle to decide who would replace him. In the case of Mohammed, however, no line of succession had been established. Mohammed is the first religious leader who set out to conquer and add territory to his lands in the name of his religion.

At the time of Mohammed's death, he not only was the spiritual leader of the Muslims, but also the leader of two rich cities and an army of followers. It was necessary to find someone to replace him who could rule the cities and provide spiritual leadership as well. His faithful follower, Abu-Bakr was selected.

The common belief in Islam made a united force out of the once-divided tribesmen. Outside economic and political factors also helped them in their conquest. One of these factors was the continuing armed conflict between the Persian and Byzantine empires which had left both empires weak and exhausted. Another factor was that Byzantine subjects had been taxed so heavily that they welcomed anyone who agreed to free them.

The first city to come under Muslim control was the city of Damascus in Syria which fell in 635. By 640 all of Syria and Canaan were under Muslim control, including the city of Jerusalem. When Abu-Bakr died, Omar became caliph. Under his leadership Persia and Egypt were added to the Muslim Empire.

The Umayyad Dynasty. Following the death of Omar, Ali became caliph. He was assassinated, however, in 655 and a new family began to rule. The new caliph made his office hereditary, setting up the Umayyad Dynasty. The Umayyad caliphs moved the capital of the empire to Damascus.

Muslim conquests continued. In the East they invaded India and controlled territory on the borders of China. In the West the Muslims took over all of North Africa and then conquered Spain. The victorious Muslim armies poured out of the Pyrenees Mountains with all of Europe spread out before them. But they were stopped at the battle of Tours, by a Frankish army led by Charles Martel.

The Muslims were ruthless when they invaded a territory. With the exception of India, however, they made little effort to convert the

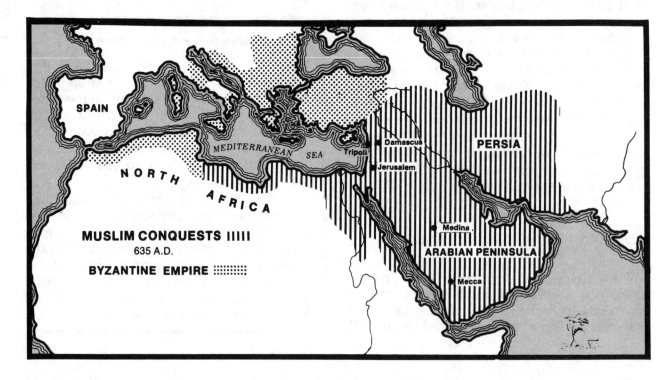

conquered people to Islam. But non-Muslims were not allowed to hold any government office and were taxed heavily. As long as the tax was paid, however, a person could worship as he chose. Many people became Muslim so they would not have to pay the taxes and so they could share in the privileges of holding office. The people in India were treated more harshly because they were pagan, rather than Christian or Jewish. We will be studying this subject in more detail in Chapter 14.

Abbasid Dynasty. By 750 A.D. the Muslim Empire had reached its height and people of many different races were citizens. These people resented the fact that the Umayyad Caliph gave special privileges to the Arabs. Finally a man, named Abbas, a descendant of Mohammed's uncle, overthrew the Umayyad

caliph and started the Abbasid Dynasty.

The Abbasid caliphs moved the capital to Baghdad, one of the world's richest cities.

Islam was a warlike faith, promising the delights of heaven to warriors killed in holy war. Here we see Muslim warriors clashing their scimitars before leaving to conquer North Africa.

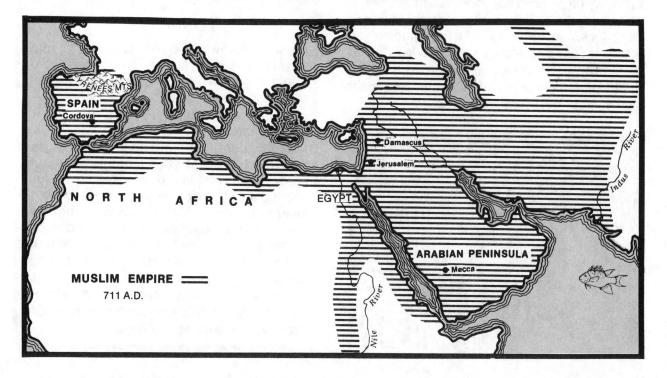

SPAIN
Cordova

PYRENEES MTS.

Damascus

Jerusalem

NORTH   AFRICA   EGYPT

Indus River

ARABIAN PENINSULA

Mecca

Nile River

MUSLIM EMPIRE ===
711 A.D.

There they set up a court similar to the ceremony and splendor of the old Persian court. The officials in this new government came from all different races in the empire.

The greatest Abbasid caliph was Haroun Al Rashid. He was the caliph written about in the *Arabian Nights*. His empire stretched from central Asia to the Atlantic Ocean. But the empire became too large to handle and after Haroun Al Rashid died, it began to split up.

In Spain the ruler, known as an *emir,* was a member of the Umayyad family. Seeing his chance, he broke away from the empire declaring himself caliph of Cordova. In Egypt a member of Fatima's family became caliph of Cairo.

The Abbasid Dynasty continued to rule for almost a hundred years. Then in 945 A.D., a new authority threatened its power. A warlike people known as the Seljuk Turks became Muslims. They took charge of the Muslim Empire just before it fell. For a time they allowed the Abbasid caliphs to continue on the throne as puppet rulers. But the Turks actually ruled and made all the major decisions.

Like an empty stage awaiting a scene from the *Arabian Nights,* this mosque in Cordova, Spain, serves as a reminder of the conquering Muslim caliphs. It was built on the site of a Gothic cathedral and today contains a museum.

Under Turkish leadership the city of Jerusalem was recaptured. This event caused the Christians in Europe to unite and go to the Middle East during the Crusades to free Jerusalem. We will study the Crusades in a later chapter.

The Muslim Influence. The Muslims have greatly influenced the history of the rest of the world. Muslim merchants were the middlemen for trade between the tribes in Africa's interior and people of the Roman and Byzantine Empires. By making the interior of Africa seem dangerous and mysterious, they prevented European interest in this continent for centuries.

Whenever the Muslims took over a civilization, they adopted much of its culture. The

---

Alchemy

Muslim knowledge of chemistry and physics resulted largely from their continuing search for a secret method of changing base metals into gold. This process of altering metals into gold is called *alchemy.*

Many people during the Middle Ages believed there was such a magic or secret process for making gold. The craze for finding an inexpensive way to make gold swept Europe. Many clever chemists swindled rich patrons out of fortunes by pretending to know the secret. Throughout history people have spent time searching for a way to get something for nothing. There always have been clever extortionists waiting to cheat anyone who is too greedy to be wise and honest.

Muslims became very interested in education, and there were schools attached to the Muslim mosques. In primitive areas where population was sparse, students learned to read and write Arabic, studied the Koran, and learned basic arithmetic. In the large cities, where more money was available for teachers, students also studied literature, logic, philosophy, law, algebra, astronomy, medicine, and other sciences.

The Muslims became known for their intellectual abilities. They invented spherical trigonometry. In astronomy the Muslims developed new methods for studying the stars. They excelled in chemistry and physics and knew more than 1,400 different drugs.

One of the greatest contributions the Muslims made to the world was the use of Arabic numerals, such as 1, 2, 3, that we use today. The Muslims did not invent these numerals, but took the idea from India and passed it on to Europe. Until the Arabic numerals were available, people had to use Roman numerals, like I, II, III. It was very difficult to do complicated arithmetic problems using Roman numerals.

Another thing the Muslims did that greatly influenced European history was to save and translate many of the ancient Greek and Hellenistic works that otherwise would have been lost. Many of these works later found their way into Europe where they had an important influence on thought.

The Muslims produced many books and there were large public libraries in the major cities. Beautiful prose and poetry was written in Arabic which became the official language of the Muslim Empire. Two of the most famous works are *The Rubaiyat* by Omar Khayyam, a famous mathematician, and *The Arabian Nights.*

The mosques built by the Muslims followed the design of Mohammed's house in Medina. The most noticeable feature of mosques is the tall slender *minarets,* pencil-like towers which rise at each corner of the building. Five times a day special criers, called *muezzins,* stood at the tops of these towers to call out when it was time to pray.

The Muslims followed strictly the Bible commandment against making any carved idols. There are no figures of any living creatures in their art. They copied the idea of mosaics from Byzantine culture, using complex designs of interwoven lines and geometrical patterns, called *arabesques.* Sometimes they used language symbols as designs and, in some mosques the ceiling is covered with selections from the Koran.

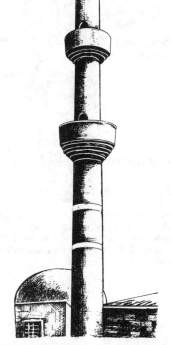

A minaret is a tall, slender tower projecting from an Islamic mosque. From its balconies a crier calls the people to prayer five times a day.

Wherever Muslim warriors went, they destroyed synagogues and churches or "converted them" into mosques. This is the minaret that Muslems built on top of the church in Joppa.

Islamic quotations are inscribed on the interior of the Dome of the Rock in Jerusalem. The decorative circular inscriptions, forming a complex design, include verses from the Koran.

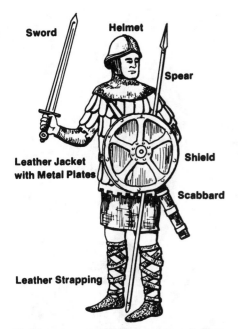

Sword

Helmet

Spear

Leather Jacket
with Metal Plates

Shield

Scabbard

Leather Strapping

Early armor consisted of a heavy leather jacket covered by metal plates. It only covered the upper body. It was not until the middle of the Middle Ages that full suits of armor were used.

Each time the Muslims captured a new city, they turned local churches and synagogues into mosques. They took down all images and pictures and painted whitewash over the beautiful frescoes. The most beautiful Muslim art objects today are jewelry, ceramics, carpets, carved ivory, and tooled leather.

It was not long before Islam became one of the world's major religions. It spread from the Arabian peninsula to Syria, Mesopotamia, Egypt, Persia, Asia Minor, Spain, Sicily, northern India, Indonesia, the Philippines, and North Africa. **Today more than 300 million people are Muslims.** The Muslim countries own some of the world's greatest natural resources, including a large percentage of the world's oil.

Muslim Muezzins

Five times a day faithful Muslims are supposed to stop whatever they are doing, bow toward Mecca, and pray. To help the faithful remember when it is time to pray, muezzins call out of their towers, summoning the people to prayer.

The call is always the same: "Allah is most great! I testify there is no god but Allah; I testify Mohammed is the messenger of Allah. Come to prayer; come to salvation (security); Allah is most great! There is no god but Allah!"

This cry is still heard in Muslim cities today. In some cases modern recorders and public address systems are used.

Feudalism

The feudal system emerged at the end of Charlemagne's rule. Europe was divided into fortified manors, each trying desperately to survive in a world of violence. Although there were some differences in the way the feudal system worked in different parts of Europe, **generally it was the same everywhere.**

A Warlike Society

Basically this was a warlike society and the best way to survive was to fight better than anyone else. When there was peace, the knights spent their time practicing the arts of war. They spent hours swinging their swords against huge, upright chopping posts or riding to the joust (knocking each other off horses with a long lance).

The System. Each nobleman was given territory to rule for the king. Before receiving his territory, or *fief,* the noble was required to swear an oath of *fealty,* or loyalty, to the king. In this oath, the noble promised to remain loyal to the king and to raise an army to help him if he went to war. The number of men that each noble was required to supply, called *knight service,* depended on the size of his fief. In exchange for the oath, the king agreed to let the noble remain in control of his territory and to protect him if he were attacked.

These nobles, also called *tenants-in-chief,* gave sections of their land to knights to hold and protect for them. Each knight had to promise the noble, who became his *liege lord,* that he would fight in his army if the noble were attacked or asked to send an army to the king. If the knight received a large fief, he might be required to furnish knight service to his lord for additional men. He might divide his fief, giving some of it to another knight, or he might have a knight promise loyalty in exchange for room and board.

If a liege lord or his son was captured in war, his sworn men were required to furnish *aids,* or money for the ransom of the captured man. Aids also were provided when the lord wanted to marry off his daughters or provide his sons with their first set of armor.

The *serfs,* or peasants, lived on the land and were not allowed to leave. If the fief was sold or given to another person, the serfs went with it. The serf had allegiance only to the knight or lord directly over him. The serfs furnished their lord with food for his castle, fodder for his animals, labor on his projects (usually one day a week or month), and men for his armies. There were so many petty wars going on that often the only people available to plant and harvest the crops were the women, children, aged, and crippled.

In exchange for these services, the lord provided protection for his serfs from outlaw knights and roving bands of thieves who looted the farms and raped the women. Under this system there was very little individual freedom. Everyone knew what his duties and responsibilities were and stayed in his place.

The nobles enjoyed riding to the hunt for entertainment. There were plenty of wild boar, deer, wolves, and foxes in the woods. To make certain there was always plenty of game, serfs were forbidden to kill any game on the lands of their lord, not even rabbits. Serfs often were executed, branded, or maimed by having a hand or eye removed as punishment for hunting on their lord's lands. The punishment was so terrible that people disobeyed only when there was a crop failure and their family was starving.

Another popular entertainment was the tourney. Both nobles and peasants gathered to watch as knights showed off their skills at war. Although there were rules to protect the fighters who fought with blunted lances, many good men were killed or wounded in this sport.

The Manor. Most people during the Middle Ages lived on manors which provided a living for both peasants and nobles. Most manors were completely cut off from contact with the outside world. They produced flax and wool, food, and tanned leather. Usually the only items brought in from the outside were iron, salt and millstones for grinding flour. An average manor usually had about 141 ha (350 acres) of farmland, including meadows, woods,

In the warlike society that emerged after Charlemagne's death, dangerous events, called *tourneys,* were staged to entertain the nobles and test the strength and ability of the combatants. Here two knights swing their deadly maces as they attack.

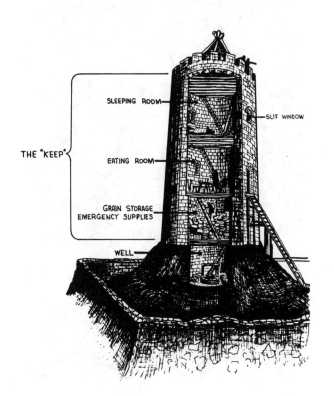

THE "KEEP"

SLEEPING ROOM

SLIT WINDOW

EATING ROOM

GRAIN STORAGE
EMERGENCY SUPPLIES

WELL

This cross-section of a medieval donjon resembles a modern silo. These towers were cramped, cold, and uncomfortable, but they provided protection against attack. The extra knights slept in the eating room, while the lord of the manor and his wife used the sleeping room.

wasteland, and the lord's private farmland. The lord's castle was usually located in the center of the manor. The village houses were built close to the castle walls as if for protection. There was always a village church, a home for the priest, and a graveyard.

The lord's family life centered around the castle. At first they had simply wooden blockhouses. By the 1000s a stone tower called the *donjon* was built. It was not until the 1100s and 1200s that huge stone castles were built.

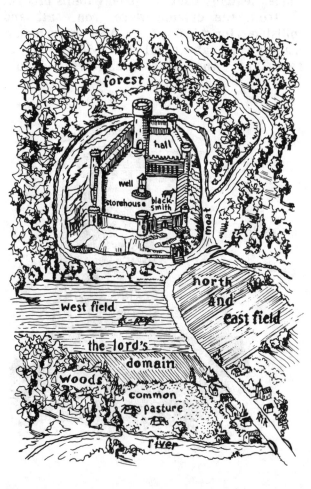

A typical manor during the Middle Ages produced everything necessary to accommodate both peasants and nobles. The lord's castle was in the center of the manor. The woods and pasture were often used by everyone on the manor. All serfs were expected to work on the lord's domain.

The donjon, in the center of the fortress, was surrounded by storerooms, workshops, and a chapel. Usually the fortress was surrounded by a *moat,* a deep ditch filled with water. The moat could be crossed by way of a drawbridge which could be pulled up in time of danger.

Life inside a castle was very uncomfortable. There were no windows to let in the warmth of the sun, and the heavy stone walls were damp and cold. Chilly drafts blew through the large rooms. The only heat came from massive fireplaces which often left smoke in the rooms. Heavy draperies were hung on walls and over doorways to cut down on the chill.

Rugs were not used as floor coverings by Europeans until after the Crusades. Until then sweet-smelling grasses, called *rushes,* were spread across the floors. The rushes were changed once or twice a year. In the main room, which was used as a dining room, bones and scraps were thrown to the floor for the dogs. Fleas, lice, and the odor of rotten food were often concealed by a layer of fresh rushes and herbs that were crushed and sprinkled over the floor.

Because of drafts, lack of plumbing, and other problems, people did not bathe more than once every three to six months. These unhealthy conditions and the constant warfare typical of this period resulted in shorter life spans among the people. A man in his forties was considered to have lived a long, full life.

The peasants' cottages had thatched roofs. They usually had one room with a table and bench. Cooking was done over a fireplace. Each cottage had a small vegetable patch, chicken yard, haystack, and stable.

The peasants were divided into two classes: serfs and freemen. Serfs were confined to the manor and forbidden to leave without the lord's permission. Their children were born serfs and there was no way to get out of this class. As long as the serf performed all his duties properly, however, he could not be evicted from his home. The lord provided a court where the serf could bring problems involving fellow serfs.

A free person paid cash rent for his land. If he did not want to perform his required work on the lord's land, he was allowed to hire someone else to do it. If he wanted to leave the manor, he merely had to find someone the lord approved of to take over his land.

The peasants provided for the manor in three ways. First, they donated up to three days labor a week for projects such as repairing ditches, bridges, and the manor. They plowed, sowed, and harvested the lord's fields before caring for their own. Second, they paid *tallage,* a tax that went to the lord. This was usually farm produce since money was difficult to come by in those days. Third, the peasants had to pay the lords for using their facilities. The lord owned the oven for baking bread, the grain mill for grinding flour, and the wine and cider presses.

Each serf had his own piece of farmland, but pastures and woods were owned by the entire village. Pigs were allowed to run free in the woods where they fed on acorns. There was a limit on how many pigs each person was allowed to feed there. Peasants were allowed to gather dead wood from the forest but they could not cut down trees.

Farming was done with very crude instruments and people did not get such large crop yields as we do today. The manor provided for everyone, as well as allowing the lord and his family to have a few luxuries. The peasants were never able to own many belongings. The peasants' lives were hard and they were "old" people, worn out by hard work, by the time they reached their thirties.

The End of Feudalism. As you study the next chapters, you will see that things got more complicated toward the end of the Middle Ages. The authority of the Church decreased and men were no longer afraid to break their oaths. In their greed to control as much land as possible, men began to swear loyalty to more than one lord.

Serfs, after traveling outside their countries to fight in the Crusades and foreign wars, returned home with new ideas. They were no longer content to be tied to the land, with little more than the rank of a slave. They had seen foreign places with wonderful luxuries and they wanted some of these things for their families.

A merchant class developed to furnish trade goods and foreign luxuries. Kings began taxing the merchants and using the money to hire soldiers. Once the kings had their own armies, they were able to break down the power of the large landholding nobles. During the height of feudalism, the nobles were often more treacherous than the kings. They constantly fought with one another which prevented strong nations from forming. By the end of the Middle Ages, feudalism had become a thing of the past. Strong nations of people who supported their king and were proud of their countries were developing.

The church of St. Nicholas represented early Christianity in Asia. Christians accepted the responsibility to take the message of Christianity--the personal relationship with Christ as Savior--to cultures around them. As people became believers in Christ, they built places of worship like this one for fishermen on an island in the Aegaean Sea. Most of the first churches were small because the Christian leaders believed that each local community should have a place of worship. Since travel was mostly done on foot, Christians built many "neighborhood churches."

Projects

1. Do a study on Stonehenge in England. Who built it? How and why was it built? What have scientists discovered about it?

2. Give a report on the life of one of the following: Queen Boudicca, St. Patrick, Olaf Tryggvesson, Eric the Red, or Lief Ericson.

3. Research several nursery rhymes. Write out the rhymes and give their historical or political meaning.

4. Make a scale model or sketch of a Viking ship.

5. Read the story of *Arthur and the Knights of the Round Table* or *Tristan and Iseult.* Tell how the people's customs and way of life in these stories differ from the history you have learned about this period.

6. Research the lives of William the Conqueror (before he invaded England) and King Harold Godwinson. What gave these men a claim to the English throne? What is your opinion of Harold's promise to William? What importance did Harold's brother have on English history? Do you like William or Harold the best? Why?

7. Do a study of the history of Greenland. The Norse were the first people to settle in Greenland. What happened to this Norse settlement? What nationality of people live there today? Draw a map showing glacier areas.

8. Find and draw at least three coats of arms. Write a report on the meaning of each one.

9. Give a report on the life of one of the following: Benedict, Bernard of Clairvaux, or Francis of Assisi. What was his background? How did he become a Christian? Tell interesting stories about your subject. What became of him?

Words and Concepts

hawking
druids
hypocrites
squire
berserkers
Saxons
Danelaw
illuminations
favor
page
" i viking"
Angles
Alfred of Wessex
convent
herald
chivalry
rickets
fjords
monastery
coat of arms
Althing
Celts

England, the Norsemen, and the Age of Chivalry

England has been mentioned, up to this point, only in connection with the history of other periods and civilizations. The development of England into a modern nation is most important to us because the English laid the foundation for American democracy. It is also important to examine England's political system to see how it differed from the rest of Europe. This chapter will take us from the Roman period through the High Middle Ages.

The Norsemen, or Vikings, who made their homes in the Scandinavian countries of Denmark, Norway, and Sweden between 700 and 800 A.D. will also be studied in this chapter. They were vital to Russian history as we have learned. Here we will examine the important part they played in European history and in settling Iceland and Greenland.

While England struggled as a nation, the Vikings raided the coastal areas of northern and western Europe. European learning and education during this time were confined largely to monasteries. There the monks copied and preserved many fine manuscripts which might otherwise have been lost. They managed, generally, to keep education alive in this confusing period of history.

The Catholic Church took an interest in the European feudal system and began to impose a strict moral code on the nobility sometime about 500 A.D. It was an attempt to make Christian knights out of Germanic tribal warriors. The result was a code of chivalry that set the pattern for the more refined society of the Middle Ages.

The Development of England

Several hundred islands, separated from Europe by a narrow strip of water called the English Channel, make up the British Isles. There are two main islands in the group. One is Ireland and the other is Great Britain, which includes Scotland to the north, England to the south, and Wales on the west coast. The peoples and cultures of each of these areas have developed independently. Even today the various peoples of the British Isles have different physical characteristics and accents. Our attention in this section will be focused primarily on the area of England.

England has a temperate climate with heavy rainfalls and thick fogs. Geographic separation from the rest of Europe has influenced England's history, but it has not protected her from invasion.

Early Settlers of England

From the early days of the Mesopotamian civilizations, Phoenician sailors traveled to Britain where they traded luxury items for tin. When the Roman Empire expanded, Roman soldiers set up a province there.

The Celts. When the Romans arrived in Britain, they found it populated with dark-complexioned people called Celts. The country was divided among several Celtic tribes who were constantly fighting each other.

The early Celts had a unique religion. They worshiped many gods, but they did not carve statues of them. Instead of worshiping in temples, they worshiped in forest groves. Their religious leaders were called *druids*. They had tremendous influence as teachers, medicine men, priests, and judges. Since the Celts did not have a written language, Celtic children were required to memorize long rituals. These were passed down from generation to generation.

The Romans. For the most part, the Romans had no trouble starting a province in Britain. Garrisons were set up along these frontiers to protect the rest of the province from raiders. There were a few uprisings, however, and some tribes on the frontiers never accepted Roman rule.

Roman citizens arrived in Britain about 50 B.C. and started building towns in the Roman style. The homes had running water and all the other conveniences developed by the Romans. They improved the Celts' farming techniques and as a result, the Celts enjoyed an improved standard of living.

Good trade relations were established between Britain and the rest of the Roman Empire. As Christianity was brought into Britain during the 300s A.D., most of the Celts dropped

---

British Druids and Caesar

While Julius Caesar was fighting the Germanic tribes in Gaul, he wrote down many interesting facts about their way of life. He reported that the druids he found in Gaul had been trained in Britain. This could mean that the area of Britain was once a religious training center for priests of the Germanic tribes in Europe. The practice of sending Germanic priests to Britain stopped after the Roman conquest. Without written records, however, we will probably never know for certain the details as to the importance of early Britain in this matter.

The Legend of King Arthur

A British leader named Aurelius Ambrosianus was a Roman. Many historians believe that he is the legendary knight, King Arthur. Ambrosianus freed England from the grip of the Anglo-Saxon invaders when he won the Battle of Badon. Legend states that King Arthur did not die and whenever England is in terrible danger, he returns to defend them.

---

their pagan religion to become Christian. Schools were established in Britain and peace was enforced under Roman rule. This made Britain one of the most pleasant areas in the Roman Empire to live.

When the Roman Empire began to decline, barbarian tribesmen threatened Rome. The soldiers stationed in Britain returned to Rome to protect their homeland. The Celts could not understand why the Romans were deserting them. They thought they were leaving them to the mercy of the vicious Picts and Scots in the north. These fierce warriors began attacking towns and farms, and the rich culture started by the Romans collapsed.

The Celts did not understand the workings of the water system and other modern conveniences built by the Romans. As these things broke down or were destroyed by raiders, they were not repaired. Soon many towns were left deserted.

The Saxon-Angles Invasion. In an effort to protect his people, the Celtic King Vortigern hired some mercenaries in 449 A.D. from the Saxon lands in Europe to help him. When the Saxons arrived, they discovered Britain was

A determined Queen Boudicca, the Celtic leader, guides her chariot forward in the march against the Romans in 61 A.D. Despite her valiant efforts, the Celts lost in their effort to win their freedom.

Clannish Celts from ancient Britain are bundled against the cold and dressed warmly in fur leggings.

Ethelbert, the king of Kent who was married to a Christian, gives his consent to Augustine to spread the gospel of Christ throughout the kingdom. It was not until later that the king himself converted to Christianity.

rich and defenseless. They sent word to this effect back to Europe. Soon a full-scale invasion against the Celts was started by the Saxons and their European neighbors, the Angles. They fought to the death against the weaker Celts.

The Christian Celts withdrew to the area known as Wales. There a training center evolved for Christians from Ireland. The Irish trained missionaries in Wales and sent them into Scotland.

Christianity Arrives in England

The Angles and Saxons gained control of Britain. A society was established similar to that of the Germanic tribes in Europe before the invasion of Rome as discussed earlier. The Angles named the island Angleland, from which the name of England came.

The people of England became known as Anglo-Saxons. Those who settled there had contacts with Christians in Europe, but they kept their own pagan religion. In 597 A.D. a Christian missionary named Augustine of Canterbury was sent to England by the pope.

St. Patrick of Ireland

A man named St. Patrick is said to have established Christianity in Ireland. As a young British lad, Patrick was captured and carried off to Ireland as a slave. He was freed and later returned to Ireland as a Christian missionary, turning people away from their pagan beliefs. St. Patrick set up churches and organized the area so that Christian beliefs were able to spread even when the Fall of Rome cut them off from contact with other Christians.

England Becomes Christian

The influence of Christianity in England has been told in a legend about Pope Gregory and St. Augustine. It tells of a group of English boys who were standing on the platform of a Roman slave market. Unlike the dark-haired, dark-skinned Italians and Greeks, the boys were blond and fair. A monk named Gregory saw them and was amazed at their light coloring. When he asked who they were, he was told they were Angles. He replied, "Not Angles, but Angels."

When Gregory learned their country was heathen, he resolved to do all he could to win it to Christianity. He was unable to go because he was appointed pope, so he sent St. Augustine to England in his place. As a result, the legend suggests England became a Christian nation.

England's Christian Kings. The most powerful ruler in England at that time was Ethelbert, the king of Kent. He had married a Frankish princess from Europe who was a Christian. For this reason, Ethelbert gave Augustine and his missionaries permission to teach Christianity throughout his kingdom. Soon the king and enough of his people were baptized and Kent became a Christian country.

When King Edwin, the much-loved king of Northumbria, became a Christian, his people followed his example. The non-Christian kingdoms fought the Christian kingdoms for more than 50 years until the island became Christian.

Culture Flourished. Then for almost 100 years, while Europe was caught up in civil wars and bloody feuds, England enjoyed a period of peace. A rich culture, centered around the Christian religion, developed. Beautiful churches were built and schools established. We have already seen that Charlemagne summoned the most famous teacher in England to run his school in the Frankish Kingdom in the late 700s. English civilization was one of the best in all of Europe until 793 A.D. Then the peace was shattered by the first of many destructive Viking raids.

The Norsemen of Scandinavia

In the north of Europe are the Scandinavian countries. They consist of two peninsulas: one is Denmark, pointing north; the other includes Sweden and Norway, pointing south. Most of the Norway-Sweden peninsula is covered by the rugged Kholen Mountains that rise to 2.1 km (7,000 feet). In Norway these mountains begin at the coast. For this reason not more than two-thirds of Norway is habitable. Sweden has fewer mountains than Norway. It has a wide, fertile coastal plain where cattle, sheep, and goats are raised.

Since Norway is so far north, the sun does not set there for two months during the summer. This may sound like fun, but the situation is reversed in the winter. Then the sun does not shine at all for two months. Since the land is not suitable for farming, the people have been forced to resort to other means of earning a living. They do have an abundance of natural resources of timber and ore. Therefore, wood pulp, paper products, and metals are among Norway's major export items. Norway also has a thriving fishing industry.

Denmark is a flat, sandy peninsula. Although the land is not good for farming, Denmark is one of the leading producers of dairy and livestock products in the world. The Danish also rely heavily on fishing as a means of earning a living.

The Early Norsemen

Many historians believe the Norsemen were descendants of Japheth. As you will recall, Japheth was Noah's son whose descendants migrated north from the Middle East about 4000 B.C. As we know, this was during the time when most of Europe was covered by giant glaciers. glacier.

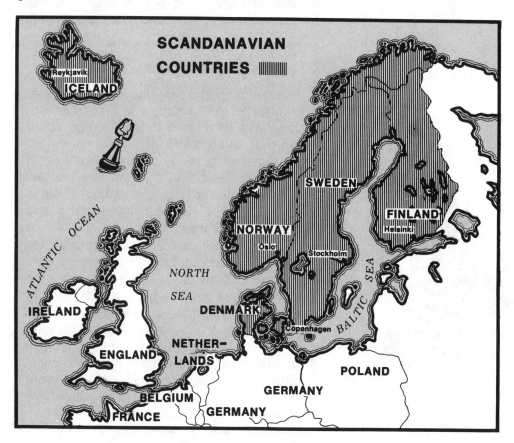

Lapland, the "land of the midnight sun." Laplanders trapped and fished in lakes and used reindeer to transport their goods. Reindeer also provided meat and milk for their diet.

A Viking man with jutting chin was crudely carved from an elk's antler.

Conditions were extremely hard for these northbound peoples. They were cut off from other groups and their tools and equipment soon wore out. They had only crude implements made of petrified wood and stone. At first they lived in caves. Later, as the glacier began to melt, Japheth's descendants moved farther north to Germany and are apparently the same Neanderthal peoples found by nineteenth century archaeologists.

As time passed and the glacier disappeared gradually, Neanderthal descendants moved northward into Scandinavia. There they built underground homes, but before long they built homes from trees. They also found metals in the

Neanderthal Living Conditions

In examining the remains of Neanderthal men found in Germany and France, scientists have been able to learn much about their living conditions and physical characteristics. X-ray techniques show us that even the children of the Neanderthal society suffered from crippling arthritis and rickets, a disease that softens and deforms the bones.

Undoubtedly such afflictions account for their stooped posture and uneven gait. Probably both diseases were common among these peoples because of poor diet and weather conditions in which they lived during the Ice Age period. Moreover, creationist scientists believe the Neanderthals were normal human beings, crippled by their environment. They were not a sub-human race as evolutionists believe.

ground to make better tools. These early Scandinavians, the Neanderthal descendants, were the people we call the Norsemen.

Norse Culture. About 2000 B.C. the Norsemen built sturdy boats. Animals and fish were their major sources of food, clothing, and shoes. Someone invented the idea of snowshoes, skis, and sleds to help them travel during the long, cold winters. Reindeer and dogs were tamed and used to pull sleds. Pictures they drew on the walls of their caves during the long winter nights still can be seen today. They carved figures in bone and made cups out of soft stone before they learned to make pottery.

Norsemen were allowed to have more than one wife at a time. As a result, families grew too large to survive on their small farms. When extra mouths to feed caused a hardship for the rest of the family, many children died from exposure.

Life was not completely grim, however. The Norse were a hearty, boisterous people and even when living conditions were hard, they often played hard and drank heavily. They enjoyed sports like wrestling and boxing that allowed them to compete in physical fitness. A favorite sport was running along a row of oars on their ships without falling into the icy waters of the *fjords,* the narrow inlets of water along the Norse coasts.

As people migrated into the Scandinavian countries, ships became important. They used them not only for fishing trips, but also for trade with peoples living south of them. We already know Swedish Norsemen traveled to Russia where they played an important role in Russian history. At the same time traders returned from England with reports of riches on the unprotected island.

The square sail was added to Norse ships at this time, and the sides were raised to carry heavier loads on open seas for long distances. They were able to navigate a great distance from the land and return to shore in the same spot. They had no equipment for navigation because it had not yet been invented. It is still a mystery how they managed to keep from getting lost.

The Vikings

Some Norsemen sailed to other territories where they attacked and looted the people. These men were called Vikings. The word Viking comes from the term "to go i viking" which means "to go raiding." Not all Norsemen were Vikings, however. There were many Norsemen who preferred trade and exploration to the uncertainties of the Viking raids.

The first Viking raids began in the early 700s.

An aging member of a monastery, armed only with a cross, defends against a sudden attack of Viking raiders. A field worker comes to his aid with a pitchfork. Churches and monasteries were constantly raided for their treasures during the Middle Ages.

Before long, these fierce raiders were attacking the unprotected coasts of Europe and England. For the most part, the Vikings were more interested in plunder than in conquering territory. The raiding bands were usually small, consisting of only three or four ships. They sailed up rivers and attacked places that did not have walls or armies to protect them. Monasteries with golden treasures in their chapels were favorite targets.

If the Vikings were faced with a defending army, they simply returned to their ships and found another place to raid. It was not a matter of being afraid, it was just that there were so many other places that could be raided without a fight. When a raid was successful, the plunder was thrown into the boats. If there was enough room, they also took the women and children and sold them as slaves.

Sometimes there were men, called *beserkers,* in a crew. These men would become temporarily insane while in battle. They would throw away their shields and armor, wade into the thick of the enemy, and try to kill everyone. Sometimes while traveling in the boat, a beserker felt a fit of insanity coming on. His friends would put him ashore so he could run wild, smashing trees with a sword or battle-axe until it passed. We do not know for certain what caused these fits, but most likely they resulted from the violent Viking life style.

The people of England and Europe learned to fear the quick lightning-like Viking raids. In fact, a prayer was added to the regular daily service of the Catholic Church which said: "From the fury of the Northmen, Oh Lord deliver us."

At first the Vikings planned their raids around their farming schedule. They planted crops

Friends with the sea, Norsemen voyagers were able to chart their course with the help of compasses such as this one.

The sleek design of this Viking ship shows the skill of the sea-going men who built these mighty vessels and sailed them across the Atlantic to America.

Alfred, king of Wessex, fought the Vikings throughout his reign. Late in the ninth century, he finally drove them out of West England.

The oldest existing Norwegian *stave*, or wood church, was built about 1050. By the beginning of the tenth century, Christianity was well established in this area and kings campaigned for more churches. The church shown here was built in 1250.

before they went raiding and then returned in time to harvest them before going out again. Later the raiders built special fortified areas in Europe where they spent the winter. It was only a matter of time before Viking attacks turned from looting raids into raids of conquest.

Viking Raids in England. In 865 Danish Vikings landed in England and began the conquest of that country. They soon controlled all of the eastern and northern parts of England. When they invaded western England, an area called the kingdom of Wessex, they were stopped by a strong king named Alfred of Wessex. Alfred fought off Viking raids during most of his reign. In 878, however, after a successful surprise attack by the Vikings, he was forced to hide in a swamp and use guerrilla warfare tactics.

Alfred was finally able to drive the Vikings out of his kingdom, but they kept control of the northeast portion of England, called the *Danelaw*. In this territory Danish customs and laws were used. Norse settlers then poured in by the scores.

The Vikings almost destroyed education and learning in England. You will remember that the English were more advanced than the rest of Europe in their schools and in the practice of Christianity. Major learning centers were located in the monasteries, which were major Viking targets as previously mentioned.

When Alfred became king, he set up a school to train the clergy, but was able to find only four educated people in his entire kingdom. Thus Alfred started a revival in learning that lasted many years after his death. Because of his victories against the Vikings and his achievements in reestablishing English learning, Alfred has gone down in history as King Alfred the Great.

He is the only English monarch to be given this title.

One of the most important results of the Viking raids in England was that Olaf Tryggvesson, the king of Norway, became a Christian while raiding England. He then returned to Norway and was responsible for both Iceland and Greenland becoming Christian countries.

In 1016 after years of fighting against the Vikings, the English asked Canute, the Danish king and ruler of the Danelaw, to be their king. He was a wise ruler, but after his death the English chose an Englishman as king. The stage was being set for the final invasion of England by a foreign power.

"London Bridge Is Falling Down"

Almost every child learns the nursery rhyme called, "London Bridge is Falling Down." This rhyme was written during the time of Viking raids on England. At that time Ethelred the Redeless (Unready) was king of England. Undoubtedly he was the most incompetent king ever to rule. He was so cowardly that when the Vikings attacked, he ran away, Olaf Tryggvesson, the king of Norway, gave him an army to drive away the Danes.

When Olaf's men tried to reach London in 1012, however, they could not get their ships past the London Bridge. They tied ropes around the bridge supports and rowed downstream, pulling the bridge down behind them.

In recent years London Bridge was moved from England to the United States. It now stands as a tourist attraction at Lake Havasu City, Arizona.

Viking Influence in Europe. While the Vikings were trying to conquer England, other groups were raiding Europe. The greatest Viking raid in history took place in France in 885. About 700 Viking ships, led by Ragnar Lodbrok, went up the Seine River to raid the rich territory of Burgundy. The city of Paris was located on an island in the middle of the Seine and the Parisians refused to allow the Vikings to pass. From November to August, the brave people of Paris fought off the Vikings who had decided to plunder Paris before attacking Burgundy.

Charles the Fat, the French king, arrived with an army and defeated the Vikings. Instead of completely wiping them out, Charles made a treaty with them and allowed them to sail south to Burgundy. This decision cost Charles the throne. His people were so angry they overthrew his government.

In 911 a strong Viking force led by Rollo landed on the coast of France. Charles the Simple, the new French king, made a treaty with Rollo. In it he granted him the rich province of Normandy in exchange for protection against Viking raids. Rollo accepted and became the first duke of Normandy.

Within three generations the Normans were more civilized than the French. They had adopted French dress, manners, languages, customs, and religion. Normandy became a major European cultural center. There many schools and monasteries had survived because they were protected from Viking attack.

Ragnar Captures A Princess

One of the most famous Vikings was Ragnar Lodbrok. This Danish Viking reportedly raided Finland, Russia, Constantinople, Ireland, and Paris. He is said to have gotten his name from the way in which he won his wife Thora, a Swedish princess. Thora lived in a castle that was surrounded by a moat filled with deadly, giant-sized adders. In order to win Thora, Ragnar had to cross the moat. He made himself pants from animal skins, covering the hairy side with pitch to protect him from adder bites. Ragnar then crossed the moat and took Thora as his wife. This is how he got the name Lodbrok, which means "hairy britches."

VIKING INVADERS
880 A.D.

ALFRED'S KINGDOM
VIKING TERRITORY
BURGUNDY

Ingolf Arnason, the first settler in Iceland, built his home on the spot where his ship drifted ashore. He called his settlement "Reykjavik" after the smell of the hot springs in that area. Reykjavik today is Iceland's capital.

In this vivid drawing of the Battle of Hastings, William, duke of Normandy, (left) is attacked from both sides as his horse rears up. Despite efforts to defend their land, the English were defeated by the Norman invaders.

The Battle of Hastings. In 1066 William, the duke of Normandy, claimed he had been promised the English throne. With the support of the pope, he invaded England and defeated the English at the Battle of Hastings. Harold, the English king, was expecting William's attack, but a Viking raid in the north forced him to take his troops inland. When word came that William had landed, Harold's tired army marched back south where it was defeated.

William's famous victory at Hastings marks a turning point in English history. Up to that time, England had been relatively unimportant. From then on, however, the English people played a major role in the history of the world. William's victory also was important because it marked the end of the Viking raids. The governments of Europe were becoming so strong they could protect their own lands. Thus it was no longer profitable for Vikings to raid them.

Norse Explorations

One of the main reasons for the Viking raids was that their small, unprofitable farms did not provide enough food to supply their large families. While some Norsemen were interested only in raiding and plunder, others set out to find new lands to settle and farm.

Iceland. Two Viking ships, which had started out on a raid, were blown off course during a storm. As a result, the Vikings discovered a new land. Later a Norse explorer, named Floki, followed their directions and set out to find this land. After spending the winter in the new region, Floki named it Iceland.

The first people to settle in Iceland were brothers, Leif and Ingolf Arnason. Leif was banished from Norway, so he and his brother decided to make their home in this new territory. By 930 some 20,000 people had settled in Iceland. While the land there was no good for farming, it made good pastureland for herds and flocks. Living conditions were very primitive, so many of these people went "i viking" to get luxury items that would make life more pleasant.

Early Government—The Althing. During the early centuries of its development, Iceland was not a colony, but an independent country. At first the country was so sparsely settled, there was little need for laws or government. If there were arguments or crimes, each family handled the problems for itself. As more people settled in Iceland, there were more feuds and bloodshed. People often tried to get revenge on someone who had injured their family.

Soon it was decided that a method other than bloody feuds was needed to settle quarrels. They established the *Althing,* an all-island governing body, and the disorders were brought under control. This government was the best democracy the world had seen since the days of Greece. The Althing made all the important decisions concerning life in Iceland. The most serious punishment the Althing could give for any crime was banishment. Sometimes people were banished for a short period of time, but returned to Iceland when their sentence was served. If a person banished for life decided to return, he could be killed by anyone who found him.

Religion. Iceland was a pagan country. Missionaries had come over from Ireland, but they did not accomplish much. If it was discovered that a missionary was winning converts in Iceland, he was asked to leave. During this time, Iceland was under Norwegian control. The people, however, remained somewhat independent.

In 1000, however, Olaf Tryggvesson, the king of Norway, decided Iceland should become a Christian country. At the time two men, Gizur the White and his son-in-law, were visiting Norway from Iceland. They met with the king who told them to go back and make Iceland a Christian nation. If they failed, Norway would invade Iceland and make Christians out of the people, they were told.

So Gizur and his son-in-law took a priest to the Althing and asked permission to conduct a service. Several Christians in the Althing insisted that the service be held. When the priest finished, members of the Althing voted to make Iceland a Christian country. It is the only country in the world to adopt Christianity through democratic processes.

Greenland. The most famous person to be banished from Iceland was Eric the Red who had killed a man. When he was banished, he decided to find the new country about which he had heard. He set out on a voyage of exploration and was responsible for establishing the first colony in Greenland.

King Tryggvesson also was responsible for establishing Christianity in Greenland. When Leif Ericson, Eric the Red's son, went to Norway, he became a Christian. His father was very unhappy when he returned to Greenland with a priest. Although Eric refused to accept the new religion, his wife and most of the people in Greenland became Christians.

America. It was in 1002 that the Norseman Leif Ericson set out on an exploration to discover new lands. He found a new territory that he called Vinland, which is now known as America. Ericson tried to establish a settlement there, but the Indians stopped him. Although the Norsemen's weapons were comparable to those of the Indians, they were so outnumbered that the Indians forced them to return. While the Norsemen never established a permanent settlement in Vinland, they returned often for timber, which was scarce in Greenland.

Leif Ericson, son of Eric the Red, is thought to be the navigator who discovered North America. He is pictured here as he steps forth upon the rocky coastline, carrying the cross symbolic of his faith.

Bronze statue from the Viking period showing Thor, the god of thunder. Thor played an important part in Norse and German mythology alike.

The Norsemen were unable to establish a permanent settlement in North America because of the Indians. The Norse were out-numbered, and without adequate weapons to defend themselves, they were driven back by the Indians.

There were two different sagas written in the 1300s about Leif Ericson's discovery of America. Apparently they were copied from earlier manuscripts which were lost and before that from word-of-mouth stories handed down from generation to generation. Most scientists thought these stories were not true, because they had no evidence of Norse landings in America. In 1963, however, Dr. Helge Ingstad

The Discovery of America

The world was amazed when proof was found that the Vikings reached America before Columbus. Arguments have raged over whether the earlier Viking visit was important since nothing apparently came of it. Historians now know that Phoenician sailors landed on the coast of South America, long before the Viking's visit.

In 1975 the newspapers carried a story telling about six old Chinese anchors that were discovered recently in waters off the California coast. This indicates that Chinese sailors reached California sometime about 600 A.D. There is an ancient Chinese legend about Fu-sang who discovered a land of strange herbs, fruits, woods, and people. Undoubtedly, it could have been America.

Most scientists agree that if the Chinese did discover America first, it was only because they were accidentally blown off course. Further reports about the anchors and their significance are being withheld until the anchors can be compared with rock quarries in China.

found ruins in Newfoundland that are unquestionably Nordic. They prove that Norsemen were in America at least 500 years before Columbus.

Summary. The Norse were a remarkable people. In only 200 years after the first Viking raid in Europe, the brave and fierce Norse warriors also had invaded most of England, built and ruled cities in Ireland, and controlled the powerful duchy of Normandy. They controlled Frisia (now called the Netherlands), raided the coast of Spain, sailed into the Mediterranean Sea, and attacked Italy and North Africa. They had provided a personal bodyguard for the Byzantine emperor, established a ruling house in Russia, settled Iceland, founded a colony on Greenland, and discovered America.

Perhaps the most important contribution made by the Norse was their passion for personal equality and individual freedom. You have seen how Iceland was run on a purely democratic basis, and Normandy was the first French province to free its serfs. As a result, freedom and equality became an important part of both the French and English heritage. This same love of freedom was passed on to their colonies in America.

The Age of Chivalry

As the Viking raids came to an end, Europe entered a period known as the Age of Chivalry. It was during the Middle Ages that a code of knighthood developed which emphasized bravery, courtesy, and honesty. This was known as the *code of chivalry* and set the feudalism of the Middle Ages apart from others. As we have seen, feudalism was not something that developed only in Europe. Almost every part of the world has used some form of feudal government at one time or another.

The Medieval Knight

The society of the Middle Ages was harsh and brutal. The knights were the same barbaric tribesmen who, only a few years before, had destroyed the Roman Empire. In an attempt to put the warrior in a more Christian setting and to slow down the brutal warfare of the period, a code of chivalry was developed.

Chivalry was the general code of conduct all knights were supposed to follow. Everything about the code of chivalry was designed especially for the knight. It set up standards for his training, his knighting, and his behavior, both in and out of battle.

Training of a Knight. Only members of the nobility could become knights. A medieval boy of the noble class remained under the care of his mother until he turned seven. Then he began to train for knighthood. A boy was sent to join another household—that of a relative, friend, or liege lord. It was believed his own parents would spoil him if he remained at home.

In his new household, the boy slept in a dormitory with other boys who also had come to train for knighthood. At first the boy served as a *page*. He ran errands for the ladies and learned manners, religion, hawking, and hunting. This period of training was designed to teach the boy obedience.

When a boy turned 15 or 16, he became a *squire* and was assigned to a knight. At that time he was taught the arts of warfare. He learned how to ride a war horse and to handle the sword, shield, and lance correctly. He also was required to care for his knight's equipment.

A *rune stone,* or telling stone, pictures life as it was in Gottland in 1000 A.D.

A medieval knight is shown wearing the symbol of his rank. His family background is on his shield and trappings of his horse. These symbols were known as coats of arms.

This medieval man feeds his domesticated hawk. Hawks were trained to kill small animals for sport and entertainment.

He served his lord and lady their meals and learned about music. He learned to play chess and backgammon, two popular games of the period.

Because there were so many petty wars between nobles, a squire usually was knighted on the battlefield after performing an act of bravery. Otherwise, a squire was considered ready for the knighthood when he reached 21 years of age.

The Knighting Ceremony. The Catholic Church was concerned about the harshness and brutality of the Middle Ages. Officials thought that knights would try harder to be honest, generous, courteous, and to treat women with respect if they took special vows when they

After spending the night guarding his arms, the knight was ready to take his vows. Kneeling before his lord, he receives the accolade while vowing to be a valiant and true knight.

were knighted. By the 1100s the Church played an important role in the knighting ceremony, giving it great moral significance.

The Church said a knight actually served God in his role as defender of the weak and helpless. He should understand it was a privilege to do so. The knighting ceremony was full of symbolism, so the knight would always remember his vows and do all he could to live up to them.

The first ritual of preparing a squire for knighthood was taking a bath. Remember in those days people did not bathe more than once or twice a year. This made taking a bath special. It symbolized the purity a new knight was supposed to maintain. Then he spent the night alone in the chapel, watching his weapons on the altar. During this night-long watch, the young man was to confess his faults to God, resolving to be a true and worthy knight.

The next day a solemn religious service was held. The squire's sword was blessed on the altar by the Church official conducting the service. The climax of the ceremony came when the young man knelt before his lord to receive a light blow on the neck or shoulder with a sword, called the *accolade*. The young knight then was told to be valiant in the name of God.

The major purpose of the ceremony was to impress upon the new knight that he was expected to be virtuous, valiant, loyal to his lord, and reverent toward all women.

Heraldry. Every lord and most knights wore symbols representing their titles, landholdings, deeds of bravery, and family background on their shields and armor. These symbols were known as *coats of arms*. A knight was known by the device called a *herald* on his shield. Some of the symbols found on a noble's coat of arms were fictitious animals, such as griffins, dragons, and unicorns. They also used lions, leopards, and different versions of the cross. Heraldry played a very important part in life during the Middle Ages.

The Role of Women. After marriage, a woman had few rights. She shared her husband's rank, was hostess to his guests, and ruled his castle and fief during his absence. Many wives successfully defended their husband's fiefs in times of war while their husbands were fighting. But men were allowed to beat or starve their wives. If her marriage was unhappy, a woman's only escape was to join a convent. The Church did not allow divorce for any reason.

The Legend of Tristan and Iseult

A favorite story during the Middle Ages was that of *Tristan and Iseult*. Tristan was a brave and loyal knight. He was sent to take the Princess Iseult to the king to be his bride.

Iseult's mother wanted her daughter to have a happy marriage, so she gave Iseult a magic love potion. Iseult and the king were supposed to drink the potion on their wedding day to insure that they would love each other passionately. Instead Tristan and Iseult drank the potion themselves while traveling to the king. Immediately they fell in love with each other.

They wanted to carry out their orders, however, so Iseult went ahead with her plans to marry the king. Love reigned supreme, however, and Iseult finally ran away with Tristan. They were never happy, though, because people scorned them for breaking their loyalty vows to the king. In the end the lovers met with tragic deaths.

Since there was little room for romance and courtship in marriage, the role of *courtly love* was a very important part of chivalry. Definite rules for love and romance outside of marriage were established. Each young knight picked a lovely woman to represent his ideal of womanhood. He carried her *favor,* usually a scarf or glove belonging to her, into battle or in a tournament. He dedicated all his victories and great deeds to her honor. He wrote songs about her and did all kinds of errands for her, protesting loudly that he was a slave of love.

Since knights were supposed to be virtuous, the relationship was never to go beyond smiles and perhaps the touch of their hands. Knights were human, however, and since there was little concern about morals until the 1800s, we can safely assume that things often went beyond the touch of hands. Romantic stories of the day tell us that when the knight and his lady went beyond the limits set out in the code of chivalry, it was considered a terrible thing. The story of Sir Lancelot in the *Tales of the Round Table* and the story of *Tristan and Iseult* are two examples.

The Medieval Church

During the Middle Ages people were divided into three classes: nobles, peasants, and the clergy. We have already discussed how the nobles and peasants lived. Now we will take a closer look at the clergy.

The Roman Catholic Clergy. In Europe the Roman Catholic Church became the major Christian Church. There were some small, independent groups, but they did not have much influence. If such groups became important enough for the Roman Church to notice them, they were usually destroyed.

The mark of heraldry, a coat of arms, was blazoned with signs and markings that told of the owner's title and brave deeds.

The Catholic Church passed a rule that clergymen could not marry. This was very important during the Middle Ages because the important Church offices were considered valuable possessions. Bishops and cardinals owned land and controlled large estates with many serfs. They lived in splendid palaces and wore expensive robes covered with jewels.

If these clergymen had been allowed to marry, they would have passed their lands, titles, and wealth on to their children. Being a Church official was supposed to be a religious experience, as well as a job and title. Making such positions hereditary would have taken away their religious significance. The position of bishop, then, would have been no different than the position of count or duke.

The Catholic Church in the Middle Ages was becoming a very powerful force. It not only concerned itself with people's souls, but with political power as well. We will see in the next chapter how the popes tried to extend their authority over kings and emperors.

A three-part society existed in a feudal system, resting equally on lord and castle, peasant and hut, monk and Church.

A position in the Catholic Church was the only means through which a peasant could step into a new life. In most cases the poor, local priests who ministered to the peasants in the different manors came from the peasant class themselves. They were trained well enough to read the Bible to their people.

In some rare cases, it was possible for a brilliant peasant to rise to a top position in the Church. This did not happen often, for usually the top Church offices were filled by members of the nobility.

Under feudalism the oldest brother inherited the entire fief. If he had younger brothers, they had the choice of staying on at the manor and serving their brother as knights or of joining the service of a rich lord. In the latter case, they hoped to eventually receive their own fief as a reward for faithful service. This did not happen often, however, and many knights were compelled to accept room and board, with a small salary, in exchange for their services. The only other opportunity for a younger son was a career in the Church.

It is sad but true that many men chose the Church as a career rather than for spiritual reasons. These men were harsh, cruel, and violent, like the secular lords. In those days Church leaders were called "the princes of the Church." It was hard to tell the difference between them and the secular lords. Church leaders were even known to lead soldiers into battle, fighting as heartily as any knight. Unfortunately, in many ways Church leaders were as wild as the secular lords, often drinking and brawling.

It is important to remember that there is a big difference in calling oneself a Christian and actually being a Christian. Many people make the mistake of thinking all Church members are

Christians, when actually they may have many non-religious reasons for being in the Church. During the Middle Ages, there were many *hypocrites* in the Church. A hypocrite is one who pretends to have beliefs, feelings, or virtues he does not actually possess; a person who is insincere.

Monasticism. From the earliest days of Christianity, believers found they could not move freely in the world without sin and violence on all sides of them. Some Christians wanted to get away to a secluded place where they would not have to worry about such everyday conflicts. They went to places where they could spend more time thinking about and worshiping God. When a group of these men joined together, they lived in a place called a *monastery*.

Later on, places were provided for women who wanted to devote their lives to prayer and serving God. These places were called *convents*. As in the case of the good monks, there were women who believed in God and wanted to help others. Also, many women were sent to the convents against their will. They resented being shut away from the glamor and excitement of the world and often did not set good Christian examples.

Most monasteries were built away from the more populated areas. They were usually built of stone and protected by thick walls. Each monastery was a self-contained unit. It was able to supply food and other needs for its members so they did not have to come in contact with the outside world.

Monasteries included a chapel, kitchen, dormitories, and a hospital. In some monasteries, each monk had his own room, called a *cell*, rather than sharing a dormitory-type room.

During the violence of the Middle Ages, it was the monasteries that kept education alive. Many precious books dealing with religion, as well as the Bible, were carefully copied by the men in these monasteries. Men spent their entire lives copying the Bible and drawing beautiful *illuminations* at the beginning of chapters and along the borders. Illuminations are artistic designs around the first letter of the first word in a chapter and the decorations of flowers and birds along the borders of the page.

Artistic monks during the Middle Ages spent many hours designing beautiful title pages for their handwritten books. This decorative page, taken from the Book of Kells, is typical of their detailed artwork.

Monks were subject to strict discipline and they all had assigned duties in the workshops and gardens or with the herds and flocks. Bells were rung both day and night to summon them to prayer and they were expected to stop whatever they were doing. Sometimes they even were awakened by bells during the night and were expected to pray. In some monasteries the monks were not allowed to talk to each other. They were expected to spend all their time thinking about their sins and praying.

Three Dedicated Monks. During the Middle Ages, men were becoming more wealthy and worldly. Even people in monasteries and churches were becoming rich and turning their backs on the teachings of Jesus. There were some men, however, who encouraged people to return to the kind of life Christians should be living.

St. Benedictine. In the 500s an Italian named Benedict saw his world in flames as barbarian tribesmen finished the destruction of the Roman Empire. Benedict believed the brutality of the barbarians was easier to accept than the conditions of Christianity in his day. The Roman Church was torn by internal problems and was unable to make strong decisions. Monks and priests roamed throughout Europe doing anything they pleased. Nobody seemed concerned about God and His plan for man.

When Benedict was 20 years old, he went to live in a cave. He stayed there for three years, praying and thinking about being a Christian. He received his food from a faithful friend who lowered it to him in a basket.

Finally Benedict left his cave and started a monastery. The monks there lived under the strictest rules of any monastery in Europe. Their lives were good examples of Christianity in a time when few people even cared about being a Christian.

Soon other Benedictine monasteries were started. The Benedictine rules for monks were followed in monasteries throughout Europe by men who wanted to get back to the basics of Christianity. Today we know the founder of the Benedictine Order of monks as St. Benedict.

Monks of the Benedictine Order lived by the most rigid rules of any of Europe's monastic orders. Following in the footsteps of their founder Benedict, these monks practiced simplicity and self=denial.

Bernard of Clairvaux. Another man who had a great impact on the Christian world was Bernard of Clairvaux. He lived in the 1100s, many years after St. Benedict. At that time even the Benedictine monks were spending more money on church decorations than on helping the poor.

Bernard joined a poor, struggling monastery which he believed followed the ideal set by Jesus. He wrote many books in an attempt to get Christians to return to the basic principles of the Bible. He even wrote to kings and popes, telling them that they had strayed from the teachings of Jesus. As a result of his writing and teachings, many monasteries turned their backs on the luxuries of life and returned to the rules established by Benedict many years earlier.

St. Francis of Assisi. The son of a rich merchant, Francis of Assisi was born in 1182. He was like a breath of fresh air in a time when even popes were engaged in political battles with emperors and kings. Francis could have lived in riches and comfort, but a deep religious experience as a young man changed his life. He then decided the most important thing in life was to serve Jesus Christ.

Francis gave up his wealth and position and tried to pattern his life after Christ's. He went to cities and villages, ministering to the sick, poor, and even to lepers when nobody else would come near them. He was dependent on gifts for his livelihood.

Other young men were inspired by what Francis was doing and began to follow his example. Franciscan friars soon became known as "little brothers." The Franciscan friars did not own property—not even a monastery. They spent their lives traveling through the country, helping others.

Summary. We have seen how the Roman Church leaders had become worldly and more concerned with power and riches than in the lives of the people. Many used the Church to gain important political positions. Through it all there were always people who trusted Jesus, believed the Bible, and tried to help others. Through them true Christianity was able to survive.

Many people were inspired by the life and good works of Francis of Assisi and spent their lives following his example. Franciscan friars such as this one roamed the countryside, helping the poor and needy.

THE DEVELOPMENT OF EUROPEAN NATIONS

Projects

1. Give a report on one of these men: Frederick Barbarossa, William the Conqueror, William Wallace, El Cid, Richard the Lion-hearted, Temuchin (Genghis Khan), or Alexander Nevsky. What did you like most about this person? What did you like least? Why?

2. Who was the last Hohenstaufen emperor? How long did he reign? What happened to him?

3. Henry II was an interesting person. Do a report on one of the following people who were close to him: Eleanor of Aquitaine, Thomas à Becket, or one of Henry II's sons. Explain how they got along with Henry II and why.

4. Compare the grand jury in the United States today with the grand jury Henry II established. How often does it meet? What is their purpose? How are people chosen to be a member of the jury?

5. Compare England's government today with the government of the United States. Who directs the English government and what selection process is used? How often do the English hold elections? Compare the House of Lords with the U.S. Senate.

6. Do a study on one of the monastic knight groups. How was it founded? What did the Knights do? What happened to the group when the Crusades ended?

7. Research the many plagues that have occurred in Europe. What were some of these diseases and where did they come from? Describe what happened during the plagues. Write a story that takes place during a plague.

8. Contact your local labor union and find out what jobs require a person to be an apprentice, journeyman, and master. How do the training programs compare with ones during the Middle Ages?

Words and Concepts

tariff
Estates General
craft guilds
grand jury
sacraments
relics
master
war of the brigands
charters
common law
shrines
excommunicated
journeyman
power of the purse
"taking the cross"
Doomsday Book
apprentice
Parliament
pilgrimage
Curia Regis
Battle of Lechfeld

Development of European Nations

The authority of the Roman Church was challenged by the rulers of European countries, as we will see in this chapter. These rulers asserted their independence and at the same time gained control over their rebellious nobles. When they were successful in their struggles, strong nations emerged. When they failed, it took many centuries for united countries to develop. In this chapter we will examine the development of Germany, Italy, England, France, and Spain during the Middle Ages.

Two other important events of this time period were the Crusades and the takeover of Russia by Mongolian forces called the Golden Horde. The Crusades, while they did not accomplish their religious goals, had a tremendous influence on European development. They affected areas of trade, growth of cities, exploration, and the downfall of feudalism. The Golden Horde, to whom Russians paid tribute, caused Russia's entire cultural outlook to become oriental, rather than European.

Twilight of Feudalism

The feudal system became outdated and the kings in Europe gained power over their nobles. In the long struggle, kings used the Church and the rising middle-class merchants to break up the power of the nobles.

Although the major struggle was between the nobles and the king, another struggle was going on at the same time between the kings and the pope. The dispute concerned the Church's authority over government and political issues as well as spiritual matters. The Roman Catholic Church was the only Church in Europe.

This was, in itself, a powerful weapon in the struggle. Christians were members of the Roman Church and the pope had absolute authority over spiritual matters. This gave him the power to control European politics as well.

Germany and Italy

The area later called Germany was made up of five powerful duchies: Bavaria, Franconia, Saxony, Swabia, and Lorraine. These duchies were ruled by dukes who were descendants of former Germanic tribal leaders. Powerful rulers tried to unite Germany into a strong country, but the common people were still more loyal to their local leaders than to the central government.

The German nobles realized they needed a ruler to act as referee to maintain peace and order. Although they wanted peace and order, they did not want a strong ruler who would interfere with the administration of their duchies. When the last of the Carolingian rulers died without an heir, the German dukes elected Conrad of Franconia as king. Germany's history is filled with political power struggles between the nobles and the rulers.

Years later, when the Germanic emperor tried to fight the pope and conquer Italy at the same time, the conflicts became too difficult to handle. The struggles continued and it was hundreds of years before Germany became a strong nation.

The Saxon Rulers. In 919 Henry the Fowler became the first Saxon duke to be elected king. Henry was a strong ruler who established authority over the nobles. He also declared war on many of Germany's enemies. He pushed the Danes back into Denmark and set up a buffer zone, called the Danish Mark, located in the neck of the Danish peninsula. He then pushed back Germany's eastern frontiers.

Henry's son Otto continued his father's policy of extending the king's power. This was done by granting titles and large amounts of land to his relatives and high Church officials. As a result, he had many strong nobles who supported his policies. Whenever a Church official died, Otto replaced him with someone loyal to the king.

Although the Vikings were unable to reach Germany in their raids, another danger lurked on the German frontier. A warlike Hungarian tribe called the Magyars was constantly raiding German territory. They invaded Germany in 955 with a great army, threatening to conquer that country. Otto completely crushed the Magyars in the Battle of Lechfeld and was hailed as the savior of Europe. This victory opened up the eastern frontier and Germanic peoples moved eastward, carrying Christianity into new areas.

Otto wanted more power than he had as elected king of Germany. When he learned that Queen Adelaide, widow of the former king of Lombardy, had been imprisoned, he used this as an excuse to gain new territory in Italy. In 951 Otto crossed the Alps with an army, rescued and married Adelaide. After this act of chivalry, he was declared king of Italy. Otto then had the pope crown him Holy Roman Emperor. As a result, the Roman Church, Italy, and Germany became united in an unnatural alliance that would later prove disasterous to all three.

The Saxon kings were the most powerful rulers in Europe at this time. They had succeeded in controlling their nobles and in defeating their outside enemies. Peace existed in Germany which rapidly was becoming the cultural leader of Europe. The people also became rich because farmers could plant and harvest without having their crops destroyed by armies at war.

The Saxon rulers, however, seemed to be more interested in Italy than Germany. Otto III, for example, did not even live in Germany. As a result, the strong leadership necessary to keep the German nobles under control weakened, and the emperor began to lose his authority in Germany. The only means he had of maintaining

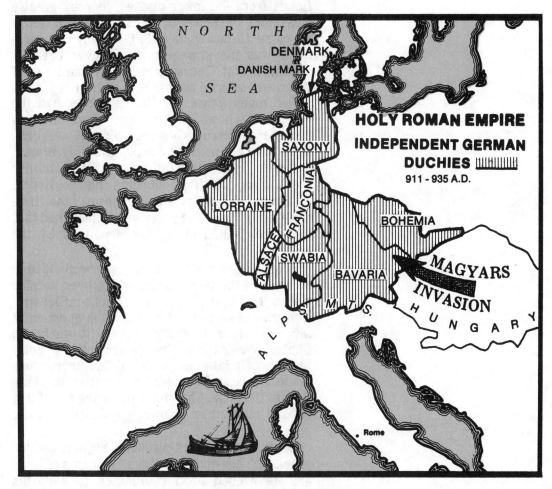

HOLY ROMAN EMPIRE

INDEPENDENT GERMAN DUCHIES

911 - 935 A.D.

control was to appoint strong, loyal Church leaders to support his cause. But when conflict arose over the right of the emperor to appoint Church leaders, the power of the emperor was destroyed.

The Holy Roman Emperors vs. the Pope. In 1024 a new line of Holy Roman Emperors came to the throne. The new rulers, called the Salian emperors, began at once to create a strongly united government. They recruited Church officials from the lower classes, thereby greatly weakening the power of the nobles. When Henry IV came to power in 1056, Germany's government was the strongest it had ever been. It appeared that Germany would become one of the most powerful nations in the world.

For many years the Italian nobles had the power of choosing the pope. The elections became so corrupt, however, that at one time three men claimed to be pope. The Holy Roman Emperor, Henry IV's father, used Constantine's method of settling conflicts and called a meeting. He ended up appointing the first non-Italian pope. For many years it seemed that the popes would always be appointed by the emperor.

When Gregory VII became pope, he decided to strengthen the power of his office over secular rulers. This brought him into direct conflict with Henry IV. The conflict involved the question of lay investiture. Gregory believed it weakened Church power for the secular rulers to appoint Church officials. He believed lay investiture made Church officials more loyal to the king than to the pope. This made imposing a uniform code of conduct on churchmen difficult for the pope.

Henry thought the king should appoint Church officials. They controlled large amounts of land, and he needed loyal churchmen to keep his nobles under control. Thus we can see how Henry used the Church to break up the nobles' power.

Henry IV was used to the idea of having authority over the pope, rather than taking orders from him. In 1073 Gregory VII ordered Henry to stop appointing Church officials. When Henry refused to obey, Gregory excommunicated him.

Powers of the Church

The power of the Roman Catholic Church rested on seven sacraments, including confirmation, baptism, marriage, confession, communion, ordination, and last rites (or supreme unction). These sacraments were considered necessary for Christians to enter heaven. All seven sacraments were performed by a Church official.

The medieval Christian believed he had to receive the sacraments from the Church or he would be cut off from God. This gave the Church great power because anyone who disobeyed the Church's authority was *excommunicated*. This meant people were cut off from the Church and could not participate in any of the sacraments. If the person died while excommunicated, it was believed he would go to hell. For this reason, when a person was excommunicated, he would do anything to get back in the Church's favor.

Today Christians who read the Bible for themselves realize their salvation does not depend on Church services or sacraments. Rather, it is their belief in Jesus Christ and the sacrifice He made when He died on the cross that saved them.

In the Middle Ages, being excommunicated was a very serious matter. People who were excommunicated were cut off from the sacraments of the Church. Nobody was supposed to give aid to an excommunicated person. Even vassals and knights were not expected to keep oaths of loyalty made to a lord who was excommunicated.

Henry IV realized his nobles were preparing to rebel and he was in danger of losing his kingdom. He had to act quickly. At that very moment, Pope Gregory was on his way to help the German nobles select a new emperor. Henry IV met him at Canossa.

For three days Henry stood barefoot in the snow, humbly asking the pope to forgive him for his disobedience. Finally Gregory was forced to reinstate Henry in the Church and he allowed him to remain in control of his kingdom. Henry never forgot this humiliation, however. Later, when he was more powerful, he captured Rome in retaliation. Gregory VII managed to escape but later died in exile.

The lay investiture dispute was settled in 1122 A.D. by a treaty called the *Concordat of Worms*. It was declared that the king could appoint Church officials and give them the symbols of their secular landholdings. The Church, however, would endow them with the symbols of their Church office. On the surface it appeared that the emperors were the winners. But the real winners were the nobles who joined the Church in an effort to completely destroy the emperor's power.

Destruction of Central Authority. There were many families who wanted to reign as emperor, so for almost 50 years there was constant civil war in Germany. As a result, Germany's strong government collapsed and culture and education declined. The peasants suffered as farms were burned and crops were destroyed by the different armies struggling for control.

While Germany was engaged in civil war, Italy was drifting away from a unified government. In the North the cities formed independent city-states. Each one was proud of its independence and was unwilling to unite under any type of central authority. As we have seen, central Italy was composed of the Papal States. In southern Italy and Sicily, a Norman knight established the kingdom of Naples and Sicily after capturing the territory from the Muslims.

A shivering Henry IV stands barefoot in the snow, waiting for the pope's forgiveness. As a result of his humility, Henry was reinstated in the Church and remained in control of his kingdom.

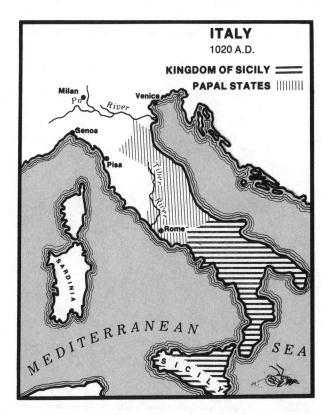

ITALY
1020 A.D.

KINGDOM OF SICILY
PAPAL STATES

Frederick Barbarossa, Red Beard, ended the civil war in Germany when he became Holy Roman Emperor in 1152. This strong ruler drowned while crossing a stream in Asia Minor on the way to the Crusades.

The Hohenstaufen Emperors. The German civil wars came to an end when the Hohenstaufens, a new ruling house, took over as Holy Roman Emperors in 1152. The first emperor from this family was Frederick I, also known as Frederick Barbarossa, Red Beard, Frederick set out to recapture his lands in Italy rather than to increase his power in Germany. To get support he was forced to grant special privileges to German nobles even though this further weakened his authority.

The Italian city-states were aware of the danger facing them so they joined together to form the Lombard League. The pope gave his support to the league, realizing a strong Holy Roman Emperor would cause the Church problems. Frederick attacked Italy twice. The first time he captured Rome, but most of his army was killed by a plague. The second time his armies were defeated in battle by the Lombard League.

Frederick returned to Germany to find rebellion and civil war. In 1190 Frederick set out to fight in the Third Crusade, but he drowned while crossing an icy stream in Asia Minor. Frederick Barbarossa was the only great Hohenstaufen Holy Roman Emperor.

After Frederick I's death, the nobles and the Church were determined to destroy this ruling house. Since the next emperors were more interested in ruling Italy than Germany, the pope openly united everyone against the Hohenstaufen emperors. The last of this family died in 1270 as a result of the pope's leadership in the wars.

The Church Authority Declines. Germany again plunged into civil war when the Hohenstaufen rule ended. The war lasted for 19 years. Several hundred years passed before the independent nobles united Germany into a strong country. The economy and culture of the area was greatly behind that of the rest of Europe as a result of civil war.

On the surface it appeared that the Church had won the long struggle. This was not true, however. The people of Europe had watched the pope use his office for political reasons, using tricks and politics to get what he wanted. As a result, they lost confidence in his position as their spiritual leader. His involvement in worldly matters eventually led people to rebel against the authority of the Church.

Because of the conflict between the Roman Church, the Holy Roman Emperors, and the

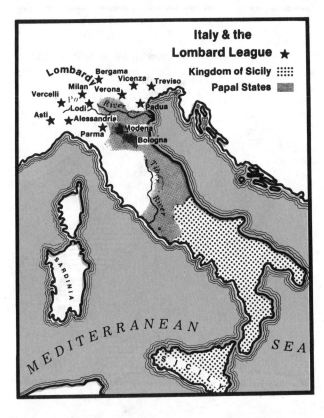

Italy & the
Lombard League ★
Kingdom of Sicily ⦂⦂⦂⦂
Papal States ▓

Lombardy
Bergama
Vicenza
Treviso
Vercelli
Milan Verona
Po
Lodi River Padua
Asti
Alessandria
Parma Modena
Bologna

SARDINIA

MEDITERRANEAN SEA

Italian city-states, it would be several hundred years before Italy united into one national government.

Norman England

When the duke of Normandy, also known as William the Conqueror, took over the crown of England in 1066, he completely changed the government. Since he had conquered the country, he claimed all the land as his personal property. He then gave sections of his land as fiefs to the knights and nobles who were part of his army. The type of feudalism established by William in England, however, was different from the European feudal system.

England Under William. William realized that powerful nobles, with their own private fiefs and armies, could cause him problems. For this reason he scattered the fiefs throughout England, making it difficult for them to unite against him. He also made every vassal in England swear primary loyalty to the king. Thus, when a noble wanted to rebel against the king, his men were not obligated to join him.

While William started many new customs, he also kept some of the old English customs. One such custom required every man in the kingdom to arm himself and fight for the king when asked to do so. Therefore, William was able to raise an army quickly without having to depend upon his nobles.

Another Anglo-Saxon custom that William used was the *Witan,* a council of leading nobles. Before William came to power, the Witan met to elect and advise kings. William began to call this group the Great Council, or *Curia Regis* (King's Council). The purpose of the council was to give the king advice and, in some cases, to try nobles who dared to break the king's peace.

William has been called "the drillmaster of England." He kept very tight control over every area of English life. William approved Church business and the decrees of the pope before they could be enforced. He also expected knight service from the churchmen who held land from him.

Shortly after taking over England, William ordered that a nationwide survey or census be made. The purpose was to determine the number of livestock and amount of property owned by the citizens as a basis for levying taxes. The results of the survey were recorded in the *Doomsday Book,* which became an official record. The Doomsday survey is important today because it gives historians a good idea of what life in England was like after the Norman conquest.

Henry II, a Dynamic King. The next three kings after William almost destroyed the kingdom established by him. The Church and nobles became so powerful that they did almost anything they wanted to do. The nobles built huge castles and raided the countryside whenever they chose.

In 1154 Henry II became king of England. He was a short, well-built man, with flaming red hair and a terrible temper. He was one of the most powerful rulers in Europe. When he married Eleanor of Aquitaine he acquired control of land on the European mainland, as well as England.

Henry II's first task was to break the power of his nobles. He passed a law requiring them to tear down their castles and he forbid them to build new ones. At first they rebelled. Henry and his army began to attack the castles. When he defeated a noble, he destroyed his castle. He traveled so fast across England that nobody

William the Conqueror was so named because he claimed all of England as his personal property after conquering it. Before the Norman conquest, English countrymen enjoyed a loosely structured way of life. William established a more structured feudal system that was different from any system Europe had ever known.

could be certain where he would turn up next, which prevented his nobles from rebelling.

Henry II and the Catholic Church. Henry was not as successful in bringing the Church under his control. One of his major policies was to provide equal justice for everyone in his kingdom. To Henry justice meant protecting the rights of the victims as well as the rights of the person accused of a crime.

The Roman Catholic Church had used its own courts since it assumed the responsibility for holding Europe together after the Fall of Rome. During those early, violent days, the only way a person could get justice was through the Church. When the strong kings came into power, there was no longer a need for Church courts. Church officials, however, wanted to keep their independence from national governments, so they claimed the right to try and punish clergy in the Church courts.

Over the years this right has been a point of conflict between national governments and the Roman Catholic Church. For one thing the Church claimed the right to decide who was clergy. During the time of Henry II, anyone who could read a certain passage in the Bible was considered to be a clergyman. Many people memorized this passage and only pretended to read it so they could be tried in the Church courts. The reason people preferred to be tried in Church courts was because the Church disapproved of bloodshed. The strongest punishment the Church court could give was a large fine. Thus it was possible for persons tried in the Church courts literally to get away with murder.

Henry II thought that a good compromise would be to allow the Church court to try the criminal. If he were found guilty, Henry II would turn him over to the state for punishment. The Church refused, however, fearing this would somehow interfere with Church power.

Henry II thought he had solved the problem when he appointed his best friend and drinking buddy, Thomas à Becket, as archbishop of Canterbury. This was the highest Church office in England, and Henry had every reason to expect his friend to support his policies. à Becket, however, changed when he became a Church official, and he was Henry's toughest opponent. One night Henry exclaimed in anger that he wished someone would rid him of this "turbulent priest." Four loyal knights took him at his word, rushed to Canterbury, and murdered à Becket in his cathedral.

Thomas à Becket, of England is viciously murdered in his cathedral at Canterbury. A former friend and later enemy of King Henry II, Becket was killed because of a misunderstanding between Henry and his knights. This "accident" brought a quick reaction from the outraged public and prevented Henry II from continuing his plan to get rid of Church courts in England.

Public opinion was outraged at this act. People did not believe Henry was blameless, and they thought of a Becket as a martyr to Christianity. Henry was forced to stop his attack on the Church. As a result, the English Church courts caused problems until England split with the Roman Catholic Church.

Henry II and Royal Justice. In addition to Church courts, every large landholder had a court where problems about his fief were solved. The fines from these cases added money to the lords' pockets. For this reason they were very unhappy when Henry II set up a new system of law.

Henry did not use the trial by ordeal or trial by combat. Instead he introduced a new system in which witnesses were sworn to tell all they knew about a case and then a judge gave the verdict. This method was much fairer than previous methods, and soon people began flocking to the king's courts for justice. The idea of using a jury to decide on guilt and innocence became a common practice.

The king had judges who traveled from county to county, hearing all the cases that had accumulated since their previous visit. In order that all people were given a fair trial, jury members took an oath. The major duty of the jury was to see that everyone charged with a crime was brought to trial. Today this type of jury is called a *grand jury*. It plays an important role in the judicial system of the United States.

The judges also began giving the same sentence to everyone who committed the same crime. As more and more trial decisions were made, the judges had more cases to draw on for sentencing. As a result, English law was called *common law,* which means that the same law was common to all. Under this system the nature of a particular crime and the punishment for it became common knowledge. The three most important accomplishments of Henry II's reign were the establishment of jury trials, the grand jury, and the common law system.

Unhappy Henry

Henry II has gone down in history as being a strong king. In his personal life, however, he was a very unhappy man. His best friend, Thomas à Becket, turned against him. Henry imprisoned his own wife because she supposedly poisoned his mistress. Two of his sons died while he was alive. His other two sons, encouraged by his enemy King Philip II of France, were in the midst of rebellion against him when he died.

King John, A Wicked Ruler. When Henry II died in 1189, his son Richard the Lion-Hearted became king. Richard was more interested in fighting in the Crusades than in ruling England. He was killed in battle in France. We will learn more about him when we study the Crusades. When Richard died, his brother John became king. John is best known as the evil Prince John of Robin Hood legend.

Magna Carta. John became king in 1199 and he was just as wicked as a king as he had been as a prince. He was cruel and greedy and soon his nobles rose in rebellion against his unfair actions. In 1215 they forced John to sign the famous document known as the *Magna Carta.*

The Magna Carta granted certain rights and protections to all freemen in England. It is important to realize that at the time it was signed, most Englishmen were serfs. The freedoms in

Houses of Parliament, pictured here as they look today, were begun by William II, son of William the Conqueror. On the right is the famous Big Ben clock tower rising 96.3 m (316 feet) into the air. It is here that the laws governing England are passed.

the Magna Carta only applied to the knights and nobles. Once the feudal system broke up, however, this document was applied to all Englishmen.

What were some of the rights covered in the Magna Carta? The king was not allowed to pass tax laws without first getting the approval of the Great Council. Nobody could be imprisoned without first being tried by a judge and a jury. It also stated that anyone, no matter how poor, had the right to seek justice in the courts when they were being abused.

As a result, even the king was forced to obey the law and could be brought to court for oppressing his subjects. Although in actual practice this idea did not always work and strong English kings often ignored the law, the Magna

Carta was still a very important document. Those countries who supported the idea that the king was subject to the law, later developed into democratic nations.

The Development of Parliament. The next two kings, Henry III and Edward I, are important, because during their reigns common men finally had a voice in government. This was a result of the establishment of the governing body called *Parliament.* You will recall that William the Conqueror's Great Council advised him on major issues of the day. At that time only wealthy nobles could attend Great Council meetings.

When Henry III was king, however, he was so unpopular that the nobles rebelled against him. To gain support for their rebellion, the nobles invited two knights from each shire and two representatives from each city to attend the Great Council meetings. They named this expanded council Parliament from the French word *parler,* meaning "to speak."

The Parliament met to suggest laws, give advice, and approve tax bills. Before long, taxes could not be levied without the consent of Parliament. Later on, Parliament suggested bills and passed them on to the king. If he refused to pass the proposed legislation, Parliament refused to approve new taxes. The pressure on the king to pass laws suggested by Parliament was called *the power of the purse.* You can see that our representative form of government, as well as many of the freedoms that we take for granted in America today, were first developed in England during the Middle Ages.

England and Scotland. England's Edward I began expanding the borders. In 1284 he conquered Wales and added it to England. To help the Welsh feel that they were part of England, Edward made his son Prince of Wales and

King John, the wicked brother of Richard the Lion-Hearted, is forced by his nobles to sign the *Magna Carta.* This document guaranteed certain basic rights to all English freemen. Part of John's unwillingness to sign the charter undoubtedly rested on the fact that he himself was now subject to the law.

declared him heir to the throne. Since that time, the heir to the English throne always has been called the Prince of Wales.

In 1290 Edward I settled a quarrel in Scotland and became Scotland's overlord. Everything was fine until Edward tried to use Scotch soldiers in English wars. Suddenly a spirit of nationalism arose and under the leadership of William Wallace, Scotland rebelled. The rebellion failed and Wallace was hung as a traitor.

You will remember that nationalism is a love of country and the desire to break away from foreign influence. Ever since the time of William Wallace, the Scotch longed to be free of English control. In 1314 Scotch forces met Edward II at the Battle of Bannockburn and defeated him. The Scotch won their independence, but fighting continued along the border for about 200 years. The Scotch often threatened to join the French during the many wars between France and England.

France—Fragmented and Frustrated

The last Carolingian king of France died in 987. The entire line of rulers had been weak and ineffective. As a result, nobles had established independent states and paid little attention to their kings.

Like the powerful nobles in Germany, the French nobles chose the weakest member of their ranks, Hugh Capet, count of Paris, to be king. His landholding was about 40 km² (25 square miles). Since it was almost completely surrounded by water, it was called the *Ile de France.*

Early Capetian Kings. When Hugh Capet was elected king, the office was not hereditary and

the nobles did not want it to be. Capet was determined to have his son rule. So he had him crowned before he died. After that, each king

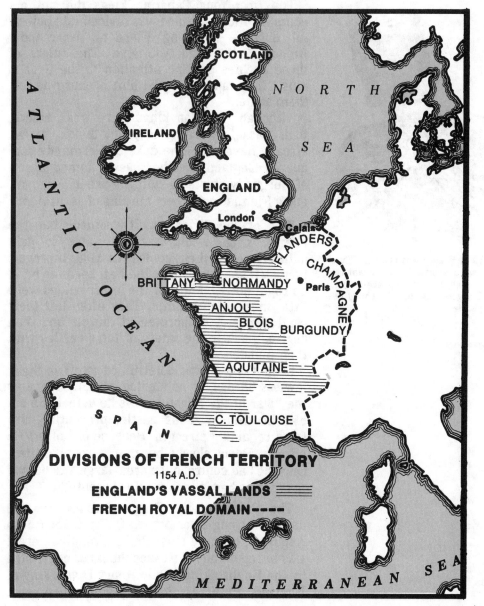

DIVISIONS OF FRENCH TERRITORY
1154 A.D.
ENGLAND'S VASSAL LANDS
FRENCH ROYAL DOMAIN----

King Louis IX of France was unusual. While other kings were known for their warlike ways, Louis was just and peace-loving. Because of his good rule he was called St. Louis by his people.

had his son crowned king while he was still alive. They were known as the Capetian kings and they continued to rule in France until 1328.

The first four Capetian kings did not accomplish much. France was divided into powerful duchies—including Flanders, Normandy, Anjou, Poitou, and Aquitaine. The rulers of these duchies paid no attention to the French king. They only tolerated him because he left them alone.

Although Capetian kings were weak rulers, their vassals were doing great things. As we already have seen, the duke of Normandy conquered England. Another vassal named Henry of Burgundy started a ruling house in Portugal, and a Flemish noble became king of Jerusalem.

War of the Brigands. It seemed that the French kings would never be able to gain authority over their nobles. In 1108, however, Louis VI, known as Louis the Fat, began to build up royal power. Many of the lesser nobles were little more than bandits. They often left their castles to strike unprotected targets and then hurried back to the safety of their castles with their plunder.

Louis the Fat was determined to crush these lawless barons, so he started what is known as the "war of the brigands." As he defeated a noble, he destroyed his castle, preventing him from regaining strength. Because of Louis VI's efforts, Paris slowly became a royal center. Once he had control of an area, large amounts of tax monies began to flow into his capital.

The Power of the King Increases. In 1180 another strong ruler named Philip II, or Philip Augustus, became king. Philip's major interest was in regaining for France the lands controlled by the English king. While Henry II was king of England, Philip II did not regain much land.

Philip did succeed, however, in making Henry's life miserable. He encouraged Henry's own sons to rebel against him by constantly stirring up devious plots. By the end of King John's reign, Philip had managed to regain almost half of the English holdings in France.

Philip II strengthened his government by recruiting able men from the middle-class bourgeoisie, rather than from the feudal nobility, as his major officials. He established a supreme court of justice to break up the people's loyalty to their feudal leaders. He also organized a treasury department and appointed a group of advisers.

Until this time all the French kings had been cruel and crafty. In 1226 Louis IX became king. Unlike the other kings, Louis IX was just, sympathetic, and peace-loving. He went out of his way to avoid war with his nobles and England. More than anything else he wanted justice for his people. With that purpose in mind, he sent investigators throughout his kingdom to see that government officials were fair.

Because of Louis IX's successful reign, the French people were convinced that the best form of government was a monarchy. So, while

---

Louis IX and Justice

Louis IX has been called St. Louis because he was such a good ruler. He tried to keep in touch with the problems of his people at all times, especially in the area of justice. Louis often sat under a tree in a field and invited people, nobles and peasants alike, to bring their problems to him. Then he personally made a judgment in each case and handled all grievances.

the English were limiting the king's power, the French were accepting the idea that a king should have absolute control over all areas of government.

The Knight's Templar. The last of the strong Capetian kings was Philip IV, known also as Philip the Fair. He was Louis IX's grandson, but he was almost the complete opposite of his saintly grandfather. Philip was a ruthless king who allowed nothing to interfere with his power. He was crafty and deceitful and never hesitated to use violence to gain his ends.

Philip IV's ruthlessness was evident when he suppressed the organization of *Knights Templar*. This was a group of knights so-named because their first headquarters was at the site of the old temple of Jerusalem. They were also called *The Knights of the Temple.* As we will see later in this chapter, several organizations of knights were formed during the Crusades. These knights took vows similar to those taken by monks in a monastery. Instead of devoting their lives to contemplation, peace, and study, men of the Knights Templar physically fought against the enemies of Christ and the Roman Catholic Church. Since they did not study the Bible themselves, they did not realize this type of activity was contrary to the teachings of Jesus. During these years of fighting, the Knights Templar became very rich from plundering cities in the Middle East. Their headquarters was in Paris, where their riches from the Middle East were sent.

As the Crusades came to an end, many knights moved to Paris where they set up a banking house. They loaned money to nobles and charged them high interest rates, a practice which made them even richer. One of the people they loaned large sums of money to was Philip IV, but he

Knights, like the one shown here, belonged to the Knights Templar, founded during the Crusades. These knights were dedicated to serving their religious military order. Later the Knights Templar organization was destroyed by Philip IV when he needed their money.

needed even more money. Philip realized that if he could get rid of the Knights Templar and take over their fortune, he would not have to repay the money he owed them. Philip also had the support of the nobles who also owed the Knights Templar large sums of money.

False charges were brought against the group, accusing them of sorcery and other evil practices. Many members were tortured and forced to confess to the false charges. They were then burned at the stake. Finally Philip eliminated the Knights Templar and took over control of their wealth.

French Government. Despite the fact that Philip was ruthless, he was a strong ruler. He chose men from the middle class for his government workers. Knowing their power depended upon the strength of the king, their every move was aimed at increasing the king's power. Philip had spies and informers all over France and knew what was happening in every part of his kingdom.

A council called the *Estates General* was established by the king to approve his tax bills and policies. The council was comprised of nobles, knights, Church officials, and representatives from the cities. This group, however, never had the power of the purse like the English Parliament. Thus they had no real power over the king.

The French King and the Pope. Both Philip IV and his contemporary Edward I of England began taxing the lands owned by the Church in their countries. Pope Boniface VIII decided to prove the power of the Church over secular rulers by threatening to depose Philip. Times had changed, however, since Gregory VII deposed Henry IV.

Philip called a meeting of the Estates General. The council decided that no more money would be sent to the Church in Rome as long as the pope continued to interfere in French politics. This meant the Church would lose all the income from the offerings made by the French people. Thus the pope was forced to back down.

Pope Boniface VIII tried to assert Church authority over the ruthless French King Philip IV. Philip attempted to have him kidnapped. Although he escaped, Boniface died shortly thereafter from the shock of the ordeal.

Boniface VIII then issued a sealed decree called a *Papal Bull* (similar to a law) in which he announced that all men were subject to the pope; otherwise, they could not go to heaven. When the bull was published, Philip IV decided to call a Church council and depose the pope. In 1303 Philip's men broke into the pope's summer house and kidnapped him. While they were taking him to France for trial, he was rescued by friends. The shock of his capture, however, was too much for Boniface and he died a month later.

Philip IV completely dominated the election for the next pope and a French archbishop was selected. The Church headquarters were moved from Rome to Avignon, a little town in southern France. The pope remained there for 67 years, completely dominated by French authority. In a later chapter, we will see how being under French domination greatly hurt the Roman Catholic Church.

The French Nation Emerges. Philip IV had three sons. Each of them was king for a while and each died without any heirs. This set the stage for a new series of wars between France and England called the Hundred Years' War. These conflicts lasted from 1337 to 1453 and brought France to the brink of disaster. We will look at the Hundred Years' War in detail in a later chapter. Nevertheless, during the reign of the Capetian kings, France had progressed from a fragmented country to the strongest monarchy in Europe.

The king spent large sums of money to improve education in France. The University of Paris became the center of learning for all of Europe, especially in philosophy and religion. French authors wrote books in French rather than in Latin, so French became the common language of the entire country.

The Christians Reconquer Spain

Spain has been mentioned previously in connection with the history of other civilizations. We know that both the Greeks and the Phoenicians had colonies in Spain. Carthage used Spain as the launching point for Hannibal's invasion of Italy. Evidence of Roman control in Spain can be seen in the roads and aqueducts which are still in use today. Two of Rome's emperors, Trajan and Hadrian, came from Spain. When Rome fell, a Germanic tribe called the Visigoths established a Christian kingdom in Spain.

Moorish Influence. As a result of the spread of Islam throughout North Africa, a group of Mohammed's followers, called *Moors,* invaded Spain. The Visigoths tried to stop them but were unable to do so. From Spain the Moors moved on to invade France but were stopped by Charles Martel at the Battle of Tours in 732. They then returned to Spain and established the remarkable Moorish Kingdom which survived for some 800 years. Only three Christian kingdoms survived in northern Spain. They were Barcelona (later to become part of the kingdom of Aragon), Leon, and Navarre. The rest of Spain was part of the caliphate of Cordova, the center of Moorish authority.

While the rest of Europe was in the midst of the Dark Ages, Spain, under the Moorish influence, was enjoying advanced learning and prosperity. The Moors had come in contact with Greek and Persian cultures and brought many of their customs and ideas into Spain. While people in France, Germany, and England were living in drafty, uncomfortable castles, people in Spain lived in beautiful palaces in their large cities. Many of the public baths and palaces had hot and cold running water. Splashing fountains, lovely mosaics, and soft Persian rugs added to the luxury of the homes of the Moorish ruling classes.

The Moors taught the Spaniards how to grow

crops and introduced rice, cotton, peaches, oranges, and lemons to that country. Scholars came from all over Europe to study science and mathematics in Moorish universities. Spain was the only European country at this time where these subjects could be studied.

A Christian Revival. In 1031 the caliphate of Cordova which ruled Moorish Spain collapsed. Twenty-one different Moorish kingdoms were established. The Christians took this as a signal to recapture Spain. A great Christian revival occurred and knights from all over Europe came in to help drive the Moors out of Spain. The territory captured by the Christians became known as the kingdom of Castile because of all the castles they built there.

When Alfonso IV was king of Castile, his most important vassal and greatest soldier was El Cid. His men conquered Valencia. El Cid is the greatest hero in all Spanish literature and the poem entitled "El Cid," written about his adventures, thrilled Europe.

Later, in the thirteenth century, other Christian forces conquered Toledo, Seville, and Portugal. Portugal was given to Henry of Burgundy as a fief to reward him for his help in fighting the Moors. In 1139 Henry's son, Alfonso Henriques, became king of Portugal. They began pushing the Moors southward in Portugal just as they had done in Spain.

The Crusades —
For Glory, God, and Unity

The Crusades is the name given to a series of eight wars that took place between 1096 and 1291 A.D. In these wars European Christians tried to take the lands from the Muslim Turks where Jesus had lived and died. The first four Crusades were the most important. The remaining ones had lost their holy purpose and were objects of ambition and greed. The Crusades themselves accomplished little. The results of the Crusades, however, affected nearly every area of Western European history, including education, trade, and social order.

Christians Unite Against the Muslims

Reasons for the Crusades. There were three major reasons for the Crusades. First, the Muslim Turks were preventing Christians from

This armor, now kept in the Topkapi Palace in Istanbul, was actually worn by a knight during the Crusades. Armor often weighed 9.1 to 13.6 kg (20 to 30 pounds) for men, and more for the horses. Heavy armor was a handicap for crusaders in battle with the lightly clad Turks.

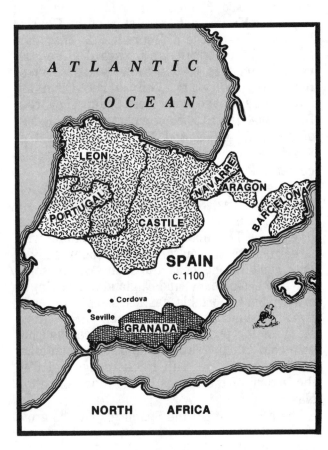

ATLANTIC OCEAN

LEON

NAVARRE

ARAGON

BARCELONA

PORTUGAL

CASTILE

SPAIN
c. 1100

• Cordova

Seville

GRANADA

NORTH   AFRICA

making pilgrimages to the Holy Land. Second, the Byzantine emperor made an appeal to the pope for help against the Turks. The third factor leading to the Crusades was the need to stop Christians from fighting each other during the Middle Ages. Leaders hoped to give them a common enemy to fight. We will examine these influences more closely.

Pilgrimages. European Christians of the Middle Ages were very superstitious. They believed many things which were contrary to the teachings of Jesus. This occurred because many heathen superstitions were brought into the new religion when entire countries became Christian all at once. Perhaps the greatest source of misunderstanding about Jesus' teachings was that people could not read the Bible for themselves. They accepted whatever their religious leaders told them. Unfortunately, as we have seen, many priests could not read the Bible either.

Going on pilgrimages was a major pastime during the Middle Ages. People believed their sins would be forgiven and they would be healed from illness by going to a holy place. They also went on pilgrimages to give special thanks for particular blessings.

People went on pilgrimages to Christian *shrines,* places where saints or martyrs had died or were buried. There *relics,* the bones of a saint or pieces of Jesus' cross, were preserved. Pilgrimages were made to shrines throughout Europe. But the most rewarding pilgrimages of all were those made to Palestine. Palestine was considered the Holy Land because it was there Jesus lived, died, and arose from the grave.

Although the Muslims controlled the Holy Land, they allowed Christians to travel freely there. All this changed, however, when the Seljuk Turks conquered the Muslims and began to murder or make slaves of Christian pilgrims.

The Call to Arms. The Seljuk Turks were threatening to conquer Constantinople. The Byzantine emperor was in need of help so he appealed to the pope in Rome. For years Church leaders trying to live Christian lives were shocked and dismayed at the violence in Europe. People claimed to be Christians but they spent a lot of time killing each other in petty wars.

The pope looked on the Turkish threat as an opportunity to unite Christians against an outside enemy. In 1095 Pope Urban II preached to a large crowd during the Council of Clermont. He called on all loyal members of the Church to go to the Holy Land and recapture Jerusalem. Those who decided to fight in the Crusades wore tunics with a large red cross on them. For this

This beautiful mosque, called the Dome of the Rock, was built by the Muslims on a site in Jerusalem considered sacred by Christians, Muslims, and Jews alike. It is the place where Abraham is said to have prepared to sacrifice Isaac; the site of Solomon's Temple; and the site from which Mohammed supposedly ascended into heaven to meet God. Crusading Christians in the Middle Ages often visited this sacred spot and other shrines in the Holy Land.

European knights, heading toward Jerusalem during the Third Crusade, are shown here in the midst of battle. They are fighting somewhere in Palestine with Turkish peoples called the Saracens. The Saracens, wielding their scimitars and daggers, were led by the mighty Saladin.

reason the decision to go on a Crusade was called *taking a cross.*

Taking the Cross. Knights went on Crusades, mainly for religious reasons. There were, however, many other reasons for a man to go on these Crusades. There was, for example, the promise of plunder and riches, as well as the opportunity to capture lands. Knights were told that if they died during a Crusade, they would go straight to heaven regardless of how wicked their lives had been. Criminals who fought in the Crusades were pardoned for their crimes.

From the moment a knight began wearing a crusader's tunic until he returned home, he was excused from paying taxes. In fact the debts of all crusaders were canceled while they were gone. Hopefully the crusader would return with enough plunder to pay off his debts. A knight did not have to worry about protecting his lands while he was gone because the Church took care of them. Serfs going on Crusades did not have to meet their manorial work obligations.

The Early Crusades. European knights dressed in heavy armor that made them hot and they were mounted on large, slow-moving chargers. They were not experienced in the fighting tactics of the lightly clad, swift-moving Turks.

The First Crusade. Although the First Crusade in 1095 was the only successful venture, the crusaders on this pilgrimage nevertheless faced many difficulties. No consideration was given to supplying the army. Thousands of men died of starvation or disease in the filthy camps or were lost in the desert. The generals quarreled constantly over who would lead the group.

In spite of these things, however, the crusaders won two great victories, capturing Jerusalem and Syria. They set up four feudal kingdoms. These kingdoms remained under

European control until 1187. Then the Muslims, led by the great Turkish leader Saladin, recaptured Jerusalem.

The Third Crusade. Many rulers joined in the Third Crusade of 1189 and as a result, it is the best known. As previously stated, the Turks had recaptured Jerusalem. Richard the Lion-Hearted, Philip II, and Frederick Barbarossa set out with armies to fight Saladin and take the Holy Land.

King Richard's Lonely Wife

Richard the Lion-Hearted, king of England, married the beautiful princess Berengaria of Navarre, Portugal. After the wedding he took her with him on the Holy Crusades in Europe. Constantly at war, Richard had little time for his wife. She is the only queen of England who never set foot on English soil.

Frederick drowned while crossing a stream in Asia Minor before joining the crusaders and his army returned home. Richard and Philip quarreled constantly about leadership of the army. Finally Philip returned to France, leaving Richard to face the wiley but chivalrous Saladin. Although Richard was a skillful leader, he was not able to win any major battles. Before leaving the Middle East, he did gain a three-year truce period in which Christians could visit Jerusalem.

The Fourth Crusade. The knights attacked the Christian city of Constantinople in the Fourth Crusade rather than face the hardships of fighting the Turks. The crusaders sacked Constantinople, and it was the first time

in her long history that she had ever been conquered. The crusaders never reached the Holy Land at all. None of the final Crusades were successful either.

The Monastic Knights. During the Crusades the knights formed three monastic orders: the Knights Templar, the Knights Hospitalers, and the Teutonic Knights. While other crusaders left the Holy Land after each war, the monastic knights remained in the area. They defended the territory that had been won during the First Crusade. These crusaders gained experience in fighting the Turks and learned to survive in the heat of the deserts. When inexperienced crusaders came to the Holy Land, the monastic knights often saved them from death.

The Importance of the Crusades. The Crusades had a great influence on Europe and future world history, even though the fighting

THE FOUR LEADERS OF THE FIRST CRUSADE.

This medieval crusader's castle is complete with moat surrounding the structure, high walls, and guard tower, all built as protection against enemy attack.

and territory captured were not significant. Constantinople was greatly weakened. By the 1400s the Turks captured this city, bringing the Byzantine Empire to an end.

The most important result of the Crusades was that they brought about the death of feudalism and set events in motion that led to the discovery of the New World. So many knights and nobles were killed during the Crusades that the kings were able to gain control over the nobility. Also, serfs who had tra-

---

The Children's Crusade

One of the most tragic things that happened during the pilgrimages of the Middle Ages was the Children's Crusade. The common people believed that the earlier Crusades were failures because the knights were fighting for lands and riches rather than for the glory of God. A French shepherd boy named Stephen gathered a band of children together and set out for Jerusalem, confident that God would help the innocent children to capture Jerusalem as the knights had not been able to do.

The French king sent the children back to their homes, but in Germany a group of more than 1,000 children stayed together. The people believed that God would take care of them as they made their way, so they were not given supplies of food, clothing, weapons, or medicine. Many of the children died of hunger, cold, and sickness. When the survivors reached the Mediterranean Sea, they expected God to open it up so that they could cross over. Instead they were captured by ruthless merchants and sold into slavery.

---

veled to foreign lands were no longer satisfied with serving their lords. They had seen the luxuries of the East and wanted to get them for their own families.

European Society Changes

A lively trade between Europe and the Middle East sprang up after the Crusades. Money began to replace produce as a means of paying for goods. As a result, cities grew larger and new ones came into existence. Kings taxed the imported luxury goods and used the money to build a standing army. Support from the cities and the army brought the power of the nobles to an end. People set out to find shorter and easier trade routes to the East. Instead, and indeed by accident, they found and eventually explored a New World. The new territory consisted mainly of the continents of North and South America. Explorers never did find a shorter route to the East because one did not exist.

The Revival of Trade

Immediately after the Crusades, the Italian cities of Venice, Genoa, and Pisa became major trade centers. These cities, with their excellent harbors, had engaged in trade during the Dark Ages, while other peoples of Europe had not. Goods from China and India were sent throughout Europe.

Since there were few cities large enough to have markets, fairs were held where people could exchange ideas as well as goods. Fairs were held only once or twice a year, but they increased the use of money, bills of exchange, and letters of credit. Instead of going to fairs, merchants began bringing their goods to city

Developed by the Church as a means of teaching illiterate people, early medieval drama centered on the Bible. Later semireligious groups such as the Craft Guild pictured here acted the "Miracle Plays."

marketplaces. People in the towns began to produce goods for merchants to sell.

The Rise of Cities. With the decline of feudalism and the revival of trade, towns and cities began to develop in Europe. Large cities influenced history by introducing a new class of people, called *merchants,* who bought and sold goods in the marketplace. Merchants were not of noble birth, but their great fortunes made them important enough to be considered by their rulers. As people crowded into cities, population increased and society became stable. This eventually led to the rise of inventions that introduced the Industrial Revolution and life as we know it today.

City Charters. Population increases affected the growth of cities in another way too. Kings discovered that it was to their advantage to support the growing middle class. They granted city *charters,* legal documents which allowed a city to be independent of the feudal lord in its district. The cities then had to answer only to the king. Another law that aided in the growth of cities allowed any serf who had escaped to a city and lived there for one year to become a freeman.

Medieval Towns. Because violence was still common, towns were heavily fortified with high encircling walls, moats, and towers similar to those around castles. The walls were built close to the city. The theory behind this was that the smaller the space enclosed, the easier it was to defend. Since every inch of space inside the walls was needed, the streets were narrow and the houses had more than one story.

The towns grew without a plan. The narrow streets wound in and out like a maze. In the larger cities the main streets were sometimes paved with cobblestones. Usually the streets

This drawing of a medieval village shows the narrow, unpaved streets in which pigs, geese, and other animals roamed freely. People sold their goods in the streets, while a criminal sat in the stocks for punishment. The unsanitary conditions in which the people lived and worked increased disease, and many died from plagues.

Drawn from medieval woodcuts, these pictures show craftsmen in their particular *guild*, or trade:

(1) the tailor, (2) the shoemaker, (3) the baker, and (4) the weaver.

were unpaved, however. Since there were no drains, people were ankle-deep in mud most of the year.

Middle class merchants often built their houses four or five stories high. Each story jutted out beyond the one below until the eaves of houses across the street from each other almost met. This caused the streets to resemble dark, airless tunnels. People threw their

The Black Death

A fear of death swept through Europe as the result of a plague called the Black Death. Nobody—rich or poor, king or serf—was safe from this terrible disease that was fatal within twenty-four hours after infecting a victim. Death carts passed daily through the streets, picking up those who had died during the night.

People were terrified and turned against their own families. When anyone complained of a headache or fever, it was immediately assumed they were catching the plague. Sick people were abandoned and left to die or to survive on their own. Houses thought to contain plague victims were boarded up so nobody could enter or leave. People were often trapped in this manner and died of hunger or thirst, though they survived the illness itself.

Large masses of people were on the move, hoping to outrun the plague, not realizing they were probably spreading it even faster by carrying germs. More than one-third of Europe's population died between 1347-50. Since that time, there has never been an epidemic of the magnitude of the Black Death.

garbage into the streets. Dogs, pigs, and geese wandered freely through the streets, eating whatever they could find.

Rats, mice, and other rodents added to the unsanitary conditions. Very few of these towns had sewage systems and infectious diseases were frequent. Between 1348 and 1350 a terrible plague called the *Black Death* swept through Europe. Black patches formed on the skin of plague victims and almost one-third of Europe's population died as a result of the disease.

Death of Feudalism. As a result of kings gaining more power and the development of cities, feudalism broke down. The Black Death plague resulted in a high death toll so there were not enough serfs to plant and harvest the fields. Landowners began offering high wages to freemen to get them to work on their lands. Serfs used the shortage of men to bargain for their freedom. The feudal system gave way to a system of property rentals, tenant farmers, and hired farm laborers. It was only a matter of time until people realized that the old feudal system would not work in their new society.

Guilds and Leagues

Many of the institutions we have today originated during the Middle Ages. We have seen how this was true in government. It also was true in the area of trade and manufacturing.

Craft Guilds. The beginnings of our modern labor unions can be traced to the craft guilds of the early 1100s. Everyone in a town who worked at the same craft, such as cloth weavers, shoe cobblers, carpenters, and potters, belonged to the same guild. Thus the townspeople had to buy goods from guild members.

There were three classes of craftsmen in a

craft guild. The *apprentice* was a young boy who lived in a master's house and learned his

HANSEATIC LEAGUE
c. 1350 A.D.
GERMAN DUCHIES ●

craft. He received no wages. Some apprentices were "sold" to their masters by their families and were not allowed to leave until their apprenticeship was completed. The apprenticeship lasted anywhere from three to twelve years, depending on the type of craft. This could seem like a lifetime to a youth who was mistreated by his master. Apprentices who were mistreated by their masters often ran away.

When his apprenticeship was completed, a young man became a *journeyman*. This came from the French word meaning "days work." The journeyman was hired by the master and received wages.

The third type of craftsman was called a *master*. To become a master, the journeyman had to prove his ability in a craft. Some crafts required him to create a "master piece" to show the best work he could do.

Merchant Guilds. Usually merchant guilds were made up of all the merchants in a town. All non-guild merchants were forced to pay tolls before they were allowed to sell their goods in a city. Their merchandise had to meet guild standards.

Guilds had their own courts where cases between merchants were handled. Uniform weights and measures were established and prices were regulated by the guilds. If a guild member was injured or killed, the guild took care of his family.

Sometimes trade leagues were formed by groups of towns to monopolize trade of certain products with foreign countries. Leagues also helped merchants to get lower *tariffs,* or taxes, on their goods. City trade leagues were especially important in Germany which had no strong national government to protect German merchants in their dealings with foreign countries.

The Hanseatic League. Seventy cities along the Baltic and North Seas formed a trade organization called the Hanseatic League. It had a strong influence on commerce and was able to put pressure on foreign governments to gain strong commercial treaties. As we shall see later, the Hanseatic League became so powerful that it played an important role in Poland's history as well as in the development of the Scandinavian countries.

Russia and the Golden Horde

The countries of Europe developed into strong national states, speaking one language and thinking of themselves either as Frenchmen or Englishmen. Meanwhile the Byzantine religion and culture had been introduced to Russia and changed the Russian upper classes. But Russia was prevented from developing into a national state by invaders from Asia. These invaders, called the Mongols, established the Golden Horde.

The Kingdom of Kiev

In studying early Russian history, it is important not to confuse it with Russia as it is today. The country did not have a large population then. The only area that influenced history was the city-kingdom of Kiev.

Kiev was located on the Dnieper River. It had a thriving trade with Constantinople and the rest of Europe. Kiev was rapidly growing larger than London or Paris. Artists and craftsmen of all kinds flocked to Kiev to put their talents to use.

Government. From 1019 to 1054, Yaroslav the Wise ruled the Kiev kingdom. Yaroslav was a Christian and did away with the barbaric trials by ordeal that were still being used in Russia. He set up a law code with fixed punishments for crimes.

Kiev and the other city-kingdoms in Russia were not under the feudal system. The king was an absolute ruler, but the freemen of the city had rights and privileges too. They were allowed to gather in a sort of town meeting where they could settle private quarrels or decide if their king should continue to rule. Some of these groups hired their kings by contract and restricted his activities.

When Yaroslav died in 1054, his kingdom was divided among his six sons. They soon began

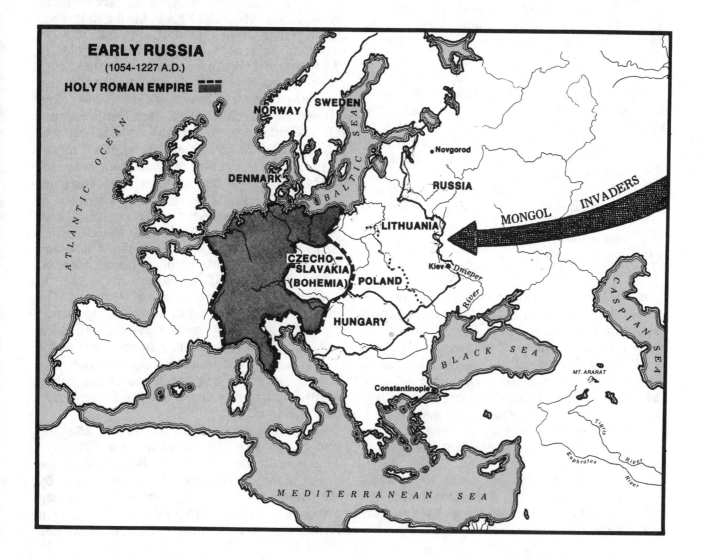

EARLY RUSSIA
(1054-1227 A.D.)

HOLY ROMAN EMPIRE

fighting each other. Through the years uncles, nephews, and cousins joined in the fighting, adding to the confusion. The nomadic tribes on the frontier were quick to take advantage of the situation by raiding the prosperous kingdom.

The Importance of Trade. Kiev had become a great trade center when Muslim forces cut off the trade route through the Mediterranean Sea. The only way goods from China, India, or the Middle East could reach Europe was by way of Constantinople to Kiev.

As a result of the Crusades, all of this changed. The Christian countries had won land and naval victories, reopening the Mediterranean Sea to trade. The Italian city-states of Venice, Genoa, and Pisa began supplying Europe with Eastern luxuries. At the same time, Kiev was being torn by civil war, a situation which caused its importance as a trade center to decline.

Mongol Invaders

At the very time the city-kingdom of Kiev was weakening, events were taking place in far-off Mongolia that would change Russia's history. A tribal leader named Temuchin united the scattered and independent Mongolian tribesmen under his leadership. Today Temuchin is known as Genghis Khan. Within five years after uniting his people, he broke through the Great Wall of China and began the conquest of China.

After conquering China, the Mongols began a campaign to take over the rest of the world. Their army was divided into two sections; while one attacked Asia Minor, India, and Persia, the other swept into the Russian steppes, a vast, fertile, treeless plain in southern Russia.

Mongolian men and their horses are inseparable.

The Golden Horde. The Russians joined forces with the nomadic tribes of the steppes to fight off this new threat. By 1237, however, a group of Mongols under the leadership of Genghis Khan's grandson Batu Khan conquered Russia.

Batu Khan realized he did not have enough men to establish a purely Mongol government in every Russian city. So he used terrorism to bring the country under his control and to keep the Russians from rebelling. Any city that refused to surrender to them was completely destroyed and the inhabitants were massacred.

The Mongols set up their stronghold at the city of Saray on the lower Volga River. The stronghold was called the Golden Horde because all the tents were yellow, the imperial color of China. The Mongolian word "horde" meant camp. From this center tax collectors were sent across Russia. As long as the tribute was paid, the Mongols allowed the Russians to continue in their Russian Orthodox religion. They also allowed Russian princes to rule the cities for them. The Russians quickly learned that any failure to pay tribute or any attempt to rebel would be handled without mercy.

Alexander Nevsky — Prince of Novgorod. The only city that did not fall to the Mongols was Novgorod. An early spring thaw had turned the area around Novgorod into a swamp, forcing the Mongols to march in a different direction. The city of Novgorod was the home of the ruling family that finally drove out the Mongols and united Russia.

The city-kingdom of Novgorod was attacked four times by fellow Christians from Europe at a time when they could have been fighting the pagan Mongols. The first attack was staged by the Swedes in 1240, but Alexander, the young prince of Novgorod, defeated them at the Neva River. Thereafter he was known as Alexander

Nevsky. Two years later Novgorod was attacked by the Teutonic Knights. Alexander, fighting on the frozen surface of Lake Peipus, again won a tremendous victory. Four years later Lithuanians attacked Novgorod, but were also driven off.

Since Alexander Nevsky was unable to fight Europeans and Mongols at the same time, he made peace with the Mongols. After Alexander's death, however, the northwestern section of Russia was captured by a group of Poles and Lithuanians, the final attack on Novgorod. The Russians believed they had been "stabbed in the back," or betrayed, by their Christian neighbors. As a result, the Russians still do not trust the good will of Europeans.

Summary. The Russians continued to pay heavy tribute to the Golden Horde for the next two and a half centuries. Almost completely conquered by these fierce and ruthless Mongols (also called Tartars), the Russian people found themselves cut off from Europe. Therefore, Russian culture, ideals, and values came from the East rather than the West.

Although they were considered Europeans, the Russian outlook on life became totally foreign to the rest of Europe. Even today people have a saying: "Scratch a Russian and you'll find a Tartar." The Russian character and attitude often differs from that of the Western World, which sometimes causes confusion and mistrust.

Mongolians have the "new" oriental look in their facial features.

Russia's Alexander Nevsky outmaneuvers the Teutonic Knights in the Battle of the Ice, fought on the frozen Lake Peipus. Nevsky (left) clashes swords with the leader of the Teutons while troops from both sides look on.

New Perspectives

Father Wilhelm Schmidt is one of those unusual men in history who step forward as leaders of thought with new ideas. He was born in Germany (Feb. 16, 1868) and died in Switzerland Feb. 10, 1954. He became a famous ethnologist as he studied communities of people all over the world. An ethnologist studies the origin and culture of people.

A scientist-ethnologist by the name of Hans Graebner introduced Schmidt to cultural studies. Schmidt had a scientist's mind; and combined evidence from geology, physical anthropology, anatomy, psychology, and archaeology to prepare his pattern of migration that he called by the German name of Kulturkreise, meaning "culture clusters."

Schmidt changed many beliefs about ancient man that even university scholars held "sacred." From his observations, Schmidt showed how every tribe (family groups) worshiped a Supreme God. Furthermore, he found records to show that earliest men and women were "monotheist." That is, the people worshiped one God in the beginning. He called this pattern, "Primitive Monotheism"and defended the writings of Moses. He believed the worship of only Jehovah God from the beginning was supported by Archaeology and Anthropology.

Schmidt showed how families migrated from a center, probably due in part, to population pressures, and referred to this movement as "Diffusion." Families carried clusters of culture with them, Kulturkreise included many and different items of culture related to their whole lives. For example, the Scythians, who began their families north of the Black Sea, were famous for their gold jewelry, buttons, and even decorations for their horses. When they migrated north and west, they carried certain shapes of pins and jewelry with them. But, as the next generations wanted to replace the objects, they had no gold. So they made the same styles in wood, or out of iron as soon as they found that metal.

Groups of people also carried family characteristics with them. A certain shape of nose, hair texture, and even length of arms became national characteristics. Family languages and belief systems stayed alive from generation-to-generation. Since migrating people expressed their beliefs, Schmidt showed the psychology of diffusion principles. He said that ethnology was a science of the mind, of both

time and space. Clusters of culture not only met physical needs, but also expressed common feelings about the basic human need to worship and serve the Creator.

Some critics said that Schmidt only studied tangible culture. Schmidt's records about man's relationships is a classic study because it helps readers understand that all cultural changes can be traced back to the point of man's creation.

Human characteristics and culture are not merely the result of man's interaction with his physical environment. Rather, they are the result of the common nature and needs that man has been created with so he can subdue the earth and exercise dominion over it.

As Schmidt recorded data from Oceania, Africa, the Americas, and from all levels of humankind in Asia and Europe, he showed how common cultural concepts bound family groups (tribes) together. By inference, modern historians observe the same kinds of common cultural concepts throughout the world today. These findings support the Biblical record that states, "God hath made of one blood all nations of men for to dwell on all the face of the earth..." Acts 17:26a.

FAR EAST AND AFRICAN DEVELOPMENTS

Projects

1. Write a report on the history of Tibet from ancient times to the present. Be sure to include the role of Tibet in the Buddhist religion and the communist takeover.

2. Find three or four poems by Li Po and Tu Fu. Read them to the class and discuss their meaning. Explain the unrest in China when these poets lived? Did these events make their poetry discouraging or depressive? Explain.

3. Read *The Travels of Marco Polo* and do a study on his experiences in China. What things would have been hard for Europeans of that time to believe? Why?

4. Give a report on either the Japanese geisha or the tea ceremony. Describe it in detail, trace its origin, and define its significance today.

5. During World War II the Japanese Air Force trained a special group of pilots called the kamikazes. What was their purpose? What made the young men willing to join? How successful were they?

6. Study how India won her independence and why Pakistan became an independent country. Draw a map showing East and West Pakistan. What are the current relations between India and Pakistan? Explain.

7. Do a report on the history of guns. Illustrate what early guns looked like. Explain how they worked. How accurate were they?

8. Research the life of Mansa Musa. How does he compare with some of the other rulers we have studied? Explain.

9. Class project. Take a field trip to your local newspaper. What type of printing press is used and how does it work? How is offset printing different from the earliest methods we have studied?

Words and Concepts

Mandingos
Urdu
kamikaze
seppuku
abstract
Songhai
Rajputs
samurai
Ainu
Manyoshu
Zimbabwe
Hsuan Tsang
shogun
cloisonne
pagoda
purdah
subsidies
jigaki
Wang An-shih
bushido

Far East and African Developments

In 627 A.D. while Europe was in the depths of the Dark Ages, China was moving into its golden age. At the same time, other Eastern civilizations were flourishing. Before the time of the Crusades, Europeans knew very little about the wealth and luxuries of the oriental East. This was because they had never traveled very far away from their homeland. When the crusaders set out for Jerusalem in 1096, however, they encountered Mediterranean traders. These merchants had been in contact with the exotic caravans from the East.

Europe's separation from Asia and Africa ended in the fifteenth century. Then European explorers (like Columbus and daGama), traders, conquerors, and missionaries began to secure footholds in areas far from their homeland. In this chapter, however, we will study Asia and Africa prior to the arrival of these Europeans.

In China two mighty dynasties rose and fell during this time and the Mongol invasion changed China's history significantly. The island nation of Japan advanced from a primitive feudal society to a cultural nation whose art and literature rivaled even that of China.

India was invaded by the Muslims in one of the bloodiest massacres in history. Even today ill feelings between the Hindus and Muslims continue to play a major role in Indian history.

In Africa several thriving civilizations came into existence just before the Europeans began to explore that continent.

China and the Mongols

As we saw in Chapter 10, the Han Dynasty controlled China from 206 B.C. to 220 A.D. At the same time, the Roman Empire and the Kushan Dynasty in India were at the height of their power. When all three of these mighty empires fell, trade between the East and West almost stopped.

The T'ang Dynasty

Centuries passed and in 616 A.D. a dynasty rose to power, conquering all the independent

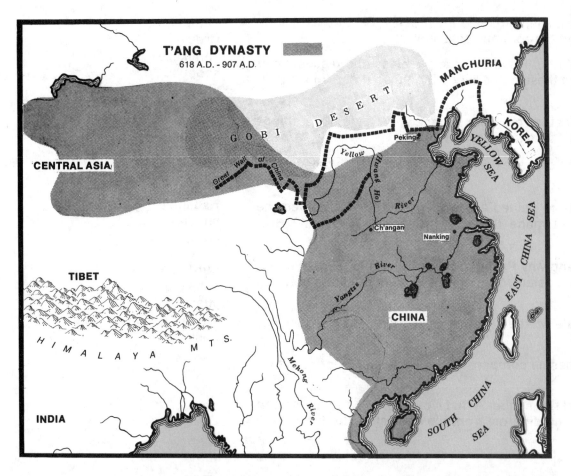

T'ANG DYNASTY
618 A.D. - 907 A.D.

CENTRAL ASIA

GOBI DESERT

MANCHURIA

KOREA

Peking

Yellow

Hwang Ho River

YELLOW SEA

Great Wall of China

Ch'angan

Nanking

TIBET

Yangtze River

CHINA

EAST CHINA SEA

HIMALAYA MTS.

Mekong River

INDIA

SOUTH CHINA SEA

kingdoms and restoring order in China. Once peace was established, the first T'ang Dynasty emperor turned the empire over to his son T'ai Tsung Tang.

T'ai Tsung. T'ai Tsung, who ruled from 627 to 650 A.D., was one of China's greatest emperors. Under his rule China became a strong and unified nation. Art and poetry were encouraged and the study of mathematics was introduced from India. Ch'ang-an, the capital city, was so beautiful that tourists came to see it from all over Asia.

Confucianism was still the major religion in China, but the Chinese also were open to new ideas at this time. The emperor allowed both Buddhist and Nestorian Christian missionaries to come into the country in search of converts. Buddhism gathered large numbers of converts, while Christianity was not accepted by the masses.

T'ai Tsung extended China's borders to India and Persia, conquering Korea, Manchuria, Tibet, and central Asia. This made China the largest existing nation in the world at that time.

Ming Huang. In 713 Ming Huang, another great Chinese emperor, came to the throne. He required Turkey, Persia, and Samarkand to pay tribute to China. During the early years of his reign, Ming Huang was concerned with improving his kingdom and was a good ruler. In later years, however, he began to care less about good government and more about his own luxury. As his government became corrupt, a Tartar general named Lu-Shan led the army in revolt. In 762 Ch'ang-an, the capital, was sacked and millions of people died.

Later Lu-Shan was killed and Ming Huang returned to his throne. Although the T'ang emperors remained in power for another hundred years, they had become too weak and frightened to rule very effectively. Large sections of the empire rebelled and broke away. A Mongolian people called the Khitan captured Manchuria, the Uigur Turks captured Mongolia, and the Thai and Tibetan people rebelled. The Arabs who were spreading Islam defeated the Chinese in a terrible battle and Turkestan also was lost.

Trade, both within China and with foreign countries, slowed down. Taxes were heavily increased as rulers became more corrupt. The great masses of Chinese people suffered terribly. Uprisings rocked the empire as strong provincial governors declared their independence. Finally in 907 A.D., the T'ang Dynasty came to an end and was followed by years of unstable government.

Architecture of the T'ang Dynasty. During the T'ang Dynasty, chinese architects designed the *pagoda,* a many-storied tower. A pagoda usually had eight sides, was built of brick on a stone foundation, and was five to thirteen stories high. It always had an uneven number of stories since even numbers were considered unlucky.

Because pagodas had religious significance, they were located in almost every Chinese town. The Chinese believed they kept away winds and floods, kept evil spirits happy, and brought prosperity to the area.

The Sung Yueh, built in 523 A.D., is the oldest pagoda still standing. The Jade Pagoda, located at the Summer Palace in Peking, is considered to be one of the most beautiful pagodas ever built. The Porcelain Tower in Nanking is probably the most spectacular and famous of all the Chinese pagodas. It was destroyed during a revolution in 1854.

Art. The T'ang Dynasty is noted for the beauty of the artwork produced during its time. Ancient

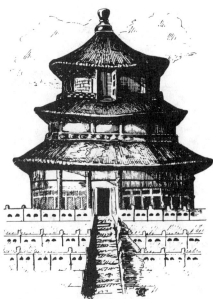

This pagoda is located in the Imperial City of Peking. The early Chinese believed pagodas would keep away winds and floods and bring prosperity.

During the T'ang Dynasty many Buddhist missionaries came to China from India. Many Chinese became Buddhists and statues like this one became common throughout the territory controlled by China.

For centuries Chinese farmers have used the same methods of growing rice. Rice cultivation is hard, back-breaking work in which farmers are forced to wade or crawl in cold water.

Chinese painting was much different from the painting of other civilizations. Until now we have studied only *realistic* painting; that is, painting that illustrated Biblical and other religious stories or showed how people lived. The artists copied or illustrated things the way they really were. Chinese painting, on the other hand, was much more *abstract*.

A Chinese artist often stood and looked at the scene he wanted to paint for many days in order to get what he called the "feel" of the subject. Then he went to a room and painted the scene. He tried to capture the inner significance of what he had seen rather than copying a perfect likeness. Very few ancient Chinese paintings have survived because they were done on silk which decays very quickly. Lei, the sister of a Chinese emperor, is said to have been the first Chinese painter.

Poetry. Li Po and Tu Fu, two of China's greatest poets, lived during the T'ang Dynasty. Tu Fu wrote poems that explained people's innermost feelings. Li Po's poetry was more down to earth and was more easily understood by Europeans. According to legend, Li Po drowned

---

Chinese Scroll Paintings

In the United States people buy paintings to hang on their walls so they can share their beauty with friends who come to visit. In ancient China paintings were done on silk and rolled into a scroll. The scrolls were kept in drawers instead of hanging on the wall. Whenever the Chinese wanted to enjoy a picture, they took it from the drawer, looked at it, and then returned it to the drawer.

---

in a puddle of water. It is said he was drunk and wanted to get close to the moon that was reflected in the puddle.

The Sung Dynasty

Between the years of 907 and 962 A.D., there was warfare and confusion throughout China. Several small, weak kingdoms which constantly warred with one another were established. Finally T'ai Tsu Sung took over the other kingdoms and founded a new Dynasty. He ruled from 1021 to 1086. His dynasty extended from 960 to 1279. T'ai Tsu was not a good ruler. He was more interested in the pleasures of his court than in ruling, so he appointed a man named Wang An-shih to run the government for him.

Wang An-shih and Strong Government. Wang An-shih was one of the most remarkable men of that time. He was very concerned about the poor living conditions of the lower classes. He passed laws, making it easier for the poor people to earn a living. Moneylenders charged so much interest that poor farmers had to sacrifice all their crops to repay loans. To ease their burden, Wang An-shih proposed a system of low interest rates on government loans.

Wang An-shih passed another law to abolish forced labor on government projects. This allowed farmers to plant and harvest their crops without having to stop and work on government projects. Many people were unemployed. Instead of having the government give them food, however, Wang An-shih loaned them free land, seed, tools, farm animals, and building materials. The new farmers were required to repay the government as soon as they harvested their first crops.

Free schools were established and everyone was encouraged to enroll their children. The government also gave pensions to old people, the unemployed, and the poor. At the same time, the government financed construction of dams and dikes to prevent flooding.

These projects cost the government a great deal of money. In order to pay for everything, the government taxed the people heavily. Even though they were all happy with the benefits of the new programs, the people began to complain about the high taxes. Wang An-shih tried to cut back expenses by dismissing the army. Instead of having a permanent army with soldiers paid by the government, Wang An-shih devised a different system. Families who had more than one man in them were required to provide a soldier whenever war broke out. Wang An-shih also raised money for the government by taking over all factories or businesses that manufactured any type of goods for sale. Their profits then went to the government.

As often happens, however, government officials running the businesses became corrupt, and taxes went still higher. Then a series of floods and droughts struck China. The people were left starving as a result of the disasters. They longed for the days when they ran their own businesses, and they blamed Wang An-shih for their problems. In order to avoid having his government overthrown, Emperor T'ai Tsu dismissed him from office. Although his ideas were not accepted during his lifetime, almost all of Wang An-shih's ideas are used today by governments around the world.

The next Sung emperor decided to enlist the aid of Manchuria to recapture some of the Chinese territory that had broken away after the T'ang Dynasty collapsed. He asked them to help him defeat the Khitan. The Manchurians defeated the Khitan, but in 1127 they turned on

northern China and captured it. They continued to rule in northern China for almost a hundred years, calling their kingdom the Chin Dynasty.

The Sung Dynasty continued ruling the southern portion of China, but were forced to move their capital from Pien Liang to Lin-an, known today as Hangchow.

Inventions and Discoveries of the Sung Dynasty. One of the most important achievements of the Sung Dynasty was the development of the printing press. Earlier civilizations used a cylinder, seal-type press, but it was too small for printing anything but letters and other brief messages. Until the Sung Dynasty, books were written by hand and took years to produce.

During the T'ang Dynasty, a printing press, similar to the ones we have today, was invented. In the Sung Dynasty, paper and ink were developed. For the first time, books could be produced in large quantities. A great revival of learning took place, as the writings of the great Chinese philosophers became available to

A printing press with movable type was invented by the Chinese during the T'ang Dynasty, almost 400 years before the Europeans. The press was not widely used until the Sung Dynasty when paper and ink were discovered.

The Giant Panda migrated and settled in China as its favorite home. It only eats certain kinds of bamboo shoots.

Temuchin, known to the Western World as Genghis Khan, is pictured here with feathered helmet.

anyone who wanted them. The oldest printed book in the world is the *Diamond Sutra* by Wand Chieh, dated May 11, 868 A.D.

Great achievements in chemistry, zoology, and botany took place between 1021 and 1127. The Chinese knew more about algebra than any other country at that time. They developed the magnetic compass and a clock powered by water. (It was not until the 1600s that a similar clock was produced in Europe.) Gunpowder, once used only for firecrackers, then was used to make bombs. The Chinese also developed an inoculation for smallpox some 300 years before it was used in Europe.

Religion. Buddhism was beginning to have an important place in Chinese thought. Confucianism, however, had another revival and continued to be the leading philosophy of China during this period. This was because a philosopher by the name of Chu Hsi turned Confucian teachings into an orderly philosophy.

Art. When China split into the northern and southern kingdoms in 1127, art in the north became very formal. Artists tried to picture everything with great realism. In the Sung Kingdom in the south, artists used lots of color and freedom of expression. Even everyday items such as pottery were created like important works of art. Each piece was crafted into a beautiful masterpiece. The potter's most beautiful product was porcelain, a clay pottery resembling glass. Porcelain glowed when baked in an oven.

Sung artists never have been surpassed in their skill with textiles, metal work, and jade sculpture. Artists began to create intricate decorations with brightly colored lacquers. Many layers of rich red and gold lacquer were applied to objects and each coat was rubbed to a deep glow. This art was later introduced in Japan where beautifully lacquered wares are still produced.

Homes and Architecture. Chinese homes during the Sung Dynasty were simple structures. Houses, palaces, and humble dwellings all had outer walls to hide them from the street. Inside the walls were courtyards where the rich people often grew lovely gardens.

The poor lived in gloomy tenements and often one wall surrounded several houses. Their homes had narrow doors, low ceilings, and dirt floors. Pigs, dogs, and chickens often shared a single-room dwelling with the family. The poorest people lived in huts of mud and straw, which gave little protection against wind and rain. A charcoal-type brazier provided the only source of heating, and both the rich and poor had to wear more clothing during the winter to keep warm. Even today most homes in China lack a central heating system.

Wealthier Chinese families had mats or tiles covering their floors. Their houses were never more than one story high. If more rooms were needed to accommodate a growing family, separate buildings were constructed rather than adding on to the original house. The only furniture consisted of hand-carved chests and chairs. It is interesting to note that the Chinese were the only oriental people to use chairs; all others sat on the floor.

The Mongols Rule China

Genghis Khan united the Mongol tribes in the 1200s. Meanwhile, Nin Tsung, the Sung emperor, sent him a letter demanding loyalty and submission to China. But the Mongols, led by Genghis Khan swept through China. In the warfare that followed, 90 Chinese cities were completely destroyed.

Genghis Khan died in 1227 before China was completely conquered, but his children and grandchildren continued fighting. They also moved westward capturing Russia and Persia, as we have seen.

Kublai Khan. The Yuan Dynasty was established in 1260 and the Mongolian Emperor Kublai Khan was its first ruler. The Yuan Dynasty ruled for 100 years. Kublai Khan, also known as the Great Khan, built his palace in the new capital city of Cambaluc, now called Peking. Most high government positions under Kublai Khan were held by Mongols. The Mongols began adopting Chinese customs and culture in much the same way the Romans had copied Greek culture.

China prospered under Kublai's rule. Seeing the cultural superiority of the peoples he had conquered, Kublai Khan wisely tolerated all religions and patronized Chinese culture. He maintained order, improved roads, and developed a postal system similar to the pony express used hundreds of years later in the United States.

Kublai Khan built canals, filled granaries, and gave government aid to orphans, the sick, and old scholars. High tax rates were necessary, however, to finance heavy government spending. Too much paper money was issued, causing the value of money to decrease. Kublai Khan's only military failure occurred when his planned invasion of Japan had to be canceled. A typhoon prevented his armies from going ashore.

The vast Mongol Empire built by Kublai Khan covered more territory than any other empire in history. After his death in 1294, however, the Russian and western Asian portions of the empire broke away from Yuan control. Seven other Yuan emperors followed Kublai Khan, but all of them were inferior rulers. The printing of money became so reckless during this time that it had to be stopped altogether. The economy was bankrupt and armed power in the territory became so weak that rulers no longer could even defend the coastal areas against pirates.

The Ming Dynasty. As the Yuan emperors

The Travels of Marco Polo

For the rich supply of information we have about China in the days of Kublai Khan, we are indebted to Marco Polo. He was the son of a Venetian merchant who traveled to China with his father and uncle in 1275. They were received there with a royal welcome and Polo was given a job in his majesty's service. The three remained there for 17 years and Marco Polo wrote a book, *The Travels of Marco Polo,* about his stay in China. It is the best account we have of Kublai Khan, his court, and his glorious reign.

When the Polos returned to Italy, nobody believed the stories they told about the wealth, comforts, and inventions in China. People called Marco "Messer Millions" because he described everything in terms of thousands and millions. Not everyone laughed at Marco Polo, however. Two hundred years later a man named Christopher Columbus read his book. Columbus then began to dream of finding a sea route that would take him to the riches of China.

Kublai Khan, grandson of Genghis Khan, was the founder of the Yuan Dynasty in China. It was during his rule that the European adventurer Marco Polo lived in China.

Mongol warriors, such as this one armed with crossbow and decorative warrior's clothing, swept across China destroying every city that stood in their way.

became weaker, nationalism began to grow among Chinese people who longed to be free of foreign rule. Finally in 1368 an ex-Buddhist priest named Hung Wu led a revolt and overthrew the Yuan Dynasty. He became the first emperor of the Ming Dynasty. Immediately he began removing all traces of Mongolian influence. He reestablished the country's defense system and repaired irrigation systems.

Hung Wu was suspicious of all foreigners, so he refused to allow any trade or other contact with the rest of the world. Chinese citizens were not even allowed to leave China. The Chinese people became convinced that their culture was superior to any other in the world. While the rest of the world was exchanging ideas, culture, and achievements, Chinese culture remained the same.

The Ming Dynasty was known for its beautiful pottery and for developing a new type of art called *cloisonne*. In cloisonne art tiny wires were used to outline a design. The spaces between the wires were filled in with tiny, multicolored mosaic or enamel pieces. When fired in a kiln, they blended together to form a pattern.

The Ming Dynasty ruled from 1368 to 1644. A new group of invaders called the Manchus poured over the Great Wall and founded the Ch'ing Dynasty. In the middle of the seventeenth century, they defeated the last Ming emperor and seized control of China. They remained in power until early in the twentieth century, as we will see in a later chapter.

Japan: Land of the Rising Sun

China's neighbors to the east are the Japanese. There are more than 3,000 Japanese islands located in the Pacific Ocean about 160 km (100 miles) from the Asian coast. They stretch from Siberia in the north to the China Sea in the south. Most of the population inhabits the four major Japanese islands of Hokkaido, Honshu, Shikoku, and Kyushu. Japan still has many active volcanoes and the Japanese islands are located on the same earthquake belt as California.

Chinese Temples are built with huge snake tails to show remembrance of snakes who rescued Noah and family.

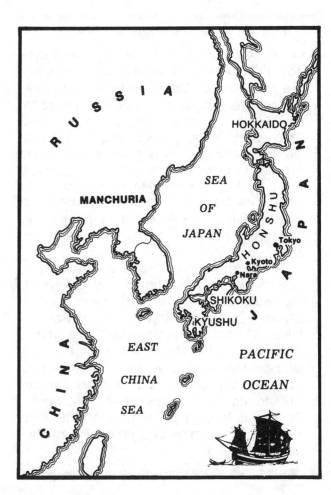

The Early Japanese People

According to historians, the exact point of origin of the early Japanese is uncertain. In prehistoric times it is believed groups of people arrived in Japan from Mongolia, Borneo, Java, the Philippines, South China, Indochina, Korea, and Manchuria. As a result of this mixed heritage, there are still marked differences in peoples who live on the various islands.

The earliest people to settle the Japanese islands were Caucasians who did not have the almond-shaped eyes of orientals. They were called the Ainu. They lived in the southern islands and were hunters. As other groups moved into the Japanese islands, the more primitive Ainu were slowly driven north. Today groups of Ainu still live on the northern island of Hokkaido.

The Earthquake Islands

Some kind of tremor or quake strikes the Japanese islands almost every day. Some of these earth movements are very destructive. In the 1603 quake, for example, 32,000 people in the city of Tokyo alone were killed.

To explain these disruptions, the ancient Japanese theorized that they were caused by a giant sleeping fish that was trapped under the islands. When its sleep was disturbed, the fish supposedly moved, causing the land to tremble. More recently, however, these quakes have been attributed to the fact that Japan's land formation lends itself to earthquakes. Also the islands are located on a major earthquake belt that runs across the Pacific Ocean.

Land of the Rising Sun

There are many different theories about Japan's name and why it is called "the land of the rising sun." At first the Japanese called their land Yamato, probably after the emperor's clan. Later on, however, the Japanese came into frequent contact with the Chinese. The Chinese called the islands *Jih-pen,* meaning "land of the rising sun."

Early in history the Chinese thought Japan was the easternmost country in the world. It was the only piece of land the Chinese could see between China and the rising sun. They undoubtedly thought the sun actually rose in the skies over Japan. They had no knowledge of the existence of land or sea any farther to the east than Japan.

At any rate the Japanese liked the name and began to use it. Later Europeans who traded with the Japanese mispronounced *Jih-pen,* calling it Japan. Another theory about "the land of the rising sun" indicates it was so-named because the sun played a significant role in the Shinto religion of the Japanese.

Even today the Japanese flag depicts a sun to represent "the land of the rising sun."

The Yamato Dynasty. The first organized society established in Japan was a type of clan feudalism. Clans ruled the land and the people owed their loyalty to the head of the clan. There

Yomei-Mon Gate, leads to the Shinto Shrine in Nikko, Japan. It has been said it would take all day to look at every piece of carving on this gate.

This armor, made from padded cloth, was actually worn by a samurai warrior during Japan's early history.

was a definite social structure. The clan head claimed to be divine. Under him were the clan warriors. Then came the farmers and artisans. The slaves and Ainus were the lowest class.

Feudalism, as we have already seen, is the best environment for warriors. From earliest times the warrior in Japan has had a high social position. The clans took over most of the Japanese islands between the first and fourth centuries A.D.

According to Japanese folklore, Jimmu Tenno, the first Yamato emperor, descended from the sun goddess and began ruling in 660 B.C. Historians believe he was only a clan chieftain at this time. The Japanese, however, claim that he established the Yamato Dynasty and that this is the oldest unbroken dynasty in the world. (Their present emperor comes from the same family.) By the early part of the first century A.D. the Yamato clan began taking over the other clans on their island.

Japanese Culture

The Chinese Influence. Japan was a rather backward country until the Yamato clan took control. They established contact with the Han Dynasty in China between 202 B.C. and 220 A.D. The Japanese soon picked up many elements of Chinese culture, including pottery-making, weaving, breeding silkworms and making silk. They adopted Chinese ideas about medicine, science, philosophy, and even military techniques.

The Japanese had no written language of their own, so they began to use Chinese writing. The Chinese had a different symbol for each word. This was because their words were short. The Japanese language has words of many syllables,

so they were forced to use a different symbol for each syllable of each word. Thus writing became very difficult for the Japanese. Finally they simplified their writing by shortening the Chinese symbols.

Japan's Religion. The earliest religion in Japan was known as Shintoism, the "Way of the Gods." According to Shinto beliefs, the land

Divine Right of Japan's Emperors

According to Japanese legend, the first emperor was Jimmu Tenno, supposedly a descendant of the sun goddess. Hirohito, a descendant of this same family, still reigns today in what has turned out to be the longest, unbroken dynasty in the world. Of course, historians do not believe that Jimmu Tenno was related to the sun goddess, but that he was a member of the Yamato clan. Like other ancient rulers, Tenno probably claimed divine descent in order to get the Japanese people to be loyal to him.

While the Chinese believed in the Mandate of Heaven, giving them the right to overthrow their emperor, the Japanese considered their emperor to be a divine being. Any rebellion against the Japanese emperor, therefore, was considered a religious crime. This prevented the Japanese from ever overthrowing their emperor. Even after World War II, many Japanese people still believed their emperor was divine. At this time, however, the victorious Americans forced him to announce over the radio to his people that he was not divine, but an ordinary earthly person like everyone else.

itself was divine. Shintoists believed that all objects and forces of nature had their own spirits. They believed that the emperor was related to the sun goddess, and he was considered divine.

Korean missionaries brought Buddhist teachings to Japan. The Japanese emperor accepted the new faith as the official court religion. He hoped the new religion would weaken the nobles' power. Buddhist teachings were a good way to introduce Chinese culture to Japan. Since Shintoism had no philosophy or code of behavior, Buddhism became an extension of the Shinto faith. Soon Buddhism grew popular and spread throughout the country. As a result, Shintoism and Buddhism existed side by side and still do in modern-day Japan.

Prince Shotoku was one of Japan's earliest Buddhist scholars. He followed Jimmu Tenno as emperor and during his 30-year reign, Chinese culture became an important part of Japanese life. Shotoku spent large sums of money building Buddhist temples. The Horiuji Temple, built by Shotoku, is the oldest temple still standing in Japan today.

The Japanese Character. Although the Japanese borrowed ideas and culture from China, they were isolated enough to remain free from foreign invasion. Because of their isolation, the Japanese people developed a strong feeling of their own importance as a nation. They had a feeling of independence toward the rest of the world.

A key element in the Japanese character is the belief that individual freedom is not important. Even during the feudal period in Europe, people were concerned with the rights and freedoms of individuals. In Japan, however, the individual was not considered important. The group to which a person belonged and the rights, freedoms, and responsibilities of the group as a whole, were the important factors.

Undoubtedly this attitude developed because Japan has always been overpopulated and crowded. Even in ancient times, the population was too large for the size of the territory. Very rigid rules of social behavior were established. Everyone had his own place in the group and the group dictated individual rights and duties. People automatically knew who their superiors were.

Japanese women wear traditional *kimonos,* or long, flowing robes with wide sashes. Women of Japan were forced to model their behavior after their Chinese neighbors and led restricted lives.

This "Red Monster" is the fierce guardian of one of Japan's Shinto shrines. The Japanese believe these frightening guards will chase away evil spirits.

In early Japan women played an important role in both the social and literary areas. There were six empresses who actually ruled the island of Japan in their own right. As Chinese influences became more widespread in Japan, however, the idea of women's total subordination to men was adopted.

Young women were forced to obey their fathers. When they married, they were under their husband's control. When both husband and father died, women were subject to the control of their sons. A man could divorce his wife if she talked too loudly or too long. If a husband treated his wife cruelly, she was expected to treat him with increased kindness. Since women were not allowed to inherit property, a man without any sons had to adopt one to be his heir.

From the earliest times the Japanese have loved art, poetry, and music. It was not unusual for warriors to compose poems while waiting to go into battle. They memorized their work and told it to others who also memorized it. Then it was passed down from one generation to the next by word-of-mouth. People always enjoyed the meaning of such poetry, but they often lost track of who wrote it.

In 951 A.D. the emperor held the first poetry contest in which people composed poems and submitted them to judges. The winning poems each year were published in government records. The *Manyoshu,* one of the oldest and most famous Japanese books, contains 20 volumes of poems which were written over a period of 400 years.

Japan's Feudal System

In order to strengthen their overall power, the Yamato emperors began copying the government used by the T'ang Dynasty in China. This new form of Japanese government was called the Great Reform. The emperor took over as the supreme authority, all land belonged to him, and all taxes went directly to him. He appointed men to govern the various areas and they answered to him for their actions. Such government positions were awarded to men of noble families rather than on the basis of merit or good qualifications.

In 710 A.D. Nara became the first imperial capital of Japan. The capital was moved to Kyoto in 784 A.D. where it remained until 1868.

Over the years the emperor became more interested in the pleasures of his court than in governing his country. He did not realize how strong his nobles were becoming. The Japanese felt it was a crime against their gods to depose or rebel against an emperor.

The Fujiwara Regents. A noble family named Fujiwara took over the government. and allowed the emperor to remain on, in Kyoto, as a "puppet" ruler. If any emperor during this period tried to regain control, or angered the Fujiwara regent in any way, he was forced to resign or go to a monastery. His son would take his place as the new emperor. Many times the emperors were forced to marry women from the Fujiwara regent clan, making the ties between their two families even closer. The Fujiwara regents kept the loyalty of other nobles by making their lands tax exempt. This only made the nobles even stronger and weakened the power of the government.

Gradually a feudal system developed, similar to that in Europe. Landowners had their own armies of professional soldiers, called *samurai,* who raided their weaker neighbors. Military power became most important and Japan was rocked by disorder and lawlessness.

As the feudal system emerged, the samurai warriors became the highest social class. *Bushido,* an unwritten code to guide the samurai's life, slowly developed. This code was similar to the code of chivalry in Europe. It encouraged discipline, strength, loyalty, and courage. A ceremonial custom of committing suicide, called *seppuku,* became a major part of this code. It was used by warriors who wanted to atone for crimes, prove loyalty to a lord, or avoid disgrace of some kind.

The Military Clans. Between 1185 and 1590, Japan's history became a time of violence. Powerful feudal lords fought each other for control of the government. This period is often depicted in Japanese movies and is idolized in much the same way as we idolize the American "Wild West" era.

Suicide—A Japanese Custom

The art of *seppuku,* a precise method of suicide with a knife, was one of the first things a young samurai was taught. Westerners know this ceremony as hara=kiri, but the Japanese consider this term vulgar and do not use it. Women and common people were not allowed to commit seppuku.

Women could, however, commit *jigaki,* the act of piercing the throat with a dagger in such a way as to sever the arteries in a single stroke. Every noble woman was carefully taught this technique while very young. Women were taught to tie their legs together before severing the artery so their bodies would not be found in an immodest position.

For brief periods of time, the two leading clans took turns controlling the government. They no longer even pretended to be ruling as regents for the emperor. They took the title *shogun,* meaning general, and ruled outright. The emperor was allowed to remain in Kyoto with his women, but he was kept out of government affairs entirely. Many times the shogun was able to maintain peace only in the territory around his capital. The rest of Japan was caught up in violence as bands of samurai terrorized farm villages and fought each other.

The most famous shogun clans were the Taira, Minamoto, Hojo, and the Ashikaga. A Hojo shogun was governing when Kublai Khan tried, without success, to conquer Japan. The Great Khan tried to invade twice, once in 1274 and once in 1281. Both times, however, his fleet was destroyed by typhoon winds. The Japanese called these winds *kamikaze,* which means "divine wind." (We will come across this name again during the study of World War II.)

Japan Under the Shoguns. Even though disorder was widespread while the shoguns ruled, Japan became a strong, highly cultural country. By 1190 Kyoto had become a great city with a population of nearly half a million people. It was larger than any European city at that time with the possible exception of Constantinople and Cordova.

The shoguns befriended artists and encouraged them by paying subsidies (cash payments) to continue working. At the same time, a merchant class was developing and strong trade relations existed between Japan, China, and Korea. Japanese trading ships and pirates sailed as far west as Siam.

The first university was established in Kyoto in the 700s A.D., but it was only for the upper

In Japan the fierce samurai warriors were professional soldiers who would commit suicide rather than bring disgrace to themselves by going against their code of honor.

classes. Gradually provincial schools were established under government control and graduates were allowed to attend the university. If they could pass certain exams after graduation, they were allowed to hold government offices.

The Muslims Conquer India

The Gupta Empire spent its last years fighting off foreign invaders. First the Hunas, nomadic tribesmen from the north, raided the frontier. Later an even greater threat arose. The Muslims, who had been expanding their empire across North Africa and Persia, began to push into India. The Guptas were the last purely Indian dynasty to rule India. For the next 500 years, India was controlled by foreigners.

The End of the Gupta Dynasty

The Gupta Empire received a terrible shock as the Hunas attacked northern India about 420 A.D. Finally the new Gupta emperor, Skanda Gupta, drove the Hunas out and restored some of the former glory of the Gupta Empire. He died after only 12 years on the throne and upon his death the kingdom fell apart.

The new emperors were too weak to control the empire, so the local governors set themselves up as kings of local feudal kingdoms. In the 490s a fresh wave of Huna invaders hit India. This time there was no strong leader to stop them. By 500 A.D. western India was ruled by Huna kings. Constant warfare among these many feudal kingdoms made it impossible for them to stay in control of the territory they had conquered. By 550 A.D. the Huna kingdoms passed from the streams of civilization.

Civil Wars. India remained in a constant state of civil war between 550 and 916 A.D. as the feudal kingdoms fought each other. In 606 A.D., however, a ruler named Harsha was able to bring about some measure of order. Harsha began to rule when he was 16 and reigned for 41 years. He had a feudal kingdom rather than an empire and spent much time traveling around keeping his nobles under control.

We know quite a bit about Harsha's kingdom because a Chinese named Hsuan Tsang visited India for several years and wrote about what he saw and experienced. From this account we

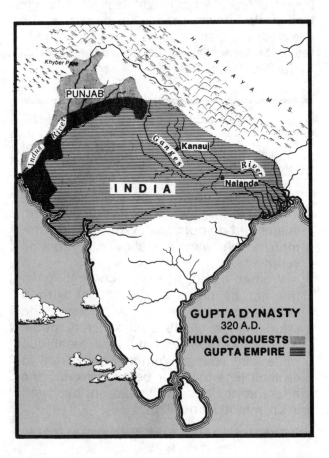

GUPTA DYNASTY
320 A.D.
HUNA CONQUESTS
GUPTA EMPIRE

know there was much disorder and lawlessness in India during this period and that Hsuan was robbed more than once.

Harsha tried to be a good ruler. He had a movable pavilion so he could sit along the side of the road and listen to the problems and complaints of his people. You will remember that Louis IX of France took a similar interest in his kingdom and was much loved by his people.

Although Harsha was a very strong Buddhist, Buddhism was no longer an important religion in India. Hinduism had adopted some of the major Buddhist teachings and the Indian people preferred it to Buddhism.

When Harsha died, he left no heirs. Immediately the kingdom fell apart. Once again civil war broke out. From 690 until 916, India remained in the grips of warring kings and kingdoms. As is always the case when civil war devastates a country, the common people trying to stay alive on their farms suffered the most destruction.

One result of all this internal strife was the introduction of child marriages. They became very common and sometimes children were married while they were still babies. The idea was to provide another family to raise the children should their parents be killed in the civil war. The girls were allowed to stay with their parents until they were 12 or 13 years old. Then the young bride was sent to live with her husband.

The Rajput Kingdoms

The Muslim Empire had now spread to the borders of India. By 916 Muslim armies had gathered on India's northwest border and were ready to attack. Many kingdoms were located in a territory known as Rajputana between the Indus and Ganges Valleys. The people in this area were a mixture of Hunas and Indians. They called themselves *Rajputs,* or sons of kings.

The Rajput kingdoms were very warlike and had developed a code of chivalry similar to that practiced in Europe. They respected women, spared enemies who were willing to surrender in battle, and tried to deal fairly with everyone. They had adopted the Hindu religion and merged into the local Indian culture.

The Muslim Conquest

The first Muslim raiders came from Afghanistan in 986 A.D. By 997 Sultan Mahmud established the practice of raiding India and returning to Afghanistan with the riches he had captured. Between 1001 and 1027, there were 17 major Muslim raids in India.

Indian kings, with the exception of the Rajput kings, were not able to unite and were defeated terribly. Indian people were divided and helpless to defend themselves, and the country lay wide open to Muslim conquest.

In 1191 a king named Prthviraja defeated the Muslim army. The army retreated from India, but returned the next year with a larger force. Prthviraja was killed in the fighting. He is the hero of many Indian folk ballads, however, and is remembered for his bravery and chivalry.

By this time the Muslims had arrived to stay. At first Muslim raiders merely collected Indian booty and left for home with it. Soon, however, they began to take over the country, setting up new governments and ruling their captive people. By 1203 all of northern India, except a small Rajput kingdom, was under Muslim control. The new ruler was a former Muslim general known as the sultan of Delhi.

Gradually the descendants of this sultan began the slow, southward invasion of the rest of India. Muslim religion and authority was widespread and by the 1300s Muslims controlled most of India. The territory was too large to be ruled from Delhi and soon the southern area broke up into smaller Muslim and Hindu kingdoms.

The Muslim Influence. Before the massive Muslim invasion, the Indian people had been able to absorb their conquerors. They influenced them to give up their old habits, religion, and customs and become Indian. Any customs their conquerors refused to give up were adopted by the Indians. Foreign religious ideas were simply added to the Hindu religion. Thus, until the Muslim invasion, foreign conquests had not disturbed the basic living patterns of the Indians.

All this changed when the Muslims invaded, however. The Muslims had always been a harsh and violent people. We have seen how they were reasonably tolerant of the non-Muslims living in the Christian and Jewish territories they conquered; but this was not true in India.

India's Hindu religion was totally foreign and contrary to the Muslims' Islamic faith. The Muslims, therefore, were fighting a "holy war," with the aim of either converting their enemies or destroying them. Hundreds of thousands of people were brutally murdered, and many beautiful temples were smashed, burned, and completely destroyed.

An example of the brutality of the Muslim conquest was their devastation of the city of Vijayanagar. Located in central India, this was one of the richest and most beautiful cities in the country. Nicolo Conti, a European visitor there, once described Vijayanagar as covering 96.5 km (60 miles) with about 100,000 homes.

When the Muslims invaded southern India, they looted Vijayanagar for five months. Anything that could not be stolen was either destroyed or burned. When the Muslims

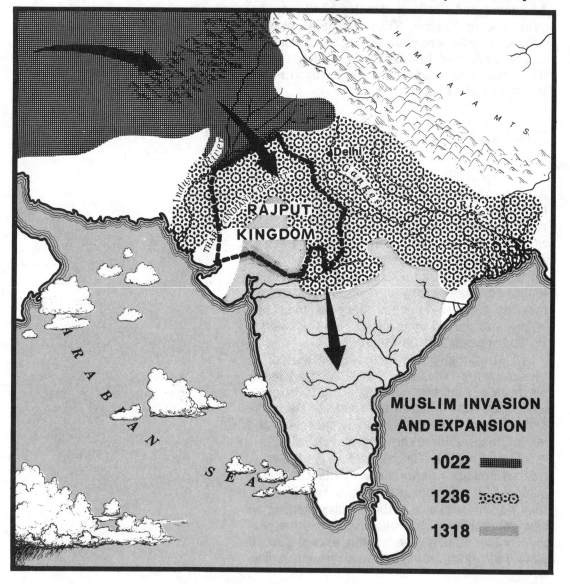

MUSLIM INVASION AND EXPANSION

1022

1236

1318

HIMALAYA MTS.

Delhi

RAJPUT KINGDOM

THAR (INDIAN) DESERT

Indus River

Ganges River

ARABIAN SEA

withdrew, the city and its population had been completely wiped out.

The Muslims then invented *Urdu,* a new language to help them govern their new subjects. This language included a combination of Persian, Turkish, and Arabic influences, while using Hindu grammar. Urdu and Hindu are still the two major languages spoken in India today.

As a result of the Muslim invasion, the position of women grew even worse than before. They were required to treat their husbands as gods. Women were not even allowed to eat with the men. They had to wait until the men were finished and eat their leftovers. They were not allowed to go to school and they were not taught anything about their religion. The wealthy families adopted the Muslim custom of *purdah* in which women were kept prisoners in a special part of the house. They were seldom allowed out-of-doors and when they were, they had to cover their faces with heavy veils.

The Muslim invasions and the resultant Muslim rule brought problems which still trouble India today. The Hindu people who resisted the Muslims were often subjected to further massacre after they had already been defeated. Many hard feelings arose as a result of this harsh treatment by the Muslims.

While many of the common people became Muslims, the upper classes clung to their Hindu faith. India became divided between these two major religions. Each hated and mistrusted the other. The Muslims, fiercely proud of their faith, maintained a separate way of life, refusing to mingle with their Hindu neighbors. The division that resulted has influenced India even today. (As we shall see, when India was granted her freedom from British rule, the fears and hatreds of these two groups tore the new country apart , forcing the people to form two separate countries: India and Pakistan.)

Muslim Influence in Africa

The Arab religion of Islam was the most important external influence in Africa between 700 and 1500 A.D. Arab traders established trade kingdoms in the African Sudan area and along Africa's eastern coast. Although these kingdoms were influenced by the Muslims, they quickly developed into black African kingdoms with typical African institutions and black rulers.

African Kingdoms Thrive

When the Islamic faith began to spread, North Africa was one of the first areas to become Muslim. At first the nomadic Berber tribesmen fought against the new religion. When they finally accepted Islam, however, they became even quicker than the Arabs to spread this religion.

Ghana. Extending from the Atlantic Ocean to the upper Nile Valley is a huge grassy plain called the Sudan. This became an area of racial mixture as the Sudanese blacks came under Muslim influence. About 400 A.D., before Islam had swept through North Africa, white Berbers had founded the state of Ghana in the western Sudan. At first this kingdom was controlled by the whites, but later on, a black dynasty took over Ghana. At the height of its power, Ghana controlled the entire area of the upper Niger and upper Senegal Rivers.

By 700 A.D. many Muslims were settling in the capital city of Ghana, which had become a great trade center. Ghana's trade and export business centered around gold. Most of the gold that was used in Europe during the Middle Ages

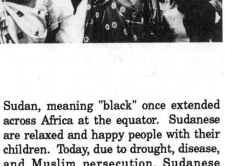

Sudan, meaning "black" once extended across Africa at the equator. Sudanese are relaxed and happy people with their children. Today, due to drought, disease, and Muslim persecution, Sudanese women suffer an eighty percent mortality rate during childbirth. A caucasian women is pictured here with Silluk women from Melut, Sudan.

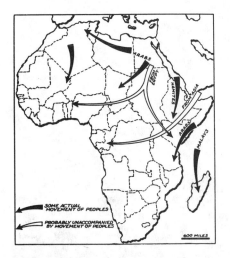

While the Mesopotamian nations were waning in power, African nations were emerging as cultural strongholds. Even as river systems were basic to strong kingdoms in Mesopotamia, the same fact was true in Africa. Notice how Hamitic people spread throughout the African continent.

Mounted Berber warriors, such as this one, helped to spread the Muslim faith across North Africa.

came from Ghana. Ghana also exported slaves, but the big need for slaves did not come until later. There were nearly 30,000 people living in Ghana at this time.

The news of Ghana's riches spread across the Sahara just as the Muslims were about to begin their military conquest of Spain. Some of the Muslims turned their eyes toward Ghana and its rich gold trade. In 1087 Ghana was plundered by the Muslims who discovered that the gold mines were not located in Ghana, but in Africa's rugged interior region. The warriors then returned to the desert, carrying their plunder with them.

Mali. In the 1000s a Sudanese tribe called the Mandingos were converted to Islam. They began to conquer their neighbors. They spread their new faith and established the trading kingdom of Mali. This kingdom was named after its capital city of Mali which was located on a branch of the Niger River.

Mali's greatest king was Mansa Musa who expanded his kingdom by conquering the trade cities of Timbuktu and Gao. Between 1200 and 1500 A.D., Timbuktu was a great trade center.

The Mali Kingdom probably covered thousands of miles, but the exact boundaries are not known today. Mansa Musa once said it would take a man a year to cross his territory. The major cities of Mali and Timbuktu were rich and beautiful. Lovely mosques and universities with famous scholars and teachers were located in both cities. They had workshops which produced goods made from iron, tin, and leather. Mansa Musa's wealth was so great that when he went on a pilgrimage to Mecca, he amazed the rulers of the countries he visited.

Because of the large size of the Mali Kingdom, people of many diverse languages and customs lived there. In addition to cities with merchants and scholars, there also were farmers, hunters, fishermen, and gatherers of foods which grew wild. When Mansa Musa died in the 1400s, his empire began to break up. The governors who had ruled the different provinces then began ruling in their own right.

Songhai. Between 1400 and 1500 A.D., a small kingdom named Songhai became the major political power in the Sudan. This was the last of the Sudanese kingdoms and its capital city was Gao. The old gold trade that had made Ghana so rich and famous continued to flourish at Gao.

The Muslim city of Morocco became greedy and wanted to take over Gao's rich gold trade. Using Spanish and Portuguese soldiers to fight as mercenaries, the Moroccans attacked Gao in 1590. The Songhai were quickly defeated

---

A Strange Method of Trading

Although Ghana was famous as the center of rich gold trade, the people of Ghana did not control the gold mines. They were controlled by primitive tribesmen from the jungles. A strange method of trading developed between merchants from Ghana and these primitive miners. The merchants went to Ghana's river boundary, where they left a pile of trade goods, including salt which was a very important item. As soon as the merchants left, the timid miners went to the river to look over the trade goods and leave a pile of gold. When the merchants returned, they could take the gold if they were satisfied with the deal, otherwise they left without touching anything. The miners would then add a little more gold. When everyone was satisfied, they all took their goods and left.

because the Moroccans overpowered them with brand new weapons called guns. Like the conquerors of Ghana, the Moroccans learned too late that the mines were located in Africa's interior. The rich trade stopped with the destruction of Gao.

The Moroccans returned home and the people of West Africa turned to farming and herding. A very small amount of gold continued to find its way into North Africa, but the Sudanese never again reached their former greatness.

Zimbabwe. We will now turn our attention to East Africa. We have already studied the civilization of Axum which was later known as Ethiopia. From as early as 700 A.D., Muslim traders sailed along the east coast of Africa and established several kingdoms.

It was during this time that Zimbabwe became an important trade state. Sofala and Zimbabwe were the two major cities in Zimbabwe. Sofala was located along the coast. Gold, slaves, and ivory were shipped from there to all parts of the Muslim Empire.

The city of Zimbabwe developed over a long period of time. The earliest buildings probably were built about 400 A.D. The city walls were 3.2 km (two miles) long and made of granite blocks about the size of bricks. The walls of the buildings were made of large granite blocks, smoothed to such perfect proportions that no mortar or cement was necessary to hold them together. The ruins of a temple with walls 3.1 to 4.6 m (10 to 15 feet) thick and 6.1 to 9.1 m (20 to 30 feet) high have been found.

The Muslim influence spread throughout Zimbabwe. Although Zimbabwe is located hundreds of miles inland, glass beads, pottery, and porcelain from Persia, China, and India have been found in her ruins.

The native language of Zimbabwe was Swahili and they used the Arabian alphabet to write their language. They began using a written

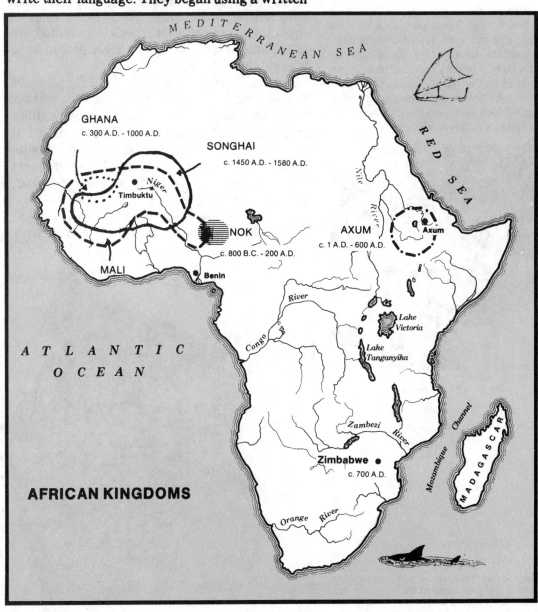

AFRICAN KINGDOMS

As Ham's descendants migrated south and west from their temperate zone, they faced the hot, humid climate of Central Africa. These people underwent phenotype changes with different skin pigmentation and thick curly hair as protection from that climate--as observed in the photo below. Only God knows why the new phenotype of these people does not reverse itself when exposed to a different climate.

language to keep trade records. Once they had a written language, a beautiful poetic literature developed. Many poems about love and religion were written at this time. Because the ruins of Zimbabwe have not been completely studied, we do not know much about how these people lived or about their history.

The Zenj. About 997 A.D. the Zenj Empire was started along Africa's eastern coast in what is now Mozambique. The capital city was Zenjibar and, like the other kingdoms we have studied, it was a trade center established by Muslim traders. This empire lasted for almost 500 years and included a lively trade between Zenjibar, Malaya, and China.

The Zenj Empire came to an end in 1497 when Portuguese explorers captured the area from

the Muslims. During the next hundred years or so, the Muslims reconquered much of the territory claimed by Portugal. The Portuguese, however, were able to retain control of Mozambique until 1975.

Ghana—The Gold Coast

West Africans look back to the period of Sudanese kingdoms with pride. In 1957, when the British Colony known as the Gold Coast won its freedom, the Africans named their new country Ghana after the first of the great Sudanese trading kingdoms.

These granite walls are all that remain of the ancient city of Zimbabwe.
Pottery, china, and trade items from distant Asia have been found in her ruins.

PRE-COLUMBUS AMERICA

Projects

1. Do a study of different types of ball games. Trace their origins and describe how they are played.

2. Give a report on at least three cultures in the world that have unusual ideas of beauty. Compare your findings with what the Mayas did to make their children "beautiful."

3. What "terrible crime" did the Aztecs commit against Coxcox. Write a fiction story about this incident.

4. The Incas used strings of wampum to keep records instead of writing them down. In North America the Indians also used wampum. Describe the various uses and purposes of wampum. Design your own wampum belt depicting your family record. Show how many members, their ages, and their sexes.

5. Do a study on messenger systems that were used before the telegraph. How did they work? Include Roman, Incan, and Greek systems.

6. Make a report on the life of Tupa Inca. Compare him with either Alexander the Great or Genghis Khan.

7. Give a complete history of the Seminoles. Include information about their peace treaty with the United States.

8. Make a model of a Pueblo, a false face, or a kachina doll. Explain what it is used for.

9. Research some of the recent conflicts involving American Indians. Include in your report one of the following subjects:
   a. Indian repossession of the sacred Blue Lake from U.S. government;
   b. Fishing rights in Washington state;
   c. The events at Wounded Knee;
   d. The Indian demonstration at Alcatraz.

Words and Concepts

Mesa Verde
Tenochtitlan
potlatch
ayllus
Mochicas
False Face Society
Chan Chan
Kachina
slash-and-burn
Teotihuacan
Nazca
The Inca
wampum
Mayapan
Topiltzin
Paracas
Huitzilopoctli
Cuzco
cacao beans
Quetzalcoatl

Pre-Columbus America

Some of the pre-Columbians migrated to North America over a land bridge in the Bering Strait as we learned in Chapter 3. These people moved south and settled throughout North America. From northern Mexico through Middle America, other groups built strong civilizations. Still other civilizations emerged in South America. We shall take a brief look at some of the many cultures that developed in the Americas.

In areas of Mexico and Peru, people learned to farm, domesticate corn, and live in larger and larger villages. Such early civilizations became the foundations for even more advanced civilizations. A few civilizations known as pre-Aztec and pre-Inca also developed.

The three major peoples we shall study are the **Aztecs, Mayas, and Incas. These** civilizations were still in existence when the first European explorers arrived in the Americas, but they were destroyed by these invaders. The Mayas and Incas both were engaged in destructive civil wars when the Europeans arrived, a fact which hastened their downfall. The Aztecs were restrained by an ancient prophecy which made them unwilling to fight the invaders until it was too late.

The only one of these civilizations that left written records that we can understand today was the Aztecs. The Incas apparently lacked a written language. Although the Mayas developed what may be the oldest, written language in the Americas, nobody has been able to decipher it. Scientists are able to read some of the dates, but there is some question about whether they are really accurate.

The Pre-Aztec Civilizations

The two important civilizations that existed in Middle America before the Aztecs became a power were Teotihuacan and the Toltecs. These pre-Aztec civilizations provided models for the Aztecs when they established their empire. The Aztecs often used Toltec artisans in much the same way as Rome borrowed the culture of Greece.

Teotihuacan

As you will remember, the Olmecs built great temple complexes where people went to make offerings to their gods. These people were not

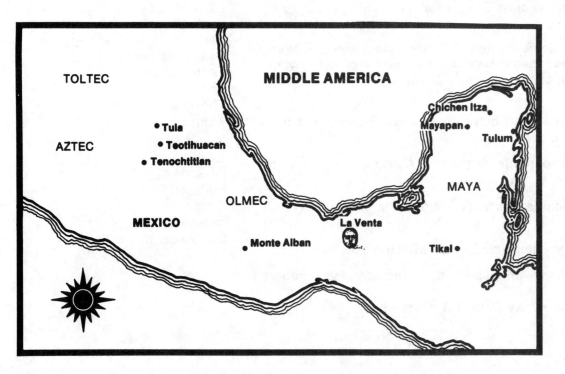

able to grow enough food to support a big city so they lived in small farm villages near the temple center.

Teotihuacan may be America's oldest true city. It was established in 100 B.C., reached its peak in 500 A.D., and fell in 750 A.D. The most important part of the city was the religious center. More than 50,000 people lived in homes in a 20.7 km² (eight square mile) area around the city's ceremonial center.

Culture. The common people lived in one-story apartment buildings that had no windows. Immediately around the outside of the temple complex were the palaces where the priests and other important people lived. These palaces had many rooms which surrounded paved courtyards. They had drains in the courtyards to help carry away rain water. The palace walls were covered with frescoes showing processions of priests, gods, and mythical animals in bright red, blue, yellow, and green colors.

As a result of trade, Teotihuacan became an important influence on the people living all over Middle America. Trade, in fact, became the source of a steadily growing culture that was spreading throughout the area.

Teotihuacan was not a warlike city. The people there did not try to conquer new territory. Their paintings show few warriors, indicating that they had a peaceful nature. We can just imagine how exciting the city must have been, crowded and bustling with visitors, their voices raised in excited tones. Solemn priests dressed in bright feathered robes and headdresses that glittered in the sun. They marched across the courts and climbed the steps of the steep pyramids to the accompaniment of deep toned drums.

The Chichimec Invasion. In 750 A.D. Teotihuacan was destroyed by a group of northern Indians called Chichimecs. These wild tribesmen wore feathers and war paint, much like the Indians who later lived in the North American plains. When they attacked the helpless city, they burned it to the ground. Its population either fled or was massacred.

For centuries after Teotihuacan, there was a period of almost constant warfare and confusion in the area. City-states developed with the warriors as the ruling class. Fighting and conquests became a major way of life. This new harsh, violent, warlike spirit began to be reflected in religion. It was a time much like that we have already studied in which the barbaric Germanic tribes invaded the Roman Empire.

Some cities accepted the Chichimec as rulers, intermarrying with them and depending on them for protection from other invaders. Some cities held out for many years before they were finally defeated. There were some cities on the outer edges of the Valley of Mexico that were never defeated and where the old culture was preserved.

The Toltecs

In 950 A.D. a Chichimec tribe founded a new city called Tula in the northern end of the Valley of Mexico. These people were called Toltecs and they established a new type of city. Tula, with its temples and residential areas, was built on top of a hill where it could easily be defended. This was important because there were tribes still raiding unprotected centers.

The Toltecs brought in skilled people who knew how to make beautiful pottery, build

Quetzalcoatl, also known as the **Feathered Serpent**, was not only one of the major **gods** of Teotihuacan, but also of the **Toltecs and the Aztecs**. He was the god who supposedly taught the Indians how to raise corn.

temples, and carve statues. They were probably survivors from Teotihuacan. Tula became a great city and all the arts that had been developed in previous civilizations were found there.

A Military City. Tula was different from other civilizations in the Americas we have studied in that she was ruled by military leaders rather than priests. Tula became the first state in the Americas to conquer her neighbors. The leaders forced the conquered peoples to send tribute. Great wealth poured into Tula from people throughout the area now known as Mexico.

The main building in Tula was the Temple of Quetzalcoatl. It was a five-step pyramid with a large temple on the platform at the top. Today all that remains of this temple are four, 4.6 m (15 feet) high stone columns shaped like armed warriors. These warriors are pictured in tall, feathered headdresses with butterfly-shaped breastplates, knotted aprons, and tasseled sandals. They are armed with stone-tipped darts, dart-throwers, and incense bags. These columns are pure Toltec and Toltec civilizations in other areas have been identified by the presence of the same style of column.

The homes in Tula were beautiful, using mosaic tiles for decoration. They also used gold, turquoise, shells, silver, stones, and feathers for wall decorations.

Religion. There were two major gods in Tula. Quetzalcoatl, the "Feathered Serpent," was thought to be the god who gave the Mexican people corn and taught them how to farm. It was said that he made it possible for men to grow enough food to sustain the population of towns. He also was given credit for the good things about the civilization.

The other god was Tezcatlipoca, meaning "the Mirror that Smokes." He was a black god—a symbol of the night sky. His followers used sorcery and he was considered to be the god of evil and death. He also was a warrior god and his followers believed he wanted to be fed the warm, beating hearts of human victims. Supposedly there was a constant struggle between these two gods for control of the Toltec Empire.

In studying the Toltecs, we find records of Topilzin, the first real flesh-and-blood person in Mexican history. He was the ruler of the Toltecs. Although many legends have been told about him, there is no doubt that he really lived. While he was a young man, he became the high priest of Quetzalcoatl, and when he became king of the Toltecs, he changed his name to Quetzalcoatl.

In 987 A.D. there was a terrible power struggle in Tula between the supporters of Quetzalcoatl and the followers of Tezcatlipoca. In the course of the struggle, Quetzalcoatl was defeated and was forced to give up his throne. The defeated king left Tula with the followers who had supported his god.

The Legend of Quetzalcoatl

When Quetzalcoatl, the Toltec ruler, was forced to give up his throne and leave Tula, he made a strange promise. He vowed to return in 532 years. Quetzalcoatl had worn a beard, and in 1519 A.D. when the bearded Spaniards arrived in Mexico, it was exactly 532 years later. It is easy to see why the Indians were unwilling to fight the Spaniards. They thought they might be representatives of their god-king, Quetzalcoatl.

Once Quetzalcoatl was defeated, the savage type of worship of Tezcatlipoca took over in Tula. By the 1100s the Toltecs had conquered all of central Mexico. After that date, however, things began going badly for the Toltecs. Droughts and crop failure weakened their empire. Then the nomadic tribes from the north began invading once again.

In 1200 A.D. these raiders burned Tula. The great sculptures were toppled over and buried in large trenches. The warlike Toltec soldiers left Tula and began setting up city-kingdoms with themselves as rulers. For the next 200 years the history of Mexico was a story of independent city-kingdoms struggling to survive. They fought each other and nomadic raiders. There would not be another powerful state in control of Middle America until the Aztec Empire in the 1400s.

The Mayas

One of the most mysterious civilizations in the Americas is that of the Mayas, which came into being about 300 B.C. Although they had an hieroglyphic writing and wrote hundreds of books, scientists have only been able to interpret the dates.

The search in America for the Mayan past is just beginning. There are more than 5,000 ruins in Mexico alone and most of them have not yet been touched by archaeologists. It is possible that there are many more cities hidden in the jungles where some of the lost books or a key to understanding Mayan writing may be discovered.

The entire area of Middle America covered by the Mayan civilization was less than half the size of Texas. It can be divided into three totally different geographic areas. One was a lowland rain forest and jungle, and another was stony with little rainfall and few lakes and rivers. The third was a mountainous area of high, fertile valleys, cool climate, enough rainfall, and swift rivers.

Mayan Society

We know very little about the Mayas. All but three of the many books that they wrote were destroyed by the Spanish. The three that do survive tell us nothing about their history. Most of what we know about the Mayas comes from archaeologists. After the Spanish arrived, however, they began keeping records about what they saw. These were written after the Mayas had passed their peak and do not give a

MAYAN EMPIRE

STONEY LOWLAND
MOUNTAINOUS
JUNGLE

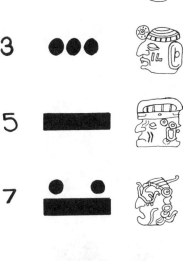

0		
3	●●●	
5	▬	
7	●● ▬	
10	▬▬	

The Mayan system of numerals combined dots and bars for counting from zero to 19. A dot stood for one and a bar for five. The Mayas had a system that was more ornate for writing large numbers, using heads of deities.

very good picture of what their civilization actually was like.

Ceremonial Centers. The Mayan civilization was built around many ceremonial centers. Apparently none of these centers served as a major political capital with authority over the others. Instead, they probably were a confederation loosely held together by trade, language, and a common culture.

The ceremonial centers that were located in the jungle areas were not like typical cities we know today. They were mostly places where people living nearby could go to worship their gods and sell their goods. The smaller centers usually had a small pyramid, a temple, a paved court, and a few stone buildings. These centers were usually deserted, except on special days when the people visited from all around the area. The priest who ministered in these centers worked as a farmer on days when the center was closed.

The larger ceremonial centers were more like cities. They were never empty. Skilled artists constantly worked on buildings, made pottery, and sewed gorgeous costumes for the priests. Young men from all over the Mayan area came to study for the priesthood. On special ceremonial days the city throbbed with excitement as people from the less important centers crowded the great paved courts.

Trade. Traders came to the ceremonial centers with goods from distant countries. Trade was very important to the Mayas. They built wide, level roads of smooth limestone blocks throughout their empire to aid the merchants and farmers in getting their goods to market. Since there were no animals to carry loads in the Middle Americas at this time, people had to carry goods on their backs.

Mayan merchants traded with the civilizations of Mexico, including the Toltecs and later the Aztecs. One of the earliest forms of money was cacao beans, which they used to make chocolate and red jade beads. Trade items included salt, incense, brightly-colored feathers, precious stones, and slaves.

The Mayas were the only great American civilization to live and trade by the sea as well as on land. Salted fish and stingray tails were in demand all over Mayan territory. Huge canoes, which carried as many as 40 people, sailed for thousands of kilometers (miles) along the Gulf and Caribbean seacoasts.

Mayan Warfare. For many years archaeologists believed the Mayas were a peaceful people because their cities were not fortified. Further studies have shown, however,

Mayan warriors were ferocious looking with plumed headdress and grotesque ornaments. Early Mayans were not interested in conquering land. They went to war to gain captives to sacrifice to the sun.

Counterfeit Beans

Cacao beans, from which chocolate is made, were used as money by the Mayas. A rabbit was worth ten beans, a pumpkin was worth ten, and a slave was worth 100.

Even in those early days, there was a problem with counterfeiting. Traders could remove the thick skins from the beans and fill them with sand or earth. These counterfeit beans were then mixed in with the good beans. A smart businessman squeezed every bean to make certain they were solid. The person in a hurry to make a sale might discover later he had been robbed. Counterfeiters were the criminals most often brought to the Mayan courts for punishment.

that the Mayas were a very warlike people. When their corn harvest was over, they spent much of their time at war with each other. Mayan warfare was different from our modern warfare in which the goal is to destroy the enemy rather than to conquer territory or destroy cities. Their main reason for fighting was to capture victims for human sacrifices.

When leaders went into battle, they were dressed in their most magnificent headgear and jewels. All the fighting was directed at capturing the enemy leader. When he was captured, the war was over and his warriors usually fled. The leader was sacrificed immediately and any other prisoners were saved for later sacrifices or to be used as slaves.

The Mayan People. The Mayas were divided into clans and every family in the clan was entitled to 37.2 m² (400 square feet) of land. Each clan worked together to farm all the land belonging to its member families. They used the slash-and-burn method of farming. When their land was no longer fertile, they were given land in a new area. They then cut down the trees, burned off the vegetation, and began planting crops.

Mayan women were about 122 cm (four feet, eight inches) tall. They pierced their ears and tatooed their bodies. Their dresses were made of a single piece of woven cloth with holes for arms and a square-cut opening for the head. Underneath their dresses they wore lightweight, white petticoats. They also wore decorated, fringed shawls over their shoulders. They nearly always went barefooted.

Girls were expected to marry when they were 14 years old. They could be divorced if they had no children. A woman could also be divorced if she failed to prepare her husband's steam bath properly. Women could own property, but were not allowed to hold public office.

Mayan men averaged 152 cm (five feet, one inch) in height. They wore nose ornaments in holes drilled through the septum. They also had holes 2.5 cm (one inch) in diameter in their earlobes for special ornaments. The men filed their teeth to points and decorated them with iron pyrites and jade. Their hair was braided and wrapped around their heads, with some hair hanging in tassels on which they tied volcanic glass mirrors. The men tatooed their bodies. Because this was a very painful process, the more tatoos a man had, the braver he was thought to be.

Mayan Customs. The Mayas had the greatest variety of foods of any primitive civilization in the world. They enjoyed corn, squash, beans, tomatoes, chili peppers, avocados, chocolate, sweet potatoes, guavas, papayas, breadfruit, and plums. In addition they grew agave for rope fibers, indigo for dye, chicle for chewing gum, and rubber. They also used calabash gourds to make cups and bowls, cotton to make cloth, and palm leaves for roofs, fans, baskets, and raincoats.

One activity that was shared by every civilization in Middle America was the ball game. The ball game was a combination of religious ritual, athletic ability, and military skill. Ball courts have been found in every Middle American civilization. The Indians gambled heavily on the outcome of these games and sometimes men lost their possessions and their freedom by gambling.

Mayan men wore a wide, cloth waistband wrapped several times around the waist. One end hung down in front and one in back. These ends were decorated with beautiful,

Mayan players combine the best of basketball and soccer for an exciting game in one of Chichen Itza's large courts. Players were allowed to use their elbows, knees, and hips when driving the rubber ball through the stone ring. But they were not allowed to use their hands. If the player drove the ball through the goal, the spectators would run. According to custom, they were required to give the scoring player all the clothes and jewels they were wearing if he caught them.

brightly colored feathers woven into the cloth. They wore large, square cloaks tied over their shoulders. The men also wore sandals of hemp or untanned deerhide.

The nobles wore sleeveless jackets, bracelets, necklaces, and perfumes. All members of the ruling class wore huge elaborate headgear. The frame of the headgear either was carved of wood or made of woven wicker. The frames were covered with feathers. Some of the headdresses were as tall as the men wearing them.

The Mayas had very different ideas about what was beautiful. The nobles wrapped their babies' heads tightly with cloths around splintlike boards to make their skulls longer. They also hung beads from a baby's forehead to create permanently crossed eyes. This was considered to be especially beautiful.

Resplendent in beads, shells, and feathers, a Mayan noble in bright costume stands before a stucco temple. His staff is made of palm wood and is carved with the symbols of his royalty.

Mayan Religion

The priests were the rulers in the Mayan civilization. They wore gorgeous costumes made of golden jaguar skins, blood-red robes, and ornaments made of green jade and beautiful multicolored, quetzal bird feathers. They wore gigantic flower-topped headdresses which were shaped like the stetson hat worn by the American cowboy.

The Mayas had thousands of gods. They believed everything in nature, including the weather, was controlled by a different god. Each day was thought to have its own god and the Mayas developed a calendar system to predict how these gods would behave. To keep all the gods happy, ceremonies were continually performed at the major ceremonial centers.

Since studying the stars, sun, and moon played an important part in their religion, the Mayas learned to predict the movements of these heavenly bodies. They knew the length of the year and developed a calendar that was so accurate that even today we can read the dates carved on their monuments and buildings.

Human Sacrifices. While the Mayas never did practice mass human sacrifices, there were times when they believed the gods required a human victim. Usually these victims were prisoners of war. They had three ways of sacrificing people. In one method, the victim was tied to a frame and people shot arrows into his chest while dancing around him.

The second way was probably introduced by the Toltecs. The victim was forced to lie across a curved, stone altar and his beating heart was ripped from his chest. The third method of sacrificing humans was used around Chichen Itza. Their large, natural limestone wells provided the only water. Some of these wells were not used for water, but only for making human sacrifices. Men, women, and sometimes children, were taken to the well and thrown in. If the victims survived for an entire day, they were pulled out so they could deliver messages to the people from their gods.

Mayan History

When Teotihuacan in Mexico first became a city in 300 B.C., the Mayan civilization was beginning to take shape. The oldest Mayan city to be discovered was Kaminaljuyu. Most of the major buildings there were made of wood. They have since decayed, but some of their beautiful stone sculpture has been found.

The earliest major Mayan site to be discovered is the city of Tikal. It seems to have been a typical city in which homes were built for 3.2 or 4.8 km (two or three miles) around the temple area. There were about 350 smaller temples and palaces surrounding the two major pyramids.

Between 300 A.D. and 900 A.D., the Mayan civilization, located mostly in the jungle areas, reached its peak. During the last half of the 800s A.D., the civlization began its decline. Building construction and religious activity stopped. No more monuments were dedicated.

For a time people continued to live in the area, making their homes in the temples. At one time, however, there had been nearly three million people living in the area, but records do not show what became of them. This is one of the great mysteries of history, and archaeologists are still searching for the answer.

After 1000 A.D. the majority of the Mayan people were living in the other two geographical areas of Mayan territory.

A terrified Mayan girl is hurled into a sacred well to satisfy the angry gods who have stopped the rain and threatened the crops. In 1960 divers found this well at Chichen Itza. It contained the bones of men, women, and children as well as thousands of artifacts.

The Toltec Influence. You will remember the story of the Toltec King Quetzalcoatl who was forced to leave his kingdom. Archaeologists now believe he moved to a city named Tobasco, which was on the Toltec-Mayan border. While he was living there, another tribe of Toltecs named the Itzas joined him.

Under Quetzalcoatl the Toltecs took over the Mayan city of Chichen Itza, making it their capital. From there the Toltecs began the conquest of the Mayan territory where the ground was covered with stones and there was little rainfall. Toltec art was revived and a new style of architecture was developed. Now the cities were built with high walls. The feathered serpent, jaguars, and eagles with outspread wings were carved on walls and monuments. These symbols all were indications of Toltec influence.

The Mayapan League. After the Toltecs settled and intermarried with the Mayas in Chichen Itza, small groups began to break away. They built other cities all over the middle territory. Finally a large city called Mayapan was built. It became the capital city of a group of cities known as the Mayapan League.

For more than 200 years, the Mayapan League and Chichen Itza struggled for control of the desert area. The people at Chichen Itza believed they were descendants of Quetzalcoatl and should be the major Mayan people. The people at Mayapan claimed to be even more closely related to the Toltecs and thought they were entitled to control the Mayan Confederation.

In 1194 Toltecs drifted into the Mayan territory after the destruction of Tula. They helped the Mayapan League capture Chichen Itza. Her golden calendar discs were thrown into the sacrificial wells. The people who survived were forced to move to the city of Mayapan to live where they could not rebel.

Civil War In Mayapan. For about 250 years the descendants of the people of Chichen Itza hoped to regain their freedom. In 1441 a major civil war broke out. The rebellion had been carefully planned to begin at a time when all the members of the Mayapan ruling family were at home. In the slaughter that followed, all but one man in the family was killed. He was on a trip to Honduras.

Mayapan's city walls were pulled down, statues of the gods were smashed, and buildings were destroyed. Mayapan had come closer than any other Mayan city to being a political capital. There never was another one. All of the Mayan peoples fought in the civil war that followed, which greatly weakened the entire civilization. As a result, when the Spanish arrived in 1517, the Mayas were too weak to fight them.

Summary. The Mayas left their mark in Middle America and their religious centers give silent evidence of their hard work. Today descendants of the Mayas live in poverty in the mountainous area of their empire. They farm in much the same way the ancient Mayas did, but they have forgotten their grand heritage. Unfortunately they are not able to shed much light on the hidden past of the ancient Mayas.

The Aztecs

When the Toltec capital of Tula was destroyed in 1200 A.D., there was continuous warfare between the many city-states in the rich Valley of Mexico. None of the city-states was able to conquer enough territory to set up an empire. Into this confusion wandered a small tribe of Chichimec nomads who called themselves Aztecs because they came from a place called Aztlan.

When the Aztecs first entered the Valley of Mexico, all the good land belonged to the city-states already in existence and nobody wanted to make room for them. Finally Coxcox the ruler of the ancient Toltec city of Culhuacan gave the Aztecs a piece of very worthless land on which to settle.

The Aztec priests were afraid their people would become Toltec, causing them to lose their power. To prevent this the priests committed a terrible crime. It made Coxcox so angry that he declared war on the Aztecs, forcing them to flee. They set up a new city in the marshes around Lake Texcoco.

The new Aztec city, called Tenochtitlan, was in a good position to become powerful. It was started on an island in the lake with three important cities around it. Since the Aztecs could only be reached by water, they were protected against sudden attack. They learned to make their island bigger by filling in the marshes with dirt and rocks. They traded ducks, fish, frogs, and other lake products for corn, beans, stone, and other necessary items.

The Aztecs Rise to Power

By 1325 the Aztecs had become a small power. Their soldiers were noted for their bravery and they fought as mercenaries in the many wars between city-states. Finally the Aztecs became a great power by taking over the three cities that surrounded their island city. They did so by helping one city in her war against another city and then suddenly changing allies in the middle of the war.

After defeating their former allies, the Aztecs demanded tribute in the form of food, clothing, weapons, and other things the growing city needed. When the Aztecs began receiving yearly tribute, their soldiers were relieved of their farming duties, making them available to fight.

The Empire Grows. Two other cities, Texcoco and Tiacopan, formed a league with Tenochtitlan. As the Aztecs of Tenochtitlan became more powerful, these cities became subject to Aztec rule and their kings served as slaves to the Aztec emperor. By the 1500s Aztec territory stretched from the Pacific Ocean to the Gulf Coasts and southward to the border of present-day Guatemala. There were 38 provinces that sent yearly tribute to the Aztec capital.

Many of these tribute cities were allowed to keep their former kings. These rulers could not be trusted, however, Aztec soldiers were put in charge of the city. Soldiers received such a post as a reward for bravery. The cities paying tribute had to provide the Aztecs with both soldiers and a yearly quota of goods.

Cities continually rebelled, however, by refusing to send tribute. The Aztecs then sent soldiers to put down the rebellions. Thus the Aztecs became a soldier society, leaving all of the work to the people they controlled.

Emperor Montezuma. In 1502 Montezuma became the new Aztec emperor. He had proved his bravery by leading many successful campaigns before becoming emperor. He took over the Aztec Empire when it was in its prime. The territory had not yet become too large to rule, and its leaders had not grown soft and corrupt.

Montezuma was a religious intellectual as well as a soldier. One matter that worried him was the legend of Quetzalcoatl, who had promised to return in 1519. As this year drew closer, strange stories began to spread throughout the empire. One told about strange men riding in

When Mexico won her freedom from Spain in 1821, Mexicans adopted this old Aztec symbol as their national emblem. Aztec legend states they were supposed to build their city where they found an eagle on a cactus with a snake in its beak. After much searching they found the right place.

white-winged boats along the eastern coast. Montezuma wondered if this was the banished god, returning to destroy the Aztec war gods. As we shall see, Montezuma's indecision prevented him from acting swiftly to stop the invasion of the winged boats which turned out to be the Spanish. As a result of his hesitancy, the Aztec Empire was doomed.

Aztec Society

By 1519 Tenochtitlan had become a magnificent city. Most of the island was man-made by Aztecs who filled in the swampland with earth brought from the mainland in canoes. The city was connected to the mainland by three huge bridges wide enough to hold eight horsemen

Temple guards stand at attention as a visiting diplomat approaches a shrine in the Aztec city of Tenochtitlan. In the background we can see the canal system which resembles those in Venice, Italy. Most Aztec cities were independent of one another. Their lack of unity made it easy for invading Spaniards to conquer them.

riding side by side, if they had had horses. When danger threatened, the bridges could be moved and the mainland was cut off from Tenochtitlan.

Near the center of the city were the emperor's palace, and the homes of the important nobles and priests. Gigantic temple-pyramids and other ceremonial buildings stood in the center of the city. Tenochtitlan was larger and grander than any cities built by the Europeans during the same time period. Between 60,000 and 120,000 homes were built there. This did not include the suburbs which supposedly housed more than 100,000 people. Tenochtitlan was almost five times larger than London.

The Aztec Religion. Aztec life centered around the worship of their god, Huitzilopochtli. When the Aztecs first entered the Valley of Mexico, they carried a wooden image of their god with them, carefully wrapped in a bundle. When they built Tenochtitlan, one of the first major buildings constructed was Huitzilopochtli's temple. When the Aztecs conquered their enemies, they offered human sacrifices to their god. They believed that Huitzilopochtli would reward them with great victories each time they brought him a human heart. Therefore, whenever the Aztecs won a war, they brought back as many captives as possible to be sacrificed to their god.

When the Aztecs conquered a new city, they carried the gods of the defeated city back to Tenochtitlan. There a temple was built for the new gods who were revered like the gods already worshiped by the Aztecs. Many of the new gods also required human sacrifice. Women were beheaded while dancing for the earth goddess and children were drowned as special offerings to a god known as Tlaloc.

Perhaps the most grisly ceremony was that for the god of spring, Xipe Totec. The sacrifice victim was tied to a frame, shot with arrows, and then skinned. The priest then danced around the altar dressed in the victim's skin. This symbolized the new coat of leaves and flowers the earth put on every spring.

Every temple had a school where priests and students lived together. Anyone, including women, was allowed to enter the clergy, but the sons of nobles attended the schools. The priests did not marry and they had high moral standards. Women were allowed to leave the priesthood and marry if they wished.

The temple area in Tenochtitlan was a noisy and bustling place. The Aztecs believed they needed to offer at least one heart to their god

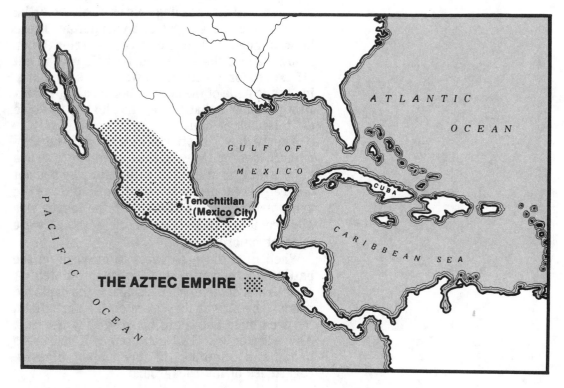

THE AZTEC EMPIRE

before starting anything new. Therefore, the stone altars where sacrifices took place were always busy. During major ceremonies the area was crowded with priests, victims, and worshipers. At other times, black-robed priests, carrying incense burners shaped like clay frying pans, walked across the pavements or climbed the steep steps of the pyramids.

A Warlike Society. Aztecs were respected for what they did, not for their social class or their wealth. All honors in Aztec society went to the bravest warriors and such honors were valued highly. Like the Spartans of ancient Greece, the Aztecs' main interest was in producing brave warriors.

When a boy was born he was dedicated to the war god. After reaching his sixth birthday, he went to live in the house of a young man. There he was taught to become a great warrior. When a boy reached the age of ten, his hair was all cut off except for one long lock which was left hanging at the nape of the neck. When he captured his first prisoner in battle, he was allowed to shave off this lock of hair.

When a boy cut off his lock of hair, he then entered two or three battles in which to prove his bravery. If at the end of that time he had not done any great deeds, he was forced to leave the army and become a farmer. He no longer was allowed to wear jewelry or clothes that were dyed or embroidered.

When men did great acts of bravery on the battlefield, however, they were promoted. A man's rank determined his share of the captured goods. The braver they were on the battlefield, the wealthier and more honored they became. Any warrior who had captured four prisoners became a member of the upper classes, regardless of his background.

The Aztecs, like the Mayas, did not enter warfare to completely destroy the enemy. The main purpose of war was to capture prisoners and sacrifice them to the Aztec gods rather than to kill people. When a city's main temple was captured during an attack, the city surrendered. The people believed that once a temple was captured, their gods were defeated and there was no reason to go on fighting. As soon as a city surrendered, negotiations began to determine how much tribute the city would be required to send to Tenochtitlan.

The warriors looked forward to dying in battle or to being sacrificed to the gods if they were captured. They believed that if they died in either of these ways, they would become companions to the eagles and spend a happy eternity. Women who died in childbirth were given the same honors as warriors who died in battle. It was believed that they both went to the same heaven.

Drunkenness was a crime among the Aztecs and a person was put to death the second time he was caught drunk. Only very old people, no longer important to society, were allowed to get drunk. The elderly indulged in heavy drinking at all Aztec ceremonies.

Aztec Social System. While the Aztec upper classes were interested in war and fighting, the common people were interested only in farming. The farmer, however, was not frozen in his class. His children could attend the temple school and become priests or noble warriors.

Every citizen was entitled to a piece of land to farm. The land did not belong to the individual, but to the state. If a man was lazy and refused to farm his land, he could lose it after three years. If he worked hard at farming, he could pass the land on to his sons when he died. Farmers always were available to do military service or to clean, repair, and build bridges and temples. All tribute that arrived at the capital was divided among the citizens. Even the farmers received their share.

The Aztecs enjoyed a variety of foods and vegetables that were not known in other parts of the world. This Aztec farmer carries his burden to market by *tumpline,* a strap slung across his forehead to support the load on his back.

Two classes of people, the craftsmen and the merchants, were totally independent of the Aztec social system. The craftsmen who carved designs on monuments and public buildings and who made jewelry and lovely feather mosaics were not Aztecs. They were descendants of the Toltecs who remembered how to produce these works of art. Their children did not become warriors or priests, but followed their father's crafts. Such craftsmen were a step above the common people in social status.

The merchants had their own gods, priests, and courts of law. Outsiders were not allowed to become merchants. They married among their own people and sometimes nobles and even the emperor married merchants' daughters. Merchants were good fighters and sometimes they were required to fight off bandits or enemy armies. They also acted as spies for the Aztec emperor when they traveled to distant cities.

Homes and Customs. Homes of the poor people were made of adobe brick and those of the rich were made of stone and stucco. Only the most important men could have two-story homes. Each home had a courtyard where children played and women could spin and weave while enjoying the sun. The courtyards were filled with flowers.

The Aztecs used very little furniture. They slept on mats on the floor. In the homes of the wealthy, a curtain was draped around the bed mat. The nobles had wicker chairs and stored their clothes and other belongings in wicker chests.

A man was not allowed to become a full citizen until he married. Each man had one principal wife and their children inherited the family property. A man also was allowed to have as many secondary wives as he could support.

The Pre-Inca Civilizations

When the Spaniards conquered the Incas in Peru, they saw many ruins of ancient cities. They asked the Incas about the ruins, but they were apparently so old that even the Incas could not remember who had built them. The many

The Paraca Indians were noted for the beautiful materials they wove. This Paracan ruler is dressed in materials covered with lovely designs.

The Mochicas made portraits of their people on their pottery. This jug has a woman's head which is so lifelike, the woman seems almost ready to speak.

ancient cultures located in the area that is now Peru are known as pre-Inca civilizations.

Early Settlers in Peru

The Indians in Peru did not have a written language, therefore, most of what we know about the pre-Inca civilizations comes from archaeologists or from stories handed down from generation to generation by the Indians. We will briefly look at a few of the small, but important cultures.

The Paracas. Between 400 B.C. and 400 A.D., a culture developed in the Paracas peninsula in southern Peru. These people, known today as the Paracas, are noted for their beautifully woven materials and their outstanding embroideries. Even with all the modern techniques of today, we do not have materials that surpass the beauty of those made by the Paracas.

Paracan designs were so intricate that they stitched only one thread at a time. They embroidered figures of fish, birds, and animals, as well as gods and mythological creatures. Their dyes were so good that today they seem as bright as they must have been when the cloth was new.

The Nazca. The Nazca people were located about 160.9 km (100 miles) down the coast from the Paracas. Although they also had beautifully woven materials, they were noted primarily for their pottery. Rather than decorating their pottery with realistic designs, they created abstract designs of fish, birds, and half-human demons or gods.

The Nazca culture was the one that in 500 A.D. built the gigantic birds, spiders, and other figures that are kilometers (miles) in length. These figures were so fantastic that today people express amazement at the skills. Now, a pre-Nazca culture has been found.

The Mochicas. The Mochicas built their civilization 804.5 km (500 miles) up the coast from the Nazcas. They developed a beautiful pottery in which they pictured every detail about their lives. Pottery has been found showing men and women of all ages, healthy and sick, in every type of work and game. The portraits on their vases look so real they seem almost as though they could speak.

Between 400 and 1000 A.D., the Mochicas began building large temples and other buildings. Their Temple of the Sun was 18.3 m (60 feet) high and covered 3.2 ha (eight acres).

A warlike people, the Mochicas took over neighboring valleys. They built roads to connect different parts of the area. They also established a courier system for sending messages from one part of their territory to another.

The Kingdom of Chimor. From 1000 to 1466 A.D., the kingdom of Chimore ruled a 965.6 km (600 mile) area along Peru's coastline. They actually controlled an even larger area. Their capital, Chan Chan, was the largest pre-Columbian city in South America. The city consisted of 20.7 km (8 square miles) and had enormous step pyramids and great walled compounds. One of the most interesting features of Chan Chan was its huge, walk-in wells. People entered the well by a ramp which led right to the water's edge.

The area where the rulers lived was large enough to hold nine football fields. The ruler was considered divine and lived in a walled-off area where he would not come into contact with the common people. When the ruler died, he was buried in this private area with all his treasures. That area then was considered sacred. The new ruler had to build his home in another area. There were nine of these rulers before Chan Chan was conquered by the Incas.

The Chimor people were skilled doctors. They were able to remove eyes and perform major surgery on a person's stomach. They also were able to remove injured or diseased internal organs. They developed the use of artificial hands and limbs. If a doctor's patient died, the doctor was beaten or stoned to death.

They knew how to make beautiful metal work, using almost all the metal work techniques that we use today. This fascinating culture came to an end in 1470 when it was conquered by the Incas.

The Incas

Like many other peoples of pre-Columbian America, the Incas left no written records. Our knowledge about the Inca civilization is based on archaeological findings, reports left by the Spanish explorers, and stories that were handed down by word-of-mouth from generation to generation by the Incas themselves.

The Inca Society

The Incas did not rule for very long. Their entire history in Peru is about 500 years long. They first moved into the Cuzco Valley where they built their capital city of Cuzco about 1000 A.D. They were a clannish people, mainly interested in agriculture.

System of Government. The common people were united in clans which were called *ayllus*. All of the people related to one another stayed in the same area. The people in each ayllu shared

their land, animals, and crops. They worked together to provide a living for the entire clan.

The Inca ayllus were different from the other clans we have studied. You will remember that usually the oldest man was the head of the family. When he died, his eldest son became the

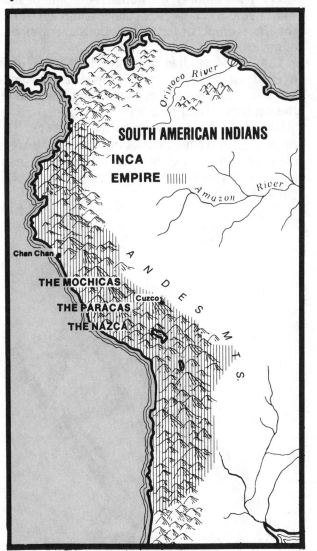

SOUTH AMERICAN INDIANS

INCA EMPIRE ||||||

The Incas did not have a written language. But they developed an interesting way to record their history and keep track of their population and crops. They used a long string with many knotted strings attached, called a *quipu*. A person who was properly trained could read the quipu's message by the way the strings were knotted. Unfortunately when the Spaniards took over the Inca civilization, these specially-trained "readers" were killed. Since that time nobody has been able to read the records.

Potatoes were raised in Peru hundreds of years before the Spaniards introduced them to Europe. Amid the terraced slopes of the Andes Mountains, Inca farmers cultivated the potato from a pea-sized tuber to its current size. Today the potato is the most important vegetable in the world.

leader. The Incas, on the other hand, elected their ayllu leader. He was guided in his decisions by a council of older men.

Several different ayllus came under the authority of a district leader. The district leaders were under the authority of one of four major rulers. These four rulers had to answer to the Inca emperor for their actions and methods of governing.

The emperor had absolute authority over everything in his empire. All the lands, precious metals, precious stones, and even the people themselves, belonged to him .

Under Inca law everyone had to work. The three most terrible crimes in this culture were stealing, lying, and laziness. Time was considered as valuable as money and laziness was punished by death.

An Agriculture Society. The farmland was divided into three portions—one for the gods, one for the emperor, and one for the people. The common people did the farming on all sections of the land, but once harvested, the crops went to the rightful owner of each land section. The finest farmland was cultivated for religious purposes. Everything that was grown on this land was burned as offerings to the Inca gods. Profits from the emperor's section were used as taxes. These crops were kept in storehouses and were given to the people only in times of war and famine.

The best lands were assigned first to the gods and the emperor. The remaining land was divided betwen the families. Each family was given enough land to provide food for itself. The farmers also planted and harvested land assigned to old and crippled people so they would not starve.

Every year the land was redivided. This way newly married couples could have a share and families with new children could have more land. The Incas learned to add to the land that was available by building terraces. They also had a good irrigation system.

In addition to farming the religious land and the emperor's property, the people of each

---

The Inca

Today we call all the Indians living in Peru the "Incas." In the days before the Spanish arrived, however, this was a title given to the emperor who was known as "The Inca." Because the Incas worshiped the sun and believed their emperors were descendants of the sun god, the Indians also called him "Son of the Sun."

village were required to do extra work for the government. This work included building and repairing the woven suspension bridges that crossed the mountain gorges, repairing roads and temples, or working in the mines. Every able-bodied man also was a member of the army and could be called into active duty whenever danger threatened. War was a serious business with the Incas and they never lost a battle until the Spanish arrived.

Architecture. Ruins of Inca cities have been found in an area extending 3218 km (2,000 miles) along the western side of South America. They have been found in all climatic regions, including desert areas, jungles, and high mountains.

Most Inca cities were built without walls, but each had a fortress where the people could go if they were attacked. The buildings in the Inca cities were huge structures, made of gigantic stones. This is even more remarkable when we consider that they were built without the help of the wheel, metal tools, or animals used as

---

Ruins in the Andes Mountains

Twentieth century mountain climbers, hoping to be the first to reach the top of the highest peaks in the Andes, have been greatly disappointed. When they got there, they discovered Inca ruins and shrines. Two peaks, more than 6705.6 m (22,000 feet) high, had stone walls at their tops. Another peak, 6309.4 m (20,700 feet) high, had an earthen courtyard that required 4,500 basketloads of earth. They must have been backpacked from the valley below.

---

beasts of burden. The huge stones were fitted together so smoothly that there was no need to use mortar. Nevertheless, many of these buildings are still standing.

The Incas did not carve decorations on their buildings and monuments like the Aztecs and Mayas. Instead the outer walls of their temples, palaces, and other major buildings were covered with large sheets of pure gold. They even used gold straw in thatched roofs of these buildings. By day the city seemed to glow as the sun reflected all this gold.

The Inca Empire

Once the Incas were well established in the Cuzco Valley, they built up an economy that supported an army. Then they began conquering their neighbors.

The Incas were different from the pre-Inca civilizations because they were able to conquer and rule large areas. This was something no other early civilization in South America had been able to do. Between 1200 and 1438, the Incas had conquered most of the territory in the surrounding mountains.

Building and Governing the Empire. When a new province was conquered, the Incas immediately made it part of their empire. The sons of the nobility in the conquered province were taken to the Inca capital as hostages. There they attended school with the Inca royal princes and were trained in the ways of Inca government. When they were older, they were returned to their cities as governors.

A census was taken in each new province to see what resources were available. The people were taught Inca farming and building techniques. Damaged buildings were replaced, and

The Incas built a wonderful highway system connecting all the parts of their empire. Since the llama was the largest animal in that area, "suspension" bridges like this one had to be built to support both men and animals. Suspension bridges were made of ropes woven from saplings and other strong fibers. Villages nearest the bridge were responsible for keeping it in good shape in exchange for not having to pay taxes. The most well-known of these bridges was built over the Apurimac River in Peru and was made immortal by Thorton Wilder's famous book, *The Bridge of San Luis Rey.*

ELONZENOINGA
GVAINACAPAC

The last great Inca emperor to rule before civil war and the Spanish destroyed the empire, was Huayna Capac. He caught smallpox and died so quickly that he was not able to appoint his successor. As a result, the Incas fought a terrible civil war. Already weakened by disease, they were easily conquered by the Spaniards.

roads were constructed. Soon the conquered province looked like the rest of the empire.

The Inca Empire was divided into four major sections and each was governed by a member of the emperor's family. All of the men working as governors were children of the emperor by his secondary wives and concubines. The emperor's primary wife was his sister. Their child would be the next emperor. As you will remember, this was how the Egyptian pharaohs kept the rule in their family.

To keep a close watch on their empire, the Incas also had a courier system. It was the fastest communication system in the world until the telegraph was invented. The Incas did not have horses and all messages were carried by fast runners. Relay stations were set up every kilometer and a half along the highways. In this way a message traveling 2011.3 km (1,250 miles) could be delivered in five days. In Rome, where horses were used, it took 47 days for a message to travel 1609 km (1,000 miles).

Pachacuti—A Great Inca Ruler. The success of the Inca Empire was due to the genius of Pachacuti, the Inca emperor. His name meant "he who transforms the earth." It was under his leadership that the Inca Empire expanded. Pachacuti's father had been forced to abandon the city of Cuzco to invading armies. But Pachacuti made alliances with several tribes, recaptured Cuzco, and then invaded his neighboring tribes.

The cities which surrendered without a fight were treated with consideration and mercy by Pachacuti. Any city that tried to fight against Inca rule, however, was treated with great cruelty. Therefore, many weak cities surrendered without a fight, hoping to receive the more gentle treatment.

By 1492 when Christopher Columbus began his

first voyage to the New World, Pachacuti had control of an empire almost as large and efficient as that of the Roman Empire at its peak. While Pachacuti ruled his empire with great wisdom, his son Tupa Inca continued to add new territory to the empire. Many historians feel that Tupa Inca was as great a military leader as Genghis Khan or Alexander the Great.

Disease, Discord, and Downfall. In 1493 Huayna Capac became the new emperor. He lived in his beautiful palace, surrounded by hundreds of wives and concubines. Meanwhile his son Atahualpa led the Inca armies in the north to conquer Ecuador. But Huayna Capac's last days were full of worry. Warnings had come in from all parts of his territory that the empire was about to be destroyed by men wearing beards. Bearded men had already been sighted along the coast in ships that looked like floating houses.

One of these ships landed, apparently carrying men with a terrible disease called smallpox. It was a new disease in the Americas so historians believe it must have come in with the men on the foreign ships. Thousands of Indians died as this deadly disease swept through the empire. In 1525 Huayna Capac died from smallpox before he could name an heir.

The priests appointed Huascar as the new emperor. The army in Ecuador claimed the throne for Atahualpa. Between 15,000 and 16,000 people were killed in a single battle as civil war broke out. The entire empire was terribly weakened by the double disaster of disease and civil war.

Huascar lost the civil war. His captors dressed him in women's clothes and forced him to watch as his family and friends were executed. Atahualpa was the new emperor, but he did not rule for long. As he began his triumphant

Supported by his retainers, an Inca emperor
rides to the capital in this decorative litter.

This Natchez Warrior wears a cloak and hat of fur. The Natchez Indians probably were influenced by the Aztecs culture.

Ecuador Vies With Peru

Atahualpa was a ruler in Ecuador where he had continued his father's conquests of that country. When he invaded Peru to claim the throne, there was bitter fighting. Although these events occurred more than 400 years ago, the hatred and hard feelings that were aroused during that time still exist today. There is still bitterness between Ecuador and Peru. In 1941, in fact, there was a border war between these two countries.

journey toward Cuzco, he received word that bearded men, riding strange animals, were marching inland. Atahualpa could have rushed to his capital and called his army together. Instead, he decided to wait for the arrival of the strangers.

There were only 180 Spaniards in the group of bearded men who arrived in Incan territory. As they marched inland, it must have been reassuring to see smoldering ruins and corpses hanging from trees as a result of civil war. They knew it would be easy to conquer a people who were fighting among themselves. We will learn in Chapter 17 what happened when these two groups met.

The North American Indians

While the most spectacular Indian civilizations were located in Middle America and Peru, we must remember that people lived in North America before the white men arrived. While we do not have time for a detailed study of each tribe, we will discuss the important ones briefly according to the section of the country in which they lived.

Southeastern Indians

The Natchez. We have already studied the Mound Builders who lived in the southeastern United States. The Natchez Indians were probably related to the Mound Builders. Undoubtedly they also were influenced by the civilizations in Middle America.

The Natchez were the only North American Indians to have a king. He had the title "The Sun" and was considered to be so sacred that he never even walked. His robes and crown were made of beautiful feathers much like the ones worn by the Toltec and Aztec rulers.

The Five Civilized Tribes. The Creeks, Chickasaws, Choctaws, Cherokees, and Seminole Indians also were descended from the Mound Builders. These tribes were so advanced culturally that the white men referred to them as "the five civilized tribes." They built permanent homes of wood, lived in large settlements, and farmed their land.

Although each separate tribe had the same language and customs, there was no overall tribal government. Each village was independent of the others and had its own chief. But the different villages of the same tribe usually did not fight each other. Whenever several tribes joined in an alliance against another tribe, they went their own way after the fighting.

Chiefs were elected and rank was given according to a man's accomplishments, rather than by the status of his family. War chiefs led the fighting. High chiefs were usually not warriors, although they probably had to prove their bravery in battle in order to become high chiefs.

Men and women alike planted and harvested crops. The women were responsible for the fields before harvest time. Women had important positions in these tribes. The husband went to live with his wife's family and he needed his first wife's permission before he could take a second wife.

The men loved wars and fighting became their main interest in life. The main reasons for their wars were to take chances, kill people, and thus win glory. Nobody wanted to end a war by completely wiping out the enemy. Warriors never fought large-scale battles. Instead they engaged in small, sudden attacks and raids on homes. At dawn they set enemies' homes on fire and then killed family members as they came out.

It was these Indians who later welcomed the white men and adopted their ways. Then they were ruthlessly forced off their land when the white man discovered gold there. The only group that was able to withstand the white man's invasion and remain in control of their own territory was the Seminole Indians in Florida.

Northeastern Indians

The northeastern Indians were divided into two separate cultural groups known as the Algonkians and the Iroquoian. The Algonkians were the original settlers in this area, but were driven out of the richer farm areas by the Iroquoian people.

The Algonkian Tribe. The territory of the Algonkian people stretched into Canada to Hudson Bay. The people had no political unity, however, and their only relation seems to be that they spoke the same language. These people did not live in large villages because there was not enough game in any one area to support and feed a large group. They rarely gathered as a people and they did not have an overall chief. Instead each small group had its own leader. The Algonkians were a peace-loving and primitive people.

The Algonkians were the Indians who welcomed the first Europeans to North America. They taught the new settlers to plant corn, bake clams and beans, make canoes, use seaweed for fertilizer, eat pumpkins and squash, and smoke tobacco. Most of these tribes were destroyed by the white men. Only a few small groups were left as the white men took their land and pushed these peaceful Indians into the territory of their warlike Indian neighbors.

The Iroquoian Tribe. The Iroquoian tribes were better known than the Algonkian. A cruel and warlike people, they controlled territory across part of Pennsylvania and a large part of upper New York. In the 1400s a league was organized by five tribes, including the Senecas, Cayugas, Onondagas, Oneidas, and Mohawks. The term Iroquois applies to this group of tribes.

The Iroquois were a farming people. Their villages were surrounded by wooden stockades. A typical feature of the Iroquois civilization was the great long houses in which several families lived. These houses were built by the men, but owned by the women. Women also owned the fields and crops.

Iroquois Customs. The Iroquois did not have a written language, but they kept records on strings of *wampum,* or beads made from a special clamshell. Since the Iroquois did not live near the seacoast, they got wampum by trading. The beads were strung on belts in such a way that each belt had its own special meaning. Messages, records of tribal legends, and historical events were recorded on wampum

The southern Indians in America decorated their bodies with tatoos. When a boy was first named, he received a tatoo. When he became a warrior, he was given a new name and tatooed again. After killing an enemy in battle, he received his final name and more tatoos. This Indian from the Florida tribe must have been very important because of the many tatoos on his body.

Masks carved by men of the Iroquois **False Face Society** looked like supernatural beings seen in dreams. Society members wore these masks and danced through the village to drive away demons of disease.

Indians of the western plains, in the years before the horse, used dogs to carry their loads. The *travois,* a platform or net attached to two long trailing poles—usually the teepee's lodge poles—were fastened to the backs of the dogs. With the coming of the horse, Indian life was greatly changed. Most territory could be covered with the travois and moving was made simpler.

belts. Specially trained men were taught to memorize what the different strings of wampum meant. Wampum was also used as money.

The Iroquois are known today for the frightening wooden masks they used in what is known as their False Face Society. The purpose of these masks was to break magic spells that caused people to become sick.

Hiawatha

One of the best-known Indians in America is Hiawatha, who was immortalized in the famous poem by Longfellow. There really was an Indian named Hiawatha, but he has no resemblance to the Indian in the poem. Hiawatha worked out all the practical details so the five Iroquois tribes could stop fighting each other and unite against their enemies. This Iroquois league lasted for some 300 years and still survives in small numbers today.

While most American Indians did not torture their prisoners as some believe, the Iroquois practiced such cruelty. They sacrificed victims to Aireskoi, their spirit of war and hunting. If they did not have a man to torture, they tortured a woman. Other tribes hated and feared the Iroquois because of the torture they practiced. If other tribes captured Iroquois, therefore, they tortured them purely out of revenge.

Although the Iroquois were cruel and savage on the one hand, they also were an advanced society. They originated beautiful legends and their ritual prayers were full of beautiful poetry.

Plains Indians

When people in the United States think of Indians, they usually picture a warrior on horseback, wearing buckskin and a long feathered headdress. This is actually only the picture that movies have given us. The truth is that the American Indians did not have horses until the explorers brought them from Europe.

According to historians, most Indians that we think of as "plains" Indians did not live in the prairies until the westward movement of the white men. They were pushed out of their homes in the western woodlands. These woodland tribes included the Ponca, Oto, Osage, Omaha, Missouri, Kansas, Iowa, Mandan, Hidatsa, Pawnee, and Sioux. They did a little farming and took hunting trips into the plains to kill buffalo.

By the 1300s these tribes had established fairly permanent homes. They were made of log rafters and had sod walls and roofs. Sometimes grass grew all over the home. The roofs were solid enough for the entire family to gather on them in good weather. Many villages were located on cliffs overlooking rivers which gave them added protection from attack. The tribes used hide tepees when they went into the plains to hunt buffalo. The tepees usually were small since the lodgepoles that held them up had to be dragged by dogs, the only beasts of burden in North America at that time.

Southwest Indians

The principal tribes in the southwest were divided into three groups. These major groups were the Pimas, the Yumas, and the Pueblos. As a general rule, these people were too busy trying to survive in the harsh, dry desert to spend time with war, elaborate rituals, or the building of great civilizations.

The Pueblos. The Pueblos were divided into several different tribes—the Hopis, Zunis, Acomas, and Lagunas. These people got their name from the special cities in which they lived, called *pueblos*.

Between 450 and 750 A.D. a basket-making culture, the forerunners of the Pueblos, developed in Mesa Verde near the Colorado border. These people were very peaceful. Between 1000 and 1200 A.D., warlike tribes began moving into the area. These early Pueblos then were forced to build their homes high on cliff ledges where they could pull up their ladders and be fairly safe.

Across the southwest are the spectacular ruins of the Pueblo Indians. It is interesting to note, however, that there are pueblos, like in Taos, New Mexico, where the Indians are still living in much the way they did centuries ago.

This area was not good farming country, but the Indians learned to use the small amount of water that was available for irrigation. Because farming was so hard, the men did the farming while the women became skilled at making pottery and weaving baskets. They wove their baskets together so tightly that they could store water in them.

Since just staying alive was a major struggle for these tribes, they did not have time for war. They did not practice rituals of human sacrifices or torture in their society. They were brave people, however, and when they were attacked they fought hard.

The Pueblos were well known for making beautiful silver jewelry, using turquois, shell, and bright stones. It was traditional among the Pueblos that a father never punished his own children. He could teach them and play with them, but all discipline was handled by the man who was the head of his wife's clan. The Pueblo Indians used dances as dramatized prayers. Every step and gesture was carefully rehearsed. One of their most interesting beliefs was in *kachinas,* special beings they believed were half men, half gods, who helped people. All the Pueblos except Taos followed the kachina cult.

The Pimas. In southern Arizona a group of Indians known as the Pimas lived. The Pimas consisted of two tribes, the Pimas and the Papagos. The Pimas lived along the Gila River where they were able to irrigate their land. The Papagos were called the "bean people." This was because their land was so barren all they could grow was beans. In order to survive, the Papagos worked for the Pimas part of the year.

The Yumas. The Yumas lived along the Colorado River on the Arizona-California border. These people were made up of the Yumas and the Mohaves. Because their land was easy to farm, the women did the farming work.

These men, with more spare time on their hands, were warlike. The Yumas had rigid rules for fighting. Often the best warriors fought individual duels before the main battle started. These people took scalps as battle trophies.

Because it was so hot, the Yumas did not wear much clothing. They were the only Indians in North America who cremated their dead.

Other southwestern Indians did not make their appearance until much later. They were the Navajos, Apaches, Kiowas, Comanches, and the Cheyennes.

Priests in many of the southwestern pueblos used doll-like images called *kachinas* in their worship and ritual. The Indians thought spirits enter the images in order to honor the dead and bless the living.

Today all that remains of the basket-making culture of Mesa Verde, Colorado, are these ruins. These people built their homes on high cliff ledges for protection against attack.

The West Coast Indians

Most of the Indians along the southern west coast of North America were poor and undeveloped. They did not have time to develop a culture because they could barely find enough food to stay alive. They grubbed for roots.

In California the Indians had a combination of cultures. Tribes hunted, fished, and wove baskets. They also gathered acorns to make flour and used shells for money. They were able to live in large communities since food was easy to find.

Colorful totem poles and wooden community houses crowd the shoreline of this village in northwestern America. Actors arrive in a carved and painted canoe to celebrate "potlatch ceremony," the main event of the winter. During this festival property was often destroyed or extravagantly given away.

There were many tribes living on the northwest coast. Some of these included the Tlingit in Alaska; the Haida in British Columbia; the Tsimshian, Kwakiutl, Nootka, Bella Coola, and Coast Salish in Washington, and the Chinook, Karok, and Yu roks in Washington and Oregon.

These people depended on fishing and hunting for seals and whales for a living. Because they learned to dry fish, they had spare time to develop an interesting culture. This fishing culture was well established along the western coast of North America when the white men arrived. They built elaborate boats covered with interesting designs.

Their houses were made of solid wood. They carved masks, chests, bowls, spoons, cradles, rattles, houses, canoes, and totem poles. They also carved large wooden boxes that were used for cooking. The box was filled with water and

The Potlatch

Almost everyone has heard the term "Indian giver." This term came from a strange custom developed by the North Coast Indians called the potlatch. The custom involved special dinners that were given to impress the guests with the importance of the host. At the potlatch, the host destroyed or gave away large quantities of valuable possessions. The favored guest was then expected to give a potlatch in which he gave away and destroyed even more. If he were unable to do this he would lose his prestige. Sometimes the entire village helped their chief throw a potlatch, fully expecting to get back more than they gave away.

then food was brought to a boil by dropping hot rocks into the water. Later these people began carving objects from bone and animal horns.

These people wore elaborate clothing to show off their rank. Although they knew how to make moccasins, they often went barefooted, even in the snow.

These tribes were warlike. Unlike other Indians we have studied, they were more interested in defeating their enemies completely. This was because their population was growing and there was not much good land available. Disagreements about fishing rights were another cause of war.

Artwork of the West Coast tribes was different from that of other Indian cultures we have studied. They did not have ritual patterns, so each artist was free to design what he wanted. They did not like to see blank spaces in their art, so they used faces or eyes to fill up the open spaces. Some of their work was so abstract in design that the forms were barely recognizable.

NORTH AMERICAN INDIANS

Explorations and Events that Impacted East and West

1. A series of stones set in perfect lines across Canada parallel Stonehenge; indicating arrival of adventurous men from North Europe or Scandinavian countries. Therefore, historians now conclude that the Americas were settled by men and women from at least three "Old World" regions: the Bering Strait, the Atlantic Trade Winds route from Africa, and Scandinavia via Greenland/Iceland.

2. European explorers traveled worldwide, starting in the 1400's.

3. Many objects now being uncovered along the Eastern coasts of (present) Central and South America closely resemble parallel objects of ancient West Africa. For example, Mayan temples parallel buildings of ancient Babylon and Egypt.

4. Since the days of Norwegian explorer Thor Heyerdahl and his voyage on the *Kon-tiki*, meteorologists who work with weather and wind currents realize how easily adventurous Hamitic Africans could have traveled within the Atlantic trade winds/currents and crossed the Atlantic Ocean at certain times of the year. When? Probably around 2000 B.C.! Newsweek, Fall-Winter, 1991, records the date of the first cities of the Olmecs (pp. 91-93) at 1500 B.C.

5. Mohammed (born 570 A.D.) determined to conquer the world for Islam. Islamic warriors conquered Arabia, Persia, North Africa, and parts of Europe c. 625.

6. The T'ang Dynasty expanded their empire in 623 to include Turkestan and Korea--Huang Gdi of the Ch'in dynasty built huge terra cotta tomb figures at the city of Xian.

7. Genghis Khan conquered the Ch'in dynasty in 1234 A.D.----Pax <u>Tartarica</u> linked East with the West.

8. The Ottoman Turks took Constantinople in 1453.

9. Ming dynasty built the Forbidden City 1403-1424.

10. By 200 A.D. Chinese naval expeditions to India, West Asia (Levant), East Africa, and Europe had linked/united most of Eurasia.

11. Arab Muslims conquered Turkestan in 751 A.D.

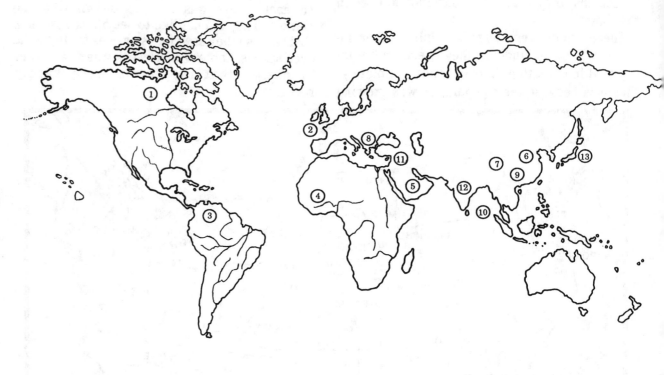

12. India was not united; Muslims invaded; Indian culture spread to SE Asia; Angkor Wat built (1100); Portuguese traders came (1498), Tamerlane Turks came (1526).

13. Buddhism came to Japan in (c. 500 B.C.) Periods: Nara--Fujiwara--Kyoto--Yoritomo--Hojo-- The Great Wing (typhoon, monsoon) destroyed Kamakura city in c. 1333 and great confusion resulted. Japan reacts to these problems with the policy of isolationism. Shogun rulers hold regional control in Japan from 1335-1850.

NATIONALISM AND THE RENAISSANCE

Projects

1. Compare the military advantages and disadvantages of the longbow and the crossbow. Make a working model of a crossbow.

2. Give a report on one of the following: Joan of Arc, Richard II, Henry V of England, Erasmus, More, Dante, Ivan the Terrible, or Isabella of Spain.

3. Compare the Battle of Bosworth Field with the Battle of Hastings. How were they similar? How were they different? Which do you believe was the most important? Why?

4. Build a model of St. Basil's Cathedral.

5. Design, plan, and write about your idea of an utopia. Include plans for a government, a work force, and a society of people that eliminate all the problems we face in our world today.

6. When we studied Aristotle we learned he was considered the most intelligent man who ever lived. Compare his life, work, and achievements with those of Leonardo da Vinci. Which do you believe was the most outstanding? Why?

7. Read *The Canterbury Tales* or *Dante's Inferno*. What was the main point the author was trying to make? What was your favorite part of the book? Why?

8. Make a report on Copernicus and his work. How did he discover the fact that all the planets revolve around the sun? Why was this idea unpopular?

9. Class project. Take a field trip to a local art gallery or museum. If there is no guide, get your art teacher to go and explain the significance of pictures displayed. Are any of them Renaissance paintings? Make a report on what you learned.

Words and Concepts

Sistine Chapel
In Praise of Folly
despots
primogeniture
Elizabeth of York
Mona Lisa
Utopia
janizaries
The Golden Bull
Divine Comedy
humanists
Battle of Kulikovo
Inquisition
Rheims
Canterbury Tales
doge
cantons
Bosworth Field

THE HUNDRED YEARS' WAR
1337 - 1453 A.D.

Nationalism and the Renaissance

The end of the Crusades brought dynamic changes to Europe, as we have seen. So many nobles were killed in the Crusades that the kings regained control of their countries. An active trade developed and cities grew. Merchants traveling from country to country brought news with them about events taking place in other areas of the world.

People began to think of themselves as citizens of a particular country and to take pride in their citizenship. They also began to take an interest in what was happening outside their local areas. Ideas and goods circulated freely between countries. Almost everywhere movements were under way to form strong national states.

A new tribe of Turks conquered Constantinople and almost took over Europe. Russian history turned in a new direction after the fall of Constantinople when the czar claimed to be the new Roman emperor. As scholars fled from Constantinople, they carried with them books containing the thoughts and wisdom of the ancient Greeks. This brought about a rebirth in study, learning, education, science, and the arts in Europe that is known as the Renaissance.

It was these events that brought Europe to the brink of the modern age. The final break came almost immediately with the questioning of the power of the Roman Catholic Church and the discovery of the New World. We shall study about these events in the next chapter.

French and English Nationalism

The two countries dominating Western Europe during this period were France and England. Although the French kings had succeeded in driving the English out of most of the French territory, the English still had a claim on much of France. The rest of France was divided by powerful nobles who had almost the same amount of power as independent kings. France did not become a strong country until later when the English were driven out of French territory. Then the powerful French nobles were brought under the authority of the king.

The Hundred Years' War

Causes of the War. The English and the Flemish Duchy had worked out an alliance that was making both countries rich. The English shipped wool to the Flemish who, in turn, made it into products to be sold all over Europe. The Flemish Duchy, however, was actually under the lordship of the French king. The king threatened to cut off this vital commerce. Since a break in the wool trade would have affected most of England's middle class, the English king did not want to let this happen.

Edward III was king of England when the last Capetian king died. When Philip VI of Valois became the new king in 1328 A.D., Edward III declared war on France. Edward claimed to be the rightful king of France because his mother was the sister of the last Capetian king. The French ignored his claim. According to their law, a woman could not inherit property, including the throne, or pass it on to her children.

The War in France. From 1337 until 1452 A.D., there was almost continuous fighting between the French and the English. Since the English were trying to take over France, all the fighting was done in France. As a result, France was greatly weakened. French peasants watched

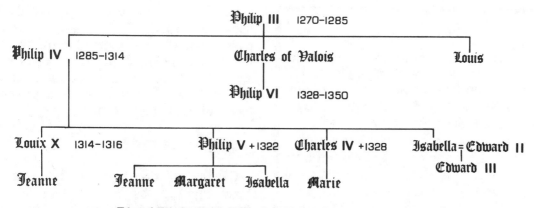

Philip III   1270-1285

Philip IV   1285-1314   Charles of Valois   Louis

Philip VI   1328-1350

Louix X   1314-1316   Philip V +1322   Charles IV +1328   Isabella = Edward II

                                                                      Edward III

Jeanne   Jeanne   Margaret   Isabella   Marie

Edward III's family tree, showing Edward's claim to the French throne. The controversy over this claim was one of the causes of the Hundred Years' War.

helplessly as their crops were destroyed and their farm animals were stolen by hungry English soldiers.

The French king was forced to collect higher and higher taxes to pay for the war. In 1358 the French peasants revolted, murdering their lords and burning their manor houses. The uprising was suppressed by violent means. As a result of this revolt, the French king took even greater control over the Estates General, the French Parliament, preventing it from ever becoming as effective an organization as the English Parliament.

Until 1482 the English armies were victorious. They won three major battles—at Crecy, Poitiers, and Agincourt. English soldiers, in a well-disciplined national army, were armed with the powerful longbow. They were far more effective than the French army which was still made up of feudal *levies,* or soldiers forced to fight in the army.

When Charles VII became king, he was in a very dangerous position. His kingdom was controlled almost entirely by the English and the powerful duke of Burgundy. He had been cut off

from Rheims where all French kings were crowned. Since he was not crowned, he did not have the loyalty of the French people.

The situation began to turn around at this time. Due to the leadership of a brave girl named Joan of Arc, the French began to win the war. Charles was crowned in Rheims and the French army was reorganized along modern lines. They began using cannons and other guns which were superior to the English longbow. The Hundred Years' War came to an end in 1453 when the English lost all their territory in France, except for the port of Calais.

Results of the War. When the war began, France was divided among powerful nobles and the king had no authority. The French people looked to their local feudal lords for protection and security. When English soldiers swept through the country, stealing food and looting homes, the French peasants soon learned that it would take the power of a king to protect them. Although France was weakened by years of warfare in her own territory, the king assumed a stronger position after the war.

Edward III's son was called the Black Prince because he always wore black armor in battle. He was one of England's greatest warriors and during the Hundred Years' War was responsible for two of England's major victories at Crecy and Poitiers. Exhausted by so much fighting, he died before his own father.

Joan of Arc, patron saint of France, symbolized the French spirit of victory. Urged by voices she believed to be divine, Joan persuaded the king to let her lead an attack against the English to retrieve the city of Orleans. Although Orleans was saved, Joan was captured by English soldiers and burned at the stake.

Joan of Arc

Joan of Arc was one of the most romantic heroines in history. As a young peasant girl, she began hearing what she thought was the voice of God, directing her to lead the armies of France to victory.

As she led the French troops to victory, the English strongholds in France fell one after another. She was captured by men belonging to the powerful duke of Burgundy, who sold her to the British. She was burned at the stake as a witch and the French king did not even try to save her. Joan's bravery in death gave the French enough faith and courage to drive the British out of France.

The war also had important results in England. As long as England had controlled territory in France, large amounts of money, men, and time were spent protecting English holdings from the French king and capturing more territory. Once these French lands were lost, however, the English devoted time, men, and money to building up their own country.

Another important result of the Hundred Years' War was the increase of power of the English Parliament. Although no fighting took place in England, the war was very expensive. The king was forced to call on Parliament to raise the money needed to continue the fighting.

Parliament used its power of the purse to get new powers from the king. They were given the freedom of speech in debating for or against proposed laws. They were given control over all bills involving money which strengthened their power of the purse. They also were assured that when they submitted a petition to the king requesting passage of a certain law, it would be passed exactly as presented in the petition. This was the beginning of the people's power to make laws. The House of Commons was given the right to decide what qualifications a person should have before being allowed to vote.

The War of the Roses

Causes of the War. While England was busy fighting the Hundred Years' War, the groundwork was being laid for a bloody civil war in England. English nobles kept small armies of trained soldiers to take with them when they went to fight in France or to leave behind to protect their property. As a result, the nobles became strong enough to force the king to abdicate, or give up his throne. This happened in 1399 when Richard II, of the York family, was forced to step down and allow his cousin Henry of Lancaster to rule.

The War of the Roses

According to legend, the duke of York and the Lancaster king were walking in the royal garden one day arguing over the throne. In the heat of the argument, the duke of York selected a white rose as the symbol of his cause, and the Lancaster king chose a red rose. Soon all the followers of the two wore roses on their crests to show which family they supported. For this reason the series of civil wars over the claims of these two men to the throne were called the War of the Roses.

From 1455 until 1485, England's history was primarily concerned with conflicts between the two families of York and Lancaster, both of whom claimed the right to rule England. Richard II's heirs were the dukes of York. Henry of Lancaster's descendants proved to be some of England's greatest rulers.

The War Begins. Three years after the Hundred Years' War, civil war erupted in England between York and Lancaster. Edward IV, the duke of York, became king since all the heirs to the house of Lancaster were dead except for a distant relative who was living in Europe. When Edward IV died, his two sons were too young to rule, so the king's brother Richard became the new king. He was named Richard III.

Edward V, the rightful king, and his younger brother were imprisoned in the Tower of London and were never seen again. The people of England suspected Richard III of murdering the two boys and they refused to support Richard III as a result. Henry Tudor, the last Lancaster heir, who had been living elsewhere in Europe, took this moment to invade from outside of England. Richard III was killed in the Battle of Bosworth Field in 1485, and Henry VII became the founder of a new dynasty called the House of Tudor.

Henry VII married a young princess named Elizabeth, sister of the imprisoned Edward V. This united the forces of the red and white roses, ending the war.

Elizabeth is unique in English history. She is the only woman who was the daughter of an English king, the sister of an English king, niece of an English king, wife of an English king, and mother of an English king.

Results of the War. The War of the Roses was important mainly because it almost completely wiped out the English nobility. Whenever a member of a different family became king, he would execute the nobility which had opposed him. Estates were confiscated and family members were forced to flee to the Continent. By the time Henry VII became king in 1485, the

The Mystery of the Missing Princes

One of the great mysteries of history concerns two little princes who were put in the Tower of London by England's King Richard III. For many months the people of London reported seeing their tiny faces peaking out of the fortress' windows.

When they disappeared, the rumor spread that Richard III had murdered them. The people challenged Richard to allow the children to ride their horses through London to disprove the rumor. But the king refused and he never denied the accusations.

The mystery was partially solved in 1956 when the skeletons of two boys were found under a staircase in the tower. Most historians believe the skeletons were those of the missing princes. Tests run on the size of the skeletons, however, have raised questions as to when they were killed.

Some historians now believe that Henry VII had the boys murdered when he came to the throne. Everyone believed they were already dead, so secretly murdering them would have been easy for Henry. Moreover it is certain that the boys were more of a threat to Henry and the new dynasty he was establishing than they were to Richard who had no heir.

The Tower of London is one of the most famous historical landmarks in England. It was used as a prison, a place of execution, and an overnight hotel for rulers prior to their coronation. Dating back to the time of William the Conqueror, the tower is now a museum where the British crown jewels are displayed.

nobility was too weak to cause the king any trouble. From then on the major check on the king's power came from Parliament, rather than from unruly feudal nobles.

France Develops Royal Absolutism

When the Hundred Years' War was over, the French King Louis XI was faced with two major problems. In the first place, the economy of France was in a bad state. For, even in times of peace, both the French and English armies lived off the land, plundering, killing, and helping themselves to whatever they wanted. In addition an enormous tax was put on the people which had been increased each year. The second problem facing the king was the struggle to gain control over the remaining powerful nobles, so he could assume the major power in France.

The King vs. the Nobles. Louis XI was faced with the job of bringing the powerful nobles under his control. The most powerful of these nobles was the duke of Burgundy who had sided with the English during the Hundred Years' War.

Charles the Bold was the duke of Burgundy when the war came to an end. He was busy adding territory to his duchy, but he made the mistake of alienating the Swiss Confederation. The confederation joined with Louis XI, and in the fighting that followed, Charles the Bold was killed. The war was continued by Charles' daughter Mary. When she died in 1482, however, her husband Maximilian made peace with Louis XI by turning Burgundy over to the French.

Louis XI and his son Charles VIII brought the remaining nobles under their control. For the first time, France became a strong and united country under the leadership of a capable king.

French Prosperity. When peace was restored, the entire country began to prosper. The king encouraged the shipbuilding industry, so that ships could be used for ocean travel as well as on French canals. The French also learned the secret of raising silkworms and a silk industry was started. France was on her way to becoming a major power and trade center.

Problem Areas of the Future. There were two problems, however, that would cause France much trouble in the years to come. To win the support of the nobles, the kings began giving them special privileges. For one thing they were exempt from paying taxes. This meant that the only people paying taxes were the peasants and the rising middle class who were involved in trade and industry.

The other problem in the provinces was the treatment of peasants as serfs. They were tied to the land and still were at the mercy of their lords. They did not yet have the same freedoms as the peasants in England. French peasants did not rebel against their unbearable living conditions until several hundred years later.

The dukes of Burgundy were almost as powerful as the kings of France. But after the Hundred Years' War, the king of France was determined to destroy their power. While Philip the Good (left) was duke, he was able to strengthen his country. His son, Charles the Bold (right), angered the Swiss Confederation that sided with the French. He was killed in the fighting that followed.

The Iberian Peninsula

The Iberian peninsula was divided into six strong and independent kingdoms—Castile, Leon, Aragon, Navarre, Portugal, and Granada. The Moors still controlled Granada, their last stronghold in Europe.

Isabella, the young queen of Castile and Leon, married the future king of Aragon in 1469. As a result of their marriage, most of what is now Spain came under their control. The nobles in Spain had become strong and independent after fighting the Moors for so many years. The first job facing the new rulers, then, was the lessening the power of the nobles.

This drawing shows the Moors' leader surrendering his sword to King Ferdinand and Queen Isabella of Spain after the fall of Granada. This victory meant that Spain was completely united for the first time since the Muslim invasion.

Love Unites Spain

When Isabella's nobles suspected that she wanted to marry Ferdinand, they did everything in their power to prevent the marriage. The nobles knew that if the couple married, their combined kingdoms would be strong enough to break the nobles' power. For a time Isabella was practically a prisoner in her castle. Armed men patrolled the roads ready to kill the young prince if he tried to enter the country.

Hoping to find Ferdinand, the nobles stopped every wealthy traveler who entered the territory. By hiding in a wagonload of straw, however, Ferdinand was able to slip into the country. He managed to rescue Isabella and they were married. Under their leadership Spain became a united country, the Muslims were defeated and driven out of Spain, and a New World was discovered by Christopher Columbus.

The Spanish Inquisition. To control the nobles, Ferdinand and Isabella initiated the Spanish Inquisition in 1480. The purpose of the Inquisition was to locate and persecute those subjects not loyal to the Roman Catholic Church. Anyone accused of being a Jew, Muslim, or witch was arrested. Confessions often were made as the result of terrible torture. Once a victim confessed, he was burned at the stake in a great public ceremony. Sometimes more than 20 people were executed at the same time. Since anyone could bring an accusation against another person, it soon turned into a system of terror. Many people left Spain rather than continue to live under the constant threat of arrest and torture.

In 1492 the Muslim state of Granada was defeated by the armies of Ferdinand and Isabella. This was the same year Christopher Columbus sailed to the West and discovered a New World. In 1516 Ferdinand conquered

Although Count Rudolf founded the Hapsburg Dynasty it was Maximilian who made the Hapsburgs the strongest force in sixteenth century Europe. He did so by marrying Mary of Burgundy, heiress of the Low Countries and by arranging for the marriage of his son to the heiress of Spain. Thus the Hapsburg territory grew vastly.

Navarre and all of Spain became a single united country.

Eastern European Nationalism

Many of the countries we are studying in this chapter developed into strong political states as a result of nationalism. We will also learn that nationalism alone was not always sufficient to bring about the formation of a strong nation. In some areas stronger forces were working against the development of a national government than those working to unite it. When this happened, the country involved remained weak and divided.

The German States

The Germans Elect an Emperor. As pointed out in Chapter 13, the area known today as Germany was left without a leader and hopelessly divided among strong nobles. This was a result of the conflict between the Holy Roman Emperors and the Roman Catholic Church. They did not bother to elect another emperor for 19 years. The nobles soon realized, however, that they needed someone with absolute authority to bring about order and to provide security.

In 1273 Count Rudolf of Hapsburg was elected as the new Holy Roman Emperor. By this time Italy no longer was considered part of the Holy Roman Empire and the emperor had no real power. Rudolf was a perfect emperor. He did not try to increase his power, but he did bring about order and a measure of peace.

When King Ottokar of Bohemia refused to recognize the new emperor, Rudolf conquered Bohemia and turned it over to his son to rule.

Rudolph wanted it ruled as private landholdings rather than as a possession of the Holy Roman Emperor. He did this because he realized his son would not succeed him as emperor. These lands, plus his own holdings in Austria and Hungary, were ruled by the Hapsburgs until the twentieth century.

The title of Holy Roman Emperor did not actually mean much at this time. The men in Germany who were elected emperor did not attempt to extend their authority and power as the kings of France and England before them had done. Even if they had wanted it, they realized they could not have gotten the support

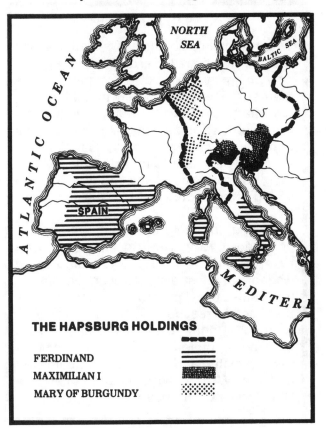

THE HAPSBURG HOLDINGS

FERDINAND

MAXIMILIAN I

MARY OF BURGUNDY

of their nobles or the other citizens. They were unable to collect taxes from the nobles or the cities to use in fighting wars. The emperor could use his own money and men to take over more territory or to increase his power. If he did this, however, his son would probably not be

---

The House of Hapsburg

From the time Albert II was elected emperor in 1438, the title of Holy Roman Emperor was almost hereditary to the Hapsburgs. They never tried to use the office to gain power, but the title did give their family an advantage in politics.

Maximilian I was responsible for the growth of the Hapsburg possessions. It was gained through marriage, however, rather than through conflict. He married Mary of Burgundy and their son, Philip the Handsome, inherited all the Burgundian estates which included: Burgundy, Franche-Comte, Luxembourg, and the Netherlands. He also inherited the Hapsburg properties of Austria, Styria, Carinthia, Carniola, and Tyrol. Philip married Joanna, daughter of Ferdinand and Isabella.

When Joanna's only brother died, she became heiress of Spain, the Aragonese kingdoms of Sardinia, Sicily, and Naples in Italy and all the Spanish territory in the New World. Her son Charles V was elected Holy Roman Emperor and ruled all this territory when he was only 19 years old. This was the most territory that any one man had ruled since the time of Charlemagne.

---

elected emperor when he died. Moreover, it was hardly worth the effort or cost.

For this reason the Holy Roman Emperors used their title and position more to expand their own personal wealth and to promote their families than to become good emperors. We saw how the Hapsburgs gained Austria as a result of being strong emperors. We saw how other families also received land in much the same way. The people of Luxembourg took over Bohemia and the Wittelbachs received Brandenburg, Tyrol, and Bavaria. They continued to rule Bavaria until after World War I.

Although the Holy Roman Empire was not important at this time, some small kingdoms were very important. Bohemia, for example, developed a strong judicial system and became one of the greatest imperial states of all while their king was Holy Roman Emperor. He also built a university in the capital city of Prague.

The Golden Bull. A few German states were well organized and had strong governments. But whenever a new emperor had to be elected, there always was a chance that civil war might erupt. There were too many states voting in the elections. In 1356 Charles IV of Luxembourg brought forth a document that allowed for orderly elections of emperors. At the same time, however, it prevented Germany from becoming a strong and unified nation.

This document, called the *Golden Bull,* defined the emperor's power and set up definite rules for electing the emperor. The document cut the number of electors to seven. Three were churchmen, including the archbishops of Mainz, Cologne, and Trier. Only four nobles became electors. They were the count of Palatine of the Rhine, the margrave of Brandenburg, the duke of Saxony, and the king of Bohemia.

The Golden Bull also required the four territories to remain completely independent of the emperor's control. These lands could not be divided for any reason; and the system of primogeniture, in which the eldest son inherited all the property, was practiced. The title and privilege of serving as an elector remained with the land. Thus, when the Golden Bull was accepted as the legal government of the Germanies, it was impossible for a single unified nation to develop.

Confederations and Leagues. Since no strong central government existed in the Germanies, there was no law enforcement and no protection available for life and property. There was much lawlessness; nobody was safe. Although the major states had fairly stable governments, many other smaller states in the Germanies had less stable governments.

The ecclesiastical states were ruled by archbishops, bishops, or abbots. There were 60 free imperial city-states and hundreds of small territories ruled by nobles or knights. Since there was no organized authority to protect them, confederations or leagues of knights, districts, or cities were formed for protection.

The Swiss Confederation. One of the first groups to be established was the Swiss Confederation, the basis for the government of modern Switzerland. At first three districts, called *cantons,* united and broke away from their Hapsburg overlords in 1315. They became basically independent of outside control. By 1513 there were 13 cantons and cities united under the Swiss Confederation. We have already seen how this confederation joined with the French king to defeat the powerful duke of Burgundy.

The Swiss Confederation worked as a defensive pact. Each canton and city was totally independent, however, and they were unable to

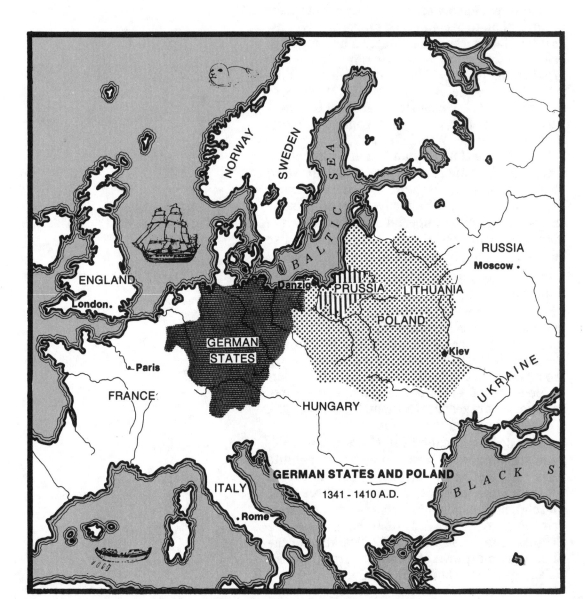

GERMAN STATES AND POLAND

1341 - 1410 A.D.

work together for any other projects. For one thing three languages were spoken in the cantons—German, Italian, and French. In addition jealousy and friction existed between the cities and rural cantons. Such frictions prevented the Swiss Confederation from growing into a strong national state.

We have already mentioned the Hanseatic League, a group of nearly 70 cities in northern Germany. These cities provided mutual protection against pirates and raiders in the northern seas. They also negotiated trade agreements with England, the Netherlands, Norway, and Russia, providing major markets for these countries.

Poland and Lithuania

Growth of Poland. Poland, as we have seen, had accepted Christianity. She had begun to attack neighbors who were still pagan or worshiped a different form of Christianity. While the Russians were busy fighting the Golden Horde, the Polish tried to take over portions of Russia.

Another pagan country was Lithuania. For many years the Poles and Lithuanians were bitter enemies. This changed, however, in 1386 when King Jagiello of Lithuania married a Polish princess. Jagiello became a Christian and Christianity became Lithuania's official religion. A few years later, Jagiello was elected king of Poland and the combined territory almost doubled the size of Poland.

In 1410 the Poles defeated the Teutonic Knights, a military order formed in Prussia during the Crusades at the battle of Tannenberg. As a result of this victory, Poland took over West Prussia. The Poles and Germans still disagree over which country has a right to this territory and the seaport of Danzig, all of which has changed hands several times since then.

Polish Society. Although Poland was one of the largest states in Europe, she did not have a strong government. The main reason for this was that her population was made up of several different racial groups. Most of the people living in the cities were German and those in the country were Slavic. Many of the people of the new territory were either Lithuanian or Russian Slavs. Because of their racial differences, it was difficult for the Poles to feel any loyalty to the state. This was because it usually takes both racial pride and patriotism to inspire nationalistic feeling.

Another reason Poland could not become a powerful state was that her elected king had little influence over the strong and independent Polish nobles. A third factor was that the Poles still used the feudal system in which the peasants' chief loyalty was to their feudal lords rather than to the king. Eventually these weaknesses caused the Polish nation to break apart.

Russian Challenge to Tartar Rule

As you will recall, the Golden Horde conquered Russia, but they allowed the Russian princes to rule their territory as long as they paid their tribute. One of these princes was Daniel, the youngest son of Alexander Nevsky, who established a new duchy called Moscow far in Russia's interior.

While this new city grew stronger, the territory along the European border was weakened by constant attacks. The Lithuanians captured most of the Ukrainian territory of

Russia, including the city of Kiev. Up to this time, Kiev had been the headquarters of the Russian Orthodox Church. Then the head of the Church was forced to flee, and in 1299 he moved to Moscow where permanent headquarters were established.

Moscow continued to grow until it became the strongest state in Russia. Russian princes continued to pay tribute to the Tartars, but they used their position as tribute collectors to conquer more territory. When the ruler in Moscow realized that the Tartars could no longer enforce their rule, he rebelled. In 1380 the Khan was defeated in the battle of Kulikovo and Moscow's "Grand Prince" became Russia's most powerful leader.

Ivan the Great. Russia was still divided into many small states in 1462 when Ivan III, known as Ivan the Great, became prince of Moscow. In the years that followed, Ivan forcibly took over all the territories where the people refused to accept him as ruler. He took the title of autocrat of all Russia. When he was powerful enough, he destroyed the remaining Tartar strongholds in Russia.

Ivan III brought many gifted artists from Italy and Constantinople to Moscow where they created numerous beautiful works of art. It was during his rule that the beautiful walled palace, known as the Kremlin, was built. Today this palace network still houses the government of communist Russia.

Ivan the Terrible. The next great ruler of Russia was Ivan IV, known as Ivan the Terrible. His reign began in 1547 and he managed to bring the nobles under his control. Ivan the Terrible was an absolute ruler with no restrictions placed upon him.

Although a harsh ruler, Ivan IV introduced a new code of laws protecting common people. As head of the Russian Orthodox Church, he made reforms in the morality of priests. Church schools provided education with Bible training and missionaries were sent out.

The beautiful onion-domed Cathedral of St. Basil was built during Ivan IV's rule. Today this cathedral still stands in Moscow's Red Square where it has been turned into a museum.

When Ivan IV died in 1584, Russia entered a period known as "the time of troubles." Russia

---

Russians Claim Heritage of Byzantine Empire

Ivan III was the first Russian leader to be called "czar," a title that comes from the Roman word "caesar." He married Sophia, the niece of the Byzantine emperor, a fact which greatly influence the Russian culture.

Ivan was a follower of the Greek Orthodox faith. When the Ottoman Turks conquered Constantinople in 1453, Ivan believed that he was the only person who could continue the tradition of the Roman Empire. Before long, Ivan adopted the Byzantine double-headed eagle as his imperial emblem and introduced the Byzantine court ceremony.

The Russians, believed they were the rightful heirs to the Byzantine Empire. They have always claimed that the territory in southeastern Europe bordering the Black Sea and the Dardanelle Strait belonged to them. This claim has involved them in more than one war over that area.

was torn by civil war for nearly 30 years as both Sweden and Poland invaded from her western borders.

The Ottoman Empire

Through the years the Muslim Empire established by the Seljuk Turks had grown smaller and weaker as various territories broke away to be ruled by local leaders. Then a new group of Turkish nomads adopted Islam and began moving into the Middle East. These people were the Ottoman Turks. Immediately they began conquering territory and building an empire. By 1354 they had captured all of the territory in Asia Minor which formerly belonged to the Byzantine Empire.

Europeans Under Attack. Turkish armies crossed the Hellespont to the European side of the Black Sea and began conquering the Balkan states. Constantinople was completely surrounded and was forced to surrender in 1453. Europeans were astonished and shocked to hear the news of the capture of Constantinople. It now seemed that the Roman Empire was completely dead and a dynamic and colorful historical age had come to an end.

Ivan the Terrible is pictured here with his eldest son whom he killed in a fit of temper during an argument. Under Ivan's leadership, Russia had one of the worst periods in her history.

The beautiful, onion-domed cathedral of St. Basil is one of Russia's most famous landmarks. It was built during the reign of Ivan the Terrible and shows the Byzantine influence on Russian architecture. Today it is a museum and is no longer used for worship.

The Turks were not satisfied with the conquest of Constantinople. Under the rule of Suleiman I the Magnificent, they went on to conquer Greece, Bosnia, Serbia, Albania, and most of Hungary. Suleiman's troops invaded Austria in 1529 and camped outside the walls of Vienna. They remained there only three weeks, however, before being forced to retreat. Nevertheless the other territories conquered by them temporarily remained under their control.

The New Muslim Empire. In addition to Europe, Suleiman I ruled all of Mesopotamia, Syria, Egypt, and North Africa. This great Muslim state, known as the Ottoman Empire, was as large and powerful as the old Muslim Empire. Instead of crusading against the Muslims, most of the European nations accepted this empire as a world power. They made treaties and trade agreements with them just as with other European countries. The ruler of the Muslim Empire was called a *sultan.*

Life Under the Ottoman Turks. The sultan was a total autocrat with absolute power over the people living under him. Mohammed II was

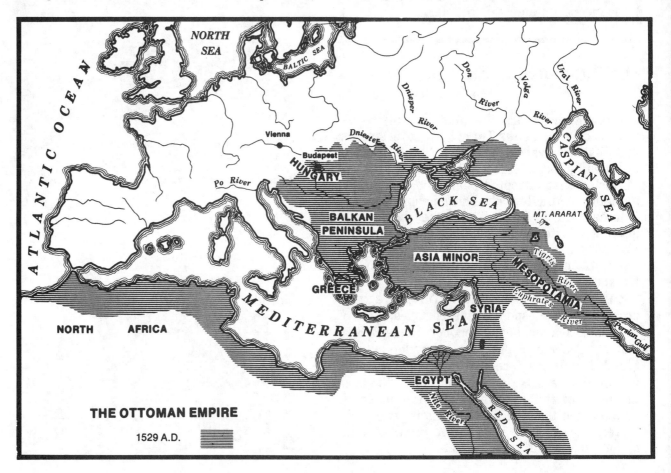

THE OTTOMAN EMPIRE

1529 A.D.

the ruler who conquered Constantinople. Immediately he changed the beautiful Christian Cathedral of St. Sophia into a Muslim mosque.

The conquered lands were divided among the military leaders who used their position to exploit their subjects. The non-Muslim people living in the Ottoman Empire were allowed to live, but they suffered from discrimination in the laws. They were not allowed to own any weapons and were forced to pay unreasonably high taxes.

The Ottoman Empire was different from any other governmental system we have studied in that slaves were used to fill all top government and military positions. The most famous of Ottoman military units were the Janizaries. The sultan's officials made an inspection every five years throughout the Balkan peninsula and selected the strongest and most handsome boys for training in Constantinople. These boys were converted to Islam and either became members of the sultan's guard or joined the Janizaries.

Pictured here is the thriving city of Constantinople, complete with its busy harbor, in the days before it was conquered by the Turks. It was in 1453 that this great eastern stronghold fell to a mighty Turkish army of some 160,000 soldiers.

These Janizaries on parade, display head-dresses representing the different branches of service. The Janizaries was an elite corps for the sultan. It was made up entirely of Greek boys taken captive and converted to Islam.

The European Renaissance

Before we can understand the Renaissance, how it came about, and how it affects our lives today, we must first know about the events in Italy that led to this movement. When the Renaissance first began, Italy was divided into hundreds of independent cities and kingdoms. These areas had become almost entirely free during the years the pope was fighting the Holy Roman Emperor.

The Italian States

The entire history of Italy during the 1300s was one of confusion, lawlessness, wars, and rebellions. For a time the Italian cities were governed along democratic lines. As some families became rich through trade and industry, however, class conflicts began to tear the cities apart. Bands of armed men roamed the streets and nobody was safe.

As a result, these cities gave up their freedom and allowed powerful men to rule in order to maintain peace and order. These new rulers, called *despots,* were entirely different from the other rulers we have studied. They were brilliant men, skilled in science, literature, the arts, and military techniques. Most of them were strong willed, ruthless, cruel, and treacherous. They would stop at nothing in order to enhance their power.

Italy During the Renaissance. By 1454 the larger city-states had absorbed so many of their neighboring states that only three great city-states and three or four minor ones were left in Italy. In addition there were two separate kingdoms, making a total of five major states in Italy. These five states were the duchy of Milan,

the republic of Venice, the republic of Florence, the Papal States, and the kingdom of Naples.

The Duchy of Milan. From her earliest days, Milan had been one of the wealthiest and most powerful cities in the Lombard League. The citizens of Milan, however, lost their freedom by 1311 when Matteo Visconti became their despot. Under the direction of this family, Milan conquered all of Lombardy and was a constant threat to the Papal States and Venice.

The Republic of Venice. Venice, located on the Adriatic Sea, was a great trading center. With the revival of trade following the Crusades, she became one of the richest cities in Europe. Since the 1200s common people had not been

ITALY'S CITY – STATES 1400's

allowed to take part in her government, which had been controlled by an oligarchy of wealthy families. They elected a *doge* (president for life), a Senate, and the powerful Council of Ten which actually controlled the government. As a result of warlike policies, Venice ruled a large amount of territory around the Adriatic Sea and part of Lombardy by 1454.

The Republic of Florence. The Republic of Florence was located on the western coast of Italy. Florence had grown rich as a result of the wool industry. Also it was one of the greatest banking centers in Europe. Throughout the 1300s revolutions and feuds racked the city. Finally in

---

The Renaissance Man

During the Renaissance a new image of the ideal man emerged. During the Middle Ages, a man's most important asset was his ability to fight. Knights were not expected to be educated and many could not even read or write their names.

The Renaissance man looked back to the city-state of Athens for his model. To be well rounded in those days, a man was expected to discuss any subject intelligently and have a variety of talents. Renaissance man was trained in music and studied old Greek plays and philosophers. He learned to write poetry, danced well, was an excellent marksman, and a supurb swordsman. He also practiced art, including both painting and sculpture. If the ruler of a city had no talent himself in the arts, he gathered many artists around his court and encouraged their work, for which he received the glory.

1434 everyone agreed to allow Cosimo de Medici, the head of a great banking family, to become despot in order to put an end to the fighting. From 1469 to 1492, the greatest Medici despot, Lorenzo the Magnificent, ruled. He was typical of the Renaissance man and many great works of art were created under his patronage.

The Papal States. The Roman Church had fallen into a period of decline after the Church headquarters was moved to France. During this period mercenary military leaders established independent kingdoms in the Papal States. During the 1400s the popes began to bring this territory under their control. As long as the popes were sincere religious men, however, this was impossible. But in 1492 the infamous Borgia Pope Alexander VI began to rule. His son Cesare Borgia was a ruthless military leader who was able to conquer most of the Papal States. Julius II, the next pope, completed the job.

The Kingdom of Naples. The kingdom of Naples was in the southern part of Italy. By 1435 the king of Aragon in Spain had managed to gain control of both Naples and Sicily.

As we can see, Italy was hopelessly divided and her people did not even think of themselves as Italians. It was centuries before their differences were settled and Italy became a unified state again.

Secularism

Until the 1400s, religion was the dominating factor in Europe. All life revolved around the Roman Catholic Church. Education was church-oriented. Artists only pictured religious subjects. Literature had pious themes. In the 1400s this changed. The switch to non-religious ideas was known as *secularism*.

Lorenzo de Medici was the so-called "despot of Florence." He was a perfect example of the Renaissance man and encouraged many artists to create masterpieces for the city of Florence.

Effects of Trade on Education. In the early 1400s, an entirely new spirit began to sweep through Europe. Prior to this time, the only reason a person needed to know how to read and write was for the purpose of studying the Bible and writings of religious leaders. For the most part, the only people who went to school were those planning a career in the Catholic Church.

This trend began to change, however, with the revival of trade and the growth of cities. Then men had to learn to read and write so they could fill orders and keep accurate business accounts. The crusaders were quick to see that the Muslims had a higher standard of living and enjoyed more luxuries than those available in Europe. Scholars began traveling to Spain to study the books accumulated by the Muslims and to attend their schools.

Soon it became obvious that Constantinople was going to fall to the Turks. So people began moving from Constantinople to Europe, bringing with them priceless manuscripts from ancient Greece and Rome. Suddenly a new world of learning opened up and people began to question their old values and traditions.

In Italy the great ruling families established schools in their courts so their children could get a better education than in the Church schools. The new court schools still taught religion, but they also taught classical literature, Greek, Latin, Italian grammar, rhetoric, dialetics, arithmetic, geometry, astronomy, music, and physical education. The purpose of these schools was to develop well-rounded citizens.

Humanism. A group of philosophers became very famous during this time, and their ideas had a great influence on European thought and history. These men were called *humanists* because they placed greater emphasis on the study and enjoyment of worldly things than on

spiritual matters. These men devoted their lives to studying the ancient writings, but they were also interested in improving conditions around them.

As leaders in the humanist movement, Petrarch and Boccaccio searched for old manuscripts in libraries, monasteries and royal courts of Europe and Asia. Unfortunately the religious organizations had not considered these documents important enough to preserve, so thousands of them were lost.

Humanism spread from Italy throughout Europe. Scholars of humanism tried to bring about reform in education and the Catholic Church. The most brilliant humanists in England lived within only a few years of one another. One of the most famous and best-loved English humanists was Sir Thomas More, who wrote a book called *Utopia.* His "utopia" was a country that had the perfect government, schools, law courts, and commercial system. By creating this utopia in his book, More was trying to encourage people to live better lives and to build better systems of government. Even today we refer to a situation or place that is too perfect to be real as a utopia. We will study Thomas More again in the next chapter.

Desiderius Erasmus of Rotterdam was a devout pietist-humanist. Entering a monastery at an early age, he soon left to begin a life of wandering. Erasmus lived in France, England, Italy, Germany, and Switzerland. His friends were among the most intellectual of the period. Erasmus was one of the early reformers who believed that the Catholic Church should return to the simple teachings of Jesus. To help people understand these teachings, he went back to the original manuscripts and published a Greek translation of the New Testament. The churchmen who were used to reading their

Thomas More, as drawn by Henry VIII's favorite painter Holbein. More, a famous English humanist, wrote a book called *Utopia* in which he invented a country where a perfect society existed. More was beheaded at the order of Henry VIII when he refused to accept Henry's first divorce.

Latin Vulgate version attacked Erasmus for corrupting the Scriptures.

When Erasmus attacked the Church and its abuses in his writings, he used heavy satire that caused people to laugh although they realized what he was saying was true. His clever style and the fact that he was the friend of so many famous and important people spared Erasmus from the wrath of the Church. His most famous book was entitled *In Praise of Folly.*

Influence of Secularism

As the spirit of secularism swept through Europe, it affected the scholars and showed up in the work of the artists as well. During the Middle Ages, all artwork was religious in nature, since most artists were commissioned by the clergy. Even the art commissioned by secular rulers had religious themes, however, unless it was portrait art.

Italian Renaissance Art. The artists in Renaissance Italy were the first to come under the influence of secularism. They painted scenes from nature. Their paintings were more realistic, using perspective, light, and shading. There was an increased market for the works of good artists. Every city-state and kingdom encouraged artists to live in their capitals and produce great artworks to make the cities more beautiful. Several of the Renaissance popes encouraged artists to produce great works of art that are today considered to be some of the richest treasures in the Vatican.

Leonardo da Vinci. Leonardo da Vinci, considered by many to be the most perfect example of Renaissance man, was born in 1452. Not only was he a great artist, but many historians also consider him to be a great genius of the

Renaissance period. His paintings of *The Mona Lisa* and the *Last Supper* are known and admired throughout the world. He was also an excellent sculptor, mathematician, writer, engineer, and biologist. In the area of science, he designed a model for an airplane centuries

The best-known humanist and perhaps the greatest scholar in Europe was Erasmus. Although his papers attacked the Catholic Church, Erasmus' writing style was so clever that he remained friends with the top leaders of the Church.

This drawing shows the wing sketch for Leonardo da Vinci's flying machine. As you can see, his notations were in a reverse writing so people could not copy his ideas.

Why did Michelangelo include horns on this sculpture of Moses? The Latin Vulgate mistranslated a verse in Scripture that said "Moses' Face Shown." The Vulgate said, "Moses had horns."

St. Peter's Basilica in St. Peter's Square in Rome. This close-up view of the building depicts Renaissance architecture at its best. The statues that line the top were sculpted by Michelangelo.

before flight was anything more than a dream. By the time he died in 1519, he had left his influence on the world for all time.

Michelangelo. Another Italian artist named Michelangelo lived from 1475 to 1564. He is considered to be the greatest painter and sculptor of all time. Although his paintings are well known, he was more interested in sculpture than painting. He paid careful attention to anatomy and, as a result, his figures are very lifelike. The *Pieta, David,* and *Moses* are three of his best known sculptures.

While Michelangelo would have preferred doing sculpture, Pope Julius II forced him to paint the ceiling of the Sistine Chapel in Rome. For four years Michelangelo had to lie on his back on scaffolding while he painted frescoes of scenes from the Old Testament. Art critics agree that these paintings have never been equaled.

Michelangelo was also a great architect. He designed the famous Church of St. Peter in Rome, the largest church ever built. Since the Renaissance was a rebirth of Greek and Roman influence, St. Peter's church is a blend of both. There are rows of columns, arcades, and rounded arches. It also contains many beautiful mosaics showing the Byzantine influence.

Other Italian Artists. Two other famous Italian Renaissance artists were Raphael, who lived from 1483 to 1520, and Titian, who lived from 1490 to 1576. Raphael was hired by Pope Julius II to paint for the Vatican. Titian worked for the Spanish court and the Holy Roman Emperor. He primarily painted portraits of famous people of his day.

European Renaissance Art. As the Renaissance spread northward into Europe, the art forms changed according to circumstances. In France, where the churches were built in the Gothic style of architecture, there were no large

wall spaces for fresco painting. In France art was used to illustrate books and most French artwork was in the form of miniature paintings. Nobles in the French court began collecting these beautiful books and artwork just like jewelry and gold plates.

It was in the Netherlands that oil painting first became a perfected art. Although the use of oil paints was not completely new, Jan van Eyck, who lived from 1390 to 1441, was the first painter to use them to their fullest potential. Besides the artwork done for the duke of Burgundy's court, there was a rich merchant class in the Netherlands. The people wanted country scenes and portraits painted for their homes and were willing to pay good prices for them. This ready market encouraged many artists to work in the Netherlands.

A German artist named Hans Holbein moved to England where he was the official portrait painter for Henry VIII's court. Although there was nothing unusual about his style, his paintings depicted some of the most interesting people of this historical period.

Renaissance Culture in Europe

Not only did the Renaissance affect art, it also influenced every area of creative life in Europe. As a result of the new ideas which emerged during the Renaissance, Europe was ready to enter the modern era.

Renaissance Music. In addition to the changes occurring in art and education during the Renaissance, major changes in music and literature were also taking place. Up to this point, music had developed as part of Church worship in the form of chants and ballad singers who traveled from castle to castle. During the

Anne of Cleves

Hans Holbein was Henry VIII's favorite and most trusted artist. When negotiations were under way for Henry to marry his fourth wife, Anne of Cleves, he sent Hans to Germany to paint the lady.

Although Anne was large and not very pretty, Hans saw something in her quiet spirit that touched his heart. He captured her "soul" in the painting rather than a photographic likeness. When Henry saw Holbein's picture, he was anxious to marry the lovely lady and the wedding plans were made.

Anne arrived in England and Henry, an eager and excited bridegroom, rushed to her side. Only minutes after meeting her, he left in sullen anger, calling her a "Flemish mare." He divorced her within six months. Thus Hans Holbein was out of favor at the English court for a while because Henry felt the artist had tricked him.

Renaissance period, a well-educated person was expected to play at least one musical instrument. Harmony and counterpoint were developed and modern choral arrangements were beginning to become popular.

Italian Literature. Perhaps the greatest breakthrough in the field of literature was the use of native languages. Before the Renaissance, books were written in Latin and sometimes in Greek. Unless a person received a classical education, he could not read them. Perhaps the earliest Renaissance writer was Dante Alighieri.

Dante, in his most famous book, *The Divine Comedy,* writes in an allegorical style about a guided tour through hell and later heaven. Virgil, the famous Roman poet, is Dante's guide through hell. During the tour Dante is surprised to find many top Renaissance religious leaders and all of his enemies in hell. As you might imagine, the book did not win him many friends. But today the book is still regarded as one of the greatest allegories ever written.

Another Italian writer was Petrarch who lived from 1304 to 1374. Instead of using the stiff, artificial style used by other writers of his day, Petrarch wrote just as he talked. Thus he has

Because of his writing style, Petrarch has been called the first "modern" writer. He is also known as the "Father of Humanism."

RENAISSANCE ART

Leonardo da Vinci/*Mona Lisa*, 1503

Rembrandt/*The Syndics*, 1661

The pictures shown on these two pages represent masterpieces of Renaissance sculpture and painting with all of their rich and realistic detail. The selections are representative of art of different countries and time periods within the European Renaissance, that reached its height in the sixteenth century. Each caption lists the artist, the name of the work, and the date it was completed.

Titian/*Bacchus and Ariadne*, 1520

Leonardo da Vinci/*The Last Supper*, 1497

Hans Holbein the Younger/*Henry VIII*, 1540

Raphael/Detail from *The School of Athens*, 1511

Jan Van Eyck/*Madonna With Chancellor Robin*, 1436

Peter Paul Rubens/*Crucifixion Altar*, 1613

been called the first "modern" writer since he introduced this new style of writing. He is considered the "Father of Humanism" because he was one of the first writers during the Christian era to say that people had a right to enjoy themselves in this life. He also championed Roman and Greek civilizations, saying their ideas were worth studying although their civilizations were pagan.

English Literature. The English were quick to see the advantage of writing in their own language. The most famous of these writers to use English was Geoffrey Chaucer who wrote *The Canterbury Tales*. His stories paint such a vivid description of English life during the last half of the 1300s that historians still find his works exciting today.

The Canterbury Tales is the story of people who set out on a pilgrimage to the tomb of Saint Thomas à Becket in Canterbury. The group is comprised of men and women from every occupation and station in life. Each of these people tells a story to make the journey less boring. From these stories we learn all about the individuals and about English life in general.

Geoffrey Chaucer was one of the most famous writers of the Middle Ages. His most famous work, *Canterbury Tales*, was a description of English life during the last half of the 1300s.

Renaissance Science. Copernicus, a Polish scientist, compiled a series of scientific papers in a book called *The Revolution of the Heavenly Spheres*. Copernicus could rightfully be called the "Founder of Astronomy." His theory that the earth and planets moved around the sun was such a revolutionary idea for that period (1543) that it was not accepted. Church leaders feared that such an idea would cause people to lose their faith in God.

Importance of the Renaissance

The Renaissance brought about many changes in the way Europeans regarded life. They were beginning to question things they did not understand. With more spare time for learning, better education, and the invention of the printing press, a new world was opening up for them. The stage was being set for two great events—the questioning of the Roman Catholic Church that resulted in the Reformation, and the discovery and exploration of the New World.

The Polish scientist Copernicus was the first to discover that the earth and planets move around the sun. Before this, everyone believed the planets moved around the earth.

THE **REFORMATION** AND A **NEW WORLD**

Projects

1. Give a report on the council of Constance. Describe in detail what happened. What were the results of these actions and why is it important?

2. Do a study on printing, from the earliest methods, including movable type and what is used today. What is the principle behind Xerox machines and other modern copy machines?

3. Research the lives of Martin Luther, Zwingli, John Calvin, John Knox, Marguerite of Navarre, Teresa of Avila, Francis Xavier, or Ignatius Loyola.

4. Today many priests and nuns are marrying. What do you think has caused this trend? Can these people remain Catholics? What is the position of the Roman Catholic Church on this subject?

5. What is meant by the Fundamentalist movement? Do a study on the World Council of Churches. Who started it? Why? Why are Fundamental churches against the Council of Churches?

6. How did the astrolabe and other early navigational equipment work? Compare with instruments now available for navigation.

7. What is the status of relations between the Roman Catholic Church and the Eastern Orthodox Church today? If the relationship has changed, when did the change come about?

8. Make a report on the life of one of the following: Columbus, John Cabot, Ferdinand Magellan, Jacques Cartier, Vasco de Balboa, Ponce de Leon, Francisco de Coronado, Hernando de Soto, Dona Marina, Hernando Cortez, Francisco Pizarro, Samuel de Champlain.

Words and Concepts

conquistadores
astrolabe
dispensations
justification by faith
The Great Schism
Northwest Passage
pluralism
Huguenots
simony
recant
Babylonian Captivity
Line of Demarcation
nepotism
predestination
The Sanction of Bourges
transubstantiation
caravel
penance
Institutes of the Christian Religion
Council of Constance
Lollards

The Reformation and a New World

Europe faced a period of great change, activity, and questioning during the period from 1300 to 1600 A.D. As we saw in the preceding chapter, there was a growth in nationalism. People were proud to belong to their countries. At the same time, the rebirth of knowledge known as the Renaissance affected art, architecture, music, philosophy, literature, science, and learning generally. It was a period of curiosity that also carried over to the areas of religion and exploration.

People no longer were satisfied with blind acceptance of ideas the pope and the Roman Catholic Church told them were right. The development of the printing press in Europe made the Bible and other books available to everyone. People began to seek their own answers to questions that bothered them. As they studied the Bible, they questioned the practices in the Roman Church which they believed were contrary to Biblical teachings. They also resented the materialistic attitudes of the Church, including the rich clothes and jewels worn by the high churchmen. People began to look back to the examples of Jesus and His disciples and they wanted to return to those ideals.

Unrest, excitement, and search for adventure also brought on the desire for exploration. While some men broke away from the Roman Church, other brave adventurers sailed away in little boats into the unknown. They discovered the New World and soon other pilgrims packed their belongings and sailed to find new homes in this wild and unexplored country.

High church officials such as this one from the 14th century were resented for the rich clothes and jewels that they wore. Many leaders of the Roman Catholic Church at this time were insincere and immoral. Eventually weak leadership caused the Roman Church to lose much of its authority.

The Eve of the Reformation

During the early years of the Middle Ages, the Roman Catholic Church challenged the Holy Roman Emperor and won. By 1294 the Church was interfering with politics, business, and the personal lives of everyone in Europe. As the Roman Church became more powerful, it also became more corrupt. Soon the problems and weaknesses of the Church caused people to question its actions and demand reforms.

Abuses in the Papacy

In the fourteenth century, the Roman Catholic Church seemed as powerful as ever on the surface. Corrupting forces from the inside, however, like cancer, were eating away at the strength of the Church. The papacy had become weak and corrupt. Many times high Church officials really were not Christians. They did not believe in Jesus or the other teachings of the Church.

People of most countries in Europe became nominally Christian along with their leaders. Common people often did not understand what it meant to be a Christian. They applied Christianity to their heathen religions, along with the practice of magic. Many of the local priests were not able to read and, therefore, were unable to teach their people from the Bible. Lack of morality was common in the Church from the highest official to the lowliest priest.

Weakness of the Papacy. For hundreds of years, members of the European nobility chose careers in the Roman Church for their younger sons. They were not concerned that their children did not understand what a Church official was supposed to do. As a result, many high churchmen had no interest in caring for the people they were supposed to serve. Since even the pope came from this unqualified background, scandals over the behavior of churchmen of all levels were common.

The strong rulers of Europe were often jealous of Church power. They resented the pope's interference in the affairs of their kingdoms. As the European rulers gained power, the idea of the "Divine Right of Kings" became widely accepted. This was the idea that kings were chosen by God to rule, as we have seen in previous chapters.

Pope Boniface VIII died when the French King Philip IV tried to have him kidnapped. The pope who succeeded was a French archbishop named Clement V. He took his orders from Philip IV and moved the papal headquarters from Rome to Avignon.

Babylonian Captivity of the Church. The city of Avignon was located just across the Rhone River from France. The papacy remained in Avignon for almost seventy years, from 1309 to 1376. This period has therefore been referred to by Church historians as the Babylonian Captivity of the Church. European rulers believed the Roman Church was a prisoner of France just as Israel had been enslaved by Babylon.

France and England were fighting the Hundred Years' War at this time. Many English Christians questioned the idea of supporting the Roman Church when she was controlled by their enemy. Pope Gregory XI realized that the rest of Europe was slipping away from the Roman Church since she was controlled by France, so he moved the headquarters back to Rome.

The Papal Schisms. When Pope Gregory XI died, the Church leaders who wanted to stay in Rome selected Urban VI as pope. Those

churchmen who wanted to return to Avignon elected a Frenchman named Clement VII as pope. This split in Church leadership also caused a conflict among the rulers of Europe. Urban VI was supported by France's enemies. France and her allies supported Clement VII.

This double papacy, called the *Great Schism,* lasted 40 years. When Clement VII and Urban VI died, new popes were appointed to take their places and the schism continued. In 1409 a Church council ordered both men to resign and a new pope was appointed. Neither of the other men accepted this ruling, so then there were three popes. It is little wonder that sincere

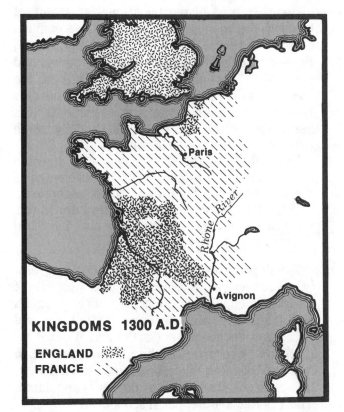

KINGDOMS 1300 A.D.

ENGLAND

FRANCE

Popes during the Renaissance were patrons of the arts and instituted many changes in churches and palaces. Some of these changes meant that religious buildings took on a secular look. In 1506 Pope Julius authorized St. Peter's basilica be replaced with one reflecting strong Renaissance style.

Christians were confused. Meanwhile, political leaders supported the pope who offered them the most advantages.

The Council of Constance. The Holy Roman Emperor at this time was Sigismund. He realized that the Roman Church was not going to be able to clear up the problem of the schism without outside help. He remembered how the Roman Emperor Constantine had called a council to settle the problem of the Arian Heresy. Following that example, Sigismund called important Church leaders to a council meeting in the city of Constance.

The Council of Constance assembled in 1414. It was the largest Christian council meeting in history. Instead of the traditional assembly of bishops, the council was organized as a convention of nations, including Germany, Italy, France, England, and Spain. Each nation had one vote. This nationalistic structure of the council was highly significant. It meant the new tendency toward nationalistic alignments was being recognized for the first time by some members of the Church hierarchy.

In April of 1415, all three popes were directed by the council to resign. Martin V was elected as the new pope and the Papal Schism came to an end in 1417. As we shall see a little later in this chapter, the Council of Constance also discussed the matter of heresy.

The Pope Loses Power. The papacy was greatly weakened as a result of the Council of Constance appointing the pope. Church councils met regularly and declared that they had authority over the pope. The Council of Basel actually took over many of the pope's duties. When Martin V ordered this council to dissolve in 1439, he was deposed and another pope was appointed. This created another papal schism.

While the pope was weakened in his struggles with the council, the king of France declared the French Church to be independent of the pope's authority. All French Church offices were to be filled with men recommended by the French king. This law was called *The Sanction of Bourges.* The Holy Roman Emperor was preparing to pass a similar law for the German Church.

The Papacy Restored. At a time when the pope's power seemed weakest, the papacy regained some of its power and prestige by an unexpected event. The weakened Byzantine Empire lost most of its territory to the Ottoman Turks. Without outside help, Constantinople was certain to be captured.

In 1439 the Byzantine emperor and the metropolitan, the head of the Greek Orthodox Church, traveled to Rome to seek help. There they both knelt before Martin V, recognizing him as the head of the united Christian Church. This recognition restored the pope's prestige and ended the second papal schism. Although this event restored the pope's authority, the union between the Greek and Roman Churches did not last. The people of Constantinople rejected the union.

Future popes were strong, ruthless, cynical, and worldly. They were vital rulers, but not true Christian leaders. Under their leadership the papacy grew ever more powerful. There was no longer any doubt that the pope was the head of the Roman Catholic Church.

Abuses in the Roman Church

While the papacy was having problems maintaining its authority, serious abuses in the Church business commonly occurred. While we are studying about this corruption, you should realize that the Roman Church was no worse than any other institutions at that time. Many abuses, such as taking bribes, selling offices, and farming out the collection of fees, were also common in government. The Church, however, should have been setting an example in honest dealings and morality. Instead Church leaders were as corrupt as the secular rulers.

Monetary Abuses. There were many corrupt ways that the Roman Church raised money. We will study only a few of them. Vacant Church positions often were sold to the highest bidder, a practice called *simony*. Church positions became so expensive that poor people had no opportunity to hold high office. Even the papacy was subject to simony from time to time.

A *dispensation* was a written permission from the pope allowing a person to do something forbidden by both the Bible and the Church law. For example, many kings and nobles got dispensations to marry a first cousin or a niece. Large donations of money accompanied dispensation requests.

Many times the Church collected money for Crusades that never took place. The money was sent to Rome and used to commission artists and for other things unrelated to Church business.

A Forgotten Purpose

The people's attitude about the Church's hunger for money might be summed up in the following comment by England's King Edward III: "The pope is commissioned to lead the Lord's sheep to pasture, not to fleece them."

The selling of *indulgences* was another practice which made people angry. The Roman Church taught that when people sinned, they needed to repent and confess their sins to a priest. They were not completely forgiven until they performed a *penance*.

A penance was an act, such as repeating prayers or doing a good deed, that was assigned to a sinner by the priest. The pope claimed he had the power to cancel a person's penance by selling him an indulgence. An indulgence did not cancel the guilt of sin, it merely canceled the penance given after sins were confessed and forgiven.

The Church began selling indulgences to raise money for her many projects. Men bid for the privilege of selling indulgences and took big commissions on the sales. Many people did not understand the nature of indulgences. They thought the Church was selling permission to sin. Many people, including members of the clergy, were strongly opposed to the entire idea of indulgences. They wanted to see this practice stopped.

Other Abuses of the Church. The Roman Church was involved in other corrupt practices besides monetary abuses. *Nepotism,* the practice of giving jobs and promotions to relatives instead of to those best qualified, was common. *Pluralism,* the practice of holding more than one office at a time also was commonplace. Although they received salaries for these positions, they rarely visited their churches or attempted to handle the responsibilities of their positions. There was much bribery and corruption in the Church courts.

Many clergymen defied their vows and lived with women even though they were not officially married. Greek Orthodox clergymen were allowed to have wives, but the Roman Catholic clergymen were not allowed to marry. There were other churchmen who were simply immoral. Their actions gave all churchmen a bad reputation.

In medieval times people believed that relics that had some relationship to saints or Jesus could bring good fortune or even work miracles. Relics were supposed to be holy and were kept in all the major churches for people on pilgrimages to see. Even bones of saints were sold or traded between churches.

But many of the so-called "holy" relics were phony. It was said that there were enough pieces of the "one true cross" to build five or six crosses. Although many were fooled by the fake relics, the highly educated people used this as a basis for attack on the Church and as an excuse to demand reform.

Early Protesters

All over Europe people were demanding reforms in the Roman Catholic Church. It was dangerous, however, to criticize the Roman Church. Many who did were accused of heresy and executed. People criticized the Church abuses, and soon were teaching ideas that were different from those taught by the Church. They believed their ideas were closer to those in the Bible.

England, Wycliffe, and the Lollards. During the Babylonian Captivity, while the pope was under the control of the French king, France and England were at war with each other. John Wycliffe, a teacher at the English college of Oxford, wrote against papal authority. He believed that since the pope was controlled by England's enemies, Englishmen did not have to be governed by papal authority.

At this time in history only a few people owned Bibles because they had to be copied by hand. Although Bibles were very rare, Wycliffe owned one. After studying it carefully, he attacked Roman Church customs which he thought were contrary to the Bible. To help his countrymen understand the Bible, he translated it into English.

Wycliffe believed the clergy had become too wealthy. He also thought the clergy should not have political control over lands they controlled. He thought churchmen should try to live the way the first disciples had lived. He attacked churchmen who led scandalous lives. He did not feel they should be able to minister to others when they were sinful themselves.

Wycliffe's followers were known as Lollards. Lollard preachers wandered across the English countryside holding meetings. As long as the pope remained at Avignon, the Lollards were free to teach throughout England. In 1376 when the pope returned to Rome, everything changed. The Lollards were persecuted as heretics and many fled from England. Some went to Europe and others moved to Scotland. As a result, their teachings continued to spread.

Although the Lollards were no longer free to teach openly in England, they continued to hold secret meetings. Many people in England agreed with Wycliffe's teachings. Wycliffe died at home in 1384, but many of his followers were burned at the stake as heretics.

Bohemia and the Hussites. Wycliffe's teachings spread to Bohemia (present-day Czechoslovakia) when the king's sister married Richard II of England. Bohemian students went to England where they studied under Wycliffe. When they returned to their country, they took the teachings of Wycliffe with them. Clergymen in Bohemia were some of the most corrupt churchmen in Europe. A great reformer, John Huss, was appointed to clean up the corruption. He began using Wycliffe's teaching against Church corruption.

As Huss continued this work, the issues changed from moral issues to questions of theology. By 1401 he was questioning the Roman Church's belief in *transubstantiation*. This is the belief that the bread and wine in Communion becomes the actual body and blood of Jesus when taken by a believer. Huss believed that Communion was to be a memorial service until Jesus returned.

Another of Huss' arguments was that Jesus, not the pope, was the head of the Christian Church. He taught people to use the Bible as a guide for their lives instead of trusting what priests or popes told them.

Although Huss gained many followers, he was excommunicated for his attack on Roman Church practices. This did not stop him, however, and he continued to preach. When the Council of Constance met to settle the Great Schism, Huss was asked to come and explain his beliefs. The Holy Roman Emperor gave him safe conduct to the meeting. When Huss appeared before the council, he refused to withdraw from his beliefs by saying his teachings were not true. In spite of the safe conduct agreement, the council had him arrested and burned at the stake in July of 1415.

Huss' followers in Bohemia were called Hussites. They separated from the Roman Catholic Church and revolted. Heretics from other countries flocked to Bohemia to escape persecution. Pope Martin V called together a Crusade against the king of Bohemia. As outside armies attacked Bohemia, the Hussites persecuted the Roman Catholics in Bohemia. Monasteries were burned and plundered and monks were murdered. The Bohemian army won some victories and for many years held off its enemies.

Other Protesters of the Church. While the Lollards and Hussites were the major protesters, people all over Europe were demanding Church reform. In France, Pierre Dubois wanted lawyers to replace churchmen in government posts. He also believed that national laws should be more important than those of the Church.

Many Franciscan friars faced the Inquisition's torture in 1323. This happened because they had taught openly that the Roman Church should not own private property. We have already seen how secularism and humanist writers were calling for reform in the Church.

The first group to separate from the Roman Church was the Moravian Brethren. They were located in Bohemia. By the 1500s they had more than 100,000 members. Today communities of this denomination exist throughout Europe, Africa, and America.

One of the major events leading to the spread of reformed ideas was the development of the printing press in 1453. It was first developed in Mainz, Germany, by a man named Gutenberg. William Caxton introduced it to England in 1476. Although the Chinese had a printing press many years before, books in Europe were copied by hand and were very rare at that time.

Few people could have read a Bible even if they could have afforded one since it was written in Latin. The printing press made it possible for scholars across Europe to translate the Bible into their native languages for the first time. The Roman Church made every effort to

Reformer John Huss is burned at the stake after being excommunicated from the Roman Catholic Church for attacking its practices. His death led to a revolt between the Church and the Hussites caused quite an uproar in Bohemia.

The Czech Bible was one of the first to be printed in the language of the common people. Bibles prior to this were written in Latin so that very few people were able to read them.

This etching of Martin Luther is by the artist Cranach. His portrait shows the determination of the man who initiated the Protestant Reformation.

keep Bibles from the common people. They did not want the Holy Scriptures to be the subject of debates in bars and taverns.

The Reformation

During this time of general protest, some of the most scandalous popes in Roman Church history came to power. Nothing was done to stop the abuses. Pope Martin V said the Church could live with corruption, but could not survive without money. Heretics were burned at the stake, and the Inquisition was in progress throughout Europe. Brave men continued to speak up for their beliefs, even though it was dangerous to do so.

Europe was on the brink of change, but it needed a leader. When that leader appeared, the dam broke and a flood of new ideas spread across Europe. At first protesters only wanted to reform the Roman Church, so their movement is called the Protestant Reformation.

The Reformation in Germany

Many European rulers opposed too much control over their churches by authorities in Rome. They were Roman Catholics, however, and did not believe anyone should rebel against Church authority. For this reason national governments cooperated with the Roman Church in punishing protesters.

It was natural, then, for the Protestant Reformation to start in Germany. Germany was divided into many territories known as duchies. Although the Holy Roman Emperor was the ruler of all these states, he had little actual authority. In Germany a protester could be protected by his local ruler in defiance of the emperor's orders. Also, if a protester was persecuted by one duke, he could find protection in a neighboring duchy.

Martin Luther's Ninety-Five Point Thesis. A prominent leader in the Protestant break from the Roman Church was Martin Luther. His father was a German copper smelter, who became wealthy by renting equipment to the mines. Martin Luther was studying to be a lawyer at the University of Erfut. He then changed his mind and became a monk.

Luther taught in the small German town of Wittenburg. This was in the territory of an independent ruler known as the Elector of Saxony. Trouble started when a Dominican friar named Tetzel began selling indulgences. When Luther found out about it, he was angry. Indulgences were contrary to his belief in justification by faith. He believed if people were saved and forgiven for their sins by the blood of Jesus, they did not need indulgences.

Luther wrote a thesis of 95 points attacking indulgences and major Church abuses. He then posted them on the Church door in Wittenburg, a practice used by scholars announcing their willingness to debate issues. The day he posted the thesis—October 31, 1517—is sometimes called the birthday of the Protestant Reformation. Martin Luther must have been surprised at the attention his work received. Soon copies of his thesis were translated into foreign languages and spread throughout Europe.

Lutheranism. At first Luther did not want to separate himself from the Roman Church. He only wanted to see Church corruption cleaned up. Like Wycliffe and Huss, however, he became more radical in his writing and debating as time passed. When he began to challenge basic Roman Church doctrine, the pope excommunicated him. Then Luther developed the basic ideas for the Lutheran denomination. He also translated the Bible into German and wrote many books.

Not all of Germany accepted Protestantism. Each duchy made the choice between joining Luther or remaining in the Roman Catholic Church. In those duchies that became Lutheran, monks were allowed to leave the monasteries to marry. Although Luther disagreed with Rome on many points, he included others with which he did agree in the Lutheran doctrine.

Lutheranism was closely associated with German nationalism so its greatest impact at first was in Germany. But it soon dominated the faith of the Scandinavians and became the spark that set Europe aflame spiritually.

The Reformation Spreads

Luther was still alive and working when other Reformation leaders established separate denominations. Within a period of 100 years, Europe changed from one unified Church to many different denominations. While religious beliefs played a major part in the Reformation, politics also played an important role. Nationalism also played a part as countries turned Protestant while fighting to be free from Roman Catholic countries.

Each country remained Roman Catholic or became Protestant, according to the wishes of its ruler. In countries where the rulers and nobility remained Catholic, the Protestants were persecuted. In Protestant countries, the Catholics were discriminated against. Until religious toleration was practiced, people tried to force their own ideas upon everyone else.

Major Points of Difference. During the Reformation it was thought to be important for everyone to think exactly alike on religious matters. There were major areas where the Protestants disagreed with each other and with the Roman Church. How a person thought on these areas of disagreement determined his denomination. We will now look at some of the more important areas of difference.

One point of difference was baptism. The Roman Catholics believed everyone had to be baptized in order to be saved, including infants. Many Protestant churches also practiced infant baptism. Some, like Calvin, believed baptism only meant membership in the Church of Geneva. The Anabaptists believed baptism was a symbol of burying one's sinful life to be born again into a new Christian life. For this reason they did not accept infant baptism.

Another area of difference was Communion. Many denominations, including the Lutherans, Roman Catholics, Anglicans, and Episcopalians, believed in transubstantiation or *consubstantiation,* a Lutheran concept in which the body and blood of Christ co-exist with the bread and wine during Communion. Others believed it was merely a memorial service. The Roman Church allowed only the clergy to take the wine. Most Protestant denominations allowed everyone to take both bread and wine.

Some denominations believed that Church and state governments should be merged. They believed everyone in the country should be a member of the state Church. Those who did not agree were persecuted. Other denominations, primarily the Anabaptists, believed Church and state should be separate and unrelated. They believed people should be free to decide for themselves whether or not they wanted to join the Church.

Title pages of two of the most famous Luther publications, printed in German and showing the popular woodcut designs of that period, are pictured here. In addition to translating the Bible into German, Luther wrote many books which formed the basis of the Lutheran denomination.

Huldreich Zwingli was the founder of the Protestant Reformation in Switzerland. Many Swiss people were not ready for such reform. A civil war broke out and Zwingli was killed in the fighting.

John Calvin, a lawyer-turned-preacher, insisted on strict obedience to the letter of the law in his Church at Geneva. This picture captures the stern and unyielding temperament of the man who played a key role in the Protestant Reformation.

The Swiss Reformation. The Swiss Confederation was made up of 13 *cantons,* or political districts. Technically they were part of the Holy Roman Empire, but the emperor had little control over them.

After Luther broke away from the Church of Rome, Huldreich Zwingli began the Swiss Protestant movement in the city of Zurich. He became both spiritual and secular leader there. The southern cantons wanted to remain Roman Catholic and the northern cantons wanted to become Protestant. As a result, civil war broke out in 1531. Zwingli and many of his followers were killed in the fighting. The cantons remained united, although each continued to worship according to individual preference.

John Calvin. The most famous Protestant leader after Martin Luther was John Calvin. A Frenchman, Calvin became a Protestant in 1533. When the French king began persecuting Protestants, Calvin fled to the Swiss city of Basel. There in 1536 he published the most in-

Switzerland—Neutral Territory

In the years immediately after the Reformation, Europe plunged into religious wars. The Catholics and Protestants each were trying to force their beliefs on each other. Having already settled their religious problems, the Swiss remained neutral during these wars. This was the beginning of the Swiss policy of neutrality.

Switzerland has stayed out of all European wars ever since. Today this country is regarded as a neutral ground for meetings, councils, and settlement of international differences.

Justification by Faith

Martin Luther confessed daily, trying to earn salvation. Once while studying the Bible, he saw the passage in the Book of Romans that said: "The just shall live by faith." Suddenly he realized his good deeds, fasting, and confession would not earn him salvation. He believed man could never be good enough to earn salvation. Salvation was a gift from God.

fluential book of the Protestant Reformation, called *Institutes of the Christian Religion.*

Calvin believed that man's chief aim was to glorify God. He also supported the Bible Scriptures concerning the teaching of Justification by Faith.

Calvin's teachings were based on the idea of the absolute sovereignty of God. From this idea of God's sovereignty comes the concept of *predestination.* This belief is the idea that before the beginning of the world, God decided which people He would save. This concept is controversial, and many Christians rejected it because they felt it contradicted the doctrine of human choice and responsibility. Because this concept is difficult to understand, many Christians have rejected it. It is interesting to note, however, that Calvin was the first Protestant leader to send missionaries to foreign countries.

Calvin had the chance to put his beliefs into practice when he was asked to head the church in Geneva. The city was a republic and the governing council wanted to run the city based on Biblical principles. Calvin believed it was the duty of any state to encourage and protect the Church, but that Church and state should be separate. He was at first troubled, and later angered, when the council tried to make Geneva a Calvinist Church state.

Laws were passed punishing people for breaking Church laws. The state imposed severe punishments for wearing bright colors, missing church services, playing cards, and dancing. For more serious crimes of heresy, adultery, cursing, or witchcraft, people were executed or banished.

Calvin was unable to persuade the council to separate Church and state. Unfortunately, today his teachings are blamed for the harsh regulations imposed by the Geneva council.

Calvin's beliefs, known as Calvinism, spread to France, Germany, the Netherlands, and Scotland. They influenced many denominations and later became the basic beliefs of the Presbyterian, Reformed, and other churches.

The Reformation Arrives in England. There were many Lollards in England who hoped the country would become Protestant; but it seemed as if the Reformation would never reach England. King Henry VIII of England was a strict Roman Catholic. The pope, in fact, referred to Henry as "Defender of the Faith" because he wrote a paper attacking Luther. Soon after that, however, a dispute arose between Henry and the pope that changed the course of English religious history completely.

Pope's Authority Challenged. More than anything else, Henry VIII wanted a son and heir to carry on the Tudor line. After 20 years of marriage, however, he and his wife, Catherine of Aragon, had only one daughter, named Mary. At the same time, Henry had fallen in love with the beautiful Anne Boleyn. He asked to pope to annul his marriage to Catherine so he could marry Anne. The pope refused because Catherine's nephew Charles V had just conquered Rome and the pope was his prisoner.

Angered by the pope's refusal to grant the annulment, Henry appointed an archbishop of Canterbury. Henry had him annul the marriage to Catherine so that he could legally marry Anne. Henry was married a total of six times, and he had the son he wanted so badly by his third wife, Jane Seymour.

Henry VIII and the Church of England. At Henry's request, Parliament passed laws denying the pope's authority over the English Church. Parliament then set up Henry as the supreme head of the new Church of England. Henry closed the Catholic monasteries and gave their lands to his favorite nobles. In turn the nobles opposed the return of Catholicism, so that Henry would not take back their lands. The pope excommunicated Henry, but the king's open defiance of the pope succeeded because he had the support of the English people. English rulers had previously tried to limit the pope's power and failed.

Undoubtedly the rise of Renaissance nationalism in England in the sixteenth century was responsible for Henry's success in starting a new Church. Englishmen now took pride in their independence. They resented the continuing interference of the Italian pope in English affairs.

Henry had been careful to get Parliament's support before acting. That way nobody could say he had forced the Church of England on his people. Although Henry VIII broke away physically from the Roman Church, he did manage to retain some of her basic philosophy.

England's Catholic-Protestant Conflict. When Henry died, his young son Edward VI became king. During his reign the Church of England became even more strongly Protestant because of the influence of his Lutheran advisors. Edward died after ruling for only six years and

Henry VIII, the pompous king of England, is best remembered for the many women he married, hoping to father a son. During the Reformation Henry was intolerant of both Protestants and Catholics, except those who furthered his own ends.

John Knox, a student of Calvin, was a leader of the Scottish reform movement. Here he is pictured with fierce intensity as he scolds his congregation.

his older sister Mary took the throne. Mary was still loyal to her mother, Catherine of Aragon, and the Roman Catholic Church. She did all she could, therefore, to revive Catholicism in England. So many Protestants were executed under her reign that she soon became known as "Bloody Mary." Her efforts failed in the end, however, because she made the mistake of marrying Spain's Prince Philip. This move made her most unpopular with the English since Spain was England's worst enemy at the time.

When Mary died, the only living heir to the throne, Elizabeth I, was crowned. The people wondered which side she would take in the Church dispute. She wisely took a middle-of-the-road stand and practiced mild religious toleration. She did not care about the beliefs of her subjects as long as they belonged to the Church of England. She controlled the Church. During her long reign, nobody was executed for religious reasons and the Church of England, also called the Anglican Church, became the official state religion. The Episcopalian denomination, as we know it in the United States today, is an off-shoot of the Anglican faith.

Reformation in Scotland. The Scottish Reformation was tied closely to politics, nationalism, and the efforts of John Knox. When Scotland's King James V was killed in battle, his French wife became the ruling regent of Scotland. She sent their young daughter Mary to France, where she later married the future French king, Francis II, who was a Roman Catholic. Mary became a Roman Catholic also and was known as Mary Queen of Scots. When this happened, the Scottish nobles were afraid Scotland would become a French province.

In 1559, however, John Knox, a zealous reformer and student of Calvin in Geneva, returned to his Scottish homeland. He began preaching and soon founded a group called the Lords of the Congregation. This was a group of Protestant nobles who wanted to overthrow the Roman Catholic Church in Scotland.

Knox drew up the Articles of the Presbyterian Church in 1560. This document abolished the pope's authority and condemned the creeds of the Catholic Church. Knox then enlisted the aid of English troops and started a religious revolution.

Mary Queen of Scots. A year later, Mary Queen of Scots returned to Scotland from France after the death of her husband. She then married a Catholic and attended Catholic worship services. Knox spoke out boldly from the pulpit against the queen's authority and challenged her religious beliefs in public debates. Mary then arranged for the death of her husband, an act which caused civil war. In the struggle that followed, Mary fled to England under pressure.

Queen Elizabeth I, Mary's cousin, considered Mary a threat to the English throne and had her imprisoned. Elizabeth believed Mary was responsible for assassination plots against her. Mary remained in prison for 19 years until Elizabeth executed her in 1587. By this time Calvinistic Presbyterianism had completely taken over in Scotland. This denomination since has spread throughout the world due to the efforts of Scottish missionaries. Upon Elizabeth's death, Mary's son became King James I of England, the first of the Stuart line.

Scandinavian Reformation. In the early sixteenth century, Lutheran beliefs spread from Germany to the Scandinavian countries under Danish control. A Swedish nobleman named Gustavus Vasa was crowned king of Sweden in 1523. For some time the Swedes had wanted their independence from Denmark. It was Vasa who finally led them to political victory over the Danes.

At the same time, Vasa wanted control over the Swedish Church as well. In 1527 he clashed with the pope over the appointment of bishops. As a result, the Church of Sweden separated from Rome. Olavus Petri, who had studied at the University of Wittenburg in Germany, translated the Bible into Swedish. He also helped to develop the Swedish Church along the lines of the Lutheran faith.

In Denmark, Roman bishops supported a move to depose King Christian III. The king, however, was able to put down the uprising and asked Luther to help him start a new state Church. Luther sent John Bugenhagen to Denmark to help translate the Bible into Danish. The Lutheran Church of Denmark then was established.

Norway, also under Danish control at this time, helped in the effort to depose Christian III of Denmark. When Christian won, however, he established the Lutheran Church in Norway, also. Since few missionaries traveled as far north as Norway in those days, the country began to slip away from Christianity, however. It was not until the 1600s that this situation improved.

The Landless Denomination. While the Calvinists and the Lutherans were splitting away from the Roman Catholic Church, many other Protestant sects were emerging in Europe at the same time.

Many of the new sects opposed infant baptism because infants could not yet understand. Historians categorize these believers in one group called the Anabaptists. They came from almost every country in Europe. This term means "those baptized again." It was used to describe the many adults who joined the Anabaptists and were baptized again as adults.

Anabaptists, as a group, had widely differing Biblical interpretations and philosophies. They felt no need for a central clergy because they believed each person should follow his own "inner light." Often they were persecuted because they questioned many of the basic beliefs of both Protestantism and Catholicism. Anabaptists were tortured and even killed in Switzerland, Germany, the Netherlands, and Austria. They did, however, find some degree of religious freedom in Russia and Poland.

Anabaptists, as a whole, believed in the separation of Church and state and opposed military service. They often refused to pay taxes in countries which were at war. Their beliefs are carried on today by the Amish, the Dunkers, the Mennonites, and the Quakers. The Baptists also have been influenced by Anabaptist beliefs.

This woodcut depicts a preacher in the Age of Reformation. The preacher seems to compare the Bible with the symbols that had come to represent the Church.

The Counter-Reformation

The development and growth of Protestant religions in Europe was called the Protestant Reformation, as we have seen. By the middle 1500s, the Protestant domination was apparent throughout Europe. Catholic leaders were more than a little concerned about this situation. They were determined to do all they could to stem the rising tide of Protestantism. Their efforts in this behalf are known as the Counter-Reformation, or the Catholic Reformation. The primary efforts of Church leaders during the Counter-Reformation involved the cleaning up of Church abuses.

Some Countries Remain Roman Catholic. Since Roman Catholic churchmen waited so

Peasants slaughtered their rich landowners during the Reformation in Germany. Although Martin Luther renounced such acts of violence, the revolt was blamed on his teachings.

long to correct the abuses, the Church was rejected almost entirely as a spiritual authority while the Reformation spread throughout Europe. Some countries did, however, remain staunchly Roman Catholic.

In France, King Francis I favored the Protestant Reformation in the beginning. French kings had struggled for years with Rome over control of the French Church. When they broke their ties with Rome, Francis was able to take over all the rich Roman Church property in France. His sister, Marguerite of Navarre, even supported the Reformation preachers.

Before Francis I made the break with Rome, the peasants in Germany rebelled against the rich landowners. Even though Martin Luther preached against the peasants, the revolt was blamed on the Protestant Reformation. So Francis I, fearing revolt in France, changed his position and sided with the Roman Church.

Geography of the Reformation

It is interesting to note that those countries which were part of the Roman Empire before 500 A.D. remained loyal to the Roman Church. These nations included Italy, Spain, Portugal, France, and Austria.

Those countries on the border of the Roman Empire were divided between Protestant and Roman Catholic beliefs. They included the Netherlands, the Rhine Valley, Switzerland, and the upper portions of the Danube River. In these countries the southern territory closest to the Roman border remained Roman Catholic; the northern areas became Protestant. The rest of Europe became Protestant.

French Protestants, called Huguenots, were persecuted. In two months during 1545, more than 3,000 Huguenot men, women, and children were massacred. Twenty-two villages were destroyed and 700 men became galley slaves. France remained a Roman Catholic country, but the Huguenot minority continued to worship in secret.

In Spain Protestant beliefs never got started because of the Inquisition. The Spanish people and their rulers remained strongly Roman Catholic.

Italy, the heart of the Renaissance, was also the heart of the Roman Church. It was almost impossible for Protestant teachings to get started there. With these Catholic countries as a base, the Roman Church began the difficult job of winning back territory influenced by Protestant teachings.

The Roman Church Reforms. In 1534 Paul II, the new pope, called a meeting of major Roman Catholic leaders at the Council of Trent to discuss reforms. Most churchmen wanted to correct the major abuses, but many wanted things to remain as they were. Despite protests from corrupt clergymen, the pope appointed a reform council. It was composed of Roman Church leaders with outstanding abilities.

Changes were immediately put into effect. Churchmen were no longer allowed to hold more than one office. Capable men were appointed to fill the extra offices. Clergymen were now required to live in the place where they performed their duties. Only qualified men were appointed to offices and there was no more simony. In this way the Roman Church reformed itself without changing any of its doctrines.

While reforms were started by the pope, movements were started also at the local level to reform the Roman Church. One such reformer was Teresa of Avila, sometimes called the most outstanding woman in Spanish history.

Teresa was given permission by her bishop in 1562 to start a new convent because the old one was not strict enough. Five years later Teresa established many convents throughout Spain. Although she was now old and in very poor health, she founded a total of 32 convents. The new convents influenced other convents and many monasteries to make changes. Rules became stricter and many worldly practices were stopped.

The Jesuits, Heart of the Counter-Reformation. Ignatius Loyola had the greatest influence of all on the Counter-Reformation. While serving as a soldier, his leg was broken by a cannonball. It did not heal properly and had to be rebroken. While his leg was healing, the only books he had to read were the Bible and biographies of Catholic saints. When he recovered, he dedicated his life to becoming a soldier for the Lord.

After a few years of fasting and prayer, Loyola entered the University of Paris to study theology. He gathered a small group of followers who became known as the Society of Jesus or "Jesuits." In 1540 the pope made them into a new order of monks.

The Jesuits soon became the heart of the Counter-Reformation. They used education, instead of violence, to win people back to the Roman Church. As a result, Poland, Hungary, Bohemia, and much of Germany returned to the Roman Church.

The Jesuits were a strong missionary organization. One member, Francis Xavier, traveled to India and Asia. The Jesuits were opposed to all forms of corruption and they helped the Roman Church with her reforms.

Summary. Before the Reformation, European Christianity appeared to present a united front to the world. After 1572, European Christianity was divided into two major groups—Protestants and Roman Catholics. The Protestants have divided into many denominations. This has given Christians the opportunity to find a form of worship that agrees with their individual beliefs.

A New World

From the time of earliest civilizations, there were trade contacts between India, China, the Middle East, and Europe. Over the years three major routes developed. One passed from the coast of China to the southern tip of India, to the south coast of Arabia, and to Cairo, Egypt. The second route passed through the Persian Gulf to Baghdad. The third route crossed the interior of the continent of Asia. None of these routes was easy or safe. There were mountains to climb, deserts to cross, storms to face, robbers on the roads, and pirates on the seas.

When the Ottoman Turks captured Constantinople, trade between Europe and the Far East stopped. Naval warfare, heavy tribute, and pirate activities in the Mediterranean prevented the Italian cities from continuing as European middlemen in Eastern trade. Other routes which bypassed the Mediterranean Sea had to be found. Explorers setting out to find a new route to the East discovered a New World which became known as the Americas.

As soon as it was certain this was indeed a new world, and not the Far East, explorers set out to learn what was there. Great civilizations were discovered and destroyed. Native populations were defeated, enslaved, and deprived of their lands. Soon floods of Europeans came to

Columbus' three ships, the Nina, Pinta, and Santa Maria, are shown here with the flagship Santa Maria in the foreground. Comparing these tiny ships to the large vessels of today, we can appreciate the courage of the early explorers who crossed the ocean and faced unforeseen difficulties.

The *astrolabe,* a medieval instrument, was used in the early voyages to the New World. With this instrument navigators could determine their latitude by taking sightings of the sun and other heavenly bodies.

the New World to live. They came to seek fortunes, to escape religious persecution, to find adventure, or to teach Christianity to the native inhabitants. They established colonies that became the foundation for the American nations.

Early Voyages

There were many reasons why the New World was discovered at this time. For many years scholars had known that the world was round instead of flat. Maps showing a round world, with

tiny oceans and Europe and Asia greatly enlarged, led sea captains to believe they could reach Asia by sailing west.

In addition, some wonderful navigational aids had been invented. Navigators could determine latitude by using an astrolabe. They also had primitive compasses.

The Portuguese Explore Africa. The Portuguese people were the first to try to find a new trade route to India. The Portuguese ruler was called Henry the Navigator because he sponsored a school where captains were taught the newest discoveries in navigation. Henry also encouraged Portuguese shipbuilding. A new ship called the *caravel* was invented. It was sturdier than earlier ships since it was designed for rough ocean voyages. Since Henry believed it was possible to reach India by sailing around Africa, many Portuguese explorers attempted to do so.

In 1486, Bartholomew Diaz became the first Portuguese explorer to circle the tip of Africa. Eleven years later Vasco da Gama rounded the tip, known as the Cape of Good Hope, and sailed

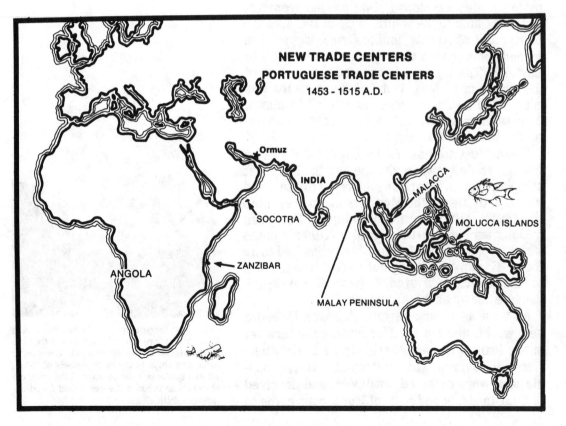

NEW TRADE CENTERS
PORTUGUESE TRADE CENTERS
1453 - 1515 A.D.

Ormuz
INDIA
MALACCA
SOCOTRA
MOLUCCA ISLANDS
ANGOLA
ZANZIBAR
MALAY PENINSULA

Fearless Adventurers

Today with all of our knowledge of geography, it does not seem to be dangerous to sail around Africa. In the fifteenth century, however, conditions were quite different. Nobody knew what Africa was like. Stories of strange monsters added to the sense of danger. In addition, while scholars knew the world was round, the sailors thought it was flat. They believed terrible sea monsters lurked at the earth's edge waiting to destroy any ship foolish enough to come near.

on to India. For nearly a hundred years, the Portuguese enjoyed a monopoly on the spice trade.

Lisbon became a great world market where France, England, the Netherlands, and the German duchies came to buy oriental luxuries. This trade constituted a government monopoly by Portugal. The ships were owned and operated by the Portuguese government although private merchants could ship goods in them. Portuguese forts and trade companies kept foreign merchants from stealing trade rights.

Spain Into the Unknown. While Portuguese ships were trying to sail around Africa, the Spanish also wanted to trade in the Far East. Ferdinand and Isabella of Spain dispatched Christopher Columbus to sail west until he reached either India or China. On October 10, 1492, one of his three tiny ships landed on a small island in the West Indies. Columbus made two more voyages trying to prove that he had, in fact, reached India.

The World Divided. Spain and Portugal began quarreling over ownership of the territory they were exploring. Since both countries were Roman Catholic, they asked the pope to settle the dispute. The pope drew an imaginary line around the world, called the *Line of Demarcation.* All newly discovered territory to the east of this line belonged to Portugal, and that to west of the line belonged to Spain.

Because of the Line of Demarcation, Portugal was able to claim Brazil when Pedro

This small, light sailing ship, called a *caravel,* was used by the Spanish and Portuguese in the fifteenth and sixteenth centuries.

The Naming of America

For a time after the New World was discovered by Columbus, it was called Columbia. Very soon after Columbus' voyages, however, an Italian navigator named Amerigo Vespucci made a number of voyages, reaching the mainland of South America first in 1499. He was the first to enter the Amazon River and also to show that America was not a part of the continent of Asia. His chart of the Atlantic and the western lands was the first to be widely used. In 1507, those lands were first called America, in his honor, and the name soon became accepted everywhere.

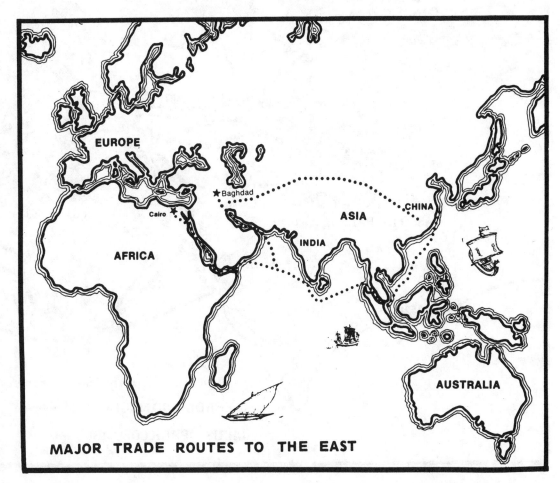

MAJOR TRADE ROUTES TO THE EAST

Cabral sighted it in 1493. This line settled problems between Spain and Portugal, but the rest of Europe refused to accept it. Soon explorers from England, France, and Holland were claiming lands in the New World.

Early Explorations

It took time for people to realize that a New World had been discovered. They found out about it from the brave men still searching for

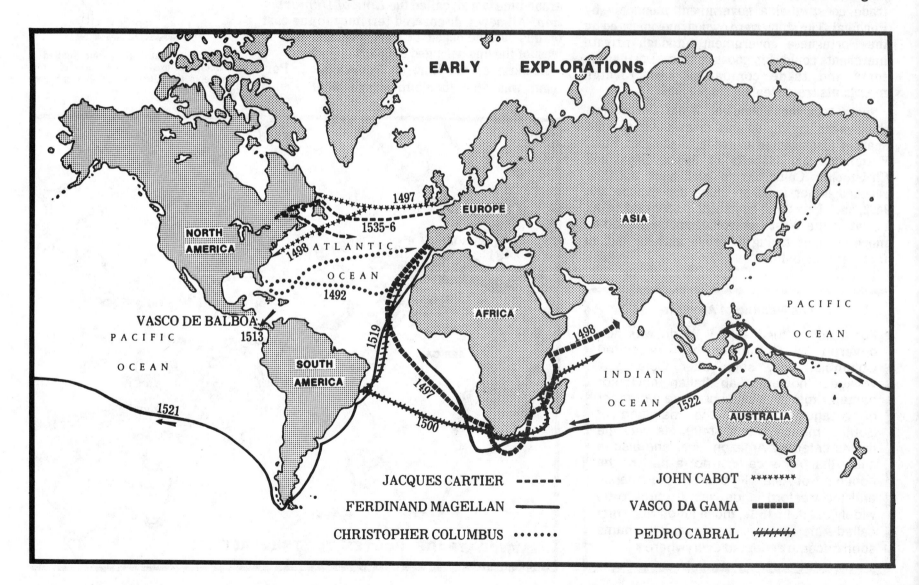

EARLY   EXPLORATIONS

JACQUES CARTIER ------

FERDINAND MAGELLAN ———

CHRISTOPHER COLUMBUS •••••••

JOHN CABOT *******

VASCO DA GAMA ■■■■■■

PEDRO CABRAL //////

shorter trade routes to the Far East. They tried to sail through and around the huge land mass blocking their way. Although they knew this was a New World, it took some time before people decided to migrate.

Voyage Explorations. It was not long before England started sending out expeditions. Ignoring the Line of Demarcation, John Cabot made two voyages along the North American coast in 1497 and 1498. Cabot was searching for a mythical shortcut to the Far East, called the Northwest Passage. England later claimed this North American territory and established colonies there.

It was 1521 before someone attempted to sail completely around the world. Sailing for Spain, Ferdinand Magellan rounded the tip of South America and sailed through the Straits of Magellan. The ocean looked so peaceful after 38 days of storms and poundings waves in the Straits that Magellan named it the Pacific Ocean.

Magellan's other ships landed in the Philippine Islands early in the spring. Magellan claimed these islands for Spain before he was killed by unfriendly natives. Finally one surviving ship, named the Victoria, arrived back in Spain. It was the first ship in history to sail completely around the world. Now there was not doubt the world was round. The entire trip took three years, however, making it an impractical route to China and India.

In 1534 and 1541 the French explorer Jacques Cartier thought he had found the Northwest Passage. After sailing for many miles, he discovered it was only the St. Lawrence River. Sailing this river gave France its claim to Canada.

Early Land Explorations. The first overland exploration of the New World was an expedition by Vasco de Balboa. He set out to reach a vast body of water by marching across Panama. In 1513, 190 Spaniards accompanied him through the jungles. As they reached the top of a hill, they became the first Europeans to see the Pacific Ocean from the Americas. As a result of Balboa's discovery, Magellan had been encouraged to make his voyage.

Leaving the West Indies, Ponce de Leon landed in Florida on Easter 1513. He named this new land after all the lovely flowers growing there. For months Ponce de Leon searched for a "Fountain of Youth" which the Indians had told him was there.

Francisco de Coronado, searching for the "Seven Cities of Gold," traveled the desert plains of the southwestern United States in 1540.

Mythical Wonders of the Americas

Today it sounds frivolous for grown men to search for fountains of youth or fabulous cities of gold. Explorers like Ponce de Leon, however, discovered a new and strange world. It was different from their European home and they did not know what to expect in this mysterious new place. The Indians, trying to please these strange visitors, made up stories about such wonderful but mythical sights as the Fountain of Youth. For all the explorers knew, the Indians' tales of wonder could have been true.

If a spaceship were to land on an inhabited planet today, we probably would believe stories told to us by the inhabitants regardless of how incredible they might sound.

Vasco de Balboa of Spain accomplished the first overland exploration of the New World by crossing the isthmus of Panama. Guided by natives through the jungle, he gets his first glimpse of the magnificent Pacific Ocean.

Pueblos in Taos, New Mexico, could be the same ones Coronado saw when he traveled the southwestern United States in search of the "Seven Cities of Gold." These adobe houses have been continuously inhabited for thousands of years.

A trusting Montezuma ruler of the Aztecs, welcomes the Spaniards to his home. When Cortez entered Mexico in the early 1500s, Montezuma believed him to be the god Quetzalcoatl whose return the Aztecs awaited. His trusting nature cost him his life. Not only was Montezuma imprisoned by the Spanish, he was later killed by his own people who thought he had betrayed them.

He discovered only the adobe villages of the Pueblo Indians. He got as far as Kansas and was the first European to see the great buffalo herds. Horses that escaped from Coronado and from later explorers, were the ancestors of the American wild horses. Remember, there were no horses in America until the Spanish brought them.

At the same time Coronado was exploring the southwest, Hernando de Soto explored the southeastern United States. He traveled from Florida to the Mississippi River in 1542 searching for treasure, but he found none. He died during the journey. His men buried him in the Mississippi River to protect the body from Indians.

Conquering and Settling the New World

As we saw in Chapter 15, the mighty Aztec and Inca Empires already were in existence when the Spanish arrived. These civilizations had cities that were larger than many European capitals. When the Indians met the Spanish, there was a clash between them that led to the destruction of Indian civilization. Once the Indians were completely subdued, European settlements began to spread throughout the New World.

The Aztecs Meet Their God. The Aztecs expected the return of their bearded god-king Quetzalcoatl in 1519. During 1518 the Aztec emperor Montezuma heard rumors of bearded men in white-winged boats along the eastern coast. He must have wondered if this meant that Quetzalcoatl was going to return.

The conquering explorers were called conquistadores. One conquistadore, named Hernan-

do Cortez, landed in Mexico in 1519 with 700 men. He burned his ships so his men would not be tempted to retreat. As he made his way inland, several tribes were defeated. They then became his allies. Cortez was helped by a young Indian woman named Malinche who acted as translator and guide. The Spanish called her Dona Marina and without her help the Spanish could not have understood the language of the Aztecs.

Montezuma, still thinking Cortez might be his lost god, welcomed him and invited him to stay in the Aztec capital of Tenochtitlan. The Spaniards were impressed with the size and wealth of Tenochtitlan.

Cortez repaid Montezuma by taking him prisoner. Montezuma was later killed by his own people who felt he had betrayed them. The Aztecs then attacked the Spanish and almost destroyed them before they escaped. Cortez, determined to get revenge, attacked Tenochtitlan. He built European-style ships to cross the lake to the island city.

The Spanish won because of their superior ships and weapons. The beautiful city of Tenochtitlan was completely leveled. A new Spanish-style city was later built over the ruins. This city, still standing today, is Mexico's capital of Mexico City.

The tremendous wealth of the Aztecs began flowing back to Spain. Settlers arrived, bringing with them European plants and seeds. The Indians were used as slave labor in the fields and mines. At the same time, the Spanish tried to convert them to the Roman Catholic faith, using force when necessary.

The Inca Empire Falls. When Francisco Pizarro crossed Panama with Balboa, he heard stories of a rich South American empire. In 1531 he sailed from Panama with 180 men and 27 horses to conquer it. When he arrived in Peru, the conquistadores were pleasantly surprised to learn the Incas had just fought a bloody civil war.

The new Incan emperor, Atahualpa, had not yet entered his capital. He decided to delay his journey in order to meet the Spaniards. Pizarro seized this opportunity to take Atahualpa prisoner.

The emperor tried to buy his freedom by filling two rooms—one with silver and one with gold. When the ransom was paid Atahualpa was given a choice. He could become a Christian and be strangled to death or remain heathen and be burned at the stake. Atahualpa was strangled, probably wondering why he had fought so hard to take the throne away from his brother.

Atahualpa, emperor of the Incas, receives the last rites before being strangled by Francisco Pizarro's conquistadores. Having betrayed his brother and stolen the throne, Atahualpa was himself betrayed by the Spanish.

Most Inca warriors had been killed during the civil war. Without a leader they were helpless and the conquistadores easily captured the Incan capital. Once the Incas were defeated, the Spanish began fighting among themselves. They were not able to set up an effective government. Meanwhile, the Incas died in great numbers as a result of European diseases and cruel treatment. It was not until after the sixteenth century that an efficient Spanish government was established.

Spanish Colonies. Major Spanish colonies were established on the islands of Haiti, Puerto Rico, and Cuba. They used the Indians as slaves to mine gold and silver in Mexico and Peru. Treasure ships began making regular runs between Spain and her New World colonies.

At first Seville was the only Spanish port allowed to handle this valuable trade. Later Cadiz was chosen to handle the trade because it had a better harbor. Ships were allowed to land at two American ports, Vera Cruz in Mexico and Puerto Bello on the Isthmus of Panama.

A fleet was sent to each of these ports once a year. Colonists who wanted to buy or sell goods had to travel to these ports. Only licensed Spanish merchants were allowed to trade in the colonies and no foreign ships were allowed to land. This monopoly allowed merchants to charge high prices on incoming goods while paying low prices on goods leaving the colonies. Although this arrangement helped the Spanish rulers and merchants, it hurt the economic growth of the colonies.

Early English and French Efforts. The Spanish New World colonies were thriving long before England and France set up colonies in North America. The English colonies became a refuge for the many religious groups which refused to worship in the Church of England. England also encouraged growth of the colonies as a market for English trade goods. The first permanent English colony was established in Jamestown, Virginia, in 1607. It was not until 1620 that the Pilgrims settled in New England.

The beginning of a new world power—Pilgrims set foot on the frozen shore of Plymouth, Massachusetts. Faced with all the uncertainties of life in a strange land, these settlers seem peacefully certain of their decision to leave the Old World.

The French colonies were late in getting started, too. The French explorer Samuel de Champlain founded the city of Quebec in 1608. Not many people were willing to move to Canada because of the cold winters. The French allowed only Roman Catholics to move to Canada. The Huguenots were willing to emigrate but they were not allowed to live there.

Portuguese, Africa, the East Indies, and Brazil

While the rest of Europe had its attention on the exploration of the New World, the Portuguese established a trade empire in Africa and the East Indies. They also started a colony in Brazil.

African Colonies. Africa was part of the territory granted to Portugal by the Line of Demarcation. The Portuguese established a colony on the offshore island of Zanzibar, and another in Angola.

The most famous Portuguese colonial governor was Afonso de Albuquerque. He realized Portugal had to either protect her new Eastern trade route or lose her monopoly. To protect her interest, he began building forts where they controlled the water route. Two of these forts were located at the city of Ormuz on the Persian Gulf and at the island of Socotra near the Red Sea.

The East Indies. Once Portuguese African interests were protected, Afonso de Albuquerque attempted to take over the East Indies. He captured the large trading center of Malacca in the Malay peninsula around 1511. Then he captured the Molucca Islands. These islands grew the finest spices and were a direct trade route to China.

For nearly a hundred years the Portuguese enjoyed a monopoly on the rich spice trade. Then in the 1590s, Dutch trading groups established bases in the islands of Malay. By 1602 the Dutch East India Company broke the Portuguese monopoly on the Eastern trade.

South America. By the 1570s, the Portuguese had a thriving colony in Brazil. African slaves were brought in to cultivate sugar cane and work the gold mines. Like the other New World colonies, the Portuguese did not allow their colonies to trade with other countries. Later Spain gained control over Portugal. Then the English, the Dutch, and the French felt free to help themselves to Portuguese territory. As a result, three South American territories, British, Dutch, and French Guiana were established near the mouth of the Amazon River.

Epilogue

In *Streams of Civilization* we have discussed two major beliefs about man's origins. We have traced the main streams of civilization from earliest times to the brink of the modern age. As civilizations developed, we have watched them merge one with another, rise and fall, and leave their mark on the world. Each new culture benefited from the learning and achievements of earlier civilizations.

Man's curiosity about the past came into full bloom during the Renaissance when Greek and Roman manuscripts became available to Europeans. In this volume we have seen the important role played by communication, and the lack of it, in the development of civilizations all over the world. With the invention of the printing press, man's awareness of the world and events around him flowered. Man's knowledge of foreign peoples and geography has brought civilizations closer together. As a result of communication and exploration, then, the world started to become smaller. The discovery of a New World brought Europeans face to face with foreign colonization and a new age.

Throughout this text we have looked at the philosophy, spirit, and religion of man and their influence on world history. From early pagan civilizations to the modern-day Christian and non-Christian religions, men around the world have searched for truth. While their conclusions have not always been accepted by future peoples, their experiences have almost always brought influence to bear on generations that followed.

In future studies you will move with the streams of civilization through the Industrial Revolution, political revolutions, two major world wars, and the Space Age. You will continue to see civilizations rise and fall; times of war and times of peace; and you will watch the world grow still smaller as technology advances.

You, the potential leader of your country, have the opportunity to examine these events closely in facing the major world crises today. By so doing you ultimately may be able to influence the direction of future streams of civilization.

CREDITS

Special permission has been granted by various individuals and institutions to reproduce the following photographs. The credits are listed according to the page on which the pictures appear. Credits for two or more pictures on the same page are listed in order of appearance and are separated by semicolons.

Names of artists who are credited for line drawings and other illustrations are listed in the Foreword at the beginning of this book.

BIBLIOGRAPHY

The books and periodicals listed below include all references used in preparing Streams of Civilization. These same materials are recommended for all school libraries so that teachers and students may have access to a fair sample of literature on the history of world civilizations.

The books listed below have been categorized according to subject matter which will enable students to readily select materials for additional reading and research on each chapter.

Africa

Bruwer, A.J. *Zimbabwe: Rhodesia's Ancient Greatness.* San Francisco: Tri-Ocean, Inc., N.D.

Davidson, Basil, *The African Genius.* Boston-Toronto: Little, Brown and Company, 1969.

Editors. *Africa: Emerging Nations Below the Sahara.* Columbus, Ohio: American Education Publications, Inc., N.D.

Editors. *Civilizations of Africa.* Columbus, Ohio: American Education Publishers, 1970.

Lengyel. *Africa: Past, Present, Future.* New York: Oxford Book Co., 1970.

Paton, Alan. *South Africa in Transition.* New York: Charles Scribner and Sons, 1956.

Thompson, Elizabeth B., *Africa Past and Present.* Boston: Houghton Mifflin Company, 1966.

Vlahos, Olivia. *African Beginnings.* New York: The Viking Press, 1967.

Wiedner, Donald L. *A History of Africa: South of the Sahara.* New York: Vintage, 1962.

Woodhouse, H. C. *Archaeology in Southern Africa.* San Francisco: Tri-Ocean, 1972.

Americas

Benson, Elizabeth P. *The Maya World.* New York: Thomas Y. Crowell Company, 1967.

Davis, Harold. *History of Latin America.* New York: Ronald Press Co., 1968.

Herring, Hubert. A History of Latin America from the Beginnings to the Present. New York: Alfred Knopf, 1961.

The National Geographic Magazine. "Lost Empire of the Incas," Vol. 144, No. 6, December 1973, p. 729.

The National Geographic Magazine. "Mounds: Riddles From the Indian Past," George E. Stuart, pp. 142-46, 783-803.

The National Geographic Magazine. "Peru's Ancient City of Kings," Michael E. Moseley, Carol J. Mackey, David Brill, pp. 143-53, 318-356.

Sellards, E. H. *Early Man in America.* Austin: University of Texas Press, 1952.

Soustelle, Jacques. *The Daily Life of the Aztecs.* New York: Macmillan Company, 1962.

Stuart, George E. and Gene S. Stuart. *Discovering Man's Past in the Americas.* National Geographic Society, 1969.

Urena, Pedro H. *Concise History of Latin American Culture.* Translated by Getdert Chase. New York: Praeger Publishers, Inc., 1966.

Von Hagen, Victor Wolfgang. *The Ancient Sun Kingdoms of the Americas.* Cleveland and New York: World Publishing Company, 1961.

Von Hagen, Victor W. *The Aztec: Man and Tribe.* New York: The New American Library, 1961.

Von Hagen, Victor W. *Realm of the Incas,* (Rev. ed.). New York: The New American Library, 1961, (paperback).

Von Hagen, Victor W. *World of the Maya,* (6th printing). New York: The New American Library, 1960, (paperback).

Ancient History

Africa, Thomas A. *Rome of the Caesars.* New York: John Wiley and Sons, Inc., 1965.

Angel, J. Lawrence. *People of Lerna: An Analysis of a Prehistoric Aegean Population.* New York: Smithsonian, 1971. (George Braziller, Inc.)

Asimov, Isaac. *The Egyptians.* Boston: Houghton Mifflin Company, 1967.

Auboyer, Jeannine. *Daily Life in Ancient India.* New York: The Macmillan Co., 1965.

Bacon, Edward. *Vanished Civilizations of the Ancient World.* New York: McGraw-Hill Book Company, 1967.

Barrow, R. H. *The Romans,* (11th printing). Baltimore, Maryland: Penguin Books, 1968, (paperback).

Baumann, Hans. *In The Land Of Ur: The Discovery of Ancient Mesopotamia,* (Translated by Stella Humphries). New York, New York: Random House, Inc., 1969.

Baumann, Hans. *The World of the Pharaohs,* (Translated by Richard and Clara Winston). New York: Pantheon, 1960.

Benoist-Mechin, Jacques. *Alexander the Great: The Meeting Of The East and West,* (Translated by Mary Ilford). New York: Hawthorne Books, 1966.

Bibby, Geoffrey. *Four Thousand Years Ago.* New York: Alfred A. Knopf, 1956.

Braidwood, Robert J. *Prehistoric Men,* (7th printing). Glenview, Ill.: Scott, Company, 1967, paperback.

Breasted, James H. *Ancient Times: Ancient Near East,* Vol. I. Boston, Mass.: Ginn and Co.

Breasted, James H. *Ancient Times: Greeks,* Vol. II. Boston, Mass. Ginn and Co.

Breasted, James H. *Ancient Times: Romans,* Vol. III. Boston, Mass. Ginn and Co.

Brune, Lester. *Ancient History to the Fall of Rome.* Tustin, Calif.: Media Masters, 1968.

Brune, Lester. *India and Southeast Asia to Sixteen Hundred A.D.* Tustin, Calif.: Media Masters, 1968.

Bulwer-Lytton, Edward. *The Last Days of Pompeii.* Garden City, New York: Dolphin Books (Doubleday Co.).

Burn, Andrew R. *Alexander the Great and the Hellenistic Empire,* (Rev. ed.). New York: Collier Books (Macmillan Co.).

Bury, J. B. *History of Greece for Beginners.* New York: St. Martin's Press, Inc. 1927.

Bury, J.B. *A History of Greece: to the Death of Alexander the Great.* New York: Modern Library.

Caesar's Gaul. Chicago, Ill.: Denoyer-Geppert, No. 20415.

Caldwell, Wallace Everett and Mary Francis Gyles. *The Ancient World,* (3rd ed.). New York: Holt, Rinehart, and Winston, Inc., 1966.

Carroll, Harry J. Jr., Ainslie T. Embree, Knox Mellon, Jr., Arnold Schrier, and Alastair M. Taylor. *The Development of Civilization: the Ancient World to 1500:,* (3rd printing). Glenview, Ill.: Scott, Foresman, and Company, 1970, (paperback).

Cary, M. *A History of Rome: to the Reign of Constantine.* New York: St. Martins, 1935.

Casson, Lionel. *Ancient Egypt.* New York: Silver Burdette Co., 1965.

Casson, Lionel. *Ancient Mariners: Seafarers and Sea Fighters of the Mediterranean in Ancient Times.* New York: Funk and Wagnalls. N.D.

Cheilik, Michael. *Ancient History.* New York: Barnes and Noble, 1969.

Chiera, Edward. *Sumerian Epics and Myths,* (Cuneiform Ser., Vol. 3). Chicago: University of Chicago Press, 1934.

Chubb, Mary A. *Nefertiti Lived Here.* New York: Crowell Co., 1955.

Chubb, Thomas C. *Slavic Peoples.* New York: World Pub. Co., 1962.

Cohen, Daniel. *Secrets from Ancient Graves.* New York: Dodd, Mead and Co., 1968.

Contenau, Georges. *Everyday Life in Babylon and Assyria,* (Translated by K.R. and A.R. Maxwell-Hyslop). New York: St. Martin's, 1954.

Coolridge, Olivia. *Roman People.* Boston, Mass.: Houghton Mifflin Co.1959.

Coolridge, Olivia. *The Trojan War.* Boston, Mass.: Houghton Mifflin Co.1952.

Cottrell, Leonard. *The Bull of Minos.* New York: Universal Publishing and Distributing Corp.

Cottrell, Leonard. *Life Under the Pharaohs.* New York: Holt, Rinehart, and Winston, Inc., 1960.

Cottrell, Leonard. *Quest for Sumer.* New York: Putnam's Sons, 1965.

Daniel, Glyn. *The First Civilizations* (The Archaeology of Their Origins). New York: Thomas Y. Crowell Co., 1968.

Daniel, Glyn, (general editor). *The Phoenicians* (Ancient Peoples and Places), (2nd printing), New York: Frederick A. Praeger, Inc., 1963, (paperback).

Daniel-Rops, Henri, (Translated by K. Madge), *Israel and the Ancient World.* (originally *Sacred History).* Garden City, New York: Image Books, a division of Doubleday and Company, Inc., 1964, (paperback).

Davidson, Marshall B. (editor in charge) and Leonard Cottrell (narrative). *The Horizon Book of Lost Worlds.* New York: American Heritage Publishing Co., Inc. (Doubleday and Co., Inc.), 1962.

Davis, William S. *Day in Old Athens,* Boston, Mass.: Allyn and Bacon, Inc.

Davis, William S. *Day in Old Rome.* Boston, Mass.: Allyn and Bacon, Inc.

Dolan, Mary. *Hannibal of Carthage.* (Abr.) New York: Avon Books.

Donovan, Frank R. *The Vikings.* New York: Harper and Row, 1964.

Dothan, Trude. *The Philistines and Their Material Culture.* New Brunswick, New Jersey.: Rutgers University Press, 1972.

Dunand, Maurice, (Translation by H. Tabet). *Biblos: Its History, Ruins, and Legends.* Paris: Librairie Adrien-Maisoneuve, 1968, (paperback).

Dunan, Marcel. *Larousse Encyclopedia of Ancient and Medieval History.* New York: Harper and Row, 1963.

Ellis, Richard S. *Foundation Deposits in Ancient Mesopotamia.* New Haven, Conn: Yale University Press, 1968.

Fairservis, Walter A. Jr. *The Ancient Kingdoms of the Nile and the Doomed Monuments of Nubia.* New York: Thomas Y. Crowell Co., 1962, (paperback).

Fairservis, Walter A. *Egypt, Gift of the Nile.* New York: The Macmillan Co., 1963.

Fairservis, Walter A. *Mesopotamia: The Civilization That Rose Out of the Clay.* Riverside, New Jersey: Macmillan Co., 1964.

Falls, C. B. *The First 3000 Years: Ancient Civilizations of The Tigris, Euphrates, and Nile River Valleys, and the Mediterranean Sea.* New York: Viking Press Inc., 1960.

Frank, Tenney. *A History of Rome.* New York: Holt, Rinehart, and Winston, 1951.

Franzius, Enno. *History of the Byzantine Empire.* New York: Funk and Wagnalls, 1970.

Foster, Genevieve (Stump). *Augustus Caesar's World: A Story of Ideas and Events from B.C. 44 to 14 A.D.* New York: Charles Scribner and Sons. 1947.

Garbini, Giovanni. *The Ancient World*. New York: McGraw-Hill Book Company, 1966.

Gardiner, Alan. *Egypt of the Pharaohs*. Oxford: Oxford University Press, 1961.

Grant, Michael. *The Ancient Mediterranean*. New York: Charles Scribner's Sons, 1969 (Michael Grant Publications Ltd.).

Gurney, Oliver R. *Hittites*. Baltimore, Md.: Penguin, 1961.

Hall, Jennie, *Buried Cities*. New York: Macmillan, 1922.

Hammond, N.G.L. *A History of Greece,* (2nd printing). Oxford, England: Oxford University Press, 1963.

Hardy, W. G. *The Greek and Roman World*. Cambridge, Mass.: Schenkman Publishing Co. Inc., 1962, (paperback).

Hatzfeld, Jean. *History of Ancient Greece*. New York: W. W. Noryon. 1966.

Hawkes, Jacquetta. *Prehistory,* Vol. I. Part I. New York: the New American Library, Mentor Books, 1963, (paperback).

Heihelmeim, Fritz, and Cedric A. Yeo. *A History of the Roman People*. New Jersey: Prentice-Hall, Inc. 1962.

"Horizon Magazine" Editors, (Narrative by Leonard Cottrell). *The Horizon Book of Lost Worlds*. American Heritage Publishing Co. Inc., Garden City, New York: Dist. by Doubleday, 1962.

Jacobs, David. *Constantinople, City on the Golden Horn*. New York: Harper and Row, 1969.

King, Leonard W. *History of Sumer and Akkad: An Account of the Early Races of Babylonia from Prehistoric Times to the Foundation of the Babylonian Monarchy*. West Port, Conn.: Greenwood Press, Inc., 1910.

Kitto, H.D.F. *The Greeks,* (18th printing). Baltimore, Maryland: Penguin Books, 1969, (paperback).

Kramer, Samuel Noah. *Cradle of Civilization,* Time-Life Book Series. New York: Time Incorporated, 1967.

Kramer, Samual Noah. *History Begins at Sumer,* (2nd printing). Garden City, New York: Doubleday and Co. Inc., 1959.

Kramer, Samuel Noah. *History Begins at Sumer: Twenty-seven Firsts in Man's Recorded History*. Garden City, New York: Doubleday and Co., Inc.

Kramer, Samuel Noah. *The Sumerians, Their History, Culture, and Character,* (3rd ed.). Chicago: The University of Chicago Press, 1967.

Lange, K. and M. Hirmer. *Egypt: Architecture, Sculpture, Painting*. Greenwich, Conn.: Phaidon Publishers, Inc., 1961.

Lissner, Ivar. (Translated by J. Maxwell Brownjohn). *The Silent Past: Mysterious and Forgotten Cultures of the World*. New York: G. P. Putnam's Sons, 1961.

Mallowan, Max E. *Early Mesopotamia and Iran* (Illus.). New York: McGraw-Hill Publishers, 1965.

Mayani, Zacharie. *The Etruscans Begin to Speak,* (Translated by Patrick Evans). New York: Simon Schuster, 1962, (Souvenir Press, Ltd.).

Mellersh, H.E. *Sumer and Babylon* (Illus.). New York: T.Y. Crowell, 1965.

Murray, Margaret. *The Splendour That Was Egypt*. New York: Praeger Publishers, 1961.

The National Geographic Magazine. "Have Excavations on the Island of Thera Solved the Riddle of the Minoans?" pp. 141-45, 702-726.

The National Geographic Magazine. "Homeward With Ulysses," Melville Bell Grosvenor I and Edwin Stuart Grosvenor, pp. 1-40, 144-51.

Oppenheim, A. Leo. *Ancient Mesopotamia: Portrait of a Dead Civilization*. Chicago: The University of Chicago Press, 1964.

Parrot, Andre, (Translated by Edwin Hudson). *Discovering Buried Worlds*. New York: Philosophical Library, Inc., 1955.

Payne, Robert. *The Splendor of Persia*. New York: Alfred Knopf, 1957.

Pfeiffer, Charles. *Egypt to the Exodus*. Grand Rapids, Mich.: Baker Book House.

Piggott, Editor. *The Dawn of Civilization*. New York: McGraw-Hill Book Co., 1967.

Reverdin, Olivier. *Crete and Its Treasures*. New York: The Viking Press, Inc.

Richardson, Emeline. *The Etruscans: Their Art and Civilization*. Chicago: The University of Chicago Press, 1964.

Riley, Carroll L. *The Origins of Civilization*. Carbondale and Edwardsville: Southern Illinois University Press, 1969.

Robinson, C.E. *Everyday Life In Ancient Greece*. Oxford at the Clarendon Press, 1933.

Samuel, Alan Edward. *The Mycenaean in History*. Englewood Cliffs, N.J.: Prentice-Hall, 1966.

Sellman, R. R. *Ancient Egypt*. New York: Roy Publishers, Inc., 1962.

Smith, Charles Edward, and Paul Grady Moorhead. *A Short History of the Ancient World*. New York: Appleton-Entury-Crofts, Inc., 1939.

Starr, Chester. *A History of the Ancient World*. New York: Oxford University Press, Inc., 1965.

Unstead, R. J. *Looking at Ancient History*. New York: Macmillan Company.

Von Der Osten, Hans H. *Explorations in Hittite Asia Minor,* (a reproduction of 1929 ed. text). Chicago: University of Chicago Press.

Weill, Raymond. *Phoenicia and Western Asia*. New York: Benjamin Blom, Inc. Publishers.

Wells, Evelyn. *Hapshepsut*. New York: Doubleday and Co., Inc., 1969.

Wells, Evelyn. *Nefertiti*. New York: Doubleday and Co., Inc., 1964.

Winer, Bart. *Life in the Ancient World*. Random House, 1961.

Woldering, Irmgard. *Gods, Men, and Pharaohs*. New York: Harry N. Abrams, Inc., Publisher, 1967.

Wooley, C. Leonard. *Sumerians*. New York: W. W. Norton and Co., 1965.

Culture

Akurgal, Ekrem. *The Art of the Hittites*. New York: Harry N. Abrams, Inc., Publisher.

Bloch, Raymond. *Etruscan Art*. London: Thames and Hudson, 1959.

Britten, Benjamin and Imogene, Hotst. *The Wonderful World of Music*. Garden City, New York: Garden City Books, 1958.

Burngart, Fritz Erwin. *A History of Architectural Styles,* (Translated by Editto Kustner and J.A. Underwood). New York: Praeger Publishers, 1970.

Chiera, Edward. *They Wrote on Clay.* Chicago: Phoenix (University of Chicago Press).

Gardner, Helen. *Art Through the Ages,* (ed. by Sumner Crosby), (4th rev. ed.). New York: Harcourt and Brace, 1959.

Ghirshman, Roman, (Translated by Stuart Gilbert and James Emmons). *Persian Art.* New York: Golden Press. 1962.

Gorsline, Douglas. *What People Wore: A Visual History of Dress from Ancient Times to Twentieth-Century America.* (4th rev. ed.) , New York: Harcourt and Brace, 1959.

Janson, H.W. (with Dora Jane Janson). *History of Art: A Survey of the Major Visual Arts, from the Dawn of History to the Present Day.* New Jersey: Prentice-Hall, Inc., 1967.

Janson, Horst W. and Dora Jane Janson. *The Story of Painting for Young People, from Cave Painting to Modern Times.* New York: Harry N. Abrams, Inc., 1962.

Kohler, Carl. *A History of Costume.* New York: Dover, 1963.

Lester, Katherine, Kerr Morris, and Netzorg Rose. *Historic Costume.* Peoria, Ill.: C. A. Bennett Co., 1961.

Lindsay, Jack. *Leisure and Pleasure in Roman Egypt.* Barnes and Noble, Inc., 1966.

Mertz, Barbara. *Temples, Tombs, and Hieroglyphics.* New York: Coward McCann, Inc., 1964.

Pericot-Garcia, Luis, et al. *Prehistoric Art.* New York: Harry N. Abrams, Inc., 1967.

Spiteris, Tony, (Translated by Thomas Burton). *The Art of Cyprus.* New York: Reynal and Company, 1970.

Tenney, Frank. *Life and Literature in the Roman Republic,* (5th printing). Berkeley and Los Angeles; University of California, 1965, (paperback).

Vilimkova, Milada. (Illus.). *Egyptian Jewelry.* New York: Paul Hamlyn (Hamlyn Publishing Group Limited)., 1969.

Volbach, Wolfgang Fritz. *Early Christian Art.* New York: Harry N. Abrams, Inc., Publishers.

Walch, J. Weston. *History of Language.* (20 posters), 1967.

Europe

Chapman, Charles. *History of Spain.* New York: Macmillan, 1960.

Descola, Jean. *A History of Spain,* (Translated by Elaine P. Happerin). New York: Alfred Knopf, 1962.

Ferguson, Wallace K. and Geoffrey Brunn. *A Survey of European Civilization, Part I.* Boston: Houghton Mifflin Company, 1958.

Wolf, John B. *The Emergence of European Civilization.* New York: Harper and Row, Publishers, 1962.

Far East—Southeast Asia

Akiyama, Aisaburo. *Chronological List of Japan and China.* New York: Paragon Book Reprintory, 1964.

Durant, Will. *Our Oriental Heritage.* New York: Simon and Schuster, 1954.

Editors. *Japan.* Columbus, Ohio: American Educational Publishers.

Elliott, Laurence H. *Climate and Men.* Manchester, Mo.: McGraw-Hill, 1969.

Fairservis, Walter A. *India.* New York: World Pub. Co., 1961.

Fessler, Loren and the Editors of "Life." *Life World Library—China.* New York: Time, Inc., 1963.

Kolevzon, Edward R. *East Asia: China, Japan, Korea.* Boston: Allyn and Bacon, Inc., 1970.

Kosambi, D.D. *Ancient India, A History of Its Culture and Civilization.* New York: Random House, 1965.

Kublin, Hepman. *China.* Boston, Mass.: Houghton Mifflin Company.

Kublin, Hyman. *India* (World Regional Studies). Boston, Mass.: Houghton Mifflin Company.

Lin, Yutang. *The Chinese Way of Life.* New York: World Pub. Co., 1959.

Rugoff, Milton. *Marco Polo's Adventures in China.* New York: Harper and Row, 1964.

Stravianos, Leften S. *China* (Cultural Areas in Perspective). Boston, Mass.: Allyn and Bacon, Inc., 1970.

Watson, Francis. *A Concise History of India.* New York: Charles Scribner's Sons, 1975.

General History

Bernstein, Paul and Robert W. Green. *History of Civilization,* Vol. I.: to 1648 , (6th printing). Totowa, New Jersey: Littlefield, Adams, and Co., 1967. (paperback).

Bernstein, Paul and Robert W. Green, *History of Civilization,* Vol. II (4th printing) , since 1648. Totowa, New Jersey: Littlefield, Adams, and Co., 1968, (paperback).

Brinton, Clinton. *Ideas and Men.* Englewood Cliffs, New Jersey: Prentice-Hall, 1963.

Broose, Jacques, et. al. *100,000 Years of Daily Life: A Visual History,* (Translated by Anne Carter). New York: Golden Press, 1961.

Bullock, Alan, et. al., eds. *World History: Civilization from its Beginning.* Garden City, New York: Doubleday, 1962.

Cantor, Norman F. and Richard I. Schneider, *How To Study History,* (4th printing). New York: Thomas Y. Crowell Co., 1968, (paperback).

Churchill, Sir Winston and Leonard Spencer. *History of the English Speaking Peoples.* New York: Dodd, Mead, and Co., 1956.

Clough, Shepard, (editor). *A History of the Western World, Ancient and Medieval,* (2nd printing). Lexington, Mass.: D.C. Heath and Co., Division of Raytheon Education Company, 1969.

Cole, William E. and Charles S. Montgomery, *High School Sociology.* Boston, Mass.: Allyn and Bacon, Inc. 1967.

Commager, Henry Steele, *The Nature and the Study of History ,* (2nd printing). Columbus, Ohio: Charles E. Merrill Books, Inc., 1966.

Coon, Carleton S. *The Story of Man: From The First Human to Primitive Culture and Beyond.,* (2nd edition rev.). New York: Alfred Knopf, 1962.

Cottrell, Leonard. *The Great Invasion.* New York: Coward-McCann, 1962.

Custance, Arthur C. *Doorway Papers.* (Abstracts of Papers). Ottawa, Canada: Arthur C. Custance, Publisher.

Davidson, Marshall, (editor). *The Light of the Past.* New York: American Heritage Publishing Co., Inc. (Doubleday and Co., Inc.), 1965.

DelMar, Alexander. *History of the Monetary System.* Chicago: Kerr Publishers, 1895.

Deuel, Leo, (editor). *The Treasures of Time.* New York: Avon Books.

Dewar, Douglas. *The Transformist Illusion.* Murfreesboro, Tenn.: DeHoff Publications, 1967.

Dorf, Philip. *Our Early Heritage.* New York: Oxford Book Company.

Durant, Ariel. *The Lessons of History.* New York: Simon and Schuster, Inc., 1968.

Durrenberger, Robert W. *Pattern on the Land.* Palo Alto, Calif.: National Press Books, 1967.

Duvoisin, Roger. *They Put Out to Sea.* New York: Alfred A. Knopf, 1955.

Gaddis, Vincent H. *Invisible Horizons: True Mysteries of the Sea.* Philadelphia: Chilton Books, 1965.

Hester, H.I. *The Heart of Hebrew History.* (25th printing). Liberty, Mo: The Quality Press, Inc., 1962.

History Teachers Association. *The History Teacher.* Notre Dame, Indiana: The History Teachers Association, University of Notre Dame., 1971, (paperback).

Hunt, Elgin F. *Social Science: An Introduction to the Study of Society.* New York: The Macmillan Co., 1966.

Irwin, Keith Gordon, (Illustrated by Guy Fleming). *The 365 Days.* New York: Thomas Y. Crowell Co., 1963.

Landis, Paul H. *Introduction to Sociology.* New York: Ronald Press Co., 1958.

Leonard, Jonathan Norton. *Great Ages of Man, Ancient America.* New York: Time, Inc., 1967.

Editors, *Life Magazine* and David Bergamini. *The Universe.* New York: Time, Inc., 1962.

McLendon, Jonathon C. *Social Studies in Secondary Education.* New York: The Macmillan Co., 1965.

Mead, Margaret. *People and Places.* New York: Bantam Books, Inc.

Mertz, Barbara. *Red Land, Black Land.* New York: Coward-McCann, Inc., 1966.

Owen, G. Frederick, *Abraham to the Middle-East Crisis,* (4th printing). Grand Rapids, Mich.: Wm. B. Eerdmans Publishing Co., 1957.

Renner, P. *Environment and Man.* New York: Haydin Book Co., Inc., 1971.

Rogers, Lester B., Fay Adams, and Walker Brown, *Story of Nations.* New York: Holt, Rinehart and Winston, Inc.. 1973.

Quennell, Peter and Alan Hodge, eds., *The Past We Share: An Illustrated History of the British and American Peoples.* New York (Buffalo): Prometheus Books, 1960.

Ross, Norman P., et al, editors of *Life, Epic of Man.* New York: Time Incorporated, 1961.

Sankowsky, Suzanne H. *Sociology for High School.* New York: Oxford Book Co., 1969.

Van Loon, Hendrik. *Story of Mankind.* New York: Washington Square Press, Inc.

Von Der Osten, Hans H. *Discoveries in Anatolia.* Chicago: University of Chicago Press, 1933.

Vernon, Glenn M. *Human Interaction: An Introduction to Sociology.* New York: Ronald Press Co., 1965.

Wallbank, Walter T., Alastair M. taylor, and Nels M. Bailey. *Civilization Past and Present.* Glenview, Ill.: Scott, Foresman and Company, 1962.

Wallbank, T. Walter and Arnold Schrier. *Living World History,* (3rd printing). Teacher's Resource Book. Glenview, Ill.: Scott, Foresman, and Co., 1969. (paperback).

Wesley, Edgar and Stanley Wronski. *Teaching Social Studies in High Schools.* Boston: C. C. Heath and Co., 1964.

Geography

Aharoni, Yohanan and Michael Avi-Yomah. *Macmillan Bible Atlas.* Jerusalem: Carta, 1968.

Association of American Geographers. *Geography in an Urban Age.* New York: Macmillan Co., 1969-70.

Boyd, Andrew and Patrick Van Rensburg. *An Atlas of African Affairs.* Maps by W. H. Bromage. New York: Praeger.

Bradley, J. H. *World Geography.* Boston, Mass.: Ginn and Co., 1971.

Freeman, Olis W. *Essentials of Geography.* New York: McGraw-Hill Book Co., Inc., 1959.

Fullard, Harold. *Cartocraft Geography School Atlas,* Chicago: Denoyer-Geppert Company, 1966.

Glueck, Nelson. *Rivers in the Desert.* New York: W. W. Norton Company, Inc., 1968.

Great World Atlas, Pleasantville, New York: The Reader's Digest Association, 1969.

Horsfield, Brenda and Peter Bennet Stone. *The Great Ocean Business.* New York: Conard, McCann, and Geoghehan, Inc., 1972.

Israel, S. (ed.), et al. *World Geography Today.* New York: Holt, Rinehart, and Winston, Inc.

Preston, E. James and Neldon Davis, *Wide World: A Geography*. (Illus.) New York: Macmillan Company, 1967.

Shepherd, William Robert. *Historical Atlas*. New York: Barnes and Noble, 1956.

World Atlas and Gazetteer. Maplewood, N.J.: Hammond, Inc., 1967.

Middle Ages

Bark, William C. *Origins of the Medieval World*. Stanford University Press, 1958.

Cantor, Norman F. *Medieval History—The Life and Death of a Civilization*. London: Macmillan Company, 1964.

Near East—Middle East

Bottero, Jean, et al. *Near East: The Early Civilizations*. New York: Delacorte Press, 1967.

Coon, Carleton S. *Caravan: The Story of the Middle East*. New York: Holt, Rinehart, and Winston, Inc., 1958.

Eisenberg, Azriel. *Eyewitness to Jewish History*. New York: Union of American Hebrew Congregations, 1970.

Ellis, Harry B. *The Arabs*. New York: World Pub. Co., 1958.

Hemple, George, *Mediterranean Studies,* (3 parts in Vol. I: Genesis of Europe Alphabet, Minoan Seals, and Hittites) New York: AMS Press, 1930.

Kirk, George E. *Short History of the Middle East*. New York: Praeger, 1964.

Mellaart, James. *Earliest Civilizations of the Near East*. New York: McGraw-Hill Book Company, 1965.

Roux, Georges, *Ancient Iraq*. New York: The World Pub. Co., 1964.

Religion

Anderson, Robert T. *An Introduction to Christianity*. New York: Harper and Row Publishers, 1968.

Baker, George P. *Constantine the Great and the Christian Revolution*. New York: Roman and Littlefield Pub., 1967.

Chadwick, Henry. *The Early Church*. Grand Rapids, Mich.: Penquin Books, Inc., 1968.

Durant, Will. *Caesar and Christ*. New York: Simon and Schuster, Inc.

Lacey, Harry. *God and the Nations*. New York: Loizeaux Brothers, 1945.

Latourette, Kenneth Scott, *A History of Christianity*. New York: Harper and Row, 1953.

Muir, James C. *His Truth Endureth: A Survey of Beginnings and of Old Testament History in the Light of Archaeological Discoveries.* Philadelphia, Penn.: National Publishing Co., 1967.

The National Geographic Magazine. "Bringing Old Testament Times to Life," G. Earnest Wright and H.J. Soulen, pp. 112-16, 833-865.

Nelson, Glueck. *Deities and Dolphins*. New York: Farrar, Stavs, and Giroux, 1965.

Pfeiffer, Charles. *Between the Testaments*. Grand Rapids, Mich.: Baker Books House, 1960.

Pfeiffer, Charles F. *Old Testament History*. Washington, D.C.: Canon Press, 1973.

Schultz, Samuel J. *The Old Testament Speaks*. New York: Harper and Row, Publishers. 1960.

Russia

Chubb, Thomas C. *Slavic Peoples,* New York: World Pub. Co., 1962.

Ellison, H. *History of Russia*. New York: Holt, Rinehart, and Winston, 1964.

Fairservis, Walter A. *Horsemen of the Steppes*. New York: World Pub. Co., 1962.

Grey, Ian. *History of Russia,* New York: American Heritage Publishing Co. (a subsidiary of McGraw-Hill, 1970.

Grey, Ian. *The Horizon History of Russia*. New York: American Heritage Pub. Co., 1970.

Riasanovsky, Nicholas V. *A History of Russia*. New York: Oxford University Press, 1963.

Rice, Tamara Talbot, *Finding Out About the Early Russians*. New York: Lothrop, Lee, and Shepard. 1964.

Scandinavia

Jones, Gwyn. *A History of the Vikings*. New York: Oxford University Press, 1968.

Klindt-Jensen, Ole, (Translated by Christopher Gibbs and George Unwin). *The World of Vikings*. Washington, New York: Robert B. Luce, Inc., 1970.

Mead, W. R. *Scandinavian*. New York: Walker and Co.

Simpson, Colin. *The Viking Circle*. West Caldwell, N.J.: Fielding Publishers.

Science

Abetti, Georgio. *History of Astronomy*. New York: Abelard, 1952.

Asimov, Isaac. *Breakthroughs in Science*. New York: Scholastic Book Services.

Barton, George A. *Archaeology and The Bible ,* (7th printing). Philadelphia, Penn.: American Sunday School Union, 1937.

Blaiklock, E. M. *Out of the Earth: The Witness of Archaeology to the New Testament*. (2nd printing). Grand Rapids, Mich.: Wm. B. Eerdmans Publishing Co., 1961.

Buried History. A Quarterly Journal of Biblical Archaeology, Vol. I, #4. Melbourne, Australia: The Australian Institute of Archaeology. Nov., 1964, (paperback).

Ceram, C.W. (ed.). (Translated by Richard and Clara Winston.) *The March of Archaeology*. New York: Alfred Knopf, 1958.

Ceram, C.W. (ed.). *The World of Archaeology*. London: Thames and Hudson. 1966.

Ceram, C.W. (ed.). *The World of Archaeology: The Pioneers Tell Their Own Story*. London: Thames and Hudson Ltd., 1966.

Chusid, Joseph G. and Joseph J. McDonald, *Correlative Neuoanatomy and Functional Neurology*. Los Altos, Calif.: Lange Medical Publications, 1962.

Custance, Arthur C. *Without Form and Void*. Seattle, Wash.: Pacific Meridian Pub. and Co.

Downs, James E. and Hermann Bleibtrece. *Human Variation: An Introduction to Anthropology*. Beverly Hills, Calif.: Glencor Press, 1969.

Freebury, H.A. *A History of Mathematics*. New York: Macmillan, 1961.

Frair, Wayne and P.W. Davis, *The Case for Creation.*, (2nd edition). Chicago: Moody Press, 1972.

Gish, Duane T. *Evolution the Fossils Say No!*. San Diego: Creation-Life Publishers, 1974.

Gropper, Rena C. *Anthropology Simplified*. New York: Barnes and Noble, Inc., 1969.

Hammond, Peter B. *Introduction to Cultural and Social Anthropology*. New York: Macmillan Co., 1971.

Himmelfarb, Gertrude. *Darwin and the Darwinian Revolution*. New York: Norton Library, 1968.

Hogben, Lancelot. *Mathematics in the Making*. Garden City, New York: Doubleday, 1960.

Kenyon, Kathleen. *Archaeology In the Holy Land*. New York: Praeger Publishers, Inc., 1970.

Klotz, John W. *Genes, Genesis, and Evolution*. St. Louis, Missouri: Concordia Publishing House.

Lammerts, Walter E. *Scientific Studies in Special Creation*. Presbyterian and Reformed Publishing Company, 1971.

Lammerts, Walter E. *Why Not Creation?*. Grand Rapids: Baker Book House, 1970.

Macbeth, Norman. *Darwin Retried*. Boston: Gambit Inc., 1971.

MacDowell, Josh. *Evidence that Demands a Verdict*. Campus Crusade for Christ, 1972.

Morris, Henry M. and John C. Whitcomb, Jr. *Genesis Flood*. Philadelphia: Presbyterian and Reformed Publishing Company, 1961.

Morris, Henry M. *Many Infallible Proofs,* San Diego: Creation-Life Publishers, 1974.

Morris, Henry M. *Remarkable Birth of the Planet Earth*. San Diego: Creation-Life Publishers, 1972.

Morris, Henry M. *Scientific Creationism*. San Diego: Creation-Life Publishers, 1974.

Morris, Henry M. *The Twilight of Evolution*. Nutley, N.J.: Presbyterian and Reformed Publishing Company, 1964.

Morris, John D. *Adventure on Ararat*. San Diego: Creation-Life Publishers, 1974.

The National Geographic Magazine. "Search for the Oldest People," Alexander Leaf and John Launois, pp. 143-51, 93-120.

Nelson, Byron C. *The Deluge Story in Stone*. Minneapolis, Minn.: Augsburg Publishing House, (Lutheran Pubs. Group), 1958.

Owen, G. Frederick. *Archaeology and the Bible*. Westwood, N.J.: Fleming H. Revell Co., 1961.

Poole, Lynn and Gray Poole. *Scientists Who Changed the World*. New York: Apollo Editions, 1960.

Reid, James. *God, the Atom, and the Universe*. Grand Rapids, Mich.: Zondervan Publishing House, 1968.

Rehwinkel, Alfred M. *The Flood: In the Light of the Bible, Geology, and Archaeology*. Saint Louis, Missouri: Concordia Publishing House, 1951.

Salzmann, Zdenek. *Anthropology*. New York: Harcourt and Brace, Inc., 1968.

Sarton, George. *Ancient Science and Modern Civilization*. New York: Harper and Brothers Publishers. 1954.

Smith, Paul E. (Revised, Carpenter and Wood.) *Our Environment: Its Relation To Us*. Chicago: Allyn and Bacon, Inc., 1965.

Suggs, Robert C. *Modern Discoveries in Archaeology*. New York: Thomas Y. Crowell, 1962.

Thompson, J.A. *Archaeology and the New Testament*. Grand Rapids, Mich.: Wm. B. Eerdmans Publishing Co., 1960.

Thompson, J.A. *Archaeology and the Pre-Christian Centuries*. Grand Rapids, Mich.: Wm. B. Eerdmans Publishing Co., 1958.

Thompson, W. R. *Science and Common Sense*. Albany, N.Y.: Magi Books, 1965.

Unger, Merrill F. *Archaeology and the New Testament*. Grand Rapids, Mich.: Zondervan Publishing House. 1962.

Unger, Merrill F. *Famous Archaeological Discoveries*. (3rd printing). Grand Rapids, Mich.: Zondervan Publishing Co., 1963.

Vos, Howard F. *An Introduction to Bible Archaeology*, (2nd printing). Chicago: Moody Press, 1959.

Wheeler, Margaret. *History Was Buried: A Source Book of Archaeology*. New York: Hart Publishing Company, Inc., 1967.

Whitcomb, John C. *The Early Earth*. Nutley, N.J.: Presbyterian and Reformed Publishing Company, 1972.

Whitcomb, John C. and Henry Morris, Jr. *The Genesis Flood: the Biblical Record and Its Scientific Implications*. Grand Rapids, Mich.: Baker Book House, 1961.

Wiseman, D.J. *Illustrations from Biblical Archaeology*. Grand Rapids, Mich.: Wm. B. Eerdmans Publishing Co., 1958.

Zimmerman, Paul A., editor. *Creation, Evolution, and God's Word*. St. Louis: Concordia, 1972.

Zimmerman, Paul A., editor (with John Koltz, Wilbert Rusch, and Raymond Surburg). *Darwin, Evolution, and Creation*. St. Louis, Missouri: Concordia Publishing House, 1959.

Zimmerman, Paul A., editor. *Rock Strata and the Bible Record*. St. Louis, Missouri: Concordia Publishing House, 1970.

Zumberge, James H. *Elements of Geology*. New York: John Wiley and Sons, Inc., 1966.

INDEX

Items listed in the General Index include people, places, things, and events. Maps, photographs, and other illustrations are listed in the index in italics.

The index is designed to provide a quick and easy reference catalogue for students and teachers alike.

Index of Maps